Photoshop® 6 Artistry

Mastering the Digital Image

▼ ▼ ▼ ▼ ▼ ▼ ▼ ▼ ▼ ▼ ▼ ▼ ▼ ▼

New Riders

201 West 103rd Street, Indianapolis, Indiana 46290

Barry Haynes

Wendy Crumpler

Seán Duggan

Photoshop® 6 Artistry

Mastering the Digital Image

By Barry Haynes and Wendy Crumpler

Published by: New Riders Publishing
201 West 103rd Street
Indianapolis, IN 46290 USA

International Standard Book Number: 0-7357-1037-6

Library of Congress Catalog Card Number: 00-104524

Printed in the United States of America   1 2 3 4 5 6 7 8 9 0

First Printing: May 2001

TRADEMARKS

WARNING AND DISCLAIMER

EXECUTIVE EDITOR
Steve Weiss

DEVELOPMENT EDITOR
John Rahm

PROJECT EDITOR
Jake McFarland

PROOFREADER
Jeannie Smith

INDEXER
Cheryl Lenser

TECHNICAL EDITOR
Gary Kubicek

SOFTWARE DEVELOPMENT SPECIALIST
Jay Payne

COVER DESIGN
Wendy Crumpler and
Barry Haynes

COVER PRODUCTION
Barry Haynes and
Wendy Crumpler

COVER PHOTO
Barry Haynes

BOOK DESIGN AND PRODUCTION
Wendy Crumpler and
Barry Haynes

A MESSAGE FROM NEW RIDERS

Every so often in the world of publishing, a book comes along that stands taller and stronger than the rest. *Photoshop 6 Artistry* is that book. This is the fourth edition that New Riders has had the honor to publish. Barry Haynes and Wendy Crumpler have given us, and all of you, a gift: quite possibly the best Photoshop book on the market. Rarely have we seen a book so embraced by its readers. Rarely do we see the type of anticipation for a new edition that *Photoshop 6 Artistry* inevitably receives. New Riders takes pride in producing great books and building great relationships with our readers and authors. To put it simply, *Photoshop 6 Artistry* is why we publish books.

We have worked with Barry and Wendy for many years now. They are great authors and great people. Their knowledge and passion have inspired hundreds of thousands of readers, and a great many editors who have had the fortune to work with them. Their dedication to their readers and this book is something special. Thank you Barry and Wendy.

This is a different kind of Photoshop book and it is for a different type of Photoshop user. This is for the perfectionist, someone not satisfied with getting close, but only satisfied with getting it right. This book will show you how to do that. This book doesn't simply teach you how to use Photoshop; it shows you how to master it. We feel that no other Photoshop book better addresses the needs of the photographer, artist, and serious student. Please let us know how you use this book and how it works for you. Because as Photoshop and its users evolve, so must this book. Thanks...

HOW TO CONTACT US

As the reader of this book, *you* are our most important critic and commentator. We value your opinion and want to know what we're doing right, what we could do better, in what areas you'd like to see us publish, and any other words of wisdom you're willing to pass our way.

As Executive Editor at New Riders, I welcome your comments. You can fax, email, or write me directly to let me know what you did or didn't like about this book—as well as what we can do to make our books better.

Please note that I cannot help you with technical problems related to the topic of this book, and that due to the high volume of email I receive, I might not be able to reply to every message.

When you write, please be sure to include this book's title, isbn, and authors, as well as your name and phone or fax number. I will carefully review your comments and share them with the authors and editors who worked on the book.

For any issues directly related to this or other titles:

    Email: steve.weiss@newriders.com
    Mail: Steve Weiss
             Executive Editor
             New Riders Publishing
             201 West 103rd Street
             Indianapolis, IN 46290 USA
             Fax: 317-581-4663
    Call toll-free (800) 571-5840 + 9 + 3567. Ask for New Riders. If outside the USA,
    please call 1-317-581-3500. Ask for New Riders. Fax: 317-581-4663

VISIT OUR WEBSITE: www.newriders.com

On our website you'll find information about our other books, the authors we partner with, book updates and file downloads, promotions, discussion boards for online interaction with other users and with technology experts, and a calendar of trade shows and other professional events with which we'll be involved. Maybe we'll see you around.

ABOUT THIS VERSION OF *PHOTOSHOP ARTISTRY*

With the release of Photoshop 6, New Riders and the authors decided a new edition of *Photoshop Artistry* was necessary. With all the new features Photoshop 6 has to offer, the realm in which the photographer, artist, and Web designer work has grown dramatically. To address this, the authors have covered the new features of Photoshop 6 with new examples and techniques, while revising the entire book to be up to date with this latest release of Photoshop. They have tweaked the design to better enable readers to quickly go back through the step-by-step examples when looking for a quick solutions, and have expanded on the great tips and techniques that have always been part of *Photoshop Artistry*.

ABOUT THE AUTHORS

Barry has been involved with photography since he was 14 using a Kodak Instamatic 104 on a trip to England. He later became a US Navy photographer and attended most of the Navy's advanced photography courses. After getting his BA in computer science from University of California San Diego, Barry spent 10 years, from 1980 to 1990, doing software development and research at Apple. It was a great time to be at Apple, and Barry was able to be a part of Apple's growth from 500 employees to over 10,000. He took a leave of absence from Apple in 1990 to set up a darkroom and get back to his photography. He soon found himself teaching Photoshop workshops and the notes for those evolved into Barry's advanced Photoshop Artistry book series, the latest of these being this *Photoshop 6 Artistry: Mastering the Digital Image* from New Riders. His books are very popular with photographers and artists who are using Photoshop to create their final artwork.

He also teaches in depth digital printmaking workshops from his studio in Corvallis, Oregon. Barry enjoys using his Photoshop darkroom techniques to print, show, and sell his own photography using Epson and Lightjet digital printers. He is currently working on a new book entitled *Making the Digital Print* which will cover all aspects of making the best commercial and art quality digital prints. Barry has given talks and workshops for the University of California Santa Cruz and Santa Barbara, the Photoshop Conference, Seybold Seminars, MacWorld, the Center for Creative Imaging, advertising agencies, design firms, photography stores and other organizations. His articles appear in Communication Arts and other photography magazines.

Wendy Crumpler has been in advertising and design since 1980. She has worked in print, television, CD-Interactive, interactive television, and computer-based training. Prior to her discovery of the computer in 1981 and the Macintosh in 1986, she was an actress and teacher. She is the Author of two versions of her popular *Photoshop, Painter and Illustrator Side-by-Side* book, from Sybex. She has done production, illustration, design, and training for a variety of clients using many applications. She has worked for Angotti Thomas Hedge, Boardroom Reports, Deutsch Advertising, J. Walter Thompson, TBWA Advertising, Wechsler Design, Wells Rich Greene, Canon, Parke Davis, and AT&T.

Seán Duggan is a photographer and digital artist who combines a traditional fine art photographic background with extensive experience in the field of digital graphics. In his imaging career, he has worked as a custom black & white darkroom technician, studio and location photographer, digital restoration artist, graphic designer, web developer, and educator. Equally at home with both low-tech and hi-tech approaches, his visual tool kit runs the gamut from primitive pinhole cameras to advanced digital techniques. In addition to providing consultation services and Photoshop training seminars, he creates illustrations and image design solutions for the web and print-based media. As an instructor for University of California, Santa Cruz Extension in Silicon Valley, he teaches regular classes on Photoshop and digital imaging for photographers. His web site can be seen at www.sdimagedesign.com.

LET US KNOW WHAT YOU THINK

There's been a lot of student and reader involvement in the shaping of this book. Listening to people who use these techniques helps us to refine and dig deeper to find solutions to our clients' and students' problems. And, we get smarter in the process. We love what we do and invite you to become part of the digital revolution with us. Let us know what you think of the book, what was helpful, what confused you. We are committed to empowering people to use their computers and their software to advance their own artistic abilities and to make a difference on this planet.

TAKE ONE OF OUR IN-DEPTH WORKSHOPS

We live in Corvallis, Oregon, an arts-oriented college town where we teach week-long hands-on workshops for up to four students at a time. These classes are tailored to meet the individual needs of those students. Barry's next book project is "Making the Digital Print", an in-depth guide for those who are making digital art prints. For more info on this book as it progresses, check Barry's web site at www.barryhaynes.com. We welcome your ideas and thoughs for this book and our other projects including Wendy's *Photoshop, Painter and Illustrator Side-by-Side* book which is now updated for Photoshop 6 and Illustrator 9. Check for the latest information about the details, times and locations for our digital imaging courses, as well as book updates, and other useful information on our Web site, www.barryhaynes.com.

WE LOOK FORWARD TO HEARING FROM YOU!

Barry Haynes Photography
Wendy Crumpler Enterprises
2222 NW Brownly Heights Drive
Corvallis, OR 97330
541-754-2219
email: Barry@maxart.com, or Wendy@maxart.com

Please check our Web site: http://www.barryhaynes.com

DEDICATION

This book is dedicated to Balance,
a most important life skill we continue
to learn about and work towards.

Balance is the essential energy:
in our lives,
on this earth,
in the universe!

ACKNOWLEDGMENTS

Each time we go through the amazing process of putting a book together, we worry. How will it be this time? Will we get the support we need, will people be competent, will they be fun? It's a difficult and daunting task to put so much effort into a book that will need to be updated again in a very short time. Not to mention the two books that Wendy and I are updating right now. But, each time we write, we're blessed with people who ease the way, straighten us out, keep us going, and make us laugh.

So thank-yous to:

Seán Duggan, for updating chapters 8, 10, 18, 36, 37 & 39, for writing chapters New Features, 32 and 38, for being a great instructor using Photoshop Artistry and for being a new Dad!

John Rahm, for always being pleasant and positive and for really liking our work and sending great complements. That really helps! Thanks for being a great editor.

Steve Weiss, for always being calm and supportive, even when Barry's not, and for doing great things to sell and promote this book. Hey man, we like the way you talk too!

Theresa Gheen for helping all of us to get everything done on time and for always being friendly while doing so.

Jennifer Eberhardt, for being there for us, always supportive and friendly when we need an extra hand.

Chris Nelson, for his help in doing a quality printing of this book, for his encouragement and for being fun to have dinner with.

Gary Kubicek, whose comments were so good we often wrote them down verbatim, and whose questions made us work harder.

Jeannie Smith, for her lovely mark-ups, her desire to get things right, for "agonizing" and telling us about it.

Jay Payne, for getting the demo versions on our disk, burning the final CD so it works on Mac and PC and for being easy and friendly to work with.

Brad Bunnin. We continue to rely on your advice and knowledge—you are such a gift. Brad's our publishing attorney but he's also now a minister, and a good one! We're looking forward to attending a sermon next time we're in Berkeley.

Jim Rich, for all your help with color and calibration, for your friendship, it's great to call up and ask "Hey Jim, what do you think of this?".

Mark Reid for starting our photography art group and for being an inspiration as well as a friend. All the members of the Corvallis Photo Arts guild for being a group of artists and friends I go to on Thursday nights, a welcome night off from writing.

Bill Atkinson, a generous and creative human being, whose fire to know and share and learn pulls us in and pushes us forward.

Charlie Cramer, a gifted artist, whose work always inspires us. Thank you so much for sharing your knowledge and friendship.

Bruce Ashley for all his wonderful images, and for his help and advice, particularly with CMYK separations.

Bruce Hodge, who is not only a wonderful photographer, but the kind of friend who would drive your station wagon all night to your new home and then hop a flight so's not to miss his daughter's recital. Was there ever better?

Nancy White, for letting us sit in on her wonderful "Photoshop for Multimedia" course, for her great help in the multimedia chapter of this book, and for being excited and eager to assist.

Ed Velandria (one of the smartest artists we'll ever meet) for his help with the Web chapters, and to Rox and Sarah for opening their home to us and being patient, loving, and fun.

Adobe's Russell Brown, Chris Cox, Mark Hamburg, David Herman, Julieanne Kost, and many others, thanks for detailed information during the beta testing, inspired creativity, and for using our book.

Bruce Fraser, Joseph Holmes, Dan Margulis and Jeff Schewe who continue to dig deeper into the possibilities of accurate color. We enjoyed working with you during the beta process, and Joe thanks for the election e-mails!

Our friends, David and Loretta, Denise and Wolf, Holly and Michael, Mark and Patty and many others for helping us through this process and their kids Jackson, Justin, Zackory, Andrew, Clara and Molly for playing with Max when we were busier than we wanted to be. Al and Mary, Bruce and Liz, Roger and Jane, all the McNamaras, Diane, Luke, Karen, and Marcella you are always there for us even though we are separated by too many miles these days.

All of the fabulous teachers and caregivers who help Max grow more fantastic every day.

Denise Haynes, a brave, wonderful, and supportive lady.

Our son, Max, for sharing his life this time with us.

Our readers, who continue to give meaning to our work.

From Barry to Wendy
I look forward to spending more time with you now that these books are done. Thanks for being a great partner!
From Wendy to Barry
Let's go to the beach!

Finally, and most importantly, our thanks to the Divine Creator for the bounty of this life and for giving us a chance to contribute in what we hope is a positive way.

TABLE OF CONTENTS

SECTION 3: OVERALL COLOR CORRECTION, SELECTION AND LAYER TECHNIQUES

Using the Lasso Tool, Magic Wand and Masks to make selections, Introduction to Levels and Curves, the step-by-step details of overall color correction in normal and problem images, using selections, layers, Adjustment layers, and layer masks to isolate specific areas of your image and change their color, retouch them, or make them lighter or darker. Many of these techniques, including color matching different color objects, spotting, sharpening and resampling for final print out, and using layers for specific color control, demonstrate the fine, artistic control that digital photography gives you. Magenta highlighted chapter names in the table of contents are essential chapters for everyone to read.

Selecting a complex object within an image using the Magic Wand, Lasso and Quick Mask, and then changing its color with Hue/Saturation to create an advertising quality, final hi-res image. Other Photoshop 6 approaches to this process are explored, including using the Magnetic Lasso with the Hue/Saturation Eyedroppers to simplify the selection and color change process.

  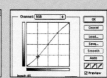 

The first things you do to a normal image after scanning it in either 8 bit or 16 bit per channel color: using Levels for overall color correction to set highlights and shadows, overall brightness and to correct for color casts; using Curves to adjust contrast; using Hue/Saturation to saturate overall and adjust specific colors; and using Curves for tweaking certain color and brightness ranges. This chapter includes a complete introduction to Levels and Curves. Fine-tuning the Banf Lake image using Adjustment layers with masks and Curves, and the Color Sampler to darken and enhance the sky and remove spots and scratches. Saving your Master RGB layered image then resampling and sharpening it separately for RGB or CMYK printer output, and for a Web image.

Overall color correction using Levels, Hue/Saturation, and Curves Adjustment layers on a problem image that has unbalanced colors and lacks a good highlight or shadow position. Using the Photoshop 6 selective Hue/Saturation features along with Color Samplers to more accurately measure colors. Make final improvements to specific off-color and dark areas using manual and Levels mask selections, Adjustment layers and Hue/Saturation tricks, dealing with out-of-gamut colors when converting to CMYK or a printer space, and the details of using the Unsharp Mask filter to sharpen an image.

Using Color Range and Replace Color to easily isolate all the yellow flowers and change their colors. Using Selective Color to fine-tune those colors after RGB to CMYK conversion. Moving Replace Color or Color Range results into an Adjustment layer's layer mask to soften or edit the mask, as well as change the color as many times as you like, without degrading the image.

Using Hue/Saturation, Levels and Selective Color along with the Color palette and Color Samplers to make sure the colors, tones and moods match between several photos of the same object(s), on a multipage spread. How to make a series of studio photos match even if they start out as different colors.

This section show you a variety of advanced color correction techniques. We discuss Duotones and their use to enhance the tonality of black-and-white images, as well as to create beautiful color images in publications using fewer than 4 colors. We show you several difficult retouching examples dealing with the fixing of damaged film and the restoration of old photographs. We also show you how to combine several different scans of bracketed photographs to get a better final result. There is also a discussion of using LAB color verses RGB for your Overall Color Correction process.

Using the Photoshop 6 Duotone features in Photoshop with custom curves, looking at separate duotone and tritone channels, printing duotones as EPS, and converting duotones and tritones to RGB and CMYK for final output.

Doing overall and final color correction and retouching of an image that has serious saturation and color problems in facial shadows, using one good channel and a Channel Mixer Adjustment layer to fix the others. Using layer masks and Adjustment layers to tweak color between several versions, retouching using Blend modes to balance facial colors, sharpening and final spotting.

 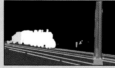 

Scanning old faded and damaged photographic prints using a flatbed scanner then using 16-bit grayscale Levels histograms and Curves to bring back the original contrast and details. Converting to 8-bit grayscale then adding local contrast enhancement Curves with masks to bring out details within the shadows and also improve flat areas. Retouching to remove scratches, damaged areas and blemishes. Converting to RGB, then adding masked Hue/Saturation adjustment layers with Colorize on to add color to a black-and-white original. Creating and addding a sky where the original was completely white paper.

  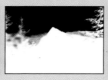

Using layers and layer masks to seamlessly combine two 16-bit per channel scans of two bracketed photos of the same very contrasty scene shot with the camera on a tripod. Learn how to line up the two scans, create a mask to separate the parts you want to use from each and how to use grouped Adjustment layers to color correct each image separately while looking at the combined results. The final touches are applied as you sharpen the combined image using my Sharpen Only Edges BH action script from the ArtistKeys action set.

Working with an image in the LAB color space involves a different perspective as we use some of the same, and also some new, color correction tools and techniques. LAB, Threshold, many more layers, Adjustment layers and layer masks are used to combine Red, Green and Highlight Bryce Stone Woman areas, creating a final image with a great red canyon as well as wonderful green bushes and trees. This example has been refined and enhanced several times to produce a very impressive final image.

SECTION 5: COMPOSITING MULTIPLE IMAGES WITH LAYERS, ADJUSTMENT LAYERS AND LAYER MASKS

The three chapters in this section focus on compositing different images together to get a totally new final effect. Rain in Costa Rica is a totally new example that uses many basic compositing techniques, including an overview of using the Pen tool, to create a final image that is far from a simple composite. The McNamaras solves a common problem of replacing some faces in a group shot of people who were not smiling or even paying attention, yet the solution involves some very advanced compositing and color correction techniques. The PowerBook example has been completely redone and enhanced for Photoshop 6.

After an introduction to the Pen tool and Paths, we use them to trace the outline of a Bus window through which we will be viewing the composite of a woman, a red car and a blue bus, all streaming by during a rainstorm on the streets of San Jose, Costa Rica. Both hard and soft edge masks are used in several innovative ways to create the final effect in this image.

Try the ultimate retouching and color correction challenge as you move six smiling heads from other exposures into this initially imperfect family portrait to end up with everyone smiling. Resizing and rotating the heads with Free Transform, blending them together using layer masks, and using Adjustment layers with the Color Samplers so you can continue to tweak the color of each head and the original group shot until they all match. Using the new Photoshop 6 Layer Sets and Locking features to organize and stabilize the many layers within this example.

Creating a prototype color ad for the PowerBook portable computer from a black-and-white Epson PhotoPC 3000Z digital camera shot of my new PowerBook G3 computer. You place screen grabs of a Tool palette and menu bar along with several background photographs into a separate setup composite. This composite is moved using linked layers from one document to another, then placed into a layer set containing a layer mask, and then Free Transformed to fit the perspective of the PowerBook's tilted screen as photographed from above. The final composite images is set up with layers so that the background, color of the computer and image on the computer screen can easily change as you show the ad and its variations to your clients.

SECTION 6: CALCULATIONS, PATTERNS, FILTERS, COMPOSITING AND EFFECTS   318

The examples in this section use Blend modes, filters, bitmaps, calculations, layer styles, shape layers, layers and other effects and techniques in combination with each other to achieve a variety of special effects, including motion simulation, drop shadows, pattern creation, glowing text, text with shadows, building an effective CD cover with effects, creating a web site or multi-media presentation, line drawings, and many others. Magenta highlighted chapter names in the table of contents are essential chapters for everyone to read.

Detailed explanations and examples of using the Blend modes in all the tools (painting tools, the Fill command, Layers, Layer Styles, Calculations, and Apply Image); the many variations and uses of the Apply Image and Calculations commands demonstrated and demystified.

Making a Web page using ImageReady, setting up the page and guides, creating slices and optimizing each slice within a page, adding the text information to your page and animations, creating animations between different images and also image positions, adding rollover states to your slices, tweening between frames of an animation, cleaning up animation and rollover interactions.

Chart of Print Display Longevity and Access Info for Wilhelm Research

(This information was unavailable at print time due to a restructuring of the Wilhelm web site. To get this very useful latest information about the Longevity of a variety of digital prints on many different papers used with the latest digital printers, go to www.wilhelm-research.com.)

FOREWORD BY BARRY HAYNES

WHERE I'M COMING FROM

Photoshop 6 Artistry is the fifth edition of the Photoshop Artistry series, which has sold over 100,000 copies. You'll discover that you can learn a lot from this book. I'll tell you a little bit about me though, because I want you to know where I'm coming from in writing *Photoshop 6 Artistry* and also as an artist. Hopefully, this will help you to decide if *Artistry* is the book for you.

After doing software design and creation since January of 1980, I took a leave of absence from Apple Computer in the summer of 1989 to persue my interests in photography. Those 10 years at Apple were quite an experience because, while I was there, Apple grew from a small company of 500 people to a large company of over 10,000 people. I got to work on the Apple II, the first really successful personal computer, the Lisa, where much of the Mac user interface was developed, the Macintosh itself and lots of other interesting projects! At the time I left, I'd already been using Photoshop for several years. Being at Apple you got all the toys, like Photoshop, often before they became real products. I've always been interested in photography and people have liked my photographs since I started at 14 with an Instamatic 104. I built a nice dark room, bought a 4x5 camera and was just going to do my art. I'd saved up a small nest egg and was going to learn how to make my living being an artist; use the other side of my brain for a change. I studied the well known Ansel Adams three book series on photography and starting taking more photographs myself. I'd been planning this life change for quite a while. During the next nine months though, an earthquake, a divorce and a group of photographer friends got me more involved in the new digital imaging which was just starting back then.

The next thing I knew I was teaching Photoshop courses at various places around the country, including the Center for Creative Imaging in Camden Main and the Palm Beach Photographic Workshops in Florida. I was learning how to be self employed...quite a different thing from the steady paychecks at Apple. As many of you know who are also artists, you often get sidetracked when trying to create and make a living from your art. In the 10 years after leaving Apple I now have a much more compatible and loving marriage to Wendy Crumpler, a wonderful five year old son, hundreds of Photoshop courses I've taught all over the country and six books that Wendy and I have written. All of this is good, yet I've not had enough time to do my art! My books and courses have helped thousands of people with their art yet I was getting frustrated that I wasn't leaving time to do my own. Since we moved to Corvallis Oregon, I've traveled a lot less, taught fewer course and actually put together a portfolio of prints that I'm starting to sell. I've got lots of great images and some fine prints too. Making sure I take the time to show and sell them is more and more important to me. That's why this book is dedicated to balance. The balance I need to write *Photoshop 6 Artistry*, and future books, in a way that still leaves me time to do my art, have a family, exercise, eat right, to be a person.

I mention this here because I know many of you are artists, some of you are very successful at spending most of your time with your art. Some of you, like me, are progressing in that direction but want to be able to do more with your art and some are just getting started as artists. I enjoy working with others, many of whom seem to be going though the same transitions I am. There is a lot that I have learned working with Photoshop, color correction and calibration over the years. This helps me have more control, to be more creative and satisfied with my own photograpy. I hope this book passes what I know on to you. Digital Imaging is a constantly changing field and one person can only keep up with so much of it. I focus on the areas that are important for my own photography work and also on things that are important for the readers of my books. I also write articles on pertinent topics, like calibration, scanning and printing since we all need to keep up on these things. There is only so much I can keep track of, however; so please contact me at barry@maxart.com when you see something the readers of this book might be interested in. I get lots of good information from my readers and I try to pass it on in new book versions and also in the Latest Tips area of my Web site at www.barryhaynes.com.

Ansel Adams, discussing the decision to make his original negatives available for future photographers to print, wrote in his autobiography that

> "Photographers are, in a sense, composers and the negatives are their scores. ...In the electronic age, I am sure that scanning techniques will be developed to achieve prints of extraordinary subtlety from the original negative scores. If I could return in twenty years or so I would hope to see astounding interpretations of my most expressive images. It is true no one could print my negatives as I did, but they might well get more out of them by electronic means. Image quality is not the product of a machine, but of the person who directs the machine, and there are no limits to imagination and expression."

Ansel Adams had a good vision for the future that we are now living. We hope this book will help you experience that vision in your photographic work.

WHERE *Photoshop 6 Artistry* FITS IN AND HOW IT WORKS

This book is evolving into what I envision to be the foundation piece of a new three book Digital Imaging Series: *Photoshop 6 Artistry: Mastering the Digital Image*, *Making the Digital Print* and *Capturing the Digital Image*. *Photoshop 6 Artistry* allows you to master the digital image by teaching you advanced Photoshop techniques. It does this in a way that beginners and intermediates can also learn yet there is plenty of information here for the advanced reader; this is an advanced book.

If you're a photographer, an artist or anyone who likes to create beautiful images, this book will help you do that using Photoshop! If you need to do it quickly and efficiently, we'll help you with that too. Understanding what you are doing and why you are doing it will turn you into a more powerful and creative Photoshop artist. If you are a beginner to Photoshop, reading this book more or less in order is the way to go. We try to introduce new ideas and explain them before we assume you already know them. If you are an intermediate or advanced user, you may learn more by reading the sections and doing the exercises in the areas of your most important interests and needs. You should also check www.barryhaynes.com for the latests tips about using new scanners and printers, our workshop schedule, as well as new techniques and examples that won't fit on the *Photoshop 6 Artistry* CD.

The examples in *Photoshop 6 Artistry* teach you how to use Photoshop 6 by working with typical situations that you encounter as a photographer, artist, or production artist. This is Photoshop for creating fine images that are sometimes high-quality reproductions of reality and sometimes fine renditions of composites and effects. Photoshop 6 Artistry has new examples about restoring old photographs, compositing and color correction. In this fifth edition, we have added all the information you will need to use the new Photoshop 6 features including color management and calibration of your monitors, scanners and printers. We give you a strategy for managing your digital images by creating a "Master Image" for each photograph. This Master Image is developed within a known color space that you can then convert using Photoshop and ICC profiles for each of your color inkjet, color laser, or dye-sub printers as well as color transparency output or compressed images for your Web sites. These same Master Images can also be used to create custom CMYK files for each of your printing situations. You only have to color correct the Master Image once, you then use color management and calibration, along with Action scripts, to generate a color compatible file for each type of output.

For each exercise, we spell out the detailed, step-by-step process and include all the steps you'll need at that point in the book. You can practice the technique yourself because the original images, masks, and progress steps, as well as the final images for each example, are included on the *Photoshop 6 Artistry* CD that accompanies the book. We have taught these examples over the past ten years to thousands of students across the country. Their feedback has helped us refine the exercises to make them easy to understand, concise, and full of special tips for more advanced users. **For example, based on reader requests, this edition shows the actual steps the reader should perform in bold.** The explanations for the steps are in normal text. This will help you more quickly go back and practice examples over and over again. In addition to student tested, step-by-step instructions, *Photoshop 6 Artistry* includes explanations of concepts like color correction, calibration, 48-, 24- and 8-bit file formats and compression, duotones, selections, masking, layers, layer masks, adjustment layers, fill layers, shapes, layer styles, blending options, history, and channels, so you really understand what you are doing and are not just blindly following directions. Understanding allows you to expand the ideas in this book as you apply them to your own situations and creations.

We start with simple examples like cropping and color correcting a photograph. We cover color correction in great depth, and then move into things that you normally would do in the darkroom, like changing the contrast, burning and dodging, removing spots and scratches, and making a nice photographic print. Before we get into compositing and special effects, we talk about the importance of having absolute control over the colors in your photographs—which you can do with ease and understanding now using the latest Photoshop 6 color management features. The masters of color photography have used contrast reduction masks, shadow, highlight and color masks in the darkroom to make very fine Ilfochrome, C, and dye transfer art prints. Now many of them have switched to digital techniques and making LightJet 5000 or Epson 2000 and 7500 inkjet prints. Using these techniques, you can make specific colors pop by increasing their saturation and changing their relationship to the rest of the photograph. *Photoshop 6 Artistry* shows you how to do all these things digitally using adjustment layers, layer masks, and multiple layers of the same image, and how to generate art-quality output to the LightJet 5000, Epson 1270, 2000 and 7500, Fugix Pictrography, and other printers, and very importantly, to the Web. We also talk about enhancing an image for output back to 4x5 and 8x10 film as well as for output to separations for printing on a press. We show you how to use the above techniques along with custom sharpening actions to get great quality prints from digital cameras, Kodak Photo CD and Pro Photo CD scans as well as scans from the better desktop film scanners and from high end drum scanners.

After we explain how to make a fine color print using Photoshop, we make extensive use of layers, layer masks, and image compositing techniques. You can do commercial compositing techniques easily using Photoshop, and we present step-by-step examples for some simple compositing jobs and then move on to some more complex examples that involve using hard- and soft-edge masks, as well as a variety of shadow effects and the features of layers, adjustment layers, and layer masks. The Apply Image and Calculations commands, the Blend mode variations and new layer styles are explained in detail along with examples of where to use them.

Photoshop 6 Artistry also includes many tips and techniques on getting the most from the Photoshop filters. We also get into creating duotones and bitmaps, adding textures to images, and other fun things.

IF YOU HAVE AN EARLIER EDITION OF PHOTOSHOP ARTISTRY

A main reason for writing *Photoshop 6 Artistry* is that this new version of Photoshop really does have some great new features, features that photographers and Photoshop Artistry readers will want to know about. Another reason for writing a new edition in the Photoshop Artistry series is that I've been printing and selling my own art prints and I've learned a lot of new techniques since *Photoshop 5 Artistry*.

Those of you who already have *Photoshop 5 & 5.5 Artistry*, *Photoshop 5 Artistry* or *Photoshop 4 Artistry* will notice that the techniques in all the *Photoshop 6 Artistry* examples have been improved to take full advantage of the great features in this new version. Many new examples have also been added to help you learn about the Photoshop 6 color calibration and color management techniques as well as making custom monitor and printer profiles, retouching old and damaged photographs, new compositing and effects examples, new color correction images and examples including working with LAB color, digital cameras, and the latest info about creating Web images. Many more new features and techniques are distributed throughout the book. You can compare this book to the Photoshop 4 or 5 versions and quickly see how to use the new features. Use our "Overview of Photoshop and the new Photoshop 6 Features" chapter, at the front of the book, to get a quick overview of Photoshop 6 and the new features. We also have reorganized the table of contents and the presentation of information to make it flow more logically for people trying to learn Photoshop by reading this book in order. This will also help instructors who are using this as a text book. The CD has an improved ArtistKeys to set up your Actions palette and to give you a great set of function keys and automated sequences for bringing palettes up and down, converting file formats, custom sharpening and large grain removal and doing other useful and repetitive tasks.

With this edition of Artistry, I changed the entire book to make it up to date with Photoshop 6. I wrote new examples where I felt new information was important. The examples in this edition that were updated from a previous edition are still here because they work well to illustrate a useful technique and they have been tested and improved by myself and thousands of Photoshop students over time. They have been improved for Photoshop 6 and will continue to be in my books as long as they are the best examples available to teach photographers and image makers what they need to know.

Photoshop is great fun! And the more you know, the better time you will have and the easier it will be to turn the images in your mind into reality. We hope *Photoshop 6 Artistry* helps you have more fun than ever before with photography and digital imaging.

Happy Photoshopping!

Barry Haynes

OVERVIEW OF NEW PHOTOSHOP 6 FEATURES

With outstanding new features and intelligent refinements to existing functionality, this is one of the most significant Photoshop upgrades in years.

In 2000, Adobe Photoshop marked its tenth anniversary. In the relatively young field of desktop publishing, a decade is a long time. In the ten years it's been around, there have been great features added to every upgrade, but Photoshop 6 stands out as one of the most significant releases in recent years. There are so many great new features and enhancements to existing capabilities, it's hard to know just where to start in listing them. If you've ever felt that Photoshop was an application you coul°d not live without, then version 6 is definitely a must-have upgrade.

USER INTERFACE ENHANCEMENTS

If you've used Photoshop before, one of the first things you'll notice about version 6 are the improvements to the user interface. The main component is the new Options bar, which replaces the Options palette of earlier versions. Although subtle, this is a excellent refinement. With the Options bar docked at the top of the screen, the options for a given tool, and in some cases, additional tools and commands, are always clearly visible. The Options bar can also be free-floating, or docked at the bottom of the screen. At the far right side is the Palette well where you can store palettes and free up some screen space. Palettes in the well can be quickly opened with a single click on their title tab. Clicking the tab again closes the palette. To move

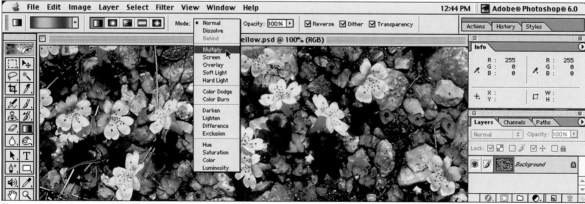

The new Options bar has replaced the Options palette of previous versions. This ensures that a tool's options, as well as additional tools, are always clearly visible. The Options bar is normally docked to the top of the screen, but it can also be free-floating or docked at the bottom of the screen. At the far right side of the Options bar is the Palette well, where you can drag and drop to store palettes and help maximize your workspace. Palettes in the well can be quickly accessed when needed by clicking on their title tab.

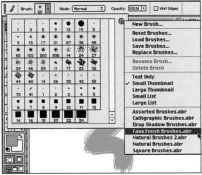

Brushes no longer have their own palette and are now accessed through a popout picker in the Options Bar. The Presets capability allows you to effectively manage different brush libraries and have them available through the Brushes drop-down menu.

a palette to the Palette well, just grab its title tab and drag it into the well.

Another change in the interface is the new pop-out pickers for items such as brushes, gradients and custom shapes. Instead of a separate brushes palette, you now access the brushes from the Options bar. If you've installed the 6.0.1 update, the brushes and gradients pickers are also available anywhere on the image canvas by using the Enter key to bring up and then dismiss the picker. Additional information on the 6.0.1 update is included at the end of this chapter. The new Presets feature (Edit/Preset Manager) allows you to store different brush libraries and other collections such as gradients, layer styles, and color swatches in a central location. Photoshop ships with a number of preset libraries and you can also create your own. Presets can be easily shared among colleagues and friends and can be quickly selected through specific Photoshop menus. This saves time and eliminates the need to navigate into nested folders in the Photoshop directory to load custom settings such as Pantone color swatches. You can find more information on using the Preset Manager in Chapter 3: "Setting System and Photoshop Preferences."

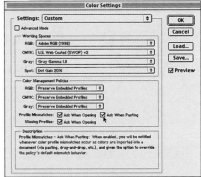

The Preset Manager allows you to manage all of your Presets from a single dialog. Presets include brushes, swatches, gradients, layer styles, patterns, contours and custom shapes.

IMPROVED COLOR MANAGEMENT DIALOGS, MULTIPLE WORKING SPACES AND SUPPORT FOR SOFT PROOFING

Photoshop's color management interface has received a major renovation, making it much easier to use and understand. Controls that were previously accessed through several different dialogs have now been combined into a single location, and you are only presented with the necessary settings; advanced options are safely tucked away, making it less likely that a novice user will inadvertently modify their settings. The location of the Color Settings, formerly found in the File menu, has been moved to Edit/Color Settings (the Preferences have also been moved to the Edit menu). Another addition that is sure to help Photoshop users understand what each of the settings is doing is informational rollovers, often an entire paragraph, that appear as you move your mouse over a specific setting or area of the dialog.

The confusing Convert Colors and Profile Mismatch warnings of Photoshop 5 and 5.5 have been improved as well. This is good news for those who were always a bit uncomfortable with the absolute, all or nothing ultimatum that these warnings presented. One reason that these warnings are easier to deal with is that Photoshop 6 now supports the capability to work in more than one color space at a time. This concept may seem confusing initially, especially if you were still coming to terms with version 5's implementation of color management, but it represents a great leap forward for a more flexible ICC color-managed workflow. If there is a profile mismatch, you no longer have to convert a document's colors to your designated workspace. You can choose to preserve the embedded profile and continue editing the file in, say, ColorMatch RGB, even if your workspace has been set to Adobe RGB. Photoshop will reference your ICC monitor profile (created with the Adobe Gamma utility or

The Color Settings dialog serves as command central for managing color in Photoshop 6. When you move your mouse over a setting, helpful informational rollovers appear in the Description area at the bottom of the dialog. The settings for the Advanced mode (top left corner) do not appear unless you choose to view them. See Chapters 3 and 15 for more detailed views and explainations of these dialogs.

In the lower left corner of the document window (Mac), or the lower left corner of the screen (PC), you can display a file's color profile. This is helpful now that Photoshop supports working in multiple color spaces at the same time.

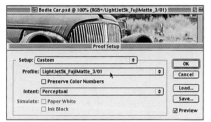

Proof Setup lets you use the monitor as a proofing device to display a "soft proof" of what your image will look like when printed on a specific device.

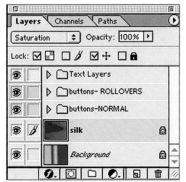

The Proof Setup dialog. Here, I've chosen a custom profile for a LightJet 5000 photographic printer. In the document window title bar, an asterisk appears next to RGB indicating I'm viewing a soft proof, and the proofing space is identified.

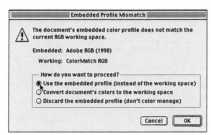

You no longer have to convert a document's colors to the current RGB workspace, but can choose to preserve the embedded profile and work in that color space, even if it is different from your workspace.

You can organize your layers with Layer sets, and individually lock transparency, pixels, position, or all three.

other profiling software) and adjust the display of the document. When you save any changes you've made, the Color-Match RGB tag will be embedded in the file, even though your working space is Adobe RGB. When opening a file with a profile mismatch, you can also choose to convert the colors to the current working space, or discard the embedded profile if you don't want the file to be color managed. Profile mismatch warnings will also now appear if you paste, or drag and drop image data from one color space into a document with a different color space. To help you keep all the different color spaces straight, you can now display color tag information in the status box located in the lower left of the document window on a Mac, or in the lower-left corner of the screen, just above the task bar on a PC.

Another welcome addition to Photoshop's array of color management features is the ability to soft proof your images and display what they will look like if printed to a specific output device. This option is available under View/Proof Setup. The default proofing space is the Working CMYK settings, but you can also load custom device profiles such as for Epson printers, film recorders or LightJet photographic imaging devices. For in-depth coverage of all the new Photoshop 6 color management features, read Chapter 14: "Color Spaces, Device Characterization and Color Management" and 15: "Photoshop Color Preferences, Monitor, Scanner and Printer Calibration."

ENHANCED LAYER MANAGEMENT

Layers, a major component of Photoshop since version 3.0, have received several enhancements that make layer management easier and expand the creative possibilities of layers. Foremost in the layer management area are the new Layer sets, which allow you to place layers into folders within the Layers palette. Layers within a set can be moved as a group, even if they are not individually linked together, and blending modes can be applied to an entire set as well. This is a great organizational tool and certainly one of the most useful features that Adobe has added to Photoshop 6. Web designers, who frequently work with files comprised of a confusing number of layers, will really benefit from layer sets. And if the old limit of 100 layers wasn't enough for you, the maximum number of layers in a file has been increased to a staggering 8000! In reality, however, you'd probably run out of system resources before ever reaching that number. Since each layer, layer set and layer effect is factored into the equation, a more probable layer limit is closer to 1000. Still, that should be enough for even the most challenging compositing job!

Far more useful in everyday tasks, and something Photoshop users have been requesting for some time, is the ability to individually lock layer transparency, pixels, position, and an overall lock that protects the entire layer. The old Preserve Transparency option is now covered by the Lock Transparency icon. Adjustment layers can now be accessed from an icon at the bottom of the Layers palette.

Layer Clipping Paths & Vector Shapes

With layer clipping paths, Photoshop has added new support for vectors and gained another tool for masking layers. Basically, a layer clipping path does the same thing as a layer mask; it controls which areas of the layer are visible. Since the clipping path is vector data, however, you can have precise, crisp edges that can be output using a PostScript printer's higher resolution, even if the image it's applied to has a much lower resolution. Layer clipping paths can be edited with the Pen tools, or the Direct Selection Arrow tool, just like any other path. You can import existing paths from Illustrator, create a clipping path from type, and even combine a layer clipping path with a pixel-based layer mask for both a hard-edged and soft-edged masking effect. The best thing about them is that after making a path, you can turn it into a layer clipping path then edit that path while watching as the edits change the mask created by the layer clipping path. This allows you to more exactly fine-tune your paths.

Shapes, another new vector feature, allow you to create shapes that can be added to your image as a pixel-based filled area of color, a new work path, or as a color fill layer with the shape defined by a layer clipping path. Standard primitives such as rectangles, ovals and lines, can be modified by using the Add, Subtract, Intersect and Exclude commands in the Options bar, enabling you to transform a basic shape into something much more complex. You can also choose from a default library of custom shapes that ship with the application or import vector artwork from Illustrator for your shapes. Using the Preset Manager you can build your own new shape libraries. Type and any path can be turned into a custom shape. Since vectors are resolution-independent, the addition of shape layers greatly extends Photoshop's capabilities as a graphic design tool. For resolution-independent PostScript output, vector information is preserved when files are saved in the EPS format. Check out Chapter 32: "Layer Clipping Paths, Shape Layers and Layer Styles," for a thorough exploration of these great new features.

Layer clipping paths and layer masks can be applied to the same layer, resulting in a masking effect that has both soft and hard edges. Here, a layer clipping path of the word "Kansas" and a gradient layer mask have been applied to an adjustment layer to create the effect of the word growing out of the wheat field.

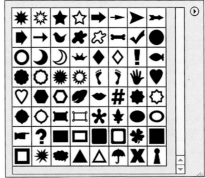

The Custom Shapes that come with Photoshop 6. Using the Preset Manager, it's easy to create your own shape libraries.

Using basic primitives as the foundation, you can use the Add, Subtract, Exclude and Intersect commands to easily transform shapes. Here, a crescent moon shape is quickly created by modifying a simple circle with another circle set to Subtract.

New Adjustment Layers & Layer Styles

The Gradient Map lets you map the luminosity (lightness) values in an image to a gradient. If you choose a purple to blue gradient, for example, shadows are mapped to the purple and the highlights to the blue, with all the tones in between taking on the corresponding hues of the gradient. This can lead to some very interesting color effects, and, with a more subtle approach, can also be used for grayscale and duotone treatments. Gradient Map can be applied as an image adjustment directly to the pixels, or as an adjustment layer. In addition to the Color Fill layer which was introduced in version 5.5, you can now create Gradient Fills and Pattern Fills. Like adjustment layers, fill layers remain editable and separate from the image pixels until you flatten your image.

The Gradient Map feature lets you map an image's lightness values to corresponding tones in a gradient. In this example, from left to right on the gradient, dark shadows are mapped to purple, three-quarter tones to a near white, mid tones to a dark gray, quarter tones to near white, and highlights to a dark blue.

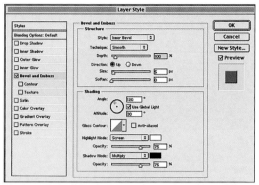

The Layer Style dialog is the new incarnation of Layer Effects.

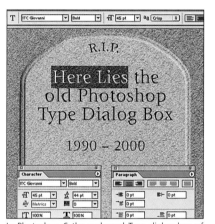

You can save any combination of layer effects as a layer style that can be used on future images.

In Photoshop 6 the awkward Type dialog box of past versions is no more. You can now enter and edit type directly on the image canvas and have access to sophisticated typographical controls such as those found in Illustrator or InDesign.

Layer effects have been greatly expanded to become layer styles and the new dialog box for this feature has an amazing variety of controls for infinite tweaking of your effects. Five new effects have been added for this version of Photoshop: Satin, Gradient Overlay, Pattern Overlay, Color Overlay, and Stroke. For some effects you can now control the shape of the edge contour, or, for metallic effects, the gloss contour. Taking a cue from the previous version of ImageReady, different combinations of effects can now be saved as a layer style so you can quickly apply the same effect on future images. Layer styles are "live" effects that update automatically as you alter the shape of a layer. Photoshop ships with several layer style libraries to get you started and you can always start making your own. Refer to Chapter 32: "Layer Clipping Paths, Shape Layers and Layer Styles" as well as Chapter 34: "Heartsinger CD Cover" for more information about these features.

A BRAND NEW TYPE TOOL

The Type tool has been completely rebuilt in Photoshop 6, from the way you interact with it, to the powerful type engine at work under the hood. The awkward Type dialog box of previous versions is gone and you can now enter and edit type directly on the image canvas. Improved typographical controls are very similar to those found in Illustrator or InDesign. The Character palette allows you to scale characters vertically or horizontally, set baseline shift and apply color and typefaces on a per-character basis. There is also a new No-Break option which controls whether a string of characters wraps as a single word. You can create point text, or paragraph text by dragging out a text box like you would in a page layout program. Paragraph text flows within the boundaries of the text box, making it much easier than in the past to contain type within a specific area. In the Paragraph palette, additional options include alignment, auto-leading, space before and after, hanging punctuation, and control over left-, right-, and first-line indents on a per paragraph basis. Extensive hyphenation and justification settings have also been added, as well as support for Adobe's latest composition engines, featuring every-line and single-line composers. The Type Warping feature allows you to distort type into a variety of forms such as arcs and waves. Warped type is still completely editable, as is type which you have scaled or distorted with the Free Transform tool. Since type is vector-based in Photoshop 6, output to a PostScript printer yields precise, resolution-independent type, no matter what the resolution of your image. All of these great new type features, however, mean that type is no longer backwards compatible with earlier versions of Photoshop. If you open a Photoshop 6 file into version 5.5, your type will still be on separate layers, but it will not be editable. For more on the new Type features, see Chapter 4: "The Tool Palette," Chapter 34: "HeartSinger CD Cover" and Chapter 35: "South Africa in Focus."

LIQUIFY

Playing around with the Liquify command (Image/Liquify) is a little like viewing your image in

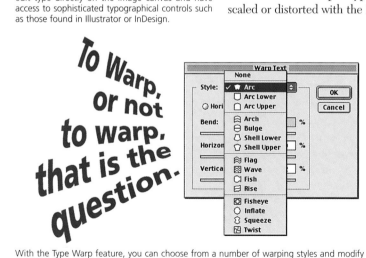

With the Type Warp feature, you can choose from a number of warping styles and modify the degree of the overall distortion. Type remains editable, even after a warping.

a carnival funhouse designed by Salvador Dali. You can push, stretch, twirl, melt, expand, shrink, reflect and warp areas of your image by using brush strokes to apply your distortions. A real-time preview updates as you make each new distortion and the actual image warping is rendered when you choose OK. You can display a mesh over the image which allows you to see a graphical wire frame view of the warping, and even "freeze" specific areas that you want to protect from distortion. Alpha channels can also be loaded to protect parts of the image. A Reconstruct tool allows you to gradually undo the warping and is very useful for selectively reverting portions of the image. The interface for Liquify takes over the Photoshop screen and displays your entire image inside its preview window. The usual zoom shortcuts don't work inside the Liquify funhouse, but you can display a close-up view of a portion of an image by selecting the area you wish to edit before you enter the Liquify command. Despite the wild, over-the-top example we have here, Liquify is also quite good for making very subtle adjustments. For more on the Liquify feature, see Chapter 34: "HeartSinger CD Cover."

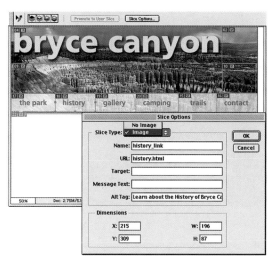

Bad night in Vegas? No, it's the Photoshop 6 equivalent to Dali's drooping watches, the new Liquify command. Despite the first comparison that may come to mind, Liquify is much more than the old Smudge tool run amok. This feature lets you push the pixels around, pinch, bloat, twirl and reflect them to apply subtle or wild distortions. A handy reconstruct tool lets you selectively restore the image to normal and you can "freeze" specific areas to protect them from distortion.

NEW PHOTOSHOP WEB FEATURES

Expanded Web production functionality includes the ability to create slices directly in Photoshop. If you only prepare the occasional image for the Web, this is very convenient, as it saves you a trip into ImageReady. Slice options include naming, assigning a URL link, target, message and alt text settings. For even greater convenience, new layer-based slices will update if you change the size of a layer. This is a great way to handle slices of text titles or graphical link names, since the actual wording can often change throughout the design process. ImageReady 3 also supports layer-based slices, as well as layer-based Image Maps. See Chapter 39: "Creating Slices, Animations and Rollovers in ImageReady 3" for in-depth coverage of image slices and other Web production tasks.

For precise control when optimizing images for the Web or multimedia, Photoshop has added Weighted Optimization to its already extensive tool kit. This feature lets you use alpha channels to vary compression settings across an entire image, producing higher quality results in important image areas while still keeping file size down. Using channels for Weighted Optimization, you can create gradual variations in JPEG compression, GIF dithering and lossy GIF settings. You can also give preference to certain colors in an image when creating custom color palettes. To learn more about this very useful new feature, read Chapter 37: "Optimizing Images for the Web and Multimedia."

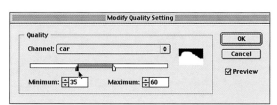

You can now create image slices for Web production directly within Photoshop.

With Weighted Optimization you can use alpha channels to vary compression and other settings in Web and multimedia images.

The Web Photo Gallery feature is back (File/Automate/Web Photo Gallery) and it has been significantly improved since it first appeared in version 5.5. You can now choose from four different gallery styles, and if you know your way around editing HTML, you can even create custom templates that will appear in the Gallery Styles menu. There's also greater control over font sizes, captions, and image and thumbnail sizing. Check out Chapter 38: "Creating Your Own Web Photo Gallery" for a step-by-step tour of automated Web publishing the Photoshop way.

AND A WHOLE LOT MORE...

BETTER SUPPORT FOR 16-BIT PER CHANNEL IMAGES

This version of Photoshop has good news for those who like to work on high-bit images with 16 bits of information per channel. Support for this mode has been expanded, and you can now use the History brush, Shape tools, as well as the Unsharp Mask, Gaussian Blur, Gradient Map, Canvas Size, Auto Contrast, Add Noise, Median, High Pass and Dust & Scratches features with 16-bit per channel images. See Chapter 17: "Steps to Create a Master Image," Chapter 19: "Overall Color Correction" and Chapter 26: "Combining Bracketed Photos or Two Scans to Increase Dynamic Range" for examples of working with 16-bit per channel images.

NEW CROPPING TOOL

The Perspective option on the new Crop tool lets you adjust the perspective of an image as you crop it. In this photograph of a Brooklyn neighborhood, the original view (top) was slightly skewed. After applying a Perspective Crop, the final image looks much better.

There's so much that's new and cool in Photoshop 6, even the humble Crop tool has received a makeover! When you drag out a crop box now, the area outside your crop is darkened with a transparent overlay, helping you visualize the final crop. Both the color and opacity of this overlay can be modified. If you are working on a layered file, cropped data can either be deleted or hidden. Whenever you have a layered document with additional hidden image data extending beyond the visible boundaries of the file, you can show all of the image data by choosing Reveal All from the Image menu.

Another new feature of the Crop tool is the ability to apply a perspective adjustment as you make the crop. This is ideal for pictures of buildings where the vertical lines skew inward due to the perspective. In the past you could have made an adjustment such as this by using the Free Transform tool prior to cropping the image. The advantage of doing it with Perspective Crop is that you can view the full image and not a low resolution proxy, and this makes it much easier to get your perspective crop lines just right.

ANNOTATIONS

The capability of adding written and audio annotations to your files is a feature that has migrated over from Adobe Acrobat. If you are not sharing working versions of complicated Photoshop files with others, then this feature may not be too exciting. For professionals exchanging project files destined for print, the Web, CD-ROM, or other high-end output, however, this is a very useful communication tool.

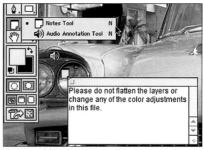

You can add both written and audio annotations to your files in Photoshop 6.

hrz_web

A Droplet for processing horizontal Web images.

DROPLETS

Droplets are self-contained mini-applications that apply an Action to an image, or a folder of images, when you drag and drop the images onto the Droplet icon. It's sort of like batch processing on auto-pilot since you don't have to set up any target or destination folders. Once you have an Action that is functioning correctly, highlight it in the Actions list (not the Button mode) and go to File/Automate/Create Droplet. For more about Actions, see Chapter 11: "Automating with Actions."

EXPANDED TIFF AND PDF FILE OPTIONS

Photoshop now supports the TIFF 7 format specifications. This means that you can now save layers, vector shapes, adjustment layers, layer clipping paths, type layers, layer styles, and annotations all in the TIFF format. You can even choose from three different types of file compression encoding with TIFF, the old LZW, and now ZIP and JPEG. With the exception of LZW compression, the new version of the Photoshop PDF format supports all of these options as well. For a detailed discussion of the main file formats and all of their capabilities, see Chapter 10: "File Formats and Image Compression."

THE PHOTOSHOP 6.0.1 UPDATE

In February 2001, Adobe released the Photoshop 6.0.1 update. This is a free download from the Adobe Web site, at http://www.adobe.com/products/photoshop/update.html, that fixes a number of problems that were not discovered until after version 6 hit the streets. None of the changes are what could be considered major, but there are some definite usability and performance improvements, especially with the way the Paint Brush Picker works, that make it worthwhile to take the time to download this update and install it. Here's a rundown of some of the main things that were fixed in 6.0.1.

When you have a painting tool active, you can now press Enter and the Brush Picker will appear at the current mouse location. Once you pick a brush, hit Enter again and the picker goes away. You can also double-click a brush to select it and dismiss the picker. The current brush is always highlighted in the picker and the current brush indicator in the Options bar always displays the actual brush size. As with previous versions of Photoshop, you can use the First Brush and Last Brush keyboard shortcuts (the left and right bracket keys), but with the 6.0.1 fix, these shortcuts work regardless of whether the current brush exactly matches a preset brush.

The 6.0.1 update: When you have a painting tool active (this also works with the Gradient tool), hitting Enter will bring up the Brushes or Gradient Picker, allowing you to choose a new brush or gradient. Hitting Enter a second time will dismiss the picker. You can also double-click a brush to select the brush and dismiss the picker. The currently selected brush is always highlighted when you return to the picker.

Other fixes include image clipping paths in TIFF and EPS files saved from version 6.0.1 can now be read by Quark Xpress. Paths exported to Illustrator, retain the path scaling. Batch file naming now works correctly. There's no slowdown in performance when files in the Open Recent list are unavailable. Showing and hiding the edges for a selection no longer requires you to press Cmd-H twice. And version 6.0.1 will remove old Photoshop temp or scratch files if the operating system is asleep at the wheel and fails to do so.

ESSENTIAL PHOTOSHOP TOOLS AND FUNCTIONALITY

SETTING PREFERENCES

NAVIGATING IN PHOTOSHOP

THE TOOL PALETTE

UNDERSTANDING PATHS, SELECTIONS, MASKS, CHANNELS, AND LAYERS

AUTOMATING WITH ACTIONS AND TRANSFORMING IMAGES

THE HISTORY BRUSH AND PALETTE

UNDERSTANDING FILE FORMATS AND CHOOSING COLORS

An unusual view of Half Dome in Yosemite I took in color with my Canon F1 and 28mm lens, scanned with a Lino Tango Drum scanner. After color correcting in Photoshop, I decided this image looked best in black and white. Matted prints are available from the Epson 2000 and 7500, check www.barryhaynes.com for more information.

1 HOW TO USE THIS BOOK ANDTHE *PHOTOSHOP 6 ARTISTRY* CD

This chapter gives you a quick preview of what you'll find in this book and some valuable tips on the best way to use it along with the images on the CD, so you can learn from creating the examples.

Photoshop 6 Artistry can help both new and advanced Photoshop users. If you read this book from front to back and do the hands-on sessions in order, it is an in-depth, self-paced course in digital imaging. If you're new to Photoshop and digital imaging, going in order may be the best way to proceed. If you are a more advanced Photoshop user, more interested in learning new techniques, you may want to read the sections and do the hands-on exercises that cover the skills you need to learn.Use the table of contents and index to find the areas you want to reference.

The book has two types of chapters: overview chapters, which contain information that everyone should learn, and hands-on chapters, where you learn by color correcting and creating images. The chapters are ordered beginning with the fundamentals and moving on to more advanced skills. Chapters highlighted with magenta color in the table of contents are essential for everyone to read. All the chapters are in-depth, and we expect most users, even experienced Photoshoppers, to learn something from each chapter. Some of the chapters toward the end of the book are very detailed and assume you already have a lot of Photoshop knowledge. You need to know the foundation skills taught in the earlier chapters before you do the later, more advanced chapters.

The first two sections of this book, "Essential Photoshop Tools and Functionality," and "Color Correction and Calibration to Create a Master Digital Image" present in-depth overview chapters that provide readers with a common base of knowledge. Everyone should read the Chapters 3: "Setting System and Photoshop Preferences," 14: "Color Spaces, Device Characterization and Color Management" and 17: "Steps to Create a Master Image," so you can set up your system and Photoshop correctly, and calibrate your monitor for working with the book and doing color output. The rest of these overview chapters go into a lot of important details. They are not introductory material by any means. If you are anxious to get your hands into the program though, you don't need to read all of these before you start the hands-on exercises with Chapter 18. You should come back to these earlier chapters later, however, to learn valuable information about the Zone System, picking colors, all the color correction tools and other important topics. The hands-on chapters generally assume you have read, and have a basic understanding of, Chapters 1 through 17.

The hands-on chapters, and some of the overview chapters, have actual steps where you are expected to do something to one of the images on the CD. These steps are **in a special highlighted format**. The steps where you are doing something are often mixed in with sentences or paragraphs of extra information that are not always essential to doing the actual steps, but are often very useful information. The first time you read through a chapter, it is best that you read the entire chapter. If you want to go back and redo a step-by-step chapter and you just want to do the actual steps, all you need to do is read and **follow the highlighted sentences**. Many readers asked for a feature allowing them to more quickly go through a chapter a second or third time. The highlighted steps should allow you to do this.

IMPORTANT DIFFERENCES FOR MAC AND WINDOWS USERS

Photoshop users, on both the Mac and the PC, will find this book beneficial. That's because in 99.9% of the cases everything in Photoshop is exactly the same for Mac and PC users. The contents of each of Photoshop's tool windows and menu bars are the same in a Mac window and a Windows window. Adobe has done an excellent job of making Photoshop cross-platform compatible in every way it can. Mac and PC users both have tested this book, and have found it valuable and easy to use. We have taught in classrooms where some of the computers are Macs and some are PCs and it works out fine.

The following sections discuss the few minor differences between Photoshop on the Mac and on the PC. I also point out any important differences that are relevant to the various topics I discuss.

MODIFIER KEYS

References in *Photoshop 6 Artistry* to keyboard modifier keys use the Option and Command keys, which are the main modifier keys on the Mac. **Windows users need to remember that whenever we mention the Option key, you use the Alt key, and whenever we mention the Command key, you use the Control key.** In those rare cases where we actually mention the Control key, you also use the Control key on the PC. To get the Fill dialog, us Shift-Delete on the Mac, but Shift-Backspace on the PC.

FUNCTION KEYS

Most PCs only have 12 function keys on their keyboards, where some Mac extended keyboards have 15. *Photoshop 6 Artistry* includes a predefined set of actions for using the function keys, called ArtistKeys, which we reference in the book. We have set these up so the ones used most often are within the first 12 keys. They should work the same for the Mac and the PC. We discuss this further in Chapter 3: "Setting System and Photoshop Preferences."

STATUS BAR

Windows users also have a Status bar at the bottom of the Photoshop screen area, which tells you what tool you are using and gives you additional information about what you are doing. This particular help information is not available on the Mac version of Photoshop.

MEMORY SETUP

For Photoshop to work most efficiently, you need to set up the computer's application memory correctly. The process for setting up memory on the Mac is a little different than on the PC. Setting up memory for both types of systems is explained in Chapter 3: "Setting System and Photoshop Preferences."

□ ▦	🗀 Photoshop
	32 items, 2.5 Ԍ

	Name
▷ 🗀	Copyright Info
▷ 🗀	Ch02.Navigating
▷ 🗀	Ch03.Preferences
▷ 🗀	Ch04.Tool Palette
▷ 🗀	Ch06.Selections
▷ 🗀	Ch07.Layers
▷ 🗀	Ch08.History and Snapshots
▷ 🗀	Ch09.Transformation
▷ 🗀	Ch11.Automating with Actions
▷ 🗀	Ch12.Color Correction Tools
▷ 🗀	Ch15.Color Pref and Calibration
▷ 🗀	Ch18.The Car Ad
▷ 🗀	Ch19.Overall Color Correction
▷ 🗀	Ch20.Correct A Problem Image
▷ 🗀	Ch21.Yellow Flowers
▷ 🗀	Ch22.Color Matching Images
▷ 🗀	Ch23.Burnley Graveyard
▷ 🗀	Ch24.Desert Al
▷ 🗀	Ch25.Restoring Old Photos
▷ 🗀	Ch26.Combining Bracketed Photos
▷ 🗀	Ch27.Bryce Stone Woman
▷ 🗀	Ch28.Rain In Costa Rica
▷ 🗀	Ch29.The McNamaras
▷ 🗀	Ch30.The Power Book Ad
▷ 🗀	Ch31.Blend Modes, Calcs, etc
▷ 🗀	Ch32.Layer Styles
▷ 🗀	Ch33.Posterize Bitmps Patterns
▷ 🗀	Ch34.HeartSinger CD Cover
▷ 🗀	Ch35.South Africa
▷ 🗀	Ch37.GIF JPEG and ColorPalettes
▷ 🗀	Ch39.Animations Slices RollOvrs
▷ 🗀	Software Demos

When you insert your *Photoshop 6 Artistry* CD on the Mac or Windows systems, the *Photoshop 6 Artistry* folder contains the set of Photoshop 6 format images for doing the book's exercises. The green folders are for the Hands-On Step-by-Step chapters and the blue folders are for In the non-step-by-step examples. In the Software Demos folder, the Photoshop 6 Artistry CD also contains demo versions of Adobe Photoshop 6, Adobe ImageReady 3 and Adobe GoLive 5.

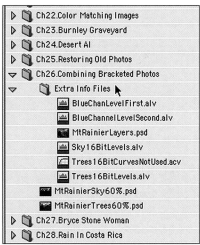

When you open a folder for one of the hands-on sessions, it contains the images and other files you need for completing the exercise. The Extra Info Files folder will contain things like the intermediate and final versions of the images along with all layers and masks for that exercise, including Levels, Curves and other settings we used along the way. You can compare these with your results if you have any questions about the way you are doing the exercise.

WHAT'S ON THE CD

The *Photoshop 6 Artistry* CD that comes with the book includes all the images you need to do the examples in the book yourself. This includes the authors' before and after versions, Levels and Curves settings, masks and so forth. Each hands-on chapter has a separate folder on the CD containing the original scan files you absolutely need for doing the hands-on exercise. The **Extra Info Files** subdirectory of each folder contains the authors' finished versions of the exercise, including layers, masks, steps along the way, Levels, Curves, Hue/Saturation and other Adjustment Layer settings. Use these files to compare your results to the authors' or to recreate the authors' results.

You can use this book and CD as a self-paced course or you can use it to teach a course at the college or professional level. When you put the CD in a Mac CD player, it will come up with the name *Photoshop 6 Artistry*, and it will look like a Macintosh directory with folders, files and icons, as well as Mac format filenames.

When you put the *Photoshop 6 Artistry* CD in a Windows machine, you will see a Windows directory named *Photoshop 6 Artistry* that contains files that have the same filenames as in the Mac directory and the appropriate three-character suffixes that the PC requires.

The directory on the *Photoshop 6 Artistry* CD opens to show you a green folder for each chapter that is a hands-on exercise. It also contains blue folders with files and images that you can use to enhance your knowledge about some of the overview chapters. Green folders are for hands-on exercises and blue folders are for overview sections. The folders are numbered with the same numbers that the corresponding chapters have.

Each hands-on chapter's folder contains the images and other information you need to complete that hands-on exercise and a folder called Extra Info Files. The Extra Info Files folder contains the authors' intermediary and final versions of the images for that exercise, as well as masks, levels, and curves settings and other pieces of information that will help you learn more and also compare your results to the authors'. We have tried to make the images printed in this book look as much like those on the CD as possible. The digital files on the disc, however, are more accurate comparisons of the progress that happens on each creation. To get the best results when viewing any of the CD files, you should calibrate your monitor and system as explained in Chapter 15: "Photoshop Color Preferences, Monitor, Scanner and Printer Calibration."

TO TEACH A COURSE

We certainly hope that other instructors will use this book to teach Photoshop courses around the world. Since 1990, Barry has used these examples to teach many Photoshop courses at the Palm Beach Photographic Workshops in Florida, University of California Santa Cruz Extension, the Santa Fe Photographic Workshops and many other places around the country. Having a professional course where the students can take home the images and exercises to practice them again later has been a main factor in making Barry's Photoshop courses so well received. We hope that you can take advantage of his years developing these exercises by using this book as the text for your Photoshop courses.

If each student purchases the book, they will have copies of all the images and step-by-step exercises for each example. The main images on the CD, in the *Photoshop 6 Artistry* folder, along with the Extra Info Files, are in Photoshop 6 format.

Most images open to about 4 megabytes in size and will grow as the exercise progresses. There are several images that are a lot bigger than that, however. For a professional course, I have discovered that using images large enough to see the kinds of details students will be working with when they are doing real projects for their art, magazines, film output and publications works best. These 4Mb Photoshop files from the *Photoshop 6 Artistry* folder are the easiest to use and give the students the most information for doing the course. If your course machines each have CD players, each student should access the images directly from his or her own CD within the *Photoshop 6 Artistry* folder.

If you plan to use *Photoshop 6 Artistry* to teach a class, please contact the authors at www.barryhaynes.com to find out about school discounts and also to get complete information regarding purchase and distribution of books and images. We also teach our own in-depth workshops; check out our site at www.barryhaynes.com for the latest course info and schedules.

USING THE DEMO SOFTWARE ON THE CD

The *Photoshop 6 Artistry* CD now contains demo versions of Adobe Photoshop 6, Adobe ImageReady 3 and Adobe GoLive 5. You can use the demo version of Photoshop 6 to try out the examples in the book and learn Photoshop, but you can not save files with this demo version. Follow the installation directions on the CD to try out each of these packages.

USING THESE IMAGES WITHOUT A COPY OF THE BOOK

We do not mind if teaching institutions or individual users use a copy of the *Photoshop 6 Artistry* images from their hard disk or over a network, as long as they have a copy of the *Photoshop 6 Artistry* book. Each person or student who uses these images to learn about Photoshop should have a copy of the book. If a school, company, institution or person gives out copies of these images to any person who has not purchased the book, that's copyright infringement. If a school, company, institution or person copies the step-by-step instructions, or copies paraphrased step-by-step instructions, and hands either of those out in class, especially when using them with the *Photoshop 6 Artistry* images, that too is copyright infringement. Please don't do this! We work hard to create these books and if you don't buy them, we won't be able to afford to continue this kind of effort. Thanks.

IF YOU HAVE PROBLEMS READING YOUR CD

When you get your book, please remove the CD from the holder in the back of the book and immediately transfer it to a solid plastic case for safe storage. The CDs are too easily scratched or made dirty by leaving them in the holder at the back of the book. If your CD has problems opening a file, clean it with a CD cleaning wipe that you can get from a computer store. This will often solve the problem.

Here is the New Riders technical support information if you need it. Mailing Address: 201 W. 103rd Street Indianapolis, IN 46290. Tech Support Phone: (317) 581-3833. To email tech support: userservices@macmillanusa.com. You can also access our tech support Web site at http://www.mcp.com/product_support/mail__support.cfm.

2 NAVIGATING IN PHOTOSHOP

How to most efficiently use the tools, palettes, and windows that Photoshop provides; make the most of big and small monitors; and use some general shortcut tips that make Photoshop more usable and fun.

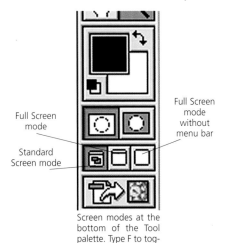

Full Screen mode

Full Screen mode without menu bar

Standard Screen mode

Screen modes at the bottom of the Tool palette. Type F to toggle between these screen modes.

Each digital image file you open into Photoshop has its own window. When you first open a file, the window will be a standard Macintosh or PC window with scroll bars and a grow box in the lower right corner, and all the rest of the standard fare. At the top of the window, in the window's title bar, is the name of the file as it was last saved followed by the zoom factor, and the color mode (RGB, CMYK, LAB, etc.) the file is currently using. The color mode has a ° after it if the file has a different profile than the working RGB profile. If you are using View/Proof Colors to proof this window to a different color space, the name of that space is shown following a slash after the color space. When you are in a layered document, the name of the currently active layer is also displayed in the title bar. This allows you to use Option-[or Option-] to scroll to the next lower or higher layer and see the layer's name without the Layers palette on the screen. If other windows cover the one you want to see, you can find it using the list of open files at the bottom of the Window menu. You can use Control Tab or Control-Shift-Tab to scroll through your open windows. You can view any of the open files in one of three screen modes, which the icons toward the bottom of the Tool palette denote. The leftmost icon denotes the standard screen mode we talked about above. The middle icon shows the Full Screen mode with menu bar and places the active, top window in the center of the screen, surrounded by a field of gray, which hides other windows from view. The rightmost icon shows the Full Screen mode, without the menu bar.

Here we see a Mac Photoshop desktop with three windows open. The active window, Young Lakes, is the window in front with its title bar striped. You will see a check mark beside this window in the Window menu. You can bring any window to the top, even a hidden one, by choosing it from the bottom part of the Window menu. In this Normal Screen mode, it is easy to accidentally click outside a window and switch to another application. Notice the new Photoshop 6 Options palette which spans the full width of the screen right below the menu bar.

THE PHOTOSHOP SCREEN MODES

Working in Full Screen mode with the menu bar offers many advantages. If you are working on a small monitor, Full Screen mode does not waste the space that scroll bars normally take up. Also, accidentally clicking down in the gray area while in Full Screen mode doesn't switch you to the Finder, or some other application. This gray area is especially useful when making selections that need to include the pixels at the very edge of the window. Using any of the selection tools or the Cropping tool, you can actually start or end the selection in the gray area, which ensures that you have selected all the pixels along that edge. When using a typical Mac or PC window, the cursor often fluctuates between displaying as the tool you are using or the arrow cursor for the scroll bar when you move the mouse ever so slightly while at the edge of the window. Even if you are not using Full Screen mode, if you are making an edit along the edge of the image, you may want to make the window a little bigger than the image. Doing so adds Photoshop gray space between the edge of the file and the window's scroll bars so you can more easily make these edge edits. As you can tell, I am very fond of Full Screen mode. It removes all other distractions from your screen and allows you to focus on your beautiful image surrounded by nondistracting neutral gray. On the PC, Photoshop has this advantage in any screen mode. That is, when the Photoshop screen area is maximized in the Windows 98 or NT user interface, it covers all other programs. On the PC you can use the Window menu to show or hide the status bar while in any of the screen modes. On the Mac, the status bar, which has additional information about the current file and Photoshop, is at the bottom of the current window and only shows up when a file is in Standard screen mode. On the PC, the Status bar gives you additional hints about how to use the current Photoshop tool. The Mac status bar doesn't have this hint information that can be useful to the beginner.

The rightmost screen mode icon, at the bottom of the Tool palette, gives you a mode similar to Full Screen mode, but with the image surrounded by black instead of gray, and the menu bar removed. We'll call this "Full Screen Mode No Menu Bar." If you are a Photoshop power user, you can work without the menu bar by using command and function keys—but I generally use this mode only for presentations. In this book, we won't be using Full Screen Mode No Menu Bar so when I refer to Full Screen mode, I'm talking about Full Screen mode with the menu bar.

Here we see Photoshop working in Full Screen mode with various palettes around the active window. We can still get to underlying windows by selecting them from the Window menu. A single press on the Tab key removes all these palettes and allows you to use the whole screen for your work. A second Tab press and all the same palettes are back in the same positions. This is a great way to see the big picture. When visible on the PC, the status bar toggles on and off along with the rest of the palettes. Shift-Tab toggles all the palettes except for the Tool palette, here on the left, and the Options palette, right below the menu bar.

Again in Full Screen mode, here we have used Command-Spacebar-click to zoom in and fill the screen with our image, a more inspiring way to work. Learn to use Command-Spacebar-click to zoom in, Option-Spacebar-click to zoom out, and the Spacebar with a mouse drag for scrolling. View/Fit on Screen (Command-0) will fill the screen with your image and it fills the entire screen if you first press Tab to remove your palettes. View/Actual Pixels (Command-Option-0) zooms to 100%. This is the most efficient way to move around the Photoshop screen, especially when in Full Screen mode or using a dialog box like Levels.

CONTROL KEYS FOR ZOOMING AND SCROLLING

There are certain keyboard shortcuts that I make everyone learn when I teach Photoshop. IT IS VERY IMPORTANT THAT YOU LEARN THESE THREE SHORTCUT KEYS! Even if you hate keyboard shortcuts and you don't want to be a power user, you have to learn these or you will find working in Photoshop a constant

7

pain. I worked on the Lisa project at Apple. The Lisa was the predecessor to the Mac and much of the Mac's user interface actually was designed for the Lisa. Larry Tesler, who was head of applications software for the Lisa project, had a license plate on his car that read, "NO MODES." A mode is a place in the user interface of a program where you can't access the tools you normally use. Programs, like Photoshop, that have a lot of modes can be confusing, especially for the beginner. Many tools in Photoshop come up in a modal dialog box; for example, Levels, Curves, Color Balance, and most of the color correction tools. When you use these tools, you are in a mode because you can't go to the Tool palette and switch to, for instance, the Zoom tool. Learning the below control keys will help you function even when you're in a mode!

ZOOMING IN AND OUT

If you are inside Levels or Curves and you want to zoom in to see more detail, which I do all the time, you can't select the Zoom tool from the Tool palette the way you usually can. Holding down the Command key and the Spacebar will show you the Zoom icon, which you can then click on to zoom in on your image. Command-Option-Spacebar-click will do a zoom out. When you zoom in and out using the Zoom tool or these control keys, Photoshop zooms by a known amount. If you are at 100%, where you see all the pixels, then you will zoom into 200% and then 300% and then 400%. You will find that the image is sharper at a factor of 2 from 100%. Fifty percent, 100%, 200%, or 400% are sharper than 66.6%, 33.3%, and so on. You can also use Command-+ and Command-— to zoom in and out. In Standard Screen mode these keys change your window size while zooming, unless you go to Edit/Preferences/General and turn off the default Keyboard Zoom Resizes Windows. You can use Command-Option-+ or — which does the opposite to the Keyboard Zoom Resizes Windows preferences setting. By default, the Spacebar zooming options do not change the window size, unless you type Z for the Zoom tool and then turn on Resize Windows To Fit in the Options bar. Control-Spacebar-click, right mouse click on the PC, gives you a pop-up menu with various zooming options. Don't forget that you can always zoom so the entire image fits in the screen by pressing Command-0 (zero). If you press Command-Option-0, the image zooms to 100%.

SCROLLING WITH THE HAND ICON AND KEYBOARD

Just holding the Spacebar down brings up the Hand icon, and clicking and dragging this icon scrolls your file. Typing an H switches you to the Hand tool. The hand tool is a good place to be when you are not using another tool because it can't accidentally damage your file and you can then scroll with just a click and drag. You can use the Page Up and Page Down keys on many keyboards to scroll the current image a page worth of pixels up or down. Command-Page Up scrolls to the left and Command-Page Down to the right. Add the shift key to any of these to scroll 10 pixels at a time. The Home key scrolls to the top left and the End key to the bottom right.

PALETTE MANAGEMENT

Photoshop contains a lot of different palettes, each of which controls a different set of functions. The Tool palette is the main palette. Its functions are discussed in Chapter 4: "The Tool Palette." The different color picking palettes are discussed in Chapter 5: "Picking and Using Color." Palettes include the Channels, Layers, and Paths palettes, which are discussed in Chapter 6: "Selections, Paths, Masks, and Channels," and Chapter 7: "Layers, Layer Masks, and Adjustment

Here we see a typical palette with its Options menu on the top right, accessible by clicking the black triangle icon. The Palette Options item shows you different ways to display the palette. You should check out the Palette Options on all the palettes that have them. Most Palettes have a close box on the top left and a similar box on the right for collapsing or opening the palette. The icons at the bottom of the palette are shortcuts for various functions associated with that palette. The name at the top is the palette's name tab. Here are some standard icons and what they mean depending on the palette they are located within:

Load Selection from Channel or Path

Save Selection to Path or Channel

New Channel, Layer, Path, Action or Snapshot

Throw away Channel, Layer, Path, Action or Snapshot

Layers." What we discuss in this chapter is how to most efficiently use all the palettes on the Photoshop screen.

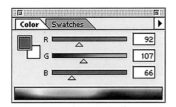
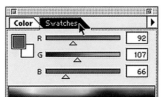
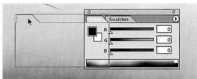

Here we see a group of palettes with the Color palette currently active. The Palette Options menu would now bring up the Color palette's options.

To switch to the Swatches palette, click its name tab and when you release the mouse, the palette group will look like the group to the right.

The Palette group after choosing the Swatches palette. Now the Swatches palette's options show in the Palette Options menu.

ACCESSING PALETTES

All palettes can be accessed from the Window menu. You can use this menu to open or close a particular palette. I recommend using the Actions palette to define function keys to bring up and close the palettes you use most often. I have created a set of function keys for you, called Artistkeys, which I show you how to install in Chapter 3: "Setting System and Photoshop Preferences." Pressing the Tab key makes the Tools palette—and all other visible palettes—disappear. Pressing Tab again brings all these palettes up in the same locations. Pressing Shift-Tab opens or closes the other palettes without changing the status of the Tools palette and Options bar. You can close any of the palettes, except the Tools palette, by clicking the close box in the top left corner of the palette on the Mac or the top right corner in Windows. If the Tab key does not make the palettes go away and come back, the cursor is probably within a text field on the current tool's Options menu. Just press Return to deactivate that field and the Tab key should hide the palettes again.

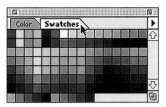

Click a palette's name tab and drag it outside the group window to put that palette within its own window.

PALETTE OPTIONS

Most palettes also have a menu that you can access by clicking the Menu icon at the top right of the palette (see Channels palette image on the previous page). You can move palettes around on the screen by clicking the title bar at the top and moving the palette to a new location. Photoshop opens the palettes in the same location at which they were last used unless you turn off the Save Palette Locations option within Photoshop's Preferences; choose Edit/Preferences/General.

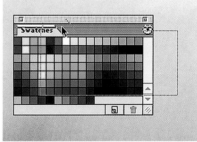

Here we see the Color palette after it has been removed from grouping with the Swatches palette. To regroup these palettes, click the name tab of one of them and drag it on top of the window of the other. The palette that is within a group window first has its name tab on the left. New palette tabs are added to the right.

GROUPING AND SEPARATING PALETTES

In Photoshop, you can group several palettes in the same palette window. You then switch between palettes in the group by clicking the name tab of the palette you want or by choosing the palette from the Window menu. If you hide any of the palettes within the group, the whole group gets hidden. Therefore, you are better off

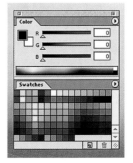

You can also stack palettes vertically. Here we dragged the Color palette on top of the Swatches palette until the gray line shows up in the gray area at the top of the window. Release the mouse at this point and you get the palette arrangement shown below.

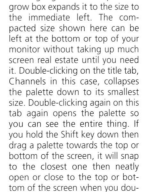

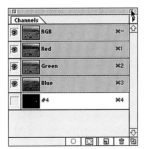

Clicking the first time in the grow box, at the top right, resizes the palette so that it just holds the things within it, like the palette on the right. In Windows systems the rightmost box closes the palette and the box just to the left of it duplicates the behavior we describe here.

Clicking a second time in the grow box, or double-clicking the title tab, resizes the palette to show just name tabs, like the palette on the right, and will also send it to the top or bottom of your monitor.

Clicking again in this palette's grow box expands it to the size to the immediate left. The compacted size shown here can be left at the bottom or top of your monitor without taking up much screen real estate until you need it. Double-clicking on the title tab, Channels in this case, collapses the palette down to its smallest size. Double-clicking again on this tab again opens the palette so you can see the entire thing. If you hold the Shift key down then drag a palette towards the top or bottom of the screen, it will snap to the closest one then neatly open or close to the top or bottom of the screen when you double-click on the tab or click the grow box.

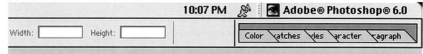

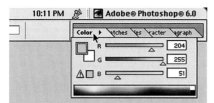

Here we have clicked on the docked Color palette's tab which pops it open. To close it, press Return, Enter or click outside this palette.

By dragging and releasing, you can move palettes into the new docking area to the top-right of the Options palette. To access one of these palettes, just click on it's tab and it will pop open as in the illustration to the right. Use the grow button in variable sized palettes, like Styles, to make it big enough for all the choices.

grouping only palettes that are used together. Sometimes you want to see two palettes at the same time that are usually used within a group. I do this often with layers and channels. When I'm working on a complicated layer document that has a lot of mask channels, I separate them to see both at the same time. To do this, click the name tab of the palette you want to separate and then drag it out of the group window to a new location by itself. To move more palettes into a group, click the name tab of the palette you want to add and then drag it over the group window. New palettes in a group are added to the right. If you have a small monitor, you may want to group more of your palettes together to save screen space. You can also compact and collapse your palettes by clicking in the grow box at the top right. This box has a minus icon on the PC. If your monitor is set to at least 1024 pixels wide then the Options palette (Options bar) will have a gray area at its right side, called the Palette Docking Area. You can drag palettes and drop them into this docking area. At that point the palette's title tab appears in the docking area and you can access the palette from there by just clicking on it. To remove a palette from the docking area, just click and drag the palette's title tab to the location you'd like to move it to.

Here we see two views of the same file. The one on the top left is a close-up of the lake shown to the bottom of the more zoomed out view to the right.

MORE THAN ONE WINDOW PER FILE

You can have more than one window open at a time for the same Photoshop document. To do this, first open a Photoshop file that gives you your first window. Next, go to the View/New View command to open a second window of the same file. Utilizing this capability, you can, for example, have one window of a section of the file up close and the other window showing the entire file. You can also use this technique to have one window display a particular channel or mask of the file, while another window shows the RGB or CMYK version. There are many uses of this feature and one of the best is to have one window showing how the image will look when printed on one printer, say the Lightjet 5000, and a second window showing you how it will look when printed on the Epson 1270, 2000, or 7500. To find out exactly how to do this, see Chapter 15: "Photoshop Color Preferences, Monitor, Scanner and Printer Calibration."

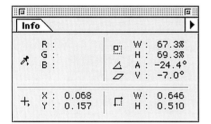

Here we see the Info palette during the Free Transform command. The contents of the right and bottom two sections change to show you information about your transformation.

USING THE INFO PALETTE

The Info palette is one of the most useful tools in Photoshop. Not only does it measure colors like a densitometer (which we will do extensively in the color correction exercises in later chapters in this book), it also gives you important measurements any time you are scaling, rotating, making, or adjusting a selection. The top right location, the size of the box you are drawing, the degree of rotation, and many other useful measurements are always present in the Info palette. This is a

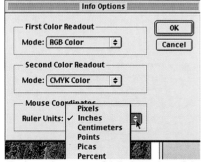

Check out the many useful display options of the Info palette as accessed from its Palette Options menu.

Chapter 2: Navigating in Photoshop

good one to keep up on the screen most of the time. See Chapter 12: "Color Correction Tools," and Chapter 17: "Steps to Create a Master Image" for a discussion of the important Color Sampler part of the Info palette. If you are using the ArtistKeys actions from the book's CD then function key F9 is used to access this palette. The built-in default Photoshop function keys use F8 for Info and you can even access it with F8 from within a Modal dialog.

RULERS, GUIDES AND GRIDS

Photoshop has rulers, guides, and grids which are very helpful for creating composite images where you need to place objects in exact locations. They are also great for Web and multimedia projects to control the alignment of buttons and action objects. The controls for rulers, guides, and grids are all located on the View menu. As you can see in the diagram on the this page, there is a different command key to turn each of the rulers, grids, or guides on and off, but you can also choose to have grids and/or guides removed when you

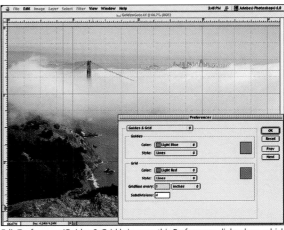

Edit/Preferences/Guides & Grid brings up this Preferences dialog box, which allows you to set the color and appearance of your grids and your guides. You can also specify how often you have gridlines and subdivisions.

use Command-H, the new global hide key. I believe Mark Hamburg, Adobe's lead Photoshop engineer, coined the term "UberHide" for the new expanded functionality of Command-H, which before had been used to hide and show selection edges. The UberSnap, Command-;, can now be used to turn off snapping to each of grids and/or guides as well as slices and document bounds. Having snapping on helps you more accurately align items, such as buttons, that need to be exactly vertically or horizontally aligned. You can also use Command-Option-; to lock guides, which will prevent accidentally moving them.

Command-R turns your rulers on, at which point you can set the zero-zero location of the rulers (the top left of the image, by default) by clicking in the top left ruler box and then dragging to the point in your image that you want to be zero-zero. To return the zero-zero to the top left position again, just double-click in the top left corner of the ruler display. You can set up the ruler unit preferences in File/Preferences/Units and Rulers.

To create a guide, just click in the horizontal or vertical ruler and drag the guide to where you want it. Clicking the horizontal ruler will drag out a horizontal guide and clicking the vertical ruler will drag out a vertical guide. You can

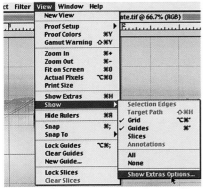

Using the View menu, you can use Command-R to turn rulers on and off, Command-' to turn Guides on and off and Command-Option-' to turn the Grid on and off. Using Show Extras Options, a selected number of these, as well as Selection Edges, Slices, Annotations and Paths, can now be turned on or off using Command-H, the "UberHide" command. As depicted below, you can use Command-;, the UberSnap command, to Snap To any or all of the Guides, Grid, Slices or Document Bounds.

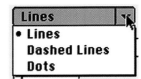

Accessed from View/Show/Show Extras Options, this dialog determines the types of items, if on the screen at the time, that Command-H, the UberHide command, will now remove.

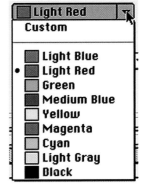

Here you see the choices you get for either grid or guide colors. Each can have a different color and choosing Custom brings up the Color Picker, where you can pick any color you want.

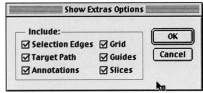

Here you see the options for grid styles. Guides can be in either the Lines or Dashed Lines styles.

Navigator palette and red View box when image is zoomed to 100% and all is visible in the image window.

Navigator palette and red View box when zoomed to 300%. Now only the area in the red View box is visible in the image window.

Dragging on the red View box to change what is visible in the image window.

Command-dragging a new box to view just the boat and water in the center. When the mouse button is released, we will zoom so this box fills the window.

Here is the small default size Navigator palette. Click in the top right corner, Minus button on the PC, to return to this size.

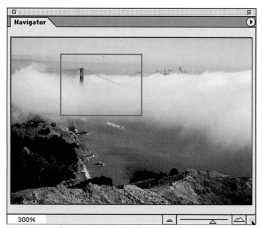

You can use the grow box in the bottom right corner to change the size of the Navigator palette. Here is a big Navigator palette.

move a guide, if Lock Guides is not turned on, by using the Move tool (V or the Command key) and just dragging the guide to its new position. Option-dragging a guide toggles it from vertical to horizontal or vice versa. Another important keyboard option for guides is to hold down the Shift key while dragging out your guides. This forces the guides to even pixel boundaries, which is critical for multimedia and Web work where precision is paramount. Take a few minutes to play with these options and you will find rulers, grids, and guides easy to learn. You can lock or unlock guides from the View menu and use the Show sub-menu of View to show or hide guides.

When working on projects where I need to measure the sizes and placements, I usually have at least rulers on. When you are drawing a selection, you can actually see the starting location as well as the current location of the mouse by following the dotted lines that show you the current mouse location along each of the rulers. For faster positioning, turn on the grid as well as Snap To Grid; then you will know that things are exactly placed. To set your own specific locations, create guides anywhere you want. You can then line up objects along these guides. When I am just color correcting a photograph, I usually turn off Rulers, Guides, and Grids and put the image into Full Screen mode so that I can see it unobstructed.

THE NAVIGATOR PALETTE

Photoshop has a cool Navigator palette (Window/Show Navigator or Shift-F2 with ArtistKeys) that allows you to zoom in and out to quickly see where you are in an image and more efficiently move to a particular spot in that image. This palette contains a small thumbnail of your entire image with a red box, called the View box, on top of the thumbnail that shows you the part of the image you can currently see in your window. As you zoom in, you will notice this box getting smaller because you are seeing less and less of the image area. You can click and drag this box, in the Navigator palette, to a new location and then your window will display what's inside the box. This is much faster than doing large scrolls with the Hand tool on the actual image window, because in the Navigator palette you always see the entire image. You do not need to guess where you want to scroll to; just click the red box and move it there. It's even faster if you don't drag the box there, but instead just click down in the Navigator palette where you want the box to be. To change the size and location of the red box, just Command-drag a new box over the area you want to see. You can change the size of the Navigator palette and its thumbnail by clicking and dragging in the grow box at the bottom right corner of the palette on the Macintosh, or click and drag on any edge when using Windows. Making the palette bigger gives you more exact positioning within your file using the bigger thumbnail. You can use the slider on the bottom right to drag the zoom factor smaller or bigger.

You can also click the smaller or bigger icon on either side of the slider to zoom in a similar way to Command-Spacebar-clicking and Option-Spacebar-clicking.

In the bottom left of the Navigator palette is a numeric text box where you can type in the exact zoom factor that you need. If you hold down the Shift key while pressing Enter after typing in a new zoom factor here, you will zoom to the new factor, but the text percentage number remains highlighted so you can enter a new value without having to click the text box again. Again, I have found that images are a little sharper on the screen when zoomed to an even multiple of 100% (25%, 50%, 100%, 200%, 400%, and so on). You can change the color of the View box from red to another color by choosing Palette Options from the Navigator palette menu.

THE ACTIONS PALETTE

Check out Chapter 3: "Setting System and Photoshop Preferences," to learn how to set up the Actions palette with my ArtistKeys command set to quickly set up function keys to show and hide any palette. You may notice, throughout the book, references like (F11 with ArtistKeys) or just (F11). These show you places where I have created shortcuts for you using the Actions feature. Actions can be used to automate a single menu choice, such as bringing up a palette, or a whole sequence of events, such as complex functions for sharpening and removing noise from an image. Please check out Chapter 11: "Automating with Actions," to learn about the wonderful ways you can automate repetitive task using actions! Most of the color separations in this book were produced automatically using actions that are included in the ArtistKeys set and explained in Chapter 12.

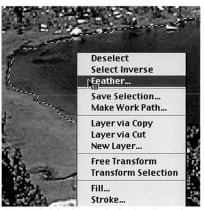

Command-click when in the Move tool gives you a menu of layers that have pixels at the location where you clicked. You can then choose the layer you want to make active in the Layers palette.

Command-click when a selection is active and you are in a selection tool gives you this Context-Sensitive menu which includes most of the choices you would want involving a selection.

CONTROL KEY FOR CONTEXT-SENSITIVE MENUS

Photoshop has a great feature using the Control key and the mouse (or just the right mouse button on Windows)! At any time, you can hold down the Control key and then press the mouse button (just right-click on Windows) to bring up a set of context-sensitive menus. What shows up in the menu at a particular time depends on the tool you are currently using and the location where you click. If you are in the Marquee tool, for example, you get one menu if there already is a selection and a different one if there is not. If you are in the Move tool, you'll get a menu showing all the layers that currently have pixels at the location where you click. You can then choose the layer you want to access from that menu. There is at least one context-sensitive menu for each tool. These are a great set of

Actions	
Tool Palette	F2
Navigator Palette	⇧F2
LevelsAdjLayer	⌘F2
Save For Web	F3
Color Table	⇧F3
CurveAdjLayer	⌘F3
Unsharp Mask	F4
Gaussian Blur	⇧F4
Hue/Sat AdjLayer	⌘F4
Duplicate	F5
Replace Color	⇧F5
Sharpen Only Edges BH	⌘F5
Apply Image	F6
Selective Color	⇧F6
RemoveSkyCrud	⌘F6
Image Size	F7
Threshold	⇧F7
History Palette	F8
Color Range	⇧F8
Canvas Size	⌘F8
Info Palette	F9
Color Palette	⇧F9
Flatten Image	⌘F9
Layers Palette	F10
Channels Palette	⇧F10
Save & Close	⌘F10
Actions Palette	F11
Paths Palette	⇧F11
Horizontal Web	⌘F11
Options Palette	F12
Vertical Web	⌘F12

Get all these built in functions, and many more, by setting up the ArtistKeys actions. These are used throughout this book and will greatly help you with your work.

tool, you'll get a menu showing all the layers that currently have pixels at the location where you click. You can then choose the layer you want to access from that menu. There is at least one context-sensitive menu for each tool. These are a great set of

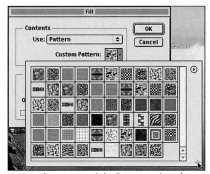

Here we have accessed the Patterns palette from a pop-up inside the Fill command. These pop-up palettes, including the Brushes palette, can be resized by taking one click to open the palette and then a second click and drag in the grow box to resize the palette so you can see all the options within the shape window you'd like. Once you change the size of a pop-up palette, you hit return to close the palette. It will remain this size until you change it again.

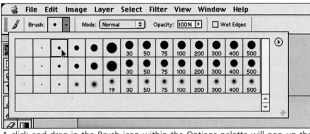

A click and drag in the Brush icon within the Options palette will pop up the Brushes palette and if you keep the mouse button down then release on the new brush you want. This allows you to choose a new brush with one click even though the palette is not always up on the screen. To edit a brush, first choose it as we just described then double click on it within the Brush icon in the Options palette. If you click once and release on the Brush icon in the Options palette, this leaves the palette open. You can then use the grow box in that palette to change its size then press Return or Enter to close that pop-up palette.

time-saving features. To learn more, see Chapter 4: "The Tool Palette" and also the step-by-step examples throughout this book.

PALETTES THAT YOU ACCESS INDIRECTLY

Some of the items don't have palettes that can be accessed from the Window menu directly. The Brushes palette used to be accessed from the Window menu in the previous versions of Photoshop but now you access the Brushes palette from inside the Options palette whenever you are using a painting tool, like the Paint Brush, Air Brush, Rubber Stamp tool, etc. To select a brush from the brushes palette, just Click and drag on top of the Brush icon at the left of the Options palette until the cursor is over the brush that you want. At that point, release the mouse button and the Brushes palette will disappear and leave you with the new brush selected. This allows you to get a new brush with only one mouse click and also without having the Brushes palette up on the screen all the time. This is a great new feature of Photoshop 6, once you get used to it. To change the shape of the Brushes palette, click on the Brush icon in the Options palette and immediately release the mouse. That will leave the palette up on the screen and allow you to go to the grow box in the bottom right corner and change the size and shape of the palette. The palette will now remain at this size. You can then choose the brush you want and then press Return or Enter to close the palette. The other palettes that don't actually occur in the Window menu are Gradients, Patterns, Contours and Custom Shapes. The Gradient palette is accessed from the Gradient Tool's Options palette, the Patterns palette is accessed from the Fill command, Contours is accessed from the Quality section of many of the new Layer Style options, and Custom Shapes is accessed from the Options palette of the Custom Shape tool. You will learn more about all these tools and palettes later in *Photoshop 6 Artistry*.

3 SETTING SYSTEM AND PHOTOSHOP PREFERENCES

Setting up your system and Photoshop's preferences to make Photoshop run more efficiently and make your work easier.

This chapter is essential for everyone to read and follow since it will set up Photoshop in the most effective way for you and also as referenced by the rest of this book. If you are new to computers or Photoshop, some of the discussions and settings here may seem a bit confusing to you. Before going on into the rest of the book, you should still read this chapter and set up your preferences as it recommends. Photoshop will run more efficiently and give you better results with your color corrections and separations. Your understanding will grow as you do the exercises and read the rest of the book. Before doing the color correction hands-on, you should also read and set up further preferences as described in Chapter 14: "Color Spaces, Device Characterization, and Color Management;" and Chapter 15: "Photoshop Color Preferences, Monitor, Scanner and Printer Calibration." Other chapters that are essential for all to read are Chapter 16: "Image Resolution, Scanning Film and Digital Cameras" and Chapter 17: "Steps to Create a Master Image."

SETTING UP YOUR MAC

You may want to read this section with your Macintosh turned on so you can refer to your screen as you follow the steps outlined here. In the System Finder, choose About This Computer from the Apple menu. An information window opens, giving you the total memory available on your Macintosh and how much memory each application currently running is using. If you check this when no applications are running, Largest Unused Block tells you the amount of space available for all your applications in megabytes. An abbreviation for 1,024 bytes is the expression One K. 1024K (1,024 x 1,024 bytes of memory) equals 1 megabyte (Mb) or 1,048,576 bytes of memory. If you had, like I do, 288Mb of Total Memory, and your system software used about 40Mb, the Largest Unused Block would display about 248Mb. Your system can use this 248Mb for the applications that you want to run concurrently.

If you are going to use only one application at a time, then you can let Photoshop have most of this remaining memory. You want to leave at least ten megabytes of space free for desk accessories to run. I often use Photoshop and Quark at the same time, so I assign 160Mb to Photoshop and 20Mb to Quark, which leaves plenty for other applications to run. If I were working on a really large Photoshop project, I would assign all available memory to Photoshop. Still, I would leave the ten megabytes for desk accessories. When the system barely has enough room to run a desk accessory, it becomes more prone to crashing.

The About This Computer window with only the system running. The spaces for System Software and Largest Unused Block don't add up to exactly Built-in Memory because the system constantly borrows small amounts of memory for various purposes.

About This Computer on my Mac with the system, Photoshop 6, Netscape, and Quark running.

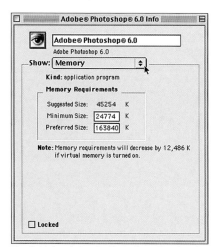

The Get Info window for Photoshop after choosing Memory from the Show pop-up. Here I have my Photoshop 6 set to exactly 160Mb of memory. 1024*160=163840.

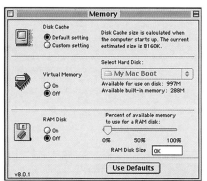

The Memory control panel and how it should be set for Photoshop. With my Mac systems that are running OS 8.6 or older, I have been leaving Virtual memory off, as shown above, but with my OS 9 and newer systems, I have been running with Virtual Memory on and that seems to work fine. Doing some Photoshop performance tests while working with large files might be the best way to determine the advantage of running either way. My systems have been so fast, I haven't worried about it.

To tell the system how much memory to assign an application, you first select the icon for the application from the Finder. You select an application icon by opening the folder that contains that application and then clicking (just once) on the application file. You need to do this when the application is not running, so don't click twice because that starts the application. Next, choose Get Info from the File menu in the Finder. An information window about that application appears. You then choose Memory from the Show pop-up menu. For every application, a suggested size and a preferred size appear at the bottom of the information window. Suggested Size usually refers to the minimum size that the application developer recommends for the application to operate efficiently. Preferred Size refers to the amount of memory this application is actually given when it runs. Some applications will still operate if you set Preferred Size to less than the Suggested Size and some will not. I would recommend an absolute minimum of at least 48Mb of memory to run Photoshop 6 on the Mac.

You can always set Preferred Size to more than Suggested Size, and that usually improves the application's performance level. Photoshop usually requires three to five times the amount of temporary space as the size of the file(s) you currently have open. It is much faster if Photoshop can put all this temporary space into real memory. If Photoshop doesn't have enough real memory for the temp space, it uses a temp file on the disk as virtual memory for its temp space needs. When this happens, Photoshop runs much slower than when everything is in real memory. Photoshop comes with its Preferred Size set to a default of about 45Mb. If you try to work on large files with so little memory, Photoshop operates very slowly. If you increase Photoshop's memory on your Macintosh, you should notice a great improvement in performance. I recommend at least 128Mb of real memory for any Mac that is going to run Photoshop. Adding more memory than that and assigning that additional memory to Photoshop will usually give you the most dramatic increase in Photoshop's performance for the money.

Several settings in the Memory control panel (Apple menu/ Control Panels/ Memory) are important to Photoshop's performance.

DISK CACHE

With OS versions before 8.5, Photoshop runs faster if you set the Disk Cache size to 96K—making it any larger just slows Photoshop down. Leave the Disk Cache set at the default value if using Mac OS 8.5 or newer.

VIRTUAL MEMORY

Photoshop has its own virtual memory system that is much more efficient for Photoshop than Mac Systems Virtual Memory. Therefore, it will make Photoshop faster if you turn off Virtual Memory in the Memory control panel. Power Mac owners get a message that system RAM requirements decrease by "x" if they use virtual memory. Still, Photoshop runs better on Power Macs with Virtual Memory turned *off*. If you don't have much memory on your system, running with Virtual Memory on may be better.

RAM DISK

Giving more memory to Photoshop using the Get Info procedure we just described makes Photoshop faster than allocating that same memory as a RAM Disk, so keep the RAM Disk off.

SETTING UP YOUR PC

When using Photoshop on a Windows-based machine, setting up your Photoshop memory usage is less complicated than on the Mac. Choose Edit/Preferences/ Memory & Image Cache from Photoshop and notice that the Memory Usage setting is 50% (which is the default). I set Photoshop on my NT system to use 80% of the available RAM. The more memory you have installed on your PC, the higher percentage you can allocate to Photoshop because there will still be enough left for Windows to run efficiently. If you don't have much memory, leave things at the 50% default, if you have lots of memory, give Photoshop a higher percentage. After setting this, click OK in the Memory & Image Cache Preferences dialog box. You need to quit Photoshop and then restart it for these changes to take effect. When Photoshop starts, it calculates the amount of available RAM in your system. Photoshop measures this RAM by taking the amount of installed RAM and subtracting any that is used by disk caching software, RAM disks and other software that permanently reserves RAM (including the Windows OS). You should have a minimum of 48Mb of RAM available for Photoshop to use. Check the Scratch Size and Efficiency box at the bottom-left of your open document to see how much RAM is available and how Photoshop is using it. See the "Plug-ins and Scratch Disk," section later in this chapter for more information on Scratch Size and Efficiency.

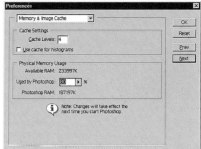

Here is the Memory Preferences dialog box from my Windows NT version of Photoshop 6. I've set this Photoshop to use 80% of the available ram. My 500 Mhz AMD Athlon K7 system has 256 megs of total RAM and it runs Photoshop very quickly.

SETTING UP THE PHOTOSHOP PREFERENCES

You access most Photoshop preferences from the Edit/Preferences or Edit/Color Settings menus. I go through setting the preferences in order and focus on the settings that are important for working efficiently with photographs. I also talk about settings that I believe should be different from Adobe's default settings. For a description of any Photoshop preferences that I don't talk about, see the Photoshop 6 manual, online Help or just hold the cursor over the preference setting and, if you have Tool Tips turned on, a yellow Tool Tips dialog will soon appear and give you a quick explanation of that item. If you are new to Photoshop, prepress or photography, you may not understand some of the concepts or Photoshop functions mentioned in this chapter. If so, just set the preferences as we recommend for now, and then reread this chapter after you study the rest of the book.

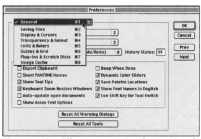

These are the different categories of general preferences. You can go to any one of them using this pop-up menu or by clicking the Next and Prev buttons. You can also use Command-1 through Command-8 to get to a particular dialog box. Command-K brings up the General dialog box and Command-Option-K brings up the last preferences dialog box you were working on.

GENERAL PREFERENCES (COMMAND-K)

COLOR PICKER

You usually want the Adobe Color Picker because it gives you more options than the Apple Color Picker. The Adobe Color Picker is the default Color Picker.

INTERPOLATION

Interpolation chooses the algorithm used when making images bigger or smaller. This process is called resampling because you are taking the current image pixels and either adding more pixels or taking some away. Bicubic interpolation is the most accurate way to resample photographs, so select it for the best quality. If you are prototyping ideas and speed is more important than image quality, you might try one of the other choices. Nearest Neighbor is the fastest, and poorest quality but can be useful for increasing the size of screen grabs of line art. It does no anti-aliasing so with screen grabs the sharp edges are not blurred with a size increase.

These are our recommended settings in the General Controls dialog box. All we do here differently from the defaults is turn off Export Clipboard which can make switching between applications faster.

REDO-KEY

Photoshop 6 gives you several choices for the way Undo and Redo work. The default setting does what Photoshop has always done by using Command-Z to continuously toggle between Undo and Redo. This is the option I recommend. If you choose the Command-Shift-Z option, then Command-Z marches back up the History palette undoing one state each time you press it and Command-Shift-Z marches back down the History palette redoing a state each time. With the Command-Y option, Command-Z marches back up the History palette undoing one state each time you press it and Command-Y marches back down the History palette redoing a state each time.

HISTORY STATES

Sets the number of History states Photoshop remembers. This is the number of Undo states you have and the default setting of 20 is a good place to start. When I am working on a very large file, I'll sometimes set this to 1 to make Photoshop faster since it doesn't have to make the sometimes costly saves of the entire file. When I'm doing retouching with the rubber stamp, I often set this to 99 to give me the highest number of undo states. See Chapter 8: "History Palette, History Brush, and Snapshots" for more information on this subject.

EXPORT CLIPBOARD

Have you ever seen the message "Converting Clipboard to Pict Format" while you impatiently waited to switch to the Finder or some other application? Turn off Export Clipboard to make switching between Photoshop and other applications much faster. You can still cut and paste inside Photoshop, just not between Photoshop and other applications.

SHORT PANTONE NAMES

Check Short PANTONE Names if you're exporting a PANTONE color as a Duotone EPS or in some other way to Quark, PageMaker or Illustrator. Make sure those other applications use the exact PANTONE names you used in Photoshop.

SHOW TOOL TIPS

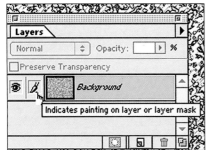

Tool Tips show up in many places and can help you learn the program and the icons.

When Tool Tips is on, you get a small yellow line of information that explains what each tool does when the cursor is on top of that tool. Displaying these tips, once you know the program, can slow Photoshop user response down. You can turn Tool Tips off here by unchecking this option. You can use the Tool Tips, for example, to get Photoshop's default explanation of each of these options, try it for the ones I don't mention in this chapter.

KEYBOARD ZOOM RESIZES WINDOWS

If this is on, then Command-+ or Command-- in Standard Screen mode will resize your window to fit the new zoom factor as you zoom in or out. Resizing windows for the Zoom tool is controlled using the Resize Windows to Fit option in the Options palette for that tool.

BEEP WHEN DONE

Setting Beep When Tasks Finish is useful if you have a slow computer or are working on exceptionally large files. It lets you go cook dinner while Unsharp Mask finishes up, for example. I used this feature a lot back when I had a Mac IIx. With my 400 Mhz G3, 288Mb of memory and fast hard disk, I don't need the beeps much anymore.

AUTO UPDATE OPEN DOCUMENTS

If Photoshop has a document open and that document is changed by some other application, like ImageReady for example, when returning to Photoshop, Photoshop would automatically read in that document again.

DYNAMIC COLOR SLIDERS

Dynamic Color Sliders allows the Color palette to show you all the possible colors, for future changes, on the fly, as you are changing one color. It is very useful to have this on when you're color correcting.

SAVE PALETTE LOCATIONS

Save Palette Locations remembers where you had all the palettes last time you shut down and restores them the next time you power up. This is very useful! If you turn it off then your palettes come up in the default state the next time you start Photoshop.

USE SHIFT KEY FOR TOOL SWITCH

If you hold the Shift key down, then typing M, for example, will toggle between the Rectangular and Oval Marquee tools, typing L will switch between the different Lasso tools. Turning this feature off means that typing M or L without the Shift key down will also toggle through the tool options with that shortcut key. Doing this without the Shift key down can often confuse the unexpecting user.

RESET ALL WARNING DIALOGS AND RESET ALL TOOLS

Various dialogs in Photoshop give you the option of no longer warning you about their particular issue again in the future. Reset All Warning Dialogs will bring all those dialogs up again until you turn them off. Reset All Tools returns all tools in the Tools palette to their default states. This may be useful if you have changed a bunch of tools to strange settings but remember that it may reset some settings you have changed specifically, like the change you'll soon make to the Eyedropper to read a 3 by 3 Average instead of a Point Sample.

SAVING FILES

IMAGE PREVIEWS

If you like to decide whether to save an Icon or Thumbnail whenever you save a file, then choose the Ask When Saving pop-up choice. You also can choose to Always Save an Icon and/or Thumbnail or Never Save one. Icon refers to the icon picture of your image you see when you are in the Mac Finder. Thumbnail refers to the preview you see in the Open dialog box on a Mac or PC. The Full Size option, mostly a waste of time and space, saves a 72dpi full size preview for applications that can use this—not many. In the Windows version of Photoshop, icons are not an option, but you can create a Thumbnail when saving an image. When you work on files for the Web, it is best to set these options to Never Save since any type of preview will increase your file size.

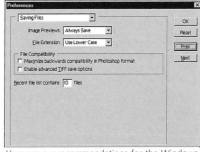

Here are our recommendations for the Windows Saving Files dialog box.

These are our recommendations for the Mac Saving Files Preferences dialog box.

Append File Extension

If you turn this on (either Always or Ask When Saving), Photoshop appends the correct three-character file extensions to files so they can be understood and opened on the Windows platform. The Mac knows the type of file you have without the extension. On the PC, the extension tells the software the type of file. Before Windows 95, Windows format files could have only eight characters in their file names before the three-character file extension (often called the 8/3 file format). If you want to make sure your file will be recognized correctly on any platform, use the 8/3 file name convention and use only lowercase letters without special characters; also, make sure you turn on Always and the Use Lower Case option.

Maximize Backwards Compatibility in Photoshop Format
(previously called: Include Composited Image With Layered Files)

I can't believe Adobe still has this on as a default! Turn this off please. The now twice renamed original 2.5 Format Compatibility option allows applications that can read Photoshop 2.5 file format to open Photoshop files with layers. If you have layers in your Photoshop files, Photoshop 2.5 format applications cannot see the layers, but they can open a flattened version of the layers whose Eye icons were on when the file was last saved. There is a BIG space cost for having this option on! Every time a file with layers is saved, Photoshop must also save a flattened version of the file in addition to all the layers. Turning off this Maximize Backwards Compatibility in Photoshop Format option saves disk space and time every time you are working on files that have more than one layer. A friend of mine, a software engineer at Adobe, didn't know about this option and was able to save several gigs of disk space by resaving all his files after turning this option off. If wasted disk space was an EPA pollution issue, Adobe would get a big fine for leaving this on as a default!

Enable Advanced TIFF Save Options

If you want TIFF files to behave the same as they did in Photoshop 5 or 5.5, then leave this option OFF, which is the default and the way I leave mine. Turning it on adds a lot of functionality to TIFF files, allowing them to save all of Photoshop's layers, save in various compression formats and more. Unless you need these added features of TIFF, leave this option off because you may create a TIFF file that some other application, like a print shop's page layout or rip software, may have trouble with. For more info on these new TIFF options, see Chapter 10: "File Formats and Image Compression."

Recent File List Contains

This controls how many files are listed in the new File/Open Recent menu. I set this to 10, whereas the Adobe default is 4.

Display and Cursors

Color Channels in Color

Leave Color Channels in Color off—it displays your Red, Green and Blue, or CMYK channels, with a colored overlay that makes it very hard to see detail. Viewing individual channels in grayscale gives you a more accurate image.

Diffusion Dither

When working on an 8-bit system, the Diffusion Dither option makes smoother transitions on colors that are not in the current palette. I like the Use Diffusion

Dither option to display 24-bit images on an 8-bit screen. I recommend leaving this option on if you will be viewing 24-bit images on an 8-bit screen.

TOOL CURSORS

The Tool Cursors settings are important! If you set Painting Cursors to Brush Size, now the default, you will paint with a circle outline the size of your brush. This setting even takes into account the current zoom factor and is very useful. I recommend this default Brush Size setting. Using the Precise option is like using the Caps Lock key, in that you paint with a cross-hair cursor. Standard uses the standard Photoshop cursors, a different cursor for each tool. I find that the standard cursors usually get in the way of seeing what I am painting. For the Other Tools option, I recommend the Precise setting, which gives you a very accurate cross-hair for all the non-painting tools.

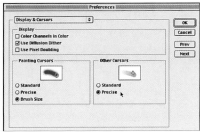

The Display & Cursors preferences. These are our recommended settings. Setting the Painting Cursors and Other Cursors settings to Brush Size and Precise is particularly important.

PLUG-INS AND SCRATCH DISK

The Plug-ins preference tells Photoshop where to find additional Plug-in filters. The default Plug-ins that come with Photoshop are already set up when you install Photoshop. On the Mac, they are in a folder called Plug-ins, directly inside the Adobe Photoshop folder that is normally installed on your boot drive. On the PC with NT, this folder is normally installed at C/Program Files/Adobe/Photoshop 6.0. You can always add more plug-ins to that folder and then restart Photoshop. Those plug-ins should appear within one of Photoshop's Filter menus, Filter/Other, or the File/Import or File/Export menu. If you want to get additional Plug-Ins from another folder that resides outside the Plug-Ins folder mentioned above, then check the Additional Plug-Ins Folder checkbox inside the Plug-Ins and Scratch Disks dialog. On the Mac, you can easily interpret the dialog box that then comes up incorrectly, or click the wrong button. When you find the folder that contains the additional plug-ins, you need to click the Choose button at the bottom right of the dialog box. Don't click the Open button at that point, like you would for most other uses of an Open dialog box, or you'll just open the folder to continue the search. On the PC you click OK after clicking on the folder that actually contains the additional plug-ins.

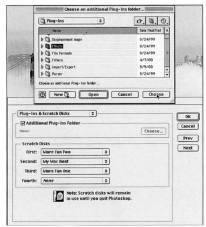

The Plug-ins & Scratch Disk preferences with the choosing Plug-ins dialog box above, which we accessed after checking the Additional Plug-Ins Folder checkbox. Make sure you click the correct Plug-Ins folder and then click the Choose button. Setting the First Scratch disk to your largest, fastest drive, not necessarily the default boot drive, is also important for Photoshop performance. Also set the Second, Third, and Fourth choice if you have that many drives.

The Scratch Disk preference tells Photoshop where to store temporary files on disk. Even if you give Photoshop plenty of memory, it also stores things on a scratch disk. In fact, Photoshop requires more scratch disk space than the amount of memory you assign to it. Use the largest, fastest disk drive you can afford for your primary (First) scratch disk. If you purchase a Mac that has a built-in drive and then later go out and purchase a very large high-performance external drive or a disk array, you probably should specify that disk array as your primary (First) scratch disk because it will be faster than your built-in original drive. You can also specify Second, Third and Fourth drives on which Photoshop can store temp files when it runs out of space on the First drive. Try to leave at least five to ten times the scratch space for the size of the file you are working on, and certainly leave much more space on the disk than the amount of memory you assign to Photoshop.

Photoshop has a scratch disk efficiency indicator. To access it, select Efficiency in the pop-up menu at the bottom-left of the top window's border when in Standard Screen mode on the Mac. This menu is at the left side of the status bar on the PC. You can bring up the PC status bar from the Window menu. The efficiency rating changes depending on the amount of time Photoshop spends swapping image data in and out of RAM from the disk. If your efficiency rating is less than 100% for most

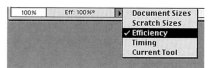

If the Efficiency is at 100%, Photoshop can do all its operations on this file without using the scratch disk. If Asynchronous I/O is working with your First scratch disk, you should see the * character to the right of the efficiency percentage, as shown here.

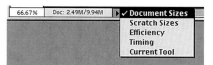

The Document Sizes option in this same pop-up shows you the flattened image size on the left (if you saved the file with no channels or layers) and the actual size including all the channels and layers on the right.

operations, you are using the scratch disk instead of RAM. You might want to add more RAM to your system to get better performance.

On the Mac, if the "*" character follows the percent display, your primary (First) scratch disk is operating with asynchronous I/O working. That is good for better performance because async I/O allows the disk to read or write while Photoshop does something else. If you don't see the "*", check the folder within the Adobe® Photoshop® 6.0/Plug-Ins/Adobe Photoshop Only/Extensions folder called "Enable Async I/O." If this folder *has* the character "~" in front of it, remove that character and restart Photoshop. This turns on asynchronous I/O for Photoshop's primary scratch disk. If you still don't see the "*" character, read the About Enable Async I/O document in the Enable Async I/O folder to learn how to set up the correct disk drivers for Async I/O.

The Document Sizes option in this same pop-up shows you the flattened image size on the left (if you saved the file with no channels or layers) and the actual size including all the channels and layers on the right.

The Scratch Sizes option gives you the amount of image data space Photoshop is using for all open images on the left and the amount of scratch memory space available to Photoshop on the right. If the number on the left exceeds the number on the right, you are using the hard disk for scratch space and likely are slowing Photoshop down. See the ReadMe file that comes with Photoshop for more information about improving Photoshop performance.

The Document Profile option shows you the color profile assigned to this file.

The Timing option will time how long it took to do the last operation. This can be useful in comparing performance on various machines or with different drives and memory configurations on a particular system.

The Current Tool option just displays the name and info about the current tool selected in the Tool palette. This information can be useful when the Tool palette is not on the screen, although I find that I can usually remember what tool I'm using and would rather have this window set to one of the other settings.

TRANSPARENCY AND GAMUT

The Transparency and Gamut preferences settings allow you to change the way transparent areas of a layer look and also what color is used to display out-of-gamut colors. The default settings work fine for us, but check them out if you want to play around some. You might want to change the settings here for certain types of images, for example, line art work where the line art has similar colors to the transparent grid.

GUIDES & GRID

The Guides & Grid preferences allow you to change the way Photoshop guides and grids appear onscreen. You can change the color as well as the types of lines (you can choose between Lines, Dashed Lines and Dots). You can also specify how often the gridlines occur and how many subdivisions each major gridline has. When working on Web and multimedia projects, I use the grid and guides to help place objects precisely. When you're in the Move tool (V or Command key), you can double-click a guide to bring up the Guides & Grid preferences, then easily change the colors and styles, and view these changes as you make them.

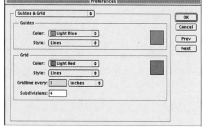

You should set the Guides & Grid preferences according to the colors of objects in the project files you are currently working on.

IMAGE CACHE

The Image Cache increases Photoshop's display efficiency when working with larger files. When Cache Levels is greater than 1, Photoshop makes several copies of the file in different sizes and uses the smaller versions to update the screen quickly when zoomed, working with layers and doing complex tasks. Leaving the Cache set to 4 seems to work quite well for both small and large files. With small files Photoshop will be so fast either way, you probably won't notice the difference and the extra memory overhead for the Cache is minimal. With larger files, you will want the extra screen refresh performance obtained using the Cache. The larger the image cache setting, the more RAM and disk space Photoshop uses when you open a file. If you don't have much memory and are working with very large files, you may want to reduce the size of the Image Cache. 8 is the largest Image Cache setting and 1 turns off the Image Cache forcing screen refresh to wait for calculations on the entire file.

We recommend leaving the Use Cache for Histograms setting off; having it on often gives you inaccurate histograms. The histogram you get with Use Cache for Histograms on depends on the current zoom ratio of your file. Leaving it off slows creating a histogram for a large file but ensures that your histograms always are completely accurate and consistent, regardless of your zoom ratio.

Leave the Use Cache for Histograms checkbox off to get accurate Levels histograms. If you turn this on, the smaller cache image will often be used to calculate the histograms. This will not be as accurate because the smaller file has fewer pixels being read. The default of 4 for Cache Levels is good.

UNITS AND RULERS

The Ruler Units setting in the Units and Rulers Preferences dialog box controls the scale on Photoshop's rulers when you go to View/Show Rulers (Command-R). It also controls the dimension display settings in the Info palette and the initial dimension display when you enter the Canvas Size command. Changing the setting in the Info palette also changes it in Canvas Size. We usually leave it set at inches, but for very detailed measurements as well as for Web and multimedia projects, we change it to pixels. There is also a Percent setting here which will display your scale, and also record your Actions using percentage of the total size. Turn this on when making Actions where proportional locations and sizes are more important than actual inches or pixels.

We usually leave the Ruler Units set to inches. When working on Web and multimedia projects, we change it to pixels to get very detailed measurements. The Units setting also controls the dimension display in the Info palette when selecting or drawing rectangles.

THE PRESET MANAGER

A new feature of Photoshop 6 is the Preset Manager. Choose Edit/Preset Manager to reach this preferences item. It allows you to set up which items you want to occur in various graphics and effects palettes, like the Brushes palette, the Styles palette, the Gradients palette and others. Some of the palettes, the Styles palette for example, give you the choice of replacing the current contents of the palette with the new Styles chosen, or appending those styles onto the list that is already there. By appending all the different Styles one by one and then Saving them to a new Style set, we've created a file called AllStyles.asl which contains all the Styles. When Styles are selected as the Preset Type within this Preset Manager dialog, you can use the Load button to load all the Styles from this file that are in the Preferences folder on the Photoshop 6 Artistry CD. We have also created AllGradients.grd, All Patterns.pat, AllShapes.csh and BarrysPhotoBrushes.abr, which you can load from the same

The pop-up menu shows the choices for palettes set up by the Preset Manager. Each of these palettes can have a variety of options chosen from them. Choose Edit/Preset Manager and then choose the Palette Type from the pop-up shown here. Notice another pop-up arrow just to the left of the Done button. This arrow gives you another pop-up menu with the available choices and options for the particular palette you are working with. You can also use the Load button to load a set of items for the palette you are currently working with or to save the items you've already set up for that palette.

In the Preset Manager, we have chosen the Swatches palette as the Preset Type. The rightmost pop-up allows us to choose a set of colors we want for the Swatches palette, the Web Save Colors this time. These sets of color choices are also available directly from the Swatches palette menu.

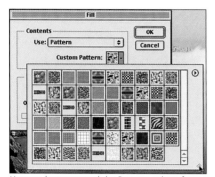

Here we have accessed the Patterns palette from a pop-up inside the Fill command. These pop-up palettes, including the Brushes palette, can be resized by taking one click to open the palette then a second click and drag to resize the palette so you can see all the options within the shape window you would like. Once you change the size of a pop-up palette, you hit return to close the palette. It will remain this size until you change it again.

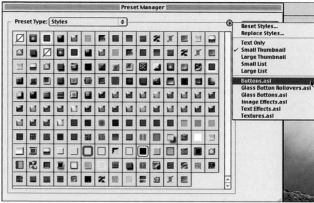

Our AllStyles.asl file contains the original styles plus Buttons, Glass Button Rollovers, Glass Buttons, Image Effects, Text Effects and Textures. It is fun to load all of these when you are playing around and learning what they do then you can later use the Style palette pop-up to load the subset you use most often. Keeping all of them loaded all the time makes extra overhead for Photoshop.

folder, provided you have the appropriate Preset Type selected. You can also load these from their perspective palettes.

PALETTES THAT YOU ACCESS INDIRECTLY

Some of the items within the Preset Manager don't have palettes that can be accessed from the Window menu directly. The Brushes palette used to be accessed from the Window menu in the previous versions of Photoshop, but now you access the Brushes palette from inside the Options bar whenever you are using a painting tool, like the Paint Brush, Air Brush, Rubber Stamp tool, etc. To select a brush from the Brushes palette, just click and drag on top of the Brush icon at the left of the Options palette until the cursor is over the brush that you want. At that point, release the mouse button and the Brushes palette will disappear and leave you with the new brush selected. This allows you to get a new brush with only one mouse click and without having the Brushes palette on the screen all the time. This is a great feature of Photoshop 6, once you get used to it. To change the shape of the Brushes palette, click on the Brush icon in the Options palette and immediately release the mouse. That will leave the palette on the screen and allow you to go to the grow box in the bottom right corner and change the size of the palette. The palette will now remain at this size. You can then choose the brush you want and press Return or Enter to close the palette. The other palettes that don't actually occur in the Window menu are Gradients, Patterns, Contours and Custom Shapes. The Gradient palette is accessed from the Gradient Tool Options palette, the Patterns palette is accessed from the Fill command, Contours is accessed from the Quality section of many of the Layer Style options and Custom Shapes is accessed from the Options palette of the Custom Shape tool. You will learn more about these tools

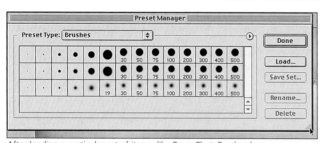

After loading a particular set of items, like BarrysPhotoBrushes here, you can use the grow box in the corner of the Preset Manager to make a window of the size and shape you want to view them. If you click and release on the Brush icon in the Options palette, shown below, you can also then use the grow box in that palette to change its size then press Return to close that pop-up palette.

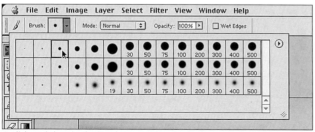

A click and drag in the Brush icon within the Options palette will pop up the Brushes palette and if you keep the mouse button down then release on the new brush you want that allows you to choose a new brush with one click even though the palette is not always up on the screen.

Chapter 3: Setting System and Photoshop Preferences

and palettes later; in this chapter you just get to see how you can use the Preset Manager to set up the initial options for them.

COLOR SETTINGS

The Edit/Color Settings Photoshop preferences are the settings that affect how Photoshop displays images on the computer screen, as well as how Photoshop does color separations. These have all changed in a major way between Photoshop 5 and Photoshop 6. Photoshop 6 is a very clean and mature implementation of what Adobe started to do with Photoshop 5. Photoshop 6 is now much more compatible with ICC profiles for different input and output devices and it actually lets you proof on the screen in RGB, CMYK and LAB what your image would look like on any device that has an accurate ICC profile. To use the power of Photoshop 6, you need to set these

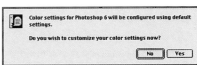

When you first install Photoshop 6, you will get this message about default color settings. These default settings are what Adobe believes people doing Web development might want. Choose either Yes or No in this dialog then set your settings as shown on the next page.

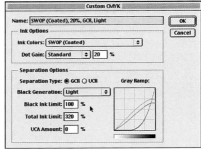

Here are starting values for the CMYK Working Space we recommend for output to coated stock. Make sure you set the Black Generation to Light and the Total Ink Limit to 320. If you have other CMYK needs those will be covered in more detail in chapters 14 and 15.

Use Edit/Color Settings to get to this dialog. Most of the settings here can be obtained directly using either checkboxes or the pop-down menus within this dialog. You need to turn on Advanced Mode, at the top-left, to get the Conversion Options and Advanced Controls shown towards the bottom of the dialog. Putting the cursor over each item will give you a short description of that item within the Description box at the bottom of the dialog. I will tell you a lot more about these in chapters 14 and 15, more than you need to know right now so go ahead and set these as you see here. To get the CMYK settings you see here, choose Custom CMYK from the top of the CMYK pop-up menu items then set your CMYK settings within that custom dialog as shown in the illustration to the right. If you don't get excited by using all these pop-ups and checkboxes, you can just click on the Load button and load the entire dialog box using the file called BarrysPS6ColorSettings.csf within the Preferences folder on the *Photoshop 6 Artistry* CD.

Color Settings preferences correctly for the type of work you are doing and for the Monitors, Scanners and Printers you are using. In this chapter we will show you the settings we recommend for working with photographs, but we are not going to explain these settings here because the explanation involves understanding a lot of background material. You should now set your Color Settings to the ones shown on the next page. After doing that, go on and finish the rest of the recommended preference settings in this chapter. To understand the Color Settings recommendations made in this chapter, you need to read Chapter 14: "Color Spaces, Device Characterization and Color Management" and Chapter 15: "Photoshop Color Preferences, Monitor, Scanner and Printer Calibration." The settings we give you here are recommended as a starting point, and in chapters 14 and 15 we will explain how to change them if you want to develop your own custom settings. If you are a beginner, we recommend that you continue to read chapters 4 through 13 in that order because you will get bogged down in color mania if you go directly to chapters 14 at this point. More advanced users, especially photographers and heavy color users, may want to read chapter 14 and 15 after finishing all the preferences settings described in this chapter. In either case, you may have to read chapters 14 and 15 several times to totally wrap your hands around the wonderful ICC color world Photoshop 6 now fully supports. By the way, we used the CMYK settings described here to create all the color separations in this book.

When you first install Photoshop 6, these are the default settings for the Color Settings dialog. They are set up to be the least offensive settings for people who don't have critical color requirements and who are probably not going to take the time to read how to set up their color. These are NOT the settings photographers and serious artists want to use. They may be the settings some web workers want to use although I imagine color management will soon become important on the web too so these may not be the correct settings for web folks either. To learn more about how to set you Color Settings, see Chapter 14: "Color Spaces, Device Characterization and Color Management" and Chapter 15: "Photoshop Color Preferences, Monitor, Scanner and Printer Calibration."

OTHER PREFERENCES RELATING TO COLOR

EYEDROPPER TOOL SETUP

Usually when you measure digital photograph values in Photoshop, you want the Eyedropper set to measure a 3 by 3 rectangle of pixels. That gives you a more accurate measurement in a continuous tone image because most colors are made up of groups of different pixels. If you were to measure a Point Sample, the default, you might accidentally measure the single pixel that was much different in color from those around it. Type I to get the Eyedropper tool and set its Sample Size, in the Options palette, to 3 by 3 Average. Setting the Eyedropper to 3 by 3 Average also sets up the Color Sampler to read a 3 by 3 average, which is what you want.

Chapter 3: Setting System and Photoshop Preferences

The last preferences items that you need to set up for color separations are the Highlight and Shadow settings, which you can reach by choosing either Levels or Curves. Here we show you how to get to them from Levels. Open the file named GoldenGate.jpg from the Preferences folder on the *Photoshop 6 Artistry* CD. Choose Image/Adjust/Levels, and double-click the Highlight Eyedropper (the right-most one). The Color Picker opens. For CMYK print work, you want to set the CMYK values to 5, 3, 3, 0, which is a neutral color for highlights. If all your other preferences are set as in this book, after you enter 5, 3, 3, 0 for CMYK, you should see 244, 244, 244 as your initial RGB settings. If this is not the case, double-check your Color Settings for RGB and CMYK Working Spaces and make sure they are the same as mine. Even if you are using different settings than ours, if your final output space will be RGB, you should make sure your RGB values all equal each other so you get a neutral highlight color when setting the highlight with the Eyedropper in RGB. Click OK in the Color Picker to return to Levels. Double-click the Shadow Eyedropper (the left-most one). Set the RGB shadow values in the Color Picker to 8,8,8 and check to make sure the CMYK values are 74, 65, 64, 92. If not, double-check your Color Settings. Click OK in the Color Picker and then click OK in Levels. To learn more about these Highlight and Shadow settings and how you use them, turn to Chapter 19: "Grand Canyon," which takes you through all the basics of color correction.

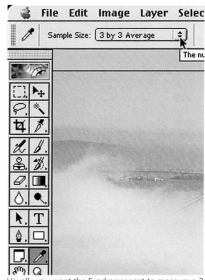

Usually you want the Eyedropper set to measure a 3 by 3 Average when measuring continuous tone color. Setting either the Eyedropper Options or the Color Sampler Options to 3 by 3 Average will set both of them to the same setting.

ARTISTKEYS TO SET UP YOUR ACTIONS

In the Preferences folder of the *Photoshop 6 Artistry* CD, we have given you a predefined set of actions, called ArtistKeysPS6.atn. You should add this set of Actions to your copy of Photoshop since we will be using them a lot in this book. To save any of your existing actions, choose Window/Show Actions and then Save Actions from the Actions palette pop-up menu. For Save Actions to work, Button mode needs to be off You have to have chosen one of the existing Actions sets and have its folder closed and highlighted. If Default Actions is the only thing there, you don't need to be concerned about saving these, since they are always available from Adobe. Now choose Load Actions, from the Actions palette menu, and pick the ArtistKeysPS6.atn file from the Pref-

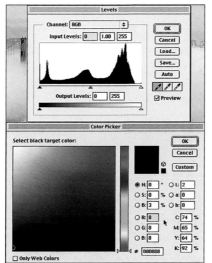

These are the shadow settings we recommend for CMYK coated stock, RGB output to film recorders, digital printers, and general overall color correction of a file. Double-click the Shadow Eyedropper in Levels or Curves to change these settings. Set the RGB values here to 8, 8, 8. If your Color Settings are set up as described in this chapter, your CMYK shadow values should now be 74, 65, 64, 92. If they are not this, make sure your Color Settings are the same as on the previous page.

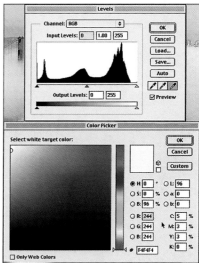

These 5, 3, 3, 0 settings are the highlight settings we recommend for CMYK coated stock. The corresponding values you get in RGB should be 244, 244, 244 if your Color Settings are the same as on the previous page. If the Red value comes in at 245, just change it back to 244 and the 5, 3, 3, 0 values should stay the same. If we were working on a document using a different RGB profile space, like ColorMatch RGB or sRGB, then the values for this same setting might change slightly.

erences folder on the *Photoshop 6 Artistry* CD. This will load Artistkeys and also leave existing actions in place. To replace all actions with Artistkeys, this is what I did, choose Replace Actions instead of Load Actions. If you choose Replace Actions you better save any actions, other than the defaults, that you previously had available. What we did to create ArtistKeys is go through all the menu items in Photoshop 6 and set up as function keys the ones that you will use most often. For example, F9

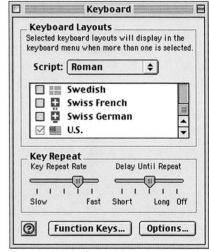

The Actions palette column (left):

Actions	
Tool Palette	F2
Navigator Palette	⇧F2
LevelsAdjLayer	⌘F2
Save For Web	F3
Color Table	⇧F3
CurveAdjLayer	⌘F3
Unsharp Mask	F4
Gaussian Blur	⇧F4
Hue/Sat AdjLayer	⌘F4
Duplicate	F5
Replace Color	⇧F5
Sharpen Only Edges BH	⌘F5
Apply Image	F6
Selective Color	⇧F6
RemoveSkyCrud	⌘F6
Image Size	F7
Threshold	⇧F7
History Palette	F8
Color Range	⇧F8
Canvas Size	⌘F8
Info Palette	F9
Color Palette	⇧F9
Flatten Image	⌘F9
Layers Palette	F10
Channels Palette	⇧F10
Save & Close	⌘F10
Actions Palette	F11
Paths Palette	⇧F11
Horizontal Web	⌘F11
Options Palette	F12
Vertical Web	⌘F12

The Actions palette with Button mode turned on and ArtistKeys loaded. In Button mode, you can click an action to play it, even if it doesn't have a function key alternative. All the actions shown here actually have function key alternatives. When loaded on the PC, the Command key functions automatically show up as Control key functions. The RGB file for this screen grab is in the Preferences folder on your CD. You can open it into Photoshop then print it on a desktop printer at a size allowing you to cut it out and tape it to the plastic next to your screen. This will help you to learn them quickly.

through F12 will bring up and close down the palettes you use most often. We tried to do this logically, so F9 is the Info palette and Shift-F9 is the Color palette. Both of these palettes deal with measuring color. F10 is the Layers palette and Shift-F10 is the Channels palette. You often use these together. I use F2 through F12 to implement single menu items (and we do mention these quite often in the book, so you will find them quick to learn). I mention these keys in context as alternatives, so you don't have to learn them if you would rather not. I consider F1, as well as F13 through F15, optional, so you can use them to reprogram other actions. You can also program many of the Command key Actions, as well as all of the Shift-Command ones.

IF ARTISTKEYS DON'T WORK

A former student from one of my Printmaking for Photographers workshop called me to complain that his ArtistKeys didn't work when he set them up on his home computer. It turns out that the problem is that, with OS 9 and possibly beyond that, there are defaults set up by the Mac OS for the function keys so they may not automatically work when you load ArtistKeys into Photoshop. If you have this problem with your Mac system, follow the directions in the two screen grabs on this page. If that doesn't solve your problem, please e-mail me and let me know at barry@maxart.com. I think you'll find the ArtistKeys function key set a valuable asset when working in Photoshop. If you ever want to use one of these function keys for something else, just Double-click the Action that is using that function key. This has to be done with Button Mode turned off in the Actions palette. Now set the Function key for that action to None then you can reassign that function key to another action. For more information about Actions, see Chapter 11: "Automating With Actions".

If your ArtistKeys function keys are not working properly on the Mac, this is more likely to happen with OS 9 and beyond, choose Apple Menu/Keyboard which will bring up this dialog. Click on the Function Keys button to bring up the dialog below.

This Mac dialog comes up after pressing Function Keys in the above dialog. To use your ArtistKeys function keys, turn on the checkbox at the bottom of this dialog labeled Function Key Settings, Use F1 through F12 as Function Keys.

Chapter 3: Setting System and Photoshop Preferences

Here we see how I have my palettes set up for Full Screen mode use on my PC. The setup I use on my Mac is similar. To get the palettes up into the docking area at the top-right of the Options palette, first drag each palette to the center of the screen using its Palette tab. That will separate it from any other palettes it is grouped with. Then drag each palette one at a time into the docking area in the order you want them to appear in that area. The first palette will be on the left and the last palette on the right. The palettes at the bottom of the screen can be opened by double-clicking on their tabs or by using the ArtistKeys function key for that palette. Double-clicking on the tab again will collapse the palette down around the edge of the screen. Using the function key again will remove the palette completely. The nice thing about learning the ArtistKeys for the palettes is that you don't have to move your mouse cursor or even think about where the palette is, you don't have to use the Window menu, you just press the right function key and the palette appears on the screen wherever you last left it.

SETTING UP YOUR PALETTES AND DESKTOP

When you have set all the preferences described so far, you should then set up your palettes the way you think you will like them. Here is one suggested setup, shown on my PC system on the next page. If you have trouble doing this, review the previous Navigating chapter to see how to work with your palettes. When you have everything set the way you like it, quit from Photoshop and the next time you start it, Photoshop will come up with all the palettes and preferences as you want them.

SAVING AND STANDARDIZING YOUR PREFERENCES

After you make major changes to your standard Photoshop 6 preferences, you should quit from Photoshop immediately. When you leave Photoshop, it saves its current state (preferences, tool option choices, palette locations, and so on) to several folders/files within the Preferences folder within the System folder named

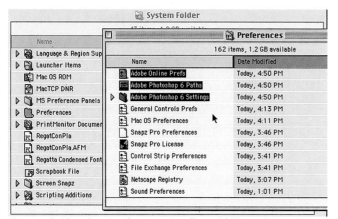

These are the Photoshop 6 preference settings files and folders and where they are saved on the Mac.

Adobe Photoshop 6 Settings, Adobe Photoshop 6 Paths and Adobe OnLine Prefs. On the PC, these files are at: C:\WINDOWS\ApplicationData\Adobe\Photoshop\6.0\ Adobe Photoshop 6 Settings. Quitting at this point ensures that Photoshop saves your preferences changes to these files. If you were to crash before quitting Photoshop, you would lose these latest preferences changes, and they would revert to the preferences you had when you last successfully quit from Photoshop

It is a good idea for everyone in your company to standardize on a set of separation and workspace preferences, especially for the same publication, and vitally important to standardize separation and workspace preferences if you are doing color corrections and separations. You can copy a standard version of these files to the Photoshop Settings folders on everyone else's machines, or print up a standards document and have your systems administrator make sure that everyone is using the same settings.

4 THE TOOL PALETTE

An explanation of each tool in the Tool palette with tips for usage and discussions of helpful, hidden features. General information about selections, cropping, painting tools, and other good stuff!

This is not an exhaustive tour of every tool with all its possibilities and applications. Several other very fine books, including the Photoshop manual, go into more detail. We try to give you all the information that you need for working with photographs. This is actually a lot of fun for us and we hope you enjoy it and take some time to play with these tools. As you begin to discover how the tools work, you can apply them to the type of images you have been creating and, perhaps, begin to discover new creative impulses.

The tools in the Tool palette are divided into groups that suggest their use. The top section of the palette contains the tools that are used to make selections, move selections or layers, or crop files. You might think of this grouping as having to do with boundaries or borders.

The second section contains image editing tools used for painting, erasing, sharpening, retouching and adding effects. If you want to manipulate the actual pixel information of a file or layer, you are probably going to use one of these tools.

The third section contains tools for dealing with vector shapes, whether Bezier curves, custom shapes, or type.

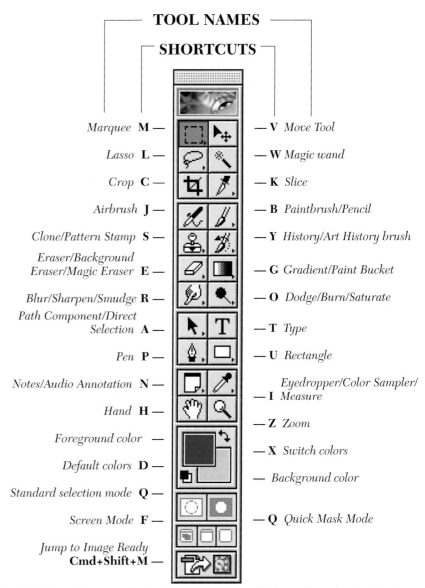

The Tool palette with corresponding keyboard commands. Copy this chart and paste it to the side of your monitor for a quick reference.

The fourth section holds tools used for viewing the file (Hand and Zoom), making annotations (Notes), and sampling color (Eyedropper).

Some of the tools in the Tool palette have a little arrow in their bottom right corners. Clicking it and holding down the mouse button shows other tools that you can access from the same icon area. Typing Shift plus the keyboard shortcut for that tool will cycle you through the available tools in most cases. I'll note exceptions in the information for specific tools. In the case of the Type tool and the Shapes tool, the different tools available show up on the Tool Options bar.

Here's the new Tool Options bar for the Gradient tool. You can see that it streamlines choosing the options you want. There's no extra verbiage here. On the far left is the "title bar" by which you can move the entire window to a new location. Next is the icon for the tool itself. Click this to reset this tool or all tools. The rest of the options available for the tool follow, and on the far right side is a docking bay for frequently used palettes. This keeps them both quickly accessible and out of the way. I really love his interface change, and I'm generally not a fan of interface changes.

THE TOOL OPTIONS BAR

Most of the tools have changeable options you view in the Tool Options bar, which is located by default at the top of your screen. This is new to Photoshop 6 and took a bit of getting used to. But both of us now find it much more convenient and less obtrusive than the old Options palette. The beauty of the new Tool Options bar is its context specificity. It's a very smart palette. If you are performing an action that does not affect an option on the current bar, that option will be grayed out and unavailable. I'll discuss the specifics of the options for each tool in that section.

If you choose a tool by either clicking or using its shortcut character, the options automatically appear in the Tool Options bar if it is present. If not, pressing Return brings up the Tool Options bar. For tools that have brushes, gradients, or patterns associated with them, you'll see an icon on the Tool Options bar with the current swatch. Click the swatch to access the options for that brush, or gradient. Click the pop-up arrow to access the palette for other swatches to choose from. Clicking either swatch or pop-up arrow on the pattern icon brings up the palette, as you cannot change options of patterns.

CONTEXT-SENSITIVE MENUS

Holding down the Control key (right mouse button on Windows) and clicking on the screen up a context-sensitive menu of commands you can execute with the current tool and/or options you can set. This is a very powerful feature because the items in this context sensitive menu may actually come from several different regular menus in Photoshop and are chosen based on Photoshop's state when you click Control. We point out these-context sensitive menus as you go through this chapter.

THE SELECTION TOOLS

The first section of the Tool palette are the three primary selection tools. In conjunction with items

This is the menu that comes up when you Control-click the Marquee tool and have no current selection loaded, but you do have selections saved in mask channels.

This is the menu that comes up when you Control-click the Marquee tool and have an active selection. See how the menu changed depending on the context?

from the Selection menu and the Pen tool (which we discuss later), you can isolate portions of your image for editing.

Marquee Tool

KEYBOARD SHORTCUT: Type the letter M. Type Shift-M to toggle between the Rectangular and Elliptical Marquees. Single Row and Single Column Marquees must be chosen from the Tool palette.

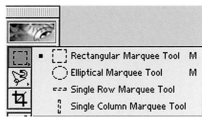

The Marquee tool pop-up menu.

You can use the Marquee tool to make rectangular or oval selections or to select a single row or single column of pixels. When you look at the Tool Options bar for this tool, you see the following areas:

SELECTION INTERACTION: The four icons after the Tool icon in the Tool Options bar control how a selection should interact with any current selection. The default is New Selection; that is, any selection you make will replace the current selection. Next is Add to Selection, which you can also accomplish using the Shift key and making your new selection. (It helps if you begin the new selection outside the old one.) Then Subtract from Selection, which you can do by using this icon or by holding down Option and dragging from within the current selection. Finally, there is Intersect with current Selection. This takes only the overlapping area of both selections and makes a new selection from it. You can also use Shift-Option-drag to intersect selections. If you use the keyboard shortcuts, you'll see the icons activate as you hold down Shift, Option, or both keys. Pretty cool, if you ask me.

Along with using keyboard shortcuts to control selection interaction, you can now choose these icons from the Tool Options bar. From left to right they are: New Selection, Add to Selection, Subtract from Selection, Intersect Current Selection.

FEATHER: The Feather option allows you to set the amount of blend on the edges of your selection. A larger feather radius gives you more of a vignette effect. The amount of feather is calculated in both directions from your selection border. For example, a 15-pixel feather measures both 15 pixels to the outside of your selection area and 15 pixels to the inside, giving you a total feather effect of 30 pixels. We rarely set a feather radius on our Marquee tool, preferring to make a selection and then use Select/Feather from the menu bar to set the feather. This way, we can change our radius if we are unhappy with the effect. Also, if you make a selection with the Rectangular Marquee and the feather is zero, you can later choose Image/Crop to crop to that selection. If you set the feather to a non-zero value, on the other hand, Image/Crop is disabled.

The Option Bar also allows you to set the Feather and Anti-aliased features.

ANTI-ALIASED: You may have noticed that the Elliptical Marquee has one other option, Anti-aliased. Anti-aliased subtly blends the edge of your selection with the surrounding area, so you usually want to leave it on. It's also available on the Lasso and Wand tools, but it is grayed out on the Rectangular, Single Row, and Single Column tools, as no smoothing is needed for horizontal and vertical lines. Keep Anti-aliased on when you want your selection edge to blend with the surrounding area. Making selections with Anti-aliased off gives you hard edges that are jagged on diagonal lines and curves.

SELECTION TOOL TIP

MOVING A SELECTION MARQUEE: After you have made a selection, you can move the Selection Marquee without affecting the underlying pixels by clicking within the selection using any selection tool and dragging.

CONSTRAINED ASPECT RATIO: The Style pop-up menu allows you to choose a constrained aspect ratio or a fixed size for either the rectangular or oval marquee. You would use a constrained aspect ratio if you were making a selection that you knew needed to have a 4:5 ratio, for example, or a 1:1 ratio for a perfect square or circle. When you choose this option, you cannot input a unit of measure in the Width or Height entry area.

FIXED SIZE: A fixed size is useful when you know exactly the size in pixels of the print you want to make and want to

Constrained Aspect Ratio allows you to click and drag until you have a crop that you like while being assured the width to height ratio will be what you need.

When you use Fixed Size for the Marquee tool you can input mixed units of measure for Width and Height, such as 3 inches by 400 pixels.

crop to that size. Here, if you click down with the Marquee tool, you get a rectangular selection of the size that you specified. By keeping the mouse button down while moving the mouse, you can move the selection around the image to find exactly the crop you desire. Of course, you can also use this option simply to select and edit an area of a specific size.

SINGLE ROW AND SINGLE COLUMN: Single Row and Single Column are just that. Single Row gives you a selection 1 pixel high all the way across your file; Single Column selects 1 pixel top to bottom. We rarely use these selection modes, but you can use them to draw straight lines or as a quick guide to make sure things are lined up. Generally, though, the Line tool is easier to use for both purposes. This option also is useful for selecting single row or column artifacts introduced by scanners or bad media and then cloning into the selected area.

MODIFIER KEYS: Holding down the Shift key while using either of these tools constrains your selection to 1 to 1; that is, you get a perfect square or a perfect circle. Make sure you release the mouse button before you release the Shift key. If, however, you already have a selection, the action is different. The Shift key causes Photoshop to add a new, unconstrained selection to your original selection.

Holding down the Option key while drawing forces the selection to draw from the center where you first click down. This can be extremely useful, as you will see later in this book.

Holding down the Shift and Option keys while dragging gives you a perfect circle or perfect square drawn from the center.

Be careful how you click in a file with an active selection. If you click inside the selection, you may inadvertently move the selection slightly. If you click outside the selection, you lose the selection.

If you press the Spacebar after starting a selection, you can move the selection while making it and then release the Spacebar again to continue to change the selection.

LASSO, POLYGON, & MAGNETIC LASSO TOOLS

KEYBOARD SHORTCUT: Type the letter L. If you type Shift-L, the tool cycles through its three states.

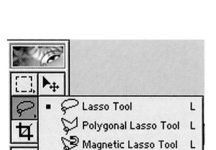
The Lasso tool pop-up menu.

Magnetic Lasso options.

You use the Lasso tool to make freehand selections. Although it's a little clunky to draw with a mouse, you'll find yourself using this tool a lot. You can always get a graphics tablet if you want to draw with a pen. Clicking and dragging gives you a line that follows the track of your mouse. After starting the selection, if you hold down the Option key and click, let go of the mouse button, and then click in a new spot, you can draw with straight lines between mouse clicks. Continue clicking this way to make geometric shapes, or you can hold down the mouse button and draw freehand again. When you let go of the mouse and the Option key, a straight line is drawn connecting the beginning and ending points of your selection, so be careful not to let go of the Option key until you finish your selection. Because the Option key in Photoshop 6 is used for deleting from a selection, you have to press Option after starting the selection to get the straight line behavior. If you prefer to use the Polygon Lasso tool, you can draw straight lines at every click, without using the Option key. In the Polygon Lasso tool, using the Option key after starting the selection enables you to draw in freehand. The Polygon Lasso tool requires you to click on the selection starting point again to complete a selection, as you also need to do

The Magnetic Lasso at work.

in the Pen tool to complete a path. With the Magnetic Lasso tool, you can set a contrast value for the edge that you're trying to capture, then draw freehand around that edge and let the Lasso decide how to draw the selection. Click the artwork to set the first fastening point. As you move the mouse, the Lasso lays down more fastening points to define the edge. You can click down at any time to manually place a fastener or hold down the Option key and either drag to access the regular Lasso or click to access the Polygonal Lasso. Draw until you reach the starting point and you get an icon that looks like the one in the Tool palette. If you let go of the mouse, the selection is made. If you double-click or press Enter before you get to your starting point, a line is drawn from the current mouse position to the starting point to complete the selection. Hold down the Option key and double-click to draw a straight line segment between the mouse position and the starting point. Needless to say, this tool works most easily where there is a good amount of contrast between the edges. But, with experimentation, you can get a pretty decent first selection using this tool, and then finesse the selection with some of the more sophisticated selection methods.

LASSO WIDTH: Set your lasso width wide enough to accommodate your drawing style but not so wide that you take in many additional areas around the edge you are trying to select. The steadier your hand, the smaller the lasso width.

EDGE CONTRAST: Edge Contrast is the minimum contrast that you want Photoshop to consider when trying to discern the edge. The lower the contrast between the edge you're outlining and the background, the lower you need to set the Edge Contrast.

FREQUENCY: Frequency governs the number of "points" that the Lasso automatically puts down to define the selection.

STYLUS PRESSURE: Check this box if you want the lasso width to respond to the pressure you exert on your stylus when using a pressure-sensitive tablet. The harder you press, the smaller your lasso width.

See Chapter 18: "The Car Ad," for more information on how to use these Lasso features as well as other selection tools.

Magic Wand Tool

KEYBOARD SHORTCUT: Type the letter W.

Whereas the Marquee and Lasso tools make selections based on physical proximity of pixels, the Magic Wand makes selections based on color values of adjacent pixels.

TOLERANCE SETTINGS: The tolerance that you set determines how close in value pixels must be before they can be selected. The lower the tolerance, the more similar the colors must be, and the higher the tolerance, the greater the range of colors.

CONTIGUOUS: You can choose whether you want Photoshop to select only those pixels within the tolerance value that are beside each other, or to search the entire image and select all pixels that fall within the tolerance. Where you click makes a difference.

USE ALL LAYERS: The Use All Layers option makes its selection based on a merged version of all the currently visible layers. Whether you want this option on

Tolerance: 32 ☑ Anti-aliased ☑ Contiguous ☐ Use All Layers

Magnetic Lasso options.

Here's the selection that I got using the default tolerance of 32 and clicking in the upper right area of sky with the Contiguous button checked.

Clicking in the same spot with Contiguous unchecked gives me a selection that would make a pretty good mask.

Use the Move tool with the Control key to find out what layers exist at a particular location in your file.

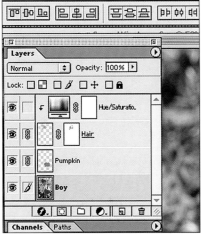

If you have linked layers and you are in the Move tool, you'll see icons for alignment.

or off depends on the type of image you are working with and the kind of selection you wish to make. If another layer affects the colors of the object you want to select, you probably want this option on. If all the colors you want to select are on only one layer, leave it off. But remember: Regardless of whether your selection is based on one layer or on merged layers, the edits that you make affect only the currently active layer.

THE GROW AND SIMILAR COMMANDS: The tolerance value that you set on the Magic Wand also affects which pixels you select when you use the Grow and Similar commands from the Select menu. The Grow command selects adjacent pixels that fall within this tolerance, whereas the Similar command selects pixels throughout the entire image that fall within the tolerance range. You can also change the tolerance setting on the Magic Wand between uses of these two commands, to select a larger or smaller range of colors.

MOVE TOOL

KEYBOARD SHORTCUT: Type the letter V or hold down the Command key.

You use the Move tool to move a selection (not the selection marquee—that you move with the Marquee tool) or the contents of a layer. Click and drag a selection or layer to move it to a new location within your document. You can also use the Move tool to drag and drop a layer from one document to another. If you are using any other tool, you can hold down the Command key to access the Move tool without deselecting the currently active tool.

Show Bounding Box shows you where the pixel information is on that layer.

AUTO SELECT LAYER allows the Move tool to activate the layer of the object that you click. This can facilitate moving objects around if the boundaries of the object you're selecting are clear. If you're having trouble selecting the appropriate layer, hold down the Control key and choose the layer from the pop-up.

SHOW BOUNDING BOX gives you a rectangle with handles that encompasses the area of that layer which contains pixels. If you move one of the handles you are immediately in Free Transform mode and the Tool Options bar will reflect that.

ALIGNMENT: Alignment options is available when working with linked layers, a selection and one or more layers, or multiple components of a single path (including multiple shapes on a single shape layer). If you have only two elements selected, you will activate only the first set of alignment icons, which allow you to align edges or entire elements with each other. If you select three or more elements, the second group of alignment icons will also activate, allowing you to distribute the space among the edges or the entire elements as well.

If you move the Bounding Box, you are in Free Transform mode and the Tool Options bar looks like this.

Chapter 4: The Tool Palette

THE CROP TOOL

KEYBOARD SHORTCUT: Type the letter C.

Before you make a selection with the Crop tool, the Tool Options bar looks like this. Here, I've clicked the Front Image button to input the dimensions of the currently active file.

Although we often use the Rectangular Marquee tool and the Image/Crop command to crop an image, the Crop tool is more powerful. To use the Crop tool, click and drag a box around the area you want to crop. The area that will be cropped from the image darkens. Click and drag on one of the handles (little boxes in the selection corners and edges) to change the size of the crop area. To cancel the crop, press the Escape key, and to accept the crop, press Return or Enter.

FRONT IMAGE: When you click the Front Image button in the Tool Options bar, the exact dimensions and resolution of the currently active image appear in the input areas. You can also enter proportions for the crop manually. Whatever crop you make will be constrained to these proportions and it will be resampled to exactly these specifications when you accept the crop by pressing Enter. Leave the resolution blank to maintain the specified aspect ratio and let Photoshop resample the file if necessary. For example, if you ask for your crop in inches, and the dimensions are larger than the area you selected, Photoshop lowers the resolution of the file after the crop but does not resample the crop area. However, if you ask for your crop in pixels and the crop is larger than the current file, it maintains the resolution of the image but adds pixels; in effect, it samples up the image. Click Clear to clear all input areas.

SHIELD CROPPED AREA: After you make a selection with the Crop tool, the Options bar changes and allows you to cover the area that you want to crop out with a colored overlay. You can choose the color and opacity. This helps you check the placement of your crop for more pleasing results.

PERSPECTIVE: Click this button if you want to change the dimensions of your crop disproportionately. This will stretch the image after the crop to fit a rectangle based on the area and shape you chose.

MOVING AND ROTATING: Click in the middle of the selected area to move the crop boundary without changing its size. Click outside the crop box corners when you see the curved double arrow rotate icon and drag to rotate the crop boundary. You can move the "center point" around which you will rotate the selected area by dragging it.

After you make a selection with the Crop tool, the Tool Options bar looks like this.

Click the Perspective button to allow irregular shaped crops. Using the Shield option colors the area to be deleted with an overlay. I've changed the overlay color to red to get a better idea of the area of the crop.

This is the result of the previous crop using Perspective.

Because I wanted to rotate my crop from the lower right corner, I moved the center point there before beginning the rotation.

The result of the rotated crop.

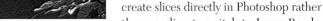

The Slice tool has few options and the style options are the same as for the Rectangular Marquee tool.

New to Photoshop 6: The Slice Tools.

SLICE/SLICE SELECTION TOOL

KEYBOARD SHORTCUT: Type the letter K.

New to Photoshop 6 is the ability to create slices directly in Photoshop rather than needing to switch to ImageReady. Slices divide an image into component sections for Web display. Each slice can have its own method of optimization that can increase download speed, and slices are the basic building blocks for animations and rollovers. For complex processing of images for the Web, you'll want to switch to ImageReady, but here's the basics that are available to you in Photoshop.

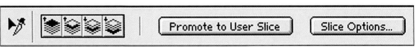

The Slice Selection tool has options that are new. First, the Stacking Order icons

Click and drag with the Slice tool.

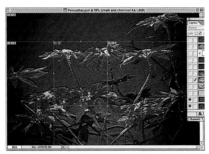

A User Slice is created where you dragged and Auto slices are created in the other sections.

The Slice tool works with a click and drag, similar to the way you use the Marquee or Crop tool. And like those tools, you can set a Constrained Aspect Ratio or a Fixed size for the slice you want to create. Before you create the slice, the only other options you need to choose are whether you want to see the slice numbers, and what color you want to use for the guidelines that delineate the slices. By the way, User slices have solid lines, Auto slices have dotted lines.

PROMOTE TO USER SLICE: Once you make the slice, Photoshop fills in the other areas of the file with Auto slices. These Auto slices regenerate as you make changes to the size or placement of User slices or Layer slices. Auto slices share the same optimization scheme, so if you want an Auto slice to have a distinctive optimization setting, you'll need to promote it to a User slice. If you double-click an Auto slice and set options for it, it automatically becomes a User slice.

SLICE OPTIONS: One of the reasons to

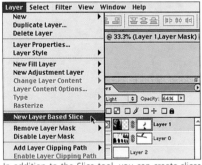

In addition to the Slice tool, you can create slices using the Layer menus.

In the Slice Options dialog box you input the URL as well as other information.

create a slice is to be able to set options for it such as a URL address. Use the Slice Selection tool, click the slice you want, and click the Slice Options button. Or, simply double-click the icon for that slice and the Options dialog box appears. The automatically generated name will appear in the Name input area. For URL, you can enter either a relative or full URL, which must include http://. If you have defined frames in your HTML document, you can enter a target frame in which the URL should open. Message text will display in the status area for that browser, rather than the URL. An Alt Tag will display on browsers that cannot use images.

Chapter 4: The Tool Palette

DIMENSIONS: If you are using User slices, you can set both the point of origin and the dimensions of a slice. Click the slice with the Slice Selection tool and use the Slice Options button, or simply double-click the slice with the tool to bring up the Options dialog box.

THE IMAGE EDITING TOOLS

Open the files CeramicFruit and Fish Art from the CD to follow the next part of this chapter.

The Pencil, Paintbrush, and Airbrush tools are the regular painting tools. The Rubber/Pattern Stamp, History/Art History Brush, and Gradient tools are more specialized painting tools. The Erasers, Blur/Sharpen/Smudge, and Dodge/Burn/Saturate tools edit existing pixels. Note also that the Tool Cursor options you set in your File/Preferences/Display and Cursors preferences control how your tool cursor appears. We use Brush Size for the Painting Cursors and Precise for the Other Cursors. Before we discuss each particular tool, we discuss the Brushes palette and some options that are pretty standard to all the tools.

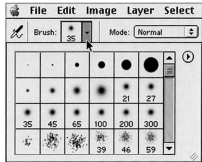
Click the pop-up arrow next to the Brush icon to get the currently loaded brushes.

THE BRUSHES PALETTE

All of the image editing tools other than the Gradient tool get their brush information from the Brushes palette. To see this window, you must be in one of the image editing tools that uses brushes, then click the pop-up arrow beside the Brush icon. The set of brushes is the same for all the tools except the Pencil tool, which has only hard-edged brushes. Each tool retains the brush and option set last used for that tool. You can add and save brushes or groups of brushes using the pop-up menu at the top right of the Brushes palette.

SETTING BRUSH OPTIONS: If you double-click a particular brush, or an area where no brush is currently defined, you get the Brush Options window, in which you can change the diameter of the brush, up to 999 pixels, the hardness of the brush, and the spacing. When you set the hardness to 100%, you get very little or no blending between the color or image you are painting and the background. A hardness of 0 gives maximum blending with the background. Try the same large brush with different hardness settings to see how it can affect the stroke. The spacing affects how closely dabs of the Paintbrush tool are placed together on the screen (the default value for this is 25%, which causes a 75% overlap of each dab, so it looks like a continuous stroke). To learn about spacing, set it to 100% and then paint using the

New Brush…

Reset Brushes…
Load Brushes…
Save Brushes…
Replace Brushes…

Rename Brush…
Delete Brush

Text Only
✓ Small Thumbnail
Large Thumbnail
Small List
Large List

Assorted Brushes.abr
Calligraphic Brushes.abr
Drop Shadow Brushes.abr
Faux Finish Brushes.abr
Natural Brushes 2.abr
Natural Brushes.abr
Square Brushes.abr

Quickly load brushes or change the look of the palette using the pop-up menu on the Brushes palette.

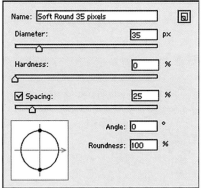
Double-click the Brush icon on the Tool Options palette to get the options for that particular brush.

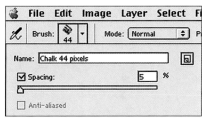
Custom brushes have only these two options.

NEW BRUSH TIP: *While you are painting, you can change the size of the brush by using the right and left bracket symbols, [and], on the keyboard. Pressing the right bracket makes the brush 5 pixels larger and pressing the left bracket makes the brush 5 pixels smaller. If you set General Preference Painting Tools to Brush Size, you can see the brush size as the brush sits over the area you want to paint. You'll see when you've reached the right size. Pressing Shift-] increases the hardness of a brush and Shift-[decreases its hardness in increments of 25%. Both shortcuts apply only to brushes created from the Brush Options palette. Custom defined brushes do not change and the shortcuts no longer cycle through the entire palette.*

Paintbrush tool with a big, hard-edged brush. At 100%, the dabs are tangent to each other on the canvas. Now try turning the spacing off (uncheck the Spacing box). With spacing off, the spacing is controlled by how fast you move the brush. Try it!

You can change the angle and roundness of the brush by typing values in the dialog box or by using the handles and arrow on the brush definition area on the lower left of the palette. The Brush icon on the Tool Options bar illustrates what that brush will look like.

DEFINING A CUSTOM BRUSH: In addition, you can define a custom brush by drawing a rectangle around all or part of an image and going to Edit/Define Brush. You can use a color or grayscale rectangular selection to define your brush, but the brush appears as grayscale in your palette. Consequently, if your brushes are built in grayscale with a white background, your results will be more predictable. When you paint with any brush, it uses the density of the gray in the brush to determine the amount of foreground color to lay down. After you have defined your custom brushes, you can use Save Brushes from the Brushes palette menu to give your new brushes distinctive names. You can save the brushes wherever you like, but if you've hit on something you think you're going to use again, save your brushes in the Photoshop/Presets/Brushes folder.

Photoshop 6 includes several custom brush palettes inside this folder already. Someone did a lot of work creating great new brushes that give you much better naturalistic results if you are used to painting traditionally or you've been using Painter. You can load these palettes or any palette you create by using Load Brushes from the pop-up options, or if you want to add those brushes to the current palette, choose Append Brushes. Reset Brushes restores the default Brushes palette.

COMMON IMAGE EDITING TOOL OPTIONS

The following options work primarily the same way for all the painting tools.

OPACITY/PRESSURE: Note the Painting mode and Opacity or Pressure settings on the Options bar. The default Painting mode is Normal and the default Opacity is 100%. Try out the different Painting modes and try painting with different opacities. You can change the opacity by typing in a number from 0–9 while using one of the brush tools (1 equals 10%, 2 equals 20%...9 equals 90%, and 0 equals 100%). If you type two numbers quickly, like 25, you can set the Opacity to that double-digit percent. Also, please note that the tools do not all handle paint buildup the same way. The Pencil, Paintbrush, and Rubber Stamp tools paint only in strokes. That is, if you lay down a stroke of color or image at a certain opacity, holding down the mouse button and moving back over that stroke has no cumulative effect. You must release the mouse and paint a new stroke to build up the amount of paint. In contrast, the Smudge tool, Focus tools, and Toning tools add paint cumulatively. Holding down the mouse button and moving back and forth over a stroke increases the effect on each pass. Finally, the Airbrush and Blur tools produce a cumulative effect whether stationary or moving. Changes continue to be applied in the mouse location until you let go of the mouse button.

FADE: The Fade distance causes color painted with the tool to fade to transparent or the background color over the number of pixels you choose for the distance. If you leave the Distance box empty—the normal setting—you get no fade-out.

STYLUS PRESSURE: You can vary the size, color, and opacity based on stylus pressure only if you have a graphics tablet instead of a mouse.

MODIFIER KEYS: If you hold down Shift when using any of the painting tools, you draw vertically or horizontally. Also, clicking once with the tool, letting go of the

To Access Specific Blend/Painting Modes	
for Macintosh Windows	
Option-Shift Alt-Shift	
plus	
Normal	N
Dissolve	I
Multiply	M
Screen	S
Overlay	O
Soft Light	F
Hard Light	H
Color Dodge	D
Color Burn	B
Darken	K
Lighten	G
Difference	E
Exclusion	X
Hue	U
Saturation	T
Color	C
Luminosity	Y
Threshold	L
Behind	Q

Chapter 4: The Tool Palette

mouse button, and then Shift-clicking somewhere else, draws a straight line between these two points with the current brush.

BLEND MODES: You can now toggle through the different Blend modes as you paint by pressing Shift-+ to move forward or Shift-− to move backward through the various modes. In addition, see the chart for the specific keystrokes for each Blend mode. These keys can also be used to change the Blend modes for layers.

AIRBRUSH TOOL

KEYBOARD SHORTCUT: Type the letter J.

The Airbrush nib looks similar to the Paintbrush except that it continues to add density as you hold down the mouse button and go over the same area again and again. If you click the Airbrush down in one spot and continue to hold down the mouse button, paint continues to be applied until you reach 100% opacity. Instead of the Opacity setting, this tool has a Pressure setting that controls how fast the density increases. Using the Airbrush is like painting with an airbrush

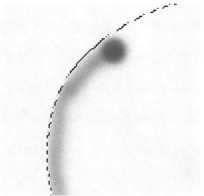

Here, I've used a soft-edge brush with the Airbrush tool. As I got to the top of the stroke, I held the mouse down and you can see that the paint built up in the shape of the brush.

Here, I've used four of the different variants of the Airbrush in Painter. More versatile, more realistic, and more fun.

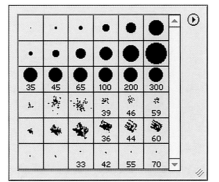

When you switch to the Pencil tool, all currently loaded brushes become aliased.

Turn on Wet Edges to have more paint applied to the edges of the stroke.

or a spraypaint can. For more of a real airbrush effect, use the Brushes options to keep the spacing and pressure low. You might also like the effect of turning the spacing off completely. Make sure you try out some of the Naturalistic brushes included in Photoshop 6 with this tool. If you want the feel of a real airbrush, I suggest you switch to Painter, which is far more realistic than Photoshop.

PAINTBRUSH/PENCIL TOOL

KEYBOARD SHORTCUT: Type the letter B. Type Shift-B to toggle between the tools.

The Paintbrush tool has anti-aliased edges that make the edge of where you paint blend more evenly with what you are painting over. When you use the Pencil tool, the edges of your drawing are jagged because there is no anti-aliasing here. Use the Pencil when you want to be sure to get a solid color even on the edge of the painted area.

When painting with the Pencil or Paintbrush, the Opacity setting from the Brushes palette is not exceeded so long as you hold the mouse button down, even if you paint over the same area again and again.

BRUSHES: Note that when you switch from an anti-aliased paint tool, such as the Paintbrush, to the Pencil tool, the brushes in the Brushes palette switch to hard-edge brushes.

For Rubber Stamp (aligned), Option-click at the pickup location...

...then click with no Option key at the location where you want to put down the clone. Notice the **+** that shows you the current pickup location, and the **O** that shows the putdown location. We have our Cursors preference set to Brush Size.

With the Aligned option on, if you let go of the mouse and move to a new location, the Rubber Stamp remembers the original location of your Option-click and maintains the relative distance.

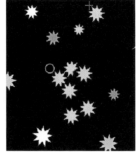

With Aligned not on, if you let go of the mouse and move to a new location, the Rubber Stamp begins cloning again from the original location.

In Photoshop 6, when you use Edit/Define Pattern you are prompted to name your pattern.

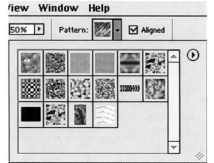

New patterns are added to the current Pattern palette, but you must save that palette with a specific name to assure you keep the patterns forever.

WET EDGES: If you turn on this option of the Paintbrush, more color is laid down on the edges of your brushstroke. It's sort of a watercolor effect.

AUTO ERASE: The Auto Erase option of the Pencil tool replaces any pixels that are currently the foreground color with pixels of the background color. You usually want to leave this option off.

RUBBER STAMP/PATTERN STAMP TOOL

KEYBOARD SHORTCUT: Type the letter S. Type Shift-S to toggle between the tools.

ALIGNED: Both tools allow you to choose Aligned if you want to paint a continuous image or Pattern, even if you let go of the mouse or stylus. With the Rubber Stamp, you can clone from an image onto itself, from one layer of an image to another layer, or from one photo to another. With the Pattern Stamp, you can lay down a pattern from the currently loaded patterns using a brush rather than the Fill command.

If you'd like to try some of the options that we show here, open the file Starry Night in the Tool Palette folder on the CD.

Aligned is the option you will use most often with the Rubber Stamp. You can use it to remove spots and scratches and also to copy part of an image from one place to another. To use it, pick a brush size from the Brushes palette, then hold down the Option key, and click at the location where you want to pick up the image (called the pickup location). Now, without holding down the Option key, click the place where you want to clone the new information (called the putdown location). As long as you hold down the mouse, information copies from the pickup location to the putdown location. Both of these move correspondingly when you move the mouse. When you release the mouse button and then move it and click down again, the relative distance between the pickup location and the putdown location remains the same, but both move the offset distance that you move the mouse. Therefore, you can clone part of the image, stop for lunch, and then come back and finish the job without worrying about misaligning your clone. This makes Aligned very good for removing spots. You can also clone from one image or one layer to another by Option-clicking in the pickup image or layer and then clicking down to clone in the putdown image or layer. See Chapter 19

"Overall Color Correction," for more information on removing spots and scratches with the Aligned option. In the Starry Night picture here, we've first been asked to clone a group of stars. The Aligned option works well for this.

You would use non-aligned (Aligned unchecked) to copy the same object into various places within the image. When you use this option, the pickup location remains the same when you move the mouse and click down in a new putdown location, which allows you to copy the same part of the image to multiple places within the image. When you want to change the pickup location, you need to Option-click again. Non-aligned would work better if you need to copy one star over and over.

PATTERN STAMP: Patterned cloning uses the current Photoshop pattern and copies it wherever you paint with the mouse. If the Align box is checked, different painting areas come up against each other; the patterns line up even if you have released the mouse button and started drawing more than once. This is the tool you want to use if you are painting wallpaper or some pattern that must match. To define a pattern, you select a rectangular area with the Rectangular Marquee and then choose Edit/Define Pattern. It is then added to the current Patterns palette. If you've added patterns that you really like and want to keep, make sure you save your Patterns into a file. In the example here, we used the file Fish Art, opened the Layers palette, and chose the Fish layer. We defined the pattern from a rectangle in the pink gill area, and then used the Pattern Stamp with Aligned on and our Blend mode set to Normal at 100%. Notice that even if you use discontiguous strokes, the pattern aligns correctly.

Non-aligned is the same as Aligned except that the patterns do not necessarily match when different painting areas come up against each other. You would not want to use this option to paint wallpaper, but by changing the Painting modes you might find that you can build up some interesting textures. Here we've used the same pattern but stroked the Pattern Stamp over the same area several times, letting go of the mouse each time. The patterns do not align. While you're here playing, try lowering the opacity or using Multiply, Screen, Dissolve, or Difference as a Blend mode to lay texture over the flat color areas. Groovy.

THE HISTORY/ART HISTORY BRUSH

KEYBOARD SHORTCUT: Type the letter Y. Type Shift-Y to toggle between the tools.

This brush works in conjunction with the History palette to give you multiple levels of Undo and multiple snapshots from which to paint. You have so many options now you can wander around painting different versions ad infinitum. My head hurts thinking about it. The quick explanation is: The position of the History Brush icon in the History palette determines the state of the file that you will paint from using the History/Art History Brush. One of the primary uses for the History Brush is to recapture effects or states that you used earlier in your work, but lost via undo or further manipulation. Although you can use layers to achieve some effects and, in general, layers give you more flexibility, learning to use the History palette effectively is often very useful. To that end we've devoted an entire chapter to its use, so make sure you read that at some point. One of the main points to remember about History is that it is layer

With the Pattern Stamp, you can paint the pattern wherever you like, including a channel.

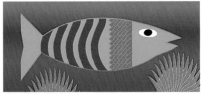
The original Fish art.

The History Brush gives you far more flexibility than the multiple undos of any other program. Here, even though we moved objects and ran filters on them, built new layers and layer masks, and changed Blend modes, we were still able to use the History Brush to paint 45% of the original Green Fan layer back into that layer for a 3-D effect.

These are the types of strokes the Art History Brush can make using the Styles pop-up.

The Art History Brush only paints in these Blend modes.

Style: [Tight Short ▼] Fidelity: [100%] ◄► Area: [50 px] Spacing: [0%] ◄►

The options for the Art History Brush.

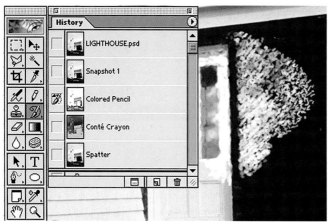

I made a snapshot of a filtered version of the file, then reverted and used the Art History Brush to paint from that version.

Mode: ● Paintbrush / Airbrush / Pencil / Block   Opacity: [100%] ►   ☐ Wet Edges   ☐ Erase to History

LIGHTHOUSE.psd @ 66.7% (Background,RGB)

The Eraser options.

The four different erasers at 50% opacity.

dependent. That is, you can only paint to a layer information that has existed on that layer. You cannot paint information from a different layer's history state.

The Art History Brush is another of Adobe's attempts to increase the capabilities of Photoshop to create artwork out of photographs. And although you can achieve some interesting results with this tool, it is unpredictable and takes a lot of playtime to discover methods that are particularly useful. My suggestion is: If you want to create naturalistic artwork out of your photos, invest in Painter.

For both the History and Art History brushes, you can use any brush shape currently loaded and you can use a Blend mode and different opacity. There the similarity ends. The Art History Brush uses Styles that control the movement of the strokes laid down, where the History Brush is completely dependent on the strokes you make with the mouse or stylus. The Art History Brush can only paint in a few of the Blend modes; the History Brush can use them all, plus Behind. The Art History brush has additional controls that specify how closely the color laid down will relate to the original (Fidelity), how large a space is covered by the brush (Area), and how different the source must be before the brush lays down a stroke (Spacing).

ERASER/BACKGROUND/MAGIC ERASER TOOL

KEYBOARD SHORTCUT: Type the letter E. Type Shift-E to toggle between the tools.

The Eraser tool erases to the background color in the background layer and to transparency in any other layer. The default background color is white but can be any color. Erasing a layer to transparent allows you to see through the erased area to the layers below it. You can choose from four options for the type of eraser nib: Paintbrush, Airbrush, Pencil, and Block. The first three give you eraser nibs that act exactly like their painting tool counterparts in respect to style, so refer to the Paintbrush, Airbrush, and Pencil sections of this chapter, respectively. The Block option is most like the eraser from early versions of the program. It does not have antialiased edges and the size of the area you erase is determined not by brush size, but rather by the magnification of the image that you are working with. The higher the magnification, the smaller your erased area, until you reach the point that you are erasing individual pixels.

ERASE TO HISTORY: You usually use the Eraser tool when you want to completely remove something in a small area. If you hold down the Option key when erasing or click the Erase to History option, you get an Eraser, which erases to the current position of the History Brush. For more information on using the History palette, see Chapter 8: "History Palette, History Brush and Snapshots."

BACKGROUND ERASER: is a much more refined tool that you will find more useful in helping to separate part of an image from the background. To those who have used Extensis MaskPro, the Background Eraser will be very familiar. The main

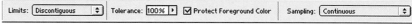

Limits: [Discontiguous ▼]   Tolerance: [100%] ►   ☑ Protect Foreground Color   Sampling: [Continuous ▼]

The Background Eraser Options.

Chapter 4: The Tool Palette

deficiency of this tool, however, is that, like the Magic Eraser, it deletes image information and replaces it with transparency. If you want to ensure that necessary pixel information is not being thrown away, you need to duplicate the image onto a new layer, as described above, so that the Background Eraser performs its deletion on the copy layer and not the original image (be sure to turn the Eye icon off for the original, so that you can see the effect of the tool). This working method preserves a back-up copy of all of your image data in case you need to fill in any areas where the eraser's choices were less than satisfactory. The downside of this is that, in making a duplicate layer of the entire image, you are effectively doubling your file size which results in more memory and disk space requirements, and on large image files, can cause Photoshop to run slower.

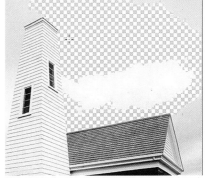

One click in the sky with the Magic Eraser and a Tolerance of 12 deleted this area. Although it's possible to delete the entire sky with this tool, you'd have to be very careful not to erase pixels of the light colors on the lighthouse as you erase light colored pixels in the sky.

The Options palette for the Background Eraser has three main settings that affect how it performs pixel deletion.

LIMITS: Discontiguous will erase the sampled color wherever it occurs in the layer; Contiguous will erase areas that contain the sampled color and are connected to one another; and Find Edges will erase the sampled color in contiguous areas, but do a better job at preserving the sharpness of object edges.

SAMPLING: From the Sampling options, you can choose Continuous to sample colors continuously as you drag through the image. This option is best for erasing adjoining areas that are different in color. The Once option will only erase areas containing the color you first click. This is best for deleting a solid-colored area. The Background Swatch option will erase only areas containing the current background color.

You may find you need to change the Limits and Sampling options from file to file or even within the same file to Use the Background Eraser effectively.

TOLERANCE: Finally, you set a Tolerance value much as with the Magic Wand tool. A low tolerance erases areas that are very similar to the sampled color, and a high tolerance erases a broader range of colors.

MAGIC ERASER: This tool functions much like the Paint Bucket tool but clears an area to transparency instead of filling it with color. Another way to achieve the same effect would be to click with the Magic Wand and then delete the resulting selection. Like the Wand and the Bucket tools, it has a tolerance setting to determine the range of pixels that are deleted, as well as Anti-Alias and Contiguous options. The Magic Eraser is useful mainly on images where there is a clear difference between what you want to delete and what you want to keep. And, true to its name, it erases pixel information, leaving you with transparency.

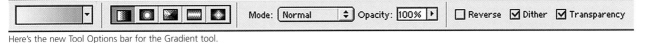

Here's the new Tool Options bar for the Gradient tool.

GRADIENT TOOL/PAINT BUCKET

KEYBOARD SHORTCUT: Type the letter G. Type Shift-G to toggle between the tools.

The basic function of the Gradient tool is to make a gradual blend in the selected area from one color to another color. A blend is accomplished by clicking and dragging a line the length and angle you want the blend to happen. The Gradient tool is often used in a mask channel to blend two images together seamlessly by making a blend from black to white. Black represents one image and white the other. If you'd like to experiment with the tool, open the files The Leaf and GrColOrPur from the Tool palette folder on the CD. You can use Select/Load Selection to load the Leaf Mask as a selection.

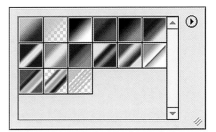

This is the default Gradient Palette. The first, second and last swatches depend on the currently selected foreground color. The first swatch is Foreground to Background and uses both of the current colors on the Tool palette.

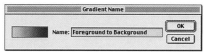

Double-click any swatch to view the name or to rename the swatch.

The TheLeaf file. Open this file if you want to play along with the Gradient tool. Now use Select/Load selection to load the Leaf Mask.

This file, called GrColOrPur, has an orange foreground and purple background. These are the colors we used to illustrate the Gradient tool. To use the same colors as you experiment, use the Eyedropper tool by itself to click the orange square and set your foreground color. Then hold down the Option key with the Eyedropper and click on the purple square to set your background color.

A blend across the selected area with the default setting…

…gives a blend from foreground to background with 50% of each color at the midway point.

A blend that begins or ends before the selection boundaries…

…will be 100% of the foreground color before the beginning of the blend and 100% of the background color after the blend line ends. When using the default settings, the midpoint, where color is 50% foreground and 50% background, will still be at the midway point.

We'll also do a few tricks with layers, so you might want to open the Fish file again. Show the Layers palette (Window/Show Layers) and click the name of the appropriate layer. Turn on the Preserve Transparency option.

You choose the actual gradient colors that you want to use via the Gradient Palette, which appears when you use the pop-up on the Gradient Color icon on the Tool Options bar. The default setting is Foreground to Background and will compute a gradient for you based on the currently selected foreground and background colors. Using the default palette, the second icon is for Foreground to Transparent. The final icon in this palette is Transparent Stripes and also uses the current foreground color as the strip color. Double-click a swatch to view its name or to rename it. Clicking once on the color swatch brings up the Gradient Editor, which is discussed later in this section.

THE DEFAULT SETTINGS: When you set the Blend mode to Normal, the Type to Linear, and the Gradient to Foreground to Background, everything from the first click on the line to the edge of the selection is solid foreground color. Everything from the mouse release to the other end of the selection is solid background color. Along the line, there is a blend from foreground to background color, and at a place 50% along the length of the line, the two colors each at 50% opacity.

GRADIENT TYPES: Photoshop 6 has five types of Gradient blends: Linear, Radial, Angle, Reflected, and Diamond. These are represented by the group of five icons on the Tool Options bar. Linear is the default and makes a blend based on a straight line that you draw at any angle. Radial creates a radial blend done as a circle. If Gradient is set to Foreground to Background, the first click of the mouse is the circle's center using the foreground color, the line length that you drag is the circle's radius, and the mouse release location is at the outside edge of a blended circle using the background color. The Angle blend gives the effect of sweeping a radius around a circle. The line you draw is the "angle" of the radius in the foreground color (or first color of the blend) that then sweeps around the circle changing gradually to the background color (or moves through the colors of your selected blend). The Reflected gradient reflects two symmetrical linear gradients outward from your starting point, and the Diamond gradient uses the line you draw as one of the corners of the diamond shape that is created.

BLEND MODES AND OPACITY: You can set the Blend mode and Opacity of the gradient you are about to create using these settings in the Gradient Options palette. We discuss the various blend modes in Chapter 31: "Blend Modes, Calculations, and

Chapter 4: The Tool Palette

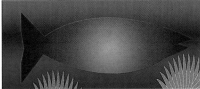

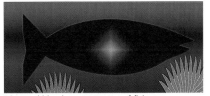

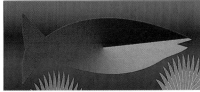

Linear blend from orange to purple, fins to mouth.

Radial blend center to top of fish.

Angle blend, center to nose of fish.

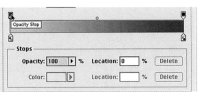

Reflected blend, center to top of fish.

Diamond blend, center to top of fish.

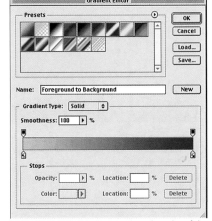

Here we made a copy of the Fish layer and then used the reflected blend shown above on the top copy. We then set the Blend mode of the top layer to Hard Light at 100% opacity.

Apply Image." However, you might want to try some of the modes, like Color, Multiply, Difference, and Hard Light as you explore the Gradient tool.

THE DITHER OPTION: Leaving the Dither option on results in smoother blends with less banding. We recommend that you leave it on unless you want a banded and uneven gradient.

THE GRADIENT EDITOR: Click the color swatch to access the Gradient Editor. The currently active Gradient palette is displayed along with the controls to create or edit any gradient. If you want to base your new gradient on an existing one, click the swatch of the existing gradient or use the Load button to load any other palette shipped with Photoshop or created by you. To modify an existing gradient, just select it and start making changes. When you have something you like, type in a name and click the New button. Your gradient will be added to the palette. If you want to save the gradient forever, you need to use the Save button and give your palette a distinctive name. Otherwise when you Reset the palette, your gradient will no longer be there. To remove a gradient, hold the Option key and click the swatch.

When you click a stop in either the upper or lower row on the color bar, you can change the color or transparency of a gradient.

Each square below the color bar represents a different color stop. You can add a new stop by clicking below the bar and you can move this point by dragging

The top row of stops are the Opacity stops. Click one to activate the controls for that stop.

The bottom row of stops are the Color stops. Click one to activate the controls for that stop. In this illustration the bottom stops use the foreground color on the left and the background color on the right. These stops look a bit different than ones you add yourself.

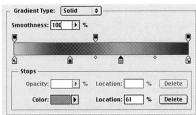

Here's a more complex gradient. The green color stop on the bottom is the currently active stop. Notice the different icons for the stops on the bottom row.

The Gradient Editor set up to adjust the color of the gradient. You access this by typing G to get to the Gradient tool, then clicking once on the color swatch on the Tool Options bar.

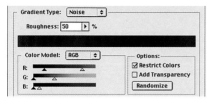

Move the color sliders to assign a range of values for Photoshop to use when computing the colors.

Here's the same gradient with the Roughness setting increased to 100%. With Restrict Colors checked the colors are not allowed to become oversaturated.

Once you uncheck Restrict Colors (especially with a high Roughness setting) the colors become very intense. If you check Add Transparency, certain values are made partially transparent or removed altogether from the gradient.

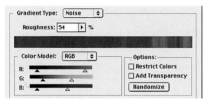

I used this Noise gradient as a Gradient Map layer to produce…

…this effect.

from left to right. The Location box tells you the location of this color as a percentage of the length of the line you draw to create the gradient. You can set a point to a particular color by first clicking that point and then either clicking the color box below and to the left to bring up the Color Picker and pick a new color or use the automatic Eyedropper to sample a color from any currently open file. The color point you are currently working on will have its triangle top highlighted in black. The little diamond points under the colored bar represent the halfway point between the color to the left and the color to the right of that diamond point. Click and drag it to have the Location window show you the location relative to the percentage of distance between these two points. The default location of the diamonds is always 50% of this distance, but you can move them left and right.

Click above the color bar to change the transparency of the gradient at points along its length. You can turn off the transparency of any gradient by turning off the Transparency checkbox on the Tool Options bar when you are using the Gradient tool. Try turning off Transparency and then using the Foreground to Transparent option. You get just the solid foreground color. The length of the bar again represents the length of the line you draw when making the gradient. You can place Opacity points anywhere along the bar by clicking above the bar. When you click a point, the top of it turns black, indicating that it is the point you are currently editing. The Location window shows you the location of this point relative to the total length of the line and the Opacity entry area shows you its opacity. The diamonds between stops show you the midpoint between the opacity stops. Bring the Gradient Editor up and play with it a bit and it will become obvious how it works.

NOISE: New to Photoshop 6 is the capability of building a gradient based on a range of colors. The application computes a gradient composed of colored bands spaced irregularly. The Roughness setting controls how radical the transitions are from color to color, with a lower setting giving you more of a standard gradient and a higher setting giving you something out of a technicolor nightmare. Use Restrict Colors to keep the colors from oversaturating. Transparency removes or partially removes colors from the gradient. Try using a Noise gradient as a Gradient Map layer. Turn on the Preview button and experiment with the sliders, buttons, and Roughness setting. As a gradient map, these gradients offer a quick way to explore color choices that would take much longer to generate as a gradient that you build yourself.

Chapter 4: The Tool Palette

PAINT BUCKET TOOL

The Paint Bucket tool does a similar thing as the Magic Wand in that it makes a selection when you click, but it also fills the selection with the foreground color or a pattern after the selection is made, then deselects after the fill. We seldom use the Paint Bucket, preferring to make the selection first with other selection tools and then, once we have the right selection, use the Fill command from the Edit menu. The Fill command (Shift-Delete) also offers more options than does the Paint Bucket. The Bucket is very useful and faster than Fill for colorizing black-and-white line drawings like cartoon drawings, animations, or solid color areas.

ALL LAYERS: If you are using several layers, you can choose which layers you want the Paint Bucket to search for the color tolerance range. If you click on Use All Layers and have the Eye icon on in more than one layer, Photoshop samples the data in every layer currently visible. The Paint Bucket fills only the currently active layer.

BLUR/SHARPEN/SMUDGE TOOLS

KEYBOARD SHORTCUT: Type the letter R. Type Shift-R to cycle through the three tools.

You can switch between the Blur, Sharpen, and Smudge tools by Option-clicking the tool, typing Shift-R, or using the pop-up. You use the Blur tool to help blend jagged edges between two images being composited, as well as to remove the jaggies from a diagonal line or just to soften selected parts of an image. You can use the Sharpen tool to locally sharpen an area without making a selection. Both tools work best when you try different levels of pressure (opacity) from the Tool Options bar, and you should start out with a low pressure, as they can work quite quickly.

The Smudge tool causes the image area you brush to behave like wet paint wet paint, You can click and drag to smear one color area into another. This blends the colors within the brush area, so the size of the blend depends on the size and softness of the brush you use. The pressure controls the amount of paint that mixes with each stroke and how far into the stroke the paint smears. At 100%, the color that you pick up is laid down the whole length of the stroke. If you hold down the Option key when you start a paint stroke or click the Fingerpaint mode, a dab of the foreground color mixes in with the rest of the colors being smudged.

USE ALL LAYERS: The Use All Layers option reads all of the layers that have the Eye icon turned on to make whatever adjustments are specific to that tool. If you are smudging colors, the Smudge tool looks at all colors in the current composite and smears them together. Ditto for Sharpen and Blur. But be aware that the Smudge, Sharpen, or Blur only occurs on the active layer, so make sure the layer that should show the change is currently active.

Sharpen tool after several applications.

Blur tool after several applications.

Smudge tool in action.

Orange foreground color mixed with the image with Fingerpaint mode.

The original image.

After dodging with the Dodge tool.

After burning with the Burn tool.

Several applications of the Saturate Sponge.

Several applications of the Desaturate Sponge.

Dodge/Burn/Sponge Tools

KEYBOARD SHORTCUT: Type the letter O. Type Shift-O to cycle through the three options.

You can switch the Dodge tool to the Burn or Sponge tool by using the pop-up Option menu, typing Shift-O, or by Option-clicking the tool. You use the Dodge tool when you want to make localized areas of your image lighter, and the Burn tool to make localized areas of your image darker. Both tools work best when you try different levels of exposure (opacity) from the Tool Options bar. Start with a low value, about 30%.

When you use the Burn and Dodge tools, you need to specify the part of the image area you are working on. Set Highlights, Midtones, or Shadows depending on the part of the image you are dodging or burning.

Truthfully, we rarely use these tools as there are better ways to burn, dodge, and saturate that are more flexible and accurate. But these tools will suffice for a minor fix.

The Sponge tool allows you to saturate or desaturate the area you brush over. It is very useful for desaturating out-of-gamut colors (colors that you can see onscreen but are unprintable) to bring them back into gamut (printable colors).

Vector Tools

The Path Component/Direct Selection Tool

KEYBOARD SHORTCUT: Type the letter A. Type Shift-A to toggle between the tools.

Photoshop 6 is far more vector savvy than any previous version of the application. If you are used to working in Illustrator, this will be a welcome change. If you're not used to the vector world, let me assure you that it's worthwhile to learn how to use the Pen tool and all its associated tools.

If you open the Fish Art file and show the Paths palette, you can click on the "fish art" path to activate it. If you use the Path Component tool and click the path in the image window, you select the entire path and can move the path by dragging it or copy the path by Option-dragging it. If you use the Direct Selection tool, you can choose a particular point to work with. Notice if you click with this tool on a point connected to a curved segment, you get "handles" that allow you to change the

To take a look at a path, click the Fish path in the Paths palette for Fish Art. When you click the path with the arrow, you'll see where the points are located. Notice the "handlebars" for the curved points.

Click the Fish path to activate the path. The icons on the bottom of the palette are for fill, stroke, make a selection, turn the selection into a path, make a new path, and delete a path.

shape and length of the curve. If you are using the Pen tool and hold down the Command key, you can also access this tool.

ALIGNMENT: The options for alignment are basically the same as those using the Move tool with linked layers. You must use the Path Component tool (there are no options for the Direct Selection tool) and all the subpaths you select must be in the same path. You cannot Shift-select subpaths from different paths. If you need to combine or align subpaths that are in different path layers, you need to copy and paste them into the same path layer. Select two subpaths to get the alignment options, three or more to get the distribution options as well.

COMBING SUBPATHS: Just as you can make multiple selections that add to, subtract from, or intersect with each other, you can combine subpaths of a path layer. However, the result depends on stacking order of the subpaths.

First, the basics. The four Combine icons are Add to, Subtract from, Intersect, and Exclude. You can choose which icon you want before you draw your subpath, or after. If you draw a single shape with the Add to icon active, your selection when you load the path will be the interior of that shape. If you draw a single shape with the Subtract from icon active, your returned selection will be the outside of the shape.

When you create a second subpath, both the stacking order and existing combine state can be important. If your first shape was a "Subtract from" shape and you create an overlapping "Subtract from" shape, you will, in effect, be adding those two shapes together. If, on the other hand, your second shape is an "Add to" shape, you will be subtracting from the first shape. Confusing for me, but those of you who understand math will get it fairly quickly.

This means that you can create two overlapping subpaths and change the selection that will occur when you load the path, by clicking different icons each time you load the path. The subpaths remain interactive with the icons unless you click the Combine button. At that point, the subpaths will always return the selection of the icon that was active when you clicked Combine, even if you select an additional subpath and use a different method to combine it. Play with the feature a bit; you'll see that it gives you much greater flexibility in making selections from paths.

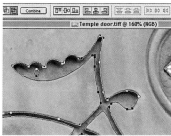

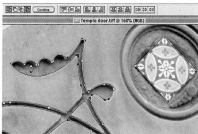

Choosing two subpaths allows you to use the first set of Alignment options to align vertically or horizontally using the edges or centers of the subpaths.

When you select three or more subpaths, you can distribute those subpaths as well as align them.

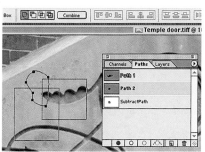

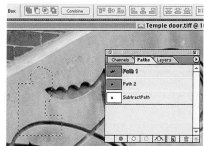

In this example the subpaths were built from left to right, so the irregular shape subpath is top in the stacking order. The first rectangle is "Add to," the second, "Subtract from" and the final shape is "Add to."

If you drag Path 2 to the Create Selection icon on the bottom of the palette, this is the selection that is returned.

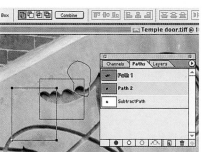

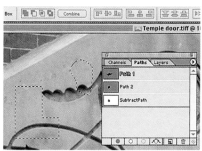

However, if you move the shapes so all three overlap...

...you get a very different selection when you load the path.

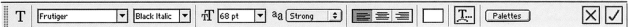

Here's the new Tool Options bar for the Type tool. The icons are for Type, Type Mask, Horizontal Orientation, Vertical Orientation. The first pop-up is for the typeface, then weight, size and amount of anti-alias. Then comes three icons for alignment, the Color square, the Warp Text button, and the Palettes button for accessing the Character and Paragraph palette.

Once you've typed in text and you select it, the Type tool Options bar changes slightly to look like this.

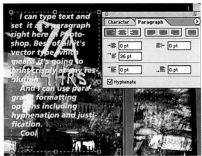

If you click and drag with the Type tool you get a bounding box in which to type Paragraph type.

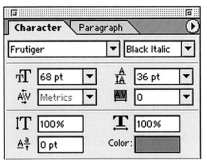

The Character and Paragraph palettes look almost identical to Illustrator's.

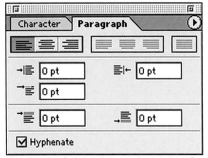

Photoshop has fairly good Paragraph controls. Unfortunately, you cannot set tabs so Photoshop is not appropriate for all typesetting jobs.

THE TYPE TOOL

KEYBOARD SHORTCUT: Type the letter T.

This is one of the major advances in Photoshop 6. Vector type that works. We use type in Chapter 34: "Heartsinger CD Cover" example, so you'll get some practice with it later. When you use the Type tool, you enter text by clicking on the image in the location where you want to insert the text or clicking and dragging to create a bounding box for paragraph type. (Text looks better if you have Adobe Type Manager installed and the Anti-Aliased option on, except for very small type). If you choose either the Horizontal or Vertical Type icon, type is added to your image as a new layer with the type surrounded by transparency. The layer is named using the characters that you just typed in, which makes identifying the layer easy. The two Type Mask tools add a selection of your type boundaries to the currently active layer. This is done by adding a "Quick mask" overlay that remains active until you hit the numeric key pad's Enter key. The regular Enter (Return) key just adds a new line for text. or click the Checkmark button on the Options bar. If a type layer is the active layer, you'll get a type mask but be unable to do much with it.

The best news is that you can edit the text onscreen. You can change the color, kern it, track it, baseline-shift it, and change the attributes character by character. If that's not enough, you can transform the layer or add layer effects and still have vector text.

The text comes in as the current color on the Tool Options bar. You can highlight portions of the text later and choose a different color in the Type Options bar. If letters on a type layer are colored differently, the color square in the Options bar will display a question mark.

Access type layers through the Layers palette, where you can modify the Opacity and the Paint mode of the layer. This cannot be done on a character by character basis.

THE CHARACTER AND PARAGRAPH PALETTES

The Character and Paragraph palettes appear when you click the Palettes button on the Type tool Options bar. Here's a quick rundown of what you'll find on these palettes.

FONT: The first entry area of the Character palette is for the font or typeface name. Sometimes the name starts with a letter that categorizes the weight or cut of the font. Generally, you look for the name of the typeface, such as Times or Garamond (we used Frutiger here), and then select the weight of the face that you wish to use, such as light, book, bold, or italic.

WEIGHT: The second entry area is for the weight of the face, which may be book, bold, light, etc. or may be prefaced by a number which describes the weight.

SIZE: The size that text appears depends not only on the size you choose in the Type tool Options bar, but also on the resolution and dimensions of the image you set using the Image/Image Size command. Luckily, if you resize your image, Photoshop sizes the type accordingly.

KERNING: Photoshop 6 allows you to kern letter pairs; that is, change the amount of space between any two characters. A positive number gives you more space between the letters; a negative number tightens the space. Click between a pair of letters you want to kern; then either type a number in the input area or use the pop-up.

LEADING: Leading is the amount of vertical spacing between the baselines of the lines of text. A positive number gives you more space between the lines, and a negative number, less space. If you set type in all capitals, a negative number usually gives better spacing between the lines.

TRACKING: Tracking refers to the horizontal letter spacing of the text. Whereas kerning is the space between any two characters, tracking is the space between more than two characters. As in kerning, a positive number gives you more space between the letters, spreading them out, and a negative number draws the letters tighter together.

SCALING: You can scale some or all of the letters vertically, horizontally or both by highlighting them and inputting values in the two areas at the top of the third section of the Character palette. Values are written as a percentage of the normal scale of the letters.

BASELINE SHIFT: Some or all of the letters may be shifted up or down from the normal baseline by inputting a value in this area. A positive number shifts the letter up; negative numbers shift the letter down.

COLOR: You can now click the Color square to change the color of the type at any time. You change the color of all the text when you click the Color square with a type layer active but no text selected. Use the Type tool and select letters to change attributes individually.

CHARACTER STYLING: You can find styles for capitalization, superscript, subscript, ligatures and faux styles in the Character palette pop-up menu.

ALIGNMENT: The first three icons at the top of the Paragraph palette (they appear on the Type tool Options bar also) are for alignment, either flush left, centered, or flush right.

JUSTIFICATION: The last four icons on the top of the Paragraph palette are for justifying paragraphs. All four justify the paragraph, only the last line is treated differently. You can align the last line left, centered, right, or (the icon that's set apart on the far right) force justify the last line. The specifications for how to justify the paragraph are set using Justify from the Paragraph palette pop-up menu.

INDENTS: The second section of the Paragraph palette controls indents. You can make left, right, and first line indents, which means you can set hanging indents. You can also set hanging punctuation from the Paragraph palette pop-up menu.

SPACE BEFORE/AFTER: The third section of the Paragraph palette allows you to control the amount of space before and after your paragraph.

HYPHENATION: If you want Photoshop to automatically hyphenate a paragraph for you, click the Hyphenate button. Hyphenation is set according to the settings you use in the Hyphenation dialog accessed via the Paragraph palette pop-up menu.

COMPOSITION: Photoshop is able to use both single-line and multi-line methods of composition. Multi-line is the default and usually gives better line breaks over the paragraph. Use single-line if you want more manual control over the breaks.

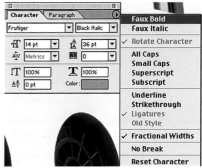
Faux styles and more are now accessed via the Character palette.

Photoshop can use multi-line composition to give paragraph text even color with fewer hyphens. To do this you select the Adobe Every-line Composer.

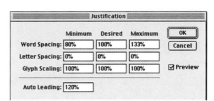
You can set desired word, letter and glyph spacing using non-justified text; minimum and maximum only apply to justified text.

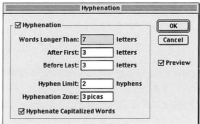
If you want to hyphenate paragraph text, Photoshop gives you control over how to do it, as you would have in a dedicated word processor.

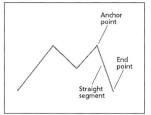

When you draw straight line segments, the anchor points and endpoints have no direction handles.

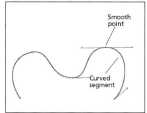

Each curved segment should have two direction points and handles associated with the curve, one at the beginning and one at the end.

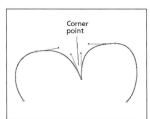

A corner point has two handles that work independently of one another.

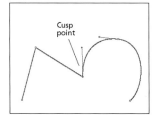

A cusp point that connects a straight line segment to a curve segment has one handle that helps define the curve.

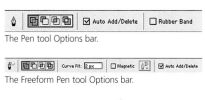

The Pen tool Options bar.

The Freeform Pen tool Options bar.

The Magnetic Pen settings..

AUTOMATIC FILL: If you have a path active in the Paths palette when you create a solid color fill layer, the color will automatically fill the paths. If you get unexpected results check the combine status of each subpath of the active path.

THE PEN/FREEFORM PEN TOOLS

KEYBOARD SHORTCUT: Type the letter P. Type Shift-P to toggle between the pens.

Photoshop 6 has added new functionality to the Pen tool, although it still "draws" just as it did in Photoshop 5.5. In earlier versions of the application, the Pen tool was used primarily for creating paths that could later be used as selections, or for painting pixels in a layer. It's still great for that. But now, you can also use the Pen tool to create vector shapes more like how you use the tool in Illustrator. Use it in conjunction with the Shapes tool, Shapes palette, and fill layers to create device-independent vector graphics.

When you begin to use the Pen tool, make sure you show the Paths palette. This is where you will name your path, fill or stroke your path, turn the path into a selection, or turn a selection into a path. You can also duplicate a path or delete a path. These options are available as icons on the bottom of the palette and from the pop-up menu. The pop-up menu is also where you can designate a path as a clipping path to be included with the file when it is placed in your page layout program (more on this later).

If you've never used the Pen tool, either in Photoshop or a drawing program, you might find it a bit confusing at first. Oh, alright, you might find it absolutely one of the most frustrating experiences of your digital life. But, we promise if you just keep at it, one day you'll have that AHA! feeling that lets you know that your hand understands something that your brain cannot and somehow you're just able to draw a path. You'll get your feet wet using the Pen Tool in Chapter 28: "Rain in Costa Rica" and Chapter 30: "The PowerBook Ad". Till then, let's talk about the basics.

The Pen tool works by placing points and connecting those points with line segments. A segment can be either straight or curved. Each segment has two points associated with it, a beginning point and an end point. (Are you with us so far?) Now, the points that control the segments can have handles. Notice that we say can. A corner point (that is, a point that connects two straight line segments) has no handles. A smooth point connecting segments in a continuous curve has two handles that are dependent on each other. If you adjust the direction of one of the handles, you affect the other handle in an equal and opposite manner. Simple enough so far. However, a corner point can also join two curve segments that are noncontinuous and abut sharply as in the two curves forming the top of this lowercase m. In that case, the anchor point would have two handles that work independently of each other. And finally, a straight line segment that joins a curve segment does so by an anchor point that has only one handle, which controls the direction and height of the curve. This type of point is sometimes referred to as a cusp.

To draw straight line segments with the Pen, click where you want to place anchor points. To draw a curved segment, click and drag. To make a corner point with handles that work independently, click and drag out a handle but after you drag, hold down the Option key to access the Convert tool. Use the tool to drag the handle in a different direction. The handle that controls the previous segment will not change but when you place a new anchor point, you'll have a corner rather than a smooth curve.

There are actually three types of pens you can use. The Pen tool works like Illustrator's Pen tool and basically the same as it has for many years. In recent versions of Photoshop there's also a Freeform Pen, which allows you to draw freehand style and place points as you go, and the Magnetic Pen (accessed from the Freeform pen), which judges the contrast between two edges to help you draw a path for use as a selection.

AUTO ADD/DELETE: All three pens allow you to automatically add or delete points on a previously drawn path simply by placing the tool over the path. If you are over a segment where no points exist, the Add Anchor Point tool appears. If you are over a point, the Delete Anchor Point tool appears. This option is on by default, and I find it easier to use when turned on. If you grew up on a previous version of the tool and find it annoying, turn it off.

RUBBER BAND: The Rubber Band option attempts to give you a preview of how the path will look before you place your anchor points. Barry uses it all the time. I think it's bogus. Your choice here.

CURVE FIT: When using the Freeform pen, Curve Fit controls how closely to your drawn path, points will be placed. You can input a value between .5 and 10 pixels. The higher the value, the fewer points will be placed resulting in smoother curves. However, if the number is too high you may find that the resulting path does not reflect the shape you drew. The default is 2 pixels, but you may find that 1 pixel works better if you draw with a very steady hand.

MAGNETIC SETTINGS: The Width is the width of the brush that covers the edge to be defined. It should be large enough to overlap the edge on both sides. The Contrast is how much contrast between values Photoshop should look for when deciding where the edge is. The Frequency is how often anchor points should be placed. If you want the brush to change size based on how hard you press, you can turn on the Stylus Pressure option (if you have a pressure-sensitive tablet). You can use the brush size shortcut keys (left and right brackets) to change the size of the brush also, and I find this easier than using stylus pressure.

The beauty of the Pen tool is that once you make a path, it is infinitely editable. You can add points or delete points, change the height or direction of curves, and even turn a curve into a straight line segment or vice versa. It may seem hard to believe if you're a Pen tool novice, but I know many Photoshoppers who rarely use any of the other selection tools. When you do learn to use the Pen, you'll have an in to the major drawing programs, and you'll understand why page layout programs are now including tools that draw Bezier curves.

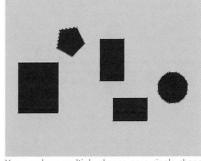

You can have multiple shapes on a single shape layer but all must be the same color.

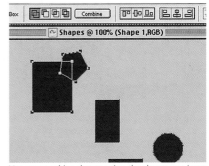

You can combine shapes using the shape area icons and the Combine button.

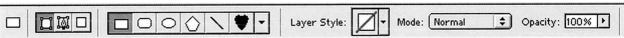

Once you've typed in text and you select it, the Type tool options bar changes slightly to look like this.

THE SHAPE TOOL

We'll go over the new Shape tool in detail in Chapter 32: "Layer Clipping Paths, Shape Layers and Layer Styles". But here's the short version. You can use shapes three different ways. You can make a shape layer, a work path, or a filled region on an existing layer. The first two shapes will be vector paths that can be edited and are device independent. The third is just like making a selection and filling it, you change the pixels and it cannot be undone later except via the History palette. These three options are the first three icons on the Tool Options bar.

The next set of icons are where you choose the shape you want. Click the shape you want and then click the pop-up menu to access the settings for that particular shape. There are especially neat settings for the Polygon and the Line shapes. The last icon in the group is the gateway to the Custom Shapes palette. Choose from the default shapes, load a larger Custom Shapes palette from the Presets folder, or create shapes yourself and save them to a new palette. If you have some cool shapes already built in Illustrator, paste them as paths into Photoshop, and then use Edit/Define Custom Shape to save them to the Shapes palette. Save the palette with a new name if you want to make sure you keep all your shapes.

These are the options for the Notes tool. The Audio Annotation tool has only Author, Color, and Clear as options.

OTHER USEFUL TOOLS

NOTES/AUDIO ANNOTATION TOOL

You can move the Note icon away from the actual note.

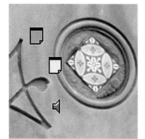

Choose different colors to quickly recognize notes from different authors.

KEYBOARD SHORTCUT: Type the letter N. Type Shift-N to toggle between the tools.

Another new feature in Photoshop 6 is the ability to annotate your files. You can use either written or audio notes but you must have either an attached or built-in microphone to record audio notes.

To attach a written note, choose the Note tool and click where you want the note to appear. You can also click and drag to create a notes box in which to input your message. Click in the input window to type your note. While you are there you can highlight the text and change its size and typeface. The color indicator on the Tool Options bar is the color of the note and the author's name. This can be changed from note to note, a quick way to identify the author. You can resize the input window and move the Window and Note icons independently of each other.

When you use the Audio Annotation tool, your options are limited to changing the author or the color. To play the annotation, double-click the icon.

To delete notes of both types, click once on the icon and hit the Delete key.

EYEDROPPER/COLOR SAMPLER/MEASURE TOOL

The Measure tool is now part of the Eyedropper/Color Sampler tool.

KEYBOARD SHORTCUT: Type the letter I. Type Shift-I to cycle through the tools.

You use the Eyedropper tool to choose the foreground and background color within an image onscreen. You can click the Eyedropper tool to use it and then click the color that you want to make the foreground color, or Option-click to get the background color. You access the Eyedropper tool by holding down the Option key when using any of the painting tools and then clicking where you want to pick up a new foreground color. You can choose to have the tool sample only one pixel to choose the color, or get an average color of 3x3 or 5x5 pixels.

AUTOMATIC EYEDROPPER: The Eyedropper tool automatically shows up whenever you are in Levels, Curves, Color Balance, or any of the color correction tools and you move the cursor over the image. This allows you to see the color values of any location in the Info and Color palettes while you are correcting and changing those values. As a preference setting for this type of use with continuous tone images, you should double-click the Eyedropper and set the sample size to 3 by 3 Average rather than the default Point Sample setting.

The Color Sampler tool allows you to place eyedropper-type samplers in up to four locations in your file. During manipulation of your image, you can watch how your changes are affecting the areas where you placed samplers. Samplers can be moved after they've been placed and can be hidden completely by using the Info palette pop-up. You can change the read-out values from RGB to CMYK, grayscale, HSB, Lab, Actual Color, or Total Ink percentages even in the middle of making adjustments to the file, by clicking the specific sampler pop-up triangle. You can delete a sampler from the screen by dragging it off the image. To see how the Color

Sampler tool can be used, read Chapter 22: "Color Matching Images."

The Measure tool measurements can now be viewed in the Tool Options bar as well as in the Info palette. If you create a line for measuring, it stays in place even when you switch tools and come back to it. The measurement does not stay after closing a file.

HAND TOOL

KEYBOARD SHORTCUT: Type the letter H.

Use the Hand tool to scroll the image. Scrolling doesn't change your document; rather, it allows you to look at a different part of it. You can access the Hand tool more efficiently by using the Spacebar on the keyboard along with a mouse click, which can be done any time. If you double-click the Hand tool in the Tool palette, the image resizes to the largest size that fits completely within the current screen and palette display.

You can set up to four Color Samplers and change the read-out at any time. Here, we've changed Sampler #3 to give us the Total Ink percentage while in the middle of a Curves adjustment.

This is the menu that comes up when you Control-click while using the Eyedropper tool.

This is the menu that comes up when you Control-click on a Color Sampler that you've placed in your image.

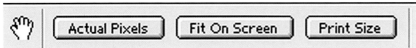

Here are the Hand tool options. These same items appear if you Control-click with the Hand tool.

ZOOM TOOL

KEYBOARD SHORTCUT: Type the letter Z.

Use the Zoom tool to magnify the image and, with the Option key, to shrink the image. The location where you click is centered within the bigger or smaller image. Using this tool is like moving a photograph you are holding in your hand either closer to your face or farther away. The actual size of the photograph doesn't change, only how closely you are looking at it. It is best to access the Zoom tool using Command-Spacebar-click to zoom in closer, or Option-Spacebar-click to zoom out further. You can use these command keys any time, even when a dialog box, like Levels, is up. If you double-click the Zoom tool within the Tool palette, the image zooms in or out to the 100% size. At 100%, the image may be bigger than the screen, but you see every pixel of the part of the image you are viewing. Use this for detailed work. The Resize Windows to Fit option resizes your normal window to surround your zoomed size, if possible. I leave it off because I don't like my windows automatically resizing.

5 PICKING AND USING COLOR

A look at RGB, CMYK, HSB, and Lab color spaces, what they are, when to use each, and how to access them from Photoshop; the Photoshop Color Picker and the Picker, Swatches, and Scratch palettes explained in detail.

There are different color spaces available in Photoshop that you can use for different purposes at different times. Instead of just working in one color space, like RGB or CMYK, it is a good idea to learn the advantages and disadvantages of the different color spaces. Photoshop has various tools for picking and saving colors. We summarize these color space issues in this chapter, mostly for how they relate to picking and choosing color. For more information on setting up and using the RGB, CMYK, and Lab color spaces in Photoshop 6, see Chapter 14: "Color Spaces, Device Characterization, and Color Management."

THE RGB COLOR SPACE

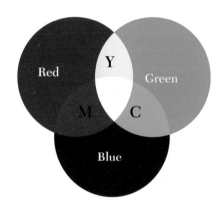

For overall color correction and ease of work, using the Red, Green, Blue (RGB) color space offers many advantages. I recommend keeping your final master files in RGB format. Red, green, and blue are the additive colors of light that occur in nature. White light consists of wavelengths from the red, green, and blue spectrums. All scanners, even high-end drum scanners, actually have sensors that originally capture the data in RGB format. You can use RGB for final output to computers, multimedia and TV monitors, color transparency writers, digital video, Web sites, and some digital printers because these are all native RGB devices. Plus, RGB files are smaller than CMYK files because they have only three components of color instead of four.

THE CMYK COLOR SPACE

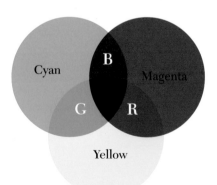

Cyan, magenta, and yellow are the complementary colors to red, green, and blue. Red and cyan are opposites, so if you take away all the red from white light, cyan is what you have left. Cyan is formed by mixing green and blue light. Green and magenta, as well as blue and yellow, work similarly; that is, they are complementary colors. When you print on a printing press, the colors of ink used are cyan, magenta, and yellow. These are called subtractive colors because when you view something that is printed, you actually see the light that is reflected back. When white light, which contains all the colors, hits a surface painted cyan, you see cyan because the cyan paint subtracts the red from the white light, and only green and blue reflect back for you to see. To print red using CMY inks, you use magenta and yellow inks. Magenta subtracts the green light and yellow subtracts the blue light so what reflects back to your eyes is red light. The cyan, magenta, and yellow dyes that make up printing inks are not pure, so when you print all three of them at the same time, instead of reflecting no light and giving you black, you get a muddy gray color. Because of this problem, the printing trade adds black ink (the K in CMYK) to the four-color process so the dark areas are as dark as possible.

THE AMOUNT OF BLACK

The amount of black ink, and the way it is used in the printing process, depends on the type of paper and press that you use. Newspaper presses typically use a lot of black ink and as little color ink as possible because black ink is cheaper. High-quality advertising color for magazines and other coated stock is printed with much more colored ink and less black. A skilled printer can create the same image in CMYK using a lot of black ink or very little black ink. You can combine the colored and black inks many different ways to get the final result.

CONVERTING RGB TO CMYK

Because of these different choices, converting from RGB to CMYK can be a complicated process. After an image is converted to CMYK, whether by a high-end scanner or by you in Photoshop, managing the relationship between the CMY colors and the black ink can be tricky. That's just one of the reasons you're better off doing your overall color corrections in RGB, so that you are taking a correct RGB file and then converting it to CMYK. You then end up with a CMYK file that has the black in the right place in relationship with the final, or close to final, CMY colors. The main reason to use the CMYK color space is that your final output will be on a printing press or a digital printer that uses CMYK inks or dyes. We discuss color correction in both RGB and CMYK as we present the examples in this book. Because you want to customize the creation of your CMYK file to the type of printing you are doing, and because colors can get lost when you convert to CMYK, you should keep your master file in RGB format, for the highest quality and versatility across all media.

THE HUE, SATURATION, AND LIGHTNESS COLOR SPACE

Another color space used in Photoshop is Hue, Saturation, and Lightness (HSL). You can no longer use the Mode menu to convert an image to HSL mode like you could in some older versions of Photoshop, but the many color tools allow you to think about and massage color using the HSL color space. Instead of dividing a color into components of red, green, and blue, or cyan, magenta, and yellow, HSL divides a color into its hue, its saturation, and its lightness. The hue is the actual color and can include all the colors of the rainbow. A particular red hue differs from a purple, yellow, orange, or even a different red hue. The saturation is the intensity of that particular hue. Highly saturated colors are quite intense and vivid, so much so that they almost look fluorescent. Colors of low saturation are dull and subtle. The lightness of a part of an image determines how light or dark that part is in

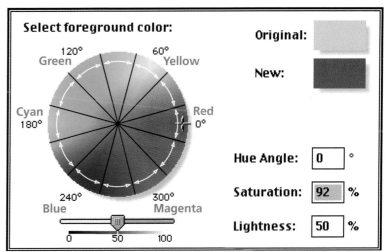

The Apple Color Picker can help you understand how Photoshop delineates Hue. I've broken the color wheel into 30° segments with black lines, and typed the names (in green) for the six true color segments. Photoshop considers Red hues to be the area from 345° to 15° with 0° being pure red. Cyan hues (red's compliment) range from 165° to 195° with 180° being true cyan. The in-between ranges (red/yellow, yellow/green, green/cyan, and so forth) are considered the fall off ranges when you adjust the hue in Photoshop.

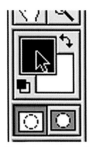

Click here to get the Color Picker and change the current-foreground color.

overall density. Lightness is the value in the image that gives it detail. Imagine taking a black-and-white image and then colorizing it. The black-and-white image originally had different tonal values of gray. The details show up based on the lightness or darkness of the black-and-white image. Removing the lightness value would be similar to taking this black-and-white detail part out of a color image. If you increase the lightness, the image starts to flatten and show less depth. If you increase the lightness all the way, the image loses all its detail and becomes white. If you decrease the lightness, the image may appear to have more depth, and if you decrease it all the way, the image becomes black. For working with the image using the HSL, you use Image/Adjust/Hue/Saturation or Image/Adjust/Replace Color. The different Color Pickers also allow you to work in the HSL color model.

THE LAB COLOR SPACE

The Lab color space is a device-independent color space that has as its color gamut the colors that the human eye can see. The Lab color space is used internally by Photoshop to convert between RGB and CMYK and can be used for device-independent output to Level 2 PostScript devices. The Lab color space is quite useful for some production tasks. For example, sharpening only the Lightness channel sharpens the image without "popping" the colors. You can work in Photoshop using Lab color, and we have converted a Lab color example, Chapter 27: "Bryce Stone Woman," for this version of *Photoshop Artistry*.

USING THE COLOR PICKER

The main tool for picking colors in Photoshop is the Photoshop Color Picker. You access the Color Picker by clicking on the foreground or background color swatch at the bottom of the Tool palette or by double-clicking the foreground or background color swatches on the Color palette. You can use this picker in Hue mode, Saturation mode, Brightness mode, or Red, Green, or Blue mode. See the diagrams here for an explanation of each

Current hue

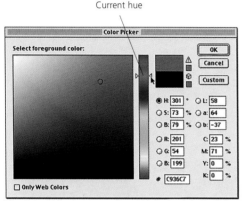

The Color Picker in Hue mode, which is the default. Sliding the color slider (shown with the arrow cursor above) up and down changes the hue in Hue mode. For a particular hue, purple here, click and drag the circle in the color box to the left to pick a particular color. As you move the cursor around in the color box with the mouse button down, left to right movement changes the saturation and up and down movement changes the brightness. You will see the values for saturation and brightness change in the number boxes to the right. You also see the corresponding RGB and CMYK values for each color. Hue is frozen by the color slider position.

Current saturation

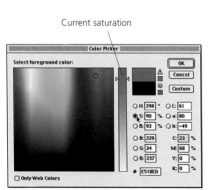

Put the Color Picker in Saturation mode by clicking on the S radio button. Now sliding the color slider up and down changes the saturation. Left to right movement of the cursor circle changes the hue and up and down movement changes the brightness.

Current brightness

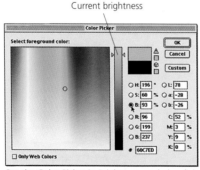

Put the Color Picker in Brightness mode by clicking on the B radio button. Now sliding the color slider up and down changes the brightness. Left to right movement of the cursor circle changes the hue and up and down movement changes the saturation. Brightness here is similar to Lightness, mentioned earlier in this chapter.

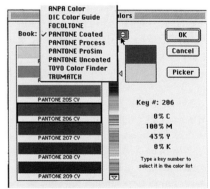

The Custom Colors picker with the different color systems that it makes available in the pop-up menu. Drag the slider or click on the up/down arrows to locate a color, click on a color to choose it, or type in the number associated with a particular color to choose that one. Choosing OK picks that color, and clicking on Picker returns you to the Color Picker where you can see and pick the RGB and CMYK equivalent to that color.

Chapter 5: Picking and Using Color

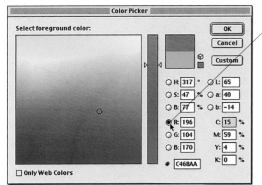

Put the Color Picker in Red mode by clicking on the R radio button. Now sliding the color slider up and down changes the amount of red in your color. For particular blue and green values, click and drag the circle in the color box to the left. Left to right movement changes the amount of blue and up and down movement changes the amount of green. You will see the values for blue and green change in the number boxes to the right. Red is frozen by the color slider position. The values for cyan, magenta, yellow, and black also change as you move around in the color box. This is a great way to see how the RGB and CMYK components change for different colors. If you are not sure how to adjust a certain color, go into the Color Picker and visually see what will happen to it as you add or subtract different component colors from it.

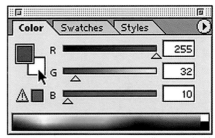

The exclamation sign shows you that the current color may be out-of-gamut (not printable in CMYK). The small swatch immediately below shows you the closest printable color. Click on the triangle sign or small swatch below it to change the chosen color to the closest in-gamut color (shown at right). See chapter 20: "Correcting a Problem Image" for a discussion of out-of-gamut colors. The cube icon indicates that the chosen color is not a web-safe color. Clicking the cube, or the swatch below it will take you to the nearest color that is web safe.

The Color palette shown as it is normally grouped with the Swatches and Styles palette. The foreground and background colors are shown to the left. You know that the foreground color is currently active because of the double line around it. If you move the sliders, you adjust the foreground color. The arrow cursor is over the background color. If you click on the background color, it becomes the active color and moving the sliders modifies it. If you click on either color square, you get the Color Picker. This palette also shows you the CMYK Gamut Warning icon.

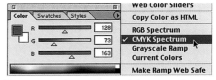

From the pop-out palette menu (click on the triangle in the upper right), you can set the display of the Color palette to Grayscale, RGB, HSB, CMYK, Lab, or Web color.

mode. In addition, you can set a specific color by typing in its Lab, RGB, or CMYK values.

The Custom button brings up the Custom Colors picker for choosing PANTONE, Trumatch, and other standard colors. You can use these as separate color channels within Photoshop's Multichannel mode, choose one or more colors for Duotone mode, set spot color channels in CMYK or RGB mode, or the color automatically converts to RGB or CMYK for painting, depending on the active color space.

USING THE COLOR PALETTES

Besides the Color Picker that you access from the Tool palette, you can also access the Color palette and the Swatches palette from the Window menu. Normally these are grouped together on the desktop, but you can separate them by clicking on their name tabs and dragging each of them to some other location on the desktop. Because the big Color Picker is a modal dialog box that you cannot access on-the-fly when using the painting tools, the Color and Swatches palettes come in very handy for getting the colors you need quickly.

THE COLOR PALETTE

In the Color palette, you can move the RGB, CMYK, HSB, or other color sliders to create a color that you like. You pick this color for the foreground or background depending on which of the swatches is chosen in the Color palette. You change the display mode in the Color palette using its pop-up option menu. You can also pick colors from the color bar along the bottom of the palette. This color bar offers different display modes to choose from using the Color palette's options. The Color palette is also useful to have around while you're in Levels, Curves, and the other color correction tools. It remembers the colors at the last location where you clicked the Eyedropper in an image, and it shows you how the

The pop-out palette menu also brings up options for how to display the color bar at the bottom of the Color palette. You can choose the foreground color by clicking on a color in the color bar; Option-click for the background color; or choose black or white from the two swatches at the right side of the bar.

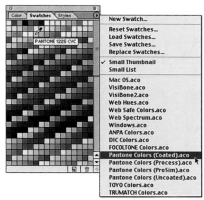

The pop-out menu of the Swatches palette contains swatch sets for PANTONE, Trumatch, and other standard color systems. Here we see the PANTONE colors loaded into the Swatches palette. When viewed as small swatch thumbnails, if you move the Eyedropper over a particular color, a small label appears, telling you which PANTONE you are about to choose.

The palette pop-out menu also gives you the option to view the swatches in a named list.

You can load and save different sets of swatches to files. If you have certain colors that you use for a particular client, you may want to save these in a file under that client's name. You can append swatches, which adds the swatches stored in a file to the ones you already have in the palette. Reset Swatches just goes back to the default set of swatches.

color adjustments you are making are changing that location. See Chapter 22: "Color Matching Images" for more details.

THE SWATCHES PALETTE

The Swatches palette gives you access to a library of swatch sets, as well as allowing you to save, and then later load, your favorite set of custom swatches. Clicking on a color swatch using the Eyedropper tool will give you a new foreground color. Option-clicking picks a new color for the background. You automatically get the Eyedropper when the cursor moves over the swatches area. To save the current foreground color in the Swatches palette, position your cursor over the empty gray area at the end of the swatches and click. Your cursor becomes a paintbucket and the new swatch is added at the end of the existing swatches. If you want to replace a current swatch with a new color, Shift-click on the swatch you want to overwrite. Pressing the Command key gives you the scissors, and clicking over a swatch with them removes it. Using the pop-up options menu, you can load custom swatch sets into the Swatches palette, including sets for custom ink colors, such as PANTONE. Remember, however, if you paint with a custom color, it is converted to the current color mode (RGB, CMYK, etc.) and does not separate as a custom color.

If you have a continuous tone 24-bit color image that has many colors that you might want to use for other projects, there is a quick way to load 256 of these colors into the Swatches palette. First, choose Image/Mode/Indexed Color to convert a copy of your image into Indexed Color mode. (Be sure to use a copy so you don't destroy your original image.) Using 256 colors, Local Adaptive Palette, and Diffusion Dither settings in the Indexed Color dialog box gives you the 256 colors most common in the image. Click on OK in the Index Color dialog box; then choose Image/Mode/Color Table to see a table of the 256 colors you have created from the image. Click on the Save button in the Color Table to save these colors in a file. In order for your saved file to be available for the Swatches palette, change the file extension to .aco. You can now use Replace Swatches in the Swatches palette menu to load these new colors, making them available for painting projects in Photoshop. You can also use Load Swatches to add these colors to the existing swatches already present. This is more of a noteworthy technique for Web work where you might commonly add 3-bit (or whatever) palettes to one another, say for an animation. For more information on 8-bit color and creating images for the Web and multimedia, see the "Images for the Web and Multimedia" section of this book.

Converting a 24-bit color image to Indexed Color to create a color table for loading into the Swatches palette. If you have more than one image open, and you want the resulting color table to be built from all open images, select Master (Adaptive) instead of Local (Adaptive) for the Palette choice.

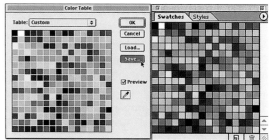

Saving your indexed color table using the Color Table editor. After saving this table (using the .aco file extension), you choose Replace Swatches from the Swatches palette pop-up menu to make this the current set of colors in the Swatches palette.

Chapter 5: Picking and Using Color

6 SELECTIONS, PATHS, MASKS AND CHANNELS

Terms and concepts for working with selections, paths, masks, and channels. Knowing the differences between each and also between these and layers.

Before you can understand all the possibilities, we first need to explain several important concepts. You need to understand the concept of a selection and how to make a selection using the Photoshop tools. You need to understand what a mask channel is, how to turn a selection into a mask channel and how to edit a mask channel using different tools to allow you to isolate the necessary parts of an image to achieve a particular effect. This includes understanding what a selection feather or a mask blur is and how these affect the edges of blended selections. We will discuss the concept of opacity, which also affects image blending. We also show you how to effectively use the Channels palette. We will talk about using paths, which are really just another form of selections. You also need to realize that a selection or a mask channel can also instantly become a layer mask for either a regular layer, a fill layer or an adjustment layer. We will discuss how selections become layer masks in the next chapter.

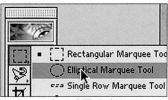

The Rectangular and Elliptical Marquees are the simplest selection tools. Click and drag in the Tool palette on the arrow in the bottom corner of the Rectangular Marquee, or type Shift-M, to change between the Elliptical and Rectangular marquee.

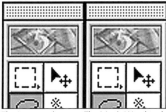

The Lasso tool.   The Magic Wand tool.

MAKING SELECTIONS

Let's start by talking about the concept of a *selection*—an isolated part of an image that needs special attention. You may want to make this part of the image lighter or darker, or you may want to change its color altogether. You might also select something in an image that you wanted to copy and paste into a different image.

THE SELECTION TOOLS

There are various tools for making selections. The simplest are the Rectangular and Elliptical Marquees, which allow you to draw a box or an ellipse around something by clicking at one side of the area you want to isolate and then dragging to the other side. This will create a box or oval-shaped selection that is denoted by dotted lines around the edge. The next level of selection complexity is the Lasso tool, which allows you to draw a freehand shape around the selected objects. Using the Lasso in Photoshop, you can draw either freehand or straight line segments, or combinations of both. Another selection tool is the Magic Wand, which allows you to click a certain color in an image and automatically select adjoining areas based on that color. A totally different way to make selections is to use the Pen tool. The Pen tool creates selections, called paths, which are mathematical descriptions of points joined by straight and curved line segments. With the Pen tool, you can create the most exact paths along subtle curved surfaces. Ultimately though, paths are converted back to normal selections when you are ready to use them to modify your image. Photoshop 5 added three

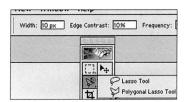

The Magnetic Lasso tool automatically traces around the edge of an object depending on the way you set up its parameters.

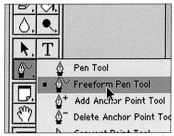

The Freeform Pen tool allows you to make Pen selections in a similar way to using the Lasso tool.

Here is the Paris Dog where we have used the Lasso to select just the dog.

The above selection after choosing Select/Inverse.

In Photoshop 6, you can also use the selection modifier icons at the left of the Options palette to always make a new selection, add, subtract or intersect with the current Selection.

Dog selection with no feather filled with green.

Dog selection with a 20-pixel feather filled with Green.

The Channels palette for an RGB image. Each of the red, green and blue channels is a grayscale image. You only see color when you view the RGB channel by choosing Command-~ or clicking the name RGB.

The Channels palette for a grayscale image with the single black channel, Gray, which is the image.

new selection tools: the Magnetic Lasso, the Magnetic Pen tool, and the Freeform Pen tool. Photoshop 6 hid the Magnetic Pen tool. It is still there but only accessible from the Options Bar as a checkbox item when you are in the Freeform Pen tool.

There are ways to increase the size of a selection and also to select all objects of similar color or brightness within the image. In this chapter, we learn about the concept of a selection and how selections fit in with the rest of Photoshop. To learn about actually using the Selection tools, go to Chapter 4: "The Tool Palette" and Chapter 18: "The Car Ad," and for the Pen tool and paths, also look at Chapter 28: "Rain in Costa Rica" and Chapter 30: "The Power-Book Ad."

WORKING WITH AND INVERSING SELECTIONS

Here you see the Paris Dog Image. We have selected the dog using the Lasso tool. If you'd like, you can open the Paris Dog image from the folder for this selections chapter on the *Photoshop 6 Artistry* CD. When the dog is selected, anything we do (painting, changing color, and so on) can happen only within the boundaries of the selected area. That is one purpose of a selection, to isolate your work to a particular object or area within the image. If you compare working on an image in Photoshop to painting a mural on a wall, selecting just the dog would be equivalent to putting masking tape everywhere else on the wall, allowing us to paint only on top of the dog. If we choose Select/Inverse, then everything except the dog becomes the selection. Now we have selected the background and not the dog. So, anytime you have a selection of an object, you also have, via Select/Inverse, a selection of everything except the object. Returning to the wall analogy, using Select/Inverse would be like removing the masking tape from the background and putting tape over the area of the dog.

CHANGING A SELECTION

Changing a selection is a lot easier than moving masking tape. You can add to any selection made using the Marquees, Lasso or Magic Wand selection tools by using any of these tools with the Shift key down when you create the new selection. You can subtract from a selection by pressing down the Option key when you define the area you want to subtract using these same tools. In Photoshop 6, you can also use the selection modifier icons at the left of the Options palette to always make a new selection, add, subtract or intersect with the current selection.

SETTING THE FEATHER VALUE

Using most of the selection tools in their default mode is similar to placing masking tape along the edge of the selection, in that there is a defined sharp edge to the selection. Such a selection is said to have a feather value of 0. The selection feather is something that determines how quickly the transition goes from being in the selection to not being in the selection. With 0 feather, the transition is instantaneous. You can change the feather of a selection using the

Chapter 6: Selections, Paths, Masks and Channels

Select/Feather command. If you change the feather of the selection to 20, the transition from being fully selected to being fully unselected would happen over the distance of 40 pixels (actually, at least 20 pixels on either side of the zero feather selection line). If you used this type of feathered masking tape to paint the selection of the dog green, the feather would cause the two colors to fade together slowly over the distance of 40 pixels.

PIXELS AND CHANNELS

A pixel is the basic unit of information within a digital image. Continuous tone digital images (scanned photographs of real objects) are a two-dimensional array of pixels. If the image were 2,000 pixels wide by 1,600 pixels high and we were printing it at 200 pixels per inch, then the image would print at 10 inches wide by 8 inches high (2000/200 = 10, 1600/200 = 8).

If we are working with a black-and-white image, each of these pixels contains one byte of information, which allows it to have 256 possible gray values. A black-and-white image has one channel in which each pixel is one byte in size. A channel is just a term referring to a two-dimensional array of bytes. If we are working with an RGB color image, it has three channels (one for each of red, green, and blue). A CMYK image has four channels. You can see these channels by choosing Window/Show Channels. In an RGB file, Channel #1 is red, Channel #2 is green, and Channel #3 is blue. There is also an imaginary Channel #~, which allows you to see the red, green, and blue channels at the same time. (This is how you see color.) The RGB channel, Channel #~, is an imaginary channel because it doesn't take up any additional space beyond that which the red, green, and blue channels take up.

SAVING SELECTIONS AS MASK CHANNELS

When you make a selection, you are making what is called a *mask*—the selection masks out the part of the image that you don't select. You can save a selection to a mask channel, which allows you to use it again later or to do further selection editing on the mask with the painting tools. This is especially useful for a complicated selection that you don't want to have to remake later. To do this, choose Select/Save Selection, or just click the Save Selection icon at the bottom of the Channels palette. The new mask channel you would create by doing the Save Selection would be named Alpha 1. When you are working with a grayscale image, Photoshop assumes Channel #1 is the image and Channels #2 and higher are mask channels. In RGB, Photoshop assumes Channels #1, #2, and #3 are red, green, and blue, and that Channels #4 and higher are mask channels. You can access a channel by clicking on its name in the Channels palette or by using the Command key for that channel (Command-1 for the top channel, Command-2 for the next channel, etc.). You can rename a mask channel by double-clicking the channel, entering the name you want, and then clicking OK. If you Option-click on the Save Selection icon, or choose Select/Save Selection, you can type in the new name right there.

Load Selection from Channel or Path.

Save Selection to Channel.

New Channel, Layer, Action or Path.

Throw away Channel, Layer, Path or Action .

Image with dog selected.

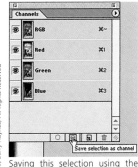
Saving this selection using the Save Selection icon.

The mask that gets saved for this selection.

The Channels palette after doing the Save selection and renaming Alpha 1 to DogMask.

65

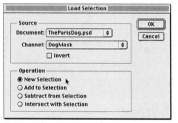

Load Selection from the menu bar.

Load Selection the quicker way; dragging the mask channel to the Load Selection icon at the bottom of the Channels palette. The quickest and best way to load a selection is to hold the Command key down and click the Mask channel you want to load. You should learn this way because it works in all cases, loading a selection from a mask channel, a layer mask or even from a regular channel, like Red.

Here are the options you have when you do a Load Selection. The Add, Subtract, and Intersect options only show up if you have an existing selection at the time of the load.

Deleting a mask channel from an RGB image using the Channels palette's pop-up window.

Deleting a channel from an RGB image the quick way by dragging to the Trash icon at the bottom right of the Channels palette.

HOW MASK CHANNELS WORK

A *mask channel* is just another channel like the others we've described. When you save a selection to a mask channel, the parts of the image that you selected show up as white in the mask channel, and the nonselected parts (the masked parts) show up as black. When you have a blend between two partial selections, it shows up as gray in the mask channel. Feathered selection areas also show up as gray. A mask channel has 256 possible gray values, just like any other grayscale image. A layer mask, which we discuss in the next chapter, is just a mask channel that is being used to mask out (remove) part of a layer. You can also save a selection to a layer mask, using Layer/Add Layer Mask, and that will usually remove the nonselected parts of that layer from view.

EDITING MASK CHANNELS

You can actually edit a mask channel just like you would edit any grayscale image. Often you may want to make a selection using one of the selection tools, save it to a mask channel or a layer mask, and then edit the selection within the mask channel. When you edit a selection in selection format, with the marching ants around its edge, you use the selection tools. When you edit a selection saved as a mask channel or layer mask, you use pixel editing tools, like the Airbrush, Pencil, Paintbrush and Gradient tools. White in a mask means totally selected and black means totally unselected. If you edit a white area to be gray, you make it less selected, or, partially selected. You can edit a black area and make part of it white; doing that adds the white part to the selected area. You may save a selection in a mask channel so you can edit it there, or you may just save it so you can use it again later.

We do many things with mask channels in this book. Sometimes we use the terms selection, mask, mask channel and layer mask interchangeably since they all refer to an isolated part of the image. To do something to the image with a mask that is saved in a mask channel, you must first load it as a selection. Choose Select/Load Selection from the menu bar or click the mask channel you want to load and drag it to the Load Selection icon at the bottom left of the Channels palette. You also can load a selection by Command-clicking on the channel you want to load. When a selection is loaded, you can see the marching ants.

Sometimes people get confused about the need to have both selections and mask channels. Remember, a selection actually masks out the nonselected areas of the currently active channel(s) and layer. After you create a selection or do a Load Selection, you can change which channel(s) or layer within a document is active and the selection remains. It just always affects what you do to the active channel(s) or layer. A mask channel is just a selection saved for later. Unless the mask channel is currently loaded as a selection, it doesn't affect any other channel(s) or layers or anything that you do to them with the painting tools or filters. You can have up to 21 mask channels in an RGB Photoshop document, plus the Red, Green, and Blue channels, for a total of 24 channels. You can load any of these mask channels as a selection at any time. A layer mask, on the other hand, is a mask channel associated with a particular layer. It is always removing the black areas of the mask from view in that layer. You access a mask channel using Command-4, Command-5, Command-6, etc. All mask channels are visible all the time within the Channels palette. Only the layer mask for the currently active layer is visible within the Channels palette and you access it using Command-\.

Chapter 6: Selections, Paths, Masks and Channels

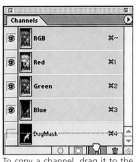

To copy a channel, drag it to the New Channel icon at the bottom of the Channels palette.

The copied channel appears at the bottom with its name being Alpha1, Alpha2, etc. If you use Duplicate Channel from the Channels palette menu, the new channel will be the same name with "copy" at the end.

To move a channel, click it and then drag it until the line is dark between the channels where you want to put it.

The moved channel appears in its new location.

COMBINING SELECTIONS

When you load a selection, you can combine that new selection with any existing selection present before the load. Command-clicking on a mask channel or layer mask loads it as a new selection and throws out any existing selection. Command-Shift-clicking on a mask channel adds this new selection to any existing selection. Command-Option-clicking a mask channel subtracts this from an existing selection and Command-Option-Shift-clicking on a mask channel intersects the new selection with the existing selection, giving you the parts that the two selections have in common. If you don't want to remember all these command options, they show up in the Load Selection dialog box, which you can access by choosing Select/Load Selection.

DELETING, MOVING AND COPYING CHANNELS

You can remove a mask channel by clicking that channel and then choosing Delete Channel from the Channels palette's pop-up menu, or by clicking the channel and dragging it to the Trash icon at the bottom right of the Channels palette. If you delete the Red, Green or Blue channel this way, Photoshop 5 & 6 will assume that you want to produce spot color plates of the other 2 channels and will give you cyan, magenta,or yellow channels, depending on which of the RGB channels you trashed. If you look at Image/Mode, you'll see that you are now in a Multichannel file.

You can copy any channel, including the Red, Green and Blue channels, by clicking on the channel and dragging it to the New Channel icon at the bottom of the Channels palette. You also can make a copy of a channel by choosing Duplicate Channel from the Channel palette's pop-up menu.

You can move a channel from one location to another by clicking the channel you want to move and dragging it until the line becomes dark between the two channels where you want to put this channel. Let go of the mouse at that point and you have moved the channel. You cannot, however, change the location of the original Red, Green, and Blue channels.

Normal state for working in RGB, Channel #~, with Red, Green, and Blue Eye icons on and the DogMask off.

USING THE CHANNELS PALETTE EYE ICONS

After you save a selection in a mask channel or a layer mask, you can then work with it in a different way than by just seeing the marching ants lines around the edge of the selection. Notice that the Channels palette has two columns. The leftmost column is the thin one that has the Eye icons in it. This column signifies the

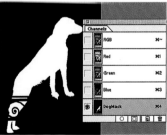

When working on a mask channel or a layer mask directly in black-and-white, you normally have its Eye icon on with its channel grayed. All the other channels have their Eye icons off and they are not grayed.

67

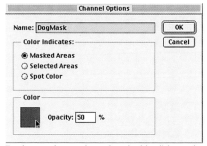

To change the overlay color, double-click on the mask channel to bring up its Channel Options, click here on the color swatch, and change its color.

You can also work on a mask while looking at the RGB image too. To get into this state, first click in the rightmost column of the DogMask channel to activate the mask and then click in the leftmost column of Channel ~ to turn on the RGB Eye icons without activating the RGB channels. Here you will be editing the DogMask channel.

If you want to work on the RGB channels while seeing the mask, first click the right-most column of Channel ~ to activate RGB, then click in the Eye icon column of the DogMask channel. Here you will be editing the RGB channels.

Use Make Work Path from the Paths palette to make a path from a selection.

Use Make Selection from the Paths palette to turn a path into a selection.

channels that you are currently seeing—the ones with the Eye icons. The right-most column is the one that has the name of the channel. Clicking in the right-most column for a particular channel highlights that channel, which signifies that you are working on it. That makes it the Active channel. Clicking in the right-most column for Channel ~ (the RGB composite channel), highlights the Red, Green, and Blue channels because Channel ~ represents all three of them. If you also have a mask channel defined, like the picture here with the dog mask, then there are different things you can do to work with that mask channel in relation to the other channels.

The Eye icons for the Red, Green, and Blue channels normally are turned on, and those channels are highlighted when you are working with an RGB image. The normal state is displayed in the first related picture on the previous page.

If you click the right-most column of the Dog-Mask channel, that channel becomes the active one. It shows up in black-and-white and if you do any editing with the painting tools, you do so in black-and-white in the DogMask channel. The Eye icons for the RGB channels turn off now. The last screen grab on the previous page shows this state.

If you want to edit the mask channel while also seeing the RGB image, do the following. After you make the mask the active channel by clicking in its right-most column, you can then click the Eye icon column of Channel ~, which turns on the Eye icons for RGB. You will see RGB, but these channels are not active. They are not highlighted, which means that you are seeing them but are still working on the highlighted DogMask channel. The parts of the mask that are black will show up with an overlay color, usually red. If you paint in black with the Paintbrush tool, you add to this black part of the mask, which would represent the non-selected area. The paint shows up in the red overlay color. If you paint with white, which normally represents the selected part of the mask or layer mask, you subtract from the red overlay color. If you want to change the overlay color, double-click the mask channel to bring up its Channel Options, click on the color swatch, and change its color in the Color Picker. Be sure to leave its opacity at lower than 100% so you can see the picture through the overlay.

If you want to, you can also view the DogMask while working on the RGB image. Click the right-most column of Channel ~, which activates the RGB channels so that when you paint with the Paintbrush, you modify the RGB image. Now if you click the Eye icon column of the DogMask channel, you see this channel as an overlay while working in RGB.

CONVERTING BETWEEN PATHS AND SELECTIONS

A path is a special selection created with the Pen tool based on points and lines that are described in an internal model as mathematical objects. A regular selection uses a mask channel, with pixels having 256 possible gray values, as its internal model. Use the Make Work Path and Make Selection commands in the Paths palette to convert between selections and paths or vice versa. To use a path, you will usually convert it into a selection and then maybe into a mask channel or a layer mask. In Photoshop 6 you can convert a path directly into a new kind of layer mask called a layer clipping path.

Chapter 6: Selections, Paths, Masks and Channels

7 LAYERS, LAYER MASKS AND ADJUSTMENT LAYERS

Terms and concepts for working with layers, adjustment layers, layer masks and layer clipping paths and for using them for prototyping and effects variations.

Since layers are now such an integral part of Photoshop, this chapter is one of the most important for you to understand. Here you will get an overview of what layers are, the different types of layers and the overall functionality you'll need to know about when working with layers and masks. You'll actually create things with layers, like the image to the right, in the step-by-step chapters.

Think of each layer in a RGB Photoshop document as a separate RGB file. Each layer has its own separate Red, Green and Blue channels. As you look at the layers in the Layers palette, imagine that the one at the bottom of the palette is a photographic print laying on the bottom of a pile of prints on your desk. Now imagine that each layer above that in the Layers palette is another photographic print laying on top of that bottom one in the order you see them

"Rain In Costa Rica"—an image with many layers. Here we see the final composite. This image is included in the Layers&LayerMasks folder on the CD; open it and follow along while reading this section.

in the palette. You have a pile of photographic prints on your desk. Now imagine that you can look at the top of this pile of photographs and see through them, seeing all of them at the same time, all the way through to the bottom of the pile. It's even better than that because, using Opacity, you can control how much of each photo you see, as a percentage of the whole, and using layer masks or layer clipping paths, you can control what parts of each photo you see. You can run a variety of effects, including layer styles and blend modes, on each photo in the pile, so the possible combinations of how you can see them all together number in the millions. You can change the order of the photos in the pile and also move them and distort them in relation to each other. All these things and more are what Photoshop layers allow you to do.

LAYERS AND CHANNELS

Layers are similar to channels in the ways you move them around, copy them, and delete them. To work with layers, you use the Layers palette, which you activate from Window/Show Layers or by using F10 with ArtistKeys. If you use layers and channels at the same time, which you often will, you will learn about them faster if you separate these two palettes from their default grouping so you can see them in different places onscreen at the same time. Just click the Layers or Channels name

The above 4 images were used, along with layers and masks, to create the composite at the top of this page.

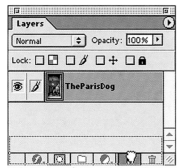

Making a copy of the Dog layer by dragging it to the New Layer icon. You could also choose Duplicate Layer from the Layers palette menu to accomplish the same result.

After the Dog Layer has been copied and named Dog Pointillize.

tab at the top of that palette and drag it to a new position onscreen. You can then hide or bring up the Channels palette with Window/Show Channels or by pressing Shift-F10 when using ArtistKeys.

Each layer is like a separate Photoshop file that you can superimpose on top of other Photoshop layers in the same document. Take a look at the "Rain in Costa Rica" image at the beginning of this chapter; we created it using four layers that were originally four photographs on one 35mm roll of film. Each Photoshop layer has its own set of Red, Green and Blue channels. When working with layers, you can use the Eye icon on each layer to view one layer at a time, several layers at a time, or all the layers at once.

LAYER MASKS AND ADJUSTMENT LAYERS

Consider the Paris Dog image we were working with in Chapter 6: "Selections, Paths, Masks and Channels". **You should open a copy of it from the Ch07.Layers folder on your CD. Make sure your Channels and Layers palettes are visible by pressing Shift-F10 and F10 (if you have ArtistKeys loaded), or by choosing Window/Show Channels and Show Layers. You start out with a simple image that has a single layer, called TheParisDog. You can make a copy of this Layer by clicking on it in the Layers palette and dragging it to the New Layer icon at the bottom of the Layers palette. Holding down the Option key while doing this opens the Duplicate Layer dialog box, where you can give this new layer a name. We will call it Dog Pointillize, because we're going to run the Pointillize filter on it.** Notice that the Layers palette now has a second layer above with the name we gave it. New layers are added above the current active layer and they then become the active layer.

Now choose Filter/Pixelate/Pointillize and run the Pointillize filter on this new layer with a value of 5. Because this layer is on top of the Dog layer, you can no longer see the Dog layer. The Dog Pointillize layer has its own set of RGB channels, so now the document is twice as big as it was when we started.

MAKING A LAYER MASK

Do a Load Selection from the DogMask channel in the Channels palette by Command-clicking that channel. Now we have a selection of the dog. Option-click on the Add Layer Mask icon at the bottom of the Layers palette to add a layer mask to this layer. Notice that the Layer Mask thumbnail now appears to the right of the Dog Pointillize Layer thumbnail and that it is black where the dog is. Also, notice that it shows up in the Channels palette as Dog Pointillize Mask. Now the Dog Pointillize layer is removed in the area of the Dog where the selection was, and you see the original dog in the layer below. If you press Command-I at this point to invert the Dog Pointillize mask, you can see the original background with the dog now pointillized.

When you first add a layer mask, it comes up in the mode in which you can edit the mask but see RGB. In this mode, the mask's thumbnail has a double border around

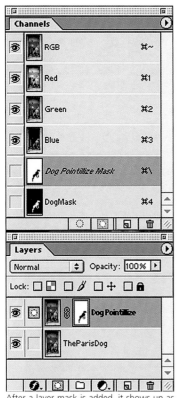

After a layer mask is added, it shows up as a thumbnail to the right of the Layer thumbnail in the Layers palette. It also shows up in the Channels palette below the Blue channel. Because the Eye icons are on for RGB in the Channels palette but only the layer mask is active, we can now edit the mask but we will see the changes in RGB.

After adding a layer mask by Option-clicking the Add Layer Mask icon. Clicking the Layer Mask icon removes everything but the selection from this layer by turning it black in the mask. Option-clicking removes the selected area. If there is no selection, clicking on the Layer Mask icon selects the entire layer and Option-clicking hides the entire layer.

it in the Layers palette and is highlighted (active) in the Channels palette. **Option-clicking this Layer Mask thumbnail in the Layers palette at this point switches you to the mode in which you can edit and see the mask. The Eye icon is now on for the mask and off for RGB in the Channels palette. Option-clicking again returns you to the original mode where you can edit the mask and see RGB. Try this on the ParisDog sample image.**

To edit the layer itself and also see it, click the Layer thumbnail in the Layers palette. For each regular layer in the Layers palette, the Layer thumbnail is the one to the left and the Layer Mask thumbnail is the one to the right. Just to the right of the Eye icon thumbnail, you see an icon that looks like a mask when you are editing the layer mask and like a paintbrush when you are editing the layer itself. The item you are editing, either mask or layer, also has a double border line around it.

Adding Adjustment Layers

Now click back on the Layer thumbnail for the Dog Pointillize layer (that is, the thumbnail on the left, not the Layer Mask thumbnail on the right). You should now see the Paintbrush icon between this Layer thumbnail and the Eye icon. Click on the third icon from the right, at the bottom middle of the Layers palette, to bring up the New Fill and adjustment Layer pop-up menu. Choose Curves to choose a Curves Adjustment layer. Click in the center of the curve line and drag to pull the curve down and to the right. This darkens the entire composite. (This darkens everything because the new adjustment layer is on top of all the others.) Choose OK, then Option-double-click on the name Curve in this new adjustment layer in the Layers palette to bring up the Layer Properties dialog box. Name it Darken Curve. Option-double-clicking on the name of a layer is what you have to do in Photoshop 6 to rename a layer. Although an adjustment layer acts like any other layer, it does not make you pay the price of adding another set of RGB channels for the new layer. The color correction adjustment you make in the adjustment layer applies to all the layers below that adjustment layer. You can turn this correction on and off simply by turning the Eye icon on or off for that particular adjustment layer. The Layer thumbnail, the leftmost one, of an adjustment layer tells you the type of adjustment layer it is. There is a different icon design for each of the 14 different fill and adjustment layers. If you double-click the leftmost icon of the adjustment layer, you can actually change the adjustment—in this case, the curve settings—as many times as you want without degrading the color in the file. If you already have a selection when you create this new adjustment layer, the adjustment layer's layer mask will be a copy of that selection and so the curve will only darken the selected area. If you have an active

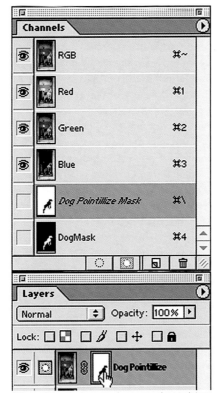

When editing the layer mask, you see the Mask icon just to the right of the Eye icon and the Layer Mask thumbnail has the highlight. In the Channels palette, the Eye icons are on for Red, Green and Blue, so you can see the results of your mask edits, but the Layer Mask channel is the only one that is actually active.

When editing the layer, you see the Paintbrush icon just to the right of the Eye icon and the Layer thumbnail has the highlight. The Red, Green and Blue channels are now the active ones in the Channels palette.

Click on this icon to bring up the above pop-up menu and add a fill or adjustment layer from these 14 choices. With ArtistKeys, you can use Command-F3, F4 or F5 to add new Levels, Curves or Hue-Saturation adjustment layers. Using these function keys, or holding the Option key down while making the above menu choice, allows you to name the layers as you go since each function key brings you into the New Layer dialog box on the way to creating the layer. Choosing Layer/New Adjustment Layer or Layer/New Fill Layer from the menu bar also brings you into the New Layer dialog box. Naming layers is a good idea since it will help you and others to later understand a complex layered document.

path before creating an adjustment layer, that path will be turned into a layer clipping path for that adjustment layer and only effect the part of the image within that path. **Click on the Darken Curve adjustment layer in the Layers palette and drag it down between the Dog Pointillize layer and the Dog layer until you see a double line form between these two layers. Release the mouse button at this point. This moves the adjustment layer down so that now it darkens only the Dog layer and not the Dog Pointillize layer.**

You now see *Darken Curve Mask* **in the Channels palette below the Blue channel because now the Darken Curve layer is active. Click back on the Dog Pointillize layer to make it active and notice that the Dog Pointillize mask is now below the Blue channel in the Channels palette. Finally, click back to TheParisDog layer and notice** that all the layer masks have been removed from the Channels palette. Only the layer mask, if there is one, for the active layer shows up in the Channels palette. Use Command-\ to access the layer mask for the currently active layer, no matter what layer it is. The DogMask channel is not associated with any layer, so it stays in the Channels palette all the time. Notice that you use Command-4 to access this channel. If there were an additional channel that was not a layer mask, Command-5 would be used to access it. Adjustment layers, and fill layers, actually have no RGB data

Here is the dog image with only the dog itself darkened using the Darken Curve adjustment layer. The leftmost thumbnail in this adjustment layer indicates that its type is a Curve adjustment layer. The white thumbnail to its right is the Layer Mask thumbnail. An adjustment layer will usually have a layer mask, although it is often totally white, showing that the adjustment is happening to the entire image area.

In Photoshop 6, you can actually click on RGB (or the Red, Green or Blue channel) in the Channels palette when on an adjustment layer and you'll even see the Paintbrush icon show up in the Layers palette but notice that you are not allowed to paint on the RGB channels for this layer because they don't exist. Within the Channels palette In Photoshop 6 you can now make a copy of the Red, Green or Blue channel while on this layer, which will give you those channels as they are modified by having this adjustment layer on.

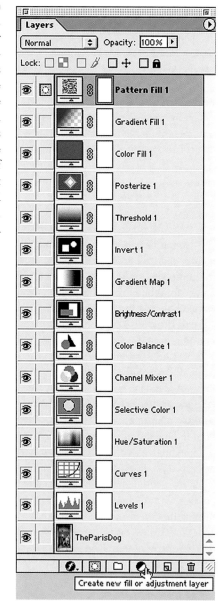

Here we see all the different icons for each of the 14 kinds of fill or adjustment layers. The type of each layer is the same as its name and icon. This is a very useful improvement added in Photoshop 6.

Chapter 7: Layers, Layer Masks and Adjustment Layers

associated with them. Regular layers each have a Red, Green and Blue channel and take up a lot of space. The purpose of fill and adjustment layers is to be able to make color, fill and pattern adjustments to all underlying layers at one time; to be able to do so in a way that can be changed as often as possible without damaging the data in any regular layers; and to make these changes in a very space efficient way. When a Photoshop file is saved, all that Adobe must save for a fill or adjustment layer is the numerical settings for that particular layer type, the layer mask and the clipping path. These can all be saved very compactly compared to a regular layer that has real Red, Green and Blue channels.

SEEING SOME LAYERS IN ACTION

Let's take a look at the Rain in Costa Rica composite image with its five different layers to see how this works. **Open the RainInCostaRicaFinal file in the CD folder named Layers, and use that file to try out the different options that we discuss here.** In the Layers palette for RainInCostaRica, you see that this image has four regular layers and one Curves adjustment layer. Currently, we are looking at all of them because the Eye icons in the left column of the Layers palette are all on. To see all the details about how this composite was created, check out Chapter 28: "Rain in Costa Rica."

Imagine that all the layers are in a pile with the bottom layer, here called Blue Bus, at the bottom of the pile. As you add layers on top of this, like Red Car, Woman and Bus Window, they are blended with the layers below them. The active layer that is highlighted, Bus Window, is the layer that is modified by changing the settings for Opacity and Blend mode at the top of the Layers palette. Click on a particular layer in the rightmost column of the Layers palette to make it active. The active layer will also be changed by anything you do with any other Photoshop tools like the Paintbrush, Levels, or Curves. If you do something to the active layer while all the other layers' Eye icons are on, you can see the changes to this layer as they are combined with the other layers, but the other layers themselves do not change.

The Channels palette shows you the Channel thumbnails and Eye icon state for the layer you are working on. What you see in the Channels palette thumbnails depends on the layer you have activated and which other layers have their Eye icons on. Notice that if you turn off the Eye icon for the Blue Bus layer, not only does the main part of the image turn into the transparency pattern, but you also see that pattern in the Channel palette's thumbnails. If you just want to work on one layer and see only that layer, you can click the Eye icons of the other layers to turn them off. A quicker way to turn them all off is to Option-click the Eye icon in the Layers palette of the layer you want to work on. Doing this also changes the RGB display of the Channel thumbnails in the Channels palette so that you see just the Red, Green and Blue channel info of the one layer. To turn all the other layers back on again, just Option-click the same layer's Eye icon in the Layers palette.

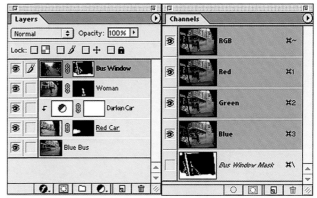

Because all the Eye icons are on in the Layers palette, the Channels palette shows you a view of the Red, Green, and Blue Channel thumbnails of all layers as a composite image. Choose Palette Options from the Layers palette menu to set the size of your thumbnails.

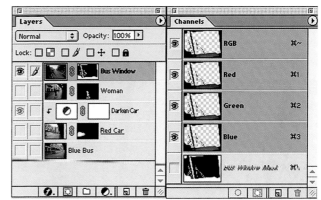

If we Option-click on the Eye icon for the Bus Window layer, that turns off all the other layers and notice that it also changes the appearance of the Channels palette thumbnails to fill the non-visable parts of the current composite with the transparency pattern.

An image with a single *Background* layer. Notice that the Locking icon is on in this layer indicating that what you can do with it is limited.

Also, the RGB channel thumbnail display in the Channels palette will once again show a composite of all the visible layers.

THE *Background* LAYER

If you open any single layer image into Photoshop, such as a TIFF file, and look at the Layers palette, you will notice that the image's layer is called *Background*. It is called *Background* in italics because the *Background* layer differs from a normal layer. The *Background* layer, when it has that name, must be the bottom layer and cannot have any transparent areas. When you choose Layer/Flatten Image, all your layers are compressed into a single layer. This single layer will be a *Background* layer. If you make a selection in the *Background* layer and clear or delete that selection, the selected area fills with the background color (usually white). If you delete a selection in any other layer, that area fills with transparency (the checkerboard pattern). Transparency is a hole where you can look through a layer and see other layers below it. You cannot move other layers below the *Background* layer or move the *Background* layer above other layers. To convert a layer from a *Background* layer into a normal layer, just double-click it and give it a new name. It then becomes a normal layer and you can move it above other layers, as well as create transparent areas in it. I usually do this when working with my images because I prefer all my layers to have the same full Photoshop capabilities, which a *Background* layer does not. The *Background* layer, or just the first layer in a document, determines the initial canvas size for your layered document. You want to make sure the canvas is large enough to encompass the parts you want to see in all your layers. Therefore, you may want to put your largest picture element, often your main background, down as your first layer. If you add additional layers that are larger in horizontal or vertical pixel dimensions than this bottom layer, you can see only as much of the image as fits on top of the bottom layer onscreen. However, you can still move these other layers by using the Move tool, V, to expose parts left hanging outside the canvas area. In Photoshop, parts that hang off the edge are permanently cropped only when you use the Cropping tool or the Image/Crop command. To expose these parts of the image, you can always increase the canvas size using Image/Canvas Size. You can have a canvas that is bigger than the bottom layer, whether it is a *Background* layer or a normal layer.

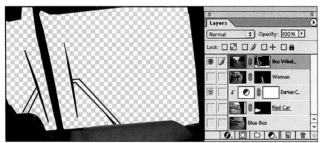

Here we see the Bus Window layer as it appears with all the other layers turned off. When you turn them back on, you'll see the other layers through the transparent checkerboard pattern.

WORKING WITH ADDITIONAL LAYERS

When you add additional layers whose contents are smaller than the *Background* layer, or if you copy a small item and do an Edit/Paste with it, the extra area around these smaller items shows up as transparent (a checkerboard pattern). Areas of an image that are removed by a layer mask also show up as transparent. When we look at just the Bus Window layer in this image, we see that it is entirely transparent aside from the frame and wipers of the bus window we are supposed to be looking out of. Through these transparent parts, when all the Eye icons are on, we will see the rainy Costa Rica street scene.

DRAG AND DROP, MOVING AND LINKING

You create additional layers in Photoshop by copying something from another image and then choosing Edit/Paste. You can name these layers by Option-Dduble-clicking them in the Layers palette or choosing Layer/Layer Properties from the main menu bar or from the Layers palette. Using the Move tool (Command key or V), you

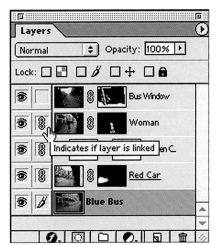

Here we have clicked on Blue Bus to activate it then also clicked on the Link columns of the three layers above it. Layers that are linked in this way can be moved or transformed as a unit. They can also all be dragged and dropped into another document.

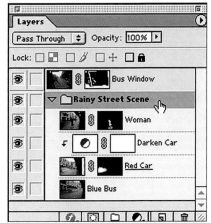

We created the Rainy Street Scene set of layers by choosing Layer/New/Layer Set from Linked after linking all the layers as they were in the image at the top of the page.

Layer sets can be closed so that group of layers are represented in the palette by a single component. This allows you to simplify complicated documents.

can also click a layer in the main document window or the Layers palette in image A, and drag and drop it on top of image B's main document window to create a new layer in image B. In Photoshop, you can also drag and drop a whole group of layers if they're linked together. Having one layer in a perspective group active, you can link other layers to it by clicking on the Link column (the one to the right of the Eye icon) of the other layers you want to link to the active layer. Layers that are linked can all be moved and transformed (scaled, rotated, and so on) together. This is a great feature of Photoshop, especially for Web and multimedia designers.

You can move a single layer, or a group of linked layers, from side to side or up and down using the Move tool. Just click to activate the layer you want to move in the Layers palette, then select the Move tool from the Tool palette (V or the Command key). Click on the layer in the main document window and drag it to its new location. If you have all the Eye icons on, you can see its relationship to the other layers change. **Click on the Blue Bus layer in the RainInCostaRica image to make it active and then click in the linking column of the Red Car, Darken Car and Woman layers above it. Now use the Move tool to drag this entire scence around inside the Bus Window layer, which doesn't move. If you drag it straight up, you can now see the woman's foot on the pavement. Now choose Layer/New/Layer Set from Linked to create a new layer set from all these linked layers. Layer sets are new in Photoshop 6 and are a great way to simplify your documents by collapsing logical groups of items into a single element. We'll learn more about these later.**

MORE ABOUT LAYER MASKS

If you want part of a layer to be temporarily removed, or made invisible, you can add a layer mask to it. The black parts of the layer mask are transparent in that layer, which allows you to instantly prototype a layer and its composite with the other layers without seeing the masked-out part. If you later decide you want to restore that part of the image, just turn off the layer mask by Shift-clicking its thumbnail. **Try Shift-clicking on the three layer masks within the RainInCostaRica image and you'll**

If you Shift-click on the Bus Window layer mask, you'll notice that the original photo this came from was quite different. Driving in Costa Rica is quite exciting, imagine going around a corner and seeing a Bus coming at you! Better to be riding the bus than in a car. Shift-click on the Woman and Red Car layers to see their original images too.

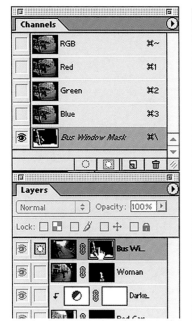

To edit the layer mask and see just the mask in the Document window, Option-click the layer mask's thumbnail. You will see the layer mask thumbnail to the right of the Layer thumbnail. The Channels palette will display the mask highlighted with the Eye icon on as above. The Eye icons are off for the RGB channels because you don't want to see them. Now Option-clicking the layer mask's thumbnail will toggle between just seeing the layer mask and then seeing the RGB channels but you will always be editing the mask until you click the Layer thumbnail again or click on RGB in the Channels palette.

To edit the layer mask while still looking at the layer, just click the layer mask's thumbnail. You will see the Layer Mask thumbnail to the right of the Layer thumbnail. The Channels palette will display the mask as above, active, with its Eye icon off. The Eye icons are on for RGB, so you see those channels, yet you edit the mask because it is active.

see what each original photo looked like before the mask was applied. When you activate a layer that has a layer mask, that mask is also added to the channels in the Channels palette. It only appears in the Channels palette while you have that layer activated. If you want to edit the layer mask while still looking at the layer, just click the layer mask's thumbnail within the Layers palette. When you paint with black in the main document window, you add the black to the layer mask and remove those areas from view in the layer associated with that layer mask.

In Photoshop, you can create a layer mask by choosing Layer/Add Layer Mask/Reveal Selection or by clicking the New Mask icon that is second from the left at the bottom of the Layers palette. If you have a selection at the time of that click, the selected area will become the only thing that is white in the mask and therefore the only visible part of that layer. If you choose Layer/Add Layer Mask/Hide Selection or Option-click the New Mask icon, everything except the selected area will now be visible and the selected area will be made black in the layer mask. If you have a path on your screen, Command-clicking the New Mask icon will create a layer clipping path that, like a layer mask, just shows you the area within the path. When you have a layer clipping path, you can later edit that path, now part of the layer, to change what you actually see. In general you should use a layer mask for any mask that you want to be able to soften or blur the edges of. When you want a very sharp edge that is mathematically accurate no matter what the image size, the layer clipping path is the way to go.

If you want to edit a layer mask while looking at the mask itself, Option-click the layer mask's thumbnail within the Layers palette. The main document window now just displays the black-and-white mask and your Layers palette has all the Eye icons dimmed out. The Channels palette now shows this layer mask channel as active with its Eye icon on. When you want to return to editing the layer itself, click the layer's thumbnail within the Layers palette.

MOVING, REMOVING AND COPYING LAYERS

You can remove a layer by clicking it, choosing Delete Layer from the Layers palette's pop-up menu or the Layer menu, or by clicking the layer and dragging it to the Trash icon at the bottom right of the Layers palette.

You can make a copy of any layer by clicking the layer and dragging it to the New Layer icon to the left of the Trash icon at the bottom of the Layers palette. You can also make a copy of the active layer by choosing Duplicate Layer from the Layers palette's pop-up menu or from the Layer menu. The copied layer will have the same name but with "copy" appended to its end.

You can move a layer from one location to another in the Layers palette by clicking the layer you want to move and dragging it until the line turns into a double line between the two layers where you want to put this layer. Let go of the mouse at that point, and the layer is moved. When you move a layer, it changes the composite relationship of that layer with the layers around it. Notice how the running woman and red car go away after you move the Blue Bus layer from the bottom upwards to just below the Bus Window layer.

Deleting a layer the quick way by using the Trash icon at the bottom of the Layers palette. If the Layer is active, you can just click the Trash icon. You can also drag any Layer to the Trash icon. If you don't want the delete warning message to come up, just Option-click.

To copy a layer, drag it to the New Layer icon at the bottom of the Layers palette. Holding the Option key down as you do this allows you to rename the copied layer. Just clicking this icon creates a new blank layer with a generic name, or an Option-click allows you to name it while creating it.

GROUPING, LINKING AND ALIGNING LAYERS

A layer can be Grouped with the layer or layers below it. The bottom layer in a group determines the transparency for the entire group. This means that if the bottom layer in the group has a layer mask that removes its center portion, that same center area will be removed from all the layers in the group. To group a layer with the one below it, choose Layer/ Group With Previous (Command-G). You can always ungroup a layer later by choosing Layer/ Ungroup (Command-Shift-G). You can also group or ungroup a layer with the one below it by Option-clicking the line between the two layers. It is obvious when layers are in a group because the bottom layer in the group has its name underlined. This bottom underlined layer determines the transparency for the group. The other layers above it in the group are indented to the right with dotted lines between them.

By clicking in the middle column of a layer in the Layers palette, that layer can be linked with the currently Active layer. When you click in this middle column, the Link icon will show up to let you know this layer is linked to the currently active layer. More than one layer can be linked together and when you activate a layer, all the layers that are linked to it will have this Link icon show up in their middle columns. If you move or scale any of the layers that are linked together, they will all move or scale together proportionately. If you drag and drop any layer that has others linked to it, those other layers will also be copied to the other document. This allows you to link together a group of layers that represent a button, for example, and then drag that button, with all its layers, to any other document. You could use this feature to make up a Photoshop library file of the buttons you use most often. When you need a particular button, just drag and drop one of its layers and they all come along

Here are three linked layers. Doing a Layer/Align Linked/Left Edges will align the left edge of the nontransparent parts of the other two layers with the left edge of the Box layer because Box is the active layer.

Before Align Left Edges.

After Align Left Edges.

To move a layer, click on it and drag it until you see the double line between the layers where you want to put it.

The moved layer appears in its new location now just below the Bus Window.

Layers before grouping.

Layers after grouping. Notice the Grouping icon where the cursor is between the Squiggle and Circle layers.

Image before grouping.

Image after grouping.

You can create a new layer set in Photoshop by clicking on the Layer Set icon at the bottom of the Layers palette. Doing this creates one, as you see here, with the default name Set 1. Creating a layer set by choosing New Layer Set from the Layer palette menu or using Layer/New/Layer Set or Option-clicking on the above icon allows you to enter your own name as you creat the set.

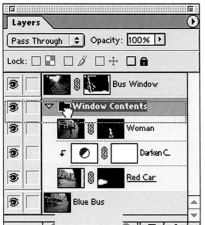

Here we have created a layer set named Window Contents and have already moved the Red Car and Woman layers into that set. We are in the process of dragging and dropping the Blue Bus layer into the Window Contents set. When the Set icon turns black, that is the point to release the mouse and have the layer enter the set.

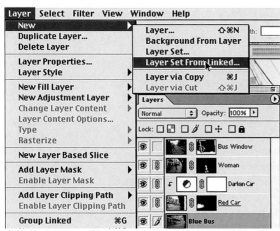

If you have a group of layers that are already linked together, you can create a layer set from them by first activating one of the linked layers then choosing Layer/New/Layer Set From Linked (Shift-F12 with ArtistKeys). When you create a layer set this way, all the layers are automatically moved into the set and the set is then closed to tidy up your Layers palette.

for the ride. This is a very powerful feature, especially for Web and multimedia people who use the same elements over and over again.

If you have a bunch of layers linked together and one of them is the active layer, you can use Layer/Align Linked to align the rest of the linked layers with the active layer in six possible ways: Top Edges, Vertical Centers, Bottom Edges, Left Edges, Horizontal Centers, or Right Edges. Remember, the results of the Align Linked command will depend on the layer that is currently active. There is also a Layer/Distribute Linked choice which will distribute the linked layers evenly in the same six ways. The Photoshop 6 Options palette for the Move tool also displays clickable icons for any of these twelve choices that apply to the currently active layer and any other layers that are linked to it. If you currently have a selection on the screen, you can use Layer/Align to Selection to align the currently active layer and any that are linked to it to the selection in the same six possible ways. For examples of how to use these

Here we see the Window Contents layer set in its collapsed state. It takes up less room and yet the layers inside the set will continue to act as they did when the set were not there and those layers were just in the Layers palette.

alignment features, see Chapter 30, "The PowerBook Ad," Chapter 32, "Layer Clipping Paths, Shape Layers and Layer Styles," and Chapter 35, "South Africa In Focus."

LAYER SETS

A great new feature of Photoshop 6 is Layer Sets. These allow you to group layers into logical sets and then collapse a finished group down into a single element within your Layers palette. This is a great feature for people who have a large number of layers and who want to be able to organize them into functional groups. Once a group of layers is combined into a layer set, the entire set can be turned on and off by just clicking on the Eye icon for the set folder. If you click on the icon for a particular set, you can use the Move tool to move the entire set, even if the layers within the set are not linked. Using the set's icon, you can also drag and drop all the layers in the set into another window. If you want to Scale or Free Transform the entire set, however, all the layers inside the set must be linked and one of those linked layers must be active. You can add a layer mask or a layer clipping path to a layer set. This applys the mask or path to all the layers within the set as a unit. A layer set also has a possible Opacity and Blend mode. When you first create a layer set, the default Opacity is 100% and the default Blend mode is Pass Through. Pass Through is a new Blend mode created for sets that has the effect that all the Blend modes in all the layers within the set will behave as they would if the set didn't exist and those

Layer sets can have both a layer mask and a layer clipping path attached to them. Here I've added a layer mask, with the soft edge, and a layer clipping path, with the hard edge, to the Window Contents set.

78

layers were there without the set. Layer sets cannot be nested; that is, you cannot have one layer set within another. Otherwise Photoshop could get as complicated as programming!

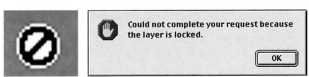

You'll see the icon to the left if you try painting on a layer that is locked. The message to the right comes up when you try to move a locked layer.

LOCKING LAYERS AND LAYER SETS

In Photoshop 6 you can finally lock layers and also entire layer sets. This is a feature I have been wanting for a long time because it can stop one from accidentally moving a layer, which can easily happen if you press the Command key, putting you into the Move tool, at the same time as moving the mouse with the button down. If you are working on a complex composite or a color correction where multiple copies of the same image have to line up exactly, I recommend that you lock any layers that you don't want accidentally moved later. Do this by clicking in one of the four lock options at the top of the Layers palette while the layer you want locked is active. You can also lock an entire layer set in a similar way. See the diagram above and to the right for details of the locking options. Once a layer is locked, you will get the universal Not symbol if you try to paint on it, and you will get a warning message that the layer is locked if you try to move it with the Move tool. Using these new features at the right times could save you a lot of grief by removing the possibility for costly accidents!

LAYER STYLES AND BLENDING OPTIONS

Photoshop 6 has combined a bunch of previous features including the former Layer Options and Layer Effects into the new and more powerful Layer Style dialog box. If you double-click the Layer thumbnail or layer name in the Layers palette, this new Layer Style dialog box comes up. You can also access it from the Layer/Layer Style menu. As a quick example of what you can do with these features, click on the Bus Window layer to make it the active layer. Click on the leftmost Layer thumbnail to make sure you are working on the layer and not the layer mask. Now Choose Window/Show Styles and click on each of a variety of styles to see the types of things you can do with the Layer Styles palette. Notice as you click on each style that the Layers palette shows you the effects applied to get this style in a list right below the layer name. If you want to explore any particular style, double-click the Layer thumbnail for the Bus Window layer and the Layer Styles palette will come up, allowing you to look at the settings in each of the effects used to create this style. All of the features in the Layer Style dialog box could fill a book in itself, so we will cover them in much more detail in Chapters 31: "Blend Modes, Calculations and Apply Image," 32: "Layer Clipping Paths, Shape Layers and Layer Styles," 33: "Pos-

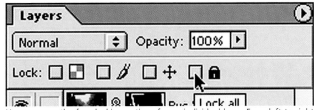

Here you see the four locking options for an individual layer. From left to right they are Lock transparent pixels, Lock image pixels, Lock position and Lock all. If you turn on Lock all, that must be turned off before you can set one of the other locking options. Lock transparent pixels stops you from painting in or changing the transparent parts of the layer, Lock image pixels does the same for the non-transparent areas and Lock position stops you from moving the layer with the Move tool. Lock transparent pixels does not stop you from painting on the parts of a layer that are made transparent with its layer mask. To stop this as well as to stop painting onto a layer mask and to stop changing a layer clipping path, you need to choose Lock all. None of the lock options stop you from moving the layer in relationship to other layers. With a layer set, the only option you can choose for the entire set is Lock all. A gray Lock icon will then appear to the right of all the layers in that set telling you that you must first unlock the set before changing the locking status of an individual layer.

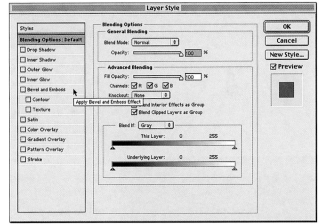

When you first double-click on a layer to bring up the Layer Style dialog box, you may think it's just the Blending Options you see here. Actually, when you click on any of the lines below Blending Options, like Drop Shadow, Inner Shadow, etc., each of these has its own special set of options that will then appear to the right. Don't just check the Drop Shadow checkbox but click on the word Drop Shadow, then you'll see all the options available for drop shadows. You can also access this dialog from Layer/Layer Style/... as illustrated below. From there you can go directly into one of the sub-options areas, like Drop Shadow, for example.

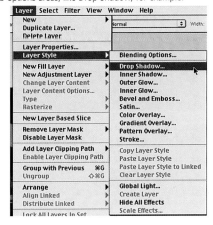

My Styles palette is set up using all the styles, as explained in Chapter 3: "Setting System and Photoshop Preferences." The Bus Window layer of the RainIn-CostaRicaFinal image, from this book's CD, is active and we clicked on the Layer thumbnail within that layer. At that point, clicking on the Styles tab, or choosing Window/Show Styles, will allow you to then click on any style available in the palette and have that style applied to the Bus Window layer. When you see one that is interesting then double-click on the Layer thumbnail in the Bus Window layer to see how that style is set up using the Layer Style dialog. You can also double-click on any particular effect listed under the Bus Window layer and the Layer Style dialog will come up showing you how that particular effect is set up.

Being in the Move tool, I held down the Control key on my Mac and clicked on top of the red car. This context-sensitive menu came up showing me that the above three layers contained non-transparent pixels at the location where I clicked. Choosing one of these will activate that layer in my Layers palette. If I were doing this on my Windows machine, I'd click with the right mouse button while in Move.

terize, Bitmaps, Textures, and Patterns," 34: "Heartsinger CD Cover," and 35: "South Africa in Focus,"

FLOATING SELECTIONS (PHOTOSHOP HISTORY)

When you have made any type of selection and it is highlighted on the screen with the dotted lines moving around it (those marching ants), you can now Command-Option-click and drag to float that selection. A floating selection is another copy of the pixels of the active layer in that selected area floating on top of the original layer below. A floating selection is sort of like a temporary layer although in Photoshop 5, 5.5 and 6 it doesn't show up in the Layers palette. To change the Opacity and Blend mode of a floating selection in Photoshop 6, you now need to use the Edit/Fade command. Before Photoshop had layers, it always had floating selections and they were more powerful. In older versions of Photoshop, all the things we do with layers today had to be done one at a time using a floating selection. You can only have one floating selection at a time, and when you deselect it by clicking outside it, choosing Select/None or by running a filter or any command on it, it becomes embedded in the layer it is floating above. At that point, you can no longer move it. A layer, on the other hand, is like a permanent floating selection; you can have many layers. Layers don't go away like floating selections do. In Photoshop 5, 5.5 and 6, you can no longer turn a floating selection into a full-fledged layer by double-clicking it in the Layers palette. If you really want a layer from a selection, just choose Command-J (Layer/New/Layer Via Copy) to create a new layer with a copy of the current selection. Floating selections had most of their power removed in Photoshop 5. (It might be simpler if Adobe removed them completely.) If you used floating selections a lot before, you should learn to do things with layers now! In Photoshop 5, 5.5 and 6, if you do a Paste on top of an individual channel in the Channels palette, you get a Floating Selection that also doesn't show up in the Layers palette and you must use Edit/Fade to change its mode or Opacity.

USEFUL CONTEXT-SENSITIVE MENUS FOR LAYERS

If you Control-click (right-click in Windows) while working in the Move tool, you will get some very useful context-sensitive menus to speed up your layer work. When using the Move tool, or with Control-Command-click if not in the Move tool (Control-right-click for Windows), you get a context-sensitive menu showing all the layers whose Eye icons are on that have pixels at the location where you clicked. You can then drag through this menu to activate the layer you want to work on. If you are in a selection tool or a painting tool, not the Move tool, you will get a different context-sensitive menu. These context-sensitive menus are great power user tools!

8 HISTORY PALETTE, HISTORY BRUSH AND SNAPSHOTS

Using the History palette, History Brush, Art History Brush and Snapshot features to give you added creative power.

The simple explanation for the History palette is that it allows Photoshop to have up to 100 levels of Undo. Actually though, the History palette allows a lot more flexibility than that. Between the History palette, the History Brush, and the way they work with the Snapshot feature, you may initially wonder if this is yet another flavor of layers. There are some important distinctions between using History with snapshots versus layers and as we will explain, they can be used in different and also similar ways, but the reasons for using one versus the other are quite distinctly different.

THE SIMPLE CASE OF USING HISTORY

Every time you do a Photoshop 6 command that changes your image, that command gets saved in the History palette. It may be creating a new layer, painting a brush stroke in your image or even using the Levels command. In the History palette, you see a list of all the commands you have done in order from the oldest on top to the newest on the bottom. As it has always been, Command-Z toggles between Undo and Redo of the last command you did. Command-Option-Z now marches back up the history chain undoing command after command. Command-Shift-Z goes back and redoes those same commands in the same order they were originally done.

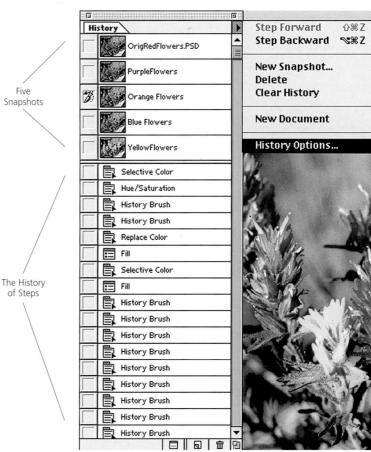

Here we see the History palette with five snapshots at the top and then a long list of commands in the lower section. In this photo all the original flowers were red. I used Selective Color, Hue/Saturation, and Replace Color to make versions of this image with all Purple, Orange, Blue, and Yellow flowers. As I did this, I made a snapshot of each set of colored flowers. I then kept changing the source of the History Brush, currently set to the Orange Flowers snapshot, as I painted with the History Brush to recolor a flower with any of the five colors. If you wanted to be able to change the colors again after saving the file, you would use adjustment layers to get a similar effect with lasting flexibility. All this history information goes away when you close or quit!

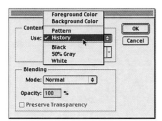

The Photoshop 6 Edit/Fill command, has the Use History option. This allows you to Fill a selection, or your entire Layer, from any previous History or Snapshot state.

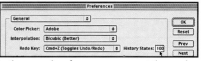

In the general preferences you can set the number of History States available in the History palette. The maximum number is 100.

You can bring up this History Options dialog from the History palette menu and use it to turn on Allow Non-Linear History, which will then no longer automatically throw away future history when you go back into the past and change the sequence of events by entering a new command.

At any time, you can create a snapshot that will remember the state of your image at that particular point. In Photoshop 6, you can have multiple snapshots and they are all saved at the top of the History palette. Photoshop is by default set to automatically take a snapshot of your image when you first enter the program. This snapshot is used to implement the Revert to Saved type commands. In the History options that are accessed from the History palette, you can also choose to have a new snapshot created whenever you save your image. In addition to being able to undo to previous snapshots and history states, you can also use them as the source for the Fill command, the Eraser, or the History Brush. This is a special painting tool that paints from your image as it existed at a particular state within the History palette. Clicking in the leftmost column of the History palette next to any snapshot or history state sets the History Brush to paint on your current image with the image as it looked at that previous point in history. See the case study with flowers later in this chapter for an example of how this is used. You are not just painting with what that particular step did; you are painting with the cumulative effect of everything you did up to and including that state. This is cool stuff because it makes certain things, like painting with any of the tools that use brushes, much more undoable, repeatable, and totally flexible.

MAKING SNAPSHOTS AND DOCUMENT COPIES ALONG THE WAY

Create a new snapshot from the current history state.

Create a new document reflecting the image at the current history state.

When you use the History palette's New Snapshot menu, or the middle icon at the bottom of the History palette, to create a snapshot, this saves not only the current appearance of your image on the screen but also its selection state and the state of the Layers palette and the rest of the file. This is a lot more than the old Take Snapshot command. You can take a snapshot whenever you want to make sure you can get back to this point within your document. If you crop your image after taking a snapshot, you will not be able to paint from this snapshot onto the current state of the document because that state will now have a different canvas size. Just like in the older versions of Photoshop, you could not Rubber Stamp from Saved if the saved file had a different crop size. Also, remember that snapshots and history states do not survive after a crash, so you should still save the file often enough to protect from any system failure. If you are in the middle of a project using snapshots and you have to close the file, you can make documents of the snapshots you want to save and then drag the opening snapshots from those documents back into the window of your original document when you reopen it. The snapshots will return to the History palette, and you can continue to paint from those snapshots as long as the image size and color mode of the snapshots are the same as the current state of the file you're working on. Or, you could make new layers and use Edit/Fill/Use History for each snapshot that you want to save.

You can click in the leftmost icon at the bottom of the History palette to create a new document showing the image at the current History state. This is like choosing Image/Duplicate, except you don't get the Merged Layers Only choice and the new document will automatically be given the name of the command you just finished doing in the current History palette. This new document will now have its own empty History palette and its own empty set of snapshots and history states, which you will develop as you start to work on it. All the layers are copied into the new document. This allows you to branch off in several directions from a particular state in the history of your image and then explore all the options, each in its own document, until you are happy with the outcome. After working in a new document, you can always go back to the document it came from and all its history will still be intact. This is somewhat subtle but very powerful, especially for creative people who like to try a lot of options.

PAINTING FROM THE FUTURE

To choose where the History Brush paints from, click in the left most column next to a particular history or snapshot state. The History Brush will then paint on your current layer from that particular past state of your file. If you click in the left column of the History palette to set the History Brush on a certain state, then click in the right column of the History palette to return the working image to a previous state prior to your History Brush state, your image returns to that previous state. If you start entering more commands, they will enter after the current history state, that previous state, and all states between the current history state and your History Brush state will be removed. The state of your History Brush stays there, sort of in the future, as long as that is the location where your History Brush will be painting from. This allows you to, in a way, paint from the future.

LINEAR VERSUS NON-LINEAR HISTORY

You can turn on the Allow Non-Linear History option by choosing History Options from the History palette. When you do this, the history system does not throw away future history states. Say you enter 10 commands so you have a History palette with 10 things in it. Normally, if you click the fifth thing to return your image to that previous state, states 6–10 disappear once you do another command. That new command appears at position 6 and states 6–10 are removed. When you turn on Allow Non-Linear History, then states 6–10 stay in the History palette, without actually appearing in your image, and that new command appears at position 11. Your actual image, however, appears as it would if you had done states 1–5 and then state 11. Still, if you click back onto

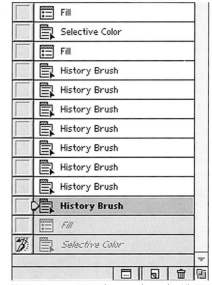

Here we see a case where we have the History Brush set on the command called Selective Color, which is in front of the current state we are working on in the History palette. This allows you to paint from the future!

1. Here we have used five strokes of the Paintbrush to paint a face. Let's say we like the head but don't like the eyes, nose and mouth. We can click back on the first Paintbrush command, which drew the head, and the other strokes will be turned off.

2. With Linear History, when we make that first paint stroke to draw the new eye, the old paint strokes for the eyes, nose, and mouth go away.

3. With Allow Non-Linear History turned on, the first stroke to draw a new eye skips the old strokes for the eyes, nose, and mouth and starts in a position beyond those. This gives you the option to return to the old face by clicking the stroke just above the currently highlighted one. It also gives you the option to use the History Brush to paint any of those old face parts onto a new face where you might want just one part from the old face.

4. Here, using Non-Linear History, I have painted a second set of eyes and a second nose; then I used the History Brush to paint the old mouth back in from the previous History state. That old mouth state would not have been there if I had not had Allow Non-Linear History turned on.

state 8, for example, the effects of states 9–11 go away and you would are where you would have been if you never returned to state 5 and then did the new state 11. Non-Linear History makes finding a state in the History palette a bit more confusing, but it always leaves you the option of returning to one of those previously removed states.

A HISTORY CASE STUDY WITH FLOWERS

I opened a photograph of some red flowers taken in the High Sierras at Yosemite. I wanted to have this same picture with multiple flower colors. (I wouldn't actually do this to one of my "true nature" photos.) Without making any selections, I used either Replace Color, Selective Color, or Hue/Saturation to change the color of all the flowers to first Purple, then Orange, then Blue, and finally Yellow. After each new color, I used the middle icon at the bottom of the History palette to create a snapshot of all the flowers at each of these four new colors. I then clicked in the left most column of the Original Red Flowers snapshot to set the History Brush there and followed that by a Fill from History to return my current state to the original red flowers. I then used one of the color change commands to change this red into yet another color. After I had the five colors I wanted, I then refilled back to all red. Next, I set the History Brush onto one of the other colors by clicking in the left most column of its snapshot. At that point, I used the History Brush to paint over some of the red flowers with flowers of new colors.

Here you can see the five different color Snapshots at the top of the History palette. I'm currently painting with the History Brush from the Blue Flowers Snapshot to change this flower from Red to Blue.

I just had to reset the History Brush source on a different color snapshot when I wanted to change colors. With this setup, I could paint over each flower as many times as I wanted and could even go back to the original red flowers at any time. The only problem is that when I close the file or quit Photoshop, my neat snapshot/history setup goes away. To see how to change the color of objects, check out Chapters 18: "The Car Ad," 21: "Yellow Flowers," and 22: "Color Matching Images." To see

The original photo with the actual red flowers.

The photo after modifying the flowers using the History palette and its snapshots along with the History Brush.

Chapter 8: History Palette, History Brush and Snapshots

how to set up this type of situation with layers so you can make changes to the flower colors even after saving the file, check out Chapter 26: "Combining Bracketed Photos," Chapter 27: "Bryce Stone Woman," and the other layer color correction examples.

HISTORY ALL GOES AWAY WHEN YOU CLOSE OR QUIT

If you are doing anything where you want several options created in a way that you can later reopen and change them, you should use layers, layer masks, and adjustment layers to give yourself that ability. By turning layers on and off, modifying layer masks and switching the settings in adjustment layers, you can make almost anything changeable in a variety of ways. You can also now do this in a sometimes simpler way with the History palette. The trouble with the History palette is that it gets cleared every time you close the file and reopen it. Also, if you made a change in the History palette, like a Curves setting, for example, you cannot go back to that history state and double-click it to see what the actual change was, like you could with an adjustment layer; you can only click that state and your image returns to where it was at that state. You can also paint with the History Brush on your current state from the image in that previous state. This History Brush feature adds a lot of power to history, snapshots, and Photoshop.

THE ART HISTORY BRUSH

Another interesting feature of the History palette is the Art History Brush. This tool allows you to paint from a history snapshot or history state just like the regular History Brush, but it adds the ability to choose from various brushstroke styles to give your image a painterly look. If you're the type of person who prefers straight photography, then this tool might not be too compelling. But if you like to take an image and explore with Photoshop to see where it takes you, then you can end up having a lot of fun while creating some very interesting effects with the Art History Bush.

Since using the Art History Brush will drastically alter your original image, it's always a good idea to work on a copy layer so you can preserve the original and keep your options open. The method I used here with the image of the man in the blue coat was to create a copy of the background by choosing Duplicate Layer from the Layers palette. I then created a new snapshot by clicking the New Snapshot icon at the bottom of the History palette. This snapshot served as the source state for all of my modifications with the History Brush. You can also use the snapshot that is automatically created in the History palette when you open a file.

My next step was to fill the duplicate background layer with white, giving me a fresh blank "canvas" to work on. In the History palette, I clicked in the column next to the snapshot I created, which specified that the Art History Brush would use that as its source state. Then I chose a brush from the new drop-down brush collection. For the Art History Brush, the irregular, rough brushes work well, since they mimic the imperfect characteristics of real-world, natural brushes. Finally, from the Options bar I chose a brush style, and set the Fidelity and Area controls.

This image was originally a black and white photo that I colorized using the History palette. After saving a copy of it, I decided to explore a painterly look with the Art History Brush.

A safe way to use Art History and still preserve your original image: Make a copy layer of your main image, then create a new snapshot. Next, fill the copy layer with white. Select the new snapshot as the source by clicking in the left hand column next to it, choose the Art History Brush from the Tool palette, choose an appropriate brush size and shape, and start creating your impressionist masterpiece!

The Options bar for the Art History Brush. Style lets you choose from ten different brush stroke styles; Fidelity controls how accurately the original colors are reproduced; Area determines the size of the area that the brush affects; and Spacing influences how close together the brush strokes are.

The Art History Brush

The rough, irregular brushes in Photoshop's default brush Presets (highlighted here) do very well when used with the Art History Brush because they mimic the imperfect characteristics of real world, natural media brushes. The middle group of brushes ship with the program and the ones at the bottom of the palette are custom brushes I created.

A series of eight custom brushes, in varying angles of 45 degrees, all made from the same shape.

ART HISTORY IN ACTION

Once you have the white-filled layer and snapshot set up, and have chosen your brush and style settings, all you have to do is start painting. As you move your brush back and forth, you'll see that Photoshop is using the source snapshot as a reference for filling in the image in the new Art History style. If you want to have an idea of what part of your image will appear next, try making the white layer partially transparent with the Layer Opacity setting. This technique, as well as setting different blend modes, can also be useful when you have finished painting with the Art History Brush and want to try combining the altered image with its original counterpart.

Since the style of brushstrokes varies greatly depending on several factors, including brush size, shape, roughness, area setting, fidelity value and brush blend mode, it's best to try experimenting so you can get the feel for how different brushes and brush styles affect the image. The illustrations at the bottom of the page will give you an idea of the tremendous variety of styles that the Art History Brush is capable of if you just dig a bit deeper under its surface.

This is also an area where experimenting with creating custom brushes can lead to many interesting results. Since the behavior of brushes is such that the orientation of the brush is always the same, no matter which direction you drag it with the mouse, you can expand your stylistic options by making a set of brushes that are the same brush shape arranged in a variety of angles. Using this approach you can follow the natural contours of image elements with much greater stroke accuracy than with a brush that has a single orientation.

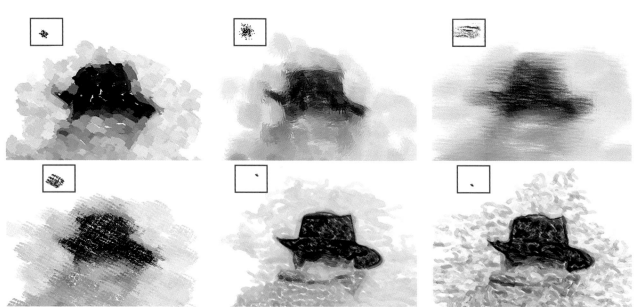

Six different results from the History Brush. The actual brushes used to create each sample are shown in the red boxes. The top row were all made using the Tight Short style, and for the third example in this row I created a custom brush. In the bottom row, the left is the Dab style, the middle is Tight Long, and the right example uses Loose Medium with a lower Fidelity setting. The lower Fidelity value is responsible for the introduction of more varied colors that were not necessarily present in the source snapshot. As is evident from these examples, a smaller brush will yield more precise detail, especially along the edges of shapes or fields of color, while larger brushes tend to have a softer, blurring effect.

9 TRANSFORMATION OF IMAGES, LAYERS, PATHS AND SELECTIONS

Using the Photoshop 6 transformation features to scale, resize and distort your images.

When I sat down to update this chapter for Photoshop 6, I started playing with Edit/Free Transform on the Square layer of the SquareButton file on the CD for this chapter. I was checking out the new features, how the numeric info is now in the Options palette, how versatile and easy to use layer styles are, and the next thing I knew, I had created a pattern I really liked, then several hundred variations of it flashed before me on the screen as I played with various layer styles! This program is awsome, what more can I say! Check out SquareButtonCreation1 in the CD folder for this chapter. Now back to reality.

In general, you want to initially scan an image at a size that will be big enough to encompass all the needs you will ever have for that image. You then color correct and spot that image to create your Master version which you archive. Later, when you want to use that image for a particular purpose, you first resample a copy of it using Image/Image Size, or the Cropping tool with a fixed target size, set to the dimensions and resolution you will need. This information about scanning and resampling your file is still important when you are going to transform an image and it is covered in Chapter 16: "Image Resolution, Scanning Film and Digital Cameras."

The Info window (F9) shows you on-the-fly progress during your transform even when the mouse is down and you are dragging a point. Use this for real-time feedback about your transformations.

This chapter talks about how you can use the Edit/Free Transform command, as well as the Edit/Transform/Scale, Rotate, Skew, Distort and Perspective commands, to distort a version of a file, layer, selection or path. The Transform and Free Transform tools in Photoshop 6 have been improved and generalized to work in a consistent way no matter what you are transforming. We will start with a simple case and then move into more complicated transforms. Let me first mention, however, that whenever you are doing a transform, the Info window and the Options palette will show you your progress with the current change in angle, position or dimensions.

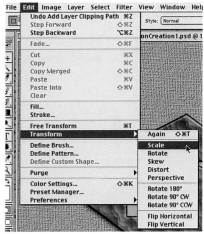

Here we see the Transform menu with all its individual options. You can choose any item from this menu to transform the image in one way at a time. While you are in the middle of a Free Transform, you can still choose any single option from this menu, which allows you to combine single transformation elements, working on them one at a time, before you have to accept any changes. This way, instead of typing in a Scale value, pressing Return, typing in a Rotate value, pressing Return, and typing in a Skew value and pressing Return, you are able to begin the Free Transform, choose each option separately, set its value, and press Return only once at the end to make all the changes you entered. This gives you more control than simply dragging handles in a Free Transform.

At any time during a transformation, you can look at the Options palette to see what changes you have done so far and to also edit those changes on the fly while you work. From left to right, the first icon just tells you that you are doing a transform, the second icon allows you to place the center point for rotation in one of nine exact locations, the x and y position values can be shown, using the arrow to the left of the Y, as relative to the position before the transform or relative to the document's zero location. Moving to the right, you then see the percent change in width and height and can click on the Locking icon to make both percentages the same. Next you see the change in rotation angle then the change in horizontal and vertical skew. All of these values can be edited as you work. A click on the X, or Escape key, cancels the transform and a click on the Check icon, or Return, completes and accepts the transform.

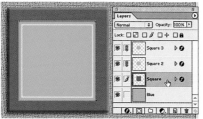

Here we see a button that has been made up of three layers. Each of these layers has had layer styles applied to give it shadows, beveled edges, and so on. Because the layers Square, Square 2, and Square 3 are all linked together, with the middle linking column in the Layers palette, any transformation done to any one of them happens to all three of them. Because each layer is an object surrounded by transparency, we do not need to make a selection before transforming the entire object. The transparency itself is assumed to be the selection.

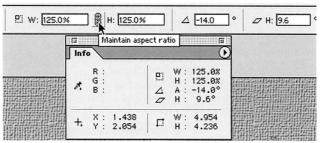

Here we see the Info and Options palettes after scaling to 125%, rotating by -14°, and skewing by 9.6°. Being able to both see and change the transform values in the Options palette almost makes the Info palette unneeded for transforms.

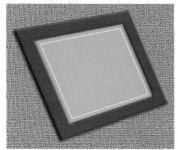

The image after scaling to 125%, rotating by -14°, skewing by 9.6°, and then applying perspective.

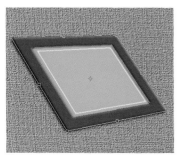

The above image after using Edit/Transform/Distort to make the bottom seem closer and the top farther away.

At any time while in the middle of the transform, you can use the Options palette to show you what you have done to the item so far and allow you to modify those changes numerically. All the Transform commands, along with Free Transform, are interrelated, and you can go from one to the other while in the middle of a transform.

Let's take a look at each of these Transform options by themselves and then we'll see how they can be combined using Free Transform and the Edit Transform menu. Take the case of the Square Button we see to the left. It is a simple shape but you will soon see that we can do a lot to it. Whatever we do to the Square Button, we could do to any image or any piece of an image that is pasted into Photoshop 6 as a layer.

TRANSFORMING A SQUARE BUTTON

To begin, open the SquareButton file in the Transformation folder of the *Photoshop 6 Artistry* CD. Type an F to put the image in Full Screen mode then type Command-Option-0 to zoom to 100%. Bring up the Info palette (F9) and the Options palette (F12) so you can see numerically what you are doing as you move the cursor during each transform. Make sure Square is the active layer in the Layers palette and then choose Edit/Transform/Scale. Click the top-right handle and drag it up and to the right. Pressing down the Shift key while dragging the corner forces the scale to be proportional. Scale it to 125% while looking at the Info palette with the Shift key down. If you can't get 125% exactly, you can actually type this number into the X scale factor of the Options palette then click the Link icon to make the Y scale factor the same. Now release the mouse, choose Edit/Transform/Rotate, and use the same top-right handle to rotate the image -14% by dragging up and to the left after clicking the handle. Now choose Edit/Transform/Skew and drag the top-middle handle to the left until the skew angle is 9.6 degrees. Finally, choose Edit/Transform/Perspective and click the top-right handle again. Drag it down until you see the dimension of the right edge decreasing from both the top and bottom at the same time. The Options palette shows you the cumulative results of the four transforms you have made so far. The Rotate and Skew angles have changed due to the effects of the Perspective command you did at the end.

Now go ahead and try Edit/Transform/Distort. This allows you to click any corner handle and independently drag that corner in any direction while leaving the other corners alone. You can also click one of the handles in-between two corners and this allows you to distort that entire side of the image as a unit. Play around with Distort for a while, and remember that if you don't like what you do, you can always exit and cancel the entire transform by choosing the Escape key or the X icon at the right side of the Options palette. If you do this though, the image returns to the original rectangular button. While you are entering the individual Transform commands, Photoshop keeps track of all of them while showing you a quick preview. When you press Escape or the X, they all go away, and when you press Return, Enter or the Check icon, they are all executed in the final high-resolution manner. This final hi-res transform may take a little longer, especially on a large file. I went ahead and used the Distort transformation to make the button appear as though the bottom of it was closer to me and the top was farther away. To do this in Edit/Transform Distort, bring the top-right and bottom-left edges toward the center and move the top left edge a bit until it looks right to you. Now go

Chapter 9: Transformation of Images, Layers, Paths and Selections

ahead and choose Return or Enter to finish the transformation and you will notice that it has a lot more detail.

If you choose File/Revert to revert your image to the square button again, I'll show you how to do this transformation all in one step. This time choose Edit/Free Transform (Command-T), which will allow you to do all the different transformations at the same time. To Scale to 125%, just click in the top-right handle and drag up and to the right with the Shift key down until you see 125% in the Info palette. Make sure you release the mouse button before the Shift key to keep things proportional. Now move the cursor a little above and to the right of the top-right handle and you should see a cursor curving to the left and down. When you see this cursor, it is telling you that if you click and drag at this point, you can rotate your object. While seeing the curved cursor, click and drag up and to the left until the angle in the Info palette is -14 degrees. To do the Skew, Command-click in the top-middle handle and drag to the left while keeping the mouse down until the delta H angle is 9.6. Don't move the mouse up or down while dragging to the left or you will also be changing the vertical scaling, and it may be hard to get the angle exactly at 9.6 without the scale changing too. When you get the angle to 9.6, you can release the Command key and you are then just adjusting the vertical scaling. Since Free Transform does many things at once, it is sometimes hard to keep a particular component of your transform exact and you may have trouble getting back to exactly 125% scaling. The way to fix this is to now release the mouse, then go into the Options palette to put the exact 125% value back in, adjust any other values and then click OK on the Numeric Transform box. You are still in Free Transform, so let's do some more transformations before we finish. To do the Perspective, hold down Command-Option-Shift and then click and drag the top-right handle down and to the right. Finally you distort by just holding down the Command key while you click and drag in any corner handle and then move it to where you want it. You can now press Return or Enter to finish the Free Transform.

CHANGING THE CENTER POINT OF A ROTATE

A new, very useful feature that was added for Photoshop 5 is the capability to change the center of rotate during a transform. Go ahead and open the original SquareButton file again from the hard disk. Now choose Edit/Free Transform (Command-T) and in the center of the button you will notice a small crosshair with a circle in the middle of it. Let's call this the rotation point. When you put the cursor on top of it, the cursor gets a small circle at its lower right, as in the diagram above. At this point, you can click and drag this rotation point anywhere on the screen. Now when you release the mouse, this moved location becomes the new center for rotation. After releasing the mouse, move the cursor to just outside one of the corner handles of the button until you see the curved rotation icon. Click and drag at that point to rotate the button and you will see that it is rotating around the center point wherever you placed it. You can even place it outside of the button's area. It is very powerful to be able to rotate around any center. You can, of course, move the center point over and over again and then rerotate around that new center point. If you want to get the rotation point back to the center of the object, just drag it to the vicinity of the center and it will jump to, and lock on, the center when it gets close enough. You can also use the Reference Point Location icon at the top left of the Options palette to exactly locate the reference point at the center, corners or middle edges. Try it!

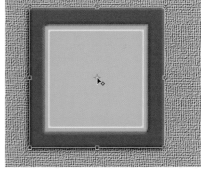

This is the default location for the rotation point, in the center of the object's area. We have placed the cursor on top of it and you can see the little black circle at the bottom-right of the cursor. This is telling you that you can now click the rotation point and drag it to its new location. Use the Reference Point Location icon at the top left of the Options palette to exactly place this rotation point in th center or on the corners or middle edges.

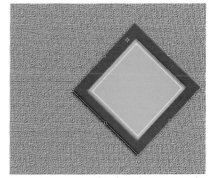

Here we are rotating the above button around a center point that was moved to the upper-right corner of the button. Now that we have rotated the button, the center point appears just to the left of the top of the button. You can see the curved rotation icon at the bottom below the center of the button.

Transforming the Contents of a Selection Versus Transforming the Selection Itself

Click the Square 3 layer in the Layers palette to activate that layer. Now Command-click the thumbnail for that layer to load that layer's transparency as a selection. Actually, the things that are not transparent are loaded as the selection. This layer has the Inner Glow effect on it to create the highlight around the green area in the center of the button. Let's say we want this area to be smaller in the center of the button. **Now choose Edit/Free Transform (Command-T), then Option-Shift-click the top-right handle, and keep the mouse button down while you drag that handle toward the center to make this center square smaller.** Remember that the Shift key forces the Scale to be proportional. The Option key makes the transformation happen symmetrically around the center of the area to be transformed. **Press Return after you have made the square smaller, as shown to the left.** We just did a Free Transform of the contents of a selection. When you have a selection, if you choose Edit/Free Transform and then do a transformation, you transform the contents of the selection within that layer, not the selection itself. To transform the selection and not its contents, you need to use Select/Transform Selection. Your selection should still be there, but if it is not, just Command-click the Square 3 layer again to reload it. **Choose Window/Show Info (F9) to bring up the Info palette. This time, choose Select/Transform Selection, which puts you in a Free Transform mode where you are working on the Selection itself. Now hold down Option-Shift while you drag the top-right handle and scale the selection inward until it is at 50% in the Info palette. Move the cursor just outside the top-right handle to get the rotate cursor and then rotate the selection up and to the left until you get -45 degrees in the Info palette.** Notice that the values in the Info palette change on the fly as you move the mouse with the button down whereas the values in the Options palette don't change until you release the mouse button. If you can't get the exact values you want in the Info palette, get it close using the Info palette then release the mouse button and edit the values inside the appropriate text boxes in the Options palette, then press Return or Enter to finish your transform. This time you have transformed the selection itself and not the contents of the selection. Again, the only difference is that to transform the selection itself, you start the process with Select/Transform Selection instead of Edit/Free Transform or Edit/Transform. **Now press I to get to the Eyedropper tool and click on the red color on the outside of the button to load it as the foreground color. Choose Edit/Fill (Shift-Delete) to fill that selected area using the Foreground Color. Your image should now look like the one to the left.**

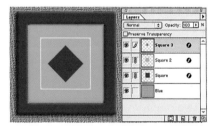

Command-clicking the thumbnail of Square 3 to load its non-transparent area as a selection.

Square 3 after making it smaller with Option-Shift-click and drag using Free Transform of the layer then Return to finish that Free Transform.

The final button after using Select/Transform Selection to create the center diamond area and then filling it with red.

Transform of a Path

Click Square 2 in the Layers palette to make it the active layer. Command-click the Square 2 thumbnail to load a selection of the non-transparent area of this layer. Now choose Window Show Path (Shift-F11) to bring up the Paths palette. Choose Make Work Path from the Paths palette menu to turn this selection into a path and choose OK when asked if you want the Tolerance set to 2.0. You now have a path of the area around the edge of this layer. **Notice that if you go to the Edit menu, the Free Transform option is still available. Type A to switch to the Path Component Selection tool then check out the Edit menu again and you'll notice that you now see Free Transform Path and Transform Path. If you have a path active, you need to be in either the Pen tool, the Path Component Selection tool, the Path Direct Selection tool or one of the Shape tools to get the option for transforming a path versus the**

Chapter 9: Transformation of Images, Layers, Paths and Selections

default of transforming the currently active layer. Now choose Edit/Free Transform Path. Now Command-click in the top-right point of the path and drag it down and to the left until that point is at the top-right highlight on Square 3. Now Command-Click the bottom-left point and drag it up and to the right until it is at the bottom-left highlight on Square 3. Press Return to complete the path transform then choose Fill Path from the Paths palette's menu to fill this area with the red foreground color. Drag the Work Path to the Trash icon in the Paths palette. You should now have the Double Diamond image to the right.

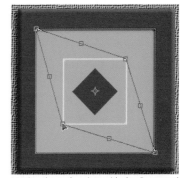

Moving the path points with the Command key down while in Free Transform Path.

LINKED LAYERS TRANSFORM AND MOVE AS A GROUP

The three layers in this example are all linked together, which you can see by noticing that the Link icon, the middle icon in the Layers palette, is on for the other two layers whenever a particular layer is active. Had we not loaded a selection to do the transformations on Square 3, all three layers would have transformed in the same way. Why don't you try this to see for yourself. **Use File/Revert to go back to the original file on the CD then click on the Square 3 layer and without loading a Selection, just choose Edit/Free Transform. You will have to first switch out of the Pen tools, type M for Marquee or H for Hand tool, to be able to access Free Transform again. Now start to scale the image and you will notice that all three layers, the entire button, scale together.** If you use the Move tool to move any of these layers, they will also all move together because they are linked. This is a very useful feature when you create an object that is made up of more than one layer and yet you want to move it or scale it as a whole. You can also drag and drop this linked object to another document and all the layers will be copied to the other document with the same names as they have in your current document. Combining all the layers that make up this button into a layer set makes this even more convinient. **Choose Layer/New/Layer Set from Linked (Shift-F12) to move these linked layers into a set named Button.** Layer sets and linking layers allows you to create component or library documents that contain your standard objects, like buttons, for example. When you need one of these objects, you just open that library document and drag and drop that component into your current working document. To get around this linking so you can move or transform a layer that has other layers linked to it, you need to first click in the Linking column of any other layers where the Link icon shows up. This unlinks those layers from the one you want to change. If there are a lot of other layers linked to this one, it may be faster to just activate one of the other layers and then click the Linking column of the layer you want to modify. This single act unlinks it from all the rest of the group. In either case, you can now transform or move the current layer. If you want to relink the layers after the change, just reclick in the Linking column of the layer(s) you unlinked before and the Link icon should show up again. You can also click and drag through a bunch of Layer's Linking columns to do a group linking in one step.

The final Double Diamond Button after filling the path with Red.

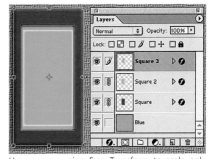

Here we are using Free Transform to scale only Square 3 and yet the other two layers are scaling too because they are linked to Square 3.

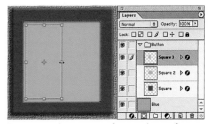

Here we see the same transform as above, after creating the Button layer set. Here only the Square 3 layer is changing because we unlinked it from the other two layers.

EDIT/TRANSFORM/ROTATE AND FLIP VERSUS IMAGE/ROTATE AND FLIP CANVAS

Edit/Transform/Rotate or Edit/Transform/Flip of a layer only rotates or flips the currently active layer and any other layers that are linked to it. Image/Rotate Canvas/Rotate or Flip rotates or flips the entire document, including all layers whether they are linked or not.

With Free Transform, you can hold the Command key down while dragging the corners across each other to create the bowtie twist look.

OTHER USEFUL EXAMPLES OF TRANSFORMS IN THIS BOOK

Check out Chapter 30: "The PowerBook Ad," Chapter 32: "Layer Clipping Paths, Shape Layers and Layer Styles," and Chapter 35: "South Africa In Focus," for real-world examples of using Free Transform in production situations.

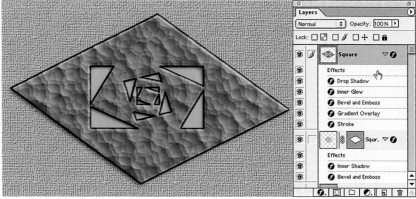

Here is the image I created after a little playing starting with the SquareButton file on the CD. Notice all the effects I added to the Square layer. To create the holes in the middle of this layer, I made rectangular selections then transformed the selected part of the layer. By rotating and shrinking these slections the holes were created. This file is also on the CD and is called SquareButtonCreation1.

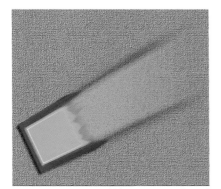

Square Button Reentry Vehicle #1. Free Transform of the button and a stretched ghost image.

Square Button Reentry Vehicle #2. The image above using Color Dodge between the ghost image and the button layers.

Here is a self portrait of me shooting into a mirror in Costa Rica. Free Transform works for photos too!

This Free Transform makes the camera look bigger.

This one makes my head seem bigger.

10 FILE FORMATS AND IMAGE COMPRESSION

*When and how to use each of the most important
file formats, and understanding Photoshop, TIFF,
and JPEG image compression.*

DIFFERENCES BETWEEN FILE FORMATS

What are the differences between file formats? When is it appropriate to use one format, but not another? Which file format should you be using? These are questions that every new Photoshop user asks, and with good reason. The long list of potential file formats in the Photoshop Save dialogs can be pretty intimidating at first. In this chapter, we'll discuss most of the formats that you're likely to use and also where one might be better than another.

Saving a file into a different format is like translating a book into a different language. In most cases, the raw data for the different formats is exactly the same; only how the data is stored or what additional information is included with the data changes. For example, an RGB file in format A may have all the red bytes stored together, then all the greens, and then all the blues. In format B, the storage might be a red, green, and blue byte for pixel 1, then a red, green, and blue byte for pixel 2, and so on. Some formats may use a simple type of compression called run length encoding, a lossless compression where, if there are 50 bytes in a row that are exactly the same, these 50 bytes are stored using a special code so they take up only 4 bytes. Another format may specify a space at the beginning of the file where extra information can be stored. The EPS file format, for example, allows you to store clipping paths, preview picts, screen angles and transfer function information within the file. In all these cases, the RGB or CMYK information in the file format remains the same. Only the packaging of the information changes from one format to another. If you save the file as a JPEG, this format does a "lossy" data compression that saves the file in much less space than in other formats. When you read the file back in, or decompress the file, it will be the same size you started with, but the actual data won't be identical. You need to be careful when using lossy compression that you do not lose important image data. We talk about this in the second part of this chapter.

The available file formats in Photoshop 6.

Name:	changes.psd
Format:	✓ **Photoshop**
	Photoshop 2.0
Save:	**BMP**
	CompuServe GIF
	Photoshop EPS
	JPEG
	PCX
Color:	**Photoshop PDF**
	PICT File
	PICT Resource
Image	**Pixar**
	PNG
	Raw
	Scitex CT
	Targa
	TIFF
	Photoshop DCS 1.0
	Photoshop DCS 2.0

OPENING AND SAVING FILES

When you open a file in Photoshop, no matter what format it was in when you opened it, the file will be in Photoshop's built-in format while you are working on it. Photoshop creates a temporary work file in memory and also, depending on the size of the file you are working with, in the free space remaining on your disk. Photoshop doesn't touch the original file on the disk until you do a File/Save. If you haven't added anything that the original format doesn't support (layers, alpha channels styles, etc.) then Photoshop saves the file using the same format in which you opened it. If you open it as a TIFF, for example, Photoshop saves it as a TIFF. As you work on a project in Photoshop, it's a good idea to save often. You should do a new save any time you have done enough work since your last save that you would be upset should your computer crash. When you choose File/Save (Command-S) to save the file, Photoshop overwrites your original file on the disk. If you have just had a file scanned, or if you want to save the original before you change it in Photoshop, you should choose File/Save As to save the file you are about to modify with a different name. This leaves your original file unchanged. When you do a Save As, the name of your window changes from the your original filename to the new name you used when you did the Save As. Doing another Save later updates the file with the new name, not the original.

INFORMATION ABOUT EACH FORMAT

Now let's discuss each of the formats that most of you will be using and when using a certain format might be best. The file formats you are more likely to use with Photoshop are Photoshop 6, TIFF, Photoshop EPS, DCS1 and DCS2, Photoshop PDF, JPEG, GIF, PICT, BMP and Scitex CT. Photoshop supports other file formats too, but these are the ones we recommend for the type of work you will be doing. If you need to know about some other format, the Photoshop 6 manual, or the online Help documentation discusses all the formats that Photoshop supports.

ADVANTAGES OF THE PHOTOSHOP FILE FORMAT

For most projects in Photoshop, we recommend that you keep your master image, or working version of your file, in Photoshop 6 format (just called Photoshop in the Save and Save As dialog boxes and having the .psd suffix). If the original file is not in Photoshop format, the first time you save the file, you should use Save As and change the format to Photoshop. Using the Photoshop format makes the program operate more efficiently because it's Photoshop's internal format and it supports everything the program can do, including image layers, vector shape layers, adjustment layers, layer masks, type layers, layer styles, channels, paths, slices and annotations. Of the other file formats available to you, only the newly expanded (and optional) capabilities of TIFF support all of these features and qualify as a viable candidate for a master file format. The Photoshop format, however, still does a much better job than TIFF at compressing images, and it saves and opens faster.

If you've opened a JPEG to work on, you should immediately Save As in Photoshop format and avoid resaving the JPEG file over and over again. Every time you save a JPEG file, it loses some information and can degrade over time. In the past, if you opened a JPEG file and added a layer to it, Photoshop would automatically save it in Photoshop format because JPEG doesn't support layers. With version 6, however, there's a new twist to this trusted behavior: if you've enabled the advanced TIFF options in the Preferences, Photoshop will automatically try to save your newly layered file as a TIFF, instead of Photoshop format. This makes no sense to me at all, since Photoshop's native format is much more efficient at losslessly compressing the image so it takes up less space on disk. There are other issues to using only TIFF as your master file format and we'll cover the new and improved TIFF a bit later in this chapter.

In addition to the standard Photoshop format, you can also save files in Photoshop 2.0 format, but this is not very useful, since it strips the file of any layers or other effects you may have added and saves it as a flattened version. Photoshop 2.0

and 2.5 did not support layers, so this is a way to save it as a psd, and still have those earlier versions of Photoshop (or other older applications) be able to open the file. To be honest, I don't know of anyone still using Photoshop 2.0 or 2.5, so that file format's inclusion in the list is more like something from the fossil record than a viable format you'll find yourself using very often.

If you're going to be sharing files with others who are using older versions of the program, it's good to know which features are supported by what versions, so here's a quick overview. Photoshop 3 does not support adjustment layers or guides and grids, but it does support regular layers, layer masks and channels. Photoshop 4 supports adjustment layers and actions, but not some Hue/Saturation and Curves features, editable type or layer effects. Photoshop 5 and 5.5 do not support the new vector shape layers, certain layer styles, slices and, most importantly, Photoshop 6 text layers. The type engine for Photoshop 6 has been entirely rebuilt and any earlier version of the program will rasterize the type if you open and then save a file. The type will still be on a separate layer, but it will no longer be editable text. This is an important thing to keep in mind if you are sharing files that contain text layers with others who have not yet upgraded to Photoshop 6.

If you are working with Photoshop 6 and you have the Maximize Backwards Compatibility in Photoshop Format option checked in File/Preferences/Saving Files (this used to be called Include Composited Image with Layered Files), then people using older versions of Photoshop, or applications that don't recognize layers, can open your layered files and see a flattened composite of the layers that were turned on when you saved the Photoshop 6 file. If the file has multiple layers, those users can't modify the file's different layers, but they can still see the results of what you intended with your layers. The cost of this backwards compatibility is an extra RGB layer the size of your entire Photoshop 6 file canvas, which will double the base size (the size of your file if it had no extra layers) of your file. That means if you started out with a 40mb scan, added layers that brought the file size up to 65mb, when you saved the file, the final size on disk would not be 65mb, but 105mb because there's that extra composited layer that weighs in at 40mb! You can save a lot of disk space by turning off the Maximize Backwards Compatibility in Photoshop Format option. (Note that these hypothetical file sizes are only approximate, since Photoshop does compress the images when it saves them to disk.)

In the Saving Files Preferences, selecting the Maximize Backwards Compatibility option will create an extra layer that is a composite of all the layers that were turned on when you saved the file. This allows users of older, pre-layer versions of Photoshop (or other applications), to be able to view your file. The drawback is that is usually doubles the base size of your file. Unless you know a reason where you need to have this on, we recommend leaving it off.

Another reason to use the Photoshop file format is that it is very effective at applying lossless compression, especially on mask channels. Consequently, files saved in Photoshop format are usually smaller than corresponding TIFF files (see the "Grid World" and "Victorians" examples later in this chapter), especially those that have a lot of mask channels. Photoshop 6 does a great job of compressing simple masks; they are often in the same file size ratio as JPEG. The RGB and CMYK components of Photoshop files are also compressed, although this compression does not make the file much smaller unless large areas in the file have the same color. The advantage of using the Photoshop 6 format to compress is that it's a fast, lossless compression.

TIFF: NEW AND IMPROVED!

The most common file format that popular imaging applications support has long been TIFF (tagged image file format). In Photoshop 6, however, it's a brand new TIFF that now supports pretty much everything that only Photoshop's native format used to support, including layers, text layers, adjustment layers, vector shape layers, layer styles, paths, clipping paths, mask channels, annotations and even slices. It's not that Adobe changed the actual TIFF file format, they just updated Photoshop

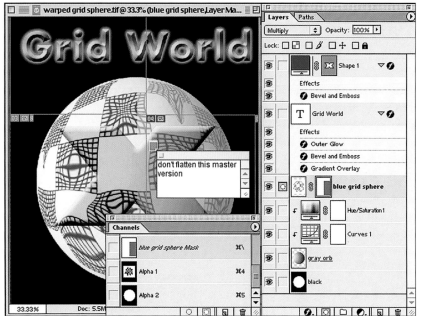

A "fully loaded" TIFF. With Photoshop 6's support for the new TIFF specifications, I was able to save the following with this file: layers, adjustment layers, layer masks, layer styles, type layers, vector shape layers, alpha channels, annotation notes, and slices. This file is 12Mb as a TIFF, but only 3Mb in Photoshop format. The large areas of solid black are compressed more efficiently in Photoshop format.

You can turn on the Enable Advanced TIFF options in the Saving Files section of the Preferences. This allows TIFFs to save most of Photoshop's features, such as all forms of layers, channels, paths, layer styles, slices and annotations. In addition to the old standby of LZW compression, there's also the option of using JPEG and ZIP encoding to compress your TIFFs.

so that it now takes full advantage of features that TIFF has evolved to support over the years. To make use of these new capabilities, however, you have to turn them on in File/Preferences/Saving Files. There you'll find a checkbox called "Enable advanced TIFF save options." Why this extra step to turn on these cool new features of TIFF, you may ask? The reason behind this is that, for years, TIFF has been considered a "safe" format that you could use pretty much anywhere without any problems. It was a simple and basic file format that was very stable, widely supported, cross-platform and rarely caused any problems during output. Since this is the first Photoshop version to adopt the new and improved TIFF capabilities, I think that Adobe is trying to ease long-time users into this brave new TIFF world, so that we're not unconsciously creating TIFFs that have layers and all sorts of other extras that TIFF didn't used to support.

That said, it's important to add that the ability of a software program, or a RIP, to correctly read the new TIFF format, depends on whether its TIFF reader is up-to-date with the current specifications. So you still may run into instances where a service provider, photo lab, or another software application cannot deal with a new, "fully loaded" Photoshop TIFF. This is not necessarily a new problem. A couple of years ago I ran across a digital photographic printer with an outdated TIFF reader that returned an error if a Photoshop 5 TIFF was saved with an alpha channel or had a color tag embedded in it. Just be aware of these issues and consult with your service provider or printer to see if their output processes and workflow supports the new "everything but the kitchen sink" breed of TIFFs.

For those who are preparing files for output to a press, the new Photoshop TIFF could be a very useful format, depending on your point of view. In the past, the working or master versions of image files were usually in Photoshop format because that was the only format that fully supported all of the possible features, such as layers, adjustment layers, etc. When it came time to place the image in a page layout document, a flattened TIFF or EPS file was generated. One problem with this was that, as concepts were revised and the master image was edited, it was possible for the final flattened placed image to be out of sync with the most current master version. In theory, the ability of the new TIFF to support layers and other Photoshop features simplifies this for publishing professionals by allowing them to use just one file, the working master image, throughout the entire process. The final placed image can now be the TIFF that has all your layers in it, but the page layout application will only see the flattened composite. In reality, however, the downside to this type of approach is that your final placed file ends up being much larger than it needs to be because of the presence of layers and any other extra features that have been saved with it. There's also the remote chance that a layered file can be accidentally modified during the final process by your output provider, or it could

Chapter 10: File Formats and Image Compression

cause output problems if encountered by an older TIFF reader, or it might not separate properly, or perhaps you just don't want to give away your secret recipe for how you made that cool multiple image composite. With a flattened TIFF you don't have to worry about these potential problems. The final placed image is distilled down to only what it needs to be for output. On the other hand, depending on the complexity of your workflow and the number of people involved, you still have to make sure that your final placed image is current with the latest revisions to your master file, but this is nothing more than good project management. In the end, you need to consider all the possible options, weigh the pros and cons and decide for yourself. Photoshop's support for the current TIFF specifications is definitely a big step forward, but I would still exercise caution when using layered TIFFs as final placed art in page layout programs, or for handing over to service bureaus for output.

As you may have gathered from the previous paragraph, the TIFF format is an excellent choice for placing images in page layout applications (the majority of the photographs and screenshot illustrations in this book are TIFFs). You can also specify a clipping path to include with a TIFF image, which some page layout programs will be able to read and/or edit. If you want to save a TIFF file, but not include any of the extras such as layers, channels, paths, etc., use File/Save As and use the checkboxes to turn off specific features. These checkboxes work with other formats, too.

The new TIFF options dialog lets you choose four methods of file compression: None, LZW, ZIP and JPEG. LZW compression has long been available for TIFFs. It typically takes longer to open and close than either standard TIFF or Photoshop compression and often causes output problems with imagesetters. When you use LZW, you usually get a file that falls somewhere between 1/3 to 2/3 as large as the original, depending on the image details in the original. LZW and ZIP compression are lossless, but JPEG is lossy, meaning it discards image and color data in order to achieve its compression. The JPEG compression option will be grayed out if the file contains any features that a normal JPEG doesn't support, such as layers or channels. I'm guessing that the reasoning behind a TIFF with JPEG compression is a way of making compressed files more acceptable to imagesetters. Since PostScript printers need to be Level 2 or higher to deal with JPEGs, perhaps encoding the JPEG compression within a TIFF file makes this output smoother. The one possible glitch here, however, is that files with JPEG encoding may not separate properly (Adobe even warns of it in their documentation), so that pretty much rules it out for dependable pre-press output. Perhaps there are specific programs I'm not aware of that also utilize this option. My recommendation is that, if you need a JPEG, save a JPEG and ignore the JPEG option in the TIFF dialog.

When working on the Mac, you should set the byte order to Macintosh. If you set the byte order to IBM PC, both Photoshop and Quark on the Mac can still open the TIFF file just fine. I've also never run into problems on a PC opening Mac byte order TIFF files, but I was using professional level programs such as Photoshop and Quark. There may be programs out there where this is an important issue, but I've never personally run across them. The Save Image Pyramid option saves multi-resolution versions within a single file, with the largest one being the actual resolution of the file. Photoshop does not currently have options for opening multi-resolution files, but Adobe's page layout program InDesign and some image servers do provide support for opening multi-resolution formats. The Save Transparency option will preserve any transparent areas in your image.

In the Save As dialog, you can choose what features will be saved with your TIFF (or any format where those features are supported). If you don't want to include an item, such as layers, simply uncheck the checkbox for it. In this example, a TIFF is being saved with layers, alpha channels and annotations; a color tag is being embedded and the full compliment of image previews and icons are also being saved with the file.

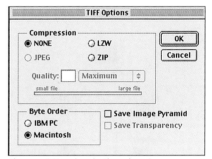

The new TIFF options in Photoshop 6.

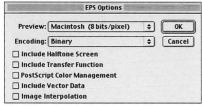

The EPS options in Photoshop 6. These are the most common choices for saving a normal file. The Include Vector Data option is new to this version of Photoshop and refers to vector shape layers and vector type.

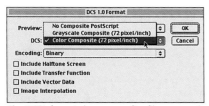

The DCS1 format always saves five files, one each for cyan, magenta, yellow and black, and a fifth file with the composite preview.

The DCS option with 72 dpi preview gives you five files. The cyan, magenta, yellow, and black files need to be in the same folder as your page layout document when you send the job to the imagesetter. The EPS preview file is used for placing and cropping in your page layout document.

Encapsulated PostScript (EPS) and Desktop Color Separation (DCS)

The EPS format, called Photoshop EPS in the file format list, is one of the most versatile formats. It's especially useful for communicating back and forth between Photoshop and Illustrator when you want to link your Photoshop file to Illustrator, rather than embed it. You can also save a clipping path from Photoshop EPS format. You choose the path you want to use as a clipping path from the Paths palette pop-up menu.

After converting your file into CMYK using the Mode menu, you can save it into EPS format in several ways. Photoshop 6 allows you to save your EPS in either a Photoshop EPS, DCS1 or DCS2 format. The Photoshop EPS format is the smallest of the three. DCS1 is the format that those of you who have been using DCS (Desktop Color Separations) are used to. It divides your EPS file into five smaller files: one file each for cyan, magenta, yellow, and black, and one composite preview file. The new format, DCS2, allows you a couple of additional options. With DCS2, you can save special alpha channels, called spot channels, which will allow you to specify a masked area as a spot color or varnish plate, and you can also choose whether to save your document as a single file, or multiple files, with or without previews. Placing just the one CMYK file directly into your page layout program is less error prone, although it does create very large files because the same file that is placed is printed. Before you save any file for final output, make sure the dots per inch (dpi) setting is correct for that final output. For a 150 line screen, for example, the setting should be 300 dpi. If you set the dpi properly, the fifth preview EPS usually is small and can read very quickly into a page layout program. Be aware, however, that all five (or more if you choose the DCS2 format) of the files must be in the folder with the layout document for the image to print correctly.

The big advantage of DCS1 is that you need to transfer only the preview EPS over the network (or, on removable media, to the desk of the person placing and cropping the pictures in the page layout application). It's much faster than transferring the entire CMYK file, which you would have to do with the EPS composite or TIFF format. The tricky thing about DCS multiple file documents is that you need to be sure to include the other four CMYK files in the same folder as your layout document and preview file when you print your layout to the imagesetter; otherwise, you get a low-quality printout. Again, you should discuss this file format choice with your service bureau and printer. Also, the Photoshop manual offers more information about the EPS/DCS file formats.

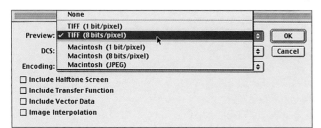

The different types of previews that can be saved with DCS1 or DCS2 format. Macintosh (JPEG) gives you a better looking preview, but older page layout applications may not be able to read the preview. Use TIFF if you need to transfer files between the Mac and a PC. Don't check Include Halftone Screens or Transfer Functions unless you are setting these things in Photoshop. Discuss all these settings with your service bureau before you send them any files.

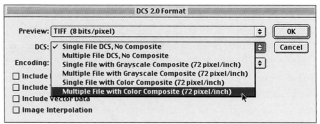

With DCS2 format, you have lots of different options as to how to save your file.

Chapter 10: File Formats and Image Compression

GIF

The GIF format (called CompuServe GIF in the file format list) is used most often for images intended for the Web. The GIF format is a lossless compression format for images of up to 8-bit color. Photoshop can create GIF files from the Save dialog boxes if the file is in bitmap, grayscale or index color format. Using the Save for Web dialog, you can create GIF format files from RGB Photoshop documents that have layers and transparent regions with much more flexibility and control. The GIF file format and the Save for Web dialog are discussed in great detail in the last section of this book, "Images for the Web and Multimedia."

PDF

You can use PDF format to send small versions of your files across networks or the Internet. These files can be RGB, CMYK, Indexed color, Lab color, grayscale, or Bitmap format. In Photoshop 6, you're given the opportunity to compress your PDF files using either JPEG or ZIP compression. Photoshop PDF files now can save every feature that the Photoshop or TIFF can support, including layers, text layers, adjustment layers, vector shape layers, layer styles, paths, clipping paths, mask channels, annotations and even slices. Of these extras, only the annotations would be editable if the file was opened in Adobe Acrobat. The annotations are a great feature for marking up proofs that you're sending to someone for review. Another value is the capability to open and print PDF files from other sources if, for whatever reason, you don't have a copy of Adobe Acrobat Reader. Photoshop 6 even speeds this conversion by an Automate command (File/Automate/Multipage PDF to PSD).

PNG

The PNG (pronounced ping) format is another Web compression format that gives you some additional options over either JPEG or GIF compression. It's a lossless compression method that allows you to choose between saving your 24-bit color information or saving indexed color information. PNG can produce transparent areas without jagged edges by saving one (and only one) alpha channel to define the transparent areas. In addition, you can store the gamma setting of your system and use two-dimensional interlacing to help your file load even more quickly. Even though it's been around for a while now, it's still not supported by all the browsers. Also, compressing large images takes a long time and the size savings are small, but PNG shows a great deal of promise once Netscape and Microsoft get on board.

PICT

PICT format is an Apple standard file format supported by automatic compression and decompression in QuickTime. I have found this format to cause some problems when placed in page layout documents and don't recommend it for that purpose. It is, however, a commonly used multimedia format, as well as the format that is used by the Mac system between applications when you copy an image from one and paste it into another. When you save in PICT format, the QuickTime compression you automatically get is lossless, but if you choose one of the JPEG options, you get a compression that isn't lossless—so beware.

BMP

This is a standard Windows graphics file format that is similar to PICT. If you're a Windows user, you're probably already familiar with this format. If you want to place an image into a Powerpoint presentation, then BMP is one of the supported formats in PC versions of that program.

The uncompressed TIFF version of the Victorians image: nine megabytes saved as TIFF and 6.5 megabytes saved in Photoshop format.

The JPEG high-compressed version of the Victorians image. This file is 640K.

SCITEX CT

Scitex CT format is sometimes used when saving CMYK files that will be processed on a Scitex imaging system. These files are generally quite large and have very few problems with moiré patterns. You can also save RGB or grayscale files in Scitex CT format, but this format does not support alpha channels. Again, your service provider will tell you if you need to save in this format.

DISK SPACE AND COMPRESSION FORMATS

In today's world of color page creation, image compositing and multimedia production, disk space is a commodity that can be used up quite quickly. Color photographs for print are items that can take up a lot of disk space. For the best quality, a color photograph has to be scanned at twice the dots per inch (dpi) as the line screen at which it will be printed. For a 5x7 color image in a 150-line screen publication, the required disk space would be: ***(5x300) x (7x300) x 4 = 12,600,000 bytes for the CMYK version of the file*** (over twelve megabytes for just one copy of the file). Usually, by the time you finish production, you may need two or three copies of each file. That could be close to 40 megabytes of storage for just one 5x7 photograph. You might want to consider using compression to reduce the size of your image files. You also use compression for sending files to a client or printer electronically and in placing images on Web pages. To find out more about GIF and JPEG compression for Web and multimedia use, please refer to "Images for the Web and Multimedia" section near the end of this book.

LZW COMPRESSION

When you save a file in TIFF format from Adobe Photoshop, you can choose LZW (Lempel-Zif-Welch) compression. It saves the 9Mb uncompressed Victorians file in 5.5Mb. When you look at the amount of time LZW compression takes versus the minimum space savings you get, LZW compression often isn't worth the effort.

JPEG COMPRESSION

Using the Joint Photographic Experts Group (JPEG) compression software built into Photoshop with the quality setting on High, the 9Mb Victorians file is compressed to 640K. You can see a real savings in data space here—the compressed file is about 1/15 the size of the original! When you use JPEG compression, you can choose how much you want to compress a file. Using more compression gives you a smaller file, but also more loss of image detail. A smaller amount of compression gives you less loss of image detail, but the compressed file doesn't save as much disk space. Depending on your publication quality requirements, you can choose a compression factor that compresses files without any visible detail loss on the final printed page.

JPEG is an industry standard file format for image compression. Many companies sell JPEG software and hardware compression products. The hardware compression boards that contain DSP chips can compress and decompress images much

📁 Victorians new compressions	Today, 12:04 PM	bytes	16.5 MB
40Victorians.jpg high	Today, 11:52 AM	421,920	448K
40Victorians.jpg high opt	Today, 12:03 PM	404,318	448K
40Victorians.jpg high prog 4	Today, 12:04 PM	402,486	416K
40Victorians.jpg high.prog	Today, 12:03 PM	405,602	448K
40Victorians.jpg max	Today, 11:51 AM	774,230	800K
40Victorians.jpg max opt	Today, 12:00 PM	764,759	800K
40Victorians.PDF high	Today, 11:57 AM	537,276	576K
40Victorians.PDF max	Today, 11:52 AM	984,451	992K
40Victorians.PDF zip	Today, 11:58 AM	5,480,158	5.2 MB
40VictoriansOrigPS	Today, 11:50 AM	6,778,333	6.5 MB

Some sizes of different compression methods. The jpg high and max files are set with the Baseline Standard setting. The jpg high.prog file uses three scans and the prog 4 file uses four scans. You can see that you start to get some savings as you use more scan passes. The PDF high and max files are using the JPEG compression method and don't give you quite the savings as a direct JPEG. The ZIP compression method gives you very little savings over the original Photoshop file. Because the Mac rounds out the file sizes, we've included the actual byte size in red.

Original file, 9Mb TIFF, uncompressed.

Maximum-quality JPEG setting, 1.2Mb.

Medium-quality JPEG setting, 352K.

Low-quality JPEG setting, 256K.

faster than they could without the DSP. DSP stands for Digital Signal Processor, which is a chip that speeds up the mathematical operations used in many image processing filters and effects, including JPEG compression and decompression.

CHOOSING A COMPRESSION FACTOR

To show you the kinds of problems to look for when choosing your compression factor with JPEG compression, we have printed the same file with different degrees of compression. For printing on coated stock or for art prints, we would recommend not compressing your file at all unless you need to. If you do need to save space, use the Maximum Quality setting when possible because it gives you the best image quality. If you can't see any data loss in your final printed image, then the loss may not be important to you. On the other hand, if you archive a digital file for use in future printed pieces, slide productions or multimedia presentations, you need to be sure that compression data loss won't show up in one of those future applications.

Another JPEG compression issue is that compressed files take longer to open and process when printing at the service bureau. Before you compress, talk to your service bureau about whether to use JPEG compressed files. Unless the service bureau owns a Level 2 or Level 3 PostScript imagesetter, they cannot download JPEG files directly. They have to re-open the file in Photoshop and save it to another uncompressed format. They may charge you more for JPEG compressed files if it will take them longer to process them on output. Other lossless compression options are StuffIt on the Mac and WinZip on the PC. With these, you need to make sure the person on the other end who decompresses the file has the right version to do the decompression. Again, you should discuss any compression option with your service provider before choosing one of them.

The original Victorians, 9Mb TIFF, uncompressed, is at the top right. Below that is the JPEG compression set to the maximum image quality, 1.2Mb. Third down from the top is the medium quality setting, 352K. Finally, in the bottom picture you see the low-quality setting, 256K. All these JPEG compressions, except for the low quality, will work for printing. For printing, I would usually use the high or maximum quality to be safe, or better yet, not compress at all unless you really must. The Medium quality is good for sending a comp to a client over the internet, and for creating web images. Avoid using the low setting. These files were compressed with the Baseline Optimized setting on in the JPEG dialog box, which should create higher color quality.

11 AUTOMATING WITH ACTIONS

Using the Actions palette to add function keys to access menu items and sequences of keys and events to automate your Photoshop production. Sharpen Only Edges, Remove Sky Crud and other useful ArtistKeys scripts are explained.

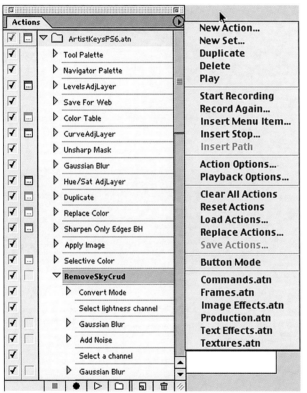

The Actions palette with Button mode turned off. This allows you to edit the actions in many ways. The Actions menu bar shows you all the things you can do with actions. We discuss these in this chapter and explain how they work. Notice the icons at the bottom of the palette that, from left to right, stop recording, start recording, play current action or command, make a new set of actions, create a new action or command, and allow you to throw an action or command into the trash.

Actions allow you to record and even edit single menu items or very complicated sequences of events. You can then run that menu item or series of events over an entire folder full of files. You can execute these events with the press of a function key on the keyboard or a click of a button onscreen. You choose Window/Show Actions (F11 with ArtistKeys) to bring up the Actions palette. To create new actions or edit them, you need to turn off Button mode from the Actions Palette menu. After you define all your actions, you can turn on Button mode, which shows you the function key associated with an action and also turns the Actions palette into a series of buttons that you can click on to play an action.

ARTISTKEYS TO SET UP YOUR ACTIONS

In the Automating with Actions folder of the Photoshop 6 Artistry CD, we have given you a predefined set of actions, called ArtistKeys. You should add this set of Actions to your copy of Photoshop since we will show you how to use them in this book. Towards the end Chapter 3: "Setting System and Photoshop Preferences," we show you how to load the ArtistKeys actions into your copy of Photoshop 6. If you haven't already done this, turn to page 27 and 28 and do it now.

What we did with ArtistKeys is go through all the menu items in Photoshop and set up as function keys the ones that you will use most often. For example, F9 through F12 will bring up and close down the palettes you use most often. We tried to do this logically, so F9 is the Info palette and Shift-F9 is the Color palette. Both of these palettes deal with measuring color. F10 is the Layers palette and Shift-F10 is the Channels palette. You often use these together. I use F2 through F12 to implement single menu items (and we do mention and use these quite often in the book, so you will find them quick to learn). I consider F1, as well as F13 through F15, optional, so you can use them to reprogram other actions. You can also program most of the Command key actions as well as all the Shift-Command ones. Most computer keyboards these days do have function keys F1–F12 with some also having F13–F15. All Macs seem to be pretty standard

If your ArtistKeys function keys are not working properly on the Mac, choose Apple/Control Panels/Keyboard, click on the Function Keys button at the bottom then turn on the Function Key Setting checkbox shown at the bottom of this dialog.

in their use of function keys, although if you have OS 9 or later on the Mac, you may have to enable the usage of function keys by the applications. If your ArtistKeys actions are not working properly, choose Apple Menu/Control Panels/Keyboard and click on the Function Keys button at the bottom of the Keyboard dialog. This brings up the dialog to the left where you want to turn on the Use F1 through F12 as Function Keys checkbox at the bottom of the Hot Function Keys dialog. Some of the function keys we've setup for ArtistKeys may have different special functions on various PC systems. On the PC side, with Windows 95, 98, 2000 and NT, as well as all the different companies that make PCs, there are too many possible special features for function keys to cover how to turn these features off. If you are having trouble making certain function keys work with your PC, either learn how to redirect the function keys on your particular model or change the function key assigned to a particular ArtistKeys action so it uses a key that your PC hasn't set up for some particular special purpose. Later in this chapter, we'll show you how to change the function key assigned to any action.

TO RECORD A SINGLE MENU ITEM ACTION

If you want to set up an action with a function key to perform any menu item, even the palette menus, here are the steps to take. Make sure the Actions palette is not in Button mode (Button Mode unchecked), by using the Actions Palette menu. While playing with actions here, create a new action set by choosing New Set from the Actions Palette menu. Name this set My Actions. Create a new action by clicking the New Action icon at the bottom of the Actions palette, or by choosing New Action from the Actions Palette menu. Either way, the New Action dialog opens, enabling you to name your action as well as pick the action set, a function key and color for it. Choose My Actions for the set, you do not need to pick a function key or color. When you click the Record button, you can record a single menu item simply by choosing Insert Menu Item from the Actions Palette menu. Doing so opens the Insert Menu Item dialog box shown here. Now choose the menu that you want to automate from the main Menu bar or from a Palette menu, and its name fills the text box. Choose OK and then click the Stop Recording icon at the bottom of the Actions palette or choose Stop Recording from the Actions menu. To play the action you just recorded, press the function key or click the action in the Actions palette and choose Play from the Actions menu, or click the Play icon at the bottom of the palette. In Button mode, clicking the button for an action plays it. The good thing about actions is that you can now record, and even edit, highly complicated sequences of events and then run them over an entire folder full of files using File/Automate/Batch or Create Droplet.

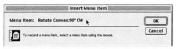

Use Insert Menu Item, from the Actions palette menu, to create an action that plays a single menu item. You can pick any menu item from anywhere within Photoshop. Also use this when you don't want the action to insert any values into the command the menu activates.

The Actions palette with Button mode turned on. In Button mode, you can click an action to play it, even if it doesn't have a function key alternative as some of the actions below Vertical Web in the ArtistKeys palette don't.

The New Action command, or double-clicking an existing action, brings up the New Action or Action Options dialog box, where you can name your action, choose an action set or function key for it, and also a color that shows up in Button mode.

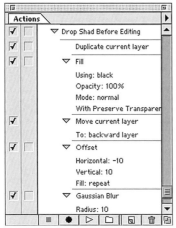

Here we see the Drop Shadow basic action prior to editing. If you play this action, the Offset command always offsets the shadow by −10 horizontal and 10 vertical. The Gaussian Blur of the shadow will always have a Radius of 10. This will not create the correct drop shadow in most cases because the size of the object will be different and the light may be coming from a different direction. You need to edit this to make it user-friendly and object-specific.

Here is the Drop Shadow action after editing to add the Stop commands as well as the breakpoints in the Offset and Gaussian Blur commands. The Stop commands were added to explain the action to future users. The Break points, which show up as icons in the middle column, allow the user to enter custom values for each invocation of the action.

RECORDING ACTIONS WITH MULTIPLE COMMANDS

To record an action with a sequence of events, you start by choosing the New Action icon or menu item. Name your action, press the Record button, and then go through the sequence of events you want in the action while working on the open file. Each recorded menu item in the sequence is now called a command. Because you want to run this sequence on many other files, you need to be aware of the state of the file when you start recording. All subsequent files will have to be in the same beginning state for the action to work properly. Actions are like computer programs; they have no intelligence to pick the right layer within the file or make sure the file was saved before you start. Take a look at the action within ArtistKeys called Drop Shad (Ob In Actv Lyr). It is meant to add a drop shadow to an object that is in its own layer surrounded by transparency. Open the file called Ball from the Automating with Actions folder on the *Photoshop 6 Artistry* CD. You will notice that the layer called Ball is currently the active layer, and the ball within this layer is surrounded by transparency. Any file that you run this Drop Shadow action on will have to first be in this state for the action to do the right thing. If you have programmed before, this will be obvious, but I know that many of you have not.

Enter the message you want displayed to give the user information about the action that is playing. Turn on Allow Continue so the action will continue when the user clicks OK.

To create this action, start with a file in this state (you can use the Ball file; you have it open anyway) then click the Record button and go through a sequence of events to create a drop shadow. This drop shadow is created in a more traditional way than some of the newer layer style techniques you can use to create drop shadows in Photoshop 6. We are just using it as an example to help explain actions. While creating an action, the Actions recording feature records the events as you do the work. If you have the Actions palette open, you can see the events recording as you work. Do absolutely nothing except this sequence of events; otherwise, you record those other things too. After you finish your sequence of events, choose Stop Recording from the Actions Palette menu or click the Stop Recording icon at the bottom of the Actions palette. You have now created the basic action! Now you need to look at the sequence of commands in this action and edit them to make sure it does the right thing when you play it back. Think about it; will you always want all the parameters to each command to be the same or will some things be slightly different for each use of the action on a different file? The great thing about actions is that you can customize them easily.

EDITING ACTIONS AFTER RECORDING

I wanted people to figure out how to use this drop shadow action without any verbal directions, so I added the Stop messages. The unedited drop shadow action is shown here to the left at the top of the page with the edited one below it. We added a Stop message by clicking the Drop Shad (Ob In Actv Lyr) line to activate it, and then clicking the arrow to the left of the name, which opens up the action and displays the list of commands in it. Choosing Insert Stop from the Actions menu opens the Record Stop dialog box. That is where you enter the text of the message you want the user to see. The message I entered just explains that to use this action, you need to start with an active layer that has an object surrounded by transparency. The Stop command now happens before the action starts, so that the user can click Cancel if the file he is running it on is not in the right state. If the user clicks Continue, the action then goes on to make a copy of the target layer, fill that copy with black using preserve transparency, and then move this new black layer below the original target layer. To turn this new black layer into a shadow, we need to now offset it from the original and then blur it to make its edges soft. I added another Stop message before the Offset command, this one explaining that the user needs to adjust the offset numbers to fit the object in question. The direction and amount of the offset will depend on the lighting on the original. To allow the user to change these values, I put a break point on the Offset command by clicking in the middle column to the left of this command in the Actions palette. Finally, I added another Stop to explain that the Gaussian Blur amount also requires editing to make sure the shadow looks right for this situation. So the user can actually edit the Gausian Blur amount, I then added a break point on the Gaussian Blur, again by clicking in the column to its left.

Throw Away Action or Command.

Begin Recording.

Create a new Action or Duplicate Current Action or Command.

Stop Action Recording or Playback.

Play Current Action or Command.

FURTHER EDITING REFINEMENTS

The preceding example illustrates the types of editing you can do to actions. After you understand how this Drop Shadow action works, you could turn off the Stop commands by clicking their check marks to turn off each check in the left most column next to each Stop command. You could also throw away the Stop commands as you can any command or action, by dragging it to the Trash icon at the bottom of the Actions palette. If you were using File/Automate/Batch to run this Drop Shadow action on a bunch of items that all have the same offset and blur values, you could turn off the breakpoints on the offset and blur steps by clicking in the middle column next to each of them. You could change the actual value of the default offset or blur by clicking that command line and then choosing Record Again from the Actions Palette menu. It will play that command line and allow you to change its default value within the action. If you want the user to always enter the values for a particular command when he uses the command, you need to use the Insert Menu Item option from the Actions menu when recording that command, and choose that command as the menu item to insert. Recording a command this way doesn't actually execute the command until the action is played, so the user has to enter the values at that time instead of having default values.

Here we have a Drop Shadow action where the Offset and Gaussian Blur were created using Insert Menu Item. These will automatically stop and allow the user to specify the parameters each time. There are no default values if you create a step using Insert Menu Item.

ADDING TO ACTIONS

After you record an action, you can add to it by selecting a particular command within the action and choosing the Start Recording menu from the Actions menu bar, or by clicking the Start Recording icon at the bottom of the Actions palette. New commands are recorded right after the command you select. You can click an existing command and drag it to the New Action/Command icon, at the bottom of the Actions palette, to make a copy of that command. You can then drag that copy, or any command, to another location in the current action or in another action. If you want to start playing an action in the middle, just click the command at the point at which you want to begin and choose Play from the Actions menu to play the action from that point forward. You can also play an action or command by clicking the Play icon at the bottom of the Actions palette.

Choose Playback Options from the Actions palette menu to bring up this dialog for your Playback options. If you have a newer faster computer, you may have to put a Pause For several seconds between each action to have time to see them as individual steps on the screen.

THINGS THAT ACTIONS DON'T SUPPORT

Some menu items in Photoshop don't do anything during the recording of an action. If, while recording, you choose a menu item or click a tool, or do anything, and a new command doesn't show up in the Actions palette, then that thing is not

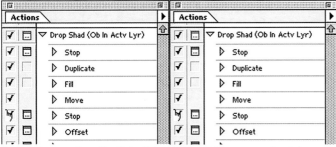

On the left we see the action that will break with each Stop command and also on the Offset and Gaussian Blur commands. On the right we have removed the Stop commands by clicking their checkmarks in the checkmark column to the left, and we have taken away the break points on the Offset and Gaussian Blur by clicking them in the break column. This is the kind of thing you might want to do to an action to prepare it for automatically running in Batch mode over a lot of files.

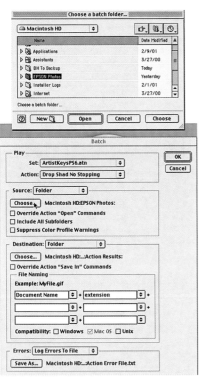

Here is the dialog box for File/Automate/Batch where you can choose the Action Set and Action, Source, and Destination for your Batch. Notice the features that let you Override Action Open Commands, Include All Subfolders, and Suppress Color Profile Warnings during the playing of an action. You are also allowed to Log Errors To a File. When you use one of the Choose buttons, for Source or Destination, this brings up the dialog box at the very top here. The trick in this Choose dialog is to click the Choose button in that dialog when the folder you want is highlighted. The dialog here is set to choose the folder called Epson Photos.

recordable. If you want to include any of them as part of an action anyway, you can choose Insert Menu Item, which will play that menu item when the action plays. You can't put default values into these commands, but at least you can get the user to respond to them.

OTHER ACTIONS FEATURES

Actions can be organized into different sets. To create a new set, choose New Set from the Actions Palette menu or click the third icon from the right (looks like an empty folder with a tab) at the bottom of the Actions palette. Use Sets to organize your actions into different functional groups. The function keys are global across all the sets, so you can't use the same function key twice for two different things without loading different actions.

RUNNING THE SAME ACTION ON A WHOLE BATCH OF FILES

The File/Automate/Batch menu enables you to specify an action along with a source and destination folder for that action. If you specify a source folder and a destination folder, Photoshop opens each file in the source folder and runs the action on the file and then saves that modified file in the destination folder. If the source folder has sub-folders, you can choose to have Photoshop also process the files in the sub-folders. You do not have to put Open or Close commands in your action; the Batch command automatically adds these at the beginning and the end. If your action has any Open commands in it, the Override Action Open Commands checkbox in the Batch dialog box allows you to tell it to ignore those commands. Another checkbox lets you tell the Batch command to ignore any Save commands. You select the action you want to perform by using the Action pop-up menu in the Batch dialog box and choosing the Source and Destination folders by clicking their respective Choose buttons. If you choose None for Destination, Photoshop leaves the modified files open. If you choose Save and Close, they are saved back in the folder in which they started, under the same name. You can also create a Multi-Batch action that records more than one Batch command. You can then play this Multi-Batch action, which allows you to batch one action after another on the same set of files, or to batch the same action over and over again on different files in more than one folder.

Photoshop also has the capability to log errors to a file, whose name and location you choose. After the error is logged, the action continues. When running actions on a large group of files within a folder, this allows the action to process the other files even if there is an error with several of them. When an error comes up, you can also choose to have Photoshop stop the action and put an error message on the screen. Let's get some action into our lives!

VERY USEFUL ACTIONS IN THE PHOTOSHOP 6 ARTISTKEYS SET

The Sharpen Only Edges BH, Remove Sky Crud and Process Color actions are very useful ones that are included with ArtistKeys, but they need some explanation. On the next page are screen grabs of each of these actions, along with large captions that explain how to use them. Please let me know, at barry@maxart.com, how useful you find these actions and if you discover any new and better variations of them.

Chapter 11: Automating with Actions

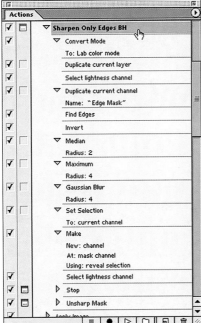

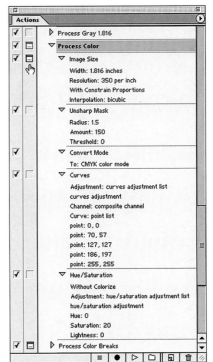

Sharpen Only Edges BH
- Convert Mode
  - To: Lab color mode
- Duplicate current layer
- Select lightness channel
- Duplicate current channel
  - Name: "Edge Mask"
- Find Edges
- Invert
- Median
  - Radius: 2
- Maximum
  - Radius: 4
- Gaussian Blur
  - Radius: 4
- Set Selection
  - To: current channel
- Make
  - New: channel
  - At: mask channel
  - Using: reveal selection
- Select lightness channel
- Stop
- Unsharp Mask

The Sharpen Only Edges BH action is one that is based on a script that I originally got from Bill Atkinson. His version, called just Sharpen Only Edges, is also in the ArtistKeys action set. They both use the Lightness channel of a LAB version of your Master Image to create a mask that applies sharpening to only the parts of the image that really need to be sharpened. MY BH version adds a step at the front that converts your image to LAB color, which does nothing if your image is already in LAB color. My version also sets up the created mask as a layer mask on a copy of the original layer. The mask that both of these sharpening actions create is made by using the Find Edges filter, followed by Invert, Median, Maximum and then Gaussian Blur to massage these edges into a mask that will sharpen only what you need. Sharpen Only Edges BH works well on images that are 50 to 150 megabytes in size to be printed at 300 to 360 dpi. If you are working on larger or smaller images, you may want to adjust the Radius settings on the Median, Maximum and Gaussian Blur filters to see if you can get better results. When using a higher dpi, you might want to increase the radius and when using a lower dpi then decrease it. The last step of Sharpen Only Edges BH, which is explained by the Stop message at the end, is to activate the Lightness channel of that copied layer, turn on the Eye icons of the other channels, then run Unsharp Mask to sharpen that Lightness channel. This allows you to change the amount of sharpening, while watching the effect of the sharpening with the Preview checkbox on within the Unsharp Mask filter. You are actually sharpening the entire lightness channel of the copy of your Master Image which is in a layer on top of the original Master Image layer underneath. The layer mask for the copy, which this action created, only shows the portions of the sharpened copy that are really necessary to sharpen the image. After finishing the Unsharp Mask you can then use black and white to further edit the mask to add more sharpness to some areas and less sharpness to other areas. This is the way I sharpen all my art prints. After running Unsharp Mask, you can also lessen the amount of sharpening by lowering the Opacity of the top layer.

Process Color 1.4
Process Color 1.816
Process Color 2.139
- Image Size
  - Width: 2.14 inches
  - Resolution: 350 per inch
  - With Constrain Proportions
  - Interpolation: bicubic
- Unsharp Mask
- Convert Mode
- Curves
- Hue/Saturation
- Play action "Save & Close" of set "ArtistKeysPS6.atn"
Process Color 2.25
Process Color 3
Process Color 4.444

This version of the standard Process Color action, shown to the right, is set up for screen grabs that will be placed into Quark at a width of 2.139 inches. Since this is a common size Quark illustration for my book, I have a special action with the Image Size set to that width and with no break-points. I can then put a bunch of screen grabs of this size into a folder and run them as a batch. Notice that the Width inside the action has been rounded to 2.14 inches. That actually works fine for Quark. I made a Process Color action for each of my more common screen grabs widths.

Process Gray 1.816
Process Color
- Image Size
  - Width: 1.816 inches
  - Resolution: 350 per inch
  - With Constrain Proportions
  - Interpolation: bicubic
- Unsharp Mask
  - Radius: 1.5
  - Amount: 150
  - Threshold: 0
- Convert Mode
  - To: CMYK color mode
- Curves
  - Adjustment: curves adjustment list
  - curves adjustment
  - Channel: composite channel
  - Curve: point list
  - point: 0, 0
  - point: 70, 57
  - point: 127, 127
  - point: 186, 197
  - point: 255, 255
- Hue/Saturation
  - Without Colorize
  - Adjustment: hue/saturation adjustment list
  - hue/saturation adjustment
  - Hue: 0
  - Saturation: 20
  - Lightness: 0
- Process Color Breaks

Here we see the Process Color Action which is in the ArtistKeys set but doesn't have a function key assigned to it. This is a generic version of the basic action I used to process all the screen grabs within *Photoshop 6 Artistry*. The Image Size command within this action has a break point attached to it which allows me to set the width I want for this particular screen grab. The other commands here will always just run and do the same thing. After resampling the screen grab to the width of its box in Quark at 350 dpi, the file is then sharpened, converted to CMYK, has a Curve run on it to compensate for contrast loss due to CMYK conversion and has Hue/Saturation run on it to saturate the colors again after the CMYK conversion. Notice that there is another similar action called Process Color Breaks that has break points on the Unsharp Mask step and the Hue/Saturation step. I use this action when I want to double-check the amount of sharpening or the amount of color saturation.

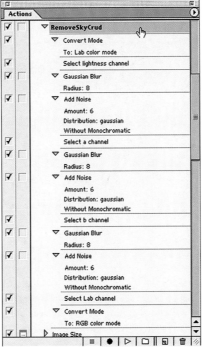

RemoveSkyCrud
- Convert Mode
  - To: Lab color mode
- Select lightness channel
- Gaussian Blur
  - Radius: 8
- Add Noise
  - Amount: 6
  - Distribution: gaussian
  - Without Monochromatic
- Select a channel
- Gaussian Blur
  - Radius: 8
- Add Noise
  - Amount: 6
  - Distribution: gaussian
  - Without Monochromatic
- Select b channel
- Gaussian Blur
  - Radius: 8
- Add Noise
  - Amount: 6
  - Distribution: gaussian
  - Without Monochromatic
- Select Lab channel
- Convert Mode
  - To: RGB color mode
- Image Size

The RemoveSkyCrud action is sometimes useful on images that have large clumpy grain in the sky. To use this action, first make a flattened copy of your Master Image then run this RemoveSkyCrud on this flattened copy. This turns the copy into LAB color mode then blurs each channel separately and also uses Add Noise after the blur to return some sort of grain pattern to the channel. When finished, this action converts this copy of your image back to RGB color using your RGB Working Space. You would then use the Move tool with the Shift key down to drag and drop this copy of your image back on top of your Master Image Layers. You then want to add an all black layer mask to this Crud Removed layer and use a soft Airbrush with a low Opacity, like 07%, to paint white in the mask only in the areas where you need to remove the clumpy grain in the sky. Depending on the amount of grain in your Master Image sky, you may want to change the Radius values, within this action, for Gaussian Blur and Add Noise.

Editing Actions After Recording

COLOR CORRECTION AND CALIBRATION TO CREATE A MASTER DIGITAL IMAGE

COLOR SPACES AND COLOR MANAGEMENT

OVERALL COLOR CORRECTION

CALIBRATION

THE ZONE SYSTEM FOR DIGITAL IMAGES

CREATING A MASTER IMAGE

SCANNING, RESOLUTION, HISTOGRAMS, AND PHOTO CD

Crater Lake Oregon is one of the clearest lakes in the world. I took this early one morning with only the boat making ripples on the water. This was taken with my Canon F1 using color transparency film and then scanned with a Tango drum scanner.

12 COLOR CORRECTION TOOLS

Overview of Photoshop's many color correction and gamma adjustment tools, which ones are most useful for what and why, and which ones are fairly useless for the professional.

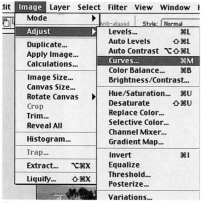

The color correction tools are in the Image/Adjust menu. When you use them from here they permanently modify the pixels they are adjusting in the currently active layer. Changing the pixels over and over again can damage the integrity of the image.

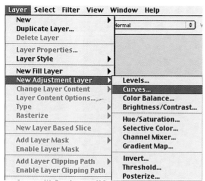

Doing a color adjustment using an adjustment layer creates a special layer above the currently active layer which allows you to change this adjustment as many times as you like without modifying or damaging the original pixels or the integrity of the image. It also keeps a record for you of the changes you have made.

Photoshop offers many tools for adjusting color and modifying image gamma or contrast. This chapter gives you a quick overview of what the different tools do and when to use each tool. The color correction tools are in the Image/Adjust menu and are also available as adjustment layers. Levels, Curves, Hue/Saturation, Replace Color, Selective Color, Color Balance and Channel Mixer are the color correction tools we use most. Auto Levels, Auto Contrast, Brightness/Contrast, Desaturate, Gradient Map and Variations are the ones we don't use as much. You will notice that *Photoshop 6 Artistry* color corrects mostly with Adjustment Layers since those corrections can be changed as many times as you like without destroying the integrity of the file. In later hands-on chapters, we actually go through the details of each tool's features and how they're used in real-world examples. Invert, Equalize, Threshold and Posterize are used more for effects and masking, which are covered in other parts of this book.

USING THE INFO/COLOR SAMPLER AND COLOR PALETTES

When you use any of the color correction tools, it is very helpful to have the Info palette, and sometimes the Color palettes, visible onscreen. Use Window/Show Info (F9 with ArtistKeys) and Window/Show Color (Shift-F9) to bring up these palettes. While working in any color correction tool, Photoshop automatically gives you the Eyedropper tool for measuring colors in the image. The Info palette shows you the digital RGB, LAB and/or CMYK values of the pixel or group of pixels you currently have the Eyedropper tool above. It shows you these values both before (left of slash) and after (right of slash) any changes you have made during the current iteration of the color correction tool you are now using. The Color palette has a subtle but important difference from the Info palette in that it displays the values of the last place where you clicked with the Eyedropper versus wherever the eyedropper might currently be located that the Info Palette displays. This allows you to click on a picture tone or color area and see how the pixel values of that particular area change as you make adjustments with the Color tool you are currenlty working with. The Color palette also has colored sliders that give you hints as to how a certain color change, like adding red, will effect the color of the location where you last clicked. The Color Sampler tool, an option of the Eyedropper in the Tool palette, allows you to click (Shift-click while in a color tool) up to four locations where you want to monitor the color of your image while working. These four color values show up in the bottom of the Info palette. This is a great feature because you can see how the color values at these four locations change throughout your color correction process. You don't have to measure them again; their values will constantly update as you work. Each open image can have up to four Color Samplers attached to it.

When adjusting a digital image, you usually want to make as few separate file modifications as are necessary to achieve the desired result. A file modification is when you click the OK button for any of the color correction tools and you are not in an adjustment layer. Each file modification changes the original data, and too

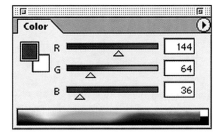

The Color palette remembers the values at the last location you clicked with the Eyedropper. If you made that click after entering a color adjustment tool, this palette will then show you how the values at the point you clicked change as you make adjustments using that color adjustment tool.

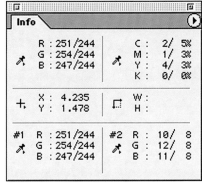

The Info palette with the before values to the left and the after values to the right of the slash. In this Info palette we have created two Color Samplers, #1 for the highlight position and #2 for the shadow position.

many changes can eventually degrade the quality of the data. Therefore, you don't want to constantly go from one color correction tool to the other frantically trying to get the effect you need. You want to use these tools intelligently, knowing what each one is good for and keeping the total number of uses to the minimum required to do the final adjustments on a particular image. If you do your changes using adjustment layers, the actual image pixels do not change until the image is flattened. Adjustment layers allow you to go back and change the color over and over again without suffering from this cumulative degrading effect on the digital values.

COMMON COLOR CORRECTION TECHNIQUES

All the color correction tools share a few things in common. When using a color correction tool, you need to turn the Preview button on to see the changes happen to the image. With the Preview button off, you are seeing the image as it appeared prior to the changes made by the current invocation of the tool you are using. You can see before and after by quickly turning the Preview button off and on. When you turn the Preview button on, Photoshop has to change the data in the file, based on the changes you have made in the color correction tool, before you can see the changes on the screen. With today's computers this happens very quickly but it still involves a lot of calculations.

In all previous versions of Photoshop on the Mac, having the Preview button off in some of the color correction tools, like Levels and Curves, would use Video LUT Animation to give you an instant preview with constant feedback as you made changes. Clicking on the title bar with the Preview off would show you an instant before version of the image. These were implemented using a feature supported on all Macintosh video cards called Video LUT Animation. Most Windows cards didn't support Video LUT Animation and now support for it has been removed from Photoshop 6 on both platforms. It did provide some useful features in some circumstances and I wonder if support of it would have been removed if it worked on Windows platforms as well? Having it work the same way now on both platforms certainly makes it easier to explain but it does seem that the world has lost some functionality here because Microsoft didn't support it.

When working with a selected subarea, comparing one window to another, or adjusting an area in one layer to blend with nonadjusted items in other layers within Levels, Curves, Color Balance or Brightness/Contrast, you usually work with the Preview button on so you can compare the changes you make to the selected area to the rest of the image. If the Preview button is on while working in a tool, clicking

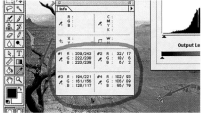

By Shift-clicking on the screen while in a color correction tool, you can place up to four Color Sampler points whose values will show up at the bottom of the Info window and will continue to update as you make color changes. These locations continue to update throughout your editing session, even as you switch tools and measure other locations with the regular Eyedropper.

the title bar doesn't give you the quick before/after toggle you used to get with Video LUT Animation.

In any of the color correction tools, you can Option-Cancel (Reset) to stay in the tool but cancel any changes you have made in that tool so far. Many of these tools also let you load and save a collection of settings. This is useful when you have many very similar images in a production situation. You could carefully make your Levels setting for the first image and then use the Save button to save those settings in a file. If you have subsequent images in the group, you can use the Load button to automatically run the same settings or load them into an adjustment layer.

LEVELS AND CURVES

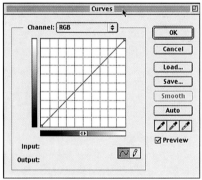

The Levels tool with its histogram is best for doing the overall color correction right after bringing in a scan or a digital camera image.

The Curves tool with a curve showing no adjustments to the image. The horizontal axis shows the original image values and the vertical axis shows these values as modified by the curve. Option-clicking on the graph toggles it between the 4x4 default divisions and the 10x10 divisions you see here.

The Levels and Curves tools have the broadest range of capabilities of any of the color correction tools. When you color correct an image from its original scan, you want to do so in a particular order. (We discuss that order in great detail in Chapter 17: "Steps to Create a Master Image," and you should read that chapter for a better understanding of this overview.) The first step after you do a scan is to do overall color correction; that is, correct the complete image without any selections. Levels is the best tool to use because it gives you a histogram of the data in the image. You can use the histogram to judge the quality of the scan and to fix many scanning problems. You can also use Levels to precisely adjust the highlight and shadow values, the overall brightness and contrast, and the color balance, while viewing the results onscreen and in the histogram. You make all these changes in one step and must choose OK only once after making all these improvements. When using an adjustment layer, you can go back in and tweak your Levels settings as many times as you like. Levels is the color correction tool we use most often.

You can also use the Curves command to do your initial overall color adjustments of the entire image. Curves enables you to do all the same adjustments that Levels does plus more specific adjustments in particular image data ranges. The Curves command has a different user interface than Levels, however. Instead of furnishing a histogram, it provides the curve diagram shown here. The horizontal axis of the diagram represents the original image values with black and shadows on the left and white and highlights on the right. The vertical axis represents the modified image values with the shadows at the bottom and the highlights on the top. When the curve is a straight diagonal, as shown here, the image has not been changed. Moving the curve down in the middle darkens the image, and moving it upward lightens the image. The endpoints of the curve are used to change the highlight and shadow values. Using Curves, you can measure individual colors, see the range of values they represent on the curve, and then change only that color range. Curves' advantage is that it allows you to independently modify specific portions of the image's tonal range in different ways with more flexibility than Levels. The advantage of using Levels is being able to see the histogram as you make changes.

Levels and Curves are the most powerful color correction tools. See Chapter 19: "Overall Color Correction," for a detailed introduction to Levels and Curves, and also Chapters 20: "Correcting a Problem Image," and 24: "Desert Al" for good discussions of using Levels and Curves in the ways for which they are best suited. Also read Chapter 13: "Digital Imaging and the Zone System" to understand how Levels histograms and Curves relate to the original photograph.

THE HUE/SATURATION COMMAND

Hue/Saturation is often used to increase the saturation of all the colors by 10% to 20% after doing the overall color correction using Levels and Curves. This change is done with the Master button on. Using the Reds, Yellows, Greens, Cyans, Blues or Magentas, you can change the hue, saturation or lightness of objects in the image that have one of these standard colors as their primary color without actually making a detailed selection. You can then fine-tune these color selections further using the Hue/Saturation Eyedroppers. You should use Hue/Saturation when you want to change the color, saturation or lightness of a particular object or color range without changing its gamma or other characteristics. The first part of the process is to select the object(s) you want to change and use the Hue/Saturation Eyedropper with plus and minus to get a model of the representative color. This model shows up in the Color Strip at the bottom of the Hue/Saturation window. This Color Strip shows changes to your representative color as you make them.

The Hue slider looks at hues in a circular fashion, sort of like the Apple color picker or a rotary color wheel type color picker. The initial hue value, 0, is the degree value where you find your initial color. To change just the color, slide the Hue slider to the right (like rotating counter-clockwise on the Apple Color Picker). If your initial color was red, then red would be your 0. A Hue change of 90 degrees would make the color green. A Hue change of –90 degrees would make your color purple. A Hue change of 180 or –180 would yield the opposite of red, which is cyan. Sliding the Saturation slider to the right makes the selected items more saturated and sliding to the left makes them less saturated. This is like moving further from the center or closer to the center on the Apple color picker.

Moving the Lightness slider to the right takes away gray values and moving it to the left adds gray values (similar to the sliding bar on the right side of the Apple color picker). See Chapter 19: "Overall Color Correction," Chapter 18: "The Car Ad," and Chapter 22: "Color Matching Images" for more information on the Hue/Saturation tool.

THE REPLACE COLOR COMMAND

The Replace Color command allows you to make a selection based on color and then actually change the color of the selected objects using sliders built into the command's dialog box. The selections are similar to selections made with the Magic Wand, but this tool gives you more control over them. The Magic Wand requires you to make a selection by using a certain tolerance setting and clicking a color, and then selects adjacent areas based on whether their colors fall within the tolerance value you set for it. If the selection is incorrect with the Magic Wand, you need to change the tolerance and then select again. This process can take a lot of time and iteration. The Replace Color command allows you to change the tolerance on-the-fly while viewing the actual objects or colors you are selecting.

The tolerance here is called Fuzziness. Increasing the Fuzziness, by moving the slider in the dialog box to the right, enlarges your selection, and decreasing it shrinks the selection. You see a preview of what is happening with the selection in a little mask window in the dialog box.

After you perfect the color selection, you then use the Hue, Saturation and Lightness sliders in the Replace Color dialog box to change the color of the selected objects. You can see this color change in the image by clicking the Preview button, and the Preview button also allows you to make further tweaks on the selection while

The Hue/Saturation tool. Usually you want the Preview button on when using Hue/Saturation. Notice the color bars and sliders at the bottom of the dialog box. These, along with the Eyedroppers allow Photoshop to do a much better job of picking a color range to modify with Hue/Saturation.

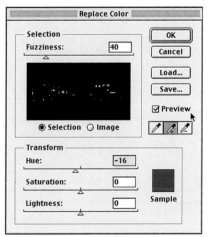

The Replace Color command has a selection capability based on object color and has some of the controls from Hue/Saturation built into it. Use it for quickly selecting and changing the color of objects. Use the sample swatch as a quick reference to see how your color will change; then use the Preview button to see the change happen within the file.

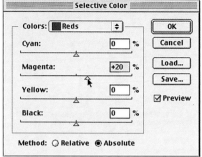

The Selective Color command is used for adding or subtracting the percentage of cyan, magenta, yellow, or black inks within the red, green, blue, cyan, magenta, yellow, black, neutral, or white colors in the selected area of a CMYK image. These percentages of change can be relative to the amount of an ink color that is already there or they can be absolute percentages.

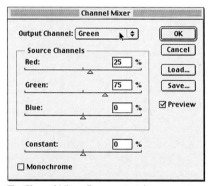

The Channel Mixer allows you to take a percentage of the color from one channel and use it to create part of another channel. Here, we are taking 25% of the Red channel and 75% of the Green channel and using it to create a new Green channel.

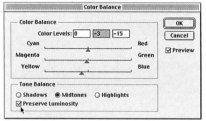

The Color Balance tool. Color levels of 0 means that no adjustment has been made. Negative values mean adjustments in the CMY direction, and positive values are adjustments in the RGB direction. Preserve Luminosity is the main feature this tool has that allows it to do something that you can't do using Levels or Curves.

actually seeing how they're affecting the color change. Replace Color changes the color of the objects it picks from the parts of the entire image selected with the selection tools before you entered Replace Color. To learn more about using Replace Color, see Chapter 21: "Yellow Flowers."

THE SELECTIVE COLOR TOOL AND CMYK

The Selective Color tool works great when you are working with CMYK images. It is a good tool for making final tweaks to CMYK colors after converting from RGB to CMYK. With this tool, you adjust the amount of cyan, magenta, yellow or black ink within the red, green, blue, cyan, magenta, yellow, black, neutral or white colors in the selected area. It's also a great tool for fine control over fixing color areas that fade a bit when converted to CMYK. For more information about using this tool, see Chapter 21: "Yellow Flowers," and Chapter 22: "Color Matching Images. "

THE CHANNEL MIXER

The Channel Mixer allows you to take a percentage of the color from one channel and use it to create part of another channel. This technique can be used to improve CMYK separations and also for the process of creating a black-and-white image from a color image. It is also very useful in reparing images where one of the emulsion layers of the film may not have been exposed properly or may have been damaged over time. You could always do this type of thing in the past using Image/Calculations or by just pasting one channel on top of another and changing the opacity; the Channel Mixer just makes this process easier and allows you to see a preview of the results as you are working. See Chapter 24: "Desert Al," where we repair a damaged color photograph, for an example of using the Channel Mixer.

COLOR BALANCE, BRIGHTNESS/CONTRAST AND VARIATIONS

You will notice that we don't use Color Balance, Brightness/Contrast and Variations tools much in this book. We consider them less precise than the other six color correction tools previously mentioned. We explain the advantages and disadvantages of using these three tools in this section. In general, they are more for color beginners and don't offer as much control as the Levels, Curves, Hue/Saturation, Replace Color, Selective Color and Channel Mixer commands.

THE COLOR BALANCE TOOL

The Color Balance tool shows the the relationship between the additive colors (red, green and blue) on the right and the subtractive colors (cyan, magenta and yellow) on the left. You move three sliders, the Cyan/Red slider, the Magenta/Green slider, and the Yellow/Blue slider, either to the left to get the CMY colors or to the right to get their complementary RGB colors. If you don't understand the relationship between RGB and CMY, this tool makes it a little easier to see. When you use Color Balance, you need to adjust your shadows, midtones and highlights separately, which can take longer than using Levels or Curves. The best feature of Color Balance is that you can make adjustments with the Preserve Luminosity button on, which allows you to radically alter the color balance of a selected object toward red, for example, without the object becoming super bright like it would if you made such a radical adjustment in Levels or Curves. There are times when this is very useful.

Chapter 12: Color Correction Tools

The Preserve Luminosity option can be useful when you need to remove a color cast from the image without changing the brightness and contrast of the image.

In general, the Color Balance tool is much less powerful than Levels or Curves because you can't set exact highlight or shadow values, and you don't have much control over brightness and contrast. If you were to use Color Balance to do the overall correction of an image, you probably would have to go back and forth between it and Brightness/Contrast several times, and that would break the rule of clicking on OK as little as possible—and you would still have less overall control than with Levels or Curves. Moreover, if you have a setting that you use all the time in Levels, Hue/Saturation or Curves, you can save it in a file and load it later to use on a similar image. This can be very useful when you want to save time and make a group of images have similar color adjustments—once again, the Color Balance tool doesn't have this option. Overall, I would say that the Color Balance tool is more of a toy for beginning color correctors and not the main tool I would recommend for imaging professionals.

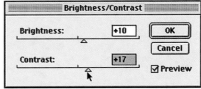

The Brightness/Contrast tool. Moving the sliders to the right increases the brightness or contrast, generating positive numbers in the respective boxes. Moving the sliders to the left decreases brightness or contrast and results in negative numbers.

THE BRIGHTNESS/CONTRAST TOOL

The Brightness/Contrast tool allows you to adjust the brightness and/or contrast of your image using Brightness and Contrast sliders. Usually we adjust the brightness and contrast using Levels or Curves because those tools allow you to also adjust the color balance and highlight/shadow values at the same time as well as allowing you to Save and Load adjustment values. Like the Color Balance tool, I would say that Brightness/Contrast is more of a toy, an entry-level tool. Most professionals use Levels and Curves. The only time you might use Brightness/Contrast is when you don't need to make any color adjustment and need only a subtle brightness or contrast adjustment.

THE VARIATIONS TOOL

The Variations tool is a neat idea, but it has several serious flaws. Variations is useful for the person who is new to color correction and may not know the difference between adding a little cyan and adding a little green to an image. When you use it, you see the current image surrounded by different color correction choices. The main problem with Variations is that you cannot zoom in on the current image or any of its new choices to see the details of what will happen when you make possible changes.

Variations works better on a 19" or 21" monitor, simply because the small images used to illustrate the changes are bigger on a larger monitor. Still, when you make the changes and say OK to Variations, you are often surprised by how the changes that looked cool in small size inside the Variations dialog box have adversely affected certain color areas. Like the Color Balance tool, you can't set precisely where the highlight and/or shadow values begin. You have to adjust highlight and shadow values separately using the radio

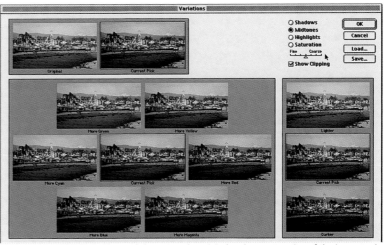

The Variations color correction tool shows you the original and current version of the image up in the top-left corner. As you change the current image, you can easily compare it here to the original. The big box in the bottom-left corner shows the current image in the middle surrounded by versions with more green, yellow, red, magenta, blue, or cyan added to it. You click one of these surrounding versions of the image if you like it better. It replaces the current image in the middle of this circle (also at the top), and then another round of new color iterations surround this new current image. On the right side, the current image is in the middle with a lighter one above and a darker one below. Again you can click one of these to make it the current image.

buttons at the top right of the Variations dialog box. You can't set the highlights or shadows to known values like you can in Levels and Curves.

In Variations, you can also adjust the saturation by selecting the Saturation radio button. The saturation, highlight and shadow settings show you out-of-gamut colors if you have the Show Clipping box checked. When shadows are going to print as pure black or highlights as pure white, these clipped areas show up as a bright complementary warning color. In Saturation mode, colors that are too saturated for the CMYK gamut show up the same way.

If you are not used to doing color corrections, Variations is a good way to prototype the corrections you want to make. Maybe you'll decide to add some yellow, darken the image and increase the saturation a bit. After you make these decisions with the aid of Variations, you probably want to go back to Levels, Curves or Hue/Saturation and make the corresponding changes there. Then you can also set the highlights and shadows more exactly and see the details of the changes you are making as you make them. We do not use Variations in this book. For more details on Variations, see the Photoshop manual or built-in Help menu.

THE AUTO LEVELS, AUTO CONTRAST, DESATURATE AND GRADIENT MAP COMMANDS

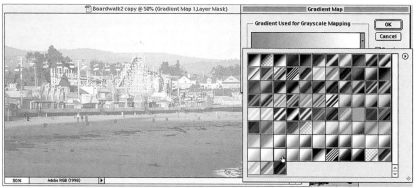

The new Gradient Map command added to Photoshop 6 is pretty cool for adding effects to an image. It converts the image using the gradient you select from the Gradients palette. There is a Dither option, which will tend to give you smoother gradients and a Reverse option which will reverse the direction of the gradient. The gradient we chose here turns this color image of the Santa Cruz boardwalk into a Duotone type effect. If you add a Gradient Map as an adjustment layer, the original image pixels are not modified and you can always go in and change the gradient at a later time by double-clicking on the Adjustment Layer icon. Thats the best way to use this tool.

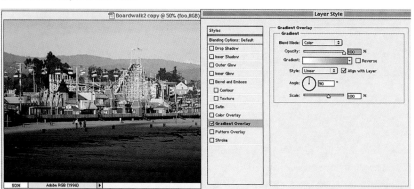

The Gradient Overlay layer style gives you a similar look to Gradient Map but has a few more options that you can play with. Here we have set the Blend mode to Color.

The Auto Levels command does an automatic color correction of your image; Auto Contrast does an automatic contrast adjustment. I would not recommend using these for quality color control, but it's okay for a quick color fix to an FPO proof.

The Desaturate command completely desaturates your image, taking all the hue or color values out of it, leaving you with a black-and-white image in RGB or CMYK mode. Desaturate does not do exactly the same thing as Image/Mode/Grayscale; with Desaturate, the image appears flatter. To convert from color to grayscale, I would correct the color image first and then choose Image/Mode/Grayscale. If you need an RGB image to send to your printer, for example, then convert this grayscale back to RGB. You get better contrast that way.

The Gradient Map command is new for Photoshop 6 and is a useful effect. It is great for getting a Duotone type look by converting the 0-255 values in your image to the corresponding values in the gradient chosen. This doesn't have the level of control that the Duotone feature has, but you could use it to quickly get standard appearances with an image that will still end up being in the RGB format when you are finished. If you like this type of effect, you might also try using the Gradient Overlay effect within the Layer Style dialog box. You get to this by double-clicking on a Layer thumbnail of a regualr layer or by choosing Layer/Layer Style/Gradient Overlay. Layer styles won't work for a *Background* layer unless you convert it into a normal layer by double-clicking on its thumbnail and then renaming it.

WHERE TO LEARN MORE

To learn more about the color correction tools mentioned in this overview, read chapters 13: "Digital Imaging and the Zone System," 17: "Steps to Create a Master Image," and do the step-by-step examples in chapters 19: "Overall Color Correction," 20: "Correcting a Problem Image," Chapters 21: "Yellow Flowers," 22: "Color Matching Images," 24: "Desert Al." Chapters 26: "Combining Bracketed Photos," and 27: "Bryce Stone Woman," also have valuable color correction techniques.

RGB to CMY Relationship

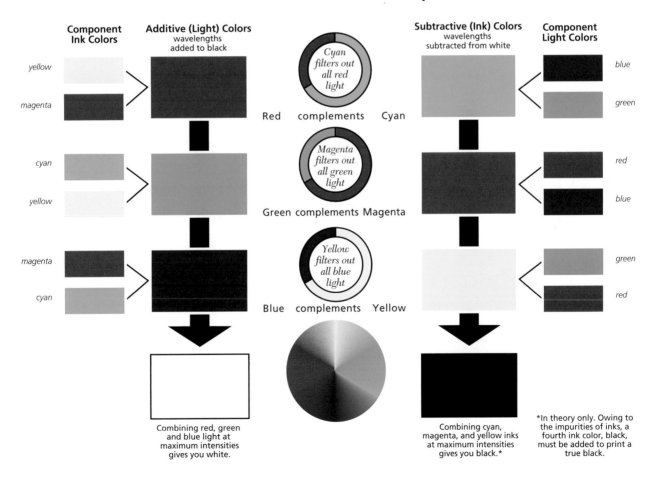

13 DIGITAL IMAGING AND THE ZONE SYSTEM

Digital imaging as it relates to traditional photography and the Zone System, and how to create a high-quality original photograph.

Images in nature that you see with your eyes have the greatest beauty because they usually are illuminated by wonderful light and have depth and texture that we can only simulate on a print or computer screen. The range of light, from the darkest black shadow to the brightest sparkling highlight, reflected from reality to our eyes is far greater than we can reproduce in any printed or screen image. Our eyes can adjust as we gaze into a shadow or squint to see a bright detail. When you look at a scene in nature, it has the best quality and the most detail. The T.V. set, which we watch so much, has the least amount of detail and sharpness. Go out and see the real world!

TRANSITIONS TO THE DIGITAL WORLD

There are many reasons to copy a scene from nature, a pretty face, or a product and reproduce the image so it can be carried around and seen again. How to do this, and get the best quality, is an important subject of this book. I give thanks to Ansel Adams, perhaps the most well-known nature photographer, and his great series of books, *The Camera, The Negative,* and *The Print,* for my introduction to an understanding of artistic photography. These titles by New York Graphic Society Books are must-reads for anyone who wants to understand how to take the best quality photographs. *Ansel Adams: An Autobiography* is also a wonderful book. Many of Adams' discussions are about black-and-white photography, but the concepts still apply to color and even digital imaging. The depth and joy of his philosophies are something all people who deal with images should have a feeling for.

Although he died in 1984, before digital imaging became easily available and popular, Ansel Adams was ahead of his time and says in his book *The Negative:*

> "I eagerly await new concepts and processes. I believe that the electronic image will be the next major advance. Such systems will have their own inherent and inescapable structural characteristics, and the artist and functional practitioner will again strive to comprehend and control them."

This chapter should help you to understand the nature of an original image and how to control and improve it in the digital world.

ACHIEVING YOUR VISUALIZATION

The Zone System, developed by Ansel Adams in 1940, gives photographers a way to measure an image in nature and then capture it on film so it can be reproduced with the photographer's intentions in mind. Adams uses the term "visualization" to explain a technique where photographers imagine what they want a photo to look like as a print before taking the photo. Once this image, the visualization, is in the photographer's mind, the photographer uses the Zone System to get the correct data on the film so that visualization can be achieved in the darkroom. Getting the right data on the film or into a digital camera is very important in the process of creating a digital image too. We use the Zone System to explain what the right data is, and then we discuss how to get that data onto film or into a digital camera. If you get the right data into a digital camera, you can transfer it directly into your computer. When you capture the image on film, you need to scan it correctly to make sure all the information gets into your computer.

CAPTURING THE DYNAMIC RANGE

When you look at an image in nature or in a photography studio, you can use a photographic light meter to measure the range of brightness in the image. On a very sunny day, out in the bright sun, you may have a very large range of brightness between the brightest and darkest parts of your image area. We will call this range the *dynamic range* of that image. Each photographic film, and each digital camera, has its own dynamic range of values from brightest to darkest that the particular film or camera can capture, called its *exposure latitude*. Many photographic films and digital cameras cannot capture the full dynamic range of brightness present in the original scene, especially on a bright contrasty day. I'm sure you have all taken photographs where the prints don't show any details in the shadows or where a bright spot on a person's forehead is totally washed out. The objective of the Zone System is to measure, using a light meter, the brightness range in the original scene and then adjust your camera so the parts of that brightness range that you want to capture actually get onto the film or into the digital camera.

DIVIDING AN IMAGE INTO ZONES

The Zone System divides an image into 11 zones from the brightest to the darkest. Ansel Adams uses Roman numerals to denote the zones from 0 to X. These zones in the printed image reference how light or dark each area will be. In a photograph, a Zone 0 area would be solid black, with no detail showing whatsoever; in a halftone you would see no white dots in the solid black ink. Zone I is still a very dark black, but it is not pure black and has no real measurable detail. If you look at a Zone I halftone with the naked eye, it still looks black without detail, but if you were to use a loupe or other magnifier, you would see very small white dots in a sea of black ink.

On the other end of the scale, Zone X is solid white. In a print this would be the color of the paper; in a halftone there would be no dots in a Zone X area. You would use Zone X to represent a specular highlight like the reflection of the sun on a chrome bumper. Zone IX is a very bright white without detail, but again you can see some very small halftone dots if you use a loupe. The range of image brightness areas that will have obvious detail in the printed image include Zone II through Zone VIII. Zone VIII will be very bright detail and Zone II will be very dark detail. In the middle of this area of print detail is Zone V. In a black-and-white print, Zone V would print as middle gray, halfway between pure black and pure white. In a color print, a Zone V area would print as normal color and brightness for that area if you were looking at it in normal lighting conditions with your eyes adjusted to it. When you set the exposure setting on your camera, areas in the image that have a brightness equal to that exposure setting are getting a Zone V exposure. We will explain this further in this chapter.

GETTING A GOOD EXPOSURE

Let's talk for a moment about how you take a picture with a camera. We will use black-and-white negative and color positive transparency as examples in this discussion. Normally, when you take a transparency picture with a camera, you measure the range of brightness in the original scene and set the exposure on your camera so as to reproduce the range of brightness on the film to look the same way it did in the original scene. The automatic cameras of today have computerized light meters that do all this for you, although you sometimes still need to do it manually to get exactly what you want. When you use a manual camera with a hand-held light meter, you need to do it manually. Even though many of you probably have automatic cameras as I do, let's describe the manual camera process so we all understand what needs to happen to take a good picture. This discussion also applies to getting a good exposure with a digital camera.

MEASURING THE BRIGHTNESS

To get a good exposure, you need to measure the brightness range of different subjects within the photograph. Let's say you were taking a photograph of a Spanish home in Costa Rica. You want to set the exposure somewhere in the middle of the brightness range that occurs naturally in the setting. That middle position, wherever you set it, then becomes Zone V. A hand-held spot light meter allows you to point at any very small area in a scene and measure the amount of light reflected from that area. The light meter measures the brightness of light, the *luminance*, reflected from the metered part of the image. Unless you plan to use filters or different film to modify the light's color, this is all you really need to measure regardless of whether you are taking a black-and-white or color photo.

In the Spanish home picture, the brightest areas are the little bit of sky at the top and the reflection of the sun in the right side of the window frame at the bottom. The darkest areas are the shadows in the bottom right corner. Measuring these with a light meter that allows spot readings might produce readings like exposure value 17 for the bright section of sky at the top and exposure value 7 for the dark shadow at the bottom. Each change in the exposure value settings on a professional light meter is equal to a difference of two in the amount of light measured.

In the building picture to the left, if we have exposure value readings from 7 in the darkest area to 17 in the brightest area, there is a difference of 1,024 times the brightness from the darkest amount of light to the brightest amount of light. This is because each jump in the exposure value represents twice as much light. Here's how we get 1,024 times as much light: exposure value 7 = 1 (the lowest amount of light), EV 8 = 2 (twice as much light), EV9 = 4, EV10 = 8, EV11 = 16, EV12 = 32, EV 13 = 64, EV14 = 128, EV15 =

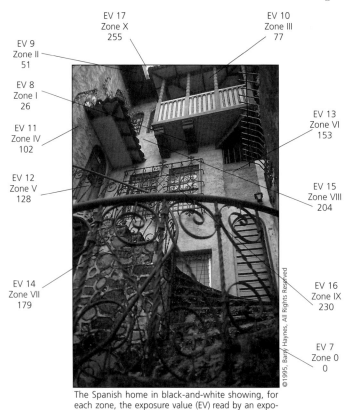

EV 17
Zone X
255

EV 10
Zone III
77

EV 9
Zone II
51

EV 8
Zone I
26

EV 11
Zone IV
102

EV 13
Zone VI
153

EV 12
Zone V
128

EV 15
Zone VIII
204

EV 14
Zone VII
179

EV 16
Zone IX
230

EV 7
Zone 0
0

The Spanish home in black-and-white showing, for each zone, the exposure value (EV) read by an exposure meter, the corresponding zones, and lastly the 0 to 255 digital value based on placing Zone V at exposure value 12 on the door.

256, EV16 = 512, EV17 (the brightest reading) = 1024. This is 1024 times as much light from the darkest area to the brightest.

PLACING THE ZONE V EXPOSURE

After measuring the range of exposure values within a scene that you want to photograph, you usually set the camera's exposure to a value in the middle of that range. The value that you set your exposure to causes the areas that have that exposure value within the scene to show up as a middle gray value on the film and print in black-and-white or as a normal middle detail exposure in color. Where you set your exposure on the camera is called "placing your Zone V exposure." Here we are placing our Zone V exposure at exposure value 12, the reading we got from the door. Usually you set your exposure to the area within the image that you want to look best or most normal. If a person were standing on the steps in this photo, you might set the exposure to a reading that you would take off the person's face.

When you decide where to set the exposure, you affect what happens to each of the zones within the image area, not just Zone V. If the Spanish home image were a transparency, it would reflect an exposure where you set Zone V based on the reading taken from the middle of the door. If the film is then processed correctly, the middle of the door in the transparency would look correct, as though you were looking straight at it with your eyes adjusted to it. When you set the exposure to the middle of the door, the areas that are lighter or darker around it, the zones above and below Zone V, become correspondingly lighter or darker on the film. The bright window, at exposure value 16, will then be placed at Zone IX and will show up as very bright and with almost no detail on the film. This is because it is four zones above, or 16 times brighter than, where we set our exposure (at exposure value 12).

If you were to set the exposure on the camera to exposure value 16, the exposure value for the bright window, you would do to the camera and film what happens to your eye when you move up very close to the bright part of a contrasty scene. The iris on your eye closes and you start to see a lot of detail in that bright area. It is no longer a white area with no detail, because

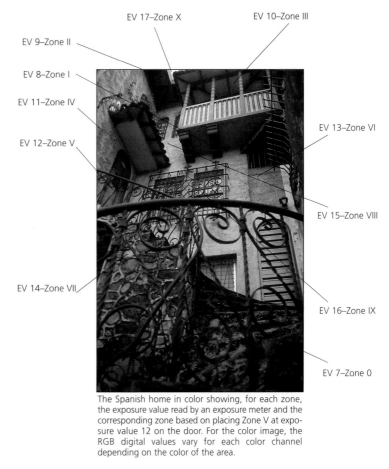

EV 17–Zone X
EV 10–Zone III
EV 9–Zone II
EV 8–Zone I
EV 11–Zone IV
EV 13–Zone VI
EV 12–Zone V
EV 15–Zone VIII
EV 14–Zone VII
EV 16–Zone IX
EV 7–Zone 0

The Spanish home in color showing, for each zone, the exposure value read by an exposure meter and the corresponding zone based on placing Zone V at exposure value 12 on the door. For the color image, the RGB digital values vary for each color channel depending on the color of the area.

the focus of your field of vision moves up and your eyes adjust to encompass just that area. If you set the exposure on your camera to exposure value 16, that bright window area in the picture would show up as a middle gray for black-and-white or a normal color in a transparency. By changing this exposure, you would then be placing Zone V at exposure value 16. Now the door would be at Zone I, 16 times darker, and everything darker than the door would be in Zone 0, totally black. This would give you details in the highlights, but you would lose the details in the darker parts of the scene. By measuring the scene and noticing that the bottom of the stairs has exposure

Zones	0	I	II	III	IV	V	VI	VII	VIII	IX	X
Approximate Digital Values	0	26	51	77	102	128	153	179	204	230	255
% Black	100%	90%	80%	70%	60%	50%	40%	30%	20%	10%	0%

A stepwedge file of the 11 zones in the Zone System with the approximate corresponding digital values and percentages of black ink. The digital values shown here fall somewhere in the center of each zone. Where the actual zone values and digital values appear for each image depends on the type of output you choose. You have more latitude where the Zone I detail begins and Zone IX details end when you print at a higher resolution and line screen. If you are printing to newsprint, all of Zone I may print as 100% black and all of Zone IX as 100% white.

If you want to know more about the Zone System and how to take the best photographs, you should read Ansel Adams' book The Negative. It contains very useful information. It also shows you some very good techniques for extending or shortening the exposure latitude of your film by under- or over-developing. Another great book on the Zone System is The New Zone System Manual by White, Zakia, and Lorenz from Morgan Press, Inc.

value 7 and the sky has exposure value 17, then setting the exposure on your camera in the middle at exposure value 12, you place Zone V there and thereby obtain the full range of these values on the film.

UTILIZING YOUR EXPOSURE LATITUDE

Different films and different digital cameras have different exposure latitudes. The *exposure latitude* of a film is the number of different exposure values it can record at once. The Zone System covers a range of 11 exposure values, a brightness going from 1 to 1,024 times as bright. Most films cannot capture detail in so broad a range of lighting situations. This range of light would be found in a contrasty scene on a sunny day with the sun shining directly on it. Some films can capture detail over a range of seven exposure values and some over a larger range. In Adams' description of his zones, detail is captured only from Zone II through Zone VIII, or over a seven-zone range. Things in Zones 0, I, IX, and X are pretty much void of detail and either black or white. Some digital cameras, like the Dicomed digital backs, have a larger dynamic range than most film. If you know the exposure latitude of your film or digital camera when taking a picture, you can determine which parts of the picture will have detail and which will be black or white by measuring the range of your image area and setting your exposure, your Zone V area, so the other zones, or brightness ranges, fall where you want them.

We could have gotten more details in the highlights in this picture by placing Zone V, our exposure setting, at exposure value 13 or 14 instead of 12, but then the shadow areas at exposure values 8 or 9, the areas underneath the roof and balcony overhangs, would have shown up as totally black. Some pictures will not be very contrasty, and you will know, by taking light measurements, that the exposure latitude of your film, or digital camera, can handle the total number of zones in the image. All you need to make sure of then is that you set the exposure in the middle of that range so all the areas of different exposure values fall within the latitude of the film or digital camera and you thus capture their detail.

The measurements and diagrams in this chapter don't accurately measure any particular film or camera. They simply illustrate how the process works.

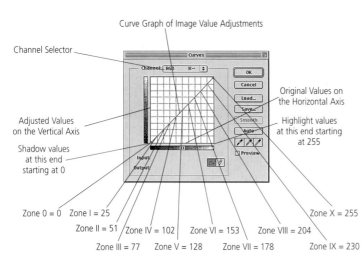

Curve Graph of Image Value Adjustments

Channel Selector

Original Values on the Horizontal Axis

Adjusted Values on the Vertical Axis

Highlight values at this end starting at 255

Shadow values at this end starting at 0

Zone 0 = 0   Zone I = 25   Zone X = 255
Zone II = 51   Zone IV = 102   Zone VI = 153   Zone VIII = 204   Zone IX = 230
Zone III = 77   Zone V = 128   Zone VII = 178

Using the Curves tool, if you want to modify the colors or brightness of the items in a certain zone or zone range of the image, this diagram points out the part of the curve you would modify to change those zones. Using the Eyedropper tool with Curves, you can measure any part of the image and the location of its values will show up on the curve as a small circle. This makes it very easy to adjust any range of values or colors using Curves.

Chapter 13: Digital Imaging and the Zone System

THE ADVANTAGES OF A DIGITAL IMAGE

Once you have captured all the information you need on the film, you want to move it into your computer by doing the best possible scan. If you have a digital camera, you don't need to scan; you can digitally transfer the image from the camera to the computer. Your objective is to make sure that your image retains all the zone detail you captured for you to play with. For more information on scanning and bringing images into the computer, see Chapter 16: "Image Resolution, Scanning Film and Digital Cameras."

When you look at the histogram of a digital image using the Levels or Curves commands in Photoshop, you see all those values, all those zones, and you can move them around and adjust them with much more precision than you would have in the darkroom.

If you are not familiar with Levels and Curves, read Chapters 19: "Overall Color Correction," 20: "Correcting a Problem Image," and 17: "Steps to Create a Master Image," later in this book.

Looking at a scan of the Spanish home image in Levels, we can actually see how many values in the image fall within each zone. Notice that in this image many values fall in Zones I, II, and III. That's because this image has a lot of dark areas. There are not many values in Zones IX and X because this image does not have many very bright areas. To move the values that are in Zone V toward Zone IV, making the image brighter, or toward Zone VI, making the image darker, you can use the Brightness/Contrast slider in Levels. To move the values in Zones I and II over to Zone 0, making the shadows darker, you can use the Input Shadow slider. In later chapters, we show you how to use these techniques with the Levels command to give you more control over the different brightness and color zones in your images. We will also show you how to use Curves to do pretty much anything you want with your image data.

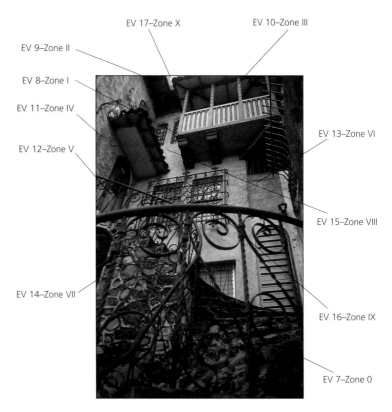

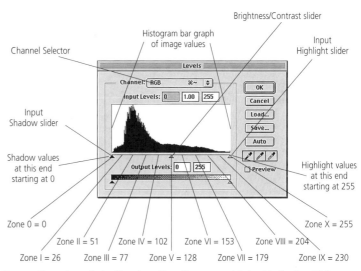

Here are the main controls of Levels and how the zones pointed out in the Spanish home image above show up in the histogram of that image. The approximate digital value, in the 0 to 255 range, is also shown for each zone. If you work on 48-bit images in Photoshop, then each pixel in each of the red, green and blue channels has 65,536 possible tonal values. If your scanner software allows you to save more than 8 bits of data per channel, save the file this way and you will capture more of the tonal variations and details from the film or digital camera.

COLOR SPACES, DEVICE CALIBRATION AND COLOR MANAGEMENT

An overview of how we see color, measure color, calibrate color scanners, monitors and printers, and what color working spaces and file bit-depths to use in Photoshop.

WHAT IS COLOR & HOW WE SEE IT

It's night and we can barely see; then the sun slowly comes up, and things begin to become recognizable. The light from the sun is allowing us to see more and more things. In that early morning light, things seem very warm and yellow. Then as the sun gets higher in the sky, that warm yellow appearance goes away and we get a whiter light. That white, midday light is made up of many wavelengths of light. Light is actually waves of excited electronic particles and those waves come in different wavelengths. When those light waves hit a surface, each different type of surface absorbs some of the wavelengths of light, and other wavelengths are reflected back toward us if we are looking at that surface. Now instead of the white light that comes from the sun, we are only seeing part of that light reflected back from a surface. The part or wavelengths that are reflected back to us determine the color of that surface.

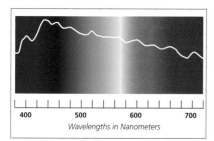

The wavelengths of light and how you see them. The white line is an approximation of daylight wavelengths.

Our eyes have sensors called rods and cones. The rods sense brightness or light intensity, but it is the cones that actually detect color, and there are three different types of cones each sensitive to a different wavelength of light. One type of cone is more sensitive to red light, one is more sensitive to green, and the third is more sensitive to blue.

AN IMAGE ON PAPER

When we look at an image printed on paper, the color we see depends on the color of the incoming light that is illuminating that paper; that incoming light supplies all or most of the wavelengths of light that we could possibly see although there might be several different types of light illuminating the paper that increases the possibilities. The color and surface texture of the paper itself will subtract some of the wavelengths from that incoming light source and give the paper a certain color. The inks or other types of color that are painted on that paper will subtract further wavelengths from that original light and reflect back different colors that are the remaining nonsubtracted wavelengths. The angle that you view the paper might also influence how much light is reflected back. When you are considering how a particular image may look on a certain printer, the digital values in the original image, the type of inks that you use, combined with the type of paper that you print on as well as the way the printer puts the ink on the paper, all work together to create a specific range of colors you can see in that one situation.

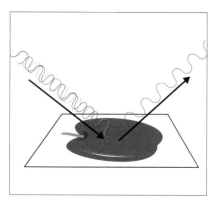

Seeing color by light reflecting back off a surface while the other colors are absorbed.

AN IMAGE ON A COMPUTER MONITOR

Color on a computer monitor comes from particle energizers, a type of light source, behind the monitor's glass that hits the coating on the inside of the monitor glass and produces different colors and light intensities depending on the numerical values that are driving the different colored light particle energizers. There is also light hitting the monitor from the outside due to other light sources within the room, and this light will have some effect on the color and brightness that you see from the internal monitor particle energizer. The way you see color on a computer monitor is quite different from the way you see color on a printed piece of paper. It is difficult to exactly match the brightness, color, and contrast characteristics of these two mediums. We will show you how to get as close as possible to a match using calibration.

SLIDE ON A LIGHT TABLE

When you see color by looking at a slide on a light table, the color you see there depends on the color of the light source behind the slide, the colors in the emulsion of the slide material, and also on the amount and intensity of the other light sources in the room.

COLOR GAMUTS

There is a very large range of colors, wavelengths of light, that the human eye can see. There are also wavelengths of light that our eyes can't see. A particular range of colors is called a color gamut. The color gamut of the human eye is described in a color space called LAB color. A color space is a description of a range of colors to be used for a particular purpose. In the 1930s, an organization called the CIE (Commission Internationale de l'Eclairage) did a bunch of scientific measurements with human observers to develop a description of the colors the human eye could see. Without filling in all the details here, this description has evolved into two very useful tools we will use in this book for measuring and quantifying color. (Note: to learn a lot more about the CIE and color history and theory, I'd recommend *The Reproduction of Color* by Dr. R.W.G. Hunt, Fifth Edition, 1995 by Fountain Press.) One of these tools is the LAB color space, that Photoshop supports, which consists of a color gamut of this range of colors that the human eye can see. The second tool is the CIE xy chromaticity diagram that shows these colors on an xy graph again representing the colors the human eye can see. This CIE xy chromaticity diagram is useful for plotting other color gamuts and comparing one against the other. When you are working on a project using the LAB color space, you won't be throwing out colors that the eye can see and you won't be working with any colors that the eye cannot see. Using the LAB color space, you can potentially be working with all the colors the eye can see; however, the eye can actually see more colors than many of the cameras and printers we work with can reproduce. Some of the step-by-step examples in this book use the LAB color space.

MEASURING COLOR

To measure color, we need to be able to measure wavelengths of light. A device called a spectrophotometer does this best, and we will be talking about how a spectrophotometer, along with various color calibration software, work together to improve our use and accuracy of digital color. We want to be able to measure the colors that a particular film can record, that a particular scanner can scan, that a particular monitor can display, and that a particular printer can print. To do this, people

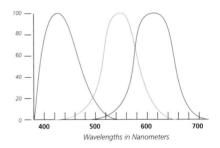

Wavelengths of light the eye can see.

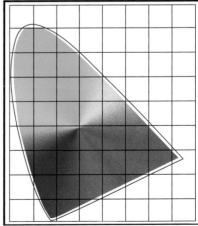

A CIE chromaticity diagram showing the LAB color space.

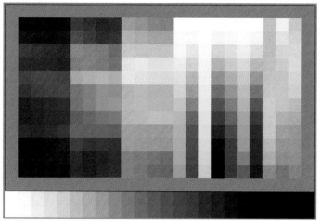
An IT8 color measuring target.

have developed test target systems, like the IT8 color target from the CIE, to measure color. In its purest form, this IT8 target consists of a group of many color swatches, light wavelength descriptions, covering a large range of colors that the human eye can see, as well as various films could capture, scanners could scan, monitors could display, and printers could print. I use the word could here because you need to know that each color device, each film, scanner, monitor, or printer, has its own color gamut. The color gamut of a device is the range of colors that particular device can detect, reproduce, or display. With a spectrophotometer, one can use the IT8 target or one of many other similar targets to measure the color gamut of any particular device.

MEASURING THE GAMUT OF A FILM

To measure the gamut of a film, you photograph a scientifically printed version of the IT8 target when that target is illuminated by a known type and color temperature light source. You then process that film exactly and use the spectrophotometer to measure each swatch in the target as it is reproduced on that film. Different film manufacturers will sell you film swatches with IT8 targets already correctly exposed on them for you to scan and measure. The film needs to be illuminated by a known light source while taking the measurements. Those measurements are then entered into a profile-making software program, which generates an ICC color profile of that film. The software program knows the empirical values each swatch is supposed to have and did have on the scientifically produced original that was photographed. Based on the differences between the original values of each swatch and the values actually recorded on the film, the ICC profile is generated that characterizes that particular film. A characterization is a description of the differences from the original empirical values, which ends up also telling you the color gamut or range of colors that film can represent. The ICC stands for International Color Consortium, which is basically a group of companies and international organizations that have agreed on a standard for specifying color. The ICC profile standard is that standard, and an ICC profile is a description of color that is in a standard format that can be recognized by many different color software applications including Adobe Photoshop 5 & 6, Apple ColorSync, QuarkXpress 4.0, Adobe Illustrator, and Adobe Indesign.

CHARACTERIZING A SCANNER

To measure the color gamut, or characterize, a scanner, you need a scientifically produced IT8 target on film, which you can get from the film manufacturer, or on a printed medium that can be scanned with the scanner. The resulting digital values that the scanner gets are entered into the profile-making software that will make an ICC profile describing that particular scanner. In chapter 15, we'll talk about several packages you can use to make custom scanner profiles.

CHARACTERIZING A MONITOR

To characterize a monitor, a scientifically created digital file of the IT8 target or some other target is measured with a spectrophotometer while being displayed on the screen in a room lit with controlled lighting conditions. Then those measurements are entered into the profile-making software to generate the ICC profile of that monitor. In the next calibration chapter, we'll show you several hardware/software packages you can use to calibrate your monitor.

CHARACTERIZING A DIGITAL PRINTER

To characterize a particular digital printer or printing press, the scientifically produced digital version of the IT8 target, or some other target, is printed on that printer or press using the standard process for outputting to that device. Then the results are measured with the spectrophotometer, and the profile-generating software creates an ICC profile from those results.

Now we know what ICC profiles are and how they are made. By the way, there are various targets that the industry uses to create ICC profiles; the Kodak IT8 is just an example, and there are various companies that create ICC profile-making software. These companies and their products include Monaco EZ Color, Proof and Profiler, Color Vision PhotoCal, Optical, Profiler RGB and Profiler Pro, Itec Colorblind ProveIt and Matchbox, Praxisoft Wiziwyg and Wiziwyg Delux and many others. Calibration products have become much more popular since Photoshop 5 first began to support ICC profiles. When you are using this process to characterize, or describe, the color gamut, or range of colors, that a particular device can record, scan, display, or print, the accuracy of this characterization is based on the accuracy of the way the test was performed and measured. When you make a profile or get a profile made, make sure it is done properly, or the profile you get might actually do you a disservice. In the next chapter on calibration, we will go through the process of making profiles using some of the more popular products now on the market.

CHOOSING YOUR COLOR WORKING SPACE

When you are working in Photoshop 6, you have the option of choosing different color spaces as your working color space. Color spaces available with Photoshop 6 use either the RGB, LAB, or CMYK color model. Each color space also encompasses a particular color gamut. So when working in Photoshop 6, you need to decide which color model, RGB, CMYK, or LAB, makes the most sense for your type of work, and then within that model, what color gamut you need for the work you are doing.

Let's first discuss the color gamut issue. For any particular body of work that involves human viewing, you will probably not need to work with colors outside the gamut of LAB because this is the set of colors the human eye can see. If you are outputting your work on color film, digital printers, computer monitors, or printing presses, you also need to consider the color gamut of those devices. It turns out that the color gamut of a CMYK printing press is much smaller than the color gamut of the human eye, the LAB color space. If you are only outputting to CMYK presses but you are working within the LAB color space, you may be constantly disappointed because many of the colors you would see on the screen could not actually be reproduced on a printing press. The color gamut of computer monitors, color film recorders and some of the new digital color printers is much larger than that of a CMYK press. So if you are also outputting to devices other than a press, you would not want to limit your gamut to colors only available on a press, especially if your goal is to produce art prints for gallery use or exciting colorful images for the Web and multimedia. The ideal circumstance would be to work in a color space that encompasses the entire color gamut of all the input scanners or digital cameras, display monitors, and output color film recorders, photographic and ink-based printers, digital printers, and CMYK or 6 color presses that you would be outputting to now and in the reasonable future. I got the term "reasonable future" from my friend Bill Atkinson, and it seems like a good term because foreseeable future could include a time when we all wear special glasses, like Geordi La Forge on Star Trek, that

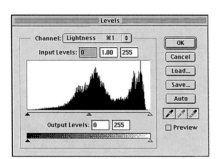

The Lightness channel in a LAB color image looks similar to an RGB histogram, but check out the a and b channels below where very small adjustments can make major changes.

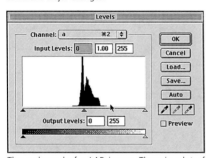

The a channel of a LAB image. There is a lot of unused space here that could be use for a more detailed spec of this color if this were a reduced gamut LAB space like LAB LH.

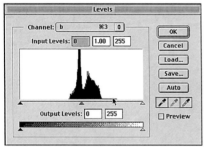

The b channel of this same LAB image.

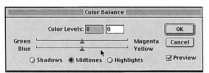

The Color Balance tool gives you different controls when working in LAB color, and you may find that you use it more in this color mode.

increase the gamut of what the human eye can see. That would complicate things too much. We could measure the gamut of each of those devices and plot those gamuts on a CIE chromaticity diagram. If we then created a color space that encompassed the gamut of all those devices, then we would be set!

Now let's discuss the Color Model issue. What we have available in Photoshop is LAB, RGB, and CMYK. In the Image/Mode menu, there are also Index color, Duotone, and Grayscale, but I would put them in the category of special case models that we only work with under certain circumstances.

THE LAB WORKING SPACE

The LAB model has the advantage that its color gamut encompasses all the colors that the human eye can see. This is a very wide gamut and would certainly encompass the devices we would be working with in the reasonable future. Bill Atkinson and Charlie Cramer, two photographer friends of mine whose work I really admire, do actually work in the LAB color space using Photoshop 6. Bill does his scans on a Tango drum scanner using Linocolor software. He uses this software on the scanner to do his overall color correction and to convert from 16 bits per channel color, which the scanner obtains, down to 8 bits per channel as a LAB file which he then uses in Photoshop 6 to do final masking and tweaking with layers. Bill's images can be seen at www.natureimages.com and Charlie's at www.charlescramer.com and both their prints can be seen at the Ansel Adams gallery in Yosemite and in Carmel. Charlie's prints are also at the Photographer's gallery in Palo Alto and the Weston gallery in Carmel among others. Charlie has also been working with LAB color but is now switching to RGB experimenting with several advanced wide gamut RGBcolor spaces. There are certain features of Photoshop that are not available when working in LAB color.

I also sometimes use the LAB color space for my art prints but the potential problems with the LAB space are that it encompasses a larger gamut than most of the output devices I will be using. These are LightJet 5000, Epson 1270, 2000 and 7500 digital prints, prints on other digital printers, output to color film via a film recorder, and display on color monitors. The other potential problem with LAB is that the tools for working in LAB within Photoshop are sometimes not as easy to work with than if I were working in RGB. In the LAB space, there are three channels: Lightness, a, and b. The Lightness channel allows you to adjust the brightness and contrast of the image as well as sharpen the image without modifying the color of the image. Using Levels to look at a histogram of the Lightness channel of a LAB image is similar to looking at a histogram of RGB, all three channels at the same time. The color values in LAB are stored in the a and b channels. The a channel controls the red/green range of color, and the b channel controls the yellow/blue range. Most of us are used to working with color using red, green, and blue along with their complements of cyan, magenta, and yellow. Using a and b takes a little getting used to, and it works pretty well in Photoshop if you start out with a scan that is very close to what you want. When you have to make major color shifts with the a and b channels in Photoshop, this can be more difficult.

Bill and Charlie have been using LinoColor, which has color controls that are more flexible in LAB, to get their colors close while scanning, then using Photoshop for all the final color tweaks, masking, spotting, sharpening, and final image production. The other thing about the a and b channels in LAB images is that if you look at their histograms, you will see that the values are usually all within the center part of the histogram. The blank parts at the left and right side of the a and b histograms represent colors that are in the very wide gamut LAB space but were not captured by the film or scanner and therefore don't get represented in most LAB images. To

Chapter 14: Color Spaces, Device Characterization and Color Management

represent a digital image in 24 bits of digital space in LAB, we have 256 possible lightness values, 256 possible a values, and 256 possible b values. The concern about LAB is that for most images, the a and b channels are using much fewer than the 256 possible range of values. The possible color range for the a and b channels is so wide that the actual range used is often covering a span of only 140 to 160 values or fewer within the center of their histograms. This brings up the concern of posterization of color values within LAB images. In a well-adjusted LAB image, one usually has a Lightness channel that has a range of values that stretches completely across the 256 possible values. According to Bill Atkinson, the Lightness channel is the one that is most important to avoid posterization. If the a and b channels contain fewer than 256 tonal values, even as few as 64 tonal values, the human eye will probably not be able to detect many more than that anyhow. Bill, Charlie and myself have not noticed any problem with color posterization when working with images in the LAB space. To address this potential problem though, LinoColor has actually defined a smaller LAB space called LAB LH that encompasses a smaller a and b gamut that is more in line with actual digital output devices, but Photoshop 6 doesn't support that space. When you are working within an RGB space, both lightness and color values are represented in each of the Red, Green and Blue channels so it is harder to adjust one without the other.

The RGB Working Space

Working in RGB is probably the most common way people work with digital images. The sensors on scanners actually scan in RGB, digital cameras capture images in RGB, most digital imaging software uses RGB as the default space, RGB is the format for images on the Web, RGB is the format used to print on the LightJet 5000 and Fugix digital printers, the preferred format for Epson and HP printers and the format to print to color film recorders. There are lots of reasons to work in RGB and it is the color model that is most fully supported by Photoshop. Photoshop allows you to also look at and work with color using other color models, like LAB, Hue/Saturation/Lightness and CMYK, and you need to learn when and why it makes sense to work with color in a model other than RGB, but for most people most of the time RGB is the color model they will become most familiar with and use most often. Working in RGB is a way to look at and interpret color data, but within the RGB world there are also different interpretations of RGB data.

If you scanned the same transparency with several different scanners, you would get different numerical results and the colors and contrast would also probably look somewhat different. Before Photoshop 5, there was not really a way to quantify those differences, all those files were just RGB files and you brought them into Photoshop and adjusted them to get what you wanted. Since Photoshop 5 and Photoshop's support of ColorSync and color management, you can actually make profiles for each of those scanners and then when you bring those files into Photoshop, you can convert them from their perspective scanner profiles to a standard RGB color space that you want to work with in Photoshop. If done properly this should make these different scans look more similar and also look more like the original transparency as you view them on the screen within your standard Photoshop working space. Photoshop 6 allows you to view each of these files on the screen in either a standard RGB working space or you can view them in the working space of the scanner itself by working on them in the color space of the scanner's profile.

When using the RGB color model in Photoshop 6, you usually want to pick an RGB working space for each file that you work with. Older versions of Photoshop, before Photoshop 5, assumed the gamut of your RGB space was the gamut of your

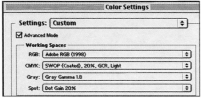

You can use the RGB pop-up in Edit/Color Settings to set your default RGB workspace; here it is set to Adobe RGB.

Gamut View

ab-Diagram

In the ab diagram above, the LAB color space includes all the colors in the diagram. The Adobe RGB space is all the colors inside the black line, ColorMatch RGB includes the colors inside the red line, sRGB the green line and the CMYK SWOP print space defined by my recommended CMYK settings is inside the blue line. The Cyan line shows the colors in a profile for my monitor, notice that it is very close to the ColorMatch RGB profile. The purple line is a profile I made with Monaco Proof for my Epson 1270 printer. Notice that the Adobe RGB color space encompasses all or most of the colors defined by any of the spaces shown here. Also notice that the three Photoshop color spaces as well as the color space of my monitor all contain many colors that cannot be printed on a CMYK press or on my Epson 1270 printer. In Photoshop 6 you can preview an image within a CMYK or RGB printing space using the View/Proof Setup dialog. It is a good idea to do this before printing to be sure those non-printable colors don't spoil the effect of your image.

monitor as described by the old Monitor Setup dialog. This caused colors outside of that space to be clipped (thrown out) even though those colors might have been printable on higher gamut output devices like color film recorders or the LightJet 5000 digital printer. With Photoshop 6, you use the Edit/Color Settings dialog in the Working Spaces RGB area to specify the gamut and other characteristics of your RGB space. You can choose an RGB color space that has a wider gamut than your monitor and Photoshop will adjust the display of your space to preview as accurately as it can on your monitor, but Photoshop 6 will not clip the colors that are outside of the monitors gamut from your RGB file. That way you will still see those colors when you print the image.

With Photoshop 6 it is easier to work with different RGB color spaces for different purposes than it was with Photoshop 5 & 5.5. The Photoshop 5 versions always displayed RGB files on the screen within one standard RGB workspace so if you opened a file that was created in a different RGB workspace than your preferences were set to, you needed to change your preferences or that file needed to be converted to your standard space for the file to be displayed correctly. In Photoshop 6, you can work on many files at the same time each with a different RGB workspace and yet each file will be displayed correctly on the screen. Photoshop 6 will also simultaneously display files in LAB color and various CMYK color spaces correctly on the screen too. The RGB Working Space that you set in Edit/Color Settings is the RGB space that will be assigned to and used to view new RGB files and is also the space that untagged files, those with no assigned profile, will be viewed in on the screen.

Using the RGB pop-up menu, you can choose from the default RGB spaces Adobe has provided. If you choose the top Custom RGB choice, you can also enter your own Gamma, White Point and Primaries values using CIE xy values. To be sure he can work with all the colors his film captures, Joe Holmes, a well-known photographer, has created his own Ektachrome RGB space which is bigger than Adobe RGB. Unless you have the tools available to measure the gamut of your input and output devices and create your own RGB workspace, you should probably pick one of the spaces provided by Adobe or something that seems to be moving toward becoming some sort of an industry standard. Of the spaces provided by Adobe, only four of them have much interest to people dealing with professional images. I will describe those here, and you can look in the Photoshop 6 manual for information about the other spaces if you want it. The four most commonly used spaces are Adobe RGB, ColorMatchRGB, sRGB, and AppleRGB.

ADOBE RGB

The widest gamut of these spaces, Adobe RGB, was originally a proposed standard for HDTV production. But more importantly, its gamut includes essentially the entire CMYK gamut and more because it also better encompasses the gamut of things like color RGB film recorders, the LightJet 5000 digital printer, various Epson and HP printers and other more advanced color output devices. If you set your RGB working space to Adobe RGB, you will be least likely to be throwing out values that you'll be able to see in most of today's digital output devices, and yet the gamut is not so large that you'll be wasting a lot of your color space and risking posterization problems. I usually use Adobe RGB when I'm working with art prints in the RGB color space. With Adobe RGB though, you will be able to see more colors on a good monitor than you'll be able to print in CMYK on a press. The technical description for Adobe RGB is: white point = 6500, gamma = 2.2, red x = .6400 y = .3300, green x = .2100 y = .7100 and blue x = .1500 y = .0600.

In the initial Photoshop 5.0 release, the Adobe RGB color space was called SMPTE-240M. Adobe renamed it to Adobe RGB, actually Adobe RGB 1998, in version 5.02 of Photoshop. If you see the name or color space SMPTE-240M, just know that it is exactly the same color space as Adobe RGB and vice versa.

ColorMatch RGB

As you can see from the Gamut View chart on the previous page, ColorMatch RGB space has a smaller gamut than Adobe RGB but a bigger gamut than sRGB and AppleRGB. This space is based on the Radius PressView monitor that has been an industry standard for quality color work. There are several advantages to the Color-Match RGB space, especially for people who are doing print work. One is that people who have been working with a PressView monitor can open their old untagged files into this space without any conversions. The other advantage is that it has a fairly large gamut, at least for CMYK print work, and it is a well-known space within the color industry. If you have been working in Photoshop 4, or earlier versions, with a quality monitor, like the Radius Pressview, calibrated to gamma 1.8 and 5000° Kelvin color temperature, the ColorMatch will give you a very similar working situation for your files within Photoshop 6. I usually work within the ColorMatch space for all the screen grabs and most of the work on this and Wendy's book where the main intention for the files is printing on a CMYK press. The technical description for Color-Match RGB is: white point = 5000, gamma = 1.8, red x = .6300 y = .3400, green x = .2950 y = .6050, and blue x = .1550 y = .0750.

sRGB

The sRGB RGB color space is the current default for Photoshop 6. This space is good for people who are primarily working on Web images and want to see what they are going to look like on a typical PC monitor. The problem with sRGB is that it is the smallest gamut space of the four, and working in this space will mean that you are potentially throwing out certain colors, even for CMYK print work, and you are certainly throwing out colors if you are planning to output to a color film recorder or LightJet 5000 type digital printer. Photographers working on art prints should certainly change their RGB working space to something other than sRGB. If you are working in a larger gamut space, like Adobe RGB or LAB, and you want

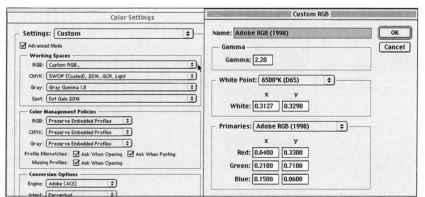

When you pick an RGB Working Space, that also sets up the default Gamma, White Point, and CIE xy primaries describing that workspace. You can then go in and modify any of these by hand by choosing Custom RGB from the top of the RGB pop-up menu. Modifying any of the values of the standard RGB spaces will change them from that space to another of your own making so be sure to change the name of the space too so you don't overwrite the standard. An example where you might want to define your own space this way would be; let's say that you measured a particular new film or digital camera that you are using and determined from its ICC profile that the Adobe RGB primaries did not contain a small portion of the film's color range. You could then change the Red, Green, or Blue xy values of Adobe RGB to extend the range of the space adding those colors. You'd want to call that Adobe RGB Plus or something like that!

to create an image for the Web, you could use Image/Mode/Convert to Profile to convert a copy of your file from the larger space into sRGB for web use. This would allow you to do your main work in Adobe RGB or LAB space and keep more colors; then use sRGB to preview the work as it will look on the average PC Web user's monitor. You can resave the file under a different name, or in JPEG format for your Web consumers, in the sRGB space that is optimized for that market. If you are a service bureau, you will probably find that you get a lot of files from the sRGB space just because it is the Photoshop 5 and 6 default and many people who don't take the time to learn about color won't bother to change this. The technical description for sRGB is: white point = 6500, gamma = 2.2, red x = .6400 y = .3300, green x = .3000 y = .6000, and blue x = .1500 y = .0600.

AppleRGB

The AppleRGB space is based on the old standard Apple 13" Trinitron color monitor. There are probably a lot of files out there in this space because older Illustrator and Photoshop versions have been using it as their default RGB space for a long time. Its gamut is not that much better than sRGB, so we really are not suggesting you use this as a current RGB working space. You will probably find it useful to use this as a Source Profile when opening old Photoshop files that were not from Radius PressView monitors, especially files from people who never changed their Photoshop Monitor Setup from the default settings. You'd be surprised how many people never change this. The technical description for AppleRGB is: white point = 6500, gamma = 1.8, red x = .6250 y = .3400, green x = .2800 y = .5950, and blue x = .1550 y = .0700.

Other RGB Working Spaces

Some photographers and imaging professionals may choose to develop their own custom RGB working space. This can be done by creating an ICC profile of a certain film that you like to work with. It can also be done by modifying an existing RGB working space to add a wider range of color in a particular area, like reds or greens for example. If you go to the top of the pop-up menu for your RGB Working Space, you can choose Custom then edit the

CMYK as a Master Workspace

The CMYK print gamut is smaller overall than the gamut of any of the RGB color spaces we just discussed above, but there are a few colors CMYK can print that sRGB and Apple RGB don't include. These days, it is not that common for people to have images that are only used in CMYK print. Even if you are using an image for just CMYK print, it is likely that you may have to print that image several times, and at several sizes and on different types of paper. For these situations, it is better if you have your master image in RGB or LAB; then when you resize the file, you can get more exact sharpening and you can also more accurately generate new CMYK separations for different papers and presses. Most of us will be using the same image in print, on the Web, and for output to several digital printers. Because the RGB and LAB spaces are both bigger in color gamut than CMYK, it makes more sense these days to leave our master image in RGB or LAB format. If you do still decide to create your master images in CMYK, remember that some of the Photoshop filters don't work on CMYK either. In any case, while viewing your CMYK images on the screen, even if the separations were done elsewhere, Photoshop compensates for the appearance of the image on the screen based on the CMYK profile the image is tagged with. If the image isn't tagged with a profile, Photoshop will display it using the CMYK settings you set for your CMYK working space using Edit/Color Settings. If you open an image that was separated to be used

In the Color Settings dialog, if you choose Custom at the top of the pop-up for your RGB Working-space, this allows you to edit the xy primaries to create a new RGB working space. This is one way that your can create a custom RGB Working space.

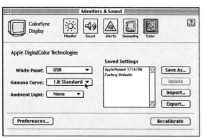

Using Apple monitor calibration software to set the hardware Gamma on my AppleVision 750 monitor, now called the ColorSync 17, to 1.8. I use a white point of D50 when I'm working on CMYK print jobs, like this book, and currently also when working on my LightJet prints. The viewing light you are using to display LightJet prints, or whatever prints you are working on, can make a difference as to where you set your monitor color temperature. You will want the whites on your monitor to match the whiteness of your printer paper when viewing that paper under your chosen viewing light. Check our Web site at www.maxart.com for my latest discoveries in the best ways to calibrate your monitor and set things up for different types of printing situations. I'm currently evaluating some new calibration products I received at the September 99 Seybold and will post my findings on our site.

Chapter 14: Color Spaces, Device Characterization and Color Management

in a 20% dot gain situation and display it in Photoshop with a CMYK working space set up for 30% gain, the image will appear too dark on the screen. When you reset the Photoshop settings to 20%, the same image appears correct again. You need to be careful when opening untagged CMYK images that your prefs are set up correctly for their display.

WORKING WITH 16-BIT PER CHANNEL SCANS AND FILES

A very useful technique, especially when working on the highest-quality art prints, is to work in 16-bit per color channel mode instead of 8-bit color. This gives you up to 16 bits per RGB, LAB, or CMYK channel of information instead of the usual 8 bits. Photoshop 6 supports Marquee and Lasso selection, Cropping, Levels, Curves, Hue/Saturation, Color Balance, Brightness/Contrast, Channel Mixer, the Eyedropper, the Add Noise, Dust and Scratches, Median, Solarize, High Pass, Gaussian Blur and Unsharp Mask filters, the Rubber Stamp and several other tools in 16-bit per channel color mode. Layers of all kinds are not supported at more than 8 bits per channel so you will not want to do all your work in 16-bit per channel mode. To convert an image to 16-bit color, just choose Image/Mode 16 Bits/Channel.

If you get a scan from a really good scanner, the scanner will be actually scanning the file getting more than 8 bits per channel of RGB information. When you adjust the curves and other controls in the scanner software, what you are really doing is deciding how to convert from the more than 8 bits of information that the scanner gets down to the 8 bits of information per channel that is in a standard RGB file. When you do that conversion, you are throwing away information that you got from the scanner, and sometimes you end up throwing away the wrong information or you want some of it back later. At this point, you may need to rescan your original to get that information. Some scanners actually allow you to save all 16 bits per channel of information exactly as it comes from the sensors on the scanner, a raw scan. This way, assuming you have a great scan from a great scanner, you might never need to scan the original again because you can always reprocess that 16-bit per channel raw scan data down to 8 bits in a different way to pull out a different area of detail.

You can actually do your overall color correction on 16-bit per channel files using Photoshop 6 to improve the histogram, colors and contrast of that original raw scan without throwing away any information. This allows you to do one raw scan and then save that and actually be able to make most of your scanner decisions later or over again without actually rescanning. In Chapters 19 and 26 of our step-by-step examples, *Photoshop 6 Artistry* will show you how to change your workflow to do your overall color correction using 16 bits per channel and get much more from your scans. Check out Chapter 16: "Image Resolution, Scanning Film and Digital Cameras" to get a lot of good ideas of things to consider when making 8-bit or 16-bit per channel scans.

PHOTOSHOP COLOR PREFERENCES, MONITOR, SCANNER AND PRINTER CALIBRATION

Here you learn how to set up your Photoshop color preferences and to calibrate your monitor, printers and output devices using ICC profiles and color management.

To fully understand this chapter, you should also read Chapter 3: "Setting System and Photoshop Preferences," Chapter 14: "Color Spaces, Device Characterization, and Color Management," and Chapter 17: "Steps to Create a Master Image." In the first part of this chapter, we will go through the Photoshop 6 Color Settings and describe each setting and our recommended choice for it and what that choice means. The second part of the chapter will explain the choices for calibrating your monitor, scanner and printer, which can dramatically effect the quality and predictability of your results.

SETTING YOUR PHOTOSHOP 6 COLOR PREFERENCES

In Photoshop, bring up the dialog to the left, choose Edit/Color Settings (Command-Shift-K). We will be working with this dialog for some time because I'm going to try and explain each of the settings, why you make a particular choice, and what that choice will mean and do to your files. Get your coffee or your Coke. Mine is right beside me, and if you are tired or bored, then just choose the settings on the left and then come back and read this chapter later. The color settings and calibration are not the most fun part about Photoshop, especially for me, but they will dramatically affect the quality and accuracy of your results. If you are not happy with the results you are getting, this chapter

Go to Edit/Color Settings (Command-Shift-K) in Photoshop 6 to bring up this dialog. Make sure the Advanced Mode checkbox, at the top left, is checked so you see this entire dialog box. Once you have all your color settings the way you want them for a particular type of project, click the Save button to save these settings in a file that can later be reloaded in one step using the Load button.

must be understood before you continue, as the problem may be your lack of understanding of what is herein.

WORKING SPACES

The top section of the Color Settings dialog is called Working Spaces. Choose Adobe RGB (1998) in the first RGB pop-up menu. After making this choice, notice that if you put the cursor on top of that same menu that the Description area at the bottom of the dialog will tell you something about the setting you have chosen. As you are learning to understand all these settings, Photoshop will give you some information about each setting in this Description area whenever you put the cursor on top of that setting. Please do that and read the description information for each of these settings as we go through them. We have now set the RGB working space to Adobe RGB. The RGB working space is the space that will be assigned to new files that you create using File/New and it is the space that you will view untagged files in on the screen even if you don't tag them with Adobe RGB when you open them. Files that are already tagged with some other color space, like some of the files on the *Photoshop 6 Artistry* CD that are tagged with ColorMatch, will usually be opened and viewed within that other color space, unless you choose to do otherwise in the next Color Management Policies section. To learn more about the Adobe RGB color space and the other default RGB spaces, see Chapter 14: "Color Spaces, Device Characterization and Color Management." If you are a photographer and don't have another default custom RGB space you want to work in, like the color space of your film or your scanner, then Adobe RGB is a good space for you to choose. If you are doing exclusively Web work, then you might want to choose the sRGB space. If you are doing exclusively work for CMYK print, then you might want to choose ColorMatch RGB. Setting your RGB working space causes certain things to happen in Photoshop in conjunction with how you set the Color Management Policies for RGB in the next section of this dialog. We'll talk about those issues there.

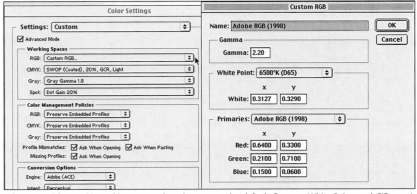

When you pick an RGB working space, that also sets up the default Gamma, White Point, and CIE xy primaries describing that workspace. You can then go in and modify any of these by hand by choosing Custom RGB from the top of the RGB pop-up menu. Modifying any of the values of the standard RGB spaces will change them from that space to another of your own making so be sure to change the name of the space too so you don't overwrite the standard. An example where you might want to define your own space this way would be; let's say that you measured a particular new film or digital camera that you are using and determined from its ICC profile that the Adobe RGB primaries did not contain a small portion of the film's color range. You could then change the Red, Green, or Blue xy values of Adobe RGB to extend the range of the space adding those colors. You'd want to call that Adobe RGB Plus or something like that!

For the second CMYK pop-up menu, I recommend that you choose the one at the top of the menu, Custom CMYK.... This will bring up the dialog shown at the top of the next page where you want to make the changes I have made. These are to set Ink Colors to SWOP Coated, change the Black Generation to Light and the Total Ink Limit to 320%. Those settings, which will be called SWOP (Coated), 20%, GCR, Light, have worked very well for me when I'm doing CMYK work. The U.S. Sheetfed Coated v2 settings also work well and may even be better. Most of my day-to-day printing is of my landscape art prints on the Epson 1270, 2000 and 7500 or the LightJet 5000. All these printers require RGB files, and in most cases I'm converting my RGB or LAB master files to a custom profile for those prints. My CMYK experience involves doing all the color separations for *Photoshop 5&5.5 Artistry*, *Photoshop 6 Artistry* and my wife's book, ***Photoshop, Painter and Illustrator Side-by-Side***. I also occasionally do

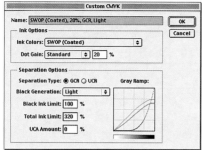

For my recommended CMYK settings, choose Custom CMYK... from the CMYK pop-up then change Black Generation to Light and Total Ink Limit to 320% then choose OK. More advanced users who want to set custom Ink Colors can get the below dialog by choosing Custom... from the Ink Colors dialog here. You can also set custom dot gain curves by choosing Curves... from the above Dot Gain pop-up. Using the above settings, I've had very good results in printing *Photoshop 5 & 5.5 Artistry* on a sheet fed press, *Photoshop, Painter & Illustrator Side-by-Side* on a web press as well as separating various brochures and magazine covers. We used the **U.S. Sheetfed Coated v2** settings, shown to the right, for the more color critical pages in this book. For newspaper presses, non-glossy papers and other printing situations, you may need to use other settings. To be sure, you should run tests with the proofing mechanism at your print shop.

Photoshop 6 provides some new CMYK default settings. We used the **U.S. Sheetfed Coated v2** settings for the more color critical pages in this book. The rest of the pages were printed with the settings shown at the top-left of this page. If the settings I recommend on this page are not working for you, you may want to try the appropriate setting for your type of press and paper shown in this screen grab. See page 161–164 of this chapter for more CMYK information. If you want even more CMYK specific information, I recommend that you check with the *Adobe Photoshop 6 User Guide* or the books *Professional Photoshop 6* and *Real World Photoshop 6*.

Most users will not need to change these. I would not recommend changing them unless you really know what you are doing or have real good recommendations. You may find more info about editing the Ink Colors in *Professional Photoshop 6* or *Real World Photoshop 6*.

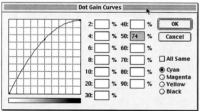

Photoshop 6 allows you to create your own custom dot gain curves. If you work in a print shop and know a lot about color separations, you may want to do this, most users won't. I would not recommend changing these unless you know what you are doing or have really good recommendations. For more info on editing these see *Professional Photoshop 6* or *Real World Photoshop 6*.

an effect for a magazine cover or advertisement and usually separate these, too. The Artistry books are printed at Graphics Art Center (Indianapolis) from Quark files containing my separated CMYK TIFF files direct to plate on sheet-fed presses. I always go to the press check for the first printing of *Artistry*; then they do a great job on reprints using the press sheets from that first printing. Wendy's *Side-by-Side* book is also printed at Graphics Art Center but on a direct-to-plate web press. When that project came up, I did some tests with the printer's Kodak Approval proofs comparing these same settings of mine with the settings normally recommended by the printer. Since this was a web press, I expected the printer's settings to work better, but my settings actually looked a bit more open on the Approval proofs. Approvals are digital proofs that actually show the dot patterns that will appear on the direct-to-plate printing plates. We decided to go with the settings shown to the left here for this web press job, too, and the results were fantastic, especially since we didn't even go to the press check. The book was printed using their standard densities on press. If you have used these CMYK settings, or any other settings from the Custom CMYK dialog, called CMYK Setup in Photoshop 5, you should expect to get the same results as you did in Photoshop 5 with these settings in Photoshop 6. For more info on Photoshop 6 CMYK settings and options, see pages 161 through 164 of this chapter and the information in the screen grabs and captions on those pages.

For the Gray pop-up menu, I'm using the Gray Gamma 1.8 option which matches the gamma that I've set my Mac monitor to and also used with grayscale images in the past. Photoshop 5 and 6 tag grayscale images with a profile showing the gamma that they have been created or adjusted with. The most important thing with grayscale images is that you stay consistent with the gamma that you use, either 1.8 or 2.2, because the appearance of the image will change dramatically if you view a gamma 1.8 image within a gamma 2.2 environment or vice-versa. There are other choices available for your Gray working space including pre-set dot gains of 10% up to 30%. You can also choose Custom Gamma to set the grayscale gamma to any custom value and Custom Dot Gain to set your own dot gain curve. You would use these options when printing grayscale images on presses and papers with different dot gain values or when you needed a gamma value other than 1.8 or 2.2.

For your Spot working space, which controls the dot gain on spot color channels, you should choose a dot gain that is comparable to the dot gain you are using with your CMYK working space. If you are adding a spot color plate to a certain print job, the dot gain for that plate should be similar to the dot gain you are getting at that printer in CMYK. I've set mine to the Dot Gain 20% setting, corresponding to my CMYK settings, but you might want to check with the print shop that is running a spot color job for you and see what they suggest. You can also choose Custom Dot Gain from the top of the Spot working space pop-up menu. This allows you to enter a custom dot gain curve, which you should only do if you know what you are doing and have specific dot gain measurements from the print shop.

In the Color Management Policies section, you have the same three choices in each of the RGB, CMYK and Gray pop-ups. For each one, I recommend that you choose the middle choice, Preserve Embedded Profiles. I also recommend that you turn on Ask When Opening for Profile Mismatches and Missing Profiles that happen when you open a file and also turn on Ask When Pasting for Profile Mismatches that happen during a paste.

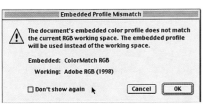

If you often work with files from different color spaces, it might be a good idea to set the info area at the bottom of your window to show the Document Profile. You will then see the profile that Photoshop has assigned to that particular document. In the case of an untagged document, that document will normally be displayed using the default RGB or CMYK working space.

COLOR MANAGEMENT POLICIES

The "Color Management Policies" section helps you deal with files that are different from what you normally expect. Photoshop 6 assumes that you will normally be working with files that are tagged with profiles from your RGB, CMYK or Grayscale working spaces. When you open or paste from a file that is tagged with a profile that is different from your working spaces or that isn't tagged with any profile, Photoshop 6 lets you choose what to do. The settings I recommend, shown here to the right, will always warn you when you open or paste from an untagged file or a file that is tagged with a profile other than your working spaces. When I'm working on photographic images, I usually have my RGB working space set to Adobe RGB, but when I'm working on a book or printing project I'll sometimes set it to ColorMatch RGB. Leaving the Color Management Policies as shown here will always give you a heads up when you are opening a file that is different from your current settings. If you always leave your working spaces set to the same values and you are always working with files in those same spaces, you should never get bothered by these settings.

If you often work with files from other color spaces, the above settings will cause Profile Mismatch dialogs to come up when you open a file or paste from a file in a different color space. The dialogs also alert you that a certain file is from a different color space or maybe doesn't have a profile at all. Since Photoshop 6 allows you to work with several files that are each from a different color space on the screen at a time, there is no need, as there was in Photoshop 5 & 5.5, to convert a file into your working space or to change your working space so a file from a different space will be displayed correctly. When you open a file from a different color space, and you get the Embedded Profile Mismatch dialog (top right), you will usually want to use the embedded profile. If you will be combining or pasting from that file into a master file that is in your working space, then it might be faster to convert this file into the working space now. Otherwise, every time you copy from or drag and drop from that file into your master file within the working space, or within

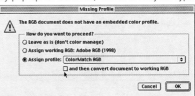

When you open a file that has an embedded profile different from your RGB or CMYK working space, you will get a dialog like the one above. If you choose Use the embedded profile, the image will be correctly displayed on the screen, taking that profile into consideration and it will continue to use that profile. If you choose Convert document's colors, the colors in the document will be converted so the document looks correct when displayed in the working space and the document will be tagged and displayed with the working space. If you choose Discard the embedded profile, the profile will be tossed but the document will be displayed using the working space. To no longer get this dialog, turn off the Ask When Opening checkbox for Profile Mismatches; you will then automatically get the behavior chosen in the Color Management Policy pop-up for that RGB, CMYK or Gray file type.

When you open a document that doesn't have a profile, you will get the Missing Profile dialog. I believe that the standard default here is to Assign the working space but this dialog is sticky. That means that if you make a particular choice, Photoshop will remember that choice and offer it next time. When working with my book, I usually assign the ColorMatch RGB profile to my screen grabs so Photoshop has remembered that and now offers it to me as the default. Notice that you can also assign a profile and then convert the file to your working RGB space. This option is useful, for example, when opening files from a scanner that doesn't save a profile with its files but that you have made a profile for and want to always convert from the scanner profile to your working space. To no longer get this dialog turn off Ask When Opening for Missing Profiles.

When you paste from a document having profile A onto a document having profile B, you get this dialog and usually you will want to choose Convert to have the colors of the pasted image look correct within the document you pasted into. If you don't convert the colors of the pasted image may look wrong!

printing project I'll sometimes set it to ColorMatch RGB. Leaving the Color Management Policies as shown here will always give you a heads up when you are opening a file that is different from your current settings. If you always leave your working spaces set to the same values and you are always working with files in those same spaces, you should never get bothered by these settings.

[Embedded Profile Mismatch dialog]
The document's embedded color profile does not match the current RGB working space. The embedded profile will be used instead of the working space.

Embedded: ColorMatch RGB
Working: Adobe RGB (1998)

☐ Don't show again   Cancel   OK

Actually, even when Ask When Opening is turned off, Photoshop will put up this dialog to let you know that the embedded profile will be used instead of the working space. Notice however that you can click the Don't show again checkbox here and then this warning message will not show again unless you click on the Reset all Warning Dialogs button in Edit/Preferences/General.

any different space for that matter, you will get the Paste Profile Mismatch dialog (bottom right) and will have to decide on doing the conversion then. Opening an image that has no profile attached will bring up the Missing Profile dialog (middle right). This dialog allows you to leave the file as is, without a profile, assign the working space profile, or assign some other profile you can choose from a pop-up menu. If you

This Conversion Options section controls some of what happens when an image is converted from one color space to another using Image/Mode/RGB, LAB, Grayscale or Image/Mode/Convert to Profile. The Use Dither option should usually be on because it will make it less likely that you will get banding when converting from one color space to another. Banding appears as a choppy gradation of subtle color changes and is not usually desirable. In Photoshop 5 & 6, I have usually left the Use Black Point Compensation option off when converting from one RGB space to another, like from Adobe RGB, or even from LAB, to an ICC profile for my Epson 1270 printer or the LightJet 5000. If you have this off and then you don't like the way your blacks and dark shadows look, try the conversion again with Use Black Point Compensation on. With my files, turning it on seems to make the blacks more muddy and gives me less snap in the shadows. The algorithm for Black Point Compensation was changed between Photoshop 5 and Photoshop 6 though, so I plan to test the Photoshop 6 version some more. What you get will depend on your image as well as how the source and destination profiles were actually created.

The Engine pop-up controls who's software actually does the conversion. Adobe (ACE) is the built-in Photoshop 6 software which you should normally use. An example where you might want to use Apple ColorSync, Apple CMM or Heidelberg CMM would be if there were a new version of one of those packages that contained a feature that ACE didn't support or where that feature was more accurate using ColorSync or some other engine.

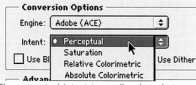

The perceptual Intent is usually what photographers want for photographs because it preserves the overall look and feel of the image. For my RGB and LAB conversions for Epson 1270 and LightJet 5000 output, I have been using Perceptual with Black Point Compensation off. Relative Colorimetric, with Black Point Compensation on, is the Photoshop 6 default. This may work well for you also, I actually like the onscreen proofs better on Relative Colorimetric with Black Point Compensation off. You may want to try that combination if the Perceptual choice is desaturating your images too much. The Saturation option is useful when you want really intense colors, like for business graphics. Absolute Colorimetric is not the choice most photographers will want since the white points of the source and destination are not compensated for. You may find it useful if trying to match the look of one media, like a Match Print for example, on another media, like an Epson printer proof.

make this last choice, you can also turn on a checkbox to convert the file from that profile you assign into the working space.

If you turn off the Ask When Opening options for Profile Mismatch and Missing Profile or Ask When Pasting option for Profile Mismatch, then you won't get the dialogs, you'll just get the behavior chosen from the appropriate pop-up menu in this Color Management Policies section. I do not recommend turning off these warning dialogs unless you are really sure you understand what you are doing and you are also bothered by the dialogs. With the warning dialogs turned off, if you choose Preserve Embedded Profiles for RGB, then when you open a file that had a different profile from the RGB working space, that file would just automatically open and be displayed correctly using the RGB profile that was attached to that file. If Convert to Working RGB was your menu choice, the file would automatically be converted to the RGB working space but you would receive no notice of this conversion. If you had chosen off for your RGB Color Management Policy then that file would be opened without a profile attached at all. If you look at the Document Profile name in the lower left corner of the window, it will be named Untagged RGB. The pixels in the file will still be viewed on the screen using the RGB working space.

On page 129 of the *Adobe Photoshop 6 User Guide*, there is a useful chart of what happens to different types of files under the three Color Management Policies, which include: Off, Preserve Embedded Profile and Convert to Working RGB, CMYK or Gray. You should check out this chart, which I will summarize again here. New documents are tagged with the current working space profile unless Color Management is set to Off, in which case they are left untagged. When opening an existing untagged document, all three options will use the existing working space for viewing and editing the document but they will leave it untagged. When opening an existing tagged document, that is tagged with the current working space. All three options view and edit this in the current working space and also leave it tagged with that space. When opening an existing tagged document tagged with a profile other than the current working space, the Off option untags the document and views it in the current working space. The Preserve Embedded option preserves the embedded profile and views it correctly in that profile's space. The Convert to Working option converts the document from the other profile space into the current working space and then retags the document with the current working space. When pasting or importing data onto an existing document, the Off option just pastes the color numbers without doing any conversions. The Preserve Embedded option converts if the data has a source profile, but if not, or in the case of CMYK data, the numbers are pasted without any conversions. The Convert to Working option converts the data to RGB or CMYK unless it comes from a source without a profile.

CONVERSION OPTIONS

At the top left we see the Conversion Options section of the Photoshop 6 Color Settings. These influence what happens when an image is converted from one color space to another using Image/Mode/RGB, LAB, Grayscale or Image/Mode/Convert to Profile. The Use Dither option should usually be on. This option makes it less likely that you will get undesirable banding when converting from one color space to another. I usually leave the Use Black Point Compensation option off when converting from one RGB space to another. If you have this option off and don't like the way the blacks and dark shadows look in your prints, redo the conversion with Use Black Point Compensation on. I believe the requirement to have this on may be to account for deficiencies in older profile generating software. It has not helped my images when working with profiles generated by Monaco or other more current sources. For me, turning this on seems to make my blacks more muddy and gives me less snappy shadows. What you get will depend on the images you are working with as well as what software and settings were used to generate their source and destination profiles.

See the screen grabs and captions to the right for information about the Engine and Intent pop-up choices. It is important to set these correctly and, in general, you will want to set the Engine to Adobe (ACE), the built-in Photoshop conversion software, and the Intent to Perceptual. Perceptual, with Black Point Compensation off and Use Dither on, is a common setting for photographers when converting an RGB or LAB master image, with a large gamut, to a CMYK or RGB print image within a smaller gamut printer space. If you find that the Perceptual setting is desaturating your colors too much, you might want to try the Relative Colorimetric setting with Black Point Compensation on or off. A good way to compare these settings is to use the wonderful Photoshop 6 onscreen proofing while comparing several versions of the same image on the screen. See the illustration above for an explanation of how to do this. For the ultimate test, you can also print several versions of the same image, converted with different Conversion Options and compare the printed results.

ADVANCED CONTROLS

Most people will want to leave the Advanced Controls off unless you are using a very wide gamut RGB space, one that is much wider than Adobe RGB. If you are using such a space, see the screen grab and caption about Advanced Controls on the bottom right of this page.

To set this up, I started with my LAB master version of this image on the left of the screen. I then did Image/Duplicate to create the copy to the right and arranged the two windows so I could see both at once. While working on the version to the right, I chose Image/Mode/Convert to Profile and picked the profile for my Epson 1270 printer. With the Preview button on, I can then choose either the Perceptual or Relative Colorimetric Intent options and also turn Use Black Point Compensation on and off while looking at a preview of the printed results in the image to the right. For this particular image, the Relative Colorimetric choice with Black Point Compensation off seemed to match my original LAB version the best. Another thing you could do is use Image/Duplicate to make several copies of the image and convert each one in a different way with different settings. You could also compare these on the screen. The final step in the test would be to make and compare test prints after converting the image with one setting versus the other. The onscreen preview should simulate the results you get in your test prints.

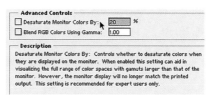

The Advanced Controls should be left off unless you are using a very wide gamut color space. Photoshop 5 has a built-in RGB space called Wide Gamut RGB. This is a very wide gamut space and was probably removed from the Photoshop 6 default list because it was really too wide to be useful in 24-bit color. If one were using such a wide gamut space, it would only be really useful in 48-bit color mode and it is unlikely the colors in that space could be accurately represented on a normal computer monitor. If you were using a large gamut space, you could turn on Desaturate Monitor Colors By to try to somehow estimate your colors on the screen. If you did this, the screen display would probably not be able to match your printed output.

Blend RGB Colors Using Gamma controls the blending of RGB colors, probably from one layer into the next. When it is turned on, RGB colors are blended using the chosen gamma. A gamma of 1 is considered colorimetricly correct and is supposed to create the fewest edge artifacts. When this option is disabled, RGB colors are blended within the document's RGB color space which matches what most other applications do.

139

Calibration of Monitors, Digital Printers and Scanners

One of the most common questions I get from the readers of my *Photoshop Artistry* books has to do with how they can better calibrate their monitors, printers and scanners. Calibration can allow you to get from your printer the same color and contrast that you see on your monitor, to get very similar color and contrast when printing the same image on a number of different printers and also to improve the results you get from your scanner. Apple ColorSync and Photoshop 6 provide an effective framework for people to accurately calibrate the production of digital images using Photoshop on the Macintosh and to also get very accurate soft proofs of printed images on the screen. Doing this calibration accurately, however, requires color measurement instruments and calibration software. When ColorSync and Photoshop 5 first came out, the only calibration and measurement products available were both expensive and difficult to use. Recently this has changed, and there is now a variety of software and hardware products to help you to calibrate. Here, I'll categorize and discuss some of those products and their effectiveness for different types of users. I'll help you understand the type of user you may be and try to match you to the calibration solution that will work best for you. These solutions include: 1. doing and buying nothing, 2. buying several of these calibration products, depending on your needs, and using them to calibrate yourself and, 3. hiring a calibration expert to do the work for you using the most expensive and accurate calibration products and also the expert's knowledge.

What Are Calibration, ColorSync and ICC Profiles?

Calibration is the process where you measure the color gamut of a particular monitor, printer or scanner and produce a detailed description of this color gamut in the format of an ICC profile. The color gamut of a device is the range of colors that device can reproduce. The ICC is an international standards organization that has developed the ICC Profile format which has become an industry standard for describing and dealing with the color gamuts of different color devices. ColorSync is a system software component that is built into the Macintosh that provides a framework for other applications, like Photoshop, Illustrator, Quark, etc., to make use of ICC profiles to accurately deal with the differences in color input and output on different devices. ColorSync and its use by other applications allows the user to get matching, or close to matching, color on each device. For calibration to work correctly, one needs to accurately make an ICC profile of each device and then correctly use these ICC profiles within a world of ColorSync-savvy applications. For color management, Windows systems can use Microsoft ICM (Integrated Color Management), but there is not as much conformity in the Windows world. One problem in particular is that most Windows video cards don't provide the necessary functionality to fully support hardware monitor calibration. ColorSync was supposed to be available for Windows 2000; the latest news I've heard is that this will no longer be happening.

Do You Need to Calibrate?

If the color on your monitor matches the color on your digital prints and if you and your clients are happy with the results of your digital image creations, you may not need to calibrate any further. Seriously! I had been using my Epson Stylus Photo 1200 to create low-cost proofs for later final output to the LightJet 5000. The LightJet 5000 is a $200,000 digital printer that prints onto 60–year, color-permanent Fuji Crystal Archive photographic paper up to 50" wide. This printer has become a standard for archival digital photographic output. With the Epson 1200 using the methods and settings described in the Latest Tips area of www.barryhaynes.com, I have been able to get images on my monitor and from this printer that were often quite close to having the same image printed on the LightJet. You may find that calibrating your monitor with Adobe Gamma, a visual monitor calibrator that comes with Photoshop, and using my or similar settings with your printer gets you close enough for your needs. This is more likely to be the case if your Epson, HP or other printer is the only output you are interested in and if you are lucky enough to have a monitor that matches the printer's output. If images on your monitor don't match your printer, then you should certainly pay close attention to the rest of this chapter. I'm interested in as exactly as possible matching my Epson 1270 and Epson 2000 prints to my LightJet 5000 prints and also in matching Epson 1270 and 2000 prints on several different papers. To do this I have found that creating my own ICC profiles for each printer and ink combination usually gets me a closer match and also a more beautiful print. I'm very picky about color so I may require more accuracy than you need. The amount of color accuracy you require will depend on the type of color user you are and also on the amount of time and money you can spend.

What Category of Color User Are You and How Much Time and Money Do You Have to Spend

There are a lot of color calibration products now on the market, and they are obviously designed for different categories of color users. I'll try to come up with some user categories to help describe who might want to go with each type of calibration solution. A "hobbiest" user is someone who uses Photoshop and other desktop applications to make prints to send to friends and relatives, to make their own Xmas cards and just for fun. If you are this type of user, you may be happy using Adobe Gamma, or some other application, to calibrate your monitor and using the Epson or HP settings described in the Latest Tips section of my web site. The hobbiest user doesn't have a lot of time and money to spend on calibration products and probably won't spend more than $300 on calibration. A "serious hobbiest" user is someone who creates digital images and really cares about more exact color control of those images. This type of user will be willing to spend some time and money on calibration products but probably won't want to spend much over $1,000 to $1,500. I'll call the next category the "professional color user." This type of user needs to have exact repeatable color on more than one output device for commercial and/or art sales of their images. The professional color user will pay considerably more than $1,500 to get control over their color and will also invest the time required to get repeatable consistent results. The highest category of color user is the "color management expert." This is a person who is in business to make color profiles and calibrate other customers' color environments. The color management expert will spend up to $10,000 and maybe more for the software and hardware needed to do the job. He or she will also spend weeks and months learning how to use these calibration products in a variety of situations. So we have the four user categories of hobbiest, serious hobbiest, professional color user and finally color management expert.

Should you Calibrate Yourself or Get a Professional to Help you?

If you are a hobbiest, then I'd say you should calibrate yourself using some of the less expensive solutions I'll describe below. Most color management experts who actually know what they are doing will charge you more than what you will be willing to pay for their services. The exception to this statement is that you might want to hire a color management expert to make a custom profile for you or try a profile from a place like ProfileCity.com, which will make a profile for you remotely. As with ProfileCity.com, some color management experts will send you a calibration file, which you print out on your printer via their instructions; then you mail it back to them and they measure it and mail you a profile. This can work if done correctly and can be as cheap as $125. I'd be willing to bet that some profiles made this way at this kind of price are not that good, but some may be, and if you find a place that makes good remote profiles, please let me know with an e-mail to barry@maxart.com.

If you are a serious hobbiest, you might want to try some of the low to moderately priced calibration solutions and calibrate your own system. If you can find a recommended color management expert who will do what you need in your price range, you may get more accurate calibration that way. The deciding issue here might be whether you will you need to calibrate more things in the future. You will probably want to make an ICC profile for each printer and paper combination that you use regularly. If you are using the Epson 1270, for example, and only the Epson Premium Semigloss Photo Paper and maybe the Epson Matte Paper Heavyweight; that will require a profile for each of these papers and calibration of your monitor and maybe a scanner. If you will be happy with those profiles for some time to come, then getting a color management expert, or a place like ProfileCity.com, to do it for you may save you time and money and get you more accurate profiles. See the downloadable articles on my web site, www.barryhaynes.com, about color calibration for references to color management experts and color consultants. There is also a small list in this chapter on page 155. If, on the other hand, you want to try Lysonic and MIS third-party inks with your Epson 1200 or 3000, use a variety of papers and are using several scanners or printers, then you might save money by purchasing your own calibration products.

If you are a professional color user, the same issues come up for you, too. I'm assuming you will have more money to spend on a solution than the serious hobbiest and that time may also be a factor for you. If you are, for example, a busy commercial photographer or design agency, you may not have the time to learn how to correctly use the calibration hardware and software products you will need to do a good job. It took me several weeks to decide which products to evaluate for last year's *Communication Arts* calibration article and then several more weeks to learn how to use the products well. To use them really efficiently in a variety of circumstances is taking me longer, and it is a constantly changing process since the products are changing and improving all the time. Your time might be better spent hiring a color management expert, who will also bring the best software and hardware to the task. One the other hand, if your organization is large and you have a lot of different color scanners, monitors, printers, inks and papers to calibrate, you might save money, make it more convenient for yourself, and have more control if you purchase your own calibration hardware and software and learn how to use it.

The color management expert is going to want to have the highest quality calibration software and hardware available and will likely have to spend at least $10,000 to get what they need. A calibration expert may also want to have several solutions available, so they can charge different amounts depending on the accuracy required by the customer and also the amount of money they can spend.

MONITOR CALIBRATION FOR FREE?

Photoshop comes with a tool called Adobe Gamma, which allows you to visually calibrate your monitor. I calibrate my monitor to a color temperature of 5000 kelvin and a gamma of 1.8, which works well for printed photographs. I've found it hard to correctly calibrate many monitors to these settings using Adobe Gamma. If you are mostly working on Web images, you may want to calibrate to 6500 and 2.2. More monitors will easily calibrate to these settings using Adobe Gamma. Most modern monitors also have buttons on the front of the monitor that allow you to set the color temperature and gamma; these are sometimes quite accurate, but often not that accurate. On Mac systems, you can also use Apple Menu/Control Panels/Monitors & Sound to bring up a control panel with a Color button that allows you to visually calibrate your monitor. With the Apple ColorSync 17" and 21" displays, this is also how you access the built-in hardware calibrator, another way to calibrate your monitor without additional expense. If you have a good eye for monitor color and some patience, it is possible to get reasonable calibration on some monitors using one of these techniques. If this doesn't work, then you should try one of the third-party monitor calibration techniques discussed later in this chapter.

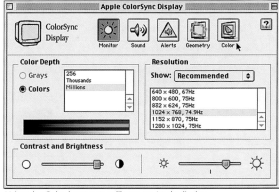

Using the Color button to calibrate an Apple display.

USING THE ADOBE GAMMA UTILITY

First, make sure the background on your monitor is neutral gray. On the Mac, go to Control Panels/Appearance in the Apple menu and set up a neutral gray desktop. If there is no default neutral gray option, as there isn't in my version 8.6 (shame on you, Steve Jobs), then use Photoshop to create a 640x480 TIFF file and fill it with the RGB value of 192,192,192. Save this file in TIFF format; then set your desktop to that image file using the Desktop tab in the Appearance control panel.

In Windows 95 and NT, click the Start button and select Settings/Control Panel. Now double-click the Display icon; then click the Background tab and select None in the Pattern and Wallpaper drop-down menus. Select the Appearance tab and click the Color button. Now choose one of the neutral grays from the pop-up swatches or click the Other button to open the Color dialog box. This dialog box gives you more color swatch selections and also allows you to choose a gray value from the Color Picker or to enter a value, like 128, for RGB in the Red, Green, and Blue settings. If you use the Color dialog box, you will have to press OK to apply the change from this dialog box; in either case, press OK from the Appearance tab to apply the changes.

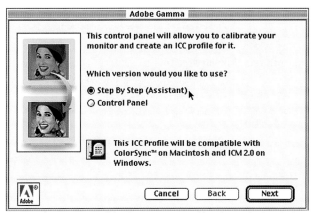

Step 1: When you open Adobe Gamma, you can either choose the Step By Step Assistant, which gives you more help along the way, or the Adobe Gamma Control Panel, which comes without much explanation. We will use the Assistant version here. You might want to try the Control Panel after more experience.

Step 2: Here you press the Load button to choose an initial ICC profile to describe your monitor. For example, if you had a Radius PressView monitor, you could probably start out using the ColorMatch RGB profile. For this monitor, I initially use the Apple 17" D50 profile.

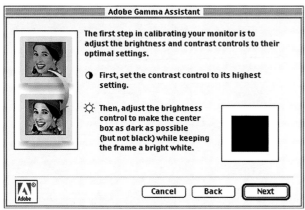

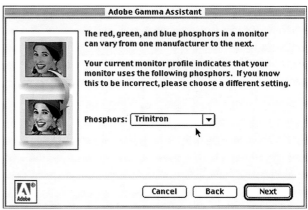

Step 3: This screen of the Adobe Gamma Assistant helps you to correctly set the Brightness and Contrast controls on you monitor. When they are correct, you should barely be able to see the smaller box in the center of the black area, and you should also have bright whites.

Step 4: Here you have to set your monitor's phosphor type. You should be able to get that information from the documentation that comes with your monitor. If you use a correct starting monitor profile, that information might also be included there. If you are not sure, try Trinitron.

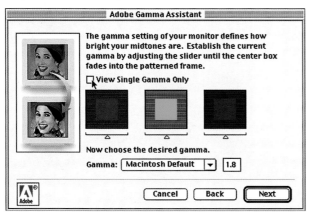

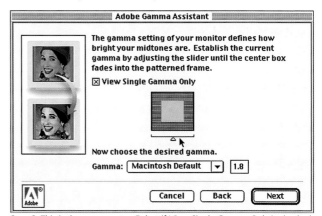

Step 5: In this step, you choose a desired monitor gamma. For print work, or for print and Web work, I would suggest setting this at 1.8. If you are doing exclusively Web work, set it to 2.2. To get the color to match correctly, sit back and squint while moving the slider until the box in the middle is least visible. If the images on your monitor have a different color cast than the printed versions, you may want to go back to this step to tweak the cast of the screen.

Step 6: This is the same as step 5, but if View Single Gamma Only is checked, you make the gray box in the middle disappear within the surrounding box. I'd try both methods to see which works best for you. When it is correct, the boxes in the middle should be least visible in both gray and color modes.

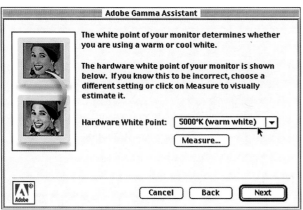

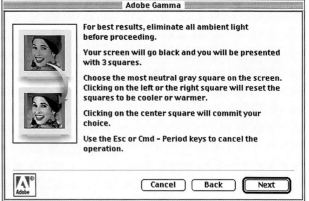

Step 7: Here you are choosing the hardware white point of your monitor. Many monitors these days have a settable white point, and if yours does, you should set it before running Adobe Gamma; then choose that setting here. For CMYK print work, you will probably want to use 5000 Kelvin although some less expensive monitors will look dull and too yellow when set to this setting.

Step 8, optional: If you press the Measure button in the last step, this screen comes up giving you directions on how to measure your monitor's default hardware white point. If you don't have a monitor with a settable white point, read these directions, then click Next in this dialog to get the next step below.

Chapter 15: Photoshop Color Preferences, Monitor, Scanner and Printer Calibration

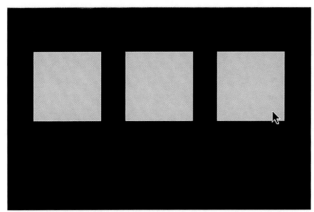

Step 9, optional: To help you judge which square is actually a neutral gray, it helps to have a Macbeth Colorchecker chart or a Kodak grayscale chart placed in your 5000° Kelvin viewing box. You can then adjust the squares here until you get a gray that matches the neutral gray on one of those charts.

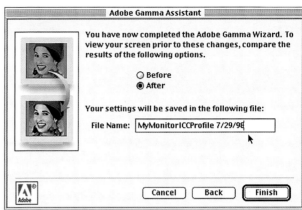

Step10: On this last step, you can use the Before and After buttons to toggle between the way your monitor was set up before and how it will be set up after this session with Adobe Gamma. If you are happy with your Adobe Gamma session, save your changes into a newly named ICC profile of your monitor. When you leave Adobe Gamma, on the Mac make sure your Color-Sync System Profile is correctly set to this new monitor ICC profile, on WIndows make sure ICM is set correctly for this profile. On either platform, this new profile should show as your Monitor RGB within the RGB pop-up menu in the Color Settings dialog in the Working Spaces area. You need to bring up the RGB pop-up to see this just above the default RGB color spaces.

To describe the use of this Adobe Gamma utility, we will show you screen grabs of the 10 steps that you have to go through, and under each grab, we'll have a caption that explains that step.

INEXPENSIVE CALIBRATION SYSTEMS

FOR MONITOR CALIBRATION ONLY

If you are unable to calibrate your monitor correctly using Adobe Gamma, which I often find it hard to do, a very inexpensive (actually excellent) visual monitor calibrator, which doesn't require an instrument, is Itec ColorBlind ProveIt for $49.95. With ProveIt and no sensor, it is possible—for an experienced color person anyhow—to do a great job visually calibrating most monitors. If you purchase an additional monitor calibration sensor, ColorBlind supports many popular models that cost around $200. This software package works very well and allows you to calibrate to any color temperature and gamma very quickly and accurately. For $299 you can purchase ProveIt with the sensor and get easy and accurate monitor calibration. Another hardware/software product that does a great job with monitor calibration is Color Vision PhotoCal. Their USB PhotoCal system, which includes the monitor calibration sensor and the software for $199, works very well in calibrating a monitor to 5000 & 1.8 or 6500 and 2.2. This is an easy-to-use product that works with the Mac and Windows; the serial interface version is $299 but if you have and older power PC Mac, it's cheaper and better to just get a USB PCI bus card which gives you two USB ports for under $100. Then you can attach other USB devices, including a USB hub, to your older Mac. If you want to be able to calibrate your monitor to any color temperature or gamma, the more expensive $399 Color Vision Optical may be the product you will want. Both Color Vision monitor calibration products use the

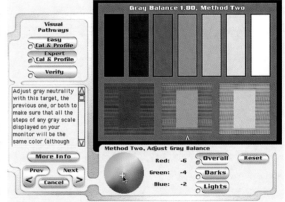

Using ColorBlind ProveIt to Visually Calibrate your monitor. This is a great visual calibration tool and it works even better and much more quickly if you purchase it with the hardware monitor calibrator!

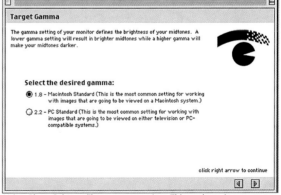

Using PhotoCal to calibrate your monitor. This package is easy to use and comes with a sensor to automatically calibrate your monitor.

Monaco EZ Color steps you through the process of calibrating monitors, scanners and printers. It is easy to use.

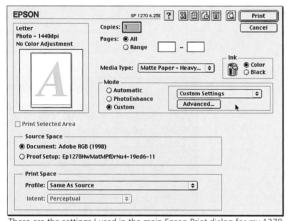

These are the settings I used in the main Epson Print dialog for my 1270 when printing both the test swatches for a profile and then later when making prints that have been converted to this profile. After you have made the profile, your document Source Space and your Print Space will both be the name of that profile. You need to use these in conjunction with the advanced print dialog settings shown below. You need to set the Media Type to the type of paper you are using.

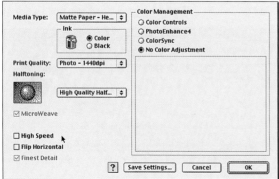

These are the advanced Epson print dialog settings to go with the above main print dialog. When making prints using your profile, No Color Adjustment is chosen here because you will have already done an Image/Mode/Convert to Profile to adjust your image for this printer and paper. Notice that I have turned off High Speed to get the most accurate print.

same hardware sensor, so if you already have PhotoCal and want to upgrade to Optical, that costs an additional $199 for the same total cost.

CALIBRATE A FLATBED SCANNER, MONITOR AND PRINTER

To calibrate your flatbed scanner, monitor and inkjet printer, there are several low-priced products I have evaluated. Monaco EZ Color, for $299 without their monitor sensor and $498 with, is the most well known of these. Monaco EZ Color developed a very smart system that uses your flatbed scanner to create a profile for both your scanner and printer. As you can see from the screen grab here, Monaco EZ Color steps you through the simple process and explains it very well. It first prompts you to print a profile from your printer. Instead of printing directly from Monaco, I recommend that you have Monaco write the profile to a file and then open that file and print that profile directly from Photoshop. This way you will be sure to use the same print options that you use when printing your profiled images. Use the print options I show here for printing the profile from Photoshop with the Epson 1270 printer; use similar options for other Epson printers. With any printer, you will want to print in a way that turns off all the color management done by the printer software.

An important thing I discovered is that the Epson inks, and some other inkjet inks, change in color if you let them dry overnight. I found that my profiles were more accurate if I let the test swatches dry overnight before reading them with the scanner or spectrophotometer and making the profile. After printing the swatches with Monaco EZ Color, you then tape an IT8 target to the indicated place on the printed swatch page. The IT8 target comes with EZ Color and is a standard set of color swatches that are produced using exact specifications. See page 126 for a picture of an IT8 target. You then place this letter size swatch printout, with the IT8 target attached, on your scanner and scan the entire thing making sure that all color management on your scanner is turned off. Due to poor software or documentation, being sure all the color management on your scanner is turned off is often hard to do and is very important as leaving the scanner's color management on can destroy the results of making a profile this way. You then save the scanned RGB file in TIFF format. Monaco EZ Color then reads in the information from this scan and prompts you to click on the four corners of both the printed swatches from your printer and also the IT8 target. Once you locate the corners of each swatch area, EZ Color can then compare the results from the scan to the empirical results of the original swatch colors. It then uses the results of scanning the IT8 target to create a profile for your scanner. With that profile in hand, it can then analyze the scan of your printer's swatches to create the profile for your printer.

I've made a number of profiles using Monaco EZ Color with different papers and Epson printers. I've found that the same image printed with the correct Monaco EZ Color profile on these different printers and papers looks very similar. This is a good solution for the price and well worth a try for the hobbiest or the serious hobbiest. Remember that when you print an image using a custom profile, you first want to use Image/Mode/Convert to Profile to convert your

Chapter 15: Photoshop Color Preferences, Monitor, Scanner and Printer Calibration

master image from your LAB or RGB color space into the space for your printer created by this profile. Then in your print dialog, you want to turn all color management off in the same way you did when printing the color test swatches to make your profile.

Monaco will also sell you IT8 targets on film so you can use EZ Color to calibrate a film scanner. These cost $40 for 35mm and $100 for 4x5 film. I have not tried this film option myself. I was not that impressed with the EZ Color system for visually calibrating a monitor. Without the monitor sensor, it didn't work much differently than Adobe Gamma and is not as useful as ColorBlind ProveIt is without a sensor. With the hardware sensor it works much better, just as well as ColorBlind ProveIt or Color Vision PhotoCal.

Another system that uses a flatbed scanner to read color swatches in the same way as Monaco EZ Color is Praxisoft WiziWYG, $79, or WiziWYG Deluxe, $599. The step-by-step process for making profiles with WiziWYG is very similar to that for Monaco EZ Color so I won't describe it in detail. I actually used Praxisoft WiziWYG Deluxe to make a profile with my flatbed scanner; the process works the same as it does in WiziWYG. WiziWYG Deluxe, which includes a hardware monitor calibrator and a profile editor, is a mid-priced calibration system that allows one to use either a flatbed scanner or a low-end spectrophotometer or colorimeter to read the color swatches and make profiles. The hardware monitor calibrator that comes with WiziWYG Deluxe did a similar job to ProveIt and PhotoCal in calibrating my monitor. Another system for making profiles using a flatbed scanner is Color Vision's Profiler RGB. This system makes the profiles without using an IT8 target. Later this year I plan to test this and re-compare it to Monaco EZ Color and Praxisoft WiziWYG. The new Epson 2000, 7500 and 9500 printers with pigmented inks are requiring new techniques to make good profiles. I will be working with these printers and software packages to determine the best way to use them for accurate color. Check www.barryhaynes.com where I will post anything new I discover.

When printing an image using a custom profile, I first use Image/Mode/ Convert to Profile from Photoshop to convert my standard master image from its default color space, Adobe RGB in this case, into the space defined by the custom profile. I then print the image using the same print dialog settings, shown on the previous page, that were used to print the sample test swatches. Depending on the image I'm working with, I may set the Intent to either Perceptual or Relative Colorimetric and I may occasionally turn on Black Point Compensation. With the Preview checkbox on as shown here, you should get an accurate screen preview to help you in making those decisions.

MID-PRICED CALIBRATION SYSTEMS

My comments in this section are based on tests I did for a *Communication Arts* calibration article that appeared in the 2000 Photo Annual. All these products update from time to time and there are always new products coming on the market. I'll be doing more tests with calibration systems later in 2001, and those results will be posted at www.barryhaynes.com or in future articles for *CA* or other magazines. The mid-priced calibration systems I've looked at are Praxisoft WiziWYG Deluxe at $599, WiziWYG Pro at $999 (this is WiziWYG Deluxe plus a ColorSavvy ColorMouse colorimeter), Itec ColorBlind Matchbox at $999 and Monaco Proof at $1,495. ColorBlind Matchbox includes a colorimeter for making printer profiles; WiziWYG Deluxe includes a hardware monitor calibrator and WiziWYG Pro includes monitor calibration and print profiling colorimeters. All these systems allow you to make profiles using either a spectrophotometer or a colorimeter, which generally provide more accurate results than a flatbed scanner. Most of the low-priced colorimeters only read one color swatch at a time. Reading all the swatches required to make a profile can therefore take an hour or two. I was very appreciative to X-Rite for lending me a DTP-41 strip reading spectrophotometer to use while I worked on a calibration article. It reads an entire strip of swatches automatically as it pulls them through its sensor. This allows you to do your readings much more quickly, and the DTP-41 is also

The main options available with Monaco PROOF.

You get a more accurate profile with Monaco Proof if you first linearize your printer. In this dialog the options for linearization are explained and you are given the option of printing the swatches directly from Monaco Proof or saving the file and printing from your application. I recommend printing from your application.

To the left you see the 29 rows of color swatches displayed. Monaco Proof flashes the row that you need to feed into the Spectrophotometer next. You put this row into the DTP-41, click on the button and the device automatically reads all 26 swatches in that row. I would not want to read all 759 swatches by hand!

very accurate. Another interesting product that I saw at the September 2000 Seybold, is the SpectroCam from Spectro Star, which costs about $1,400. It is a very versatile spectrophotometer that allows you to calibrate your monitor, is a strip reader for doing quicker printer calibrations and also has other uses. I hope to evaluate the Spectro-Cam later this year.

The Monaco Proof product, which I used a fair amount, appears to be a subset of Monaco's higher-end product, Monaco Profiler 3.1. The spectrophotometer I used to make profiles with Monaco Proof was the X-Rite DTP-41, which costs $2,500. Monaco Proof allows you to make profiles for monitors, scanners and printers and also contains MonacoTweak for editing profiles that you and others have made. Although not as useful as the Gretag Macbeth Profile Editor's Gamut View, shown later, Monaco Proof's View Gamut feature allows you to see 3D pictures of profiles and compare several of these on your monitor. Monaco Proof has an optional $249 sensor to calibrate your monitor, which is the same sensor you would get with Monaco EZ Color.

Monaco Proof gives you the option to linearize the profile first, which is the best thing to do. Linearization prints a small set of swatches which you then read with your spectrophotometer allowing Monaco Proof to determine the linear response of your output device. This information is then used to create a more accurate set of color swatches for the next set of measurements. Higher-end profile making packages tend to have this optional extra linearization step. To linearize you turn on the Linearize option and have Monaco write the linearization target out to a file. You then open that target and print it from Photoshop, using the same no color management settings as you will later use when printing with a profile. There is a screen grab of these settings above in the description of Monaco-EZ-Color. I found that the profiles come out better if you let the linearization target then dry over night to be sure the ink colors have completely stabilized. The next day, using the DTP-41 or another spectrophotometer or colorimeter, you read the values from this target into Monaco Proof. The Linearization swatches contain three rows and 36 swatches total. The software prompts which strip of the target to read next. To read a strip you put it into the DTP-41; then push its only button which causes all the swatches on that strip to be read. The Monaco software then inputs those swatch values, which are sent to your computer over the serial port by the DTP-41, and then prompts you to read the next strip.

After reading the linearization values, Monaco Proof uses them to create a large set of color swatches. This set of color swatches is written to either 7 letter size page files or three tabloid size files so you can print them from Photoshop. You can actually print the swatches directly from Monaco but to duplicate the exact process I use when making a photographic print, I printed them from Photoshop using the same settings, shown above, I use when printing images. You want to let this second set of swatches dry overnight, so when you read them and make the final profile you'll actually be working on the third day of this process.

Chapter 15: Photoshop Color Preferences, Monitor, Scanner and Printer Calibration

This second set of swatches contains 29 rows of 26 swatches each, and a last row that only contains 5. That is 759 swatches in all! Can you imagine clicking on each of them, one at a time, then waiting a couple of seconds while each swatch is read? That is why I like the DTP-41, which still took about 25 minutes to read the 759 swatches. All I had to do was line each of the 30 rows up correctly; then the DTP-41 did the rest. The ColorBlind Matchbox Colorimeter takes about 2 hours to read the 300 swatches in the Matchbox swatch pattern, but then it comes with Matchbox included in the $999 price versus about $4,000 for Monaco Proof plus a DTP-41.

After reading all 759 swatches into Monaco Proof, you are now given quite a few options for making a profile. There is an option to add contrast to your profile; I left this off. You need to choose your rendering intent, choose Perceptual for photographs, and there is also an option to neutralize any color casts caused by the paper. I found the profiles made with this Neutralize Paper Color option on did a better job making neutral stepwedge grays actually print without a cast and also did better at matching the same image printed on the LightJet 5000. Once you have chosen your options, you are then asked to name the profile you will make; then Monaco Proof creates the profile. At this point, without having to reread all the swatch data, you can go back to the step where you chose the profile making options and make another version of the profile having different options. I was quite impressed with this package and the Epson 1270 profiles I made with it and the DTP-41. These profiles have been the most accurate and pleasing ones I was able to create so far.

The process for making profiles with WiziWYG Deluxe is similar to that of Monaco Proof. WiziWYG Deluxe did not support the DTP-41, however, but only supported the $550 ColorSavvy ColorMouse and X-Rite Digital Swatchbook, which are less expensive measurement devices that read one color swatch at a time. Since I didn't have one of these devices attached, WiziWYG would not give me the option of printing out the color swatches for a higher-end device to read. If you do have one of these cheaper devices, then Deluxe prints 512 swatches for you to read with it. Since I didn't have one of these, I had to choose the option for printing the swatches and reading them on my flatbed scanner, as I could have done with regular WiziWYG and did with Monaco EZ Color. It seems that for $599 WiziWYG Deluxe should support the DTP-41 and Gretag higher-end swatch readers. The more expensive Monaco Proof, on the other hand, only supported more expensive readers, like the DTP-41 and Spectrolino, but did also support ASCII data files. Why didn't it support the less expensive devices? Praxisoft also has a more expensive product, the $1,949 Compass Profile, that does support the more expensive devices and has more features like Monaco Proof. Calibration packages can be expensive, and you need to make sure the software and hardware products you plan to use will work together.

To compare these profiles, I printed the same six images with each profile. The six different images each tested particular types of color situations. The profiles made with the DTP-41 and Monaco Proof showed the most variety of colors and produced the most pleasing prints. I rate second the profiles made with Monaco EZ Color using my flatbed scanner as the measurement device. I actually have quite a good

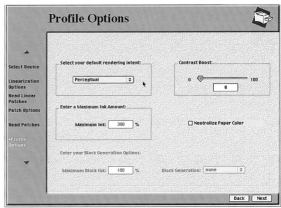

After reading all the 759 swatches, you get these options for creating the profile. You should use the Perceptual rendering intent when working with photographs. I didn't turn on any of the contrast boost since I want the printer to emulate what is on my screen. The Black Generation and Maximum Ink options refer to CMYK profiles and I did my Epson profiles as RGB profiles. I did like the profile generated for the Matte Paper Heavyweight better when the Neutralize Paper Color options was turned on. It did a better job of creating neutral grays on my stepwedge that I usually add to the border around my prints. You can actually generate more than one version of the profile without rereading all the swatches. To do this, you click Next here and create a profile, then use the Back button to come back to this Profile Options screen, change the options then go on to create a second profile with different options.

Measurement devices and input formats supported by Monaco Proof version 3.0.

Using WiziWYG Deluxe is similar to using Monaco EZ Color or Monaco Proof. I found that Monaco Proof had more details in its PDF electronic manual than the very short WiziWYG PDF manual.

flatbed scanner, the Lino Saphir Ultra 2, although I have heard from color experts at Adobe that Monaco EZ Color works well with most flatbed scanners, even many of the cheaper ones. The profiles I made with my scanner and WiziWYG Deluxe did not appear to do quite as good a job printing my files as the ones made with Monaco Proof or the ones made with Monaco EZ Color. They were a bit darker and the color not as close to neutral. I wasn't able to extensively test WiziWYG Deluxe, however, or make higher-end profiles with WiziWYG Deluxe since it didn't support the DTP-41.

I have heard good things about the Itec ColorBlind Matchbox product and have several photographer friends who have been happy with the profiles it makes. I've tested Itec ColorBlind ProveIt and am very impressed with it! I'll be testing ColorBlind Matchbox soon since I recently received a copy, so check my Web site for more up to date test results. The ColorBlind Matchbox product is a great deal since it comes with profile making software, a colorimeter (the sensor for making printer profiles) and also a profile editor all for $999. The included colorimeter only reads one swatch at a time so it takes longer than the DTP-41. It is also a colorimeter and not a spectrophotometer so may not be quite as accurate as the DTP-41. Still, for $999 total this is a solution well worth looking at! This product appears to have similar functionality to WiziWYG Pro which also costs $999.

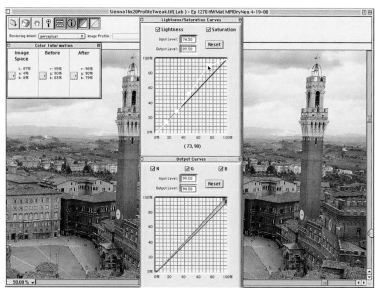

Monaco Tweak shows you the before image on the left and the after image on the right. With a well calibrated monitor, both images give you accurate RGB monitor soft proofs of how your images will look when printed with this profile. The edits you can make with Monaco Tweak include Lightness, Saturation, Red, Green and Blue with each control being a curve. You can place the cursor anywhere within either image and see the before and after values. Make sure you give Monaco Proof more than the default memory on the Mac to see an accurate display of your images.

EDITING PROFILES

Once you make a profile, or have one made for you, it is possible to edit the profile to change it and fix small areas you are not happy with. According to my friend Bruce Bayne, a color management expert, it is very common to have to make small edits to many of the profiles that are created. You will want to have this capability even if someone else makes a profile for you. Many of the profiles I made were essentially good except for some minor flaw, like having a magenta cast in the 20% and 10% highlight areas. I was able to improve these profiles using a profile editor. Monaco Proof contains a profile editor called Monaco Tweak, Praxisoft WiziWYG Deluxe contains a profile editor called TweakIt, and ColorBlind Matchbox also contains a profile editor; the ColorBlind one I have not tested so far but have heard it is good. Monaco Tweak and WiziWYG TweakIt both work in similar ways and have similar options, although I found the options on Monaco Proof's Tweak give you better control over specific ranges of color. All the controls in Monaco Tweak use an interface similar to the Curve tool in Photoshop. The controls in WiziWYG's TweakIt all looked like the Color Balance tool in Photoshop, except with fewer options, so they didn't allow you to, for example, only add greens to the highlights.

Monaco Tweak allows you to adjust Lightness, which does not effect color but only brightness and contrast, color saturation, giving you the option of, for example, saturating or desaturating the more saturated colors without affecting the neutrals. It also provides a curve for each of Red, Green and Blue.

WiziWYG TweakIt's controls included sliders to adjust the overall color balance between Red and Cyan, Green and Magenta, Blue and Yellow; there is also a control to saturate or desaturate all the colors or any particular of the six colors separately; and finally there are controls to increase or decrease brightness or contrast.

The process for editing a profile in both applications is very close to the same. You first tell the application which profile you want to edit and then you open a file; it's best to use several files that are typical of the type of work you will be doing with these profiles. Monaco Proof was able to open either LAB or RGB format TIFF files whereas WiziWYG TweakIt would only open RGB format TIFF files. I downsampled the 60 meg files I was working with to about 20 megs so these applications could deal with them when I assigned each program 80 megabytes of application memory to work in. When you open the file, you can display a before and after version of the image, with before on the left and after on the right. As you make changes to the profiles those changes are previewed on the right side of the screen within the image you have open.

Here are the controls for WiziWYG Deluxe TweakIt. As you can see, all the controls here are sliders, like in Photoshop ColorBalance, so you can't change what is happening in a particular range of values within an image, like you can in Monaco Tweak. WiziWYG Deluxe TweakIt did have faster feedback of changes and scrolls than Monaco Tweak but ultimately it is the amount of detailed control possible that is most important. What we are seeing here is the before and after images from TweakIt on the left and in the middle. The rightmost image here is this same file opened in Photoshop. Having Photoshop open in a window underneath allows you, with both Tweak and TweakIt, to compare Photoshop's soft proofing to that of your profile editing application. This image was in LAB color and I found Photoshop's display of it to be almost identical to that of both profile editors. Monaco Tweak can read a LAB format TIFF file directly but to open this file into WIziWYG TweakIt, I had to first convert it to an RGB TIFF format in Photoshop then resave it in that RGB format.

These profile editing packages are giving you RGB soft proofs of how the image you have open will print on your printer when using the profile you are editing. I found that the screen display of the Monaco Proof profile I made, with the Neutralize Paper Color option on, most closely matched my Photoshop display of the image and also my print. Both applications also allow you to read the before and after digital RGB or LAB values of any point within the image you have open. This is helpful especially if you are trying to adjust neutral gray step wedges to print as exactly neutral. During these tests, I always added the StepWedge file from the Calibration folder of the *Photoshop 6 Artistry* CD to the edge of any image I was printing. If neutrals don't print as neutral, that is a good sign that your profile is not correct.

Monaco Proof's controls were not very responsive and sort of clunky. When you moved a slider to scroll the images or entered a point on a curve, the visual feedback was too slow. To enter curve points accurately, I found it best to click on the curve, drag it somewhere so the point actually stayed on the curve, then actually type in the Input and Output values I wanted, separated by tabs. The slow visual feedback on the screen showing the changes appeared to be quite accurate, however, and matched my printed output from a particular profile quite well. WiziWYG's controls and screen feedback were more responsive although the screen display of the images was initially very poor. This problem was easily solved, however, by assigning more memory to the application. The online PDF manual that came with Monaco Proof was much more detailed than the very brief manual that came with WiziWYG Deluxe.

Editing Profiles

Expensive, "Professional," Calibration Systems

The professional color user and the color management expert would probably want an X-Rite DTP-41 or the even more expensive $6,000 Gretag Macbeth Spectrolino spectrophotometer with the SpectroScan X-Y table. The Spectrolino is a spectrophotometer which can take readings from your monitor, a swatch printed on paper and also through film. The SpectroScan X-Y table allows you to place a page of swatches on the table, hook up the Spectrolino to its holder on the table then automatically read all the swatches on the page without any further user intervention. If you are in the business of making profiles and you have to make a lot of them, this is the professional tool of choice. If you are a professional color user and you need to make a number of printer profiles, only then may the DTP-41 be a more cost effective solution for you that still allows for some automation. X-Rite also makes more advanced versions of the DTP-41 which allow you to take readings from both film and paper.

The professional level software packages include Gretag Macbeth's Profilemaker 3.0 for around $3,500, Lino's $1,595 PrintOpen, $1,595 ScanOpen and $895 View Open (bundled for $3,795), Monaco Profiler for $4,250, Praxisoft CompassProfile for $1,949 and Itec's ColorBlind Professional for $4,799. These are the products that the color calibration expert will want to check out. I have not evaluated these products myself so far but hope to do so in the future. I recently received a copy of Monaco Profiler and am looking forward to working with it when *Photoshop 6 Artistry* is finished. I do believe that the professional color user will find they can get very good printer profile results using Monaco Proof with an X-Rite DTP-41 as I did for my 1270 profiles.

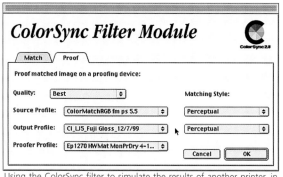

Using the ColorSync filter to simulate the results of another printer, in this case the LightJet, using an Epson 1270 printer.

Using Your Printer to Simulate the Results of Another Printer

Another thing you can do with ColorSync and a good profile for your printer is to use the ColorSync filter in Photoshop to simulate the results of another printer using your printer. To do this within Photoshop having ColorSync installed, go to Filter/ColorMatch/ColorSync Filter and enter the following information. The ColorSync filter does not work with LAB format files so I had to convert the image I wanted to print to RGB first. Although I do a lot of my work in LAB, when I have to convert a file to RGB to work with an application that doesn't understand LAB, I have Photoshop's RGB setup set to either ColorMatch RGB or Adobe RGB; then I do the conversion with Image/Mode/RGB. For these tests I actually used ColorMatch RGB and got pleasing results when printing on my 1270. Once you get into the ColorSync Filter, choose the Proof tab and set Quality to Best. Set the Source Profile to the profile that represents where your image came from. If this was an image that had been scanned from a scanner that I had a profile for, I would use that scanner profile as the Source Profile, assuming I hadn't modified the file after the scan. Since this file had been heavily modified by me in LAB color and I then converted it to ColorMatch RGB to use this filter, I set the Source Profile to ColorMatch RGB. Set Output Profile to the profile of the printer you are trying to simulate. I used the LightJet 5000 profile from Calypso Imaging, where I have been sending my LightJet files. Set Proofer Profile to the profile you have made for your printer; in this case, I used the Monaco Proof profile I made for my Epson 1270. Set both of the Matching Style pop-ups to Perceptual and then choose OK. The filter will transform your image and you then want to print it using the same No Color Adjustment settings used to print the swatch tests. If you have a different printer than the 1270, you will need to figure out how to make prints on that printer without the printer software doing any color adjustments. The settings for most Epson printers are quite similar to those for the 1270; the print dialogs may look a bit different and the No Color Adjustment option may show up within a pop-up menu in the advanced dialog instead of as a separate option. I found that printing to simulate the output of the LightJet gave me prints that were very close to the LightJet with most images. Printing using my Monaco Proof profile directly also gave me prints that were very close. The only images that looked significantly different were ones that used a part of the color gamut that was very different between the two printers. That leads us into our next topic, which is comparing the color gamuts of different printers.

COMPARING PROFILES OF DIFFERENT PRINTERS, PAPERS AND INKS

Once you have made profiles for all the different color devices you work with, you can compare the color gamuts of these devices. This first diagram compares the profiles of the LightJet 5000 and the Fujix Pictrography 3000 with the Epson 1270 using both Epson Premium Glossy Photo Paper and also Epson Matte Paper Heavyweight. You can see that the LightJet and Fujix have a larger gamut in the deep blue and purple areas. I have one print that is a close-up of the solid blue color from Crater Lake in Oregon. This print is a deep, saturated, almost purplish-blue when printed on the LightJet. It looks more cyan and not as saturated when printed on the 1270 using the Monaco Profile. Notice, however, that based on these profiles, the deep blues and purples are the only color areas where the color gamut of the LightJet and Fujix exceed the 1270. Most nature prints I've tried on the 1270 can appear to match the colors of the LightJet quite well. Notice that the gamuts of the Fujix and the 1270 using Premium Glossy Photo Paper are larger in the cyans and greens than those of the LightJet and 1270 with the Matte Paper Heavyweight. I compared my Monaco Proof 1270 Premium Glossy Photo Paper profile to one that Bruce Bayne made using Color-Blind and they both are very similar. This is also a useful technique to help validate a particular profile.

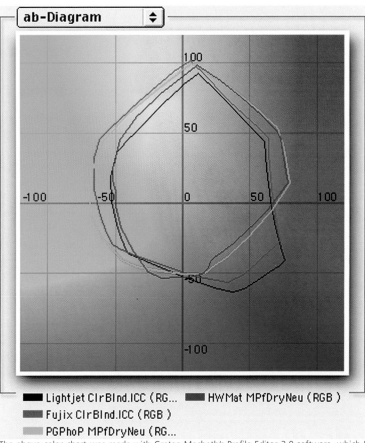

The above color chart was made with Gretag Macbeth's Profile Editor 3.0 software, which I found best for comparing profiles. The black graph is from a LightJet 5000 on Fuji Crystal Archive paper with the profile made using ColorBlind software, the red graph is from a Fujix Pictrography 3000 on its Fuji paper also made with ColorBlind. Thanks to Calypso Imaging and Bruce Hodge for printing the color targets and to Bruce Bayne for making these profiles. The green graph is from the Epson 1270 on Epson Premium Glossy Photo Paper with a profile I made using Monaco Proof and the DTP-41. The blue graph is from the Epson 1270 on Epson Matte Paper Heavyweight with a profile I made using Monaco Proof and the DTP-41.

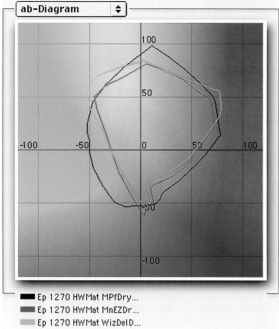

Ep 1270 HWMat MPfDry...
Ep 1270 HWMat MnEZDr...
Ep 1270 HWMat WizDelD...

The black graph is a profile made with Monaco Proof and the DTP-41, the red graph was made using Monaco EZ Color and my flatbed scanner and the green graph was made with Praxisoft WiziWYG Deluxe and my flatbed scanner.

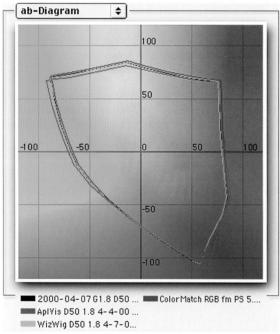

2000-04-07 G1.8 D50 ...   ColorMatch RGB fm PS 5....
AplVis D50 1.8 4-4-00 ...
WizWig D50 1.8 4-7-0...

In this comparison, the black graph is a profile made of my Apple ColorSync 17 monitor made with ColorBlind ProveIt using ColorBlind's sensor. The red graph is a profile of the same monitor using the built in monitor calibrator. The green graph is a calibration of this monitor using WiziWYG Deluxe and the sensor that comes with it and the blue graph is a graph of the ColorMatch RGB color space from Photoshop 5.5. Notice how similar they all are!

COMPARING PROFILES OF THE SAME MONITOR OR PRINTER CREATED WITH DIFFERENT PRODUCTS

It is also useful to compare profiles of the same device made with different products. In the next illustration we see a comparison of the Epson 1270 printing on Matte Paper Heavyweight using profiles made with Monaco Proof, Monaco EZ Color and Praxisoft WiziWYG Deluxe. Both the Monaco EZ and WiziWYG Deluxe profiles are generally smaller than the Monaco Proof profile. The images printed with the Monaco Proof profile showed a wider range of colors and more openness. Notice the similarity in shapes of the two profiles made using my Lino Saphir Ultra 2 scanner versus that made with the DTP-41. It would be interesting to try the same software packages using other scanner and spectrophotometer input devices and see how those effect the profiles. All this is possible when you can view and evaluate the profiles you have created. You should also check out the illustration below comparing the graphs of three different calibration techniques used to profile the same monitor and also the ColorMatch RGB color space. They are all very close to the same!

SUMMARY OF CALIBRATION PRODUCTS

In this chapter I've tried to take a look at some of the software and hardware products available to help us calibrate our color environments. I hope the process for calibrating is now clearer to you and you have some ideas about the path that is right for you. Calibrating can be inexpensive and easy using products like Monaco EZ Color, Praxisoft WiziWYG, Color Vision PhotoCal and Profiler RGB and ColorBlind ProveIt. You can spend more time and money to get more control and better results with midrange products like Monaco Proof, WiziWYG Deluxe or ColorBlind MatchBox. You can also hire a color management expert to do the work for you using the highest end solutions.

There now exists, and are about to be, many more serious hobbiest and professional color users than the current smaller number of high-end color users willing to spend up to $10,000 on a calibration solution. I believe the calibration solutions company that sells a complete color calibration software package for under $1,000 and also provides a bundle with an easy to use sensor, like the DTP-41 or SpectroCam, but a cheaper solution for an additional $1,000, will be the winner in this relatively new color calibration market. The high-end hardware and software products that sell for $3,000 each and up will not be purchased by large numbers of users. Photographers and other more critical color users need products with more functionality at a lower cost. The market for calibration of color scanners and printers is about to explode. If I were the president of Monaco, Praxisoft, X-Rite, Greytag-Macbeth, Lino, Color Vision, SpectroStar or Color Solutions, I would provide more complete products for less money knowing that higher sales volume would justify providing more features at a lower price.

My tests of these particular software and hardware products have not been exhaustive, so I plan to continue to learn more about them. You should look at my results as giving you information that will help you make some choices, but not as absolute judgements of these products. You should also read articles by others and check out the products themselves. Check out each company's Web site for more information. Look at the Web site of Robin Myers, the inventor of ColorSync, at www.rmphoto.com, for his existing and future color management product tests. I will continue to test and work with color products and keep you posted at my Web site on what I find.

I'd like to thank Bruce Bayne of Alder Technology for all the help and advice he has give me in writing this chapter. The profiles he made for me were also very helpful. Robyn Myers and Jim Rich have also been a big help with phone discussions and e-mails and the great info on their web sites. For further information, you can reach these color calibration experts at the locations listed on the right. My longtime photographer friends Bruce Ashley, Bill Atkinson and Bruce Hodge have also been a big help. Thanks, you guys!

COLOR MANAGEMENT SYSTEMS AND HOW THEY FIT INTO THE PHOTOSHOP 6 ENVIRONMENT

Color management systems, like ColorSync, take an image that you have corrected on your computer screen and remap that image based on the color gamut of the particular output device it is being printed on. The color gamut of an output device is the set of colors and brightness ranges that the output device can print. Each different output device, such as a digital printer, CMYK proofing system, transparency writer, and so on, has its own specific gamut. If you take the same digital file and print it, unmodified, on a number of different output devices, each print will look different—from each other, and also probably different from the image on your screen. The purpose of a color management system is to adjust for these differences so the same image will look as close as possible on different computer monitors and will print as closely as possible on different types of output devices.

The monitor calibration technique we used to use with older versions of Photoshop showed you how to calibrate your monitor to make it look as much as possible like the output of one particular output device, but then you had to do this calibration routine separately for each output device. A color management system measures the difference between different types of output devices and creates a device profile for each device. Photoshop and ColorSync use ICC profiles to characterize devices. When you send an image to a particular device, the color management system changes the image, using that image's device profile, to try to make it print in a standard way on that device. If you print the same picture on many devices, the color management system does its best to make all those pictures look as close as possible to each other. I say "does its best" because you cannot always get the same colors on one device that you can on another. Each device has its own color gamut, the range of colors that device can scan, display or print.

Apple's ColorSync color management system is a generic one that allows many other third-party companies to contribute device profiles for their specific products. I have, for example, an Epson Stylus Photo 1270 inkjet printer. I love the photographic quality prints it gives me. But if I took the digital file that produced a print on my Epson printer and printed the same file, unmodified, on someone else's Epson printer, you would see subtle differences between the two prints. The other printer might have a different batch number on its inks, it might be slightly out of alignment,

COLOR MANAGEMENT EXPERTS:

Bruce Bayne of Alder Technology
(They make remote profiles for you for $200 each)
13500 SW 72nd Ave, Suite 200
Tigard, OR 97223
503-603-0998 or 1-888-318-8230
fax 503-443-4609
www.aldertech.com
bruceb@aldertech.com

Robin Myers
(Robin has a useful web site)
3887 Yosemite Court North
Pleasanton, CA 94588-4934
925-484-1065
myers@rmphoto.com
www.rmphoto.com

Jim Rich
Rich and Associates
4601 North Park Ave, Apt. 301
Chevy Chase, MD 20815
301-652-7266

COMPANIES MENTIONED IN THIS ARTICLE:

X-Rite
3100 44th Street S.W.
Grandville, Michigan 49418
www.x-rite.com
888-826-3059

Monaco Systems
100 Burtt Road, Suite 115
Andover, MA 01810
www.monacosys.com
978-749-9944

Praxisoft
1400 Shepard Dr., Suite 200
Sterling, VA 20164
www.praxisoft.com
800-557-7294

Itec - Color Solutions
15175 Innovation Drive
San Diego, CA 92128
www.color.com
858-613-1300

GretagMacbeth
617 Little Britain Road
New Windsor, NY 12553
www.gretagmacbeth.com
914-565-7660

Color Vision
1430 Vantage Court, Suite 101
Vista, CA 92083
800-554-8688
www.colorcal.com

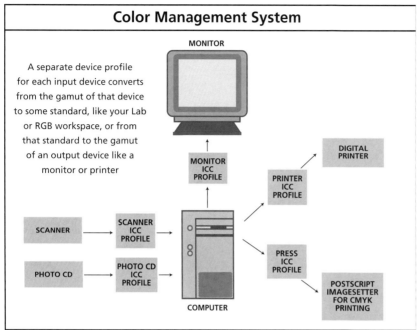

Color Management System

A separate device profile for each input device converts from the gamut of that device to some standard, like your Lab or RGB workspace, or from that standard to the gamut of an output device like a monitor or printer

The standard file format your files are stored in, on your computer and in Photoshop, should be either Lab or your default RGB working space. The ICC profiles will then translate files into that standard space, from a scan or digital camera, and out of that space, to display on a monitor or print on a printer of some kind.

the temperature and humidity at the other printer's location might be different, and for whatever reason, there may be other subtle differences.

To solve this type of problem, a color management system needs to be able to measure the output from your particular device and create a custom ICC device profile for it at any particular time. That is what we have been talking about doing in the above sections of this chapter. Color management systems can characterize different types of scanners and film input types, different types of monitors, and other factors that affect color production along the way to final output. Given the great many variations in what can happen to the colors, it's no wonder color calibration and correction often prove so difficult.

Color management systems can help you deal with the differences in the gamut and characteristics of different types of input and output devices, and they are improving all the time. Some color management system marketing implies that these systems can automatically scan, correct, and output images so that they print like originals. It's usually not that easy and it needs to be done carefully and correctly. Although color management systems can be adjusted to give you a high degree of calibration and control between devices, doing this correctly still requires a lot of careful measurement and control of every part of your color production system.

GETTING ACCURATE ONSCREEN SOFT PROOFS OF YOUR OUTPUT TO RGB PRINTERS, CMYK PRINTERS AND PRESSES

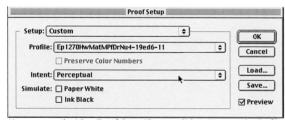

Here we see the View/Proof Setup/Custom dialog. You use the Profile pop-up menu to select the printer profile for your printer then the Intent menu to select your rendering intent.

One of the best features added to Photoshop 6 is the ability to accurately preview your printed images using your monitor. To do this for an RGB device, like a LightJet 5000, Fuji Pictrography 3000 or Epson 1270, 2000 or 7500, you will need an accurate ICC profile of your RGB printer when printing using a particular ink and paper combination. The profile can be made using one of the techniques discussed in the above sections. You can compare the way the image will look when printed using this profile to the way it looks within your LAB or RGB working space. Start by choosing View/New View to give you an alternate window on your image. This is not another copy of the image, like you would get with Image/Duplicate; it is just another way to look at the same file you have open. Now arrange the original window of the image and the New View of it so their windows are next to each other and you can see them side by side. After doing that, choose View/Proof Setup/Custom, which will bring up the Proof Setup dialog, allowing you to choose the Profile you will use when printing to your printer and also the rendering intent you want for this image. With

Chapter 15: Photoshop Color Preferences, Monitor, Scanner and Printer Calibration

the Preview box checked, you can actually try out several profiles and rendering intents and see which settings come closest to matching the image, in the other view, in your LAB or RGB working space. For color correction perfectionists, like myself, this feature alone makes Photoshop 6 worth the upgrade price. You can then use View/New View again to create a third view and set that one up to do a soft proof to a different printer. This would allow you to compare how the image will look on a LightJet 5000 versus your Epson 2000 versus the original in Adobe RGB or LAB. With a well calibrated system, as mine is, the images on the screen are a very accurate simulation of what the print will look like. This is a great way to compare one profile to another, one rendering intent to another or even to decide if you want black point compensation on or off! To use it accurately with RGB printers you will need an ICC profile for your printer and an accurate calibration of your monitor.

Here I have used View/New View and View/Proof Setup/Custom twice so I can compare this image on two separate printers to the original in its LAB workspace. The original is on the left, in the middle we see it as printed on my Epson 1270 using the profile I made with Monaco Proof and the DTP-41 and on the right we see it as it looks when printed on a LightJet 5000 using a profile I got from Calypso Imaging in Santa Clara California, the LightJet service bureau I use.

USING PROOF COLORS AND GAMUT WARNING

To get soft proofs for your RGB files and how they will look on CMYK printers or CMYK presses, you can just choose View/Proof Colors (Command-Y) and Photoshop will show you how the file will look and print in CMYK. If you have already converted the file to CMYK, then you are already seeing it as it should print on your CMYK device, provided you are calibrated correctly. It is very important that your CMYK settings in the CMYK working space area of Color Settings are set correctly when using Command-Y to preview RGB files as they will look within CMYK. If you open an existing CMYK file, it should be displayed correctly on the screen provided that the file has an embedded ICC profile and your screen and output devices are correctly calibrated.

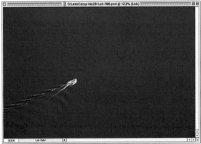

Here is my Crater Lake image as shown on my screen in LAB color. This image has very deep saturated blue colors, as does Crater Lake, one of the clearest lakes in the world.

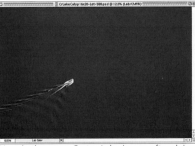

Here is the same Crater Lake image after doing Command-Y to get a CMYK preview. Notice that the title bar at the top of the window has changed its name from LAB to LAB/CMYK.

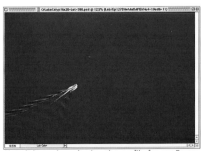

Here it is previewed using the profile for my Epson 1270 printer on Matte Paper Heavyweight. This deep blue is way out of the CMYK gamut and also partially outside of the gamut for my Epson 1270. The prints of this image on the LightJet 5000 do show this deep blue because it is within the gamut of that printer printing on Fuji Crystal Archive paper.

157

You'll notice that when you initially look at View/Proof Setup the default is that, when you use Command-Y to see Proof Colors, Photoshop will show you how your RGB file will look when separated into CMYK using the current CMYK settings within the CMYK working space inside the Color Settings dialog. If you choose View/Proof Setup/Custom, as we mentioned, you can change that default for the current file to show the preview using an ICC profile for your printer or other output device. When you choose View/Proof Setup/Custom while working on an open file, this sets the preview on a file by file basis or actually on a window by window basis, as shown in the illustration here. If you open Photoshop and then immediately go into View/Poof Setup/Custom, while no files are open, this sets the default proofing environment for Photoshop, which is normally set to Working CMYK when you install Photoshop. You can change this setting to that of an ICC profile for your RGB printer, or some other profile, by setting it when no files are open and then quitting from Photoshop right after making that setting. When you later restart photoshop, you will notice that Command-Y now shows you how your RGB file will look when printed on your printer using that profile.

Using Command-Shift Y to get a Gamut Warning for a CMYK version of Crater Lake, you see that the entire blue image is out of gamut.

A Gamut Warning with the ICC profile for the Epson 1270 using Matte Paper Heavyweight shows that many blues are out of gamut but not as many as with CMYK. This is one of only a few of my images that has a gamut problem with this printer and paper combination.

Even on the LightJet 5000 using Fuji Crystal Archive paper, there are a few colors out of gamut in the water highlights around the boat. I often print images with small gamut warnings anyhow and they usually look fine. Using Command-Y to get the onscreen preview often tells you the most about whether you will like the image using a particular printer, ink and paper.

Notice that if you choose View/Gamut Warning (Command-Shift-Y), Photoshop will show you the colors in your RGB file that are outside the gamut of the profile that is currently set in View/Proof Setup to be your proofing profile. If you want that to show the out of gamut colors for your current CMYK settings, then View/Proof Setup should be set to Working CMYK. If you want it to show you the out of gamut colors based on the ICC profile for your RGB printer, then you need to use View/Proof Setup/Custom to set proofing to the ICC profile for your printer.

CALIBRATING YOUR OUTPUT DEVICE

Many issues arise in attempting to get quality output to a digital printer, film recorder, or imagesetter. First among them are calibration issues. You must calibrate the output device and keep it calibrated. When your output device is not calibrated and consistent, any calibration and correction you do on your computer is less useful. The job of a digital printer, for example, is to print exactly the same way every time. If you change the batch of ink or the type of ink or paper, that may change the results of the printer and require you to recalibrate. The supplier of your inks and papers must have strict controls to keep them consistent or else you will have to recalibrate every time you get new inks or papers even if you are using the same type of ink or paper. Some printers, like the Fuji Pictrography printers, have a built in system to calibrate the printer itself whenever the paper and chemicals are changed. This ensures that the output of the printer is consistent; then all you have to do is make a profile for that printer. When calibrated correctly you should be able to send some known, good test output to your output device and compare that output print to previous versions of that image on that printer with that ink and paper and the result should be the same.

When you scan an image or have it scanned or put onto Photo CD, you need to be sure to get the best scan and it would be very helpful to have an ICC profile of your scanner. If you are not doing the scanning yourself, you need to know how to check the scans that others have done to make sure that the maximum amount of information is available. And, you need to understand how to make the most of the information that you have. We cover the scanning part of the process in Chapter 16: "Image Resolution, Scanning Film and Digital Cameras."

Trying to calibrate your monitor or perfect your process of making color corrections doesn't do any good unless the output device you are sending to (imagesetter, color printer, film recorder, or whatever) is consistent and is calibrated. A good way to test this calibration is to send a group of neutral colors to your output device. I have created a file, called the StepWedgeFile, for use as a test file for calibrating your output device. The StepWedgeFile consists of wedges of neutral gray that have a known value. Two issues are involved in calibrating your output device. The first issue is whether the device will print the correct density. If you send a 50% density value to the device, it should measure and look like 50% when it prints. All densities should print as they are expected. The second issue is getting colors to print correctly. Using all its colors, if you get the output device to print these neutral gray values correctly, it's a good sign that it will also print colors correctly. You want the densities on the gray wedges to be correct, and you also want each wedge to continue to look gray since when you see a cast in your printed grays, that cast usually gets added to all color correct images. The original StepWedgeFile was created using an older version of Photoshop and it wasn't tagged with an ICC profile. In that version of Photoshop, I was working in a gamma 1.8 RGB working space similar to ColorMatch RGB but that was before Photoshop used ICC profiles. With Photoshop 5 and now in Photoshop 6 I'd noticed that, depending on the color space I was working in, the density readings from the Info palette could change when reading neutral values from the untagged StepWedgeFile. To make them simpler to use with Photoshop 6, I've now included three versions of the StepWedgeFile within the Calibration folder on the CD. The StepWedgeFileUntagged is the same StepWedgeFile I've included with previous versions of *Photoshop Artistry*, which contains correct neutral grayscale values but is not tagged with any particular profile. The StepWedgeFileGamma1.8 and StepWedgeFileGamma2.2 are explained in the caption on this page which you need to read and understand before using these files!

CHECKING RGB PRINTER OUTPUT OR PHOTOSHOP CMYK SEPARATIONS ON YOUR RGB OR CMYK PRINTER OR A CMYK PRESS

I have created a Photoshop Printer Test file from some of my prints and the StepWedgeFile. It is called PS6ArtistryCalibrationImage.psd and is included in the Ch15.ColorPrefs&Calibration folder on the *Photoshop 6 Artistry* CD and also printed on the next page. This RGB file in ColorMatch RGB space can be used to test output to your RGB printer or other RGB output device. Before doing any

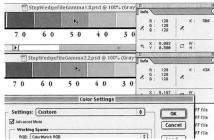

In the Calibration folder on the CD are the grayscale StepWedge files. You can use them to test your printer and see if it is printing neutral grays as neutral. I usually open one of these, then copy or drag and drop it onto the white canvas edge of a print. Then I print the image and see if the grays come out neutral in all density areas. If they don't then you know the part of your printer or profile that needs further calibration. There is a file called StepWedgeFileGamma1.8 which you should use with RGB or grayscale images that are in a grayscale or color space like ColorMatch RGB that has a gamma of 1.8. The file called StepWedgeFileGamma2.2 should be used with images that are in a grayscale or color space like Adobe RGB that has a gamma of 2.2. When you use the matching gamma stepwedge file then the RGB values will read correctly in the Info palette after that file has been pasted on top of another grayscale or RGB file.

The Info palette readings that you get from these grayscale files, and from RGB files that they are pasted on top of, will depend on the RGB working space preference that is currently in place. In the illustration above, two info palette readings are shown from the 50% gray swatch when the RGB working space is set to Color Match RGB. In this case the RGB values for the Gamma 1.8 and 2.2 files will both be 128, 128, 128, the LAB values will both be 61, 0, 0 and the black(k) values will be 50% for the Gamma 1.8 file but only 43% for the Gamma 2.2 file. If we change the RGB working space to Adobe RGB that makes the RGB values in both files be 145, 145, 145 and both the Lab values are still 61, 0, 0 and black(k) values are still 50% for the gamma 1.8 file and 43% for the gamma 2.2 file.

Since a Gamma 2.2 environment is more contrasty, 43% black there will look the same as 50% black in the Gamma 1.8 environment. The data in the gamma 2.2 file was converted from gamma 1.8 to gamma 2.2 so the files will match on the screen, when used within their correct gamma environment, and should match when you output them after correctly using profile conversions to your printer's color space.

When you convert either of these two grayscale files to ColorMatch RGB, the resulting RGB value of the 50% swatch will be 128, 128, 128, the Lab value 61, 0, 0 and the K value 50%. When you convert either file to Adobe RGB, the RGB values will be 145, 145, 145, the Lab values 61, 0, 0 and the K values 50%. Again, in a gamma 2.2 space, an RGB value of 145 will look the same as an RGB value of 128 would look in a gamma 1.8 space.

Play around with these two files as your change the Info palette readouts between RGB, Grayscale (K), and LAB and also as your change the RGB working space and make sure you are aware of the differences that can occur in the Info palette readings.

Calibration Image from Photoshop 6 Artistry. All Images © 2001, Barry Haynes, All Rights Reserved

100 98 95 90 80 75 70 60 50 40 30 25 20 10 5 2 0

You are given permission to print this to calibrate your output devices only. Large Archival prints of these and other images by Barry Haynes are available for sale at www.barryhaynes.com.

This is the new *Photoshop 6 Artistry* printer calibration image. It can be used as an RGB test image to check your screen calibration and your printer output to an Epson RGB printer, LightJet 5000 or Fuji Pictrography printer and a variety of RGB devices. The Photoshop file is in ColorMatch RGB format and can be converted to a printer profile for print tests using Image/Mode/Convert to Profile as described earlier in this chapter when talking about making printer profiles and printing using those profiles. If your monitor is calibrated correctly and you have a controlled lighting monitor viewing space then this image should match your prints when viewed on the screen using View/Proof Setup/Custom correctly set to your printer's profile which was used to make your prints. When you open this file, it will be rotated to vertical orientation which allows the printer software to output the file without further image rotation processing.

To use this file to test CMYK output, make sure your Photoshop 6 CMYK preferences are set up for the type of CMYK press and paper you will be using then choose Image/Mode/CMYK to convert this file to CMYK. If you are calibrated then this image on screen, after converting to CMYK, should look like your best press proof from your printer.

tests, be sure to set up your Color Settings preferences as shown at the start of this chapter. If you are doing CMYK output to a CMYK printer or printing press to see if your Photoshop color separation settings are working well, we will show you how to use this image to create a Photoshop separation test.

To make your own test image, create an 8.5x11 canvas in RGB mode, fill it with a neutral gray background, and save it as MyPrinterTest or something like that. Now use Image/Mode/RGB to convert the grayscale StepWedgeFile, in the Ch15.ColorPrefs&Calibration folder on the CD, to your RGB working space and then paste it into your test file. Next, find some color corrected RGB images that are typical of your normal work. Copy these images and paste them into your test file. Save the final RGB version of your RGB test file.

Use your test image, or ours, to output to your RGB printer or device in the way that you would normally use that device. If you have a profile for the printer, then use Image/Mode/Convert to Profile to convert a copy of the test image to that color space. Then print the image using printer settings that do no further color management or changes since the profile should have done that for you. If you are not using a color profile, then use whatever settings you would normally use with your printer. The PS6ArtistryCalibrationImage prints well on most Epson printers on an 8.5x11 sheet of Epson paper if you use Image/Image Size to set the Resolution of the file to 380 Pixels/Inch with the Resample Image option turned off. This will not actually resample the file; it just sets the print size to one that will work with most Epson printers. Depending on the Epson printer that you have, check out my recommended printer dialog settings for printing with no profile at www.barryhaynes.com in the LATEST TIPS section. There I have recommendations for using the Epson Stylus Photo EX, 1200, 1270 and 2000. If you have another Epson printer of similar vintage to one of these, you should be able to get the same settings in your print dialog; they might just be in different places. If you have an Epson Stylus Photo 870, 875DC or 1270 or HP Deskjet 970c or 1220c, then download the "Digital Printers for Final Art and Commercial Output" article from my Web site in PDF format. When comparing your test print to the image on your monitor, make sure you view the test print in the lighting you have calibrated for and the image on the screen should be previewed using View/Proof Setup using the profile you made for your printer. If you are not using a profile, then just view the image on screen using your normal LAB or RGB working space. I view my art prints under halogen floods with a color temperature of around 2700K since that is the light source used in most galleries. When working on a book that will be printed on press, I view proofs from the printer using my Soft View D5000 Transparency/Print Viewer which lights them a 5000K, the standard for most press rooms in the USA. The light you view your print under will make a big difference in the way it looks!

If converting the test file to CMYK for a CMYK printer or a press, make sure your CMYK Color Settings preferences are set correctly for the type of printer or paper and press your are using. If you normally use Image/Mode/CMYK to convert from RGB to CMYK, do just that with your separation test. If you use someone else's separation tables, do it that way. If you normally save your files as EPS/DCS from Photoshop and then put the file into Quark, do the same thing in your test. Save your final CMYK version of the file under a different name than the RGB version. Whenever I'm going to print a new version of *Photoshop Artistry*, I always have the printer make a set of proofs using their current best color proofing system. Lately, Graphic Arts Center has been using Kodak Approval proofs, which are digital proofs that can be printed on the actual paper the book is being printed on. The paper of your proof can also make a difference in the color.

When evaluating your test image, the densities should look correct in the gray stepwedge and they should also look gray. If the stepwedge densities are not right, or if they have a cyan, magenta, or some combination of color casts, it's a sign that either the RGB or CMYK output device, imagesetter, platemaker, or proofer isn't calibrated or something's not right about the way you created this output. You should not have altered or color corrected the stepwedge file using your monitor, so it should be gray. If it doesn't look gray or the densities are not correct, you will have to calibrate your printer, or for CMYK adjust your separations to solve this problem. If the stepwedge looks good and this test prints with the correct densities and no color casts, you know your output device is calibrated.

MORE ABOUT THE CMYK WORKING SPACES

Photoshop 6 has a lot more options for controlling CMYK separations than previous versions of Photoshop did, and you should expect the built-in separations in Photoshop 6 to work a lot better than those in Photoshop 4 or previous versions. The display of CMYK images on the screen in Photoshop 6 should also be more accurate than even Photoshop 5 or 5.5 when you have your system set up correctly. There are two main types of choices for how to specify your CMYK Model in Photoshop 6. You can choose an ICC profile directly from the CMYK Working Spaces pop-up menu, and Photoshop 6 has provided seven new canned CMYK ICC profiles that I have heard work quite well but have not extensively personally tested. The Euroscale Coated v2 and Euroscale Uncoated v2 are the settings to use with European inks and presses for either coated (i.e. glossy), or uncoated stock. Japan Standard v2 is the setting to use when printing with standard inks in Japan. The US Sheetfed Coated v2, which we used for the cover and section divider pages of this book, and US Sheetfed Uncoated v2 are new Adobe separation settings to use with sheetfed presses when using either coated or uncoated paper. The US Web Coated (SWOP) v2 and US Web Uncoated v2 are new Adobe settings to use with web presses, with the Coated (SWOP) one being for the SWOP web press printing standard.

When you choose Custom CMYK, you get a set of controls that are identical to the previous built-in CMYK options for Photoshop 5. These should give you the same good results you could achieve with Photoshop 5, provided you make the correct choices.

These are the canned CMYK ICC profiles that Photoshop 6 provides. Choosing one of these, or adjusting your Photoshop 6 CMYK settings yourself using Custom CMYK should all give you good results provided you choose the right setting for your print job, paper and press. To print this book, we used the U.S. Sheetfed Coated v2 settings for the section divider pages and for the cover because these seemed to give slightly cleaner separations with more saturated color than the settings described on page

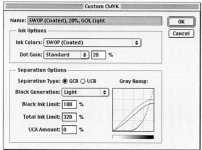

For my recommended CMYK settings, choose Custom CMYK... from the CMYK pop-up then change Black Generation to Light and Total Ink Limit to 320% then choose OK. More advanced users who want to set custom Ink Colors can get the below dialog by choosing Custom... from the Ink Colors dialog here. You can also set custom dot gain curves by choosing Curves... from the above Dot Gain pop-up. Using the above settings, I've had very good results in printing *Photoshop 5 & 5.5 Artistry* on a sheet fed press, *Photoshop, Painter & Illustrator Side-by-Side* on a Web press as well as separating various brochures and magazine covers. We used the **U.S. Sheetfed Coated v2** settings, shown to the right, for the more color critical pages in this book. For newspaper presses, non-glossy papers and other printing situations, you may need to use other settings. To be sure, you should run tests with the proofing mechanism at your print shop.

INK OPTIONS

INK COLORS: This setting tells Photoshop the types of inks you will be printing with on a press. You will notice that the number of preset values in Photoshop 6 and also Photoshop 5 here has been changed from the old Photoshop 4 to those that really relate to press conditions. Because printing inks are fairly standardized, you will probably find it unnecessary to change this setting after you pick the right ink. For printing this book on a sheetfed press, I used the SWOP coated setting. You would want to choose the SWOP Newsprint for newspapers or the SWOP Uncoated for uncoated paper. If you are printing with Toyo inks, which I was impressed with the time I used them, you would pick one of those settings. You can also choose Custom and enter the xyY values or LAB values in the case of special custom inks. When you convert from RGB to CMYK, the actual CMYK values you get for a given RGB value depend on a combination of the Color Settings in RGB working space, CMYK working space, and also where and how you set your highlight and shadow values in Levels or Curves. For magazine-quality output to coated stock, you should start out using the SWOP Coated setting here.

DOT GAIN: The Dot Gain setting adjusts how dark Photoshop displays an untagged CMYK image on the screen as well as how dense Photoshop makes each of the CMYK separation channels when you convert from RGB to CMYK. The Dot Gain value represents how much the printing inks will spread when printed on certain papers. If you set the dot gain to 30%, Photoshop will separate each CMYK color with less density and display the colors of untagged CMYK files on the screen darker than if the dot gain were set to 20%. As a general setting, you should start with a dot gain setting of 20% or less for coated stock. You should talk to the press expert at the printshop you will be using to find the exact Dot Gain settings for the press and paper combination you will be using. Most print shops are familiar with Photoshop settings these days, although the new settings that Photoshop 6 offers may be new to them. Photoshop 5 and 6 allow you to use this dialog to specify each of the Cyan, Magenta, Yellow, and Black dot gain curves separately instead of just picking one dot gain value to use for all four. Again, you should discuss the expected dot gain with your printer and set the Photoshop Standard single value or the new dot gain curves accordingly.

SEPARATION OPTIONS

The Separation Options further control RGB to CMYK conversion values. The Gray Ramp is a curve diagram showing how cyan, magenta, yellow, and black are generated for neutral colors as the image goes from highlights on the left to shadows on the right. There is more ink used in the shadows, and black ink gets used only in the darker half of the color ranges. If you adjust the settings for Black Generation from Light to Medium, or Dark, you can see how the black setting affects the Cyan, Magenta, and Yellow curves. You can also choose Custom for the Black Generation curve, and this will bring up a curve dialog that allows you to manually modify the black curve. You cannot manually modify the Cyan, Magenta, or Yellow curves here, although you can now modify their dot gain curves. Changing the Black Ink Limit, Total Ink Limit, and UCA (Under Color Addition) also affects all the curves shown in the Gray Ramp. The Separation Type lets you choose between GCR (Gray Component Replacement) or UCR (Under Color Removal) separations. Our recommended settings for Separation Type are GCR (Gray Component Replacement) turned on; for Black Generation, Light; for Black Ink Limit, 100%; and for Total Ink Limit, 320%. If your were printing on a web press, your total ink settings would probably be somewhat lower, around 280, and for a newspaper press, they would be lower still. Each newspaper press is a little different. We are leaving the UCA (Under

Color Addition) amount set to 0, but you can increase the UCA value if you find that the GCR separations are removing too much colored ink in the nonneutral areas. Again, if you are not happy with the results you are getting, the best thing to do here is talk to your print shop and run some tests with different settings until you get the results you like. If the Custom CMYK controls don't allow you to get what you want, you can also use profile making software to create a custom profile for a particular press, paper and ink combination; then choose that ICC profile as your CMYK working space.

USING AN ICC PROFILE FOR SEPARATIONS

When you set your CMYK Working Space to an ICC profile, you will set the Profile to a special ICC profile for your press and paper conditions. There are standard profiles available for particular presses and inks, and you might want to ask your printer or service bureau if they have any of these to recommend. In theory, though, the best thing to do is to make a custom profile for your particular press, paper and ink condition. To do this, as described earlier in this chapter, you have to first choose the profile making software and hardware you are going to work with or a color management expert in the business of creating color profiles for you.

The process would be to print a standard test target, made up of many swatches of color and neutral values, on your press using standard ink densities and printing conditions. This test target would then be measured with a spectrophotometer to see how these standard color swatches printed on this press with this paper and ink. Those measurements would be entered into a software package, like Monaco Proof, which would then create the ICC profile for that press, ink, and paper combination. That profile would then be chosen as your CMYK Working Space. When you printed those separations, it would be expected that you would get the best results when printing using the same standard ink densities and printing conditions that were used to make the profile.

When you use a profile for your separations, your results will be based on three things. These are the accuracy of the printing test proof that was used to take the measurements from, the accuracy of the person and equipment making the measurements from that proof, and finally, the quality of the software making the ICC profile from those test results. If the persons running the test printing and making the profile do a good job, you might get the best possible results from this approach; however, if it doesn't work that well, you may have less control over any changes you need to make unless you actually own all the software, equipment, and knowledge to make further tests and correct the situation.

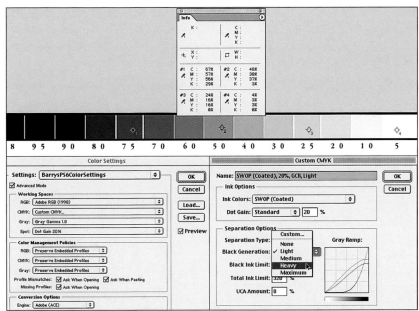

Here is the setup to use the Info palette to measure what you actually get, after influence from Ink Colors, Dot Gain settings, and Separation Options, when making a separation. Change some of the settings, and you can measure the differences using the Eyedropper and Color Sampler tools, and Info palette. You need to make sure the Preview button is on in the Color Settings dialog to be able to see the changes in the Info palette. Here we have four Color Sampler settings to measure the values at 5%, 25%, 50% and 75% within a Stepwedge file that comes in the Calibration folder on the *Photoshop 6 Artistry* CD. When we change any parameter seen here, including the Dot Gain curves, Black Ink Limit, Total Ink Limit, UCA Amount, and so on, we see what separation values those changes will actually give us in the five measured areas. You should be able to use this technique to tweak the Built-in separator to get very close to what your press person wants for a particular press. First though, I'd try the built-in Photoshop seps we talk about above, and you might find that even if the numbers are different than what you normally get, the results are much better than they were in Photoshop 4 or in older versions. You can also use this type of measuring technique to compare the CMYK values you would get using different ICC profiles including the new built in Adobe separations for US Sheet Fed, US Web, etc.

More About the CMYK Working Spaces

USING SEPARATION TABLES FROM OLDER VERSIONS OF PHOTOSHOP

If you are happy with the color separations you were getting from an older version of Photoshop and want to continue to use them with Photoshop 6, here is how you can do that.

1. Go to your old version of Photoshop, in this case Photoshop 4 or older, and make sure your Monitor Setup, Printing Inks Setup, and Separation Setup settings are correct for the tables you want to move over to Photoshop 6 as an ICC profile.

2. Go to File/Color Settings/Separation Tables, and click the Save button to save your old tables.

3. Quit from your old Photoshop and start up Photoshop 6. Now go to Edit/Color Settings then choose Load CMYK from the CMYK Working Space pop-up.

4. After you have these old tables loaded, choose the Save CMYK menu item from the CMYK Working Space pop-up and resave them into the ColorSync Profiles folder, within the System Folder, on the Mac. On the PC, save this ICC profile into the folder where your particular Windows versions saves ICC Profiles. You will now be able to choose this as an ICC profile setting from the CMYK Working Space pop-up menu within Color Settings. When you add ICC profiles to the ColorSync Profiles folder, depending on the system you are using, you may need to quit from Photoshop 6 and then restart Photoshop 6 for those profiles to show up within Photoshop 6

5. In general, you should find the Photoshop 5 and 6 separations better than those from older versions of Photoshop, so I would not recommend just using your old tables. However, if you were happy with your old tables and you just got Photoshop 6 and need to do some work before having time to test the new Photoshop 6 separations, you can load your old tables and use them until you set up the new Photoshop 6 stuff the way you want. I do really encourage you to use the new Photoshop 5 and 6 separation engine, however, because it is much better when you get it set up correctly for your needs.

OTHER PREFERENCES RELATING TO COLOR

EYEDROPPER TOOL SETUP

Usually when you measure digital image values in Photoshop, you want the Eyedropper set to measure a 3 by 3 rectangle of pixels. That gives you a more accurate measurement in a continuous tone image because most colors are made up of groups of different pixels. If you were to measure a Point Sample, the default, you might accidentally measure the single pixel that was much different in color from those around it. Click on the Eyedropper tool and set its Sample Size in the Options palette to 3 by 3 Average. You can also do this by Control-clicking, right mouse button on the PC, in an image when the Eyedropper is the active tool which will bring up a context-sensitive menu allowing you to change the dropper options. Setting the Eyedropper to 3 by 3 Average also sets up the Photoshop 6 Color Samplers to read a 3 by 3 average, which is what you want.

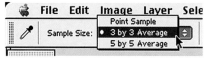

Usually you want the Eyedropper set to measure a 3 by 3 average when measuring continuous tone color. Setting either the Eyedropper Options or the Color Sampler Options to 3 by 3 Average will set both of them to the same setting.

HIGHLIGHT AND SHADOW PREFERENCES

The last preferences items that you need to set up for color separations are the Highlight and Shadow settings, which you can reach by choosing either Image/Adjust/Levels or Curves. While in Levels or Curves, double-click the Highlight Eyedropper (the rightmost one). The Color Picker opens. For CMYK print work, you want to set the CMYK values to 5, 3, 3, 0, which is a neutral color for highlights. If all your other preferences are set as in this book, after you enter 5, 3, 3, 0 for CMYK, you should see 242, 242, 242 as your initial RGB settings if your RGB workspace is ColorMatch RGB, and you will see 244, 244, 244 if your RGB workspace is Adobe RGB. If this is not the case, double-check your Color Settings values. For the ColorMatch RGB case, you may also need to change the initial 241 Green value to 242 and for Adobe RGB the initial 245 Red value to 244. Even if you are using different settings than ours, if your final output space will be RGB, you should make sure your RGB values all equal each other so you get a neutral highlight color when setting the highlight with the Eyedropper in RGB. Click OK in the Color Picker to return to Levels, double-click the Shadow Eyedropper (the leftmost one). Set the RGB values in the Color Picker to 8, 8, 8 and check to make sure the CMYK values are 74, 65, 64, 92. If not, double-check your Color

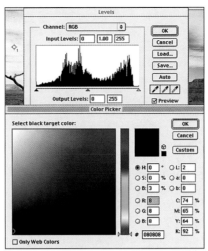

These are the shadow settings we recommend for CMYK coated stock, RGB output to film recorders, digital printers, and general overall color correction of a file. Double-click the Shadow Eyedropper in Levels or Curves to change these settings. The RGB values here should always be all the same, a neutral color will be 8, 8, 8 whether you choose Color-Match RGB, Adobe RGB, or sRGB as long as your Color settings are the same as this book's settings. I have used shadow settings between 2, 2, 2 and 8, 8, 8 depending on how dark I want my blacks to be and where I am setting my black. A value of 8, 8, 8 may want to be set in an area of the image that represents the darkest place where you want any detail, a value of 2, 2, 2 or even 0, 0, 0 would be set where you want absolute black.

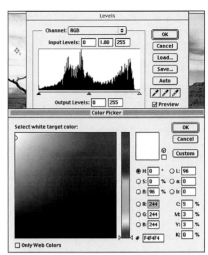

These 5, 3, 3, 0 settings are the highlight settings we recommend for CMYK coated stock. The corresponding values you get in RGB will depend on your chosen RGB workspace and also on your CMYK Setup settings. Initially, 242, 241, and 242 are the RGB values you get with your RGB workspace set to ColorMatch RGB and with the other settings we show in this chapter. If you are using ColorMatch RGB as your workspace, double-click the Green 241 value and change it to a 242; the 5, 3, 3, 0 values should stay the same. If we change the RGB workspace to Adobe RGB or sRGB, the RGB values will change to 245, 244, 244 with these same CMYK settings. You can then change the Red to 244. For RGB output to the Web, film recorders, and digital printers, and general RGB overall color correction of a file, you should make sure the RGB values shown here are neutral and around 244, 244, 244. Double-click the Highlight Eyedropper in Levels or Curves to change these settings for different output devices or situations.

Settings. I have actually used shadow settings between 2, 2, 2 and 8, 8, 8 depending on how dark I want my blacks to be and where I am setting my black. A value of 8, 8, 8 may want to be set in an area of the image that represents the darkest place where you want any detail; a value of 2, 2, 2 or even 0, 0, 0 would be set where you want absolute black. Changing the RGB values to 2, 2, 2, only changes the CMYK black value to 97 instead of 92. If that is still not dark enough for you, try setting your CMYK values to 95, 85, 83, 95 which are the values my previous *Artistry* books used. This will force your RGB values to 2, 2, 2 but you may find this black setting a bit too dark. You can certainly adjust the black setting depending on the type of output you are doing and how dark you like your shadows. Click OK in the Color Picker and then click OK in Levels. To learn more about these Highlight and Shadow settings and how you use them, turn to Chapter 19: "Overall Color Correction," which takes you through all the basics of color correction and shows you when and how to use the Eyedroppers.

SETTINGS FOR COLORSYNC ON THE MAC

If you are working on a Macintosh computer, you want to have ColorSync installed. ColorSync comes with the Mac OS and you can also get free updates for ColorSync from the Apple web site. If you are using Mac OS version 8.6, then you want to be using ColorSync version 2.6.1 and when you go to Apple/Control Panels/ColorSync you will want the ColorSync dialog to look like the one to the right with your Monitor's ICC profile in the System Profile area. If you are using Mac OS 8.6 then you don't want to use ColorSync version 3.0.1 and also the ColorSync Workflow choice, within the Settings pop-up at the top of the Photoshop 6 Edit/Color Settings

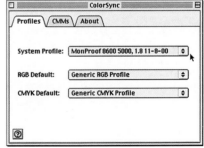

If you are using ColorSync 2.6.1, all you need to do is make sure your current monitor profile is set here within the System Profile pop-up.

Other Preferences Relating to Color

The built-in ColorSync Workflow setting which I do not recommend. It is better to set all your Photoshop Color Settings manually as described at the beginning of this chapter.

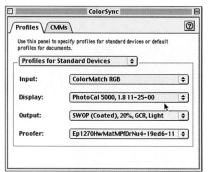

The ColorSync 3.0.1 Profiles for Standard Devices section. Here you would normally set Input to a profile for your scanner and Display to the latest calibration profile for your Monitor.

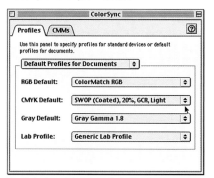

The ColorSync 3.0.1 Default Profiles for Documents as set up for ColorMatch RGB, SWOP (Coated) 20% GCR Light, and Gray 1.8. Photoshop 6 can get these Working Space settings from here.

If you choose ColorSync Workflow, you will probably want to set your Engine back to Adobe (ACE).

If you choose ColorSync Workflow, you will probably want to turn Use Black Point Compensation off.

If you choose ColorSync Workflow, you will probably want to set your Intent back to Perceptual.

dialog, won't work properly. Just set all your Color Settings manually as we talked about at the beginning of this chapter.

If you are using a version of Mac OS 9, I still don't recommend using the ColorSync Workflow choice in the Settings dialog but you can get it to work if you do it carefully. This setting gets Photoshop's Monitor, RGB and CMYK Working Space settings from ColorSync but there are potential pitfalls in doing it this way as we will explain. It is safer to explicitly set these things in the Color Settings dialog as I mentioned earlier in this chapter. If you do use the ColorSync Workflow setting then you need to do the following.

Don't use ColorSync version 3.0 but get the free upgrade, off Apple's web site, to ColorSync 3.0.1 or a later version. Make sure the version you use is compatible with the Mac OS you are using. After installing ColorSync 3.0.1, choose Apple Menu/Control Panels/ColorSync and choose Profiles for Standard Devices from the top pop-up menu in the Profiles section. Set Input to the profile for your scanner, if you have one. Set Display to the ICC profile for your Monitor. This ICC Profile will be created by the monitor calibrator that you use, or by Adobe Gamma, and placed in the ColorSync Profile folder in your System Folder. When you go into the Color Settings dialog for Photoshop 6, you monitor's profile should show up in the pop-up menu for RGB Working Space to the right of the title Monitor RGB. If the correct profile does not show up here then Photoshop may not be giving you accurate on screen proofs.

Now change the ColorSync pop-up menu to Default Profiles for Documents. Set RGB Default to the RGB Working Space you want to use. If you are using a standard space, then this will probably be ColorMatch RGB or Adobe RGB. Set CMYK Default to the ICC profile for your CMYK separations. If this doesn't show up in the ColorSync pop-up, you may have to first go into Photoshop 6 and save your current settings by choosing Save CMYK from the CMYK Working Spaces pop-up. Set you Gray Default to the setting you want. To make this choice available, I had to first choose Save Gray from the Photoshop 6 Gray Working Space pop-up to save the Gray Gamma 1.8 setting as an ICC profile.

If you save all these changes when you quit from the ColorSync control panel, then the Display setting, RGB Default, CMYK Default and Gray Default from ColorSync should appear in the correct places when you choose ColorSync Workflow from the Settings menu at the top of the Color Settings dialog. **The problem with doing this is that it also automatically sets the Engine to Apple ColorSync, the Intent to Relative Colorimetric and it turns on Use Black Point Compensation. You then need to remember to go down to the Conversion Options section of the Color Settings dialog and set these back to the settings you prefer.** See the screen captures and captions here for my recommendations about resetting these Conversion Options.

For specific information about setting up ColorSync with Mac OS 10, look at Apple's web site for documentation on ColorSync and OS 10. I have not converted to OS 10 at this point and don't have a big reason to do so.

SAVING AND STANDARDIZING YOUR PREFERENCES

After you make major changes to your standard Photoshop 6 preferences, you should quit from Photoshop immediately. When you leave Photoshop, it saves its current state (preferences, tool option choices, palette locations, and so on) to several files within the System/Preferences/Adobe Photoshop 6 Settings folder on the Mac (on the PC with Windows 98, these files are saved at: "Windows/Application Data/Adobe/Photoshop/6.0/Adobe Photoshop 6 Settings. Photoshop also creates an

Adobe Photoshop 6 Paths file in the same location and also folders called System/Application Support/Adobe with a bunch of folders inside it on the Mac and on the PC in Windows 98, these are saved at: "C:\Program Files\Common Files\Adobe\Calibration". Quitting after changing preferences ensures that Photoshop saves your preferences changes to these files. If you were to crash before quitting Photoshop, you would lose these latest preferences changes, and Photoshop would revert to the preferences you had when you last successfully quit from Photoshop.

It is a good idea for everyone in your company to standardize on a set of separation and workspace preferences, especially for the same publication, and vitally important to standardize separation and workspace preferences if you are doing color corrections and separations. You can copy a standard version of these files to the Photoshop Settings folders on everyone else's machines, or print up a standards document and have your systems administrator make sure that everyone is using those settings.

CREATING CUSTOM SEPARATION SETTINGS

If you want to calibrate Photoshop separation settings for a newspaper, a particular type of web press, or other custom CMYK output, you can do this using Photoshop 6. First, you need to find out the correct CMYK values for the full range of neutral colors in a stepwedge file, like the one included in the Calibration folder on the *Photoshop 6 Artistry* CD. The press expert at your print shop should know this information. Next, you adjust Custom CMYK, as well as the way you set highlights and shadows, using the techniques described in the illustration on page 163 of this chapter, until you get the CMYK values closest to the CMYK values from your press expert for neutral colors in the stepwedge file. Using those settings in Photoshop usually gets you very close to the separations that you want. That's basically what we did to get our settings using the following table of desired values for coated stock.

	Neutral RGB 0...255 values			Sample Target GCR type CMYK values to print these as neutrals			
	Red	*Green*	*Blue*	*Cyan*	*Magenta*	*Yellow*	*Black*
highlight	243	243	243	5%	3%	3%	0%
1/4 tone	192	192	192	25%	16%	16%	0%
midtone	128	128	128	50%	39%	38%	4%
3/4 tone	64	64	64	69%	58%	58%	30%
shadow	13	13	13	76%	66%	65%	85%

Actual CMYK values (plus or minus 1) when separating the unmodified StepWedgeFile using our Photoshop Separation settings

	Cyan	*Magenta*	*Yellow*	*Black*
05% highlight	5%	3%	3%	0%
25% 1/4 tone	24%	16%	16%	0%
50% midtone	49%	37%	36%	3%
75% 3/4 tone	67%	57%	56%	29%
95% shadow	75%	65%	64%	84%

The preference settings we chose don't exactly match the values in the target CMYK table, but they give the closest overall settings to these values, which also are the most useful starting point settings.

Newspapers and Other Custom Settings

Our default highlight and shadow values usually are good for most RGB output purposes including output to film recorders and also for CMYK separations to coated stock. If they are not working for you, use this process to change them. Newspaper presses tend to vary much more than web or sheetfed presses for coated stock. If you are doing output for newspapers or some other special process, first get a set of correct values for printing neutral colors from your press person. It should look like the preceding table but with different numbers. For newspapers, start out with Custom CMYK set to SWOP (Newsprint) with a Standard Dot Gain of 30%. Set the Separation Type to GCR, Black Generation to Medium, Black Ink Limit to around 85%, and Total Ink Limit to around 260%; again, get these values from your press person. Set the Highlight and Shadow preference values in Levels initially as your press person recommends for the brightest and darkest place that can still carry a dot or not be solid black on your press.

Bring up the StepWedgeFile, which starts out as a grayscale, and convert it to your RGB working space using Image/Mode/RGB. Bring up the Info palette and and use Color Samplers to measure the RGB and CMYK values you get at different density areas along your stepwedge. Compare the CMYK numbers with the ones you got from your press person. Change the Dot Gain (remember, you can now use the Curves setting to adjust each curve separately and exactly if needed), Black Ink Limit, and Total Ink limit settings in Custom CMYK until you get values that are as close as possible to those your press person gave you. You can also change the Black Generation curve between Light, Medium, and Heavy as well as create a custom Black generation curve by choosing Custom. Photoshop doesn't give you direct control over the Cyan, Magenta, or Yellow generation curves, but you can affect them via changes you make to the Black curve. You can also separately adjust each of the dot gain curves by choosing Curves from the Dot Gain pop-up.

You will have to play with all these settings until you get a feeling for the relationship they have with each other. The settings we have recommended for coated stock have worked quite well in producing this book and for many other projects that I have done. We don't recommend particular settings for newspapers because they tend to vary from paper to paper. For more information on output to black-and-white halftones, you should get *Photoshop in Black-and-White: An Illustrated Guide to Producing Black-and-White Images with Adobe Photoshop Version 5.0* by Jim Rich and Sandy Bozek.

You can also load a custom ICC profile to run your separations. This custom profile would decide for you how to convert from RGB to CMYK. There are companies that sell custom separation tables and ICC profiles for Photoshop. If you have another color separation system that you would like to import into Photoshop, like from Scitex or some other high-end system, you can do that also by converting that to an ICC profile.

Hardware Monitor Gamma Versus Working Space Gamma

Another thing you need to consider when working in Photoshop is the hardware gamma your monitor is calibrated to and whether you work in an RGB workspace that is 1.8 or 2.2 gamma. If you are using your monitor to work with images that are for CMYK print output, you may be better off if your monitor hardware gamma is set to 1.8, which is the standard gamma of Mac systems. If you are doing primarily output to the Web, you may want to set your monitor hardware gamma to 2.2, which is the typical gamma of PC systems. Now the gamma of your RGB workspace is a different story. Regardless of what you have your monitor gamma calibrated to, Photoshop will compensate for a different gamma in your RGB working space if necessary to give you a correct display of your images on the monitor.

An RGB working space that has a gamma of 2.2 does a more even job of displaying the values in a histogram and allows you to see more separation in the shadows. Your shadow detail will less likely be posterized. Many people in the print world are used to working with the ColorMatch RGB workspace with their gamma set at 1.8. In general, more people who work in print have been working with a workspace having a gamma of 1.8, and people who use the Web or work on the Web are more likely use a workspace with a gamma of 2.2. If you open a file that has been color adjusted in a gamma 1.8 space into a gamma 2.2 space without converting, the file would seem darker and more contrasty. Similarly, if you initially corrected the file in a gamma 2.2 space and then opened it into a 1.8 space without converting, the file would seem too flat and light. Whatever space you adjust your files in, you will get used to and make the appropriate choices as to your color adjustments. It's just when you open or print that file into a different gamma environment without compensation, you will notice a problem.

Open an image that was corrected and tagged with a gamma 1.8 workspace, like ColorMatch RGB, and then choose Image/Mode/Assign Profile and assign a gamma 2.2 profile, like Adobe RGB, to this file without conversion. See how this changes the appearance of the file?

16 IMAGE RESOLUTION, SCANNING FILM AND DIGITAL CAMERAS

Here you learn how to make 8- or 16-bit scans at the appropriate resolution and file size, how to use histograms to evaluate and improve scans, how to compare film scans on popular multiformat scanners, and how to make the best use of digital cameras.

WHAT ARE BYTES, BITS AND DPI?

To learn how to make a good scan, you need to understand resolution and the issues involved in determining what size to make the scan. Because we're going to be talking about size in bytes, let's take a minute to talk about bytes, bits, and dpi. A *byte* (8 bits) is the most common unit of measurement of computer memory. All computer functionality is based on switches that can be turned on and off. A single switch is called a *bit*. When a bit is off, it has a value of 0. When a bit is on, it has a value of 1. With a single bit, you can count from 0 to 1. With two bits lined up next to each other, you can count from 0 to 3 because now there are four possibilities (00=0, 01=1, 10=2, and 11=3). Add a third bit, and you can count from 0 to 7 (000=0, 001=1, 010=2, 011=3, 100=4, 101=5, 110=6, and 111=7). When there are 8 bits, or a byte, you can count from 0 to 255, which is 256 possible values. When there are 12 bits, you have 4,096 possible values and when there are 16 bits you have 65,536 possible values.

A grayscale 8-bit digital image has one byte of information for each value scanned from the film. A value of 0 is the darkest possible value, black, and a value of 255 is the brightest possible value, white. Values in between are different levels of gray, the lower numbers being darker and the higher numbers being lighter. You can think of these values like you would think of individual pieces of grain within a piece of film: the more values you have per inch, the smaller the grain in the digital file. Also, the more of these values that you have per inch, the higher the resolution (alias dpi [dots per inch] or samples per inch) in your file. An 8-bit RGB color digital image has three bytes of information (24 bits, one byte for each channel of red, green, or blue) for each value scanned from the film. And CMYK files have four bytes per pixel. A 16-bit per channel grayscale file has two bytes and 65,536 possible tonal values. A 16-bit per channel RGB file, 48 bits in all, contains 65,536 possible tonal values per color channel. With today's scanners, scanning 12-bit per channel or even 16-bit per channel images is something well worth considering.

If you have an enlarger in the traditional darkroom, you can make a 20x24 print from a 35mm original. Its quality will not be as good as a 20x24 print on the same paper from a 4x5 original of the same type of film, because the 4x5 has more film area with which to define the image. If you were printing on different types of paper, the paper's grain would affect the look of the final print. It's the amount of grain in the original film that makes the difference when you project that film on the same paper to make a traditional darkroom print.

When you make a print on a printing press, the line screen of the halftone is somewhat analogous to the grain in the photographic paper. When you make a print on a digital printer, the dpi (dots per inch) of the printer is analogous to the grain in the photographic paper. The dpi of a digital printer is the number of individual sensors, or ink jets, or laser spots, that the particular printer can put down per inch. Each digital printer has its own maximum possible dpi, based on its own specific physical limitations. The relationship between the dpi of a scan and the line screen or dpi of a digital printer is analogous to the relationship between the grain size of film in the enlarger and the grain size of the paper you are printing on in a traditional darkroom. A scan of 100 dpi will print on a digital printer that can output at 720 dpi, but it won't look as good as a 300 dpi scan of the same image for the same printer. Similarly, a print on photographic paper from ASA 1600 (large grain) film won't look as good as a print on the same paper from ASA 25 (small grain) film.

How Big Should I Make a Scan?

When you are having an image scanned, you should know the intended purpose of the scan well ahead of time. When you have more than one purpose and image size, scan the image at the maximum size you would use it or at the maximum optical dpi of your scanner. Scanning at higher than the optical dpi of your scanner just means that the scanner software is upsampling your file. Photoshop can usually do as good a job or better upsampling as your scanner software can so there is usually no need to scan at higher than the scanner's optical resolution.

The formula for calculating the required byte size for a scan of a 6x7 image to be printed at 300 dpi is (6x300 dpi) x (7x300 dpi) x 3. This file would be 11,340,000 bytes in size. (The final factor represents the number of bytes for each pixel in the image; 3 is the number for an RGB color image.) If you were saving the complete file after scanning at either 12- or 16- bits per channel, or anything more than 8 bits per channel, you would end up with a 16-bit per channel file in Photoshop which would double the above file size making this final factor be 6. For an 8-bit CMYK scan, the factor is 4 instead of 3 because there are 4 bytes for each pixel in a CMYK image. If you do a black-and-white scan, you can remove this factor because they require only one byte per pixel, two bytes for a 16-bit grayscale scan. Here's the general formula for the required byte size of final publication scans:

Scan Size = ((height of image) x (2 x line screen dpi)) x ((width of image) x (2 x line screen dpi)) x 3 (for 8-bit RGB) or x 6 (for 16-bit RGB)

If you scan a file for output to a digital printer, such as the Epson Stylist Photo 1270, 2000 & 7500 or the LightJet 5000, you don't need to do the scan at the same dpi as the resolution of the printer you plan to use. After scanning the file, the resolution can be set to different values depending on the printer you are using for that print. For output to the LightJet 5000, which has a resolution of 120 pixels per centimeter (304.8 dpi), the formula and byte size would be (6x304.8 dpi) x (7x304.8 dpi)

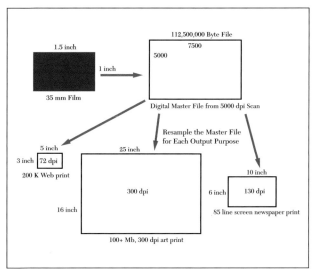

If you will use the scan for more than one purpose, make the original scan for the size of the biggest file you will need. Do your overall color correction, image enhancement and spotting on this biggest master file. You can then resample that corrected file down to whatever resolution and file size you need. Above you see some sample uses. When scanning most files on a high end drum scanner, you will find that you will not get anymore detail information from the film by scanning it at more than 5000 dpi. If you scan at a higher dpi than this, you probably will not get any better data than just resampling up the 5000 dpi file. A file of this dpi can certainly be resampled down with Image Size or the Cropping tool to 72 dpi for the Web, 300 dpi for a digital art print, 170 dpi for a newspaper print, or anything else you need.

If the image is to be published as a halftone on a printing press and you want the best quality, you need to scan it at a dpi (dots per inch or scan samples per inch) of at least twice the line screen of the publication. For example, if you are printing a six-inch by seven-inch photograph in a 150-line screen publication, you should scan it at 300 dpi for the number of inches you're printing it at.

x 3 = 11,705,783 bytes. Most dye sublimation digital printers (Fargo, Tektronics, Mitsubishi, GCC, et al.), and also the IRIS inkjet printer, have a printed dpi of 300. The Epson Stylist Photo 1270, 2000, 7500 & 9500 have printed dpis of from 720 to 1440. The way the Epson printers use dots, however, is different from digital printers like the dye subs and the LightJet 5000. I have found that for these types of Epson printers, you get good results if you use a file of about 360 dpi or higher. I recommend scanning your film at the highest optical dpi of you scanner, up to around 5000 dpi (5760 with the Imacon scanner and 35mm film), then color correcting this large master file. You can always downsample the master file for smaller uses. If you have the option of scanning at 12 or 16 bits per channel and actually saving all that information in your file, you will be able to do more with that information when color correcting in Photoshop 6.

If you scan a file for output to a film recorder, such as the Kodak LVT (Light Valve Technology), or Cymbolic Sciences' LightJet 2000, remember that they require a very high dpi. If you want the output to have the same quality as original film, the dpi can be around 2000 or more. Outputting a 4x5 RGB transparency at 2,000 dpi requires a file size of (4x2000) x (5x2000) x 3, or 240,000,000 bytes. For film recorders, the dpi of the file needs to match the maximum dpi of the film recorder for optimal quality. If you don't have a file that large, you may still be happy with the film recorder output, you should ask your service bureau for their recommendations.

If you have trouble remembering formulas and don't want to bother with a calculator, there is an easy way to calculate the file size you will need: by using the New command in Photoshop. Choose File/New, and then enter the width and height dimensions in inches for the largest size you expect to print the image you are scanning. Based on the current discussion, set the resolution in pixels/inch to match what you will need for your line screen or printer resolution. Now set the mode to Grayscale, RGB, or CMYK, according to the type of scan. The image size that shows up at the top of the dialog box is the size in megabytes that you should make your scan. Now you can cancel from this dialog box; Photoshop has done the calculation for you. If the scan you are making will be 16 bits per channel, then double the file size that File/New gives you.

The formulas for file size that we present here are the ones you would use to obtain the best quality on a printing press. Making even larger scans than these is unlikely to improve the quality on a press but definitely increases the time necessary to work with and output the files. Making smaller scans than these most likely reduces your quality but also decreases the time necessary to work with and output the files. When working with digital printers, like the Epson 2000, 7500 and 9500, picky photographers may notice a quality improvement when printing at dpis up to 480. Some artists I know also print their 16-bit per channel color files directly to their Epson printers and claim the quality is better than when printing 8-bit versions of the same files. It usually doesn't hurt to have more optical data in a scan, you can always reduce it later if you don't need it and that is often much easier than rescanning.

If you scan small files, usually measured in pixel dimensions, for Web sites or multimedia applications, you often can get better results if you scan a simple factor larger in each dimension. I recently did some Web images where the final spec for the GIF file size was 180 by 144 pixels. I scanned the files at 720 by 576 and did all my color corrections and masking at this larger, more detailed size. One of the final steps before creating the GIF files was to scale the corrected and sharpened files to 25% of the larger size. This 25% scale factor is a simple ratio that allows for very accurate scaling. See Chapter 37, "Optimizing Images for the Web and Multimedia" for the details of this process.

Use File/New to calculate the size of the scan you will need.

Chapter 16: Image Resolution, Scanning Film and Digital Cameras

If you need some digital files to prototype a project, you don't need to start with the large scans we describe here. I find that RGB scans of about four megabytes usually provide plenty of screen detail for any prototyping I do. When you decide on the final dimensions for the images in your project or printed piece, you can do a final scan for the intended output device at those final dimensions. When you get a big final scan, archive the original digital file as it was scanned and use copies of it to do color corrections, color separations, and crops, so that you can go back to the original if you make a mistake and need to start over. Happy scanning!

EVALUATING HISTOGRAMS TO MAKE THE BEST SCAN FROM ANY SCANNER

Now that you know how big to make the scan, you need to know how to make a good scan and also how to do a good job of bringing an image into Photoshop from Photo CD. The key to these techniques is learning how to use the histogram in Levels or in the scanner software to evaluate scans. This section presents a few histograms and talks about what they reveal about the images they are describing. By the way, some of the Levels histogram screen grabs from this chapter and others are from earlier versions of Photoshop. We usually only update screen grabs if the features in the tool or the tool's layout have changed. The features have not changed in Levels; Photoshop 5 and 6 just use the newer platinum appearance.

A *histogram* is a bar graph of the samples of each possible setting in the 0 to 255 range in the entire image. This range may actually be a 0 to 65,535 range when working with 16-bit images. The diagram above shows you some of the useful information that a histogram can provide. When you have normal subject material, the best possible circumstance is to have an original image, transparency, or negative that has a good exposure of the subject matter and shows a full range of values from very dark to very bright and some detail in all areas. Chapter 13: "Digital Imaging and the Zone System," tells you how to create a high-quality exposure with a camera. If you have a high-quality image that contains values in all zones and has been scanned correctly, you often see a histogram like the one shown to the right.

A histogram, like the one above, is the graph you get of an image when you look at it in Photoshop's Levels or in various scanner software interfaces. For more information on levels and histograms, turn to Chapter 19: "Overall Color Correction," where we furnish a detailed introduction to levels. Also refer to Chapter 13: "Digital Imaging and the Zone System" to see how histograms relate to traditional photography and light.

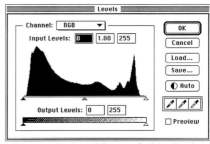

A histogram that has a full range of values. The shape of the histogram in the middle is different for each image.

When you scan a normal full brightness range image, you should aim to get a scan that has a full range of the values present in the original. For most common commercial uses of photography, you want a histogram that has similar traits to the one shown here.

> *You may not want the shadow values to go right down to 0 and you may not want the highlight values to go right up to 255, depending on the range of values in the original image and on the intended output device.*

SCANNING SHADOWS AND HIGHLIGHTS

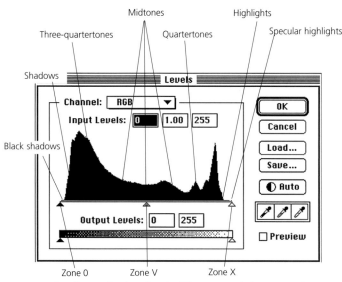

Here is a diagram showing what the different parts of a histogram refer to.

When you scan an image, there are several areas in which you need to be careful what values you obtain. There can be places within the scanned image that are totally black. These should occur only if the original has areas that are totally black (*black shadows*, Zone 0). Then there are the regular shadows, which are the darkest places in the image that still show texture or detail when printed (Zones I and II). On the other end of the spectrum are specular highlights, which are areas in the original that are totally white, such as the reflection of the sun in the chrome bumper of a car (Zone X). Next, there are regular highlights, the brightest areas of the image where you still want to see some texture or detail (Zones VIII and IX).

To some extent, we can call everything between the regular highlights and the regular shadow areas *midtones*. At the dark end of the midtones, are the *three-quartertones* (shadow areas where you can see a fair amount of detail) and at the bright end of the midtones, the *quartertones* (highlight areas where you should also be able to see a fair amount of detail).

ADJUSTING THE SCANNER TO GET THE RIGHT VALUES

When you do a scan, the values that you want to obtain for the shadows and the highlights may depend on the type of output device you are directing the final image toward. If you are not sure of the output device or if you might be using different output devices, the highlights (Zone IX) should have a value in the range of 245–250 and the shadows (Zone I) should have a value in the range of 5–10. With an original image that has a full range of colors in each of the red, green and blue channels, you need to adjust the scanner to get these types of highlight and shadow values. If you get the highlight and shadow values correct, the values of the quartertones, midtones, and three-quartertones usually fall between these endpoint shadow and highlight values. When you get this type of scan, the histogram starts out looking like the good histogram mentioned earlier. With this complete scan, you can always adjust the image in Photoshop to get different highlight, midtone, and shadow values, as well as different contrast, and you will know that you started with all the information from the scanner. I usually start out doing my scans with the normal default scanner settings. Some scanners allow you to add a curve that adjusts the image as you scan it. I generally don't use a preset curve in the scanner because I'd rather do the adjustments myself in Photoshop. My objective with most scanners is to get all the information out of the film without throwing any of it away. When the file you are saving is an 8-bit per channel file, the scanner software will often have to decide how to convert the 12 or more bits of information the scanner is actually getting down to 8 bits per channel in the file that will be saved. When you are doing this, it is important to use the settings in the scanner software to optimize how the scanner converts from the higher bit depth down to 8 bits.

Chapter 16: Image Resolution, Scanning Film and Digital Cameras

Scanning up to 16 Bits Per Color Per Pixel

Many scanners these days scan a lot more than 8 bits of information per color per pixel. The scanner gets this information out of the film and then the scanner software uses a curve or other scanner settings to reduce this down to 8 bits per pixel when it gives it to you in Photoshop. If you later decide you are not happy with the 8 bits of information you got, you will have to rescan the image to get a different set of values. For example, the scanner may actually pull more shadow range information from the film but, due to the fact that 8-bit files are limited to a total of 256 tones per color, the software throws out a lot of this shadow info when it reduces the file to 8 bits. Since Photoshop 6 has much better support for actually working with files that have more than 8 bits per color, it would be much better to have the option of getting all the information the scanner gets from the film before the scanner software reduces it down to 8 bits. That way you could save this info on disk and modify it many different ways without having to rescan the image. Photoshop 6 allows you to work with up to 16 bits of information per channel using many of its tools, including Levels, Curves, Hue/Saturation, Brightness/Contrast, Color Balance, Equalize, Invert, and Channel Mixer. You can also Crop, Rubber Stamp, Image Size, Unsharp Mask, Gaussian Blur and Rotate, as well as use the History Brush with 16-bit channel files. Most scanners these days allow for the saving of files with more than 8 bits per color channel, but many, even some very expensive ones, don't. This is now an important feature to check for when buying a scanner to use for high-end color work. I wouldn't purchase a scanner that didn't allow me to write the full information the scanner's sensors get to a file.

My preference is to save the full bit depth from the scanner into a file and then use the Photoshop Levels, Curves and Hue/Saturation adjustments, which usually give me more control than the scanner software, to do the adjustments on the 12-or 16-bit per channel file. The hardware sensors on many scanners actually do whatever they do without much adjustment possible; the software controls in most scanners adjust how the data from the scanner's hardware sensors is converted from 12 or 16 bits down to 8 bits when the file is saved. Saving the data directly from the scanner's hardware sensors into a 16-bit per channel file allows you to use the more accurate Photoshop tools to readjust that scan as many times as you would like without ever having to rescan the file. This is the strategy that makes the most sense for fine artists and people who want to tweak their images to the max. If you are a service bureau or doing production scans for a magazine or newspaper, then you probably want the scanner software to do as much of the work as possible and just give you an 8-bit file you can place and print, maybe even a CMYK file.

Scanning Step by Step

Whenever I scan in Photoshop, using any scanner, I always use the same simple technique. First I set up the default brightness, contrast, and color balance controls on the scanner. I remove any pre-set curves that would change the contrast of the scan from the scanner setting. I make sure that I set the scanner for the correct type of film. I then do a prescan, which shows me the image in the scanner's preview window. Using the scanner software, I set the crop of the image to scan the area I want to scan. For evaluating the histogram of this scan it is best if this crop does not include any black or white borders around the edges of the film. In the Imacon scanner dialog box at the top of the next page, the prescan and crop are shown with the image preview in the center. If the scanner software doesn't have an accurate histogram display, I set the scanner to do about a 4Mb test scan. I usually don't tell scanners to sharpen the image, because sharpening works best when customized to each

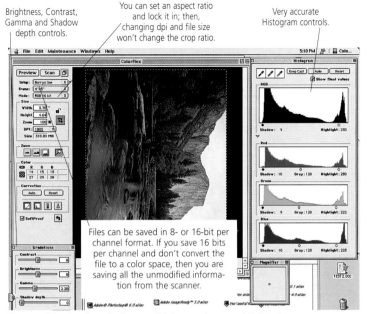

Brightness, Contrast, Gamma and Shadow depth controls.

You can set an aspect ratio and lock it in; then, changing dpi and file size won't change the crop ratio.

Very accurate Histogram controls.

Files can be saved in 8- or 16-bit per channel format. If you save 16 bits per channel and don't convert the file to a color space, then you are saving all the unmodified information from the scanner.

Scanner dialog box from the Imacon. This is a good scanner interface because you can create the cropping box in the prescan window in the center, and set its dimensions and its dpi independent of each other. You can also see accurate histograms, like those shown here, curves and many other controls. See the scanner comparison section at the end of this chapter for more information about the Imacon scanners.

final image size and I can usually get better sharpening with the Photoshop Unsharp Mask filter and the Sharpen Only Edges BH Action. If I get a good focused raw scan from the scanner, I know Photoshop sharpening can do a great job. The next step is to evaluate the histogram based on the scanner software preview or do a 4Mb scan at the default settings and look at the histogram in Photoshop. It helps to have a scanner that has a Photoshop plug-in allowing it to scan directly into Photoshop. This saves a lot of time over scanning into another package, saving the file, and then having to reopen it in Photoshop.

Next, I evaluate the histogram using the scanner software itself or using the 4Mb scan with Levels in Photoshop to look at the image. You want to have cropped any black or white borders before you look at the histogram because they distort the accuracy of the histogram. Later in this chapter, I show you some sample histograms and explain their problems and how to correct them by adjusting the scanner.

Keep on doing scanner previews or small 4Mb scans and adjusting scanner settings each time until you get the best histogram you can for this particular image. Once you get the histogram to look correct in the scanner software or on the small 4Mb scan, use the same scanner settings for exposure and color balance, and increase the size of the scan to give you the final number of megabytes that you will need. If the scanner software allows it and you want to get the most detail and control from your scans, I suggest doing the final scans at more than 8 bits of information per color channel and saving all that information to your file. The Imacon scanner, for example, does scans at 16 bits per channel, the Nikon LS-2000 does them at 12 bits. Both allow you to save all this scan info into your file. It is always best to get a good-looking histogram from the scanner before you make corrections to the histogram in Photoshop. If you aren't personally doing the scan, you at least now know how to evaluate the scans you get. When you cannot improve the scan using the scanner itself (you didn't do the scan, you don't have the scanner, or you already did the best that the scanner can do), the next step is to get the histogram correct using Photoshop's color correction utilities and the Overall Color Correction process. I cover this process after the next section.

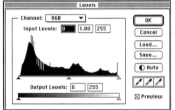
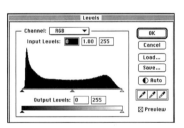
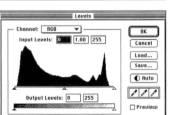
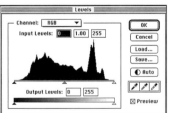

These could all be good normal histograms. Generally, the important characteristic in a good histogram of a typical photograph is to have values that go all the way from one end of the histogram to the other. This histogram would represent an image that has values from black, Zone 0, all the way to white, Zone X. The way the graph actually looks in between these two endpoint areas varies with the particular image. **For some images, such as soft fog on a mountain lake after sunset, or a subtle snow scene, there may not be bright highlights or dark shadows, and then you wouldn't have values that go all the way from one end of the histogram to the other. That is OK for that type of image.**

GETTING THE RIGHT HISTOGRAM

Time and again I am asked in classes, "What is a good histogram?" Let me ask a question in response. If you have three different photographers take a picture of a basket of apples, which would be the "good" photograph: the one that is dark, moody and mysterious; the one that is light, delicate and ethereal; or the one that is an accurate representation of a basket of apples in the sunshine? In actuality, any or all of the three may be excellent photographs. Judging a histogram is similar, in that many different histograms could be the "right" histogram for a given photograph, depending on the artist's interpretation of the subject.

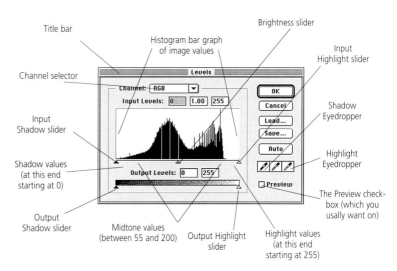

Study this diagram to learn the various controls of the Levels tool.

COMPARING THE HISTOGRAM TO THE ORIGINAL

The histogram cannot be viewed separately from the original slide or photo. A good histogram of the original is one that accurately reflects the amount of information in the original. A good histogram of the final output accurately represents the artist's visualization. Never does the adage, "garbage in, garbage out" apply more fully than in digital imaging. If you have an original with no highlight detail, there is absolutely zero possibility that even a high-end scanner can give you something to work with. A good scan of a good original, however, gives you a full range of information that can be manipulated digitally, just as you would manipulate information traditionally in the darkroom.

If you start with a very low contrast original, your histogram will have a shortened value scale; that is, the representation of the pixel values will not stretch across all the values from 0 to 255. In general, as you color correct this scan, you force the values of the pixels in the scan to spread out along the luminosity axis all the way from deep shadows (between about 3 and 10) to bright highlights (around 245)—notice that we say "in general." If the effect that you wish to achieve is a very low contrast image, say, a photo that appears ghosted back, you may need to do very little adjustment to the histogram. It all depends on what you are visualizing for the final output. Just as you use the Zone System to set where the values of the actual subject matter will fall on the film, in digital imaging you choose (by manipulating the histogram) where the values of the scan will fall in the final output. Therefore, you must view the histogram in the context of the original input and the desired output. You must ask yourself, "What is actually there?" and "What do I want the audience to see?"

MODIFYING WITH LEVELS AND CURVES

Once you get a good scan with a good histogram, you can modify it with Levels and Curves to get your visualization of that image for your final print. If you move the Levels Input Highlight slider to the left, you move your Zone VIII and IX values toward Zone X, brightening the highlights. If you move the Output Highlight slider to the left, you move your Zone X, IX, and VIII values toward Zone IX, VIII, and VII, respectively, dulling the highlights. Similarly, you can use the Shadow sliders to move the zone values around in the shadow parts of the histogram. If you move the Input Brightness slider to the right, you move Zone V values toward Zone IV or III, making the midtones darker and more contrasty. If you move the slider to the left, you move Zone V values toward Zone VI or VII, making the image lighter and brighter.

The Curves tool allows you to make even finer adjustments to values in specific zones. Read Chapter 19: "Overall Color Correction," Chapter 20: "Correcting a Problem Image," and Chapter 24: "Desert Al" to try out these techniques and see how digital imaging gives you more power to realize your vision. As Ansel Adams says in his book *The Negative,* "Much of the creativity in photography lies in the infinite range of choices open to the photographer between attempting a nearly literal representation of the subject and freely interpreting it in highly subjective 'departures from reality.'" Many people think of Adams' prints as straight photos from nature. Actually, Adams did a lot of adjusting with his view camera and in the darkroom to create the visualization of the image that would bring forth his feelings and impressions from the original scene. I believe he would enjoy digital imaging and all the extra control it would give him.

WORKING WITH PHOTO CD IMAGES

Photoshop 6 now has some pretty good built-in support for Kodak Photo CD. First let's talk a little about Photo CD. When you get an image scanned onto Photo CD, there are two possible formats: Regular and Pro Photo CD. Regular Photo CDs have five scans of different sizes of each image. The five pixel dimensions are 192x128, 384x256, 768x512, 1536x1024, and 3072x2048 pixels. For about $1 to $2 a photograph, you get all five sizes of scans of each photograph. The largest of these is an 18Mb file, which is useful for a 10"x6.8" print at 300 dpi. With these 18Mb files, I have actually made some very high-quality 11x17 prints by using a ProofPositive dye sublimation printer (no longer available), resampling up the images, and sharpening them. I have also made great prints from Photo CD scans on my Epson Stylist Photo 1270 printer.

Kodak also offers Pro Photo CD scans. These scans have the same five resolutions as above, plus a sixth resolution that is 4096x6144, or up to 72Mb in size—big enough for 11x17 by 300 dpi without resampling up the scans. I have made high quality 16x20 LightJet 5000 prints from 4x5 Pro Photo CD scans. The Pro scans cost about $15 to $20 each and they seem to be very good as long as you give them a proper original exposure. I have been getting my Photo CD and Pro Photo CD scans done at Palmer Photographic and have been quite happy with the results. Unfortunately Palmer Photographic is now closed. When getting Photo CD scans, it is important to find a service bureau that you can trust with your film and also who does good work. Palmer always handled film carefully and I've always heard praise about the scans he did for many of my friends and *Artistry* readers. Please let me know if you find another Photo CD service bureau that is as good as Palmer's was. Sorry that I don't have another one I have used myself at this point and so won't recommend someone until I know they consistently do good work as Palmer's always did.

If you have a difficult negative—one that is improperly exposed, too dark or too light—and you want to get the absolute most out of the scan, you may do better with a high-end drum scan or a scan from one of the scanners we discuss at the end of this chapter. On the other hand, if the original is a good exposure with a full range of data, and you make sure that you tell the people doing the Photo CD scans the type of film you are sending them, it is possible to get very usable scans. As with any scan, however, the operator of the scanner and the quality control of the service bureau doing the scans is going to affect the results. If you are not happy with the results at your service bureau, try a different Photo CD scanning location.

The Photo CD scan puts your image onto a CD. A regular CD, be it an audio CD, multimedia CD, or whatever, can hold up to 650Mb of digital information. The Photo CD scans are compressed so that even if a file is 18Mb when you open it, it takes up only 4Mb to 6Mb of storage on the disc. That means you can get about 100 to 120 regular Photo CD scans on a single CD. The Pro format takes much more disk space; you can only get about 30 of them on a single CD.

BRINGING PHOTO CD INTO PHOTOSHOP

Photoshop 6 has very good built in Photo CD support available from the Open dialog that allows me to open Photo CD images in an ICC profile compatible way. To Open a Photo CD file from the File/Open dialog, choose File/Open then use the Open dialog to navigate to the numbered files within the PHOTO_CD/IMAGES folder on the Photo CD disk. You will have to use the little printed picture directory that comes with your Photo CD to decide which image to open because the images just have numbered names on the CD. Double-clicking one of the numbered images brings up the Kodak PCD Format dialog to the right. Use the Source Image Profile pop-up to set the ICC profile that describes the "Film Term" used to scan your type of original. There is usually one for E-6 scans and one for Kodachrome scans. Set the Destination profile to RGB or LAB 8- or 16-bit files. If you choose an RGB choice, the file will be converted into your RGB working space as it is opened. Choose which of the 5 (or 6 with Pro) Pixel Sizes you want and then click OK to bring up the image into Photoshop.

I have a trusted recommendation from a skillful photographer friend that one can get good Photo CD Pro scans from a placed named Imagers. Their web site is: http://www.imagers.com and you can set up all the information for a scanning order there. Try it and let me know, at barry@maxart.com, how they worked for you.

Here are the controls for the built-in Photo CD Opening software that you access from File/Open. This dialog allows you to specify an ICC profile for the Source Image and the Destination Image. The Source Image specification is an ICC profile that you should get from your Photo CD provider. The name they seem to use for it is a film term, which will describe what the Photo CD scanner will do with a particular type of film. There is usually one film term for Kodachrome and another for E-6. The Destination Image Color Space should be set to your RGB working space or Lab. If you choose RGB 8 bits/channel or RGB 16 bits/channel, then this dialog wil convert your file into your RGB working space. With the LAB choices it seems to open the file without doing a conversion at the end. I have had very good results opening my own and various students' Photo CD files into LAB color. When you have an accurate Source and Destination profile, this version of Photoshop appears to give you pretty good results with Photo CD scans.

When opening Photo CD files, you want to navigate to the numbered files within the IMAGES folder within a folder called PHOTO_CD inside your Photo CD icon on your desktop.

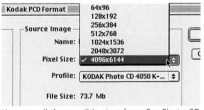

Here are all the possible sizes for a Pro Photo CD scan. Regular Photo CD scans have all the same sizes except for this biggest 4096 x 6144 choice.

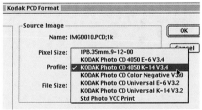

Here we see some typical choices for the Photo CD Source Image Profile. KODAK Photo CD 4050 E-6 V3.4 is the film term I have been using for film processed in E-6, KODAK Photo CD 4050 K-14 V3.4 is the film term I have been using for Kodachrome. These seem to work especially well when the Image Info Product Type, at the bottom left of the dialog, is set to Film Scanner 405. The Color Negative film term here also seems to work well but I haven't used it a lot since I shoot mostly transparencies. The version 3.2 E-6 and K-14 film terms seem to be older versions that I have not used lately. These may work better with older Photo CD scans.

Poor Scans and Their Problem Histograms
(Different types of problems require different scanner adjustments)

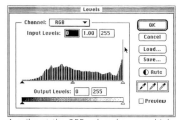

A spike at the 255 value shows no highlight detail. Rescanning with a lower exposure setting may fix this problem.

The image is too bright, obscuring the detail in the clouds and other highlights.

This scan has quite different ranges for each of the Red, Green, and Blue channels. Best to rescan and adjust each channel separately.

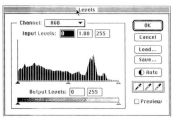

A spike at the 0 value shows no shadow detail. Rescanning with a changed shadow setting on the scanner may fix this if there was actually any shadow detail in the film.

No matter what we do in Photoshop, we won't be able to bring out shadow detail because it was lost in the scan.

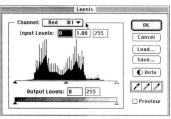

The Red channel for the scan above. Rescan with more exposure on red, and a different black value.

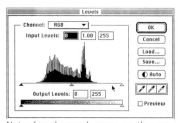

Not a broad enough range on the scan. We could correct this in Photoshop by bringing in the Highlight and Shadow sliders, but then we would end up with a gappy scan like below. We are better off rescanning with more exposure and a different shadow setting.

The highlights and shadows are way too dull.

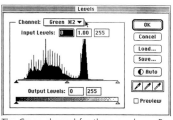

The Green channel for the scan above. Rescan with larger exposure for green; black is okay here.

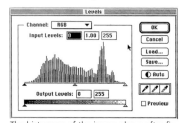

The histogram of the image above after fixing it in Photoshop; it now has a bunch of gaps in it that represent lost tonal values. You will get more detail in the printed result by rescanning.

The corrected image with the gappy histogram still prints better than with the uncorrected histogram above.

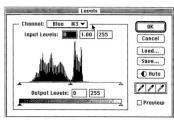

The Blue channel for the scan above. Rescan with a much larger exposure and possible black adjustments.

Corrected Photographs and Their Good Histograms
(Values in the middle of a histogram look different for each photo)

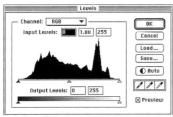

The correct scan and print for the sample image on the previous page. Lots of ¾ tones on the dark parts of the beach. The large number of ¼ tones are probably in the sky and the waves.

Santa Cruz sunset from the boardwalk.

Young Lakes.

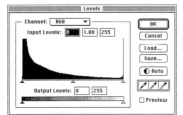

Lots of very dark areas and very bright areas, even totally black and white, are OK in this photo.

The Paris Cafe.

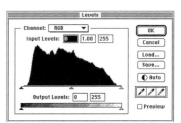

Lots of values everywhere across the full brightness range.

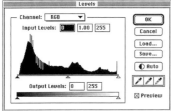

This histogram has lots of dark shadows in the trees and the fence. The spike at the far right is the white buildings.

The Burnley church.

Shells in Costa Rica.

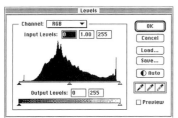

Notice the small spike for the dark shadow areas that are small but so important in the photograph.

Man on the beach at sunset.

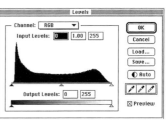

This histogram probably is so smooth because all the objects have a similar range of colors and subtle tones.

The Santa Cruz California beach boardwalk image which is a 35mm original.

The Bandon Oregon harbor image shot with 4x5 inch film.

COMPARING SOME CURRENT MULTIFORMAT FILM SCANNERS

Since digital imaging began, I have been waiting for a cost effective multiformat film scanner that actually did really good scans. Back in the early 90's the Leaf Scan 45 was a good choice but I didn't have an extra $15,000 to spend on this scanner. Now there are quite a few relatively inexpensive flatbed and multiformat film scanners that will do a pretty good job on 4x5 inch film and maybe even 6x6 cm film but many of these, especially the flatbed models, have not done that well with 35mm scans. For a less expensive solution, one could get a Nikon LS-2000 for 35mm and then use a better flatbed for 6x6 cm and 4x5 inch scans. Luckily for me, I have a good friend, Bill Atkinson, who has a Lino Tango drum scanner and lets me scan with it from time to time. Since I moved up to Oregon though, the Tango scanner in California is a long way away. I've been wanting my own film scanner and would probably pay up to $5,000 for a solution that would do really quality scans. I bet that many readers of this book are in a similar situation.

For *Photoshop 6 Artistry* and also for a mid year 2001 article I'm writing for *Communication Arts* magazine, I've decided to take a look at some of the multiformat film scanners that are currently on the market. I've been scanning several 35mm images, some 6x7 shots and also some 4x5s. For this discussion though, we'll be looking mostly at two images, both transparencies. The first one is a 35mm Kodachrome 25 photograph of the Santa Cruz beach and boardwalk that was shot from the Santa Cruz pier with a great Canon 50mm lens using my trusty old Canon F1 mounted on a tripod. This is a very sharp and low grain photograph which I can print sharply at 25 inches wide on the LightJet5000 when scanning with a Tango drum scanner at 5000 dpi. The second image I'll be working with is a 4x5 inch original of the harbor in Bandon Oregon shot on Kodak Ektachrome with my 4x5 camera using a 210mm Nikor lens. Both of these images are very sharp originals that have a broad range of values going from bright white down to dark black and lots of sharp details that are good for measuring scanners.

In this discussion we'll be comparing the following scanner issues:

1. Highest resolution scan in each film size
2. Sharpness of focus, very important to me
3. Maximum film density range the scanner can capture
4. How well highlight and shadow details are captured
5. Bit depth of scans and ability to save files of up to 16 bits per channel
6. Price
7. Ease of use
8. Speed of scans
9. Useful, irritating or missing features

The scanners we will be looking at include the Imacon FlexTight Precision II, Epson Expression 1680 and 1640 XL, UMax PowerLook 3000, Polaroid Printscan 45 Ultra, Polaroid Sprintscan 120, Microtek Artixscan 4500t and the new Nikon 8000. We will also use scans from the Lino Tango drum scanner and the Nikon LS-2000 as a high-end and low-end references for comparison. The computer I'm using to drive the scanners in this section is a Macintosh PowerPC 8600/300 with a 400 MHZ Sonnet G3 accelerator, 288 megs of memory and 36 gigs of hard disk space. The scanners are attached using that computer's built in SCSI connector or the USB interface I've added via a PCI card.

You may notice that I don't go into great lengths about the details and features of the software on each of these scanners. I've found over the years that scanner vendors try to sell their scanners by wowing people with all the features of the scanner's software or the bundle of toys that come with the scanner. Many of these features duplicate things that Photoshop 6 can do just as well and often better if you can just figure out how to get all the data out of the scanner. If you just get the raw scan from any scanner and are able to save this as a 16-bit per channel file, then you can use Photoshop's Levels, Curves and Hue Saturation tools, among others, in a standard way to get great results from many different scanners. If you are saving 8-bit per channel files from the scanner, then you need to rely on the scanner's software not to damage the data, and also to optimize it, as it transforms that data from 10, 12, 14 or 16 bits per channel that the scanner hardware gets, down to 8 when saving the file. My main philosophy in this article is to get up to 16 bits per channel of info from the scanner then do most of your corrections in Photoshop. People who are doing hundreds

Here are some of the more important controls on the Imacon Precision II scanner using its ColorFlex software. In this 320 meg 48-bit scan of the Bandon 4x5, notice the very exact histograqms within Imacon's Histogram dialog to the right. You can keep this dialog up all the time and the histograms get updated every time you make a new Preview or new crop. As you can see me doing with the cursor in the top-most RGB histogram, you can exactly adjust the highlight and shadow points for RGB, which adjusts all the settings, and you can also adjust each color separately. When doing a 16-bit per channel scan, one can afford to be conservative and adjust the histograms so no values get lost from the highlights or shadows. When I do my scans in this way with a great scanner like the Imacon, I probably will never need to scan that piece of film again. That scan got all the useful data out of the film and I can reinterpret the original 48-bit scan data as many times as I like before converting to 8 bits per channel color. One can then bring the 48-bit scan into Photoshop and fine tune those highlight and shadow points while zoomed in to look at the highlight and shadow details you care the most about. You can adjust one version to keep the extreme highlight details and another version for the midtones and shadows. These can be combined in Photoshop with layers and masks after converting to 8-bit per channel color.

of batch scans daily will want to use their scanner's software to automate this process. Using the scanner's software for that purpose is not really the focus of this section. This is about using a scanner to get the most information from your film with the goal of using Photoshop 6 to create the most detailed color correct master image starting with a 16-bit per channel scan.

IMACON FLEXTIGHT PRECISION II

The Imacon FlexTight Precision II scanner is at the high end of the non drum scanners. At $14,995, it is the most expensive scanner to be tested here. It has a dynamic range of 4.1 and can scan a 35mm at 5760 dpi, a 6x6cm at 3200 dpi and a 4x5 inch at 1800 dpi maximum optical resolution. It uses a unique mounting system where the film is placed and lined up on one of four thin metal backing holders, one for each film size. After you line up the film, a hinged magnetic flap is dropped down over the film to hold it in place. The scanner is shipped with holders for 35mm, 6x6cm, 6x7cm and 4x5 inch film. A hole is cut in the metal backing holder and also in the magnetic flap allowing you, and the scanner, to see the film through this holder. After the film is mounted, one frame at a time, the holder is then placed on a light table attached to the front of the scanner. The holder snaps in place and is held in place by magnets. After setting the correct preferences for the type of film you are using and the type of scan you want, pressing the Preview button in the scanner's ColorFlex software creates a preview of the scan which you then crop as you

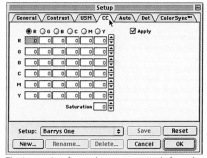

The Imacon's software has many controls for color correction that could be quite useful if one were saving 8-bit scans directly from the scanner. When doing large volumes of production scans, these can allow the experienced operator to do the corrections on the 16-bit data before saving the corrected file in 8-bit. When doing 16-bit per channel scans, I almost always leave all the color correction until I bring the file into Photoshop and can use Photoshop's familiar and powerful color correction tools.

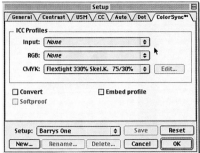

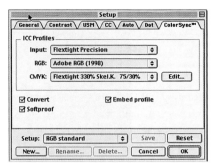

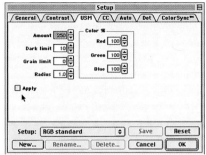

Using these Imacon ColorSync settings allows you to save the raw unmodified information from the scanner. The file is not tagged with any profile and it is not converted before saving. Once you are in Photoshop, this allows you to use Image/Mode/Assign Profile to retag the original unmodified scan with any profile, like a newer and better custom scanner profile you made even long after the scans were made. Once you tag the file, you can still use Image/Mode/Convert to Profile to convert it to your working space and you can do the conversion using the Photoshop conversion choices that work best for this image. For the artist who wants to have the most flexability to tweak their images later, saving without a profile, or tagging with a custom scanner profile and not converting, leaves one with all the options on the original unmodified scan.

ColorSync support with the Imacon software is great. You can choose an Input profile describing the scanner then automatically convert the file, with that Input profile as the Source, to your RGB Working Space as your save the file. That is a good way to work if you are trying to get a lot of scans done quickly and you want the scans already in a standard working space before you enter Photoshop.

The Imacon's software has very flexable Unsharp Masking functions which can save time in volume production situations. For the fine artist, I recommend scanning with sharpening turned off, as it is here. You then do your sharpening on the final corrected, spotted and resampled image in Photoshop using Filter/Sharpen/Unsharp Mask along with selective masking using techniques like the ArtistKeys Sharpen Only Edges BH action.

would like. To actually do the scan, the FlexTight Precision II film carrying mechanism bends the holder, and the film within it, so they are wrapped around a drum as they are drawn into the scanner. The drum in this scanner is actually two metal bands that contact the holder on each side and bend the holder and the film into a position so it doesn't buckle and is a consistent distance from the scanner's CCD sensor. It's like bending the film around a real drum scanner drum but with no actual drum surface, just air, where the film passes over the sensor. This is a great idea because you don't have to clean the drum and attach the film to it, you don't have to surround the film with liquid and remove any bubbles, you don't have to touch anything to the emulsion or base of the film. It is much easier to do than real drum scanning, and yet you get some of the same benefits in the way the film is bent into a known plane of focus. With a real wet mounted drum scan, there are some benefits to having the film surrounded by liquid since the liquid will fill many scratches and imperfections that might be on the film's surface. The disadvantage to wet mounting though, is that your film must be cleaned before and after the process. It is best to have clean and dusted film for any scans but wet mounted drum scans put your film through more torture, and are more work for the scanner operator, than most other scanning processes.

Here we have the Imacon's general setup controls set for the 1800 dpi maximum optical resolution on 4x5 film. We are set for a 16-bit per channel RGB scan of a transparency. Imacon recommends leaving the Enahnced shadow detail setting on.

An Imacon tip that wasn't in the manual is that you can tweak the focus calibration on the Imacon using the Descreen funtion that you see in the middle of this dialog. A setting of zero gives you the focus setting that was saved the last time you calibrated the focus. A setting in the positive or negative direction will either make that focus slightly more blurry or possibly slightly sharper, only if the calibrated focus was off. I found that calibrating the focus with the calibration target that came with the Imacon actually made it worse at times but I was able to dial directly in on the grain by tweaking this descreen setting until the grain was as in focus as possible.

To preview a 35mm slide on the Imacon takes about 15 seconds after pressing the Preview button. To scan a 35mm at 16 bits per pixel a the highest 5760 dpi optical resolution takes about 12 minutes to produce a 237 megabyte file. Scanning this same image at 8 bits per pixel takes 13 minutes and gives you a 118 meg file. You can scan 6x6cm film at a maximum of 3200 dpi. Scanning a 4x5 at its highest 1800 dpi optical resolution takes 14 minutes and produces a 315 meg file. We would get a 158 meg file and also take 14 minutes if scanning at 8 bits per pixel.

As you can see from the screen grabs and discussions on this and the previous page, the Imacon's Setup dialog gives you a lot of options. Take a look at each of the screen grabs and read its caption describing how you can adjust Color, ColorSync output options, Unsharp Mask, Focus and the rest of the Imacon's general settings.

The Imacon manual suggests that usually the factory focus is accurate and it encourages you to only refocus the scanner about once every three months and then only if you are unhappy with the focus. When any good scanner is focused correctly, you should be able to see the grain on the film. If it is very low grain film, this may be sometimes harder to do but if you zoom into 100%, 200% or even up to 400% while looking at the scan in Photoshop, you should be able to scroll around and find some grain somewhere. If you can't ever find this then your scans may be out of

Chapter 16: Image Resolution, Scanning Film and Digital Cameras

focus. The Imacon has a focusing target containing straight lines that you put into the 6x6 holder when you want to refocus the scanner. You then choose a special focusing dialog from the menu bar. I found this focusing process to not always be consistent. The first time I calibrated the focus, my scans were actually more blurry than before I recalibrated. After several tries I was able to get the scanner back to its original sharpness but I'd have to say that recalibrating the focus was not a sure thing type of process. If you recalibrate the focus and wish you hadn't, there is a way to get back to the factory settings. You'll have to contact Imacon tech support to find out exactly how, though, since Imacon only lent me their scanner for a limited time and I've forgotten the exact process. Even if the focus is correct, Imacon tech support suggests that, to fine tune it, you may want to use different Descreen tweaks for different film emulsions. The Descreen option in the General area of the Setup options (see the screen grab on the previous page) allows you to tweak the focus ever so slightly in either a positive or negative direction. To do this, rescan a small section of film over and over again with different settings for Descreen (like -3, -2, -1, 0, 1, 2, 3) until you find that setting where your film grain is as focused as possible. Now use that setting with that type of film and that film size to get the most accurate focus. Of course, you'd have to redo these tests whenever you recalibrated your focus.

Even though you have to remove your slides from their transparency holders to make a scan, Imacon's 35mm film holder crops some of the image from around the edges of the film area, as did the 4x5 holder. For extra money, they will sell you a 35mm one that doesn't have this problem. For $14,995, I think that holder should come for free. You can also get an optional holder that will allow you to leave the film in its original 35mm transparency holder. The small attached light table with horizontal and vertical lines on it is helpful to make sure your film is lined up before you scan. The current design has this mounted at an angle sloped away from the scanner. If the table were flat, one could actually lay the film on the table while the flap were lifted up and reposition the film using the lines on the light table. With the slope it currently has, it is easy for your film to slip out when you move it with the flap even partially up. Because of this design, I usually mounted my film on a differnt light table and found the built-in one not as useful as it could be. To find out more about these options, see the Imacon Web site at www.imacon-usa.com.

UMax PowerLook 3000

The UMax PowerLook 3000 is a higher-end flatbed scanner that is focused towards the professional user and especially towards scanning film. With an MSRP_of $7,695, it is not an inexpensive device. It has an overall optical resolution of 1220 and with its second lens, an optical resolution of up to 3048 x 3048. This second lens is great for scanning film with the high resolution of 3048 x 3048 and the scanner has an internal 14-bit per channel bit depth allowing you to write all that information into 42-bit TIFF files. This scanner automatically focuses on the film and produces pretty sharp results even with 35mm scans. The time it takes for a 35mm scan at 3048 dpi and the highest 42 bit output is about 5 minutes for a 70 meg scan.

My tests trying to scan a 4x5 with this scanner were frustrating. First of all, I discovered that the maximum dimension for scanning in the 3048 dpi mode is 3.4" x 11.7". This means that to get non interpreted scans of more than 1220 dpi, you can't scan anything in the one dimension larger than 3.4". You can't get more than 1220 dpi on a 4x5 and be able to scan the entire 4x5! This is a big problem with this scanner although it can scan 35mm, 6x6cm, 6x7cm and 6x9cm at the full 3048 dpi, which is actually almost as high as the Imacon dpi for medium format cameras. Only being able to get 3.4 inches out of your 4x5, though, may be a problem if you are an avid

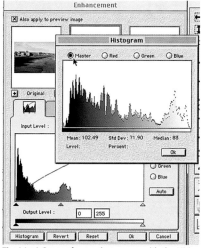

The MagicScan software that comes with the UMax PowerLook 3000 has a very useful histogram feature similar to the Imacon's. After moving the Red, Green and Blue highlight sliders to the left, as I would in Photoshop to get a full range of values, I was able to click on the Histogram button in the lower left and see the new modified histogram chart at the top right. Getting this feedback that the histogram now looks correct is great.

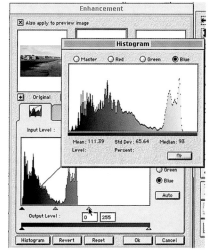

If you really want to keep all the highlight detail, I found that it was best to set the highlight point on the MagicScan histogram back 10 or 20 points from what this histogram display showed as actually being the brightest point. When the files were brought into Photoshop, there were sometimes a very small set of values beyone those points.

Comparing Some Current Multiformat Film Scanners

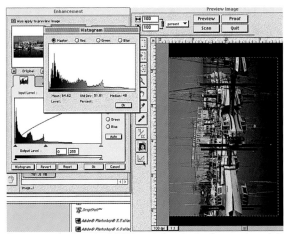

Here we see the PowerLook 3000 controls and setup for scanning a 4x5. As you can see, I'm able to get the full 5" in one dimension but only 3.4" in the other dimension. To bring up the histogram controls, you click on the color controls icon, where the black cursor is in the middle of this diagram. MagicScan, which is also shipped with other UMax scanners, has a nice set of color controls, though it took me a couple of minutes to find them via this icon.

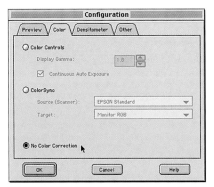

With the Epson Twain Pro software, I used the Color settings in Configuration and the Unsharp Mask setting in Destination to turn off the scanner software's automatic color correction and sharpening of the scan. I like to do these things myself in Photoshop 6 where I get a little more control and I can make the changes in the same way no matter where the scan is coming from. All the scanners I tested actually do a reasonable job of auto color correcting a file, and for people who do a lot of production scans, this may be the way you want to scan. Doing the adjustments manually in Photoshop just gives you ultimate control over highlight and shadow values as well as other decisions.

4x5 photographer. I tried to scan the 3.4" x 5" of my Bandon 4x5 image at 3048 dpi and found that nothing was happening after quite some time so I canceled that scan. The manual gave me the impression, although it was not totally clear on this point, that if I scanned at some even multiple of 3048, I'd still get an optical scan without interpolation. I tried 2286 dpi, 3/4 of 3048, and after 30 minutes of scanning the scan dialog claimed there was still 89% of the scan left to do. I canceled this scan too. I then tried 1524 dpi, 1/2 of 3048, and after 45 minutes of scanning the dialog claimed there was 81% left to scan. At this point I called the product manager, and UMax sent me new PROMs which were supposed to make the scans five times faster…

The new PROMs (programmable roms) arrived and I installed them. With the new proms installed it still took this scanner two hours and 25 minutes to scan a 4x5 at 1524 dpi, which is half of the maximum 3048 dpi. Besides the slowness of the scan, I was only able to scan 3.4 x 5 inches of the 4x5 at that resolution. This seems way to slow to me and I'm usually willing to wait a while for a good scan. The scan that I did get was quite sharp but it had some neuton rings in it, mostly in neutral areas. After waiting that long for a scan, I wasn't about to see if there was a way to get rid of the neuton rings. For a flatbed scanner, the Umax PowerLook 3000 makes quite sharp scans of 35mm film, 120 film and 4x5 but it seems too slow when making larger scans and the main reason for buying it, as it seems to me, would be to get larger scans from 120 and 4x5 film. If you have to do a lot of batch production scans of 35mm, 4x5 and 120 film formats, and the 120 and 4x5 scans are not usually over 1220 dpi then you may find this scanner good for that purpose. I'd test it and time it for your particular needs before buying it though!

EPSON EXPRESSION 1680

The Epson Expression 1680 is the recent update to the popular Epson Expression 1600 flatbed scanner. The new features of note are increased dynamic range to 3.6, and a higher color bit depth of 48 bits. The MSRP for the Pro model, which includes the transparency scanner, is $1,149. It allows you to scan at an optical resolution of up to 1600 x 3200 dpi, although I've found that these unbalanced optical resolutions usually do their best job at the lower balanced number, which would be 1600 x 1600 dpi. The reason for the imbalance in many flatbed scanners is that the scanner's CCD actually gives you only the lower resolution in one direction but the stepper motosr that

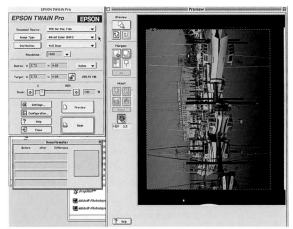

These are the control settings I used to scan the Bandon 4x5 at 1600 dpi with the Epson 1680. Notice that I did the scan a 16 bits per channel, 48 bits total. As with the scans I did with all the scanners, I scanned here with sharpening turned off. I do my sharpening in Photoshop after color correction is finished using Unsharp mask and the Sharpen Only Edges BH action from the ArtistKeys actions set. It took only 10 minutes over the USB bus to scan this 250 meg file directly into Photoshop 6.

Chapter 16: Image Resolution, Scanning Film and Digital Cameras

moves the CCD over the image can actually step at the higher value. With this scanner, we are getting 1600 dpi from the CCD and 3200 from the stepper motor.

This scanner scans the 4x5 Bandon image at 1600 dpi and 48 bits in just 10 minutes to bring the image directly into Photoshop. The time for scanning a 35mm at 1600 and 48 bits was 1 minute and 45 seconds. It took 2 minutes and 18 seconds to scan a 35mm at 3200 dpi. One nice thing about the film holders that come with this scanner and the Epson 1640 XL was that they didn't cut much, if anything, from the edges of the image area. A great thing here was that I was able to scan the full frame of the 35mm shot and very close to the full frame of the 4x5. The film holder for 35mm film did a fine job of keeping my film flat but the one for the 4x5 inch let the film sag a bit in the middle which can give inconsistent focus across the film area.

The Twain software that you see here did not include any histogram options but the SilverFast software, which also comes with both these Epson scanners, does include histogram support. Both the Epson Expression 1680 and 1640 models come with some very useful software bundles. They both come with the Twain and SilverFast software, for scanning, Monaco EZ Color, for making colorsync profiles of your scanner, as well as Photoshop 5 LE. You won't need Photoshop LE if you already have the full version of Photoshop but it does make this scanner bundle a full imaging system for a beginner. The Monaco EZ Color in both scanner packages comes with the IT8 target for making reflected scanning profiles and the Epson 1640 also inclues the 4x5 film IT8 target for making profiles for film scanning. Making a Monaco EZ Color scanner profile will make it easier to have your scan files initially match the colors on your original film.

The problem I've always had when trying to scan film from a flatbed scanner is getting sharp scans. Unlike the Powerlook 3000, many flatbed scanners don't actually have a focus mechanism to focus on the grain of the film, they simply rely on depth of field, making things that are placed either on the glass, or in this case within the supplied film holders, sharp. I have not found a flatbed scanner yet that gives scans as sharp as a film scanner with a good focus mechanism. This Epson 1680 also falls into that category with the film scans not being that sharp compared to the ones on the Imacon or the Nikon LS-2000 for 35mm film. I tried scanning the 35mm sample in the mounted transparency holder, in the

The same area shown below, from the Imacon, left sharpened at 150, 1, 3, and the PowerLook 3000, right sharpened at 150, 1.0, 0.

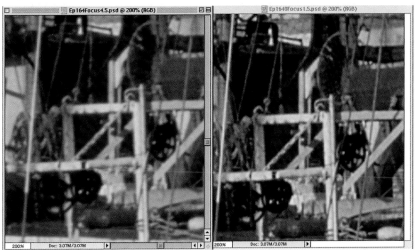

Both these images were sharpened with the Photoshop 6 Unsharp Mask filter after their scans. The image on the right was the best focused scan and the image on the left was the worst focused scan from the Epson 1640 XL. Having the manual focus control on the 1640 did help me to get a sharper scan than the 1680 and also to zero in on the focus position where the image was the sharpest. I didn't find that the auto focus function always optained the sharpest focus point. By trying different settings on a small section of the image, and looking at those sectional scans in Photoshop, I was able to come up with a sharper focus. The software focus comparison tool built into the Twain scanning utility didn't allow me to zoom in close enough or easily pick the point I wanted to focus on. Still, having the additional hardware focus control that the 1640 has was helpful in achieving sharper scans.

The image on the left was scaned at 3200 dpi, the image on the right was scanned at 1600 dpi and resampled up to 3200. Notice the jaggies on diagonal lines in the leftmost image. If you are using the 1680 or 1640 to scan film, especially 35mm film, I find you get better results when scanning at 1600 dpi and then resampling that scan up in Photoshop to 3200 dpi than just doing the scan at 3200 dpi. Diagonal lines have fewer jaggies that way.

strip film holder and directly on the glass and none of these options produced scans anywhere near as sharp as those from the Nikon LS-2000 or the Imacon. The scans from the UMax PowerLook 3000 were also sharper because it has an auto focus mechanism that actually focuses on the film. I also tried scanning using the 1680 with Auto Color Correction and Unsharp Mask turned on during the scan and, although this gave me a pretty good looking image, it still didn't give me anything as sharp as what I was getting from the other scanners. If you scan a 4x5 piece of film with this 1680, or maybe even a 6x6cm image, you can get prints that will appear quite sharp and acceptable to many people. If you compare these scans to ones done with the Imacon scanner, you will definately see that the Imacon scans are considerably sharper. The Imacon does cost 13 times more, however!

EPSON EXPRESSION 1640 XL

The 1640 XL is an A3 size scanner with a maximum scan area of 12.2 x 17.2 inches for flatbed scans and 11.4 x 16.5 for the transparency adaptor. My main interest was in scanning 35mm, 6x6cm and 4x5 inch film so the larger possible size of scans didn't matter much to me. The reason I looked at this scanner, which is very similar to the 1680 in functionality and quality of scans, was that the 1640 has a more adjustable focus than the 1680. The 1640 has an automatic focus mechanism, which didn't really seem to work that well, and it also has a manual focus mechanism whose user interface was also not that useful since it was hard to see the difference between one focus and another. What did help, however, was trying several different focus settings on the same small area of an image by scanning this area about four times with different focus settings. This can be time consuming but the extra sharpness can pay off. Even though I was able to get scans from this scanner that were a bit sharper than the 1680, both these scanners were still not as sharp as any of the other scanners I tested. This doesn't mean though, that you cannot make beautiful prints with these scanners. Several people in my local Photo Arts Guild have the Epson Expression 1600, an earlier version of the 1680, and are very happy with the prints they are making with it. I have also been impressed with their work. If money were no object or if Imacons were cheap, I'd get an Imacon because with it you get sharp detailed scans with very little effort. These two Epson scanners are a lot cheaper and they allow you to do a variety of things besides just scanning film. Another possible approach that is more cost effective is to get a dedicated 35mm film scanner for that smaller film then use one of these Epson scanners for scanning 6x6cm and 4x5 inch film.

Another useful feature of the 1640 is having the larger scanning bed for scanning prints. Some of my friends in the Corvallis Photo Arts guild are making beautiful black and white prints by first making a good 8x10 or 11x14 print in the darkroom then scanning that print on a UMax or Epson scanner. That scan of a print, which these scanners do a great job of, can then be further improved in Photoshop. Let's say for example you shoot a 4x5 original on film and then make an 11x14 very sharp and high quality black and white print from that film in the darkroom. Now you could scan that 11x14 print at 1600 dpi on the Epson 1640 or 1680 scanner and get

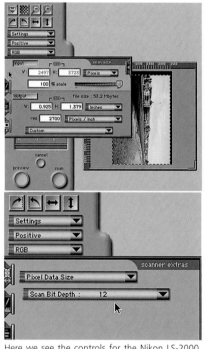

Here we see the controls for the Nikon LS-2000, mentioned on the next page, which is a good 35mm scanner if 2700 dpi is enough to meet your needs. It will certainly scan 35mm sharper than all the flatbed scanners we looked at in this section. The top screen grab shows the controls set for the maximum scan size. The bottom screen grab shows the settings for a 12-bit scan that gives you a 16-bit per channel file in Photoshop as does any scan with more than 8 bits per channel. The other setting that is important with this scanner is the one that tells it to do more than one scan, I usually like four, and average the results for more accuracy.

Chapter 16: Image Resolution, Scanning Film and Digital Cameras

a great scan. After improving the digital file in Photoshop, you could then make a great print with it without resampling and at 300 dpi, this print could be up to 58x75 inches in size. If you wanted to output the image at 600 dpi to an image-setter, this would give you a black and white digital negative at 29x37 inches in size, which you could then very easily contact print back onto darkroom paper. My friend Dave McIntire has been making wonderful black and white prints this way using his Epson 1600 scanner. See the Epson 1680 section above for a list of the software bundle that comes with both Epson scanners.

NIKON LS-2000 SUPER COOLSCAN

This scanner has been around for several years and it only scans 35mm film. I would have bought one long ago except I wanted something that could scan at more than 2700 dpi, which is the maximum for this scanner. I have used quite a few of these however and find that for the money they make really good scans. If you Option-click on the Focus control, you can then click down on the preview of the image to focus on the part of the image that you would like. Doing this or just the general focus on this scanner gives a scan that is often focused quite well on the film grain. Since this section is really about multiformat film scanners, I'm not going to say a lot about this scanner but I am mentioning it because it does do good scans of 35mm, probably better than all the flatbed scanners in this article, and it does this for a pretty good price. If you don't have a lot of money to spend on scanners, a good way to go might be to use the LS-2000 for 35mm scans and then resample these up, if you need to, using the Genuine Fractals software. I've heard that you get better results if you resample the file up using Genuine Fractals after the file is color corrected but before the file is sharpened and then don't do more than a 200% enlargement. If I have time, I'll try this and compare it to the better scans, like those from the Imacon. First I'll scan with the Nikon LS-2000 at 12 bits per pixel using its feature that allows a multi-pass scan. This does several scans and then averages them to get the best results. The option of four scans seems to work well. Then I'd do my overall color correction in Photoshop. Then I'd resample the file up using Genuine Fractals. I'd only sharpen the file at the end using Unsharp Mask or my Sharpen Only Edges BH action script.

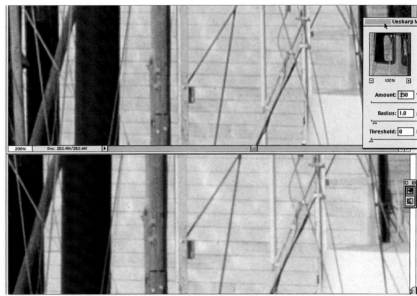

The top image is a section of the Bandon 4x5 image as scanned on the Epson 1640 with the best focus I could get and then sharpened by 350, 1 and 0 using Photoshop's Unsharp Mask. The bottom image is the same section with no sharpening from the Imacon. You can get very useful 4x5 scans from the Epson 1680 or 1640 but you do have to sharpen them a fair amount to get similar sharpness to that from the Imacon without any sharpening. When you sharpen flatbed scans that much, diagonal lines are not quite as natural and you can lose subtle things that were available in the original film. I'm seeing these differences, however, when comparing the two at 100% or 200% on a computer monitor. The average person and, even some photographers I know, comparing prints made from the two may not notice these subtle differences. If you are not sure about the quality you will need, get some sample scans from these different scanners and compare them yourselves.

This is a small section of the Santa Cruz 35mm image that was scanned with the Epson 1640 at 1600 dpi and then sharpened using the Sharpen Only Edges BH action. Using this type of scanner, you will need to do extra sharpening to blow small sections of 35mm up this large.

Comparing Some Current Multiformat Film Scanners

MORE INFO ON OTHER SCANNERS

I'll also be looking at the Microtek Artixscan 4500T, the Polaroid Sprint Scan 45 Ultra, the Polaroid Sprint Scan 120 and the Nikon 8000 for the scanner article I'm writing for the Photo Annual of *Communication Arts* magazine which comes out in late July to early August. Look there for more information on the latest film scanners.

Criteria	TANGO Drum Scanner	NIKON LS-2000	IMACON Precision II	EPSON 1680	UMAX PL3000	POLAROID 45 Ultra	MICROTEK 4500T	NIKON 8000	EPSON 1640 XL	POLAROID Sprintscan 120
35mm Res	9000	2700	5760	1600x3200	3048		2571	4.000	1600x3200	4,000
6x6 Res	9000	N/A	3200	1600x3200	3048		2571	4.000	1600x3200	4,000
4x5 Res	9000	N/A	1800	1600x3200	3048		2571	N/A	1600x3200	N/A
Sharpness	10 Auto	9 Auto	10 Fixed/ Manual	5 Fixed	8 Auto				6 Auto/ Manual	Auto
Density Range			4.1	3.6	3.6		3.9	4.2	3.6	3.9
Scan Bit Depth		12/36	16/48	16/48	14/42		14/42		14/42	14/42
Max File Bit Depth		12/36	16/48	16/48	14/42		14/42		14/42	14/42
Price		Under $900	$14,995	$1,149	$7,695			$2,995	$3,200	$2,795
Ease of Use	7	9	9	9	8		Not Rated Yet	Not Rated Yet	9	Not Rated Yet
35mm Speed	+Mount time		12 mins @ 5760DPI 48 Bit	1 min 45 sec @ 3200 PI 48 Bit	5 mins @ 3048 PPI				1 min 45 sec @ 3200DPI 48 Bit	
4x5 Speed	+Mount time	N/A	14 mins @ 1,800 DPI 48 Bit	7.5–10 min 1,600 DPI 48 Bit	2.5 hours for 1524 DPI				7.5–10 min 1,600 DPI 48 Bit	2 minutes for 6x6@4,000 DPI
Interface	SCSI	SCSI	SCSI	SCSI, USB, IEEE 1394 Firewire Optional	SCSI		SCSI-2	IEEE 1394 Firewire	SCSI, USB, Firewire Optional	SCSI-2, Firewire
Overall Rating	10	8	10	6		Not Rated Yet	Not Rated Yet	Not Rated Yet	7	Not Rated Yet

1 2 3 4 5 6 7 8 9 10   N/A= Not applicable

SCANNER COMPARISON TABLE

Some of the values in this table have not been filled in since they were not available at publication date. For more final information, check my extensive film scanner article that will appear in the August Photo Anual issue of *Communication Arts* magazine and also check the Latest Tips area of my web site at www.barry-haynes.com. Please e-mail me at barry@maxart.com if you have discovered other scanners Photoshop Artistry readers would like to know about.

Chapter 16: Image Resolution, Scanning Film and Digital Cameras

A close up of a section of the 35 mm Santa Cruz boardwalk image scanned at 5760 dpi with the Imacon and zoomed to 100% within Photoshop.

The same area scanned at 2700 dpi with the Nikon LS-200 and zoomed to 200% in Photoshop. All images on this page have been color corrected.

Scanned at 5000 dpi with the Lino Tango Drum scanner zoomed to 100% within Photoshop and color corrected within Photoshop.

A Photo CD Pro scan done at Palmer's at 4000 dpi zoomed into 100% in Photoshop and color corrected in Photoshop.

The same area scanned at 3048 dpi with the UMax Powerlook 3000 and zoomed to 200% in Photoshop, color corrected by me in Photoshop.

The same area scanned at 3200 dpi with the Epson 1680 and zoomed to 200% in Photoshop also color corrected by me in Photoshop.

Each of the images above was scanned with the perspective scanner at the stated dpi without any sharpening turned on in the scanner. The amount of sharpness that you see here is a factor of the focus and scanner optics without software Unsharp Masking. Each of these images can be further sharpened using either the scanner's sharpening software or Unsharp Mask in Photoshop. Looking at the unsharpened files gives you a way to compare the hardware and focus on the scanners. Even my friend Bill with his Lino Tango Drum scanner does his sharpening in Photoshop using his Sharpen Only Edges action script; included in ArtistKeys.

Working with Digital Cameras

I have not used a lot of digital cameras myself, probably based on my early experience with digital cameras and the thought I always have, when taking a photograph, that I might want to blow up the image to make a larger print. My first digital camera was purchased for about $10,000 back around 1988 and was a Canon 760 Still Video camera. I was doing digital research at Apple at the time and had a nice budget for buying the latest toys. That toy looked and felt like an SLR but the pictures it took were not impressive at all. Why pay that much money to get images that you could get with a much cheaper video camera? I'm glad that digital cameras have improved a lot since then! Still, even today, only the most expensive digital cameras can match the quality and detail I can get with a 200 meg 16-bit per channel drum or Imacon scan from a 35mm original. If that original were a 6x6cm or a 4x5 inch piece of film, most digital cameras can't touch that detail. The ones that can are very expensive scanning back types of cameras that usually don't stop motion. Digital cameras are improving all the time but the cost of the camera is usually far greater than what it costs to get the same or better results from a film camera. When your output process requires a digital file, however, then you do need to add in the cost of scanning that film into the computer. From what we have seen here, depending on your quality needs, that cost can be up to $14,995 for an Imacon scanner. Add to the cost of a possible scanner purchase, the cost in time spent processing and scanning, and the environmental chemical impact when processing film.

There are a lot of very useful digital cameras, especially for the studio photographer. This type of photography either doesn't require stopping motion and doesn't require the large print size with minute details that a landscape photographer, like myself, would demand. Digital cameras in a studio make sense for a number of reasons. When you have to shoot many images during a day's work, a digital camera saves you the time and money it takes to process and scan all that film. You know as soon as you have shot it whether you got the shot you needed, since you can bring it right up on your computer screen. The client can also potentially walk away with the required digital files at the end of the shooting session instead of waiting for film processing and scanning. There are several books about digital cameras; the trouble is though, the camera models and features change so quickly, the books become outdated soon after they are printed.

My First Useful Digital Camera, the Epson PhotoPC 3000Z

Lately my interest in digital cameras has been increasing. I read an article that compared digital cameras costing less than $1,000. That article rated the Epson PhotoPC 3000Z with the best overall rating, although it also had much praise for the Nikon 990. I've heard good reports from photographer friends about the 990. Epson was kind enough to lend me an evaluation unit of the 3000Z and using it has shown me several very good reasons to have a digital camera. First of all, THEY ARE FUN! You shoot pictures and then get to see them right away using the viewing screen on the back of the camera. This is great for photos of kids and family events. I found that with the Epson I shoot pictures with no concern about running out of film, having to get the film processed or even if it would make a good shot. Because of this attitude change, I have more fun and get some great shots I would otherwise not take. When I've filled the camera's CompactFlash memory, if I still need to take a picture or two, I can look through the photos I've taken, using the built-in screen, and delete the ones I don't like to make room for a few more.

The Epson PhotoPC 3000Z, and many other digital cameras, do a better job than film capturing low light situations. I've also been carrying around a compact Canon Sure Shot Z90W, which is one of the smallest 35mm pocket zoom film cameras. The Epson 3000Z is able to capture many low light images that the Canon, with ASA 100 film, cannot. This is all casual hand held shooting I'm talking about. I know film can often capture in low light when you are shooting with a tripod and using a camera with absolute manual controls and a good light meter. It's nice to be able to capture these low light images, as I can with the 3000Z, just handheld and often without a flash.

I like being able to hook the 3000Z up to my Apple PowerBook G3 and very quickly download the entire 16 megs of images from the camera over the built-in USB interface. Once that is done, I can flush the camera's memory with two button presses and I'm ready to shoot more images. I have been using this camera with the 16 meg CompactFlash card that comes with it. It allows me to shoot about 32 of the 2048x1536 jpeg images that I find most useful or up to 150 640x480 images. One can mix all four of the built-in image sizes at will until the memory is full. If you need to shoot more, you can get extra CompactFlash cards or buy larger ones . The rechargeable batteries that come with this camera seem to retain their charge for a large number of shots and are easy to recharge with the included battery charger.

I have been having a lot of fun with the Epson 3000Z and getting some great shots. My only suggestion is that I'd like the cycle time between shots to be faster. This camera has three resolutions that I've found useful. The 640x480 size has a very fast recycle time, and is a great size for Web images, but really is too small for most print purposes. The next two resolutions are 2048x1536 pixels with either a medium or high quality jpeg compression. The medium compression is better for shooting because the highest quality compression takes longer between shots. If you have the time, then the higher quality compression is still useful and will give you a better image. There is an even bigger size of 2544x1904 but this takes even longer between shots since the camera is resampling up from the 2048x1536 size. I can resample up using Photoshop, which seems to make more sense than waiting for the camera to do it, so I don't use this biggest format. Finally, you can photograph an uncompressed 9 megabyte TIFF file but this takes very long for the camera to process and uses up 9 megs of the camera's memory. Maybe I'd use this in the studio when photographing a still life but that is about the only time I'd use it. For the photograph I took of my PowerBook, which you open and use in Chapter 30: "The PowerBook Ad", I used the higher quality 2048x1536 jpeg setting. This camera also allows audio annotations of your shots. I was taking some photos on the beach, wanted release info from some people in the shots and I didn't have a pen or paper. That was a good time to use the annotation feature. The 3000Z will even take video clips of up to 30 seconds; I haven't tried that feature yet.

Digital Cameras Versus Film

Many photographers who attend my workshops have also brought in great images shot with the Nikon 990, the Nikon D1, and the Kodack DCS 5000, among others. One could write a separate book on all the digital cameras then many of them would become outdated by the time the book reached the stores. For doing landscape photography, I'm planning to use film for now and give digital cameras another few years to evolve. For family photos and studio work, digital cameras are there now and have a lot of advantages since you don't have to take the time or make the expense of getting your film processed and getting prints made. I can make very nice quality 8x10 prints and maybe sometimes larger with the 3000Z images I've been taking. I'm sure once this book is finished, I'll be spending time doing exactly that. This is not a comparison of digital cameras or a recommendation of any in particular. I am quite happy with the Epson PhotoPC 3000Z but I haven't really tried its competitors. If I do try any other digital cameras, I'll let you know what I think about them on my web site in the Latest Tips section at www.barryhaynes.com.

The Fitness Center images below show a comparison between the Epson PhotoPC 3000Z, on the right, and the Canon Sure Shot Z90W on the left. Both cameras were mounted on a tripod while taking these shots. I took the picture of the Corvallis Fitness Center because of the sharp contrasty colors, lines and text. The 3000Z was set at the highest quality 2048x1536 jpeg setting and the Canon Sure Shot Z90W was using ASA 400 Fuji film. Even with the 400 ASA film, notice that the blow up of the signs, at the bottom of the page, show the extra detail captured on the film. If I had used Fuji Velvia, ASA 50, or some of the other new fine grain films, and/or a more expensive 35mm camera, I'd be able to make a much larger blow up of a 35mm film image than one shot with this, or any, 3.3 megapixel digital camera. For a nice 8x10 print of this building, though, the digital camera shot was available right away and if the photo was poor, I'd know right away and could reshoot it. I could have had that print within five minutes of taking the photograph. That often means a lot to a lot of people including myself.

The Canon Sure Shot Z90W with ASA 400 Fuji Film.

Epson Photo PC 3000Z with best jpeg setting giving a 2048x1536 file.

Zoomed in on a Small Section of the Canon Sure Shot image above.

The same area of the above digital file.

Chapter 16: Image Resolution, Scanning Film and Digital Cameras

Blue Egret and reflections in water.

Clouds and blue sky reflections with green water plants.

Grass and Sky Reflections.

Silver Reeds.

Sunset at Swamp. Taken hand held after my friend no longer had enough light to shoot with his film camera on a tripod.

Sunset at Swamp version two. Also taken hand held after my friend no longer had enough light to shoot with his film camera on a tripod.

These images were all taken by Barry Haynes with the Epson PhotoPC 3000Z digital camera while shooting pictures during the Fotofusion conference at Palm Beach Photographic Center in Del Ray Beach Florida. These images were all taken at the 2048x1536 size and were later color corrected in Photoshop.

STEPS TO CREATE A MASTER IMAGE

Choosing your color working space, the color correction process, archiving the master and then targeting resampled versions for different uses, sharpening, soft-proofing, device-specific tweaking, and saving final output files.

CHOOSING YOUR MASTER COLOR SPACE

Versions of Photoshop before version 5 assumed the gamut of your RGB working space was the same as the gamut of your monitor. Photoshop 5 allowed you to choose an RGB or Lab workspace that is not limited by the gamut of a particular monitor or device. You need to decide which RGB working space, or the LAB space, you are going to use as your default color working space. To help you in making this decision, you should read Chapter 14: "Color Spaces, Device Characterization and Color Management." This chapter is an overview of the workflow we suggest you use to create master images within your default color working space, and then color correct those images, archive the final color correct master and, finally, output copies of it to several different device-specific color spaces, like CMYK, the LightJet 5000 color laser printer, the Epson 2000 inkjet printer, a film recorder, and also to the Web.

GETTING AND CONVERTING YOUR SCAN OR DIGITAL FILE

I create my master digital photographs from scans that are big enough to make the largest print that I might want. In scanning 35mm color transparency film, experimentation has shown that a scan from a good drum scanner of around 5,000 dpi will get all the information from the film. Good scans from an Imacon scanner or some of the new higher resolution desktop scanners, or even correctly done Photo CD Pro scans, at 4,000 dpi, also do a pretty good job. For larger film formats, like 4x5 for example, a smaller dpi will often give you as big a file as you will need. Many scanners these days allow you to obtain a file with more than 8 bits of information per channel. If you want to get the most information from the scanner, start with a file of up to 16 bits per channel. If getting your work done as quickly as possible is your goal, then letting the scanner software convert the file down to 8 bits per pixel will probably save you time. When working with a digital camera, one would use either the largest resolution the camera could get or the resolution needed for the job at hand. See Chapter 16: "Image Resolution, Scanning Film and Digital Cameras" for more information about scanning, resolution, file sizes, etc. It would then usually be best to use the scanner software or Image/Mode/Convert to Profile to

Here we see the Image/Mode/Convert to Profile dialog showing a conversion from a Nikon LS 2000 scan into the Adobe RGB color space. For images one would usually use the Perceptual Intent but if you are not happy with that, you could also try Relative Colorimetric and you could try turning on Use Black Point Compensation if you are not happy with the way the shadow areas of the image are converted.

convert the scanner output file from a source ICC profile that describes the color gamut of the scanner into the destination color gamut of your preferred RGB or Lab working space. Depending on where I get the scan, I usually use either the Adobe RGB color space or the LAB color space to do my color corrections and create my master images. When I'm working with an image that is exclusively for CMYK presses, I may choose ColorMatch RGB as my RGB working space. I use the word master image because once this image has been color corrected, I should not normally need to color correct it again to be able to print it with the same, or very similar, color on a number of different devices.

COLOR CORRECTING YOUR SCAN OR DIGITAL CAMERA IMAGE

Even after getting a great scan or digital camera image, you usually need to do some further color correction work. The first step in color correction is to work some more on the histograms until you get them as close to perfect as you can given the data available. Before you start the color correction process, make sure that your Photoshop preferences are set up correctly for all the color spaces you will be working in for this project, that is, if your RGB working space is Adobe RGB, but you will print a version of this image in CMYK on a sheet fed press, you need to be sure your prefs are set up correctly for your RGB working space and your CMYK working space for that press and paper. The parts of the preferences that affect color correction and the appearance of images onscreen are all described in Chapter 15: "Photoshop Color Preferences, Monitor, Scanner and Printer Calibration." You should usually do your color correction in a specific order following a recipe you will become very familiar with. The next few pages offer an overview of the order and steps you should use in making color corrections and in creating a master image, and your device-specific images. Chapter 19: "Overall Color Correction" goes into much greater detail, as it follows this process step-by-step while working on a photograph.

GETTING SET UP TO COLOR CORRECT

The first step in color correcting is to bring up the Info palette by choosing Window/Show Info (F9). The Info palette shows you the RGB and CMYK values of the current location of the Eyedropper tool while in Curves, Levels, Hue/Saturation or any color correction tool. It also shows you how your color correction is modifying these values by displaying before values on the left of the slash and after values on the right. When you move the cursor into the Levels or Curves dialog boxes, the values in the regular Info palette go away, but you can use a Color Sampler to keep track of values at specific locations you choose or you can use the Color palette to keep track of values at the last location you clicked with the Eyedropper. The Color Sampler tool is grouped with the Eyedropper Tool pop-up menu in the Tool palette. To add a color sampler value to the Info palette, just click on the image using the Color Sampler tool or Shift-click when in the regular Eyedropper tool. The Color Sampler values, up to four per image, show up at the bottom of the Info palette. It is useful to always have the Info palette and, sometimes, the Color palette showing when you are making color corrections. When you click in a particular location with the Eyedropper, the values in that location show up in the Color palette. These values change only when you click in a new location or use Levels, Curves or Hue/Saturation to make a color adjustment that affects the location where you last clicked. When you use all color correction tools, the color values at all the color sampler locations are updated to reflect any changes in color.

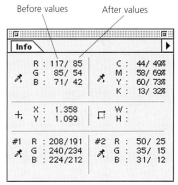

Before values   After values

Here we see an Info palette with the standard RGB and CMYK readouts as well as two of the possible four Color Sampler readouts. The Info palette shows you the original values, upon entering the tool, on the left of the slash. On the right, after the slash, it displays the values resulting from the tool's adjustments since you entered it this time.

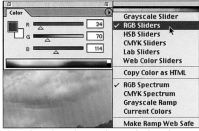

The Color palette shows values at the last place you clicked. You can see how the values at that location change when you make an adjustment using one of the color correction tools. The color bars in the Color palette give you hints as to how adding or subtracting one of the color components will change the color of the last place you clicked. The Color palette can display color bars in grayscale, RGB, HSB, CMYK, LAB and Web colors. You can use the spectrum at the bottom of this palette to pick a new color by clicking on it. That spectrum can be in the RGB, CMYK, Grayscale ramp or Current Colors space. Current Colors gives you a ramp from the current foreground color to the current background color.

Before you start any color correcting, make a copy of the original scan and color correct the copy, so that you can return to that original if you make any mistakes. You also want to make sure your original scan is scanned for the biggest possible usage for that image. For example, I make 16x25 prints of my 35mm transparencies. For this type of print, I scan at 5,000dpi, which also gets all the possible info from the film and gives me about a 100Mb file. I do my color corrections on this file, which becomes my master image after it is corrected. I can then resample the file down for smaller prints, this book and for my Web site. The basic order for color correction when starting with an RGB scan is as follows:

OVERALL COLOR CORRECTION
(16-BIT IMAGE/ADJUST-SAVE, 8-BIT ADJUSTMENT LAYERS)

Step 1.   Go into Levels.
    a.   Set the Highlight.
    b.   Set the Shadow.
    c.   Adjust the overall brightness of the image.
    d.   Go into the Red, Green or Blue Levels channel and remove color casts, being especially careful that neutral colors stay neutral and don't have a cast.
    e.   Save your Levels or Curves settings in a Levels or Curves adjustment layer, so you can change them later without image degradation.

Step 2.   If needed, use the RGB channel of Curves to adjust the overall contrast of the image and the Red, Green or Blue channels to adjust color casts in particular color ranges within the entire image.

Step 3.   Use Hue/Saturation to increase or decrease overall saturation. Make adjustments to the hue, saturation and lightness of specific color areas. (At this point, use Image/Mode/8-Bits/Channel to convert 16-bit image to 8–bit.)

COLOR CORRECTION OF SPECIFIC AREAS USING MASKS, SPOTTING

Step 4.   Make color changes to specific image areas using Levels, Curves, Hue/Saturation and other adjustment layers each with a mask to isolate its target correction area. There can be as many of these as needed to get the job done.

Step 5.   Remove Spots and Scratches from your Master Image and do any required retouching.

Step 6.   Save and archive your Master Image on disk and then to a CD. Make a copy of important CDs and put them at an off-site location.

RESAMPLE A COPY, SHARPEN, CONVERT, FINAL TWEAKS

At this point, you have a color-corrected Master RGB or Lab image. You will archive this Master Image and then resample a copy of it down, or sometimes up if needed, for each different specific usage of that image. After the copy image is resampled to the final size, you will do a final sharpening and spotting. You can print resampled copies of this image directly to RGB printers, or output to an RGB film recorder to make transparencies. If you have a profile for the output device, you would first do Image/Mode/Convert to Profile to convert the specific copy from your RGB working space into the space for that printer. You can use a specific copy for

Web and multimedia projects and as the final file if you use a third-party method to convert your images to CMYK on-the-fly from Photoshop or Quark. You can also use Image/Mode/CMYK to convert an image to CMYK using Photoshop for separations.

Step 7. Resample each copy of the image to final size and do final sharpening, and after the sharpen, a final spotting.

Step 8. If you are going to output files to a LightJet 5000, Epson 1270 or other RGB printer that you have an accurate ICC profile for, use Image/Mode/Convert to Profile to convert to that RGB color space. Photoshop will then give you a soft proof of what your converted image will look like in that color space on that device. If you need CMYK, convert to CMYK using Image/Mode/CMYK. This will automatically soft proof the converted file using the simulated CMYK colors on your screen.

Step 9. Make minor color adjustments to specific color areas using Hue/Saturation, Curves and Selective Color with or without selections. This is often not needed.

OVERALL COLOR CORRECTION DETAILS

USE 8 BITS/CHANNEL OR 16 BITS/CHANNEL FILES

When color correcting your image, it is helpful to do as many of the color correction steps as possible using adjustment layers. Each new step is added as a new adjustment layer on the top of the Layers palette with the bottom layer being your original scan which remains unmodified as long as you do all your work with Adjustment layers. If you are working with a file from your scanner that has more than 8 bits per channel of color information, you will not be able to use layers or Adjustment layers with that file until you convert it to 8 bits per channel. Whether your scanner saves 10 bits, 12 bits, 14 bits or 16 bits per channel of information, as long as it is over 8 bits per channel, it will show up in Photoshop at Image/Mode/16 Bits/Channel. You will not be able to use layers or Adjustment layers with this larger bit depth file until you convert the file to 8 bits per channel using Image/Mode/8 Bits/Channel.

When working with a 16-bit per channel file, you will often do your overall color correction steps, steps one through three, using Image/Adjust/Levels, Image/Adjust/Curves and Image/Adjust/Hue/Saturation. Each step done this way will modify your original background permanently versus steps in an adjustment layer that don't modify your original background layer. When using Image/Adjust/..., you should click on the Save button before choosing OK in Levels, Curves or Hue/Saturation. This will allow you to save the settings you used for that step so you can change them later if you are not happy with the results. To change them though, you would have to go back to your original, unmodified scan and start over versus just double-clicking and changing an adjustment layer. The advantage of doing your first three overall color correction steps on a 16-bit file is that a 16-bit file has up to 65,536 tonal values per color channel, where an 8-bit file only has 256 tonal values per channel. You can make many color adjustments and mode conversions to a 16-bit file and yet, when you convert it down to 8-bits of information, you still get a very accurate 8-bit file with a great histogram. If you make many color changes or mode conversions on 8-bit files, they start to loose details.

After doing the overall color correction steps, one through three, on a 16-bit per channel file, you will use Image/Mode/8 Bits/Channel to convert that file to 8 bits per channel. If you plan to convert the file from LAB to Adobe RGB or from your scanner's RGB space to Adobe RGB, or ColorMatch RGB, you might want to do that conversion while still in 16 Bits/Channel space, and then convert down to 8 bits per channel. That will make it less likely that your 8-bit file will have lost information due to the mode conversion.

Steps 4 through 8 in creating the master image will usually be done in 8 bits per channel color, so you can do them using adjustment layers and masks.

STEP 1-A, SETTING THE HIGHLIGHT

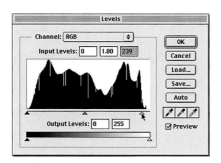

It is often hard to distinguish what point is the brightest on the computer screen. You can find the highlight by holding down the Option key while moving the RGB Highlight slider to the left. The first area to turn white on the screen is usually where you want to look for the highlight. Make sure you move the slider back to 255 when you see where the highlight is. For this to work with Photoshop 6, you need to do it with the Preview checkbox checked. Photoshop 6 no longer supports Video LUT animation on the Mac or PC so the way you did it with earlier versions of Photoshop on the Mac having the Preview checkbox off no longer works.

With a 16-bit per channel file, go to Image/Adjust/Levels (Command-L); with an 8 bit per channel file you will create a Levels Adjustment layer. Creating a Levels Adjustment layer can be done using Layer/New Adjustment Layer/Levels, from the pop-down icon at the bottom of the Layers palette, or by using Command-F2 with ArtistKeys. Within the Levels dialog, you work in Channel RGB, the composite channel, to set the highlight and shadow. The *highlight* is the brightest point in the image where you still want to have texture. Everything brighter than the highlight prints totally white, with no dots. The RGB values here should read somewhere in the range of 240 to 250, depending on your device. Remember that after you set the highlight, everything brighter than the highlight location will usually print totally white. Setting the highlight also removes color casts from the whole highlight part of your image. You need to set the highlight at a place you want to be white in the end, a place that was white in the original scene as well as at a location you want to print as a neutral value. You want to pick a spot where the detail or texture is just fading but is not completely gone. This usually falls at the brighter end of Zone IX in the Zone System. If you Shift-click at the spot where you want to set your highlight, this will place a Color Sampler there and allow you to follow the color values of this spot throughout the entire color correction process...a very useful thing to do. Now, using the rightmost highlight Eyedropper, click at the location where you want to set the highlight (where you just set your Color Sampler), and at the same time, watch how the Info palette shows the values (before and after in RGB and CMYK, or LAB). When you click, the after values should change to the default preference white point values or very close to those values. Because not all images have a good white point, you can also set the highlight by going into each of the Red, Green and Blue color channels and moving its Highlight slider separately. The Highlight slider is the rightmost slider in the top set of three sliders. We'll show you exactly how to find and set these highlights in the step-by-step examples starting with Chapter 19: "Overall Color Correction."

STEP 1-B, SETTING THE SHADOW

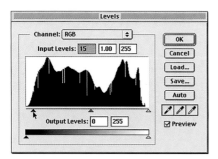

It is often hard to distinguish what point is the darkest on the computer screen. You can find the shadow by holding down the Option key while moving the RGB Shadow slider to the right. The first area to turn black on the screen is where you want to look for the shadow. Make sure you move the slider back to 0 when you see where the shadow is. For this to work with Photoshop 6, you need to do it with the Preview checkbox checked. Photoshop 6 no longer supports Video LUT animation on the Mac or PC so the way you did it with earlier versions of Photoshop on the Mac having the Preview checkbox off no longer works.

Now pick the point where you want to set the shadow. The RGB values here should read about 5 to 10. It should be at a location you want to print with a neutral shadow value. This location would be at the darker end of Zone I in the Zone System. Everything darker than this point usually prints as totally black after you set the shadow. If you want a lot of totally black places in your image, set the shadow at a location that isn't very dark, say 15, 15, 15. Everything darker than that location goes black. If you want a lot of shadow detail in your image, set the shadow at a location that is as close as possible to 0, 0, 0 in RGB. If you Shift-click at the spot where you want to set your shadow, this will place a Color Sampler there and allow you to follow the color values of this spot throughout the entire color correction process.

Chapter 17: Steps to Create a Master Image

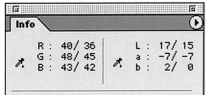

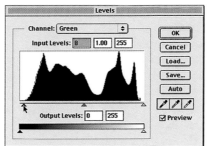

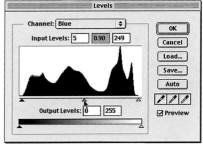

R : 40/ 36   L : 17/ 15
G : 48/ 45   a : -7/ -7
B : 43/ 42   b : 2/ 0

Here we can see the unbalanced values in the Color Sampler number 2. The green value is more than red or blue.

Make the change using the Shadow slider from the Green channel while looking at the values in the Color Sampler in the Info palette.

Now the Color Sampler shows the correction implemented to neutralize the shadow value in green.

Using the leftmost shadow Eyedropper, click at the location where you want to set the shadow (where you just set your Color Sampler), and at the same time, watch how the Info palette shows the values (before and after in RGB and CMYK (or LAB)). When you click, the after values should change to the default preference black point values or very close to those values. Because not all images have a good shadow point, you can also set the shadow by going into each of the Red, Green and Blue color channels and moving its Shadow slider separately. The Shadow slider is the leftmost slider in the top set of three sliders. We'll show you exactly how to set these in the step-by-step examples starting with Chapter 19: "Overall Color Correction."

These initial RGB highlight and shadow values vary somewhat from image to image. The purpose of setting the white and black is to normalize these values to neutral grays and also to set the endpoints of detail in the reproduction. Some images do not have a good point at which to set the highlight and shadow with the Eyedroppers. See the Chapter 20: "Correcting a Problem Image" and Chapter 27: "Bryce Stone Woman" for examples of how to deal with that situation.

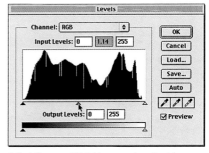

Adjust the overall brightness and contrast by moving the middle slider using Channel RGB.

Step 1-C, Adjusting the Overall Brightness

Use the RGB channel of Levels again for this step. Move the middle slider, in the top set of three sliders, to the right to make the image darker. Move it to the left to make the image brighter. Move it around until the image has the level of brightness that you want. If the image is too flat or too contrasty, you will adjust that in your next tool by adding a contrast adjustment curve. When working with an image in LAB format color, you would do all the work we've covered so far using only the Lightness channel.

Step 1-D, Adjusting the Overall Color Cast

If the overall image seems too green, use the Channel pop-up to go to the Green channel in Levels and move the top middle slider to the right. This will add magenta to the midpoint values in the image and remove the green cast. Moving it to the left would add green. If the image is too blue, go to the Blue channel and move the middle slider to the right to add yellow to the image. You just need to remember that the Red channel controls red and its complement, cyan; the Green channel, green and magenta; and the Blue channel, blue and yellow. When adjusting an image for color casts, try to remove the worst color cast first and then move on to the lesser ones. You do it in this order because removing one cast will change the appearance of the others. The middle sliders of each channel are going to mostly affect the midtones as well as the quartertones and three-quartertones.

The rightmost Highlight and leftmost Shadow sliders should have already been adjusted correctly when you set the highlight and shadow earlier, but you can always

Now deal with color casts by adjusting the middle slider in the color channel that affects the color cast.

Overall Color Correction Details

tweak them after setting the middle slider if you need to. If your highlight and shadow Color Sampler positions are no longer neutral (the same value in Red, Green and Blue), that is a sign that you may want to tweak them. Sometimes you can get a color cast in the highlight or the shadow if the point at which you set the highlight was not a neutral location. Some images do not have neutral locations. Use the High-light or Shadow sliders for the color channel(s) that are out of adjustment to correct the numbers in the Color palette or Color Sampler. Afterward, you may have to go back to readjust the midtone sliders to slightly adjust the midtone color cast again.

You should modify all these corrections in the Levels dialog box as one step. You don't want to click on OK until you complete all these steps. If you choose OK too many times in the Color Adjustment dialog boxes, you can degrade the image, espe-cially when you are not using adjustment layers. You don't want to go into Levels or Curves repeatedly. Do it all in one step if possible, and then go back and tweak it later if you did it with adjustment layers. If you are working with 16-bit per channel files, and therefore not using adjustment layers, you should click on the Save button in the Levels dialog to save your settings in case you want to redo this process with a tweak here or there later. After you finish all the above color correction steps in Levels, and only then, choose OK in the Levels dialog box. To have the ability to modify your changes over and over again when working with 8 bits per channel, do this step with an adjustment layer. For hands-on examples using these techniques, see Chapter 19: "Overall Color Correction," Chapter 20: "Correcting a Problem Image," and Chapter 24: "Desert Al." If you find that doing a color shift by moving the middle slider of a color channel in Levels affects the brightness and contrast too much, you can use the Color Balance tool with Preserve Luminosity turned on. This will change the color without changing the brightness or contrast. If you were work-ing in LAB color, you would make these cast changes using the A and B channels of a LAB image and they would not affect the brightness or contrast.

STEP-2, ADJUSTING THE OVERALL CONTRAST AND SPECIFIC COLOR RANGES

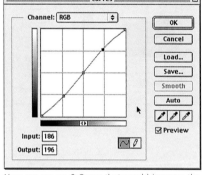

Here we see an S-Curve that would increase the contrast in the file it was applied to.

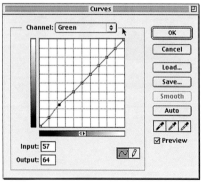

Here we see a lock down curve to pop the greens in the three quarter tones.

Use the RGB Channel of Curves for this step with Image/Adjust/Curves for 16 bit per channel images or Layer/New Adjustment Layer/Curves for 8 bit per chan-nel images. If your image is too flat or too contrasty, Option-click inside the curve graph until you get the graph with four sections each, horizontally and vertically. Place a point at each of the three intersections along the diagonal line going from the bottom left to the top right. To make the image more contrasty, move the top right point up and to the left and move the bottom-left point down and to the right. This creates a curve that looks like an S. To make the image less contrasty, move the top-right point down and to the right and move the bottom-left point up and to the left. This creates a reverse S curve. If you need to enhance a specific range of color within the entire image, Option-click within the curve graph until you get the graph with 10 sections each, horizontally and vertically. Go to the color channel that will most affect the color you want to change. This would be the Red channel for red and cyan, the Green channel for green and magenta and the Blue channel for blue and yellow. Click on the intersection of every graph point along the line going from bottom-left to top-right. This will lock down the curve in each place. Now put the Eyedropper cursor over the color area you want to modify and with the mouse button held down, move the cursor over the range of color you want to change. A larger circle will appear on the curve diagram showing you the range of values in that color channel that affect that part of the image you want to change. Remove the lock down points from the graph within that range by clicking on each point and dragging it entirely

Chapter 17: Steps to Create a Master Image

outside the Curve dialog box. Now click a new point along the diagonal line in the center of that range and drag it up and to the left to add red, green or blue, or down and to the right to add cyan, magenta or yellow. Don't make too radical of a curve adjustment or you'll notice that the colors will become posterized. Choose OK if you are in an adjustment layer, or Save, to save your Curve settings, and then OK if you are not in an adjustment layer.

Step 3, Making Overall and Selected Changes to Hue, Saturation and Lightness

You often want to increase the overall saturation or colors using the Hue/Saturation tool, especially if you had to brighten the image in Curves or Levels. With 8-bit per channel images, do Layer/New Adjustment Layer/Hue/Saturation. With 16-bit images do, Image/Adjust/Hue/Saturation. To increase the overall saturation, move the Saturation slider to the right with Master selected in the Edit pop-up menu. You can also selectively correct color if a certain color range in the image is off. For example, if the reds in the image were too orange, you could make them redder by first selecting Reds from the Edit pop-up and then moving the Hue slider toward the left. This operation would add magenta to only the red areas of the image. This method differs from adding magenta using Levels or Curves because the latter method usually adds magenta to all colors in the image.

When the Red Edit menu item is selected, only the parts of the image that are red have their color changed. If these parts were unsaturated, you could add saturation to just the red items by moving the Saturation slider with Red selected. Similarly, you could add or subtract lightness in the reds. If your image contains different tones of red, and you only want to adjust some of them, you can use the Eyedroppers in the Hue/Saturation dialog to fine-tune the range of reds you want to adjust by adding to the default red tones using the +Eyedropper tool, and subtracting from the default red tones using the –Eyedropper tool. Choose OK if you are in an Adjustment layer or Save, to save your Hue/Saturation settings, and then OK if you are not in an Adjustment layer. The Color Range, Replace Color and Selective Color tools are also good choices for tweaking colors and you could use them at this point in a similar way.

If you are working on a 16-bit per channel image at this point, you should choose File/Save or Save As to save the 16-bit version; then choose Image/Mode/8 Bits/Channel to convert the file to 8 bits per channel color. Now Save the 8-bit version using a different name so your 16-bit version will still be there. If you were already working on an 8-bit per channel image, you will just continue to add more adjustment layers in the following steps.

Color Correcting Specific Area Details

Step 4, Making Color Changes to Isolated Areas Using Selections, Layer Masks, and Adjustment Layers Along with Levels, Curves, and Hue/Saturation

The color corrections I have discussed so far have been overall color corrections to an entire image. If a particular area is the wrong color, too light or too dark, too flat or too contrasty or if you want to tweak it in one of thousands of ways, you now should make a selection of that area using Photoshop's selection and masking tools. Then you may want to adjust the colors in that area using Levels, Curves, Hue/Saturation, Color Balance, etc., but in all cases doing this with an adjustment layer gives you the ability to change the correction or the mask, which determines exactly what gets corrected.

When you have a selection on the screen, creating an adjustment layer at that point automatically sets up the selection as the layer mask for that adjustment layer, so only the selected part is adjusted. The selection's marching ants go away and are replaced by white in that adjustment layer's layer mask. After making the adjustment, you can later go back and tweak the mask, and thus exactly what is being adjusted, by using the painting tools. Painting with white adds to the adjusted area and painting with black takes away from it. You have much more fine control when painting in a mask using the painting tools than you do when editing a selection using the selection tools. You often want to use the selection tools to create an initial rough selection, then edit the corresponding mask with the painting tools to make your selection perfect. Each new adjustment layer you add will tweak a particular part of the image and should usually be added to the top of all the other adjustment layers you have created so far.

Go through Chapter 20: "Correcting a Problem Image," Chapter 27: "Bryce Stone Woman" and Chapter 24: "Desert Al," for a complete description and some hands-on practice in using these techniques to change isolated areas.

STEP 5, SPOTTING THE IMAGE

You will want to clean up your master image by removing spots, scratches and other blemishes with either the Rubber Stamp tool or the Dust and Scratches filter. You will usually do this to the bottom layer in your Layres palette, which will be your original scan. If you have to do some complicated retouching, you can do that on a copy of your original scan layer or a section of your original scan layer. That way, if you make a mistake, you won't have damaged your original scan layer. You can also merge all your layers into a new "Merged" layer at the top of all your existing layers and then spot that. If you spot the original scan at the bottom of the Layers palette, you won't need to respot if you later change any of your adjustment layers. This does make permanent changes to this layer, however (although you could spot a copy right above the bottom layer). If you spot a "Merged" layer on top of all the others, as we do in Chapter 24: "Desert Al," you will have to respot this if you make any changes to the adjustment layers underneath. Still, you save time by spotting the master image because you only do that once; then the spots that have to be removed after you sharpen each resampled version later will be a lot fewer or possibly none. Many of the step-by-step examples show you how to spot your with different techniques.

STEP 6, SAVING YOUR MASTER IMAGE

After spotting, your master image is ready to be saved and archived. You can now use this image for any future projects or prints to RGB printers, film recorders, CMYK print jobs, Web or for multimedia use. For any of these uses, you will make a flattened copy of the master, rename it, resample it to the size needed and convert it to the format needed for this particular purpose.

RESAMPLE COPY, SHARPEN, CONVERT, TWEAK DETAILS

STEP 7-A, MAKING RESAMPLED COPIES FOR EACH USAGE

With your master image opened, you can choose File/Save a Copy to save a flattened version without extra channels on the disk. This can then be opened, resampled and saved for a particular project. You can also choose Image/Duplicate and turn on Duplicate Merged Layers Only to make a nonlayered copy of the master that

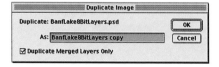

You can use Image/Duplicate Image to make on screen copies of your Master image, one for each usage. Choose Duplicate Merged Layers Only to compress all the layers in the master into just one layer in the duplicate.

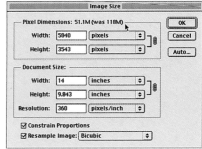

The Image Size dialog in the illustration to the right does not allow you to crop and resample your image at the same time. To do that, you want to use the Cropping tool with Fixed Target Sizes as shown here.

is already open and on your screen. After you have one of these copies up on the screen, you need to choose Image/Image Size, or use the Crop tool with a fixed Height, Width and Resolution to resample the image to the size and resolution you need for this particular project. See Chapter 16: "Image Resolution, Scanning Film and Digital Cameras" or Chapter 19: "Overall Color Correction" to learn the details of this resampling process. Just remember that you will get better results when you take a big image and sample it down, than if you take a small image and sample it up. If you had already scanned your original at 5,000 dpi from film, or if your original is the highest resolution from your digital camera, then sampling up is certainly a viable choice. When you scan film with a good scanner at more than 5,000 dpi of optical resolution, it is unlikely you will get any more real information.

Make sure the image Width, Height, and Resolution are set correctly for your layout dimensions and line screen when printing on a press. You don't want Quark or Pagemaker to resample your image. For best results, place it into other apps at 100%. For Web images, change the Inches pop-up to pixels before typing in your pixel dimensions.

STEP 7-B, SHARPENING THE IMAGE

As a final step, on each resampled version of your image, you will want to use Filter/Sharpen/Unsharp Mask to sharpen the image. You will have to run some tests to determine the type and amount of sharpening that works best for your different categories of images and output devices. It is sometimes useful to run tests on a section of the image and do side-by-side comparisons. Select a section of the image that represents the entire image using the Rectangular Selection tool, and then make a copy of it. Next, choose File/New and create a new file. Because you just made a copy, the new file will be the size of the copied section. Choose OK in the New dialog box and then do an Edit/Paste. To compare different parameters of the Unsharp Mask filter, you can repeat this or use Image/Duplicate, until you have several files that you can place next to each other onscreen.

Let me explain the three parameters of Unsharp Mask.

AMOUNT: Controls the overall amount of sharpening. When you compare sharpening effects, zoom the image to at least 100% so you can see all the detail. Compare different copies of the same image area using different settings for Amount and you will notice that the larger the amount, the sharper the image becomes, but at some point the more the grain gets enhanced also.

RADIUS: Photoshop sharpens an image by looking for edges in the photograph and enhancing those edges by darkening one side of the edge and lightening the other side. *Edges* are sharp color or contrast changes in an image. The Radius setting in the Unsharp Mask filter controls the width of pixels along an edge that are modified when you sharpen the image. Again, try running the filter with different settings, as well as comparing two copies of the same image side to side.

THRESHOLD: When you set the Threshold to 0, everything in the image becomes a candidate edge for getting sharpened. At a setting of 0, an image can easily be made to look too grainy by sharpening because even the changes caused by the grain will get shapened and increased, which is especially noticeable in skys and clouds. If you set the Threshold to 10, Photoshop finds and sharpens an edge only if there is a difference of at least 10 points (in the range from 0 to 255) in the pixel values along that edge. Areas, like clouds, will not be sharpened and the grain there will not be increased. The larger value you give to the Threshold setting, the more contrasty an edge must be before it is sharpened, and the more you are just sharpening the edges. I usually set my Threshold values at between 3 and 5 depending on the image. When

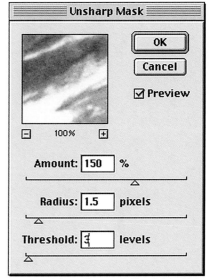

Here we see the Unsharp Mask filter dialog with its three parameters of Amount, Radius and Threshold.

you find the correct Unsharp Mask values, use them to sharpen the entire file. See Chapter 20: "Correcting a Problem Image" for a detailed, hands-on example of using Unsharp Mask. For more control over your sharpening, you can also use the Sharpen Only EdgesBH action from the ArtistKeys actions that come on the *Photoshop 6 Artistry* CD. This action builds an edge mask so only the parts of the image that really need sharpening are affected by the Sharpen filter. This allows you to sharpen those areas even more and yet not get unwanted grain effects in skys, clouds and other areas that don't improve when sharpened. Using this filter is described in Chapter 26: "Combining Bracketed Photos".

STEP 8, CONVERTING FROM YOUR RGB OR LAB WORKING SPACE TO THE FINAL OUTPUT COLOR SPACE

If you are working on an image for output to an RGB printer, like the LightJet 5000 or the Epson Stylist Photo 1270, 2000 or 7500, you can leave the resampled and sharpened image in your RGB or Lab workspace and still get a soft proof on the screen of how the image will look when printed to that output device. To do this, you choose View/Proof Setup/Custom and pick the ICC Profile for your printer from the Profile pop-up menu. The Imaging Intent will usually be Perceptual or Relative Colorimetric, you can try each one while looking at the soft proof of the image on your screen. After choosing OK from this dialog, Command-Y will toggle between showing you a soft proof of the image as it will look on this printer, and as it looks in your working space. See pages 156-158 of Chapter 15: "Photoshop Color Preferences, Monitor, Scanner and Printer Calibration" for more information on the best ways to set this up. This is a very useful feature, check it out!

If this will be a CMYK-specific version of your image, make sure that your CMYK preferences are set up correctly for the type of press and paper you will be using; then choose Image/Mode/CMYK Color to convert the image from RGB or Lab to CMYK. If you don't correct the RGB or Lab file before converting to CMYK, Photoshop could create the Black channel on your CMYK file incorrectly. Unless your scans are done directly into CMYK, you should do overall color correction on your master RGB or Lab file before converting to CMYK. Scans made by high-end scanners in CMYK should already have had overall color correction done for you by the trained scanner operator.

STEP 9, MAKING FINAL SUBTLE COLOR ADJUSTMENTS

When you are comparing the image on your screen to a print from a particular RGB printer, you want to compare the Lab or RGB version of the image onscreen with Proof Setup set to the ICC profile for your printer. There are colors that will show up on an RGB monitor, and in your RGB or LAB workspace, that may not be able to be printed with your RGB printer. When comparing a CMYK print proof with the image onscreen, you want to be looking at the CMYK version of the image; in which case, Photoshop automatically soft-proofs the CMYK colors on the screen, based on the ICC profile stored within the CMYK file. If you are working with CMYK files that don't have embedded ICC profiles, files that may have been separated elsewhere, you need to be sure that your CMYK working space preference values are compatible with the type of CMYK separation you have or the file may not be displayed correctly on the screen.

Because the CMYK or RGB Soft Proof image onscreen more closely matches the image on a press or your printer than your Master RGB image, you may need to do final subtle color corrections in CMYK or RGB Soft Proof mode. For some images, the CMYK or RGB Soft Proof version will look the same on the screen as

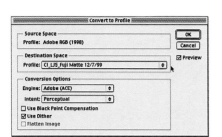

Here we are using Image/Mode/Convert to Profile to convert a file from Adobe RGB to the ICC profile for a LightJet 5000 printer. Depending on the image, set the Intent to either Perceptual or Relative Colorimetric. I usually leave Use Dither on and Use Black Point Compensation off. If you don't like the way your blacks look, try turning Use Black Point Compensation on.

Chapter 17: Steps to Create a Master Image

the Master RGB version, depending on the colors in the image and the gamut of your device. Certain colors, for example bright saturated red or deep blue, may get duller or change when you convert to CMYK. Also, the shadow or highlight areas may require a slight modification to be sure the correct balance is achieved in the neutral areas. To add contrast to CMYK images, you may want to run a curve or increase the black midtone values. You can make these final color adjustments using Curves, Levels, Hue/Saturation, Replace Color or Selective Color. See Chapter 11: "Automating with Actions" for a discussion of the actions we use when processing all the CMYK files for our books. They usually apply an S-Curve, to increase contrast, and a Hue/Saturation adjustment after converting each file to CMYK.

If this version of the image is destined for the Web, you might want to use Image/Mode/Convert to Profile to convert the image from your regular RGB or LAB working space to the sRGB space. Now you should see an accurate example of how this image will display on the average PC monitor. If you save this copy of the file at this point, it will now be tagged with sRGB, which may be best for a Web image for general industry consumption.

SAVING THE DEVICE-SPECIFIC IMAGE

For output to a press or imagesetter, especially if printing directly from Photoshop, you might need to go into Page Setup in the File menu to adjust some of the settings. You should talk to the print shop or service bureau doing the output and ask them if you need to set Negative or Emulsion Down. Also, ask the service bureau how to set the Halftone Screens. Often, they will want you to not set either value in Photoshop because they will set them using Quark, the imagesetter or platemaker. You really should coordinate with the printer or service bureau concerning who's going to set what. Also ask the service bureau whether they want you to save the images as Photoshop EPS, use one of the DCS options or use CMYK TIFF, or use some other format because this varies according to the type of output device that particular bureau uses. For our books, which we lay out in Quark, we usually use the CMYK TIFF format which works well and is simple and compact to save in.

If you save the image in Photoshop EPS format for input into Quark, you will most likely use the settings in the dialog box here. You should check the Include Halftone Screen box only if you set up the screen angles and frequencies using the Screens dialog box (which you access from the Page Setup dialog box). If the screens are going to be set in Quark, leave the Include Halftone Screen checkbox unchecked. Good luck with your color. If you have any questions or comments about these techniques, please email us at www.maxart.com or reach us via our contact information at the end of the book.

If you are outputting to an RGB printer, like the LightJet 5000 or an Epson printer that you have made a custom profile for, make sure the correct ICC profile is embedded in the file. You can see the profile that is embedded in the file by setting the pop-up menu at the bottom-left of the window to Document Profile.

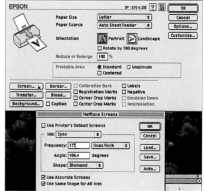

The Page Setup dialog box and its Halftone Screens dialog box. When separating files for use on a press, check with your service bureau for how to set the screens and other settings here. They usually want you to leave these unset in Photoshop as they are often planning to set them in Quark or some other layout application at the print shop.

If you set this pop-up menu, at the bottom left of your Photoshop windows, to Document Profile then the profile that is assigned to your document will be displayed to the left of the pop-up menu. The profile displayed above is of a CMYK document using the CMYK defaults recommended in this book.

OVERALL COLOR CORRECTION, SELECTION AND LAYER TECHNIQUES

MAKE DETAILED COLOR SELECTIONS AND MASKS

OVERALL COLOR CORRECTION

REPLACE COLOR, COLOR RANGE AND SELECTIVE COLOR

SHARPENING AND SPOTTING

COLOR MATCH IMAGES

CORRECTING A PROBLEM IMAGE

My trusty companion Chumley, center, with his friends Tiger, left, and Dusty. I took this with my Canon 35 mm camera while my friend Angelika kept the dogs entertained. This is a Photo-CD pro scan which I color corrected in Photoshop.

18 HANDS-ON SESSION: The Car Ad

Using the Magic Wand, the Lasso tool, Quick Mask mode, the Magnetic Lasso tool and Hue/Saturation capabilities to select the red car and change its color.

STEP 1: The original perspective Acura ad with the red Acura.

STEP 1: The Magic Wand tool options with its tolerance set to 75 and the Anti-aliased and Contiguous checkboxes on.

STEP 1: This is about as much of the selection as you should try to get with the Magic Wand. Now use the Lasso tool.

Suppose the image for an ad has been created and the clients love it. They are ready to run the ad, when the art director and the boss enter insisting on a purple car. You try to explain to them that red really looks better because the background is mostly purple, but they insist on a purple car. You don't want to have to go out and reshoot the car—that never happens in the digital world—so you simply change the color of the car.

Making selections is one of the most basic Photoshop tasks, but also one of the most important. Often the difference between work that looks polished and work that looks hack is dependent upon how well you make your selections. Here we'll show you a couple of different ways to achieve the same result. With practice, you'll find which tools you're most comfortable with and which give you the type of accuracy and flexibility you need.

SELECTING THE CAR

STEP 1: **Open the RedAcura.psd file from The Car folder. Select the Magic Wand tool and in the options bar, set its tolerance to 75. Make sure Anti-aliased and Contiguous are checked.** The larger the tolerance, the more adjacent colors the Magic Wand selects. Having the Anti-aliased feature on makes edges of the selection blend easier with their surroundings. The Contiguous setting will restrict the selection to areas that are contiguous to the pixel you click on. **Click on the bright red color just to the right of the Acura emblem above the bumper to select most of the front of the car. Now Shift-click the reddest part of the hood, in the middle.** Holding the Shift key down while making a selection adds the resulting selection to what you have already selected. **Change the tolerance to about 45 and then continue to Shift-click unselected red areas with the tolerance set to 45.** If adding any new area makes the selection lines go outside the area of the car, choose Edit/Undo (Command-Z) to undo that last part of the selection. Your previous selections should still be there. After you select most of the red areas of the car without going beyond its boundaries, your selection should look like the one pictured here. If you lose your selection at any time, you can reselect using Select/Reselect or Command-Shift-D.

STEP 2: The Lasso tool and its options.

STEP 2: **Double-click the Lasso tool, make sure its feather is set to zero, and make sure that Anti-aliased is also on. Again, hold down the Shift key and then circle areas that you didn't select with the Wand.** While adding to the selection with the Lasso tool, you should zoom in closely to the area you are working on. Make sure that the Shift key is down or you might accidentally move the selection instead of adding to it. When you hold down the Shift key, the cursor appears as either a crosshair or the Lasso, depending on how your preferences are set up. In either case, you will see a little plus to the bottom-right of the cursor to tell you that you are adding. When the Shift key is not down, the cursor looks like a white pointing arrow with a selection box. Clicking and dragging inside the existing selection at this point will move the selection. If you do this by accident, immediately choose Edit/Undo (Command-Z), or if you notice that you moved the selection a few steps ago, use the History palette to back up to a state where the selection had not been moved. Use Shift with the Lasso tool to circle all the areas not selected. When adding to the selection, first put the cursor on top of an area already selected, and hold the Shift key down. Next, press and hold down the mouse button while circling the areas you want to add. **If you accidentally select something along a border that you don't want to select, move the cursor into an area nearby that isn't selected, hold the Option key down, press the mouse button down, and use the Lasso to circle the part of that border area you want to deselect.** When you hold down the Option key, you see a minus to the right of the cursor signifying a subtract from the selection. When doing selections along a border with the Lasso tool, you have to trace the edge pixel by pixel. The Lasso tool has no intelligence to detect where color or brightness changes, so this is a hand-eye coordination exercise. Be sure to select everything that is part of the red car, even the reds that have a purple tone or are almost black. If they're part of the painted car, you should select them. Just like an auto body shop that is putting masking tape on the chrome and other areas for a paint job, you need to make sure that all areas to be painted are selected and all areas not to be painted are not selected. Pretend that the unselected areas have masking tape on them

STEP 2: No Shift key down, so white arrow cursor moved selection. Choose Edit/Undo (Command-Z) immediately if this happens.

After you have started a Lasso selection, addition or subtraction, the mouse button is down and you are drawing with the button down. At this point, if you hold the Option key down, you can release the mouse button and draw straight line segments between mouse clicks. If you want to draw in freehand again, hold the mouse button down again while drawing. In any case, either the Option key or the mouse button needs to remain down until you are done with this selection change, because when you release the Option key and the mouse button at the same time, the two end points of the selection will join. The hand-eye-mouse coordination in this maneuver can be tricky! Let's go through the most difficult case, when you are subtracting from the existing selection. First press the Option key and hold until you click down on the mouse button. Starting with the Option key down tells Photoshop you want to subtract. Next, you click the mouse button and hold it down while drawing in freehand. Now you can release the Option key as long as you keep the mouse button down. If you want to draw straight line segments, press the Option key again after its initial release. Now each time you mouse click, you are defining a corner point and straight lines will be drawn between clicks. To draw in freehand again, press and hold down the mouse button while drawing. When you have looped

STEP 3: Click on the Save Selection icon to save your selection.

STEP 3: To load your selection again, click on the channel and drag it to the Load Selection icon at the bottom left area or just Command-click on the channel.

STEP 4: The sample swatch in the Tool palette changes to purple when you move the Hue to –70. With the Preview button on, the selected area will change also.

STEP 5: Unless your selection was perfect, you might have a red border around the edge and you might notice other areas that are still red after you turn the car to purple. Zoom in using Command-Spacebar-click to see selection edges closely.

around what you wanted to subtract, release the Option key and the mouse button, and the end points of this selection will be joined. Remember, this works for both adding to (Shift key starts) and subtracting from (Option key starts) a selection.

SAVING AND LOADING YOUR SELECTIONS

STEP 3: After you work on this for a while, you might get nervous, fearing you could lose all your hard work with a random mouse click. Remember, if you click without holding down the Shift key, you make a new selection and will lose the selection you have worked on so hard. If this happens by accident, choose Command-Z or use the History palette to Undo. Another way to protect against this happening is to save your selection into a mask channel. To do this, **bring up the Channels palette, Window/Show Channels (Shift-F10 with ArtistKeys), and click the Save Selection icon (second from the left) at the bottom of the palette.** A new channel is created; it's white in the areas that were selected and black (or masked) everywhere else. **If you want to save your selection a second time after you work on it some more, choose Select/Save Selection, and then choose Alpha 1 from the pop-up Channel menu and the Replace Channel option.** This new selection overwrites the old saved selection. To retrieve your selection from the mask channel, choose Select/Load Selection of a New Selection and set the Channel pop-up to Alpha 1. A shortcut for doing Load Selection is to hold the Command key down and click Alpha 1 in the Channels palette. That selects the white parts in the channel. The mask channel CarColor is a completed selection that you can use to check the accuracy of your selection. Leave this mask channel on the palette until the end, and then compare your finished selection to it for an idea of what you need to improve, if anything. If you have questions about how channels or the Channels palette works, see Chapter 6: "Selections, Paths, Masks and Channels."

CHOOSING A NEW COLOR

STEP 4: **When you think you have finished the selection process, choose Command-H with your selection loaded and active to hide the selection edges.** This operation removes the marching ants and lets you see the edges of your selection as you change the color of the car. If your selection is not correct, problems usually show up along the selection edges. **Now choose Image/Adjust/Hue/Saturation (Command-U) to bring up the Hue/Saturation dialog box.** While you are in a color correction tool, the Eyedropper is automatically selected from the Tool palette. **Click down with the Eyedropper on the red area of the car just above the Acura emblem.** The Foreground color swatch in the Tool palette or the Swatches palette will show this red. To use the swatch as a preview, you need to first set it to your starting color, as we just did. **Move the Hue slider, the top one, to the left until the number reads –70.** Notice that the swatch changes from red to purple, indicating that making the change would make your reds purple. If the Preview button is selected, the car will also change to purple after a brief delay. When you are working on a large file, this delay can be longer, so you might want to move the Hue slider back and forth with the Preview button off, and use your swatch to get the new color in the ballpark of what it should be. The swatch will change instantly. When the swatch seems correct, click the Preview button to see your selection change color. If the Preview button isn't on yet, turn it on now.

WORKING WITH QUICK MASK SELECTION MODE

STEP 5: **In the Hue/Saturation dialog box with the Preview button on, use the Space-bar to scroll around the edge of your selection, making sure all the red areas of the car have changed to purple**. You might notice a red edge around the car and in other areas, such as on the Acura emblem, which indicates that your selection isn't perfect. **If you find some leftover red traces, press the Cancel button in the Hue/Saturation dialog box** to return the car to red.

Quick Mask mode selector (Quick Mask icon)

STEP 5: The Quick Mask mode selector is toward the bottom right area of the Tool palette. Here we see the color swatch in the Quick Mask Options dialog box. Note: As a shortcut, you can also use (Q) to toggle back and forth between the regular and Quick Mask modes.

Now you're going to use Quick Mask mode along with the Paintbrush tool to clean up your selection. **In the Tool palette, double-click the Quick Mask mode icon toward the bottom right of the palette to bring up your Quick Mask options. Click the color swatch, and set it to a bright green.** The default color for this swatch is red, which won't work here because we have a red car. The default for Quick Mask mode is that the masked area, the nonselected

STEP 5: In the default Quick Mask mode, the Quick Mask icon has gray on the outside, a white circle on the inside, and a semitransparent green mask that overlays the nonselected areas. Painting with black here subtracts from the selection.

area, is covered by a colored semi-transparent layer. This is like seeing a rubylith in traditional masking. The selected area is not covered. When you're in Quick Mask mode, you use the painting tools to add or subtract from your selection by painting with a brush. This gives you finer pixel-for-pixel control than you can get with the selection tools.

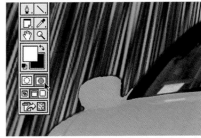

STEP 5: In the Selected Areas Quick Mask mode, the circle in the Quick Mask icon has gray on the inside. The green mask area overlays the selected areas. Painting with black here adds to the selection.

Type a D to set the default black and white colors. When the masked areas are overlayed, which is the default, painting subtracts from the selection and adds to the masked area. The default Quick Mask icon is gray on the outside. If you Option-click the Quick Mask icon, it changes so the gray is on the inside and the selected areas are overlayed with green. When you paint in this mode, painting adds to the selection. Put yourself into this mode by **Option-clicking the Quick Mask icon until the circle in the middle of it is gray and the outside is white.** Now the green overlay will be wherever your selection was.

STEP 6: Notice that the Channels palette displays an extra channel called *Quick Mask* when you are working in Quick Mask mode. This is temporary and goes away when you return to Normal Selection mode.

STEP 6: **Using the Paintbrush tool, in Normal mode, with 100% opacity in the Paintbrush options, choose a 5-pixel brush, third from top left, in the drop-down Brushes palette.** If you see a red border around the edge of your selection, paint this border area with the brush. You may need to pick a larger or smaller brush. You can use the left and right bracket keys to change your brush size without moving the cursor to the Brushes palette while painting. You can also click the Brush icon at the left side of the options bar to change the size and attributes of the selected brush. If you are not sure how to pick brush sizes and options, see Chapter 4: "The Tool Palette."

Paint any red areas that still show up so they are overlayed in green. If you accidentally paint beyond the edge of the red area, you can Option-click the Quick Mask icon and invert the overlay; then you're subtracting from the selection instead of adding to it. **A faster way to erase mistakes is to type an X, which exchanges the foreground and background colors and allows you to paint with white.** While you're

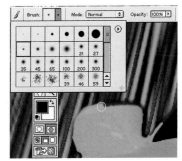

STEP 6: Using the Paintbrush tool to remove the red border from around the edge of the red car selection by adding to the selection.

213

in Quick Mask mode with selected areas overlayed, painting with black adds to the selection and painting with white subtracts from the selection.

When you have perfected your selection, the selection overlay should look like the illustration here. You shouldn't have a red border protruding around the overlay edge. Be sure to check the Acura emblem and the red roof of the car. For an area where the red color fades into another color at the edge, you can use less than 100% Opacity on the Brush to blend the selection of the red into the other edge colors.

Working in Quick Mask mode can be confusing if you load selections or work with the selection tools at the same time. For now, use the Paintbrush and other painting tools to edit in Quick Mask mode.

RETURNING TO STANDARD MODE

STEP 6: What the edge should look like with a perfected selection, before switching back to Normal Selection mode.

STEP 7: At this point, **Option-click the Quick Mask icon so that the masked areas are overlayed and the icon appears gray on the outside and white on the inside. Then click the Standard Mode icon to get the marching ants back around your selection.** If you leave the icon gray on the inside and white on the outside when you save a selection, your masks will be inverted. The selected part will be black instead of white. This may confuse you. Believe me, it has confused many of my students! **Now use Select/Save Selection to update your selection in the Channels palette.**

MAKING THE CAR PURPLE

STEP 7: What the Quick Mask icon should look like (gray on the outside with a white circle inside) after switching back to Normal Selection mode. Option-click the Quick Mask icon to return it to this state after you are finished with your Quick Mask edits.

STEP 8: **Choose Select/Feather and put a 1-pixel feather on the selection border before going into Hue/Saturation**. This may blend away very fine reddish hues along some edges of the car.

STEP 9: **Now choose Command-H to hide the edges of your selection. Go back to Image/Adjust/Hue/Saturation (Command-U) and move the Hue slider back to –70.** Your purple car should now look great and have no red edges. If it looks great, choose OK from the Hue/Saturation tool. If it still isn't perfect, choose Cancel in Hue/Saturation (or choose Edit/Undo if you already said OK), and go back to Quick Mask mode for more fine-tuning with the Paintbrush tool. When you're done, choose File/Save As to save your final purple car under a different name.

STEP 9: The final purple Acura, after the Hue/Saturation color change.

After your save, reopen the original TheCar.psd file from the CD and get ready to do this example again using the Magnetic Lasso tool and a different, more flexible approach with the Hue/Saturation capabilities.

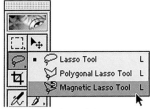

STEP 1: The Magnetic Lasso.

THE MAGNETIC LASSO: MAKING THE INITIAL SELECTION

STEP 1: We are going to use the Lasso tool again, but this time we'll use the Magnetic Lasso option. This tool creates selections based on color and contrast differences between the element you are selecting and the background. **Type Shift-L until you see the icon for the Magnetic Lasso; then go to the Options bar and set your Feather value at 0 and turn Anti-aliased on. Start with 10 as the width setting.** This gives you a brush size large enough to cover the edge between the car and background, but not so large that you include a lot of the background streaks. The **Frequency** is how often the Lasso will put down anchor points to anchor the selection marquee. **We're going to use 40. For Edge Contrast, type in 20%.**

Before we actually begin the selection, it's important to note that the Magnetic Lasso is sometimes not as ideal a selection tool as it might seem. The accuracy of its selections depend not only on the settings that we discussed in the paragraph above, but also on the particular image and specific edge that you're working on. In the photo of the red Acura, for example, the colored streaks surrounding the car can cause difficulties for the Magnetic Lasso when it tries to determine the correct edge to follow. For this image, the Magnetic Lasso is probably not as fast as the Magic Wand for making a basic selection of the car and, like the Wand, it should be thought of as a tool that will help you create a good starter selection that you can then modify with more precise refinements.

STEP 2: The Magnetic Lasso places anchor points as you move along the edge. Click once to place an anchor point manually. Hold down the Option key and click to draw with the Polygonal Lasso as we did here around the windshield.

STEP 2: Let's **begin at the lower left corner of the car. Click once to set the first anchor point and start the Magnetic Lasso selection; then begin to guide the mouse around the edge of the car. You do not need to have the mouse button pressed down after the initial mouse click.** If you have your cursor preference set to Brush Size, keep the middle of the circle over the car's edge. If you see that the selection is being drawn into the car's body or into the background, you can move the mouse back over the previous selection, retracing your steps until you get back to the last anchor point that was laid down. If you've placed the last anchor point in a poor position, you can delete that anchor point by pressing the Delete key. Continue to retrace your path, pressing the Delete key until you get back to a place where you like the path you've drawn. Continue forward again, clicking once to add an anchor point where you feel one is needed. (Photoshop will continue to add automatic anchor points, but it's nice to put some down where the curve changes directions sharply, such as around the mirrors, or where the background and the color of the car are too closely matched for Photoshop to place accurate anchor points.) If at any time you become hopelessly entangled in Lasso lines, you can press the Esc key to quit drawing and start again. **When you reach the windshield area or the bottom of the car, you might find it useful to switch to the Polygonal Lasso tool. You can access the tool while in the Magnetic Lasso by holding down the Option key and clicking from point to point, releasing the mouse button between points.** (The Lasso will draw the line but not

STEP 2: The selection marquee from the Magnetic Lasso. Don't worry about the areas where the path is incorrect. We'll fix those later.

place anchor points.) To switch back to the Freehand Magnetic Lasso, click the mouse and release the Option key to continue drawing. Once you are sure the tool has resumed its magnetic behavior, you can release the mouse button and continue to guide it along the edge.

Finish the selection by drawing all the way back to your starting point. You'll see the Magnetic Lasso icon again, with a little circle at the bottom-right, which means that when you click, the selection will be closed. The selection will also close if you double-click at any time or press the Enter key.

STEP 3: **To subtract areas from the selection, use the same Magnetic Lasso tool and settings but hold down the Option key before you start to draw.** For the headlights, I brought the Lasso Width down to 7 and the Contrast down to 10%. Use this technique to take out the four round headlights, the license plate, and one of the yellow turn signal lights. **Leave the other signal light and the Acura emblem in the selection for now.**

STEP 3: Use the Magnetic Lasso with the Option key to subtract from your selection just as you would with the regular Lasso.

ADDING AN ADJUSTMENT LAYER

STEP 4: When we did this example before, we built a channel, loaded it as a selection and then used Hue/Saturation to change the color of the car directly on the *Background* layer. We're still going to change the color of the car, but this time we'll do it via an adjustment layer. This will keep all the pixel information of our original intact and give us more flexibility to change the hue again and again, without risking degradation of our file. Because you've already worked in Quick Mask mode, you'll quickly grasp editing the adjustment layer mask. But, if you have trouble or find it confusing, read Chapter 27: "Bryce Stone Woman" or Chapter 26: "Combining Bracked Photos or Two Scans to Increase Dynamic Range."

Create the adjustment layer while your selection is still active by clicking on the new Adjustment Layer icon at the bottom of the Layers palette. From the pop-up menu, choose Hue/Saturation. In the Layers palette. You'll see that you now have a new layer above the Background layer, which consists of a layer showing the adjustment icon and an attached mask thumbnail. **In the Hue/Saturation dialog, we'll make the same modifications as before: Change the Master hue setting to –70 and click OK.**

STEP 4: Clicking on the new adjustment Layer icon at the bottom of the layers palette while your selection is active will give you an Adjustment layer with a layer mask. If you hold down the Option key before you click the icon, you'll be able to give the adjustment layer a name and choose grouping, opacity and blending options.

STEP 5: Now go back to the car and take a look at edges to see how good your mask is. You'll probably see areas that you want to include in your adjustment layer mask and others that you want to exclude. Remember the turn signal that we didn't knock out of the original selection? Let's work on that first because it's easy to see the change there.

The Hue/Saturation layer should still be the active layer in the Layers palette. Choose the Paintbrush (B) and a medium size brush (10–13 pixels). Type D and then X to make Black your foreground color. When you begin to paint, you'll be painting on the Layer mask for the adjustment layer. Painting with black will mask out (remove the color change) from any of those areas that you've just changed with the Hue/Saturation adjustment layer. As you paint the turn signal, you'll see the original color from the Background layer return. If you want to see how your painting is affecting the adjustment layer mask, Option-click either the adjustment layer thumbnail or its Layer Mask thumbnail. Option-click again to return to a normal view and continue to paint with black any areas that should remain the original color. **Switch to white by typing X while in the mask to paint any areas that should be purple.** When you used

STEP 5: After you've changed the hue, it's pretty easy to paint out the areas that shouldn't be adjusted by painting directly on the adjustment layer mask with black.

Quick Mask mode, you were doing essentially the same thing, only this time you're editing the adjustment layer mask and therefore your changes are saved automatically. Plus, you don't have to remember to get out of Quick Mask mode to go back to Selection mode.

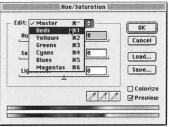

STEP 6: After you've perfected your edges, you're probably itching to get to the Acura emblem to finish your job. But wait! We're going to go a little further with the Hue/Saturation tool and let Photoshop do some of the really hard work for us. Double-click the Hue/Saturation layer's Adjustment icon to bring up the Hue/Sat dialog box again. **Hold down the Option key to get the Reset button and reset the colors to their original hues. Now use the Edit pop-up to switch to the Reds.** This way, you'll be editing only the red pixels in the selection and the Acura emblem, even though it is not currently masked out, will be unaffected by the change. **With the Edit pop-up menu set to Reds, move the Hue slider to –70 to once again change the car to a purple color.**

STEP 6: After resetting the Master to 0, use the pop-up to select only the Reds in your selection.

STEP 7: **With the Hue/Sat dialog still open, use the Command key and Spacebar shortcut to zoom in close and check the area around the Acura emblem to see if there are any errant red pixels hanging out there.** More than likely, there will be. Photoshop didn't consider these pixels "red" enough to change them during your Hue/Saturation adjustment of the reds. **With the Reds still selected in the dialog, click the +Eyedropper because we're going to add those straggler red pixels to the range of reds that we are editing. Click one or more of the red pixels.** Notice how the colors quickly come into line with the other purples around them. Check other areas of the car, especially the highlight areas, for pixels that still appear red to you and include those pixels in your red range. If you look at the range indicator (the darker gray rectangle between the two color bars) in the Hue/Sat dialog box, you'll see that the range is now larger because you've added those shades.

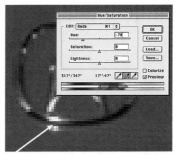

STEP 7: Use the +Eyedropper to click on the red pixels that still appear near the Acura emblem to add those colors to the red range being modified.

The beauty of using the adjustment layer method is that you can now go back and change the color of the car again and again without risking any degradation to the pixels in the file. You can also return and fine-tune your adjustment layer mask as often as you want. Fast, clean, flexible…who could ask for more?

STEP 7: Notice that the range of colors you are editing (denoted by the central, dark gray slider) is now larger than the original range.

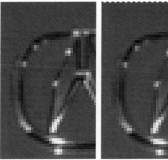

STEP 7: Selecting only the red colors with the Hue/Saturation adjustment layer tool, you can continue to add to or subtract from the range of colors you are editing to fine tune your changes.

19 HANDS-ON SESSION: Overall Color Correction

Introduction to Levels, Hue/Saturation and Curves
for overall color correction and the fundimental steps
in creating a master image.

In Chapter 3: "Setting System and Photoshop Preferences," we showed you how to set your Photoshop preferences for doing high quality color correction. This Overall Color Correction chapter is done using those Color Settings and, specifically, the RGB working space set to Adobe RGB and the CMYK working space set as in Chapter 3. If you didn't already do so, go through Chapter 3 before doing this exercise or any of the other color correction exercises. Before you proceed, also read Chapter 14: "Color Spaces, Device Characterization and Color Management," Chapter 15: "Photoshop Color Preferences, Monitor, Scanner and Printer Calibration," Chapter 16: "Image Resolution, Scanning Film and Digital Cameras," and Chapter 17: "Steps to Create a Master Image." These chapters give you an overview of the entire reproduction process, show you how to calibrate your monitor and give you a further understanding of the Levels, Curves and Hue/Saturation tools you will be using here. You should calibrate your monitor before proceeding with this chapter.

INTRODUCTION TO LEVELS

Before you start actually color correcting the Banf Lake image, let's take a tour of the Levels tool and explain its different parts and functions. Levels contains two sets of controls, which can make the image lighter or darker as well as change its contrast: Input Levels and Output Levels. The Input controls on top include the histogram, the Input Levels numbers and three sliders. The Input Shadow slider, on the left, darkens shadows as you move it to the right. The Input Highlight slider, on the right, lightens highlights as you move it to the left. The Brightness slider, in the middle, adjusts the brightness of the image. The Output controls on the bottom of the Levels dialog contain the Output Levels numbers and two sliders. The Output Shadow slider, on the left, makes shadows lighter as you move it to the right. The Output Highlight slider, on the right, makes highlights darker or duller as you move it to the left. The names "Input" and "Output" are chosen by comparing what happens with the Levels Highlight and Shadow sliders to what happens in Curves when you move the end points of a straight

The initial uncorrected Banf Lake image. Notice the overall flatness of the image.

curve either along the horizontal (Input) axis or along the vertical (Output) axis. This might seem a bit obscure at this point, but maybe it will make more sense to you after you read the entire chapter.

STEP 1: **From the OverallColorCorrection folder on the CD, open the BanfLakeOrigScanRes.psd file into Photoshop**. If your RGB working space is not set to Adobe RGB, you will get the Embedded Profile Mismatch dialog. In that case, you should make the Use Embedded Profile choice to leave this file in the Adobe RGB space and work on it in that space. That way the Info palette numbers and Levels histrograms will look the same as in the book. **Type F to get Full Screen Mode and then press the Tab key to get all your palettes off the screen. Type C to get the Crop tool and use it to crop the black borders from around the edge of the image. Click and drag to draw a box around the entire outside of the image, then click on two of the diagonal corner handles and drag them inward to remove the black borders from around the end of the original transparency. You'll notice that as you try to move the corner handle close to the corner, it will snap to the edge of the image. While holding the mouse button down on the corner handle, press the Control key and hold it. This will turn off the snapping to the picture edge and allow you to exactly place the corner handle to remove the black crud around the edge of the image without removing any extra info. When you have the corner handle where you want it, release the mouse button and the Control key. You can now zoom into any of the handles to check their exact location before cropping. To do the crop, press Return.** Use File/Save As BanfLakeResLayers.psd in Photoshop format on your hard disk; it is always good to save things in Photoshop format while you are working on them because it saves all your channels and layers.

STEP 2: **Bring up the Info palette from the Window menu. If you have loaded ArtistKeys, the predefined set of function keys explained in Chapter 3, press F9 to bring up the Info palette. Be sure to set up the Info palette's Options to show you both RGB and CMYK values.**

STEP 3: **Choose Image/Adjust/Levels and then click and drag the Levels title bar, at the top of its dialog box, to move the Levels dialog box out of the way as much as possible. You want to see as much of the image as you can while color correcting it. Use the Levels Overview diagram on this page as you review or learn the basic functions covered in steps 4 through 9. Make sure the Preview button is turned on.**

STEP 4: **Move the Input Highlight slider to the left and observe that the highlight areas in the clouds get brighter and the Input Levels number on the right decreases from 255. Move the slider until the number reads about 200. Let go of the slider and move the cursor over an area of the image where the clouds have turned completely white.** When you use any of the color correction tools, you automatically get the Eyedropper tool when you move the cursor over an area of the image. The Info palette shows you two sets of values for this white area. The values to the left of the slash are the original values at the Eyedropper location when you first entered Levels, and the

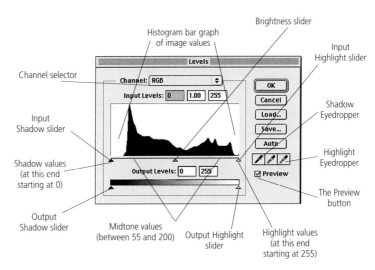

Study this Levels Overview diagram to learn the various controls of the Levels tool.

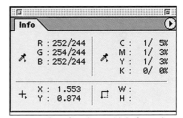

STEP 2: The Info palette with before values on the left of the slash and after values on the right.

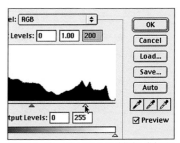

STEP 4: Move the Input Highlight slider to the left so the right Input Level reads about 200.

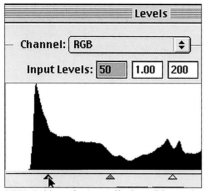

STEP 5: Move the Input Shadow slider to the right so the left Input Level reads about 50.

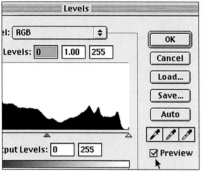

STEP 6: Leave the Preview checkbox checked in Levels and other color correction tools to see your changes as you make them. To see the image as it looked before this round of changes, uncheck the Preview button. When you are working in an adjustment layer and you are entering the Levels dialog for this layer for a 2nd or 3rd time, having Preview checked shows you the changes since the last time you entered Levels and unchecking shows you how the image looked with your previous set of Levels adjustments. To see the image without this Levels adjustment layer altogether, turn off the Eye icon for this layer in the Layers palette.

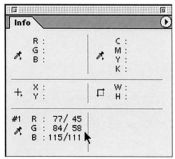

STEPS 6 AND 7: A Color Sampler shows up at the bottom of the Info palette. It will always show you the before and after values at that location even when the cursor is inside the Levels dialog.

values to the right of the slash show you what your levels changes have done to the digital values at the Eyedropper location. You can now see that moving the Input Highlight slider to the left makes the highlights brighter, but it also causes you to lose detail in the highlights if you move it too far. The original RGB numerical values that were in the range of 220 to 240 have now all changed to 255, which is pure white and prints with no color or detail—and you don't want that.

STEP 5: **Move the Input Shadow slider to the right until the Input Levels number on the left goes from 0 to about 50 and the shadow areas of the image darken. Move the Eyedropper over a dark area and measure the changes in the Info palette.** The RGB values originally in the range of 0 to 50 have all moved to 0 and have become totally black.

STEP 6: **Move the cursor to the title bar at the top of the Levels dialog box. You'll notice that when you click down on it with the Preview checkbox unchecked, nothing happens.** In previous Mac versions of Photoshop, when you clicked on the title bar and held the mouse button down, the image returned to the way it looked before you changed anything in Levels. To do this, Photoshop used a feature available on the Mac and not on most PCs called Video LUT_Animation. Photoshop 6 no longer supports Video LUT Animation on either platform, so now you always have to have the Preview checkbox checked to see the changes in the image as they happen in Levels or any color correction tool. To see the image the way it looked before any changes were made in the current invocation of Levels, or any tool, uncheck the Preview checkbox.

Now, **hold down the Option key and click the Cancel/Reset button.** The Cancel button changes to Reset, and clicking it restores the levels to their starting values when you entered Levels this time. All your changes are removed, but you don't leave Levels. Calculating the Levels histogram can take a long time when you're working on large files, and this Reset feature saves time when you want to start over.

Notice that the values in the Info palette disappear when you move the cursor back into the Levels dialog box. Move the cursor out over the image, while holding the Shift key down, and click on the image area. Notice that a new set of numbers appears at the bottom of the Info palette. This is called a Color Sampler, and the Info palette will always show the values at this location no matter where the cursor is located, even if the cursor is inside the Levels dialog. When you want to precisely set the digital values at a certain location, Shift-click there to create a Color Sampler; then go back into the Levels dialog and move the controls until you get those values at that location. Using the Color Samplers lets you remember the values at a particular location and see how a change in Levels modifies those values.

STEP 7: **Choose Window/Show Color to bring up the Color palette. Use the Eyedropper tool to click a midtone value in the Banf Lake image; clicking in the lake itself will work great. When you press down on the mouse button, the values in the Color palette change. Now Shift-click the lake. This creates another Color Sampler at the bottom of the Info palette that will always show you the values at that location. Now move the cursor back into Levels; notice that these values in the Color palette and Color Sampler don't go away, even when you're in the dialog box. Press down on the Input Brightness slider, the middle one, and move it to the left; the image gets brighter and the numbers in the Color palette and Color Sampler get smaller. Move the slider to the right, and the image gets darker, while the numbers in the Color palette and Color Sampler get larger. Also, observe that the middle number (the**

Chapter 19: Overall Color Correction

gamma) in the Input Levels numbers boxes is changing. **When you move the Bright-ness slider to the left, the gamma goes above 1.0, and when you move it to the right, the gamma goes below 1.0.** If the Input Levels numbers read 0, 1.0, 255, you know you haven't changed the Input Levels. When you click another area of the image, the Color palette's values will change to show you the reading at that new location. The Color Sampler you created before will not move or change, however. If you Shift-click in a new location, a new Color Sampler, up to four per image, will be created at that location. To move an existing Color Sampler, you need to Shift-click on top of the old sampler location and drag it to a new location. **Hold the Option key down and click on the Reset button, formerly the Cancel button, to move the Input values back to 0, 1.0 and 255.**

STEP 8: **Move the Output Highlight slider to the left until the Output Levels number on the right reaches 200. Then measure the brightest cloud values; notice that values originally in the 200 to 220 range have all dropped below 200.** You changed the Output Levels number from 255 to 200, and the difference of 55, or close to it, has been subtracted from all these highlight values, darkening and dulling your highlights.

STEP 9: **Move the Output Shadow slider to the right. Notice how doing that makes the shadows lighter and duller.** If you measure the changes with the Eyedropper and Info palette, you will notice that moving this slider increases the shadow's numerical values (which makes the shadows lighter).

SETTING THE HIGHLIGHT AND SHADOW VALUES

Step 10: Steps 4 through 9 show you the basic functions of the different parts of the Levels tool. It is important to use those functions in the right order and to take careful measurements of your progress using the Info palette, Color Samplers and Color palette. We will start out working with the Highlight and Shadow Eyedroppers to set the highlights and shadows on this image—a very important step in this process. All reproduction or printing processes, including sheet-fed presses, web presses, newspaper presses, digital printers and film recorders, have certain end points to their reproduction process defined by the highlights and shadows. Many newspaper presses can't show detail for shadow values that are more than 85% to 90% black, and some newspapers are even worse. Sheet-fed presses, on the other hand, can sometimes show detail in areas with more than 95% black. In a digital file, these percentages are represented by numerical values ranging from 0 (100% black) to 255 (white, or 0% black).

When you color correct an image, you don't want that image to contain areas that the output medium you are using can't reproduce. Setting the highlight and shadow values correctly for your output device ensures that this won't happen. You also want the white parts of your image to print as white (not with a color cast of yellow, cyan or magenta) and the black parts of your image to print as black (not dark gray with a green cast). You can ensure this by setting your highlights and shadows correctly. When you set the highlight, you are setting the brightest point in the image that is a neutral color, white, and that still has a dot pattern or some ink (doesn't print as pure white paper). The highlight would be the brightest part of Zone IX in the Zone System. Any point brighter than the highlight will print as totally empty paper with no dots or ink. When you set the shadow, you are setting the darkest point in the image that is a neutral color, black, and that still has a dot pattern. The shadow

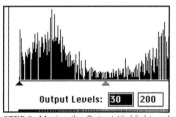

STEP 8: Moving the Output Highlight and Shadow sliders and looking at the Output Levels numbers.

would be the darkest part of Zone I in the Zone System. Any point darker than the shadow will print as totally black ink with no white holes to give detail.

STEP 11: **To start the actual color correction of this image, Option-Shift-click on any Color Sampler points you set to remove them from the Info palette. Press the Cancel button to leave the Levels tool. Close the Color palette and choose Window/Show Navigator to bring up the Navigator palette. Move it mostly off the screen on the right side, but leave enough of it so you can see your zoom factor number in the bottom left of this palette. All you need on the screen is this small piece of the Navigator and the Info palette in the bottom right corner.** The image we are working on here was scanned at 16-bits per color channel, using an Imacon Flextight scanner. The original scan was over 200 megs in size and scanned at over 5700 dpi. I have resampled down the file so it would fit on the CD and be a good size for this book. If you are starting out with a 16-bits per channel scan, you will have to choose Image/Adjust/Levels to get into the Levels dialog for the first color correction step. Photoshop does not support Layers with files that are more than 8-bits per channel. Doing this example with an 8-bit per channel image, you would want to get into a Levels adjustment layer using Layer/New Adjustment Layer/Levels. **Choose Image/Adjust/Levels to start your Overall Color Correction.**

Photoshop allows you to decide where you want it to set the highlight. The highlight should be the brightest neutral point that still has detail. **Double-click the Highlight Eyedropper button, the rightmost Eyedropper inside the Levels dialog, and make sure that the CMYK values in the Color Picker are 5, 3, 3, 0 and the RGB values 244, 244, 244.** If you are using a different RGB workspace, you may have slightly different RGB values here. These are the neutral values you would want your highlight to have for a sheet-fed press on coated paper, and they also work for most other purposes including the LightJet 5000 and most Epson printers. Due to the impurities in printing press inks, you get a neutral color by having more cyan than magenta or yellow. Because this is a highlight, there is no black. Click the OK button if you need to change any of the values.

STEP 12: **Now double-click the Shadow Eyedropper and make sure the shadow values are 74, 65, 64, 92 in CMYK and 8, 8, 8 in RGB.** If you have different values than these, compare your settings to those in chapters 3 and 15. As discussed in chapters 3 and 15, the shadow preference values should be somewhere between 2, 2, 2 and 8, 8, 8 depending on how dark you want your shadows to be. Click the OK button if you needed to change any of the values.

SETTING THE HIGHLIGHT

Step 13: Next, you use the Highlight Eyedropper to click on a highlight, which should be the brightest white area in this image. You want the highlight to be a neutral white area—the last possible place where you can see a little texture. The RGB values in the Info palette should be in the 240 to 255 range and the CMYK values in the 0 to 10 range. If you have specular highlights (the sun reflected off a chrome bumper, for example), these will not have detail and should have values of 255. You're looking for something just a hair less intense than that. **Move the Levels dialog box out of the way so you can see the entire clouds and snow area. To find the correct place for setting the highlight, with the Levels Preview checkbox checked, hold down the Option key and move the Input Highlight slider to the left. The whole image area first turns black and then, as you move the slider to the left, brighter and eventually white areas appear. The first white area that appears in the snow on top** of the mountains at the left is the area you should set as the highlight. Remember where that location is in the window. Now move the Input Highlight slider back to 255 because you were only using it to locate the brightest point.

Zoom into the area of the snow on top of the mountain until you are zoomed in about 400%. Click the Highlight Eyedropper in the Levels dialog box. Now move this Eyedropper up to that bright place in the snow, and move it around in the area while looking at the RGB values in the Info palette for the highest set of numbers. When you find those numbers (I chose 255, 255, 25), Shift-click once to set a Color Sampler at the spot where you want to set your highlight. Now move the cursor back on top of the circle where you set the Color Sampler and, when the cursor disappears, click without the Shift key to set your highlight value at that point. When the cursor disappears, you have the Color Sampler and the location for setting your highlight lined up exactly. The numbers to the right of the slash in the Info palette at your #1 Color Sampler location should now display 244, 244, 244 for RGB at that exact spot where you clicked. By setting the highlight here you have actually lowered the brightness of this snow to a value that will still have a dot when printing on a press and will actually get some ink dots when printing with a digital printer. If you wanted this snow to be a specular highlight, you could adjust this value to 255. As we go through this example, you can watch this Color Sampler location and you may notice the values get a bit higher than 244, 244, 244. You will be able to decide if this snow prints as pure white paper at 255, 255, 255 or still has a bit of detail by printing a smidge darker.

Now go to the Preview checkbox and turn off Preview. When Preview is off, you see the original image. When Preview is on, you see the image after the highlight change. Notice that this process of setting the highlight has darkened the image somewhat. As we go through the color correction process, click the Preview on and off from time to time to see what has happened to the image. **Turn Preview on again for now.**

Setting the highlight actually moves the highlight sliders in each of the Red, Green and Blue channels, which in turn moves the highlight part of the histogram in the Levels Channel RGB display to the left or to the right. **Press Command-Z once to undo and then Command-Z again to redo this change while watching the RGB histogram and the white color or the sky. See the differences? Use the Channel pop-up menu at the top of Levels to look at each of the Red, Green and Blue channel histograms. The Output Highlight slider in each of them should have changed to 244 or thereabouts. Clicking on the snow with the Highlight Eyedropper caused each of these Red, Green and Blue sliders to move. To change your Color Sampler highlight value to other than 244, 244, 244, you could just manually move any of these Red,**

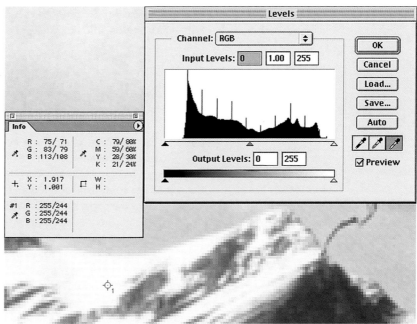

STEP 13: The before and after values for the highlight. Notice how the totally white snow was replaced by the 244, 244, 244 values by clicking using the Hightlight Eyedropper. You can increase the brightness of these 244, 244, 244 values, and thus the snow, by going into each of the Red, Green and Blue channels and moving the Output Highlight sliders back to the right. After moving the Output Highlight sliders back to the right all the way, moving the Input Highlight sliders to the left will make the image even brighter.

Setting the Highlight and Shadow Values

Green or Blue Output Hightlight Eyedroppers. Move the Channel pop-up back to RGB, which you can also do by using Command-~.

SETTING THE SHADOW

STEP 14: Now we are going to use the Shadow Eyedropper to click a shadow. The shadow should be the darkest neutral area where you still want a little detail or you may want your shadows totally black. This depends on the image you are working on, where you click with the Shadow Eyedropper and the actual numerical values you use for your shadow. When looking for a location to set your shadows, the RGB values in the Info palette should normally be in the 1 to 10 range, but they may be higher than this for a particular scan like they are with this image. **Move the Levels dialog box to the top of the screen and zoom out so you can see the entire bottom half of the image. To find the correct area for setting the shadow, hold the Option key down while moving the Input Shadow slider to the right. The whole image area first turns white, and then as you move the slider to the right, black areas appear. The first black area to appear, in the upper tree to the lower left, is the place where you should set the shadow. Now move the Input Shadow slider back to 0 because you were only using it to locate the darkest point. Click on the Shadow Eyedropper, the leftmost Eyedropper, in the Levels dialog box to select it. Now move this Eyedropper up to that darkest place, and then move it around in the area while watching the RGB values in the Info palette. You might want to zoom in to that particular area to around 400% before you pick the darkest spot. When you find the right spot, Shift-click there first to place a Color Sampler, then click once again without the Shift key in exactly the same location. You know that you are exactly on top of the Color Sampler when the cursor disappears.** The numbers for the #2 Color Sampler in the Info palette should now display 8, 8, 8 (or very close to it) for that exact spot where you clicked. The location you click will get a value of 8, 8, 8, or whatever preference value you have set for Shadow Eyedropper. If the point you click for the shadow is the darkest point in the image, then you won't lose any shadow detail that wasn't already in your scan, even if you set this to 0, 0, 0. On the other hand, if you click at a place that wasn't the darkest place in your image, you may end up removing some of the shadow detail from the scan. Be careful where you click to set your highlight and shadow values. **Now you can turn the Preview checkbox on and off to see the changes made to this image so far. Leave it on when you are done.**

SETTING THE OVERALL BRIGHTNESS OF THE IMAGE

STEP 15: As you look at this image, notice that it's pretty dark at this point. **Move the Input Brightness slider to the right until the middle Input Levels number reads about 1.44.** This opens up the image and makes it even a bit flat looking. If you think back to our discussion

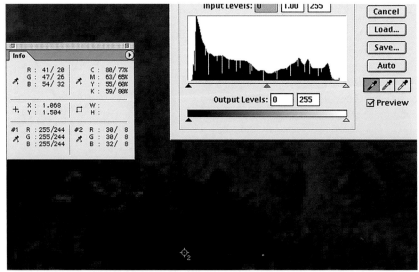

STEP 14: The before and after values for the shadow. Notice that the shadow CMYK values to the right are not the same as the 95, 85, 83, 95 default values you entered, but you should get exactly 2, 2, 2, or very close to it, in RGB.

STEP 14: Setting the shadow in the dark area at the top of the tree. As you can see with the #2 Color Sampler, the initial values at this point were 30, 30, 32 but after we set the shadow that changed them to 8, 8, 8. Right after clicking on your Color Sampler point with the Shadow Eyedropper, use Command-Z to toggle back and forth between having the new shadow value set and right before that. As you do that, notice how the shadow part of the RGB histogram on the left moves back and forth as each of the Red, Green and Blue shadow values are changed when you click with the Eyedropper.

Chapter 19: Overall Color Correction

of the Zone System, you can equate the initial location of the Brightness slider with Zone V, the middle gray values. Moving the slider to the left moves Zone V down toward Zone III or IV, depending on how far you move it. What was a Zone IV value now becomes a Zone V value; lighter, and possibly a bit flatter. This effect is similar to the one you would get by setting the original camera exposure at Zone IV or lower, except moving the Brightness slider by a zone or two wouldn't change Zones I and IX as much. Notice that the RGB values for your #2 Color Sampler have changed to be around a value of 15 instead of 8. If you leave them here, this will make your shadows look washed out. Since the shadows in this image don't have much detail anyhow, it is better to make sure they are black than have them end up a muddy gray. **Go into each of the Red, Green and Blue channels and move the Input Shadow slider to the right until that channel has a value of around 6 to 8. Try to match the value, within 1 point anyhow, to get a neutral shadow. Once you click in the Input Shadow slider and move it a bit, the leftmost Input number is highlighted. At this point you can use the up and down arrows in the lower right of your keyboard to nudge the number up or down by a single digit.** This nudging works with all number entries in Photoshop and is often more accurate and less tedious than using the slider with the mouse button down.

CORRECTING FOR COLOR CASTS

STEP 16: **All adjustments so far have been done with the Levels Channel selector set to RGB (Command-~). You can now use the Channel selector in Red (Command-1), Green (Command-2) and Blue (Command-3) modes to control the color balance of the image and to correct for color casts. You can switch between channels by clicking the pop-up menu and dragging up or down, or by using the key combinations Command-~ through Command-3.** The Red channel controls red and its complement, cyan; the Green channel controls green and its complement, magenta; and the Blue channel controls blue and its complement, yellow. Try to commit this set of complementary colors to memory. To learn more about the complementary colors, refer to the RGB/CMYK table at the end of Chapter 12: "Color Correction Tools." This image has a slightly blue color balance, which makes it seem a little cold. **Use the Channel selector or Command-3 to move to the Blue channel. Move the Input Brightness slider far to the right until the middle Input Levels number reads about .5 and notice how yellow the image is. Now move the same slider far to the left to about 1.5. Notice how blue the image is.** You can use this middle slider to control the color balance of the midtones. Remember that when the Brightness value reads 1.0 for any channel, that is the position where you haven't made any changes. **Move this slider back to the right until it reads about .94 and notice the subtle differences in the color.** You have added yellow to remove the blue cast in this image.

STEP 17: **Press Command-2 to switch to the Green channel. As you move the middle slider to the left, you add green, and as you move it to the right, you add magenta. Move this middle brightness channel to about 1.04 to add a little green to the entire image and improve the look of the trees.** Now when you turn the Preview checkbox on and off, you are seeing the difference all the Levels changes have made in this image.

If you press Command-1, you can use the middle slider to move between red and cyan. I didn't change this one. You may make these adjustments differently depending on your preferences for color and your monitor. So long as you have calibrated your monitor and your output devices, you should be able to obtain results

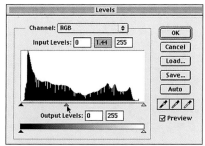

STEP 15: Move the Input Brightness slider to the left to about 1.44 to open up this image.

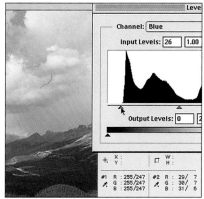

STEP 15: Here we are moving the Red, Green and Blue Input Shadow sliders to the right to darken and re-neutralize the shadows.

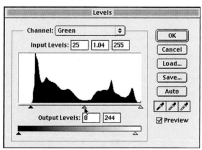

STEP 16: Here we are adjusting the color cast by moving the Green Brightness slider to 1.04 which adds green to the midones of the entire image

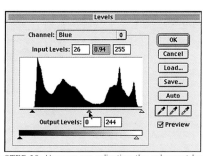

STEP 16: Here we are adjusting the color cast by moving the Blue Brightness slider to .94 which adds yellow to the mitones of the entire image.

STEP 17: Here we see the Banf Lake image after making all the initial Levels adjustments.

that you like. Whenever you make major cast changes to any particular channel, go back to RGB (Command-~) and then double-check your overall Brightness adjustments. **Since we are working with a 16-bit per channel image, and we can't automatically save our changes in an adjustment layer before leaving Levels, click on the Save button to save these changes in a file named BanfInitialLevelsChanges. Now click the OK button to complete all the changes you have made in Levels.**

At this point, choose File/Save As and save this as BanfLakeAfterLevels48bits.psd in case you want to revert to this version of the image later. Now choose Image/Mode/8 Bits/Channel to convert this image to 8 bits per color channel for a total of 24 bits. We wanted to do this initial adjustment in 48 bits then convert to 24 bits so we have the best quality histogram in 24-bit mode. If we had done the Levels adjustment after the conversion to 24 bits, we'd now have some gaps in our histogram. We could actually do the next two Curves and Hue/Saturation steps in 48-bit color as well, but that wouldn't give us as much flexibility later if we wanted to redo any of those steps. We'll go ahead and do Curves and Hue/Saturation in 24-bit color using adjustment layers so we can tweak them as many times as we want. If you are going to do 48-bit scans, your initial Levels adjustment at the least, should also be done in 16-bit per channel mode as we have just done. **Choose File/Save As to save the 24-bit version of this file as BanfLakeLayers.psd.**

INTRODUCTION TO CURVES

This section shows you how to adjust specific color ranges using Curves. Before you start making further adjustments to the Banf Lake image, take a moment to examine the Curves tool and its different parts and functions.

Curves is a graph of input and output values with the input values at the bottom of the graph on the horizontal axis and the output values to the left of the graph on the vertical axis. When you use Curves, the input values are the original unadjusted values before you invoked Curves. The output values are the adjusted values and depend on the shape of the curve graph.

In Levels, the histogram is a picture of the actual data that makes up the particular image. In Curves, you see a graph of how this curve would modify any image, but you don't actually see the data that is part of the image. That is why I recommend using Levels first, after you do a scan, because you can see how the scan worked by looking at the histogram and then use Levels to create

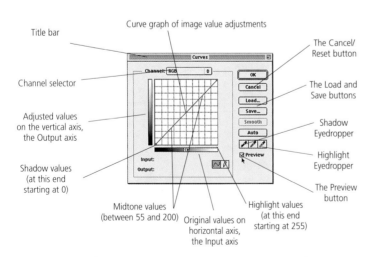

Study this diagram of the Photoshop 6 Curves dialog to learn the controls of the Curves tool.

the best possible histogram from the scan you started with. Many of the controls in Curves are the same as those in Levels, but with Curves you don't see a picture of the data in this particular image. Both tools provide an OK button, which you press when you want the changes to become permanent, and a Cancel button, which you press when you want to leave the tool without any changes taking effect. If you hold the Option key down and then press Reset, you stay in the tool, all changes are undone and the curve goes back to the

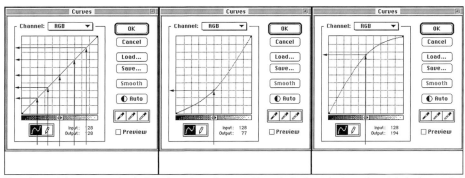

To understand the curve graphs, look at these three diagrams. Along the horizontal axis are the original values, called Input, with 0 (black) on the left side and 255 (white) on the right side. On the vertical axis of the curve, to the left side, are the modified values, called Output, with 0 (black) on the bottom and 255 (white) at the top. Imagine that the original values are light rays that travel straight up from the bottom of the diagram. When they hit the curve graph, they make an immediate left and exit the diagram on the left side. When the curve is the straight default curve, the values go out the same as they come in, as you can see by the leftmost curve above. When the curve is dragged downward, like the middle curve, a value that comes in at 128 hits the curve sooner so it will go out at 77. Because lower values represent darker numbers, pulling the curve down makes the image darker. When the curve is dragged upward, as in the right curve, the input value of 128 doesn't hit the curve until it gets to 194, and that is the brighter output value.

default straight curve. Both Levels and Curves also have Load and Save buttons that you can use to load or save settings to the disk.

If you particularly like a curve that corrected one image, you can click Save to save it, go into Curves while working on another image and click Load to run those saved settings on the other image. Curves, also like Levels, has Highlight and Shadow Eyedropper tools to set the highlight and shadow the same way you do in Levels. In fact, Curves uses the same preference values for the highlight and shadow numbers as you set in Levels. These preferences are systemwide. The curve graph is just a picture of what happens to all the values from 0 to 255. To move the curve, you click it and drag it to a new position. When you let go, Photoshop leaves a point along the curve graph, a point that causes the entire curve to move. To get rid of a point, click and drag it outside of the Curves window. When you do this, the curve bounces back to where it would be without that point. Let's experiment a bit now with Curves before you make final adjustments to the Banf Lake image.

STEP 18: Using the same image you saved at the end of Step 17, choose Image/Adjust/ Curves (Command-M) and look at the Curves dialog box. If the Curves graph area is divided into only four sections, both horizontally and vertically (the default), you can get a more precise grid. Move the cursor to the middle area of the Curves graph, and Option-click in this center area. Now the Curves graph will have 10 sections in each direction. Option-clicking again will get you back to 4 sections in each direction. To get a bigger Curve window, where you can enter more points with greater precision, click in the box at the top-right area of the Title bar, the middle right box in Windows. Clicking in this area again will go back to the smaller curve diagram. Make sure that the Preview button is on so you can see your changes as you work with Curves.

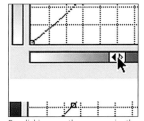

By clicking on the arrows in the middle, you can make the horizontal axis have shadows on the left or the right. Leave the shadows on the left, like on the bottom here, for working with this book.

STEP 19: Now click in the middle of the curve and move the mouse up and down, left and right, and notice how the curve shape changes. Also notice the corresponding changes to the image. Try all the curves

By default in Curves, the horizontal axis shows the shadows on the left. The grayscale on this axis is a hint at this, which is easy to remember because Levels does the same thing. Some curve diagrams show the shadows on the right. If you click the arrow in the middle of the grayscale, you can flip this curve to put shadows on the right. Doing this turns everything else in the curve adjustment into a mirror image of what it was. Therefore, we recommend leaving shadows on the left. When you set the shadows on the right, the Input and Output values read as percentages between 0% and 100%. If you are more comfortable reading percentage values than the 0..255 values, you can make your Curves tool work this way. Just remember, though, that if you flip your curve orientation, the curves in this book will be opposite to yours.

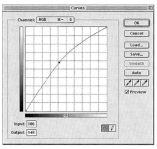

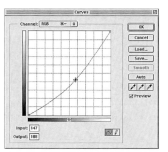

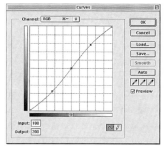

STEP 19: This curve makes the image lighter and brighter. To do this in Levels, move the Input Brightness/ Contrast slider to the left.

This curve makes the image darker. To do this in Levels, move the Input Brightness/Contrast slider to the right.

This S-curve makes the midtones more contrasty and the shadows and highlights less contrasty. You can't do exactly the same thing in Levels.

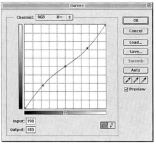

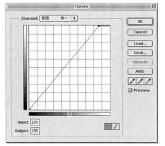

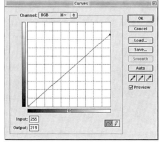

STEP 19: This backward S-curve makes the midtones flatter and increases contrast in the highlights and shadows. You can't do this exactly in Levels.

This curve makes the highlights brighter. This is similar to when you move the Input Highlight slider in Levels to the left.

This curve makes the highlights duller. This is similar to when you move the Output Highlight slider in Levels to the left.

in the diagrams above and on the previous page. Option-Cancel between each one to reset the curve to the original, straight diagonal. Make sure you understand why each curve changes the image the way it does. Remember that each input value has to turn instantly to the left and become an output value as soon as it meets the curve. Trace some values for each of these examples, and I think you will understand how the curve graphs work. You need to understand these curve graphs because they come up all over the place in Photoshop (in Curves, Duotones, Custom CMYK, and Transfer functions), as well as in many books and other applications dealing with color.

CHANGING CONTRAST WITH CURVES

STEP 20: **Use Window/Show Layers (F10) to bring up your Layers palette. Choose Layer/New Adjustment Layer/Curves to add a Curves adjustment layer to your image. The New Curves dialog will come up and you should name this layer Overall Contrast and press OK to bring up the Curves dialog. For this curve, you will want the curve diagram with 4 section dividers. If you currently have a graph that is divided into 10 sections, Option-click in the middle of the curve graph until you get only 4. Click once on each of the 3 intersections along the diagonal line, across the curve, which will place a point on each of those points. Move the bottom point down and to the right, the top point up and to the left and leave the middle point where it was.** This will create an S shape curve that will make the image more contrasty. The values we used for the bottom point were Input of 66 and Output of 55 and the values for the top point were Input of 185 and Output of 195. After clicking on any point, you can either drag to move the point, type in a new value for Input or Output, or you can use the up and down arrows on your keyboard to move any point up or down in value. **If you don't like the way the image looks with these values, move the points around until you get what you like.** The bottom point has more control over the shadow areas, the top point the highlights and the middle point controls the midtones. If you move the middle point up and to the left, the midtones will become lighter. Moving it down and to the right darkens the midtones. If any location in the image actually appears on the curve, click on that point in the image and hold the mouse button down; you will see a circle on the curve showing the values relating to that point. You could now move that part of the curve and the contrast of that point, and similar ones, will change. With Curves you have a lot of control! **Press Return (OK) when you are happy with the contrast of the image.** Since you did this curve as an adjustment layer, notice that the Layers palette now contains the Overall Contrast curve on top of the Background layer.

ENHANCING COLOR WITH HUE/SATURATION

STEP 21: Now you are going to create another Adjustment layer of type Hue/Saturation. **Choose Layer/New Adjustment Layer/ Hue/Saturation or use the pop-up menu at the bottom of the Layers palette, as illustrated to the left, to create a new Hue/ Saturation adjustment layer.** Using the Master selection in the Edit pop-up menu at the top, the Hue/Saturation tool allows you to adjust the hue balance and color saturation of the entire image. Using this tool, you can add contrast and drama to an image without losing shadow detail. **In Master, move the Saturation slider to +20 to increase the saturation of all colors and move the Hue slider to the right to +2 to make all the colors a bit more magenta.** When you saturate all the colors, mainly the midtones change; the highlights and shadows remain the same. You can verify this by looking at the values in your highlight and shadow Color Samplers in the Info palette.

    Now change the Edit pop-up to Greens and saturate the greens even more by an additional +7. When Greens is selected, only parts of the image that contain green will change in color. **Now move the Green Hue slider to the right to +5, which should make the lake and clouds look more bluish.** The color of the lake in this image may seem a bit strange, but this lake in the Canadian Rockies is filled with water from a melted glacier and it actually does have this unusual color. When the Edit menu is not in Master mode, you can use the Eyedropper tools at the bottom to fine-tune the definition of that particular color. The colored bars at the bottom of the dialog show you all the colors with the darker gray slider in the middle, showing you what the current definition is of Green, for example. This darker gray bar represents the range of colors you will be changing here with the lighter gray bars on either side showing you colors that will be modified in a lessser way as the effect of the change tapers off. If you first click in the Eyedropper plus tool, and then click and drag over an area of the image with that tool, that area's colors will be added to the definition of the greens that will be changed. Removing some greens from the colors to be modified can be done by clicking and dragging over the colors you want to remove. **Try working with the Eyedropper tools here, by clicking**

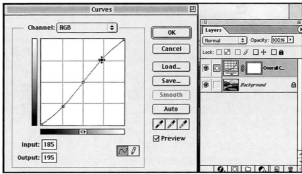

STEP 20: Here you see the Overall Contrast curve that we have added as an adjustment layer on top of the *Background* layer in the Layers palette. After choosing OK and closing this Curves dialog, you can go back to it and even change it as many times as you want to by double-clicking on the little curve graph which is the leftmost layer thumbnail for this Curves adjustment layer. When you change an adjustment layer, you are not permanently modifying the values in the background layer as you did in the first adjustment that you did with Levels where you didn't use an adjustment layer. Adjustment layers also keep track of your changes for you.

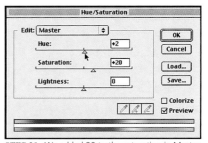

STEP 21: We added 20 to the saturation in Master, which will saturate all the colors. We also moved the Hue to the right by 2 which makes the colors a bit warmer and more magenta. Notice that if you move the Hue to the left, the image looks more green.

STEP 21: After adjusting Master, we switched the Edit menu to Greens and saturated them even more by moving the Saturation up to +7. We also moved the Hue slider to the right by 5 which puts more blue into the lake and the clouds.

STEP 21: Another way to create a new adjustment layer is to click on the circular icon at the bottom of the Layers palette. This brings up a menu showing each type of adjustment layer. Choosing one this way brings you directly into the Hue/Saturation dialog so if you want to give this layer a custom name, like Overall Hue/Sat, then you will have to later Option-click on its layer thumbnail which is how you rename an existing layer.

STEP 21: Here I'd initially chosen Greens for the Edit mode but after using the Eyedropper plus tool to add this cyanish green to my color definition for Greens, photoshop changed the name of Edit to Cyans. When making my green adjustments, I first moved Saturation to +7, then moved Hue to +5 then I clicked down in this area of the image because I wanted to change its tonal value. At that point further changes in the Hue or Saturation would now be changing that new range of green colors.

and dragging with the Eyedropper plus tool over greenish areas in the image to change the definition of the greens you are changing. Remember, you can always use Option-Cancel to return this tool to where it started before you made any changes. If you just want to see the effect of the additional green changes, first make the suggested changes to Master and then choose OK. Now double-click on the leftmost Layer thumbnail for this Hue/Saturation layer to bring up the Hue/Saturation dialog. Now move the Edit pop-up to Greens and go ahead and make your green changes. Since you made the changes to Master within the initial invocation of this dialog, turning the Preview checkbox off will now show you the image with just the Master changes applied. Turning the Preview checkbox on will show you the image with the Master changes and the **Green changes.** The Preview checkbox, for this second invocation of the tool, now just shows you the changes you added for the Greens. To see your changes as you work, make sure the Preview checkbox is checked while working in this tool and all color correction tools.

Now switch the Edit menu to Blues and notice that moving the Hue slider in Blues to +3 gives some shadow parts of the image a slightly more magenta tone. Adjust the Blues to a point where you like the image best.

Move the Edit menu to Reds and notice that moving the Hue slider to the right to +15 makes the dirt in the foreground appear more greenish-yellow. Moving this Hue slider to the left to -15 makes the dirt have a more magenta color. Notice that these moves also change the tones on the sunlit mountains to the top right of the image. I liked the Red tones the way they were, so I left the Red Hue at 0 but it is interesting to look at and understand the possibilities. Choose OK when you are happy with the image's Hue and Saturation.

STEP 22: The Layers palette after adding the Overall Color layer set. Make sure the order of the layers stays the same inside the set with Hue/Saturation on top of Overall Contrast.

STEP 22: We have now finsihed the Overall Color Correction steps (Levels, Curves and Hue/Saturation), in this case we did the Levels step on the 16-bit per channel version of the image. We will group these steps into a layer set. **Choose Layer/New/Layer Set and call this new set Overall Color. It will appear on the top of the other layers in the Layers palette. Click on the Layer thumbnail of the Overall Hue/Saturation layer and drag it until the cursor is on top of the Overall Color layer set icon. At that point you can release the mouse and the Hue/Saturation layer will become part of that set. Do the same thing with the Overall Contrast layer until your Layers palette looks like the one to the right.** Layer sets give you a way to group your layers and organize your work. Clicking on the arrow to the left of the Overall Color layer set will collapse this set so all you see is the folder showing that other layers are inside. Clicking on this arrow again will open this and show you the layers that are in this set. Layer sets are a very useful feature added for Photoshop 6.

ADJUSTING SELECTED COLOR AREAS USING MASKS

STEP 23: During the Overall Color Correction steps, which we just completed, the goal is to correct the overall image without using selections or masks to fine-tune the color, or contrast adjustment, of any particular areas. We are looking at the entire image and trying to make the largest areas of it look correct. Now that we have completed those steps, we should have a histogram for this image that we are happy with having correct and neutral highlight and shadow values, an overall brightness and contrast that we like and also a good overall color saturation. Now we want to find the isolated parts of the image that can be improved even more, but will require a selection or mask to improve those areas. In this step we are going to enhance the look of the clouds.

Here is the Banf Lake image after completing the Overall Color Correction steps. Compare this to the version on the first page of this chapter.

As shown on the top of this page, make sure that the active layer in the Layers palette is the topmost OverallColorCorrection set. The active layer is the one that is highlighted, you can click on the name of a layer to highlight it. We are going to create a new Curves adjustment layer which will appear on top of the OverallColorCorrection set and that means this new layer's corrections will happen after the overall color corrections have already occurred. Choose Layer/New Adjustment Layer/Curves or just press F3, if you have ArtistKeys installed, to make yet another adjustment layer which you should name DarkenClouds. Click a point in the center of the diagonal line and drag it down and to the right until the clouds have more drama and you like the way they look. We chose a point at Input 141 and Output 118. Don't worry about the rest of the image looking too dark, just get the clouds to look the way you want them.

Choose OK to finish your curve adjustments and notice that the Curve adjustment layer in the Layers palette has two thumbnails associated with it. The leftmost one is the Layer thumbnail and it contains the little icon that looks like a curve diagram, which shows you that this is a Curve type adjustment layer. The rightmost thumbnail is the Layer Mask thumbnail and it is completely white, which means that right now this adjustment is happening to the entire image. **Choose Image/Adjust/Invert to invert this Layer Mask thumbnail, and the layer mask, to completely black. Now this curve change doesn't apply to any of the image. Type a B, to switch to the Paintbrush tool and select a 200 pixel soft brush from the Brushes palette at the top left of the Options palette at the top of your screen. Type a D, for default colors, which will make your foreground color white and your background color black. Make sure the Opacity for your brush is set at 100%. Now paint over the entire area of the clouds with this soft brush. Notice that as you paint, the darken curve is again applied to the areas where you painted in the mask with white. Don't bring the brush too close to the tops of the mountains, as you don't want them darkened by this Curves adjustment. If you accidentally paint too close to the mountains and they get darkened, you can use Command-Z to undo the last brush stroke or use the History palette (F8) to remove several brush strokes. You can also just type an X, for Exchange, to**

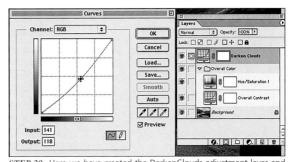

STEP 23: Here we have created the DarkenClouds adjustment layer and are setting the curve point at 141, 118.

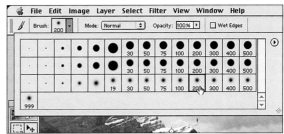

STEP 23: After typing B to get the Paintbrush, click and drag in the Brush pop-up at the left of the Options palette until you are on top of the 200-pixel soft brush. Releasing the mouse button at this point will close the Brush pop-up and select that brush. The brushes shown here are BarrysPhotoBrushes which we show you how to set up in Chapter 3.

Adjusting Selected Color Areas Using Masks

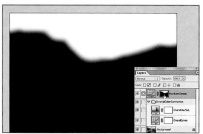

STEP 23: Here I have Option-clicked on the Darken-Clouds Layer Mask thumbnail to show my final clouds mask. Option-clicking a second time will show the image again.

switch the foreground color to black. Painting over the mountains with black will again remove the curve adjustment from the black painted areas. Type X a second time to switch back to white.

If you Option-click on the Layer Mask thumbnail for this DarkenClouds layer, you will actually see the mask. If you left any black holes within the clouds area, you can paint them white while looking directly at the mask. To see the image again, just Option-click on the Layer Mask thumbnail again.

FIXING CLOUDS AND REMOVING SPOTS

STEP 24: Now we are going to fix the top left and top right of the image where the lens shield of the camera removed some image area from this 28mm wide angle lens. **Click on the word Background in the Background layer to activate that layer. Type an M to switch to the Rectangular Marquee tool. Shift-M will toggle between the Rectangular and Oval marquee, by the way. Use this tool to select all of the clouds area**

STEP 24: Select this area with the Marquee to start the process of fixing the clouds

of the image as shown in the illustration here. Now choose Layer/New/Layer via Copy to turn this selection into a new layer right above the Background layer. You will work on this copy of the clouds so if you make a mistake, the original undamaged clouds will still be in the background layer below. **Click on the Lock Position icon at the top of the Layers palette to lock the position of this layer so you don't accidentally move it with the move tool. Type an S to switch to the Rubber Stamp tool, called the Clone Stamp tool in Photoshop 6, and choose the 100-pixel soft brush from the Brush pop-up in the Options palette at the top of your screen. Move the cursor over some good-looking clouds, a bit below and to the left of the dark top-right corner area. Option-click at the spot where you want to copy the clouds from. Now release the mouse button and move the cursor over to the top-right corner where you need to replace the black area with good clouds. Click and hold the mouse button as you drag across the black area and see it replaced by good clouds.** While the

STEP 24: This is what it should look like in the Rubber Stamp tool with the mouse button down as you replace the black area with good clouds. The + shows you where clouds are being copied from and the circle shows you where the clouds are being copied to.

mouse button is down, you'll see a + where Photoshop is copying new cloud data from and a circle where the data is being copied to. Do this slowly and over and over again until you understand what is happening and get some good-looking clouds in the top-right corner. You can always choose Command-Z to Undo one step, then try it again. If you really mess up the area, bring up the History palette and click back before you started using the Rubber Stamp tool. **When you have fixed your clouds, Option-double-click on the default Layer 1 name for this layer and rename it to Fix Clouds. Turn the Eye icon off for the Background layer for now, so you are just seeing image data from this Fix Clouds layer.**

Now zoom the image into 100% by choosing View/Actual Pixels (Command-Option-0) then zoom in one more time, using Command-Spacebar-click, to get the image to 200%. Press the Home key on your keyboard to scroll the image to the top-left corner then choose the third brush from the top left in the Brushes pop-up. You should still be using the Rubber Stamp tool, now the Clone Stamp tool. You can now press the Tab key to remove all your palettes from the screen. If you are still in Full Screen Mode, you will just see a close-up of the top-left corner of the screen. You now want to scroll through your image one full screen at a time and remove any dust or spots until you have a totally clean image. When you see a dust spot, or a larger piece of dirt, move the cursor next to the spot on top of an area that matches the color and contrast where the spot is. Hold the Option key down and click once where you want to copy image data from to fix the spot. Release the mouse button.

STEP 24: Locking the position of the Fix Clouds layer so it can't be accidentally moved.

STEP 24: A spot to the left with the Option key down and cursor on the right. Option-click next to the spot to show Photoshop where to pick up color and detail.

STEP 24: Click the spot without the Option key down. The cursor should look like this before you click, and the spot should be removed when you click using the pixels from where you Option-clicked before.

STEP 24: The circle and the crosshair that you see while cloning with the mouse button down. Photoshop picks up detail from the crosshair and places it down at the cursor circle.

Now move the cursor on top of the spot and click without the Option key down. The data will be copied from where you Option-clicked to where you clicked without the Option key. If you hold the mouse button down and drag, you'll see a + where Photoshop is copying from and a circle where it is copying to.

Once you initially Option-click then click without the Option key, sets up the spacial relationship between where Photoshop copies from and where it copies to. If Aligned is on in the Rubber Stamp's options, this spacial relationship will stay the same until you Option-click again, so you don't have to use the Option key each time. You can just click and data will always be copied from the left, right, bottom or top of where you click, depending on your initial set of Option-click and then click. **To remove a big spot or piece of dust, you'll have to click multiple times, or hold the mouse button down and drag, until the spot is gone. You only need to Option-click again if the color of where you are copying from no longer matches where you are copying to.** If you are having trouble getting the Rubber Stamp tool to work

STEP 24: This long piece of dust with 3 straight sections can actually be removed in about 3 short steps. Option-click to the top left of the dust to pick up clean sky from there then Click at the top of the dust as shown here, which will remove the top end of the dust. Release the mouse button and move the cursor down the straight piece of dust and Shift-click just before the dust piece curves to the left. Shift-clicking will clone from where you first clicked in a straight line to where you Shift-click. You can repeat this process for the 3 straight sections of this strip of dust to remove it more quickly.

SCRATCH REMOVAL A: First, Option-click below the left end of a scratch using a brush slightly bigger than the scratch.

SCRATCH REMOVAL B: Second, click the left end of the scratch, centered on the scratch, directly above where you Option-clicked before.

SCRATCH REMOVAL C: Third, Shift-click the right end of the scratch, centered on the scratch. The scratch should disappear! You can use this technique to remove scratches made in film by the film processor. After the initial removal, you may need to do some further Rubber Stamp cleanup on some parts of the scratch.

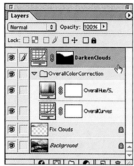

STEP 24: The final Layers palette for this master image.

correctly, look at page 42 of Chapter 4: "The Tool Palette" for more details about how it works.

When you have removed all the spots from this section of the screen, you can use Command-Page Down to scroll one screen full to the right. Now you remove the spots from this section and continue to scroll to the right until you reach the right side of the screen. At that point you can press the Page Down key on your keyboard to scroll one full screen down. Now you are fixing a full screen, then choosing Command-Page Up to scroll a full screen to the left. Move through the entire Fix Clouds layer until you have removed all the spots in this layer. Now use Tab to bring up your palettes again and click on the word Background to activate the background layer. Press Tab again to remove your palettesand then continue stepping through screens of the background layer until you have removed all the spots there, too.

SAVING AND ARCHIVING YOUR MASTER IMAGE

STEP 25: **Now that you have spotted your master image, you need to save this file and go ahead and make a test print to be sure you are happy with the color. We will show you how to prepare the test print in Step 26 and beyond. After making the test print, you may need to come back to one or more of your adjustment layers and tweak the color before you achieve a final print. To tweak an adjustment layer, just double-click on its Layer thumbnail, which will bring up that layer's Levels, Curve or Hue/Saturation dialog and show you the adjustments you already made. You can then make subtle changes to what you have already done based on what you want to change in the print. When bringing up an adjustment layer a second time, turning the Preview checkbox off shows you the image based on the first set of adjustments; turning on the Preview checkbox shows you the image with the further changes you have added after bringing it up the second time. To see the image without this adjustment layer at all, you need to turn off this layer's Eye icon in the Layers palette. When you are finally happy with all your adjustments to this image, save and archive this as your master layered image to a CD or some other permanent backup storage.**

RESAMPLING AND RETARGETING COPIES OF A MASTER IMAGE FOR DIFFERENT SIZE PRINTS AND OTHER USES

MAKING AN RGB OR CMYK PRINT VERSION

STEP 26: **After saving your master layered file, choose Image/Duplicate (F5) to make an onscreen copy of your master image. Turn on the Duplicate Merged Layers Only option in the Duplicate dialog and enter a name for this image of LakeTest 300 dpi 4x6. Choosing Merged Layers Only in Photoshop 6 will blend all the layers in this copy into one Photoshop background layer. Press F for Full Screen mode and then Command-0 to fill the screen with this copy. Go into Image/Image Size (F7) and turn off the Resample Image option at the bottom of the dialog.** This allows you to play around with numbers to see what you will get without resampling your image. If you don't need to resample, that is better, and when you do resample, you want to resample down and make a larger image smaller, rather than resample up. **Set the resolution to 300 dpi, which is the resolution you would use to print this on a 150-line screen press, your typical glossy magazine. With the resolution set to 300 dpi and Resample Image off, you can see that this image has enough information to print over 6 inches wide and over 4 inches high. If you wanted a 4x6 test print, you now know you can do this and resample down instead of up. Turn Resample Image back on and set the width to 6 inches; notice that the height now says 4.319. Your numbers may be slightly different, depending on how you did your initial crop.** The point here is that the Image Size dialog is showing you that with the width set to 6 inches, you have a little more height than you need. If you look at Pixel Dimensions, at the top of the dialog, it is also showing you that the image is going to be a little smaller if we resample to 300 dpi at 6 inches wide. **Choose OK to Resample the image.**

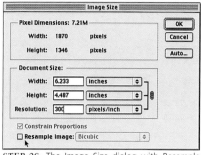

STEP 26: The Image Size dialog with Resample Image off and the dpi set to 300, which allows us to see how big of an image we can get at that resolution we want without resampling. If the WIdth and Height shown here are bigger than what we need, we know that we will be resampling down and not up, which is what we want. To test print this on an Epson printer, I'd probably just set the pixels/inch to 310 and not resample.

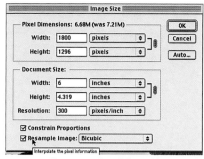

STEP 26: The Image Size dialog with Resample Image turned on again after we have typed in an exact width of 6 inches and set the resolution to exactly 300 pixels/inch. When placing the image in a page layout application, the size and resolution need to be exact. Notice how the Pixel Dimensions at the top of the dialog show the before and after sizes.

STEP 27: Now we need to sharpen the image because it is at its final size and we have not sharpened it before, even while scanning. You will get better sharpening results if you don't sharpen the image till it reaches its final resample size. **Choose View/ Actual Pixels (Command-Option-0) to zoom the image to 100% and then do Filter/Sharpen/Unsharp Mask (F4).** The details of the Unsharp Mask filter are explained in the next chapter, but what you need to know here is that you will use different settings in this filter, depending on the size of the image and also on the particular image. Also, you are usually best judging the results of a sharpen or a blur while looking at the image at 100%. **For this image, I have decided to use the 100, 1.0 and 5 setting. Start with these values and then you can play with the settings and see what they do to the image, as long as the Preview button is on in the Unsharp Mask dialog.** Again, we will go into the details of what each setting does in the next chapter. You may want to check and respot your image after the final sharpening; there should be little additional work! **Do Command-S to save your image in RGB format. If you were going to make a test print on an Epson or other RGB printer, this would be the image you'd test.**

STEP 28: **If you were going to print this as a CMYK press proof of some sort, make sure your CMYK working space in the Color Settings preferences was correct for this print job, then you'd choose Image/Mode/CMYK to convert this image to CMYK. Depending on your monitor calibration and your other preferences setup, you might notice a certain color and/or contrast shift after converting to CMYK. You can use Command-Z to toggle back and forth between RGB and CMYK to help you decide if you need to make adjustments after converting to CMYK. When View/Proof Setup is set to the default of Working CMYK, you can actually do this and make the adjustments in RGB mode by turning on View/Proof Colors to see what your RGB file will look like when converted to CMYK.** Because I don't usually adjust my RGB master files based on how they will look in CMYK, my normal workflow is to go ahead and

Resampling and Retargeting Copies of a Master Image For Different Size Prints and Other Uses

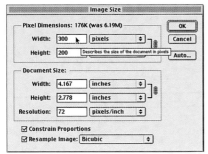

STEP 29: Here we made a much smaller Web image by setting the pixels/inch to 72 and the Pixel Dimensions to 300 wide by 200 high.

do the conversion to CMYK and then fix any problems in that particular CMYK version at that time. This is my preference because the main focus of my images is my larger art prints that are destined for RGB output devices, like the LightJet 5000 or Epson 7500.

MAKING A WEB VERSION

STEP 29: **Use the Window menu to go back to your BanfLakeLayers master image; then choose Image/Duplicate again with Duplicate Merged Layers Only on naming this file BanfLakeWeb300x200. Choose F for Full Screen mode and View/Fit On Screen (Command-0) to fill the screen with this image. Type C to switch to the Crop tool, and press Return to bring up its options. Set the Width to 3 and the Height to 2; then draw the crop box across the full width of the image. Release the mouse and then click in the center of the crop box and drag down to center the crop area, so an even amount is cut from the top and bottom of this image. Press Return to actually do the crop. The Crop tool will have now forced the image to the aspect ratio you have chosen. Now choose Image/Image Size (F7) to bring up the Image Size dialog again and set the top Width, in the Pixel Dimentions area, to 300 pixels; then set the dpi to 72 making sure the Pixel Dimentions still read 300 pixels at the top. Press OK to resample your image for the Web. Now choose Command-Option-0 for 100% and then press F4 for Unsharp Mask and use the 200, .5, and 0 settings.** Larger amounts and smaller Radius values seem to work better for the small Web images. **Now choose File/Save As and save this file in JPEG format with the Quality set at High (8) and Baseline Optimized On.** These JPEG settings are explained in great detail in the last section of the book: Images for the Web and Multimedia.

In previous versions of this book, we had used an image called the Grand Canyon for this initial Overall Color Correction exercise. For *Photoshop 6 Artistry*, I decided to move on to a new image with a slightly different approach. The Grand Canyon image however, is a great image to illustrate that setting the highlights and shadows to neutral values can do a lot towards the color correction of many images. **To gain extra understanding of what we are doing here and why, you might also want to go through the Overall Color Correction process described in this chapter using the Grand Canyon image, which is still on the CD for this chapter.**

STEP 29: Here is the JPEG version of this image we made in step 29 but printed at 300 dpi.

STEP 29: The final version of the Banf Lake image after sharpening and resampling to 6 inches wide. For my final art print of this image, I also removed the people and the post in the front right of this image. Doing that is a bit advanced for the first exercise in this book. Later in this book, you'll learn to do that type of thing and more.

20 HANDS-ON SESSION: Correcting a Problem Image

Overall color correction using adjustment layers on a problem scan without good white or black points. Using advanced selections and adjustment layers with Curves, Hue/Saturation and Unsharp Mask to finish color correcting a problem scan; learning about Preview CMYK and fixing out-of-gamut colors.

The initial Kansas Photo CD scan.

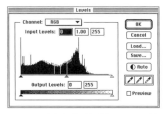

STEP 2: Original RGB histogram with lack of highlight values.

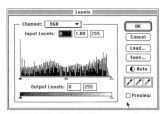

STEP 2: Final RGB histogram data is spread from 0 to 255.

In this example, you will do overall color correction but use some different techniques than in the Banf Lake session because the histogram of this scan looks different. For the purposes of this example, we assume that you have done the Banf Lake example.

SETTING HIGHLIGHTS WITH CHANNELS

STEP 1: **Open the file KansasRawPhotoCD from the chapter 20 folder on the *Photoshop 6 Artistry* CD.** This is a 4Mb Photo CD scan of a Kodachrome shot I took while driving through Kansas during a summer vacation when I was in college in 1977. Old Kodachromes tend to fade! In the Crop tool, delete the Option palette values in Width and Height if they are still there from the last exercise. **Use the Crop tool to crop the copyright notice from the bottom. Choose File/Save As and save this file as KansasLevels. Put the image in Full Screen mode (F) by clicking the middle icon at the bottom of the Tool palette. Bring up the Info palette (F9 with ArtistKeys), and then choose Image/New Adjustment Layer/Levels (Command-F3) to enter Levels giving this adjustment layer the name Overall Levels.**

STEP 2: Look at the original RGB histogram pictured here and notice that the values don't go all the way to the right (highlight) side, which is why the picture looks dull. **Press Command-1, then Command-2, and then Command-3 to look at the Red, Green and Blue channels, respectively.** I always do this when I first look at a scan to see if it has any potential problems. In this image, all the channels have dull highlights, but each of them has highlight detail that ends at a different point on the histogram. **Press Command-~ to go back to RGB and then hold down the Option key while dragging the Input Highlight slider to the left.** Remember, the Option key technique only works if you have the Preview checkbox on. You would normally set the highlight at the first area to turn white. In this photo, there is no good, neutral place to set a highlight, which should be pure white after that setting. The "white" buildings aren't really that white, and the brightest area is actually somewhere in the blue clouds. That's a sign that the Eyedropper may not be the best way to set the highlights in this image. **Type Command-1 again and move the Red Input Highlight slider to the left until it reaches the first real histogram data, at about 213. Do the same thing for the Green (189) and Blue (171) channels, and then press Command-~ to return to RGB.** Notice how much brighter the image looks now and how much more complete the RGB histogram looks. We have set our highlight for this image.

STEP 3: Notice that the shadow values in the Blue channel suddenly drop off a cliff on the left side, unlike those in the Red and Green channels, which taper off like they should. This is a sign that the scanner did not get all the shadow detail in the Blue channel or that there was no more detail in the film. Because this is a Photo CD scan, we have to live with it or buy our own scanner. When this happens to you, look at the original transparency and see if there was actually detail in this area. If there was, you might be able to get better results by rescanning with a high-end, drum scanner, a better scanner or just better scanner settings. **However, in the real world, we often have to correct problem images and scans, so hold the Option key down and move the Input Shadow slider, the top-left slider, to the right to test for a shadow point. There are some good shadow locations on the right side of the wheat, at the bottom and also within the big green tree by the house. Move the Input Shadow slider back to 0. Measure these shadows with the Eyedropper until you find the darkest neutral spot (I found a few in the wheat that had initial values of 5, 5, 5) and then Shift-click on that spot to create Color Sampler #1 in the Info palette. Go into each of the Red, Green and Blue channels and move the Input Shadow slider to the right until the Color Sampler for your shadow point reads around 2, 2, 2 and your black shadows look neutral. If they don't, click a new neutral darkest spot until your shadows look and measure neutral. Now you have set your shadow. Turn the Preview checkbox off and on to see what you have done to the image so far.**

BRIGHTNESS, CONTRAST AND COLOR CAST

STEP 4: **Move the Input Brightness/Contrast slider in the RGB channel until the overall brightness of the image looks correct. I moved it to the left to 1.15 to bring out a little more shadow detail in the foreground wheat and in the dark trees around the house. You can't bring out more detail in an area that is totally black, so don't go too far on this shadow detail thing.**

STEP 5: Because we moved the highlight sliders differently on each of the color channels, we need to go into each channel and correct for color casts, which is easiest to do if you try to fix the most annoying cast first, and then fine-tune the other colors and casts that appear along the way. The wheat in the foreground seems to have a greenish cast. I often have a hard time with these greenish casts because they're

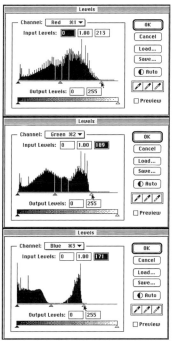

STEP 2: Move the Input Highlight sliders of the Red, Green, and Blue histograms to the left until they touch the beginning of the data. This moves all the data to the left of that point all the way to the right, spreading out the values in each histogram.

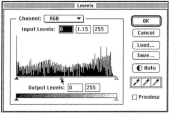

STEP 4: After setting highlight and shadow, set overall brightness and contrast. Move the middle slider to the left in RGB.

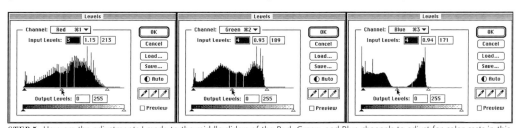

STEP 5: Here are the adjustments I made to the middle sliders of the Red, Green, and Blue channels to adjust for color casts in this image. Because the wheat is the major component here, getting that to look good was the main goal. Other parts of the image can be fine-tuned later.

STEP 5: Kansas, after all the Levels adjustments.

sometimes both green and cyan. This one looks greener, so go to the Green channel (Command-2) and move the middle slider to the right to add magenta; that should improve the situation and make the wheat look more golden. Move the slider until the wheat looks too magenta, move it back until you start to see the green again, and then add just a little magenta. If the image still has a greenish tinge, it might be that there is a cyan problem too, so move to the Red channel (Command-1) and add a little red by moving the middle slider to the left. Finally, add a little yellow by moving the middle slider in the Blue channel a little to the right. The color choices you make may be different than mine depending on your taste. That is certainly fine! When your color appears correct, look at the RGB values of your Color Sampler for the shadow in the Info palette. If they are no longer neutral, you can go back into each color channel and move them back where you want them using the Input Shadow slider for that channel. When you're happy with the color, you should click OK to complete your Levels changes. Since you have your Levels changes in a Levels adjustment layer, you can turn these changes on and off using the Eye icon for that Layer, which is above the Background layer in the Layers palette. Choose File/Save to save your changes so far. Now you have done the initial Levels adjustment on this difficult image. In this example we are using adjustment layers for all the overall color adjustment steps since we started with an initial 8-bit per channel scan. Had we started with a 16-bit per channel scan, we would have done this initial step using Image/Adjust/Levels since adjustment layers don't work with 16-bit per channel images. It is always better to use adjustment layers when you can.

SATURATING COLORS

STEP 6: After the Levels adjustments, you could add a Curve adjustment layer to change the contrast of this image with an S curve. We are first going to saturate the colors using Hue/Saturation and see if that gives us enough contrast. We could always insert a Curve layer between the Levels and Hue/Saturation layer afterward. **Choose Layers/New Adjustment Layer/Hue/Saturation (Command-F4), calling this layer Overall Hue/Saturation then press OK. Make sure that the Preview checkbox is on when you reach the Hue/Saturation dialog.** For flexibility later, unless you are working on a 48-bit image, you should create a Hue/Saturation adjustment layer, as we just did here, instead of just doing Image/Adjust/Hue/Saturation. **When you first enter Hue/Saturation, the Edit Master menu is selected. Any master changes you make apply to all the colors at the same time. Move the Saturation slider to the right to about 15, making all colors more vivid.**

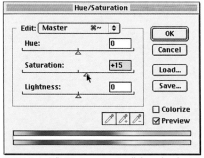

STEP 6: In Edit Master, saturate all the colors by 15.

STEP 7: **Because the wheat is mostly composed of yellow, this is an important color to tweak. Choose the Yellow Edit menu to restrict the changes you make to apply only to the yellow parts of the image. Move the Saturation slider to the right by 15 and move the Hue slider a little to the left toward red; –1 makes the yellows a little warmer and more intense.** The changes you make might be a little different depending on your personal taste and exactly how you have adjusted your version of this image so far.

STEP 8: **Chose the Red Edit menu and move the red Hue toward the left by –3, add magenta and saturate the reds also by 5. Choose the Cyan Edit menu and move the cyan Hue toward the right (blue) by 5, and saturate them by 10.** The cyan changes mostly affect the sky. When you choose OK in this Hue/Saturation dialog, your changes are archived in a Hue/Saturation adjustment layer that you can tweak as many times as you like, without damaging the original image, even after saving the file. We will learn a lot more about the many advantages of adjustment layers as we go through this book—it's just important that you get used to using them as soon as you can.

STEP 9: In color correcting this image so far, we have made the corrections we are going to make without creating selections. **Choose Layer/New/Layer Set and create a set, which you name Overall Color Correction. Move the Levels and Hue/Saturation adjustment layers into that set by dragging each of their Layer thumb-**

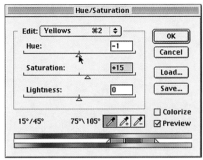

STEP 7: In Yellow, saturate the yellow colors by 15, and move yellows slightly toward red.

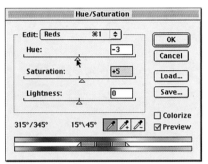

STEP 8: Red Hue/Saturation changes.

STEP 9: The Layers palette so far after adding the Layer set.

STEP 9: Kansas, after Levels and Hue/Saturation adjustments using adjustment layers.

nails on top of the Layer Set thumbnail, and then releasing them there. After the Levels and Hue/Saturation layers are inside the Overall Color Correction layer set, click on the Layer set to make it active. That way new adjustment layers will be added above that set. Your Layers palette should now look like the one on the previous page. Use Command-S to save the image at this point.

IMPROVING SELECTED COLOR AREAS

STEP 10: **Type a W to switch to the Magic Wand tool and look in the Options palette at the top of your screen to make sure that the Tolerance is set to 32 and that Anti-aliased and Contiguous are on; these are the defaults.** You are going to select parts

STEP 11: Create the selection of the green field with the Magic Wand and Lasso tool.

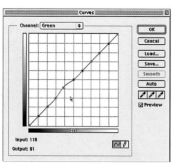

STEP 11: My final adjusted Green curve.

STEP 11: If you Option-click on the Green Field layer mask thumbnail, the rightmost thumbnail, you will see the mask created from your Wand selection. That is the only thing adjusted by this adjustment layer. Option-clicking a 2nd time will return you to the display of the composite image.

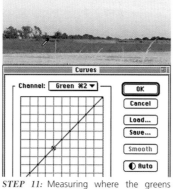

STEP 11: Measuring where the greens occur in the green grass. Command-Shift-click to add a point to the Red, Green and Blue curves at the same time or just Command-click to add a point at the corresponding location in the curve you are currently looking at, as we did with the Green curve.

of this image and improve their color balance and/or density. **Notice that when you move the cursor over the image, you get the universal Not Allowed icon. Photoshop 6 isn't allowing a selection when you have a Layer set active. Click back on the Overall Hue/Saturation adjustment layer to make it active and notice that the Not Allowed icon goes away. Start out selecting the green strip of grass that separates the field from the sky; you will have to Shift-click on it several times to get the entire green field. This whole area seems a bit magenta to me. Click the grass and then Shift-click to add to the selection until you have selected all the grass. If you accidentally select something that you shouldn't, choose Edit/Undo (Command-Z) and try again. You can also use the Lasso tool (L) with the Shift key to add to the selection, or with the Option key to subtract from the selection. After you select the entire area, choose Select/Feather and enter 1 to create a 1-pixel feather. This feather will blend the color changes you will make along the edge of the selection.**

STEP 11: **Choose Layer/New Adjustment Layer/Curves and name this new adjustment layer Green Field, and then press OK in the New Layer dialog. Use the pop-up at the top of the dialog to go to the Green Channel, and then press the Load button in the Curves dialog to load the LockdownGreen curve from the Lockdown Curves folder within the Ch03.Preferences folder on the *Photoshop 6 Artistry* CD.** This places points all along the curve so you can make changes to a selected part of the curve. You could have placed these points manually, but the Lockdown Curves save you time. **Click on the image with the Eyedropper and hold the mouse button down**

242

Chapter 20: Correcting a Problem Image

in the area where the green grass seems a bit magenta. Look at the circle that appears on the curve. move the cursor around a bit in the green area, while holding down the mouse, until you can see where an average magenta/green area is. At that point, Command-click on the image and Photoshop will place a point on the curve representing the place you clicked. Move that point in the curve diagram up and to the left to add green to that part of the curve. If you click in the box at the top right of the Curves dialog, you will get a bigger dialog that makes it easier to place more detailed points. When you are happy with your color changes, choose OK. Now drag this Green Field adjustment layer above the Overall Color Correction layer set; you'll see a black line when you can release this layer and actually have it end up on top of the layer set.

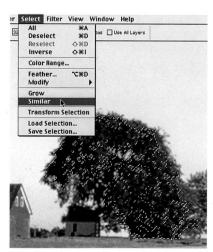

STEP 12: **Use Command-Spacebar-click to zoom in on the trees; then select the darker parts of the big tree with the Magic Wand (W), as shown in the illustration below right. Now go to Select/Grow and notice how this increases the size of that selection with that local area. Use Command-Z to undo the grow; then do Select/Similar and notice how this selects similar areas throughout the entire image, but with the Wand tolerance at 32, this selects too much. Use Command-Z again then press Return, then 12, then Return again and notice that the Wand's tolerance is now set to 12. Now try Select/Similar again and you should see a selection that is like the one at the bottom** of this page. **You want to have the trees and bushes selected, but not the shadow areas in the foreground. Type an L to switch to the Lasso tool and use Option-Spacebar-click to zoom out so there is gray area surrounding the image. While holding the Option key down, circle the area shown in red in the illustration below and the Lasso tool will remove those foreground shadows from the selection. Now choose Command-F3 to create a new Curves adjustment layer and use the Curves dialog to brighten up the shadow areas and also the green color of the trees and bushes.** Don't over do it here, you want small subtle adjustments like those shown to the right; otherwise, your trees will look posterize. When you are finished, you should have a Layers palette that looks like the one you see here. **Now choose File/Save (Command-S) to save your work on this example so far.**

STEP 12: Here we see the tree selected as we did using the Magic want tool. Now we are choosing Select/Similar after setting the Magic Wand's tolerance setting to 12.

STEP 12: After using Select/Similar to select the other dark green parts of the image, you then use the Lasso tool with the Option key held down to circle the area seen in red above here. When you release the mouse button, this part of the selection will go away and only the trees and bushes will remain.

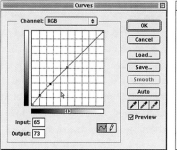

STEP 12: My RGB curve for step 12.

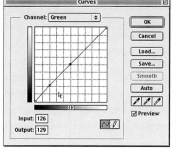

STEP 12: My Green curve for step 12.

STEP 12: How your Layers palette should look after step 12.

STEP 13: Close-up of the Barn selection. Don't let the selection go down into the yellow field because that does contain some red and the change won't work as well.

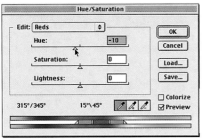

STEP 13: In Edit Reds, move the Hue slider to -10 and you'll notice that the barn gets a new paint job.

STEP 13: **Now we'll show you a useful tip you can use when selecting areas of isolated color. Type an L to switch to the Lasso tool and press the Return key to select the Lasso's feather value. Type in a 2, then press Return again to accept the feather change. Using the Lasso tool, make a very loose selection around the red barn, like you see to the left. Use Command-F4 to get a new adjustment layer of type Hue/Saturation and call it Barn Hue/Sat. Now move the Edit menu to Reds and then move the Hue slider to –10, which will make things that are already red look like they just got a new coat of paint.** Since there is no red component to the sky or green grass, this works well and saves you from making a detailed selection of the barn. Setting the Lasso feather to 2 before you started makes the edge of this selection soft, which aids the process of not making it visible in the areas we don't want changed. **Choose Command-S to save your file.**

STEP 14: Notice that each time you create a new adjustment layer, your Layers palette grows toward the top. Also notice that these last four adjustment layers have mostly black Layer Mask thumbnails in the Layers palette. **If you Option-click one of these thumbnails, you will notice that you see a mask and that mask is black everywhere except the area that was selected before you created the adjustment layer. When you create an adjustment layer when having a selection, Photoshop assumes the selection is the part you want to adjust and creates a mask that is white only in that area. Only the white parts of the masks are actually changed in color or contrast by the adjustment layer. The two adjustment layers in the Overall Color Correction Layer Set have totally white Layer Mask thumbnails because those layers adjust the entire image. If you type a B for brush, then a D for default colors and then pick the third brush from the top left in the Brushes palette, you can now paint 100% white over the top of the red roof on the small building at the left of the green field. You should ctually be painting white into the layer mask for the Barn Hue/Sat adjustment layer, and this will make that red roof a more saturated red just as it did for the barn.**

STEP 15: Looking at the Red, Green and Blue channels to decide which one to copy to make a mask.

STEP 15: **Use Command-0 to zoom out until you can see the entire image. Now bring up the Channels palette (Shift-F10) and click on each of the Red, Green and Blue channels, one at a time, until you find the one with the most contrast between the sky and the rest of the image. Click on the word Blue in the Blue channel and make sure the Eye icons are off for RGB, Red and Green.** The Blue channel has the most contrast in this image, so we are going to use it to create a mask separating the sky from the rest of the image. This is a useful technique that I use all the time, but it is quite often a different channel than Blue that has the most contrast. **To make a copy of the Blue channel, drag the Blue channel down to the New Channel icon next to the Trash icon at the bottom of the Channels palette. You should now just be working on this grayscale channel called Blue copy, so choose Image/Adjust/Levels and move the Input Highlight and Input Shadow sliders towards the center to increase the contrast between the sky and everything else. As you move the Input Highlight slider left, you will notice the sky being etched away. Moving the Shadow slider right makes the buildings and foreground turn towards black. An ideal mask would be a pure white sky, with everything in the foreground being pure black then a subtle gray along the horizon, which will blend any change in the sky seamlessly into the rest of the image.**

244

Move the Input Brightness slider, the middle one, to the left to make the transition darker, and to the right to brighten it up. Zoom into the horizon area, especially in the area of the buildings and trees and turn the Preview button on and off to see how accurately the horizon is captured by the mask. Notice how changing the three Input sliders changes the makeup of the horizon. When you have the mask as close as possible in Levels, choose OK. Type B to get the Paintbrush, then use a large, solid brush to paint black anything that is still gray in the foreground, and paint white anything, like large dust, that is not white in the sky. The horizon line should have some gray transition values.

Command-click on the thumbnail for the Blue copy channel that you have been working on in the Channels palette. This will load the white areas of this channel as a selection. Using Command-click is the universal way to load a selection and you will find it is the easiest and most useful, so make it a point to learn. Now click on the word RGB at the

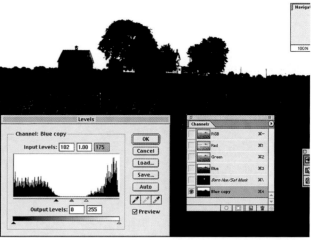

STEP 15: Here is the setup for creating the mask for the Darken Sky layer. You are using Image/Adjust/Levels on a copy of the Blue channel in the Channels palette. Notice the positions of the Input Shadow and Input Highlight sliders.

top of the Channels palette and the color image should come back into display. Make sure the Barn Hue/Sat layer is the active layer and choose Layer/New Adjustment Layer/Curves (Command-F3) to create a Curves adjustment layer you should call Darken Sky. Move the Eyedropper around in the sky while the mouse button is down and notice the areas of the curve diagram the sky values take up. Click a point in the center of that sky area on the RGB curve and drag the curve down and to the right to darken the sky. Choose OK when you are happy with your darker sky. At this point, this mask of the sky is saved in the layer mask of the Darken Sky adjustment layer, so you can now drag the Blue copy channel, in the Channels palette, to the trash if you would like. Do Command-S to save your file.

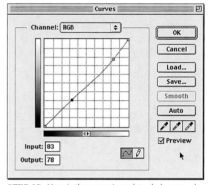

STEP 15: Here is the curve I used to darken my sky.

STEP 16: To further modify any of your adjustment layers, double-click the Layer thumbnail of that adjustment layer and your old modifications will come up, allowing you to change them again and again without slowly destroying the integrity of the original image. **One thing you should do to the** *Background* **layer, however, is use the Rubber (Clone) Stamp tool to remove all the spots and scratches. Click the** *Background* **layer to activate it and then use the Rubber Stamp techniques you learned in the last chapter to spot this image, especially the sky.** Another easier way to spot skys is to use the Dust and Scratches filter. You only want to use this filter on soft skys, and you need to use it correctly so you don't lose the grain pattern in your sky, but only the spots. **Command-click on the Layer Mask thumbnail of the Darken Sky adjustment layer to reload this mask as a selection. Choose Select/Modify/Contract and use a contraction value of 10 pixels. This moves the selection away from the horizon so the filter doesn't blur any details along the horizon. Use Command-Option-0 to zoom in to 100%, then Command-Spacebar-click to get you up to 200% while looking at the sky in the area behind the buildings. This allows you to see the details while you are working on your Background layer. Choose Filter/Noise/Dust & Scratches and set the Radius to 2 and the Threshold to 0.** Notice that all the scratches and clumpiness in the sky is removed, but so is the natural grain pattern. The Radius is the number of pixels around a spot or scratch that Photoshop will change to get rid of the spot. **Leave the Radius at 2, but increase the Threshold to around 4 or 5. Your grain pattern returns, but the large clumps, spots and scratches are now removed. Choose Command-H to hide the selection edge and see how this sky blends with the**

Improving Selected Color Areas

STEP 16: The Kansas image after specific color corrections using selections and adjustment layers and before sharpening.

horizon at the bottom. **Turn the Preview button in the filter off and on to see the sky as it was before and after the filter. This is a good way to save time spotting skys! You may still have to do a few large dust spots with the Rubber Stamp tool. First, do a Command-D to deselect the selection so you can work anywhere in the file. Do another Command-S to save the latest changes.** This would actually be your master layers version of this image, so this is the one you would archive for future uses and different sizes. Note: My editor, John, keeps reminding me that the Rubber Stamp tool is now called the Clone Stamp tool. I'm sure in this book, you'll see it referred to as the Rubber Stamp tool a lot because I've been thinking of it with that name for over 12 years.

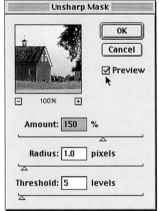

STEP 17: The Unsharp Mask filter dialog box with the settings I used to sharpen my KansasVersion1 file.

Another technique for sharpening very saturated files is using Image/Mode/Lab Color to convert the file to Lab Color mode and then sharpening the L channel. This method prevents your saturated colors from popping as much during the sharpening. You can actually print to an Epson printer directly from Lab color so you don't need to convert back to RGB. Another sharpening option is to just sharpen one of the RGB channels.

THE UNSHARP MASK FILTER

STEP 17: If you are going to resample your image by either adding pixels to make it bigger or removing pixels to make it smaller, you should do that first before sharpening your file. In the Image/Image Size dialog, if you are just changing the Pixels/Inch with the Resample Image option turned off, this should not affect the sharpening of an already sharpened file as you are not adding or removing pixels.

Choose Image/Duplicate (F5) to make a copy of this master layers file called KansasVersion1, turning on the Duplicate Merged Layers Only option and then choosing OK in the Duplicate dialog. Type an F to put this single layer copy in Full Screen Mode. Now you will use Filter/Sharpen/Unsharp Mask to sharpen your image for final output. The Unsharp Mask filter has three different settings (Amount, Radius, and Threshold) that affect different parts of the sharpening process. You will have to run some tests to determine what value to use in each of these settings. It is often useful to compare tests on a small section of the image. Photoshop does have a Preview button in the Unsharp Mask filter that allows you to see the filter of a selected area of the image, but it doesn't allow you to compare one group of settings to another. Once you get familar with the amount of sharpening you like on your various types of prints, you can turn the Preview button off in the Unsharp Mask dialog and on while trying different settings to decide the amount of sharpening you want. Turning the Preview button off and on will change the part of the image that is visable on your computer screen from not sharpened to sharpened. The small window inside the Unsharp Mask filter will always show part of the image as sharpened, but if you click down and hold inside that little window, that part of the image will toggle to unsharpened. Click anywhere in your image to reset what acutally shows within this window inside the Unsharp Mask filter.

A good way to compare different sharpening settings is to use the Marquee (M) to select a section of the image that can represent the entire image, and whose sharpness is most important, and make a copy of it using Edit/Copy. (See the images on the next page to see what I selected from this photograph.) Now choose File/New (Command-N) to create a new file. Because you just made a copy, the new file will be the size of the copied section. Say OK to the New dialog box and then do Edit/Paste (Command-V). Repeat this action several times, until you have five or six small files that you can place next to each other on the screen for comparison. Now run different tests on each file to see what each of the three parameters of Unsharp Mask do. Speaking of those three parameters, here is what they do:

AMOUNT: This setting controls the overall amount of sharpening. When you compare sharpening effects, you want to zoom in to the image, to at least 100% to see all the detail. Compare different copies of the same image area using different settings for Amount. You sharpen an image by looking for edges in the photograph and enhancing those edges by making one side of them darker and the other side of them lighter. Edges are sharp color or contrast changes in an image.

RADIUS: This setting controls the number of pixels along an edge that you modify when you sharpen the image. Again, try running the filter with different settings and compare several copies of the same image side by side.

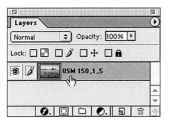

STEP 17: If you name the layer in your document with the sharpening value you used, that information will help later if you decide the sharpening amount wasn't correct.

THRESHOLD: When you set Threshold to 0, everything in the image becomes a candidate for being an edge and getting sharpened. If you set the Threshold to, say 10, then an edge will only be found and sharpened if there is a difference of at least 10 points (in the range from 0 to 255) in the pixel values along that edge. The larger value you give to the Threshold setting, the more contrasty an edge needs to be before it is sharpened.

When you find the correct Unsharp Mask values, use those to sharpen the entire file. If the original image is very grainy, I might increase Threshold, which lessens the sharpening of the grain. If the image is very fine grained, I might decrease Threshold, which allows me to sharpen the file a bit more, without getting more than the normal grain appearance in the final image. You have to be careful not to over-sharpen. If your final output is a halftone, you can get away with more sharpening than you can for a transparency film recorder, or even a digital print output, because the screen angles and dots in a halftone tend to lessen some sharpening artifacts. All artifacts show up if you output to a color transparency film recorder, however. We usually use the Unsharp Mask filter instead of the other Photoshop sharpening filters because Unsharp Mask provides much finer control over the many different types of images.

Another way to sharpen your image, which I usually use on mine, is the Sharpen Only Edges BH action script. This is explained in Chapter 11: "Automating with Actions;" you should check it out, as it is very useful.

Image with no sharpening. We need some!

Unsharp Mask 150, 1.5, 0. Too much grain!

Unsharp Mask 450, 1.5, 0. Too much sharpening and grain!

Unsharp Mask 150, 4.5, 0. Too large a Radius for a real look.

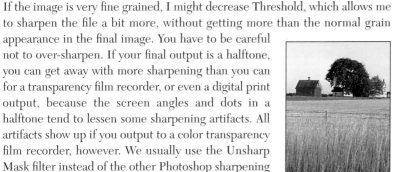

Unsharp Mask 150, 1.5, 8. I used to use this a lot but now I experiment more on each image.

Unsharp Mask 300, .5, 4. Compare this to the ones on either side.

Unsharp Mask 500, .5, 8. Let's see how this prints.

RESPOTTING WITH THE RUBBER (CLONE) STAMP

STEP 18: After you sharpen any image, you should zoom in to at least 100% and then go through each section of the file, checking for spots that appeared after sharpening. Sharpening tends to enhance spots that may not have been obvious before, which is why you should double-check the spotting of your Master file after any final

247

sharpening. The procedure is the same as the spotting work demonstrated in Chapter 19: "Overall Color Correction." Do another File/Save (Command-S) to save your final spotted file.

OUT-OF-GAMUT COLORS

Step 19: You can see many vivid colors on the computer screen in RGB or Lab that won't print in CMYK on a press. If you are working in RGB to send your final output to a film recorder and color transparency film, you can get more colors on film than you can on a press. If your final output is some Web or multimedia presentation, you can also get the colors there. You need to realize that each different type of computer monitor or digital color printer, or even press and paper combination, might have a different color gamut. The gamut of your output device is the range of colors it can actually print. For more information about these issues, see Chapter 14: "Color Spaces, Device Characterization and Color Management." If you are going to print this file on a press in CMYK, or if you are using View/Proof Colors to soft proof RGB output devices, you might want to check your out-of-gamut colors and see if you need to correct them. This might be a good time to review the discussion of View/Proof Colors and View/Proof Setup in Chapter 15: "Photoshop Color Preferences, Monitor, Scanner and Printer Calibration." **Choose View/Proof Setup/Working CMYK for now as we go through this discussion. Now choose Select/Color Range, and then choose Out-of-Gamut from the Select pop-up at the top of the dialog box. Click OK to see a selection of all the colors that you can see in RGB, but which won't print exactly the same in CMYK or on your RGB device when Proof Setup is set to soft proof for an RGB output device. Choose View/Hide Edges (Command-H) to hide the edges of this selection.**

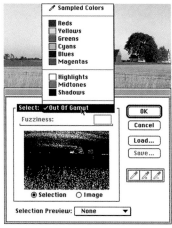

STEP 19: In Color Range, selecting out-of-gamut colors.

STEP 20: Some out-of-gamut colors, like red, often look quite different, and usually muted, when printed in CMYK. In many other colors, you might not notice the difference. **Choose View/Proof Colors (Command-Y) for an estimate of what the image will look like when printed in CMYK while you are still working in RGB or Lab. If you made the red barn really bright, you will notice it fades a bit.** How many other changes did you see in the image? The sky might look a bit duller. **Now choose View/Gamut Warning (Command-Shift-Y), and all these out-of-gamut colors will change to gray or whatever color you have set in Preferences as the gamut warning indicator. Remember that you have a selection, which you made using Color Range, of all the colors that are actually out-of-gamut. With Gamut Warning on, you can use this selection in conjunction with the Hue/Saturation command to fix much of the gamut problem.** Colors often are out-of-gamut because they're too saturated. **Choose Command-U for Hue/Saturation and move the Saturation slider to the left. Notice that the Gamut Warning areas get smaller the more you desaturate the selected out-of-gamut area.** You might want to desaturate your out-of-gamut colors in several stages, or use the Sponge tool from the Tool palette, so you don't further desaturate colors that have already come back into gamut. To desaturate in stages, move the Saturation slider to the left, to –10. Choose OK and then choose Select/None. Now go back to Color Range (see step 19), and choose the new smaller set of out-of-gamut colors. Reduce the saturation on these, also, by –10. Continue this iterative process until you have no more out-of-gamut colors, or until the out-of-gamut areas are so small they won't show.

STEP 21: Gamut Warning is a very useful tool for seeing colors that are going to be difficult to reproduce in CMYK, or on your RGB output device when soft proofing to an RGB device. However, if you always desaturate all your colors so that no Gamut Warning areas show up, you may end up with duller colors on press or your device than you would have gotten if you were a little less strict about desaturating all your RGB colors. I compared two conversions to CMYK of this image. The first had been pre-adjusted, via steps 19 and 20, to remove out-of-gamut colors, and the second was of the same image without the out-of-gamut adjustments. The pre-adjusted image didn't change much at all when converted to CMYK, which is good. The image that I hadn't pre-adjusted for out-of-gamut colors did change and got a little duller, as with the red barn, but overall was a bit brighter and more vivid in CMYK than the pre-adjusted image was. **So if you work in RGB and use bright colors, even out-of-gamut ones, you might get brighter color results by going ahead and converting these to CMYK. You know that some bright colors may get a bit duller, but you can deal with those dull or changed colors when you are in CMYK mode, instead of dulling them ahead of time by desaturating based on Gamut Warning and possibly desaturating them too much. Do some tests to see what works best for you!** When printing on an RGB device, like the LightJet 5000, you might find you lose a few less details in your extreme saturated areas if you bring things into gamut with the device a bit, before sending a file to the printer. Again, you should experiment and see.

CONVERTING TO CMYK

STEP 22: Now you have your final color corrected version of the RGB image for this particular job. If your final output device is an RGB device, such as a film recorder or a video screen, your work is done. If you use a color management system or printer software that automatically converts your file from RGB to CMYK as you output it, you also are done. If your final output device is CMYK and you are going to do the conversion from RGB to CMYK in Photoshop, you need to make sure all the preferences are set up correctly for CMYK conversion and for this particular print-

ing project. **Choose Image/Mode/CMYK to convert the image to CMYK.** When in CMYK, Photoshop automatically adjusts the image display on the monitor to try to simulate your actual CMYK printed output. Consequently, some of the brighter colors may get duller or change slightly. **You might want to do additional small color tweaks now that you are in CMYK, using the same tools you used in RGB. You can also use the Selective Color tool and other tools to tweak CMYK colors, as explained at the end of Chapters 21: "Yellow Flowers" and 22: "Color Matching Images." When you are happy with your CMYK image, save it as KansasFinalCMYK.**

STEP 21: The final RGB version of Kansas after all color corrections and using the Unsharp Mask filter.

21 HANDS-ON SESSION: Yellow Flowers

*Using Color Range and Replace Color
to change the colors of flowers and to
enhance those colors; using Selective Color
to improve the CMYK version.*

Original version of the flowers picture. We will select the flowers and change their color.

In this session, you use the Color Range and Replace Color tools to select the flowers and change their color from yellow to orange. You then use the Selective Color command to enhance the color of the orange flowers. This image is tagged with Color-MatchRGB and was created in a ColorMatchRGB workspace. Using a different workspace to do this example might yield slightly different measured values.

ABOUT COLOR RANGE AND REPLACE COLOR

The first thing you do in this example is select all the flowers. There are two similar tools for making selections based on color in Photoshop 6. Select/Color Range allows you to specify a color using the Eyedropper tool and then shows you a mask of all the areas in the current selection that contain that color. You can add to or subtract from that mask using + or – Eyedroppers, so that when you leave Color Range, you have a selection that contains the final colors you specified. Another command that is similar to Color Range is Image/Adjust/Replace Color. It lets you make selections similarly and also change the colors of the selections at the same time, using controls that are like those in the Hue/Saturation command but not quite as powerful. You can load and save color selection sets between these two tools, so you need to understand the subtle but important differences between them.

The Color Range tool always returns a selection, which you can then use as you would any other selection to modify the selected areas using an adjustment layer or other Photoshop tool. Because Color Range lets you make selections, it furnishes some very useful features for seeing exactly what you have selected. When you choose

The Color Range tool lets you make selections based on these different color choices. When you use the Sampled Colors choice, you click on the colors you want to select within the image.

the Sampled Colors option from the Select pop-up menu in Color Range, you select colors by clicking on them with the Eyedropper (you do the same in Replace Color). You can add to the colors that you select by using the regular Eyedropper and Shift-clicking, and you can subtract from the selected colors by Option-clicking. Also, the + and – Eyedroppers always add to or always subtract, respectively, from the selected areas. You see what colors are selected by looking at a black-and-white mask window in the dialog box. Here, white shows you the selected areas. To see the selected items in the most detail, choose the Quick Mask option in the Selection Preview pop-up of Color Range, and you will get a Quick Mask overlay on top of the unselected areas in the Actual Image window. If you choose the correct color for your Quick Mask (notice the purple in the diagram here), you can see when your selection is complete. You choose the color for your Quick Mask by double-clicking on the Quick Mask icon at the bottom of the Tool palette. (You need to do this before you enter Color Range.) See Chapter 18: "The Car Ad" for a discussion of Quick Mask mode. You can also choose no preview in the image area, or a Grayscale, Black Matte, or White Matte preview. These can also be very useful in different types of situations. Try them all and see what works best for you. By the way, the other options in the Select pop-up allow you to select all the reds, yellows, greens, cyans, blues, magentas, highlights, midtones, shadows, or out-of-gamut colors in the part of the image that you selected before you entered Color Range. The out-of-gamut colors option can be very useful (see Chapter 20: "Correct a Problem Image"). Although Replace Color doesn't give you these other Select options, you can get them by using the Save button in Color Range to save selections made with these options, and you can use the Load button in Replace Color to load these selections.

The Replace Color tool also allows you to select colors with the Eyedropper in the same way as Color Range, but it has no Quick Mask Preview mode and no Select options. Replace Color doesn't provide as many options for selecting the colors or for seeing the selection as Color Range does, but after you make a selection in either one, you can click on the Save button to save the description of the selected colors. This feature allows you to select similar colors in other images or make the same color selection in the current image from Color Range or from Replace Color by going into either tool and using the Load button to load that color selection description. When you have the selection you want, the Replace Color tool allows you to change the color of the selected items by using the Hue, Saturation, and Lightness sliders at its bottom. The Preview box here shows you the color changes happening in the image on the screen. For changing color, Replace Color is even better than a selection preview because you see whether the selection is correct as you actually change the colors you want. So, when you use Color Range, you are selecting a range of colors in an image and ending up with a selection. When you use Replace Color, you select a range of colors and replace those colors simultaneously. Now, let's try this out!

USING COLOR RANGE TO SELECT THE FLOWERS

STEP 1: **Open the FlowersYellow image in the YellowFlowers Example folder. Put Photoshop into Full Screen mode by pressing F or by clicking on the middle icon at the bottom of the Tool palette. Double-click on the Quick Mask icon, click on the colored square, and then set the color to medium blue or purple. Find a color that has no yellow in it so that any flower parts not selected show up easily. Make sure the Opacity is set to 50%. Say OK to these dialog boxes and click back on the regular Selection icon to the left of the Quick Mask icon. Now press the Tab key to remove all the tool windows from the screen. Choose Select/Color Range. Set the Fuzziness to 40. The**

Preview set to Quick Mask   Preview set to None

In the top part of this illustration, the Selection Preview is None and you see the image. At the bottom of the illustration you see the purple Quick Mask preview, which is very useful.

The Quick Mask icon   Click here to change the Quick Mask color.

Click on the Quick Mask icon to get the Quick Mask Options dialog box, and then click on the color square and select a new color with the Color Picker.

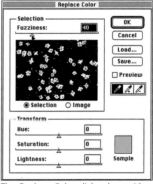

The Replace Color dialog box with a mask showing the flowers selected.

STEP 2: Part of the flower on the right is covered by purple. Shift-click on it to add it to the selection.

Fuzziness, which works the same in Replace Color and Color Range, is like the Tolerance on the Magic Wand; the higher the Fuzziness, the more similar colors are selected. Unlike using the Magic Wand, you can move the Fuzziness after you make a selection to change the range of selected colors. **Set Select to Sampled Colors and set Selection Preview to None, for now. Use the Eyedropper to click on the yellow flowers and you will notice that wherever you see a flower, you should get some white showing up in the mask window. Hold the Shift key down and click on different areas of the flowers, adding more to the mask. If white areas or spots show up in the mask window where there are not any flowers, press Command-Z to undo that last Eyedropper click. When you think you have selected all the flowers—and no areas that are not flowers—set the Selection Preview to Quick Mask.**

STEP 2: **In Quick Mask, you will notice a see-through purple layer covering everything not selected by the mask. That's the Quick Mask preview. If you notice that parts of the flowers are covered by purple, Shift-click on them to add them to the selected areas. If you select a really bright part of the flower or a really dark part of the flower, you may also notice the purple overlay coming off other areas of the image that are not flowers. If so, you have selected too much, and should press Command-Z.**

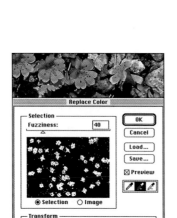

STEP 2: Here we have selected too much. You can see the mask coming off things that are not flowers, like the green leaves to the left of the flowers. Use Command-Z or the –Eyedropper to fix this.

STEP 3: **When the purple mask doesn't cover any flowers but still covers everything not a flower, you have done what you can do with Color Range to select the flowers. You might want to try the Grayscale, Black Matte, or White Matte Selection Preview modes to see if there are any errors that show up there. If so, just use the + or – Eyedroppers to fix them. Click on the Save button and save this set of colors as ColorRangeToRC. Click on OK now and you end up with a selection of the flowers.** If you wanted to work on these selected items with one of the other color correction tools, such as Hue/Saturation or a filter, you could have used this procedure to get a selection of the flowers. We had you do the first part of this exercise in Color Range so that you could see the differences between it and Replace Color. You could have done the whole session in either Color Range or Replace Color. Just so you know, you can click inside the preview window itself with the Eyedropper tools to add and subtract in Color Range. This may not be accurate enough for this difficult selection, but it can be faster in simpler selections.

USING REPLACE COLOR TO SELECT AND CHANGE THE COLOR

STEP 4: **You are now going to use Replace Color for the rest of the exercise. Choose Select/None (Command-D) because you're actually going to improve on this selection using Replace Color. Double-click on the Eyedropper tool and set the Sample Size to Point Sample. Choose Image/Adjust/Replace Color, and click on the Load button. Select the ColorRangeToRC file you just saved from Color Range.** This will give you the same selection you just had, but this time you only see the black-and-white mask in the dialog box. As an alternative to loading the selection you created in Color Range, you can also just create a new selection using Replace Color. **If you want to start over using Replace Color, just initially click down within an average yellow color within one of the flowers. If you are doing the selection over again, then you want**

STEP 4: The Replace Color dialog box previewing yellow to orange.

to switch to the + Eyedropper tool and click with it in various places within the flowers until you have clicked on bright, medium and shadow yellow flowers. When you believe you have created a selection of all the yellow flowers, either by loading one from what you did in Color Range or by starting over using Replace Color, then choose the middle + Eyedropper tool and click on a yellow flower at a place that is a middle yellow color. This color should be a shade of yellow that best represents the flowers as a whole. Notice that the sample box at the bottom right of the Replace Color dialog now has the yellow color you clicked on in it. Getting the color into the sample box is why you clicked here with + Eyedropper. This tool adds a color to the color selection range instead of starting a new selection range. **Now go down to the Hue slider and move it to the left to –20. The yellow sample is now orange. When you click on the Preview button, all the selected yellow flowers will turn orange.** This is the one type of selection preview that you can't do in Color Range, and it is very useful. **If most of the flowers look orange but have a little bright yellow around their tips, you have 'em right about where you want 'em. If all the flowers are orange without a trace of yellow, you should look around the rest of the image and make sure you didn't change the color of anything else that had some yellow in it but wasn't totally yellow, such as the green leaves on the ground.**

The flowers, after changing them to orange.

STEP 5: **Now you need to change the yellow in the tips of the flowers to orange. Since the Eyedropper is set to Point Sample, this will allow you to select minute color differences that are only one pixel in size. Zoom in (Command-Spacebar-click) on any flowers that still have too much yellow around the tips of their petals. Zoom in close enough so you can see individual pixels at about 400%. Carefully click on those yellow tip colors and add them to the color set. As you do this with Preview on, the tips of other flowers also turn orange. You can also increase the Fuzziness; you will notice that more little dots show up as selected in the mask. This may also improve the blending of any remaining yellow in the flower tips. Some of the brighter tips may actually just be highlights, so you don't need to change every last one. They just need to look natural as orange flowers. Some of the flower petals tips, which look almost white, were originally burned and dried on the yellow flowers, so don't try to get them to turn orange also. If you do, you will make the Color Set too large and change colors where you shouldn't.**

Click the Save button in Replace Color and save the final Color Set as YellowFlowerSet. Later in Step 9, you will use YellowFlowerSet to learn about a more advanced way to do this that gives you more control over your flower color details. **For now though, click on the OK button in Replace Color when you are happy with your flowers. It may be faster to change the dried tips using the Rubber Stamp tool, cloning color from another flower or another part of the same flower. You still will want to do this with Aligned turned on in the Rubber Stamp options using either the Normal or Color Blend mode.**

STEP 6: **Use File/Save As to save the file as FlowersOrange, and then open the origi**nal Flowers file and compare the two images. The flower colors and tones should

Using Replace Color to Select and Change the Color

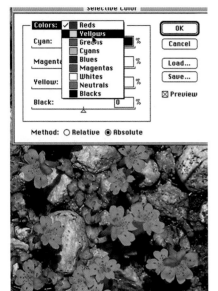

STEP 7: After measuring the orange flowers, we notice in the Color palette that this orange color is made up of 97% yellow and 52% magenta. You may get slightly different values. We then choose yellow as the color to change in the Colors pop-up.

look as natural in orange as they did in yellow. Bring back the Tool palette by pressing Tab, and then double-click on the Eyedropper tool and set the Sample Size in the Options palette back to 3 by 3 Average.

USING SELECTIVE COLOR

STEP 7: **When you are happy with the RGB version of this image and have saved it (in Step 6), you should convert it to CMYK using Image/Mode/CMYK. You may notice a slight dulling of the flowers when the image converts to CMYK, although this particular orange color converts to CMYK quite well. When in CMYK, it is best to use the Selective Color command to make further subtle tweaks on colors. This command changes a particular color based on the respective amounts of cyan, magenta, yellow and black that comprise it. Bring up the Color palette using the Window menu (Shift-F9 with ArtistKeys). If you had this palette in the palette well at the top right of the Options palette, drag it onto the screen using its Color tab. Use its Palette Options pop-up menu to change it to CMYK Display mode. Now choose Image/Adjust/Selective Color to bring up the Selective Color tool.** With this tool, you have to select the main color that you would like to change using the Colors pop-up menu at the top. The choices are Red, Yellow, Green, Cyan, Blue, Magenta, White, Neutral and Black. If you want to change the orange flowers, you'll probably notice that orange is not one of these colors. **Use the Eyedropper and click on an orange flower in a shade of orange typical of the orange color of all the flowers. Notice in the Color palette that this bright orange consists mainly of yellow and magenta. Because yellow is the main component of this orange color (it's around 97% yellow, in fact), you should now choose Yellow from the Colors pop-up. Next, you change the percentages of the other colors that make up your yellows.**

STEP 8: **Notice that the orange color already is very close to completely saturated in yellow but that the magenta component is only 52% saturated. On the top left side of the Color palette, you see a swatch of the color where you last clicked. The Magenta bar in the Color palette shows that if you add magenta to this color, the flowers will look a deeper orange, and eventually reddish, in color. If you take away magenta, the flowers will become more yellowish. Move the Magenta slider in Selective Color (not in the Color palette) to the right, to +20%. In our example, the Method radio button at the bottom of the dialog box is set to Absolute, which should mean that you're adding 20% magenta ink to the 52% magenta already in the yellows, resulting in 72%.** If you were to set Method to Relative, you would add 20% of the 52% of magenta already there, which should

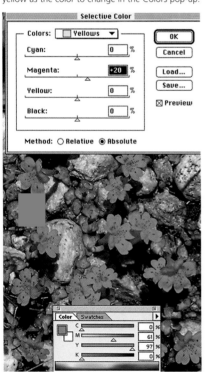

STEP 8: The orange flowers after adding 20% magenta. Notice that the Magenta value actually changes from 52% to 61%.

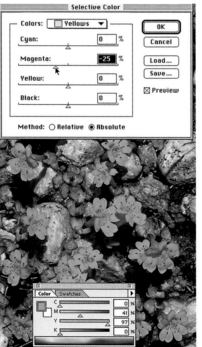

STEP 8: The orange flowers after removing 25% magenta with Selective Color. If you click on a sample color after entering Selective Color, the Color palette shows you the actual new CMYK percentages as you make adjustments in Selective Color.

bring it up to about 62%. In reality, Absolute mode brings the 52% magenta up to 61%, and Relative mode brings it up to 57%. **If you are trying to add a specific percentage, you should measure the results you actually get using the Color palette rather than assume the percentages in the Selective Color dialog box will be exact. Now subtract 25% magenta from these orange flowers to get the lighter, more yellowish orange you see in our third Selective Color illustration.** These operations are examples of how you use the Selective Color tool to make subtle tweaks in specific color ranges. When you set Colors to Neutral, Selective Color is also very good at removing color casts in the neutral areas. Photoshop is good at identifying which colors should be composed of equal quantities of cyan, magenta and yellow.

A MORE FLEXIBLE WAY TO SET THIS UP

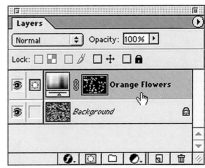

STEP 9: For a more advanced way to set this up, try this. **Re-open the original FlowersYellow image from the** *Photoshop 6 Artistry* **CD. Choose Select/Color Range, use the Load button to load the YellowFlowerSet that you saved in Step 5, and click on OK. You now have a selection of the parts of this image that you want to change. Now choose Layer/New Adjustment Layer/Hue/Saturation, name this new layer Orange Flowers, and then click on OK. This adds a Hue/Saturation adjustment layer above the existing yellow** *Background* **layer. Now you are in the Hue/Saturation dialog box, so set the Hue to –20.** Your flowers will now change to orange and only the flowers will change because your selection will have been automatically put into the layer mask of this Hue/Saturation adjustment layer. When an adjustment layer is active, you are automatically working on this layer mask. **With the adjustment layer active, you can now use Gaussian Blur and the painting tools to fine-tune the adjustment layer's built-in layer mask, and you can double-click on the name of the adjustment layer (Orange Flowers) at any time to change the color of the flowers. I found that a Gaussian Blur of 1 on this adjustment layer's mask improved the color**

A MORE FLEXIBLE WAY: The Layers palette for this more flexible way to change the color of the flowers and leave your options much more open.

change blend. Do Filter/Blur/Gaussian Blur (Shift-F4) and set the Amount to 1. Try Command-Z several times to Undo and Redo this Gaussian Blur and notice how the darker reddish-orange spots on the flowers look more natural and less pixelated after the Gaussian Blur is added to the mask. You can also turn the Eye icon on and off on the Orange Flowers layer to see that the tonality of the orange flowers with the blurred mask matches the tonality of the original yellow flowers more closely. This solution allows for an infinite number of changes to the color and also to the mask without degrading the image. See the Yellow/ Orange Layers file in the Extra Info Files folder for this chapter and try this out for yourself!

The flowers with the burned petals have to be fixed with the Rubber Stamp tool.

The orange flowers after the color correction choices have been made with Selective Color.

255

22 HANDS-ON SESSION: Color Matching Images

Measure and adjust the color of objects so differently colored items can be changed to match, and do subtle color tweaks after CMYK conversion to deal with faded CMYK hues.

The long shot is a red car, and you need to end up with two matching red CMYK images.

The close-up shot is a green car; you need to change its color to match the red car to the left.

Imagine that you want to create an advertisement using two photos of the Acura Integra. One of the photos is of a red Integra and the other is a green one. You need to convert the green car photo so that its color matches that of the red one. You also need to convert both cars to CMYK and do some final color matching there. **The files in this example were saved using the ColorMatchRGB settings and the example was done with ColorMatchRGB as the RGB working space. Your numbers should come out very similar if you leave your files in the ColorMatch space for this example, but you might get somewhat different numerical values if you choose to convert these original images to another RGB workspace.**

CHOOSING THE COLOR MATCH SPOTS

STEP 1: **Open the RedAcuraCM and GreenDetail files from the Color Matching Cars folder.** Find a spot on the red car where the color appears to be an average, intermediate color that could represent the color you want for the whole car. Both of these photos have highlight and shadow areas that you are going to want to match also. I've found that if you can locate a good midtone area in both images and get those midtone areas to match, the rest of the image will also match pretty well. I used the area on the front of the car to the right of the chrome Acura emblem, just above the word Integra embossed in the red bumper. Because this spot exists—and the lighting on it is similar—in both photos, you can use this

STEP 1: Here is the color match spot in the red car.

STEP 1: Here is the color match spot in the green car.

location on both cars to get the colors to match. We call this location the color match spot. Bring up the Info palette (F9) and set the top- eft viewing area to HSB mode. Type an I to choose the Eyedropper tool; then Shift-I to switch to the Color Sampler Eyedropper. This tool was added in Photoshop 5 and it allows you to place a measurement location within an image and then see how the values at that location change when you make color adjustments. You can place up to four Color Sampler locations in each image that you have open. **If you now press Return, this will bring up the Options palette for the Color Sampler and you should make sure the Sample Size is set to 3 by 3 average. Put the Eyedropper over the color match spot and click to take a measurement. Hold the mouse button down and measure around a bit to make sure the spot you are using as this first measurement is an average measurement for this area. I used the area just above the E in Integra. When you release the mouse, the Color Sampler added to the bottom of the Info palette will remember values for that location. Change the current display of those values for that Color Sampler to HSB and write down the HSB values within the Red image. I got 358 for the hue, 89 for the saturation and 81 for the lightness, but slightly different values will work also. We will now match these in the green image.**

STEP 1: Choosing the Color Sampler tool and setting the Sample Size to 3 by 3 Average.

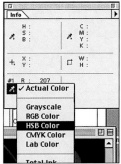

STEP 1: Setting your Color Sampler readings to HSB.

STEP 2: **Switch to the green car and find the same location right above the embossed E. Click here to create a Color Sampler reading in this image, too. Change the Color Sampler display of this spot in the Info palette to HSB.** If you ever have trouble seeing the Color Sampler part of the Info palette, which is at the bottom, you can always choose Hide Color Samplers followed by Show Color Samplers from the Info palette's options and this will bring all your Color Sampler values back into view. **Choose Image/Adjust/Hue/Saturation (Command-U) to bring up the Hue/Saturation color adjustment tool. Move the Hue slider so that the Hue value in your color match spot for the green image matches the one you wrote down for the red image. You need to have the windows open on the screen so you can see both cars at the same time, and you might want to zoom in so that you see this part of both cars at the same time. Now move the Saturation and Lightness sliders back and forth until you get saturation and lightness values in the Color Sampler that match the numbers you**

STEP 2: Adjusting hue, saturation, and lightness to get the green color match spot to match the values in the red car.

wrote down for the color match spot on the red car. The Color Sampler continues to show you how the color match spot, where you set it in the green car, has changed based on the Hue/Saturation slider movements. Try to get all three numbers to match exactly, but don't worry if one of them is off by one point in either direction. The Saturation and Lightness settings influence each other as you move them. As you change one, the other also changes, so you must tweak both of them for a while until you get as close as possible to what you had in the red car. When you are happy with the adjustments, click the OK button in Hue/Saturation. You could have also made a Hue/Saturation adjustment layer if you wanted to easily go back and modify these settings again later.

STEP 3: **Now click and drag the little Eyedropper pop-up menus in the Info palette to convert the Color Sampler displays for both images to RGB mode. Write down the Red, Green and Blue values from the color match spot in the original red car. My values were 207 for Red, 23 for Green and 29 for Blue. Switch to the green car, now converted to red, and choose Image/Adjust/Levels (Command-L). Go into the Red**

Choosing the Color Match Spots

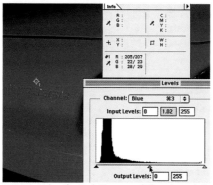

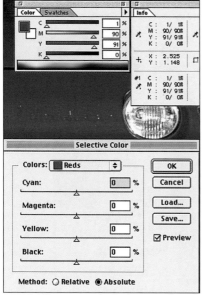

STEP 3: Using the Red, Green, and Blue channels in Levels to match the green car's RGB values to the red car's values.

STEP 5: When you put the Eyedropper tool exactly over the color match spot, the circle and crosshair will disappear and you will just see the number 1 that denotes Color Sampler number 1's position. At this point, you can click and get all the values to match exactly between the different palettes.

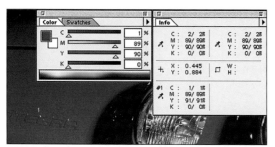

STEP 5: Sometimes, even when everything appears to line up correctly, the values will not match exactly between the different palettes or even between two readouts from the same palette. Just get things as close as possible.

channel (Command-1) and move the Input Brightness/Contrast slider, the middle slider, until the Red value in the Color Sampler matches the Red value you wrote down for the original red car. Switch to the Green channel and do the same thing until the Green value matches on both. Finally, do the same thing for the Blue channel. Now the two cars should match fairly well.

CONVERTING TO CMYK MODE

STEP 4: **Now bring up the Color palette (Shift-F9), which is useful here because it shows you, with its colored sliders, how to adjust colors to get more of what you want.** In older versions of Photoshop, I always used the Color palette for all my matching color situations. Now the Color Sampler in Photoshop 5 and 6 gives you the advantage of remembering the location of the sample point and also having up to four sample points for each image. It is good to know the trade offs between using the Color Sampler and the Color palette and here we'll learn them. **Using its Palette Options menu, convert the Color palette to CMYK mode. Also convert all your Color Sampler readouts to CMYK. Type Shift-I twice to switch the Tool palette back to the regular Eyedropper tool. This is the tool you will use for getting measurements into the Color palette.**

STEP 5: **Make sure your File/Color Settings/CMYK Setup settings are set correctly, and then use Image/Mode/CMYK Color to convert both cars to CMYK mode. Based on your CMYK preference settings, the colors onscreen should now be as close as possible to your printed colors. You might notice the intense red of these cars fades somewhat as you convert to CMYK. Now we'll use the Selective Color tool to do subtle, final tweaks of your red colors in CMYK mode. Selective Color is a great tool for doing subtle adjustments to particular color areas in CMYK. Switch to the original red car, the long shot, and make sure you can see both the Info palette and the Color palette. Now go into Image/Adjust/Selective Color (Shift-F6). Make sure that Colors is set to Reds because you're going to be adjusting the red colors in the car. Set the Method to Absolute, so that you can make the color adjustments more quickly. Move the cursor until it is exactly on top of the color match spot; at that point the circle and crosshair will disappear. At this exact point, click to take another measurement at the color match spot on the car and notice that when you click, the values come up in the Color palette. Values only change in the Color palette when you click or take a reading with the mouse button down. The values in the top-left area of the Info palette change whenever you move the mouse, and the values in your color match spot in the Info palette will only change when you change the color of that color match spot. These values should now match the values in the color match spot within the Info palette, although, as we show you in the illustration, the match might not be completely exact.**

STEP 6: **Notice that the color consists mostly of magenta and yellow. The colors of the sliders on the Color palette show you how the color at the color match spot will change if you add or subtract more cyan,** magenta, yellow or black ink. If the cyan value is greater than 0, subtract cyan using the Selective Color slider, until the cyan value reads 0 in the Color palette. You should also now see the 0 value in your Info palette Color Sampler reading. This maneuver adds red to the car color. Add magenta with Selective Color until the magenta value in the Color palette is about 99 to make the car a deeper, richer color. Adjust the yellow until the yellow value in the Color palette reads about 94. To get a slightly darker, richer color, add some black until the black value in the Color palette reads about 4. The colors in the Color palette's sliders will give you hints on what to do to improve the CMYK color of the spot you are reading in your image. You don't have to use the exact same numbers that we have; just adjust the cyan, magenta, yellow and black percentages on the color match spot until you like the car's shade of red. Write down these final, adjusted CMYK values from the Color palette.

STEP 7: **Switch to the image that was originally green and then again enter the Selective Color tool. Press down on the mouse button while taking a measurement of the color match spot in this image. The values in the Color palette should now match those in the color match spot for this image in the Info palette. Now adjust the cyan, magenta, yellow and black inks, using the sliders in Selective Color, until the percentages match the final adjusted percentages you just wrote down from the other image.** We used Cyan = 0, Magenta = 99, Yellow = 94 and Black = 4, but your values can be different. You just want the two red colors to match and both to look the way you like them. This method is a good way to match the colors of objects that start out differently, but have to end up the same.

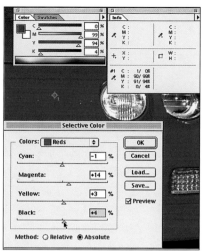

STEP 6: Here are the final Selective Color adjustments we made to get the 0, 99, 94, 4 values for the car that was originally red.

The final green car after converting to red and CMYK adjustments.

The final long shot of the original red car after conversion and adjustment in CMYK.

ADVANCED COLOR CORRECTION AND RESTORATION TECHNIQUES

USING DUOTONES FOR HIGHER TONAL RANGE

RESTORING OLD PHOTOGRAPHS

WORKING IN LAB VERSES RGB

USING MASKS FOR VARIED COLOR CORRECTION

COMBINING BRACKETED PHOTOGRAPHS TO INCREASE DYNAMIC RANGE

RESTORE DAMAGED FILM AND RETOUCH FACES

This photo of a church in the countryside near the town of Burnley, England, was taken in 1985 with my Canon F1 during a trip to visit my many English relatives. Both my parents were born in England then immigrated to Canada, where I was born, after WWII.

HANDS-ON SESSION: Burnley Graveyard

How to work with duotones, how and why to adjust duotone curves, and how to save and calibrate your duotone output.

STEP 1: The BurnleyGraveyard image printed as black and white using only black ink.

Duotones are used when printing black-and-white photos on a press to get more tonal range. Black-and-white (B&W) digital images can have up to 256 tones in digital format, but you can't get those 256 tones on a printing press with just the single black ink. If you use two or more inks to print B&W images, part of the tonal range can be printed by the first ink and part of it by the second ink. Many of Ansel Adams' well-known B&W posters are actually duotones. Besides giving you a larger tonal range, duotones allow you to add rich and subtle color to your B&W images.

Typically, you use black ink for the dark shadows and a second color, a brown or gray, for the midtones. You can add a third and even a fourth color to enhance the highlights or some other part of the tonal range. Many books are printed with two colors, black for the text and a second color, such as red or blue, for text section titles, underline, and other special colored areas. If this type of book has photographs, you can often make them more interesting by using duotones instead of just B&W.

CREATING A DUOTONE

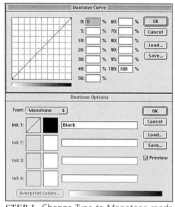

STEP 1: Change Type to Monotone mode and start with a straight curve.

STEP 1: This photo was originally a color transparency, but I felt a B&W or duotone printing of it would better convey the feelings I have about this stark graveyard where my grandfather and uncle are actually buried. Before using Image/Mode/Grayscale to convert the image to B&W, I did the overall color correction with Levels to get the best version of the RGB image I had scanned. It is usually best to do overall color correction before converting an image from RGB to either B&W or CMYK. After converting to B&W, I edited the contrast of the sky and the foreground separately to bring out the drama of the scene. I also fixed a section of the sky which was blown out due to the high dynamic range of the original photo. I plan to add the full step-by-step process for this image, including the color work and conversion and then masking in black and white, to my future book: *Making the Digital Print.* **Open and crop the BurnleyGraveyard image from the Ch23.Burnley Graveyard folder on the CD. Choose Image/Mode/Duotone to start working with the Duotone options. Start with the Type set to Monotone and the curve for Ink 1** straight. If the curve is not already straight, click on the **Curve box (the leftmost one) for Ink 1 and bring up the curve. Click and drag any extra points in the middle of the curve to outside the dialog box to remove them.** The horizontal axis of the curve diagrams in Duotone Options has the highlights on the left and the shadows on the right; the opposite of the default for Levels and Curves. The numbers in the boxes represent a percentage of black. Box 0, for the brightest highlight, should read 0, and box 100, for the darkest shadow, should read 100. All the other boxes should be blank when you have a straight curve. **Click on OK in the Duotone Curve dialog box. The Ink box for Ink 1 should be black and Black should be its name. Change the Type to Duotone to activate Ink 2 with a straight curve. To pick the color of Ink 2, click in the Color box (the rightmost one) for Ink 2 to bring up the Custom Colors picker, and then select a PANTONE, Focoltone, Toyo, Trumatch or other color from one of the Custom Color Systems.** Look in Chapter 5: "Picking and Using Color," if you need help using the Custom Colors picker. If you were going to print your duotone on a two-color book job or a job with a spot color, you would probably use one of these color systems. **We selected PANTONE Warm Gray 10 CVC for Ink 2. You now have a black ink and a medium gray ink, both with straight curves. Make sure the Preview button is on in the Duotone Options dialog box to give you a preview of what it should look like with the current inks and curves.** Printing two inks, both with straight curves, is like printing the image in black and then printing the exact same image again with the second ink color. When printing with halftone screens, the second ink will be printed with a different screen angle to add some additional tonality over using one ink. Printing the two inks using the same curve will cause the image to have too much density and seem very dark. This is not taking advantage of the real possibilities for duotone improvements.

STEP 1: The BurnleyGraveyard image created in Duotone mode as a duotone with black and PANTONE Warm Gray10 CV inks, both having straight curves, and later converted to CMYK for this final output.

ADJUSTING YOUR DUOTONE CURVES

STEP 2: **Click on the Curve box (the leftmost box) for Ink 1. You want to adjust the black ink to make it prevalent in the shadows, but less prevalent in the midtones and highlights. To do this, click on a point in the middle of the curve and drag that point downward to remove black from the midtones and highlights. Now click on the shadow end of the curve (to the middle right) and drag it up to add a little more black to this area of the image. See the illustration of the black curve here. Click on the OK button for black and then click on the Curve button for Ink 2 (middle gray) so you can work on its curve. Because we want the dark areas of the image to be represented mostly by black, we need to remove the gray from the shadows. Click at the top-right of the curve and drag it down to about 55. Now you need to put the gray back into the highlights and midtones, so click a couple of points in the middle of the curve to pull it up so it looks like the curve here. When the Preview checkbox in Duotone Options is on, you should be able to see these changes as you make them. You have now made the basic adjustments for your duotone curves. Now change each curve just a little bit, one curve at a time. Tweak these curves until you are happy with your duotone; then choose OK to Duotone Options and use File/Save As to save the image as BurnleyGraveyardDuo.**

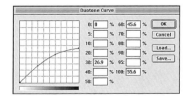

STEP 1: Picking the second color by clicking on the rightmost color square for Ink 2.

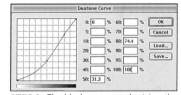

STEP 2: The black curve emphasizing the shadows.

STEP 2: The midtone curve for Ink 2, lowering this color in the shadow areas.

STEP 2: The BurnleyGraveyard image created in Duotone mode as a duotone with black for the shadows and PANTONE Warm Gray 10 CV for the midtones and highlights, after adjusting the curves for those two colors, and then converting to CMYK.

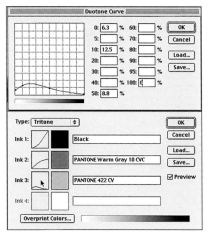

STEP 3: Final tritone values with details of the highlight curve. Notice how this curve actually starts above 0 on the Y axis. This adds density in the very brightest areas.

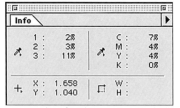

STEP 4: The Info palette measuring a highlight in Tritone mode.

STEP 4: Set the Info palette to Actual Color for duotones.

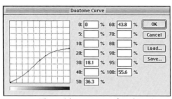

STEP 5: The midtone curve for the tritone with a small dip in the highlight area and a bigger dip in the shadows.

CREATING A TRITONE

STEP 3: To further enhance this image, you can add a third ink for the highlight areas to alter them in subtle ways. Before doing so, however, take time to make a copy of the two-ink version of the image so you can compare them onscreen. **Choose Image/Duplicate (F5) and name this copy BurnleyGraveyardTri. Choose Image/Mode/Duotone, and select Tritone from the Type menu in Duotone Options so that a choice for Ink 3 will be added. Click on the Ink Color box and choose a lighter gray for the highlights. (For Ink 3 we chose PANTONE 422 CVC.) Adjust the curve for this highlight color so that it has ink only in the brightest part of the image. Here is the curve we chose for the third ink. Notice how we moved the 0 position of the curve up to 6.3 instead of leaving it at 0.** This strategy actually adds some density to the brightest parts of the image; that is, in the clouds and where the sun reflects off the gravestones, two areas that previously were pure white. Here, we are using a third ink to subtly fine-tune the main image created by the first two maininks.

STEP 4: **You may want to measure some values on the screen using the Eyedropper. When working with duotones, you want to set the top left area in the Info palette to Actual Color, so that it will give you measurements of the ink density percentage of each color. If you measure one of the highlight areas in the clouds, you can see that there is no density there from Inks 1 and 2, but that Ink 3 has 6% density in that area. If you measure a shadow area, the maximum density there will be from Ink 1, black. There will be some density from Ink 2 and there will be no density from Ink 3 because its curve specifies no ink in the shadow areas.**

STEP 5: **You have added a third color specifically for the highlights; therefore, you may want to go back to Ink 2 and remove some of the midtone ink from the highlight areas. Click on the Curve box for Ink 2 and lower its curve in the highlight areas by clicking a point there and dragging it downward. Here is the final curve we used for Ink 2 in the tritone. Our final tritone image appears on the next page.**

STEP 6: **Go back and try some different colors and different curves for this duotone or tritone. Try some blues, greens, purples, magentas, yellows—lots of wild things. Experiment with some radical inverted curves to discover the great range of effects you can achieve with the Duotone options.**

CALIBRATING AND OUTPUTTING YOUR DUOTONES

If you are not having any particular calibration problems, especially if you are converting duotones to CMYK for final output, we recommend that you leave your calibration and preferences set up the same as those for your CMYK Working Space as described in Chapter 3: "Setting System and Photoshop Preferences."

When you output your duotones, you have several choices to make. If you actually print with PANTONE or some other custom spot color, you need to save the file as a duotone in Photoshop EPS format. You can set your screen angles for the duotone in Photoshop using the File/Page Setup/Screen button, or you can set your screen angles in QuarkXPress or PageMaker if you are placing your duotone into one of those page layout applications. Talk to your service bureau about how and where to set your screens and what screen angles and frequencies to use; they may be different depending on the type of imagesetter or plate maker your service bureau uses. You may want to use the Short PANTONE Names option in Edit/Preferences/General. It removes an extra C at the end of some names. This option may make the PANTONE names chosen in Photoshop more compatible with those specified in PageMaker, Quark, Illustrator and other layout and graphic applications. The important thing is to make sure the name of each color is exactly the same (including upper- and lowercase letters) in your page layout application; otherwise, your duotone may be output as CMYK. To save from Photoshop as a duotone, leave the Mode menu set to Duotone, choose File/Save As, and then set the Format to Photoshop EPS. In the EPS dialog box, set the Preview to Macintosh (8 bits/pixel) and the Encoding to Binary, and then click on the Include Halftone Screen checkbox only if you have set your screens and frequencies using Page Setup in Photoshop. On Windows, you may want to set the Encoding to ASCII, depending on the page layout application you're placing the duotone into. Check with that Application's manual.

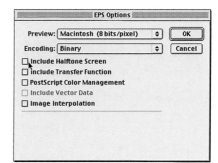

The dialog box and settings for saving the file as EPS Duotone.

If you want to convert the duotone to CMYK to output it with process colors, use the Image/Mode menu to convert the image to CMYK color. For more information on the options for saving CMYK files, see Chapter 17: "Steps to Create a Master Image." You can also convert your duotones to RGB format if you want to composite them with other images for Web or multimedia use, or for output to a film recorder or some other RGB device, like an Epson printer. To do the conversion to RGB, just select Image/Mode/RGB.

Converting a file from Duotone to CMYK format for output to process colors.

When you work on a duotone or tritone, the Channels palette displays a single channel—your original black-and-white image. When you print the tritone, this same black-and-white channel prints three times, and each time the separate curve for the particular tritone color is used to modify it before it goes to the printer. If you want to see each of these three-color tritone channels as they will look after the curves are applied, switch the Image/Mode menu to Multichannel. The Channels palette will now show you three channels: Channel 1 for black, Channel 2 for PANTONE 10, and Channel 3 for PANTONE 422. You can then click on each channel in the Channels palette to see how that channel will look on film. If you wanted to edit each of these channels separately, you could do so now, but after doing that, you could not convert them back to Duotone mode. These three channels would now have to be output as three separate black-and-white files. If you were just looking at the three channels and not editing them, you would choose Edit/Undo Multichannel to undo the mode change and put things back into Duotone mode.

The final BurnleyGraveyard image created in Duotone mode as a tritone with black shadows, PANTONE Warm Gray 10 CV midtones, and PANTONE 422 CV highlights, then converted to CMYK for final output.

Calibrating and Outputting Your Duotones

24 HANDS-ON SESSION: Desert Al

Color correcting this difficult exposure and scan and using color channel swapping, adjustment layers and intralayer blending to produce a print with natural, consistent and pleasing tones overall.

The original uncorrected image.

One of my favorite pictures has always been this photo of my best buddy Al, taken on a desert trip we made together back around 1980. I always wanted to make a print of it, so when I got my Epson Stylist Photo printer, I had it and many other favorite pictures put onto Photo CD. When I brought in the photo from the CD, it was obviously oversaturated in the shadow areas of the face. Because this is not a major area of the image, the first step to correct it is to do Overall Color Correction to get the rest of the image to look right. This file was saved using ColorMatch RGB so if you want your values and histograms to look the same as in the book, leave this file in the ColorMatch RGB space.

OVERALL COLOR CORRECTION

STEP 1: **Open the OrigAl file from the Color Correcting Al folder on the CD. Crop any areas from around the edge of the image that are not going to be in the print. In this case, my copyright notice is the only thing you need to crop. Double-click on the Background layer and name it Original Al; then click on the Lock Position icon, second from Right at the top of the Layers palette, to lock the position of this layer. Use F9 to bring up the Info palette and Shift-F9 to bring up the Color palette. Now use Command-F2 to create a Levels adjustment layer and use the steps outlined in Chapter 19: "Overall Color Correction" to set the Highlight, Shadow, overall Brightness and finally the color cast. Here are the Levels settings I ended up with for Al. To set the highlight, I used the Highlight Eyedropper in Levels and set it to the white area on the tip of Al's right shoulder (on the left side of the image). For the shadow, I used the Shadow Eyedropper and set it to the shadow on the black tuft of hair below Al's ear and behind his neck. I then adjusted the overall brightness, as well as the color balance. When you are done with your basic color corrections, choose OK to save your Levels adjustment layer.**

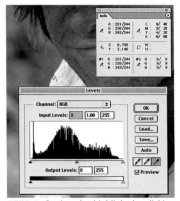

STEP 1: Setting the highlight by clicking with the Highlight Eyedropper on the whitest area of Al's shirt.

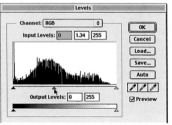

STEP 1: The overall corrected RGB histogram.

STEP 2: **Use Command-F4 to add a Hue/Saturation adjustment layer above the Levels Adjustment layer. Here are the settings I made in Hue/Saturation. The goal was to saturate all the colors, as I normally would do, but then to not add more saturation to the reds in the face. To get the set of reds that I wanted to desaturate in the face, I first used the Hue/Saturation Eyedropper and dragged it over the**

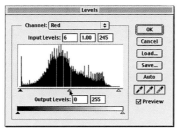

really saturated areas of his face because these are the ones that need desaturation. I then used the –Eyedropper to subtract away

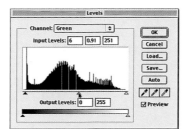

STEP 1: The overall red adjustments.

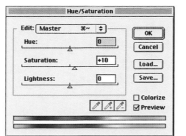

STEP 1: The overall green adjustments.

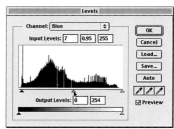

STEP 1: The overall blue adjustments.

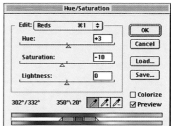

the normal red flesh tones by dragging over them and then the +Eyedropper to add any too saturated colors back in. As you are doing this, notice that the range of reds that are selected changes based on the width of the gray slider bars between the two rainbow color bars in the Hue/Saturation dialog. Try my settings and feel free to modify them and make your own to improve the image. Don't try to fix the red shadow areas around the eyes here, just desaturate them a little bit. They should still look a bit too saturated when you finish with Hue/Saturation.

FIXING THE OVERSATURATED AREAS WITH CHANNEL MIXER

STEP 3: Use Shift-F10 to bring up the Channels palette; then click on the word Red to look at the Red channel. Make sure the Eye icons are off for the RGB, Green and Blue channels. Now look at just the Green and just the Blue channels in the same way. This will tell you if one of the channels has a noticeable pattern within the oversaturated area on Al's face. The Levels and Hue/Saturation layers actually have no Red, Green, and Blue channels themselves because they are adjustment layers, but this is showing you what each of these channels will look like when the layers you've created so far are merged. You can see that the Green channel is very dark, magenta, in all the saturated areas. Make sure the Hue/Saturation layer is active; then Option-click on the New Layer icon at the bottom of the Layers palette to add a new layer above it and name it Color Merged. Hold down Option and leave it down while choosing Merge Visible from the Layers palette menu and while the calculations are happening. This maneuver merges the effects of the Levels and Hue/Saturation adjustment layers into the new Color Merged layer. Lock the position of this new layer. Option-drag the Color Merged layer to the New Layer icon and call this copy Color Merged Fixed. Drag this layer to just below the Color Merged layer and Option-click on the Color Merged Fixed Eye icon

STEP 3: Al's RGB before using the Red channel to fix the saturated areas.

STEP 3: The Red channel we will use to fix the Green and Blue channels.

STEP 3: The unfixed Green channel is dark in all the saturated areas.

STEP 3: The Color Merged Fixed layer after fixing the Green and Blue channels.

267

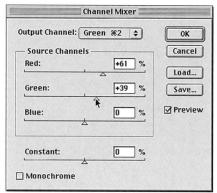

Channel Mixer

Output Channel: Green ⌘2

Source Channels
Red: +61 %
Green: +39 %
Blue: 0 %

Constant: 0 %

☐ Monochrome

OK
Cancel
Load...
Save...
☑ Preview

STEP 3: Here we see the Channel Mixer settings for the Green channel.

STEP 4: Al before retouch and sharpening.

to just work on and see that layer. **Choose Layer/New Adjustment Layer/Channel Mixer and choose Group with Previous Layer so the changes just affect the Color Merged Fixed layer.** Channel Mixer is a feature in Photoshop 5 and 6 that makes this kind of operation much easier and more flexible than it used to be. We are going to use the Red channel to fix the oversaturation problems in the Green and Blue channels. **Make sure the Preview button is on in the Channel Mixer dialog; then set the Output Channel to Red and leave the Source Channels set to 100% Red. Now set the Output Channel to Green; then change the Source Channels to about 61% Red and 39% Green.** This will change the Green channel to actually be made up of 61% of the Red channel and you will notice more detail returning to the saturated areas of Al's face. **Now set the Output Channel to Blue; then set the Source Channels to about 47% Red and 53% Blue.** You can change these percentages as many times as you like, and as you do, you will notice small changes in color balance and the amount of detail in the saturated areas of Al's face. To fix the Green and Blue channels, you want to use the least amount of the Red channel that both repairs the dark areas and keeps a compatible color balance that will be flatter than the Color Merged layer, since much of the detail is coming from the Red channel. **Compare my Color Merged layer (with its layer mask off) to my Color Merged Fixed layer to see the relative color balance and lightness I used. My final version of this example is in the Extra Info Files folder of the Ch24.Desert Al folder on the CD.**

BLENDING THE TWO LAYERS

STEP 4: **Click on the words Color Merged to make the Color Merged layer the active layer. At the bottom of the Layers palette, click on the second from left Layer Mask icon to add a layer mask to the Color Merged layer. Use the Air Brush (J) at about 05% Pressure with soft brushes and paint black in the Color Merged layer mask. Doing so lets you slowly remove dark and oversaturated parts of the Color Merged layer to reveal the lighter fixed version of the Color Merged Fixed layer underneath. You want to have the Eye icons on for both layers while doing this. Don't worry if the color balance of Color Merged Fixed isn't exactly right; just work on getting the saturation down in the damaged areas. You want to paint with black very lightly to get a gray value in the layer mask so just barely enough of the Color Merged Fixed layer is revealed. Painting too darkly in the mask is the most common problem students have in getting this example to work for them.** If you are having trouble making this work, see the Extra Info Files folder to check out my layer mask for the Color Merged layer. **When you are happy with the basic detail that you have added with the layer mask, click on the Channel Mixer layer to activate it again. Then use Command-F2 to add a new grouped Levels Adjustment layer above it. To have this adjustment layer be grouped, you need to turn on the Group with Previous Layer checkbox in the New Layer dialog. Now you can change the color balance and contrast of the Color Merged Fixed layer while watching how these changes affect its composite with the Color Merged layer. You should find that you can get Al's face to look much better when you match the color and brightness of the two. Now activate Color Merged and click back on its layer mask. Use black or white with the Airbrush to make further changes to the mask and fine-tune the face composite.**

When this is looking as good as you can get it, Option-click on the New Layer icon to add a new layer above the Color Merged layer, named Final Retouch. Make sure that the Eye icons are on for Color Merged Fixed, the Channel Mixer

and Levels adjustment layers above it, Color Merged and this new layer. Then choose **Merge Visible with the Option key held down to merge the four lower layers into this new layer.** Using a new Merged layer for retouching allows you to just retouch a single layer and to also have the option of throwing this layer out and starting over again if you make an undoable mistake.

CLEANING UP SOME BLEMISHES

STEP 5: **Now use the Lasso tool to select the white part of Al's left eye. Use Select/Feather to put a one-pixel feather on this selection. Go into Hue/Saturation (Command-U) and try to brighten the white of Al's eye and to make it more white. I added +10 to the lightness in Master mode, and then I moved the Hue to +8 in Reds mode, all of which made the eye stand out a little better and removed some of its red tint.**

STEP 6: **Now use the Rubber Stamp tool with different size soft brushes and opacities to remove any blemishes and to tone out areas that are too magenta.** If you set the opacity to 30–50% and then clone from an area next to the one you want to fix, it's easy to even out color areas that aren't quite right without losing the original detail in that area. You can also clone with the Blend mode set to Color to change the color of something without losing its original detail. **Remember that you can change the opacity by typing a number on the numeric keypad between 0 and 9. Zero is for 100%, 9 for 90%, 8 for 80%,…1 for 10%, or even 25 for 25%. You can also use the bracket keys, [and], to move to the next smaller or the next larger brush.** Make sure that you use Edit/Preferences/Display & Cursors to set the preferences for Painting Cursors to Brush Size so that if the cursor is over your image, you can see the brush size relative to your image and zoom factor as you change the brush size with the bracket keys. **Be careful not to blur the facial detail with too much cloning. To see what is possible with retouching, turn the Eye icon off then on again in the Final Retouch layer of my AlAllFinalLayers file from the CD.**

STEP 7: **Option-drag the Final Retouch layer to the New Layer icon and name the copy USM. Go into Filter/Sharpen/Unsharp Mask (F4) and use the techniques demonstrated in Chapter 20: "Correcting a Problem Image" to find the right sharpening settings for Al. I used 150%, 1.5 and 3. You may want to rename this USM layer with the sharpen settings you used. This will help if you need to change them later. After doing the sharpen, you may want to do another quick sweep at 100% to check for spots that the sharpen might add. I did my sharpen in a layer that is a copy of Final Retouch to give me the option of later trying a different sharpen amount!** Save the file as your final RGB version of Al, and call it AlFinalRGB or something like that. You want to save the flattened version under a different name to preserve the layered RGB version for later use.

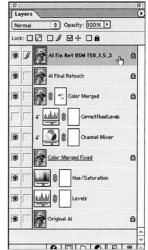

STEP 8: The final Layers palette for this example. Check out my version in the Extra Info Files folder on the *Photoshop 6 Artistry* CD.

STEP 8: The final version of Al, after retouching and sharpening.

269

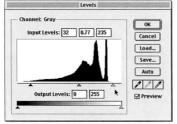

25 HANDS-ON SESSION: Restoring Old Photos

Techniques for restoring and colorizing old photographs are explored as we restore a black and white photo of the Cochrane train station taken in the thirties by Arthur F. Lynch, Jr. and provided for use in this book by the Adams Collection.

Since I have been teaching the Printmaking for Photographers workshop in my studio, various students have brought in old photographs they wanted to restore. I am very impressed with what we have been able to do to restore these old black and white as well as color photographs so I decided to add a restoration example to *Photoshop 6 Artistry*. I had been looking for the right photograph to restore and mentioned this during one of my courses. A student at the course, John Adams, happens to collect old photographs so he sent me this as a possible candidate. It is a great shot, taken in the thirties by Arthur F. Lynch, Jr., and is just what I was looking for. Thanks to the Adams Collection for providing this photograph for use in this book. You can gain access to the Adams Collection via their web site at www.adamscollection.com.

The original faded and scratched photograph was not that different from this size.

SCANNING THE ORIGINAL

STEP 1: Scanning an old photograph can be done quite well using a flatbed scanner. This one was scanned on the Epson Expression 1640 XL at 1600 dpi. This scanner does a great job scanning prints and has a large bed, allowing you to scan prints up to 12.2 x 17.2 in size. The file you will be working with here is 25% of that 1600 dpi scan. The important thing to do in making a scan of an old photo is to try to get all the detail out of the photo. Try not to lose any highlight or shadow detail that is in the original print. It is important to have the focus right on, which is usually not a problem when scanning prints using a flatbed scanner. I scanned this at 16 bits per channel. **Your first step will be use File/Open to Open the file CochraneOrigScanAt25%.psd from the Ch25.Restoring Old Photos folder on the *Photoshop 6 Artistry* CD. This is a 16-bit per channel grayscale image so use Image/Adjust/Levels to do the intial adjustment. The settings I used are shown to the left. Choose OK in the Levels dialog then choose Image/Mode/8 Bits/Channel to convert this to an 8-bit grayscale image.**

STEP 1: The Levels settings I used on the 16-bit per channel grayscale file.

ADDING CONTRAST

STEP 2: **Create a Curves adjustment layer using Layer/New Adjustment Layer/Curves (Command-F3). Use Option-click in the Curves graph area until you have a graph with just four divisions in each direction. Now make an S-curve like the one to the right to increase the contrast of the scene. Make sure the shadow detail in the train and on the station platform doesn't get too dark.** You may notice that the shadow detail in the train wheels and also on the station platform is sort of plugged up. What we need to do to solve this problem is create a curve that increases contrast in these areas but then only apply that curve to these areas. **Use Command-F3 to create a second Curve adjustment layer called Add Contrast to Shadows. While looking only into the shadow areas, adjust the curve until you add contrast to these areas. We are going to isolate this adjustment to these areas so it doesn't matter a whole lot what this curve does to the rest of the image. Choose OK in the Curves dialog, and then choose Image/Adjust/Invert (Command-I) to invert the layer mask on this adjustment layer and make it totally black. Now this adjustment is doing nothing...for the moment. Type J to switch to the Airbrush tool and set the Pressure, in the Options bar, to about 7 percent. Pick a soft brush of about 30 to 50 in size, and then type D to get the default colors of a white foreground and a black background. Paint on your layer mask in the shadow areas of the train wheels and the station platform to reveal the extra contrast and detail only in those areas. The longer you hold the Airbrush down, the more paint is applied and the more contrast you'll see in these areas.**

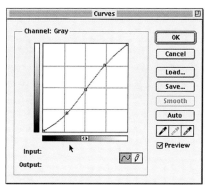

STEP 2: The initial S-Curve to increase contrast. Notice that these curves have their shadows to the left. You can use the double arrows in the middle to display your curves with shadows on either side.

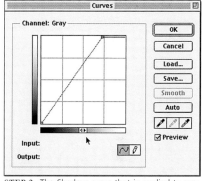

STEP 2: The Shadow curve that is applied to specific areas using the mask below. This increases the slope of the shadow areas, making them more contrasty but it also pulls the curve up, making those areas brighter.

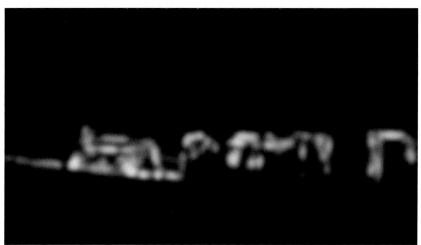

STEP 2: The Shadow curve mask that applies the Shadow curve only in the areas where the mask is white.

DARKENING THE BRIGHT WASHED-OUT AREAS

STEP 3: We want to do a similar, but opposite thing to darken the bright and washed-out areas and also add some contrast to them. **Use Command-F3 again to make another Cuves adjustment layer named Fix Highlights. Adjust this curve to make the flat, dull highlight areas on the station roof and in the tracks area darker and more contrasty. The curve pictured to the right worked well for me. While making this curve, only look at those areas of the image. When you choose OK to the Curves dialog, then choose Command-I to invert the mask and make it totally black. You now want to paint white with the Airbrush in the areas you want to enhance.** This will take a while but it is worth the effort. The images on the next page show you

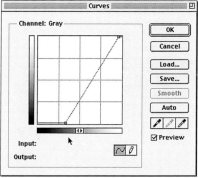

STEP 3: The curve used to darken the bright and washed out areas. Since the slope of the curve in the highlights is increased, that adds contrast to these flat areas. Pulling the curve downward also makes those areas darker.

STEP 3: The Cochrane station before we darken the roof and foreground with the mask to the right.

STEP 3: The Cochrane station after we darken the roof and foreground with the mask to the right.

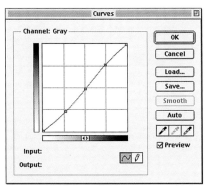

STEP 4: A final more subtle S-Curve was added to the entire image to add just a little more overall contrast.

STEP 5: The Layers palette after making the RetouchCopy layer. Notice that I have locked four of the layers against accidental movement.

the before and after versions of this photo. These curves adjustments can have a dramatic effect on an image. Use File/Save As to save your file as CochraneLayers.

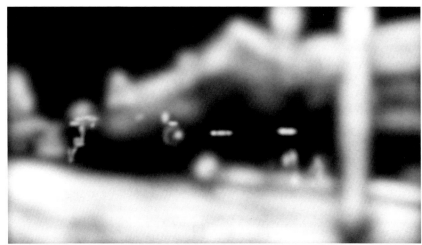

STEP 3: Where this mask is white, its accompaning curve makes the bright areas of this image darker and more contrasty.

A FINAL CONTRAST TWEAK

STEP 4: **My image still looked a bit flat overall so I used Command-F3 one more time to add another more subtle S-Curve to the entire image. This curve is pictured to the left. Depending on the curves you created so far, you may or may not need this step.**

SPOTTING AND RETOUCHING

STEP 5: This image obviously has a lot of spots, scratches and other blemishes. We want to fix them but also be able to make sure we don't destroy the original integrity of the image while doing so. Doing these fixes on a copy of the original image allows us to keep the original as a backup and also to look at it from time to time to double check that we are really making positive progress. **Double-click on the *Background* layer to turn it into a real layer and name it Orig Scan. Drag this Orig Scan layer to the New Layer icon, to the left of the trash, and make a copy called RetouchCopy. This RetouchCopy layer should now be next to the bottom of the layers palette. See the illustration to the left to make sure you have it correct. Lock the Orig Scan, RetouchCopy, Add Contrast to Shadows and Fix Highlights layers so they can't be accidentally moved with the Move tool. Make sure the RetouchCopy layer is active, and then type an S to switch to the Rubber Stamp tool. Check in the Options palette to be sure the Opacity is set to 100%, that Aligned is turned on and that Use All Layers is turned off. Pick the third brush from the top-left in the Brushes palette as a starting point. Make sure you are in Full Screen mode, type the Tab key to get rid of all your palettes, use Command-Option-0 to zoom into 100%, and then press the Home key to scroll to the top-left corner of your document. You may want to use Command-Spacebar-0 to zoom in to 200%. Now you need to spot, remove scratches and retouch each section of this image. The big spots in the sky and elsewhere are fairly easy to remove. It's the fingerprints and tiny scratches in the station and station platform area that you can spend a lot of time on. Be patient and don't get carried away with the rubber stamp tool. Fix one section at a time and you may find**

Chapter 25: Restoring Old Photos

that you don't need to fix every last blemish to make the photo look a lot better. Since the Orig Scan layer is underneath the RetouchCopy layer, you can turn the Eye icon for the Retouch-Copy layer off and on again from time to time to see how much you have improved it over the Orig Scan layer in the area you are working.

SHARPENING

STEP 6: **When you have finished spotting and retouching the RetouchCopy layer, choose File/Save (Command-S) to save your final layered file. Now choose Image/Duplicate (F5) to make a copy of**

Step 5: Before retouching, you can see the scratches in the top right of this part of the building and there is also a fingerprint slightly above left of the Cochrane sign.

Step 5: After retouching with the Rubber Stamp tool. It took me about an hour to retouch this entire image. It's still not perfect but looks a lot better.

your master layered file and make sure Duplicate Merged Layers Only is checked in the Duplicate dialog. With this flattened copy of your file, choose Filter/Sharpen/ Unsharp Mask (F4) to sharpen it. I did an overall sharpen of 150,1 and 0. This improved the image somewhat and also added a normal grain pattern. Now go to the Channels palette and make a copy of the single grayscale channel by dragging it to the New Channel icon next to the trash can at the bottom of the Channels palette.

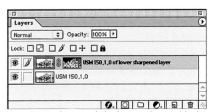

Step 6: We sharpened the bottom layer with the Unsharp Mask filter at 150,1,0. We then copied this sharpened version in the Channels palette and used that to make the mask with the modified Sharpen Only Edges BH action. We also copied the sharpened verison as a layer and sharpened it again at 150,1,0 but applied it through the edges mask as shown here.

Press F11 to bring up your Actions palette and turn Button Mode off using the pop-up Options menu in the Actions palette. Open up the Sharpen Only Edges BH action and turn off the steps shown to the right. This modifies the action so it will just run on this new channel you just made in the Channels palette. Play the action on this extra channel and when the action is finished, turn those steps back on again so the action will work normally next time you use it for a color image. To load it as a selection, Command-click on the Mask channel you just created with the Sharpen Only Edges BH action. Click back on the top channel in the Channels palette to activate it again. Now switch to the Layers palette and drag a copy of your single layer to the New Layer icon to make a copy of this layer. You should still have the selection loaded from the sharpen mask so now choose Layer/Add Layer Mask/Reveal Selection to turn this into a layer mask on this top layer. Click on the Layer thumbnail for this top layer so you will be sharpening the layer and not the mask. Now use F4 again to go back into Unsharp Mask and sharpen this top layer. I used the same value of 150,1 and 0 but this time only the areas that are white in the mask are going to be adding sharpness. The final setup for the sharpening is shown above. Use File/Save As to save this as CochraneUSMLayers. Use Image/Duplicate (F5) again to make a flattened copy of this and name that copy CochraneColorLayers. Choose Image/Mode/RGB to convert that image from black and white into color. You will now have a Red, Green and Blue channel in your Channels palette instead of just a single grayscale channel.

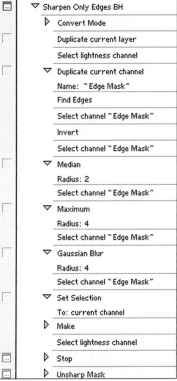

Step 6: The modified Sharpen Only Edges BH action so it will work on a channel by itself. After sharpening the channel, turn the other steps back on. You could also start out by just dragging this entire action to the New Action icon at the bottom of the Actions palette. This will make a copy of the entire action. Rename the copy to Sharpen Only Edges BH Grayscale. Now you could just remove the steps you don't need by dragging them to the trash. This will leave you with a Sharpen Only Edges action that you can use on any channel. To sharpen any RGB image, this new action could be used on one of the Red, Green or Blue channels of that RGB image instead of converting that image to LAB color as the Sharpen Only Edges BH action does.

Step 7: For each of the adjustment layers in the below layers palette, we have done a similar adjustment with the Colorize checkbox on in Hue/Saturation. The difference between each one is where we moved the Hue and Saturation sliders. That will determine the color created as we colorize this black and white image. These are the settings for the first HueSatBrown layer. You can open my final color version of this image, including all the layers by looking in the Extra Info Files folder on the CD.

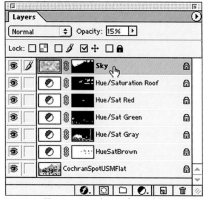

Step 7: Here is the mask for the Hue/Sat Gray layer shown below. We wanted the train engine to be a darker blue-gray than the other areas so we painted using 100% white. The Opacity of the Paintbrush was changed in the other areas to get the shade of blue-gray we wanted. The straight tracks were done by clicking at one end then Shift-clicking at the other end, which draws a striaght line between the two ends.

STEP 7: The Layers palette after adding all the Hue/Saturation Colorize adjustment layers to create the image at the right.

COLORIZING

STEP 7: The process for colorizing the image involves creating various Hue/Saturation adjustment layers and turning on the Colorize option in each one. The final layers palette for my colorized Cochrane image is at the bottom of the page here. **First I chose Command-F4 to create the HueSatBrown adjustment layer. Using the settings shown to the left, this gave the entire image a brown sepia tone effect. Using the Paintbrush, I painted black in the mask for this adjustment layer at either 100% or a lower Opacity to remove this effect from the windows of the station. I next used Command-F4 again to create a Hue/Saturation adjustment layer with a blue-gray color. I used Command-I to invert the mask on this Hue/Sat Gray layer so it wasn't affecting anything. Then I used the Paintbrush painting in the adjustment layer's mask with white at either 100% or a lower Opacity to add this color to the train engine and other parts of the image. Next I created a Green then a Red Hue/Saturation layer, inverted each of their masks, then painted white in each mask where I wanted that color in the image. The final Hue/Saturation colorizing layer was the Roof one, which I used to give the roof of the station a more gray color. The only problem left now was the sky with no color or detail in it. To create a sky, I used Layer/New Layer to make a new normal layer at the top of the Layers palette. I went to the color picker and picked a sky blue color then filled this layer with that color. I then chose Filter/Render/Clouds, which creates a sort of cheesy cloud effect. Setting the Opacity of this layer to 15% made this effect somewhat believable. I turned off the Eye icon for this top layer, then clicked on the Hue/Sat Roof layer to make it active. I then looked at the Red, Green and Blue channels in the Channels palette and made a copy of the Blue channel, then used Levels on that copy and then the Paintbrush to make a mask that was white only in the sky. I Command-clicked on that mask to load it as a selection then clicked back on RGB in the Channels palette. I then went back to the Layers palette and clicked on the Sky layer to reactivate it. I then choose Layer/Add Layer Mask/Reveal Selection to add this sky mask as a layer mask to the Sky layer.** For more details on how to make this type of sky mask, see Chapter 20: "Correcting a Problem Image."

The final colored version of the Cochrane train station after making the initial improvements to the black and white version, sharpening and then finally colorizing as explained above.

HANDS-ON SESSION: Combining Bracketed Photos or Two Scans to Increase Dynamic Range

26

Taking two bracketed photos and/or two 16-bit scans to get the full range of detail in a high-contrast image; then using layers, adjustment layers, and layer masks to color correct the image by combining the two versions into one final print.

In June of 2000, I went on a trip with my photographer friend, Dave McIntire, to Mount Rainier and found it to be an incredible mountain and surrounding park. If you are ever in Washington state, Mount Rainier should certainly be on your list of photography stops. It was hard to photograph the mountain since it was covered with snow and very bright in the full sunshine we were lucky enough to have during our stay there. This mountain, which is 14,410 feet high, is often covered by clouds and therefore impossible to photograph at all. With my Canon EOS 10s on a tripod, I bracketed three exposures of this shot of Mount Rainier we will be working on here. Even with the full stop bracketing (one stop over, one stop under and one stop at the meter's reading), the exposure in the shadow areas of the trees was still very dark. I did get a good exposure of the white snow on the mountain without losing any highlight detail. Using the UMax PowerLook 3000 scanner, I scanned this at the highest 3048 dpi and at 16-bits per channel in a way that made sure I didn't lose any of the highlight detail. On the CD, in the Ch26.CombiningBracketedPhotos folder, is a 60% scaled down version of this scan called MtRainierSky60%.psd. For the second scan, I chose the exposure that had the most possible shadow detail, although I wish I had an exposure that had even more shadow detail. When scanning this second exposure, I did the scan in a way that would keep the most shadow detail and without worrying about losing highlight detail since I was going to get that from the other exposure. On the CD is a 60% scaled down version of that scan called MtRainierTrees60%.psd.

DOING INITIAL COLOR CORRECTION ON 48-BIT FILES

STEP 1: **Open the MtRainierSky60%.psd and MtRainierTrees60%.psd files from the Ch26.CombiningBracketedPhotos folder on the *Photoshop 6 Artistry* CD. In this example, we'll call these the Sky and Trees images respectively. Since these are both 16-bit per channel scans, we can't combine them using layers until we convert them to 8-bit per channel. Before doing that, we want to do the initial Levels color adjustments to adjust the histograms so we can get the most out of each of these images when converted to 8 bits. Bring the Sky image to the foreground and type an F to put it into Full Screen mode. Use the Tab key to get rid of your palettes, and then type Command-0 so you can see the entire image on the screen. Type C to get the Crop tool and use it to crop black border from the top and left of the image. Remember that, while the mouse button is down and you are dragging one of the cropping handles, you can use the Control key to turn off**

STEP 1: This exposure, the Sky image, was taken to get the most detail on the snow covered mountain. I was happy with this exposure and scan.

STEP 2: This exposure, the Trees image, was taken to get more detail in the tree and shadow areas. The averaging meter I used here still swayed this exposure too much towards the very bright snow covered mountain so I didn't get as much shadow detail as I would have liked. I should have used my spot meter and taken some spot readings of the trees and dark shadows here. We'll show you how to get as much as possible out of this situation.

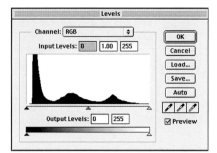

STEP 1: The initial histogram for the Sky image shows us that we haven't thrown out any highlight detail on the right side but that the shape of the shadow area shows a lot of values very near to black.

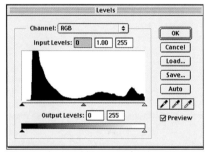

STEP 1: The initial histogram for the Tree image shows the subtle highlight details missing on the right and also how the shadow values and midtone values are spread out over a much wider area.

Photoshop's feature that locks you to the edge of the image when you are close to it. Don't crop any more than what you need to remove the black borders on the top and left edges. Switch to the Trees image and crop it in the same way, being careful to just remove the black border on the left side.

Even though these were shot using a tripod, with 35mm film and the scanner we used it was hard to scan them so we got exactly the same image area and even degree of rotation. I'll show you how to line them up after they sit on top of each other as layers. **I'm assuming both these images are now in Full Screen mode so use the Window menu to switch back to the Sky image. I usually keep my Navigator palette (Shift-F2) hanging off the right side of the screen so I can just see the zoom factor and with my screen set to 1024 x 768, a 50% zoom factor allows me to clearly see most of this image. Use the Window menu or F9 to bring up your Info palette and type an F for Full Screen mode. Type an H to put you into the Hand tool then click and drag the image so you can see the entire sky and the main mountain area is visible on your monitor. Note that the Layer menu is grayed out since this is a 16-bit per channel, 48-bit total, image and Photoshop doesn't support layers with this type of image. What we want to do here in 16-bit mode is adjust the Sky image so it isn't losing any highlight values and so the snow area is best adjusted in overall brightness values to where you might want it to be in a final composite. We can make small adjustments after converting to 8 bits per channel but we want to make any large moves right here.**

Choose Image/Adjust/Levels to enter the Levels tool. The Levels settings I used on this image are in the Extra Info Files folder and are called Sky16BitLevels.alv. You can use the Load button to load them and take a look if you'd like. To create your own settings, Option-click on the Cancel button which will put everything back to their starting values. With the Preview checkbox on inside the Levels dialog, hold down the Option key while dragging the Input Highlight slider to the left until you see the first area to turn white. This is the brightest area within the snow image and would be a good place to set your highlight. Move the slider back to 255 and then use your Highlight Eyedropper to find the brightest point in this area, with the largest set of RGB numbers. When you find this point, first Shift-click to set a Color Sampler there and then click again without the Shift to set the highlight there. After converting to 8-bit, you may want to make this a bit brighter, but for now the Eyedropper highlight will give you a good value here and also adjust for any color cast gained during the scan.

Now go into each of the Red, Green and Blue channels and move the Input Shadow slider to the right until you get to where the large amount of shadow data starts. Since most of the important shadow detail will be coming from the other scan, one does not have to be as careful with the shadow settings on this one. This image will, however, control how the shadows will look in the area of the snow covered mountain. Go back to the RGB channel and move the middle Brightness slider to the left until the mountain is not quite so contrasty. I moved it to about 1.40. When you are happy with your Levels settings, click the Save button to save them in a file, then choose OK to complete your Levels adjustments. With your settings saved to a file, you can look at them later if you decide to try a different approach. When you can't create an adjustment layer, that is the next best way to remember what you did.

STEP 2: **Switch to the Tree image and go into Levels. The settings I used on this are called Trees16BitLevels.alv, so load them from the Extra Info Files folder and check them out. What I was trying to do here was make the shadow areas close to neutral**

Chapter 26: Combining Bracketed Photos or Two Scans to Increase Dynamic Range

without losing any possible shadow detail, open up the 3/4 tones and midtones a lot and not be too concerned about the highlights since they are mostly coming from the Sky image. First I went into each of the Red, Green and Blue channels and moved the Input Shadow sliders to the right until where the graph started to have values and then maybe moved them back a bit to the left to be sure I'm not throwing anything out. Next I went back to the RGB channel and moved the slider way to the left to open up the 3/4 and mid tones. Finally I went into each of the Red, Green and Blue channels again and moved the middle slider to give the trees the approximate color balance I would want in the end. I purposely left the image a bit light and flat so I'd have a full range of values once I got to 8-bit mode and could tweak them after compositing the two images together using a layer mask. Now Option-Cancel to reset my Levels settings and go through the process of making the Levels adjustments yourself. Use the Save button to save your Levels settings and choose OK when you are finished with this step. Don't forget to Option-drag the Input Shadow slider, with the Preview checkbox on, to find the darkest shadow area and mark this with a Color Sampler so you can keep an eye on its color balance as you color correct the image.

While still having 16 bits per channel, this image looked so flat the first time I color corrected it, I decided to run a small S curve on it to increase its contrast a bit. I was concerned that it might be better to leave this until I converted to 8-bit but to see what I did choose Image/Adjust/Curves and use the Load button to load the file called Trees16BitCurves.acv from the Extra Info Files folder. The risk with doing this here is that we may permanently throw out a little shadow detail that we'll wish we had later. When working without adjustment layers, it is harder to go back and try many variations so you want to give it your best shot in 16-bit then make the complicated moves in 8-bit where you can use masks and adjustment layers. I later redid this color correction step and omitted this S curve in 16-bit mode so you should probably do the same and cancel from the Curves dialog at this point. I'm mentioning this here because these are the types of decisions that can determine whether you get any shadow detail at all on a difficult image like this. Save each of your images with a suffix named 16bit because we are going to convert them to 8-bit in the next step.

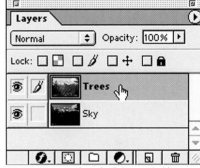

STEP 3: You now have both images inside a two-layered document with the Trees layer on top and the Sky layer on the bottom.

CONVERTING TO 8-BIT, COMBINING AND ROTATING

STEP 3: **Choose Image/Mode/8 Bits/Channel on each of the two opened images to convert them to 8 bits per channel. Use the Window menu to bring the Trees image to the top, and then type F until you convert it to normal Window mode where you can see the titile bar at the top of the window and the scroll bars at the side. Move this window over so you can see the Sky image underneath, which should still be in Full Screen mode. Type a V to switch to the Move tool; then hold the Shift key down while you click on the center of the Trees image and drag and drop it, releasing the mouse when the cursor is over the top of the Sky image. This should drop the Trees image on top of the Sky image as a centered layer. Bring up the Layers palette (F10) then Option-double-click on the names of the layers to rename the top one Trees and the bottom one Sky. The first time you Option-double-click on the bottom layer, it will just be called Layer 0 and the Layer Properties dialog will not come up allowing you to rename it. This is because it is being converted from a Background layer to a normal layer. Option-double-click a second time and then you can name it Sky. Choose File/Save As and save this as MountRainierLayers. We will be working on this file for the rest of the exercise.**

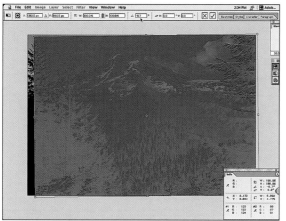

STEP 3: This is what your zoomed out screen should look like when you are rotating the Trees layer to align it with the Sky layer. You want the Options bar on the top and the Info palette in the corner.

STEP 3: When properly aligned, the center of the two image overlay should look like this.

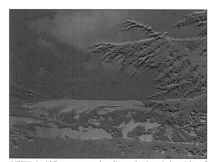

STEP 3: When properly aligned, the right side of the two image overlay should look like this. The alignment between the trees on both sides may not be perfect at this point.

Now we are going to line up the two layers. Type a 5 to set the Opacity of the Trees layer to 50%. This should allow you to see both layers at once. With the Move tool, click on a spot on the screen and move it around until you are sure which image represents the Trees layer. That will be the one which is moving around. Now drag the Trees layer until the spot where the Move cursor is located lines up with the same spot on the Sky image underneath. Release the mouse button. That should have made the two images fairly close to being aligned. Now use Image/Adjust/Invert (Command-I) to invert the Trees layer. If the images are not perfectly aligned, you will see an embossed effect along the misaligned edges. With the cursor over the image, you can now use the Arrow keys on the keyboard to move the image one pixel at a time up, down, left or right. Do this until the center of the image is as closely aligned as possible. At this point the embossed effect in the center should be minimized.

If you zoom out, however, you'll notice that the embossed effect is greater at the left and right of the image. This shows us that the rotation of the two is not the same. Since the two were shot on a tripod, this difference in rotation must have happened during the scan. Now choose Edit/Transform/Rotate and zoom out until you can see the handles in the corners of the image. Move the cursor up to just outside a corner and when you see the curved arrows, click and drag to start the rotation. When the image is closer, you can type fractional rotation changes into the angle text box of the Options bar, pressing Return, ONLY ONCE, to get the cursor out of the text box. If you move the cursor back on top of the image again, you can still use the arrow keys to move the image one pixel at a time up, down, left or right. Don't put the cursor over the little dot in the center of the screen as that will move the center of rotation. Do this rotation process slowly and carefully, zooming into different areas to check them and scrolling around with the Spacebar down to give you the Hand tool. If your machine is not the fastest, give Photoshop time to update the screen after making a movement. My rotation seemed to work best at –0.7 degrees but I also had to use the arrow keys a few times to move the image a pixel or two one way or the other and also up and down. When you are happy with the alignment and rotation, press Return to complete the process. If you need to get

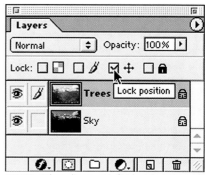

STEP 3: When alignment is finished, lock the position of both layers by activating each then clicking in the Lock position checkbox for that layer.

out of Rotate to start over, press the Escape key to exit from the Rotate. When your Trees image is rotated and aligned as best as possible, use Image/Adjust/Invert to bring the image back to a positive and type a 0, zero, to bring the Trees layer back to 100% Opacity. Now lock the position on both the Trees and Sky layers in the Layers palette, and then choose Command-S to save your work on this file so far.

SEPARATING MOUNT RAINIER FROM THE TREES

STEP 4: Type C to switch to the Cropping tool, zoom out so you can see the entire image on the screen then press Tab to get all your palettes out of the way. Crop the

Chapter 26: Combining Bracketed Photos or Two Scans to Increase Dynamic Range

two-layer image to just include the rectangle that is common to both images. Remember that you can zoom into the corners and the crop handles to see how the edges line up with more detail. Save the image again after the crop. Turn off the Eye icon for the Trees layer and click on the word Sky to activate the Sky layer. In the Channels palette look at each of the Red, Green and Blue channels to decide which one has the most contrast between the mountain and the trees. The Eye icons for RGB and the other channels should be off when looking at a particular channel. I decided to use the Blue channel as the candidate for separating the mountain and sky from the trees. In the Channels palette, click on the word Blue and drag this channel down to the New Channel icon just to the left of the Trash icon at the bottom of the Channels palette. This will make a copy called Blue copy. Now choose Image/Adjust/Levels to go into Levels and increase the contrast of that copy. I did this with a two-step Levels adjustment. First I entered the values 26, 1 and 245 into the Input Levels text boxes, then I chose OK for my first step. I then chose Image/Adjust/Levels (Command-L) again, entered the values 64, 1.58 and 210 and then chose OK again. This gives you a good start for a mask; you will have to hand edit it the rest of the way. If you chose the Red or Green channel to start your mask, you will probably have to use different values in Levels to separate the mountain from the trees.

STEP 4: Deciding which channel to use as the starting point for your mask. Don't forget to copy the Blue channel before going into Levels.

Go ahead and Command-click on the thumbnail for the mask you made; in my case, it is called Blue copy. This will load this mask as a selection and actually selects the whiter areas of the mask, which will be the sky and mountain. Now click back on the word RGB in the Channels palette and then click on the word Trees in the Layers palette. This shows you color again and makes the Trees layer the active one. Choose Layer/Add Layer Mask/Hide Selection to add a layer mask to the Trees layer which will remove the mountain and sky area from this layer revealing the better one from the Sky layer below. It won't look too good until you edit the mask. Type a B to get the Paintbrush and a 0, zero, for 100% Opacity, and then pick a big hard-edge brush and Option-click on the Layer Mask thumbnail which is the rightmost one in the Trees layer in the Layers palette. This will show you the now inverted mask which you should clean up with the brush by painting the sky and mountain area totally black and the trees area totally white. You

STEP 4: Adding the layer mask to the Trees layer to remove the mountain and sky. You will have to edit this mask to make it look correct.

can close the Channels palette at this point to get it out of the way.

At this point what you are trying to do is quickly cut a rough mask using the Paintbrush tool. Be careful not to damage any of the subtle edge detail on the trees or the tops of the smaller tree covered mountain in the foreground. After cutting this rough mask, you will do the Overall Color Correction on each of the Trees and and Sky layers using a set of Grouped adjustment layers on each of these real layers. This Overall Color Correction process is described in detail in Chapters 19 and 20 so you can review them now if you

STEP 4: Here we are rough editing the area where we see Mount Rainier through the silhouette of the dark foreground trees. Be careful not to change the edge detail on the trees.

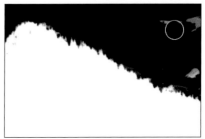

STEP 4: Here we are rough editing the area of the white Mount Rainier being careful not to change the sawtooth edge of the smaller treed mountain in the foreground.

STEP 4: This is how my mask looked after finishing the rough cut process. I won't do any more work on the mask until I'm finished with the Overall Color Correction of the two layers.

need to. Once each of the Trees and Sky layers is color corrected separately, then you will do further work on this mask to seamlessly blend them together. Since the color correction of the two layers will add contrast and change the color of each, it is better to wait until that is done before doing the final mask tweaking.

OVERALL COLOR CORRECTION OF THE TREES AND SKY LAYERS

STEP 5: You now have a rough cut mask that allows you to see the two layers as they will have to work together. The edges around the silhouetted trees may not yet be sharp and there may be other areas of local strangeness but you can see the major components of the Sky layer, which are Mount Rainier and the sky, and the major compenents of the Trees layer, which are the smaller mountain in the center foreground and the trees in front of and to the sides of it. **When working on this type of composite, I usually come up with a quickly made mask, then color correct each of the components, then fine tune the mask once I have the final, or close to final, brightness, contrast and color of each of the components set. Click on the word Trees to make the Trees layer active then choose Layer/New Adjustment Layer/Levels (Command-F2) and create a Grouped adjustment layer named Tree Levels. At this point the Trees layer looks pretty flat compared to the darker mountain. We have kept it that way so we can avoid losing too much shadow detail in the trees.**

You will have to decide which parts of this layer you are willing to let go totally black and which parts you want to keep some detail in. This particular scan has some very dark areas in it that don't have much detail anyhow. When you were actually looking at this scene, Mount Rainier was very bright, brighter than how I actually color corrected it in this composite, so one wouldn't notice a lot of shadow detail when looking at an overall image having that large bright area at the top. If you marked a shadow Color Sampler position while working on the 16-bit per channel version of this image, you will have to remark that position now since it was lost when you dragged and dropped this Trees layer on top of the original Sky layer. Notice that the Color Sampler point that you marked for the highlights is still there since that was actually marked on the original *Background* layer of this file. Option-drag the Input Shadow slider and remark the darkest area in the Trees with a Color Sampler as your shadow position. My approach here was to slowly darken and adjust the contrast and color balance of the trees so they seemed natural to me and made a pleasing composite with the mountain. If you open my version of MtRainierLayers from the Extra Info Files folder on the CD, you can look at the adjustments I made at each adjustment layer step along the way. Following the overall color correction steps described in detail in Chapter 19, I then added a Grouped S curve adjustment layer and a Hue Saturation adjustment layer to the Trees layer. The S curve increased the contrast of the Trees layer and the Hue/Saturation layer saturated its colors. Do the overall color correction steps on your own version of this composite getting the Trees layer to look as good as you can in the process.

At this point, I activated the Sky layer and began the overall color Correction process on it. After adding a Grouped Levels, Curves and Hue/Saturation adjustment layer to the Sky layer, I was happier with the way Mount Rainier looked but again

STEP 5: My Highlight Color Sampler, #1 top left, and Shadow Color Sampler, #2 bottom left, are marked in these positions and allow me to keep track of the brightness and darkness and also the neutrality of these positions as I go through the color correction steps.

Chapter 26: Combining Bracketed Photos or Two Scans to Increase Dynamic Range

found parts of the Trees layer to be flat. I also found parts of Mount Rainier to have a blue cast to them. Check this out again by looking at my version of MtRainier layers from the *Photoshop 6 Artistry* CD. Mount Rainier actually does sometimes have a blue cast when you look at it with the deep blue sky reflecting off the white snow. Still, I don't want this to be so obvious in my photo.

USING MASKS TO CORRECT SPECIFIC PARTS OF THE TREES AND SKY LAYERS

STEP 6: I now added another Grouped Hue/Saturation adjustment layer to the top of the other three layers already created to correct the Sky layer. In this layer, I lowered the Saturation value for Blues by –24. I chose this value by looking at the blue casts in the snow and desaturating with the Edit pop-up set to Blue until these casts were completely gone. After choosing OK and adding this adjustment layer, I then chose Image/Adjust/Invert (Command-I) to invert the Layer mask of this adjustment layer to be completely black. This stops the layer from desaturating the blue in the sky and parts of the image where I don't want to desaturate blue. You then want to type J to switch to the Airbrush and 05 to set its Opacity to about 5%. Type a D for default colors to set your foreground color to white then paint over the areas in the snow where you see the blue casts. Hold the mouse button down and move the mouse around until the cast is just gone. You are slowly painting with white to apply just enough of the effect of this Desaturation adjustment layer to remove the blue cast only where needed.

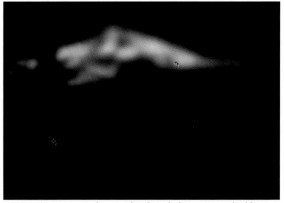

STEP 6: Here you see the completed mask that removes the blue cast from the white areas of Mount Rainier. The cast is only changed where the mask is not totally black.

With parts of the Trees layer also being flat, you might want to add a Grouped Curves adjustment layer on top of the Trees Hue/Saturation adjustment layer and create an S curve the makes the flattest areas of the Trees layer as contrasty as you want then choose OK to add the adjustment layer. There may be other parts of the Trees layer that are now way too contrasty but that is OK because you are now going to again use Command-I to invert the mask of this curve so it is now applied nowhere. Again using the Airbrush (J), slowly paint with white using a soft brush over the areas in the Trees layer where you want to increase the contrast. This allows you to apply only the amount of contrast you need in just the areas where it is needed. This layer is called TreeFixFlatAreasCurve within my version of this image.

At this point you may notice that some the shadows within parts of the Trees layer don't have much definition. Concern that this might happen was why I didn't do the S curve on the 48-bit version of this image back at the end of step 2. It will be hard to fix this by adding another adjustment layer above the existing Tree adjustment layers since those layers have darkened the shadows a lot and probably lost a lot of their detail. What we need to do is make a copy of the original Trees layer by clicking on its Layer thumbnail and dragging it to the Copy icon at the bottom of the Layers palette. This creates a layer on top of Trees called Trees copy but moves the adjustment layers that were grouped with Trees to now be grouped with Trees copy. The quickest way to solve this grouping change is to now Option-double-click on the Trees layer's name and rename the Trees layer to Shadows. Now Option-double-click on the Trees copy layer and rename it back to Trees. This leaves all the adjustment layers grouped where they need to be. Now drag the Shadows layer up to the top of the Layers stack and make sure it is the active layer. We are going to create a very radical Grouped Curves adjustment layer (Command-F3) that has a very steep slope

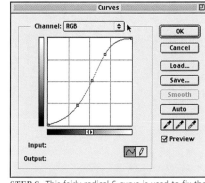

STEP 6: This fairly radical S curve is used to fix the flat areas of my Trees layer but it is only applied by its layer mask, shown below, where needed.

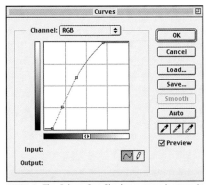

STEP 6: The Brings Out Shadows curve is steep in the areas of darker shadows where more definition is needed. It is applied using the mask below.

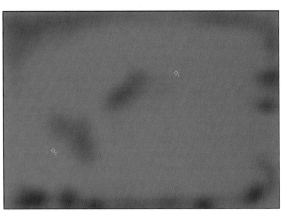

STEP 6: This is my Burn&Dodge layer showing that I'm burning in areas around the edges and also several areas that were too bright within the image. The Blend mode on this layer is set to Soft Light.

in the areas where the shadows lack definition. After typing Command-F3 and naming this layer Brings out Shadows, you should be in the Curves dialog. Put the cursor over the parts of the shadows that don't seem to have enough definition and hold the mouse down while moving the cursor over these parts of the image. This will show you where they are within the curve diagram. You want to create a curve that is very steep in those areas and to some extent, you are not too concerned with what this curve does to other parts of the image because you are only going to apply it in those areas. The curve to the left adds a lot of contrast to the shadows and also makes them lighter and somewhat flat in places so you want to be very careful to only apply it in a very subtle manner. Your shadows will now have a lot of contrast and the rest of your image will look really bad. Choose OK to Curves then click on the word Shadows in the layer underneath to activate the Shadows layer. Choose Layer/Add Layer Mask/Hide All to add a layer mask to the Shadows layer that hides all of it. You need to hide all of this layer because you only want to use it in the areas where you want to add some definition to the shadows. Now use the Airbrush (J) again to paint white with a soft brush into this Shadows layer mask where you want that small amount of shadow definition added. In some places, I had to set the pressure on the Airbrush to 02% or this effect was applied too quickly to my image and it made that shadow area look flat. The mask to the left shows you where this effect was applied in my version of the image. You can look at my MtRainierLayers file on the CD for a more detailed look at each of these steps.

Now that you have all these adjustment layers in place, you can double-click on the Layer thumbnail of any of them to tweak the color balance, contrast or color saturation. You can also lower the Opacity of any layer to lessen the effect of that layer versus all the others. When I'm doing this process with an art print, I'll usually make a test print at this point and then tweak the adjustment layer values to make slight changes in the color printout. You can also estimate this by using View/Proof Colors.

Choose Layer/New Layer to add a layer on top of the entire Layer stack called Burn&Dodge. Choose Edit/Fill to fill this with Use 50% Gray at 100% Opacity in normal Blend mode. Now set the Blend mode of this layer to Soft Light and you'll notice that it now has no effect on the underlying layers. Using the Airbrush again you can paint in this Burn&Dodge layer with a large white brush to lighten areas and a large black brush to darken areas. I usually do this as a last color correction step and I darken areas that are too bright and distracting, especially areas at the edge of the image, and I lighten areas that are too dark.

FINALIZING THE MASK SEPARATING THE SKY AND TREES LAYERS

STEP 7: Now that the color correction proces is complete, it's time to go back and work on the layer mask attached to the Trees layer. This is the mask that separates the Trees image from the Sky image and we can now work to perfect that mask. The silhouetted trees on either side of the image may have strange highlights on them due to a slight misalignment of the rotated image and also due to the difference of contrast between the dark subject matter in the Trees layer and bright snow, mountain and sky of the Sky layer. An easy way to start blending these two together is to use Gaussian Blur to blend them. Click on the layer mask of the Trees

Chapter 26: Combining Bracketed Photos or Two Scans to Increase Dynamic Range

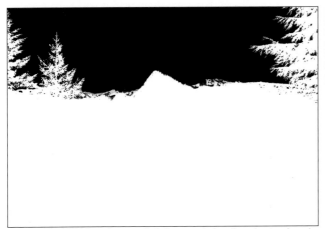

STEP 7: The initial Trees layer mask that we created earlier using Levels and some quick editing with the Paintbrush tool.

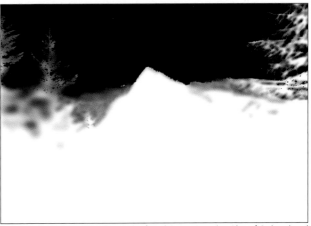

STEP 7: The final Trees layer mask after doing a Gaussian Blur of 2 then hand editing using the Airbrush to blend the transition areas of the two images together.

layer to activate it. Zoom into 100% and scroll so you are looking closely at some of those trees along either edge of the composite. Choose Filter/Blur/Gaussian Blur and set the Blur amount to about 2. This should improve the blending of the trees and other edges into the brighter background of the Sky image. Swich to the Airbrush (J) and paint at about 7% Opacity with white where you want to see more of the Trees image and with black where you want to see more of the Sky image. Some areas along the border between the two will come partially from the Trees layer and partially from the Sky layer. You will find that getting this blend correct can be tricky. Take a look at the mask in my version of the master image called MountRainierLayers.psd in the Extra Info Files folder inside the Ch26.CombiningBracketedPhotos folder on the CD.

STEP 7: Here we Gaussian Blur the Trees mask by 2 to blend the edges of the trees and other areas with the brighter background.

Spotting the Sky and Trees Layers

STEP 8: Use Command-Option-0 to zoom into 100% then type an S to give you the Rubber Stamp tool. For spotting, I usually start with the brush that is third from the top left then use the left or right Bracket key to adjust the brush size from there. Click on the word Sky in the Sky layer to activate that layer. Scroll through the document one full screen at a time and remove any spots you see in that area. You'll find that most of your spots are in the sky. You can use the Tab key to get rid of all your palettes then the Home key to get you to the top-left of your image. The Page Up and Page Down keys move the image up and down one full screen at a time and Command-Page Up moves the image to the lef,t with Command-Page Down moving it to the right. For a review of how to spot your images, see chapters 19 and 20. When I'm finished with spotting, I usually Option-double-click on my main layers, the Sky and Trees layers here, and add the word Spotted to their name. That way I know they have been spotted. Use Command-S to save your master image after you are finished spotting it. Once you have made test prints and are happy with the color and contrast, this will be the master image that you can archive to use in making future prints to different printers and of different sizes.

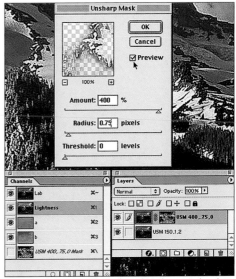

STEP 9: The Layers, Channels and Unsharp Mask palette and dialog setup for using the Sharpen Only Edges BH action script discussed on the next two pages.

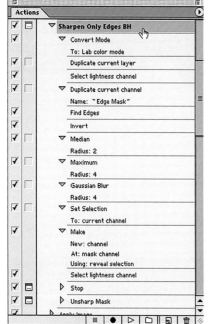

The Sharpen Only Edges BH action is one that is based on a script that I originally got from Bill Atkinson. His version, called just Sharpen Only Edges, is also in the ArtistKeys action set. They both use the Lightness channel of a LAB version of your master image to create a mask that applies sharpening to only the parts of the image that really need to be sharpened. My BH version adds a step at the front that converts your image to LAB color, which does nothing if your image is already in LAB color. My version also sets up the created mask as a layer mask on a copy of the original layer. The mask that both of these sharpening actions create is made by using the Find Edges filter, followed by Invert, Median, Maximum and then Gaussian Blur to massage these edges into a mask that will sharpen only what you need. Sharpen Only Edges BH works well on images that are 50 to 150 megabytes in size to be printed at 300 to 360 dpi. If you are working on larger or smaller images, you may want to adjust the Radius settings on the Median, Maximum and Gaussian Blur filters to see if you can get better results. When using a higher dpi, you might want to increase the radius and when using a lower dpi then decrease it. The last step of Sharpen Only Edges BH, which is explained by the Stop message at the end, is to activate the Lightness channel of that copied layer, turn on the Eye icons of the other channels, then run Unsharp Mask to sharpen that Lightness channel. This allows you to change the amount of sharpening, while watching the effect of the sharpening with the Preview checkbox on within the Unsharp Mask filter. You are actually sharpening the entire Lightness channel of the copy of your master image which is in a layer on top of the original master image layer underneath. The layer mask for the copy, which this action created, only shows the portions of the sharpened copy that are really necessary to sharpen the image. After finishing the Unsharp Mask you can then use black and white to further edit the mask to add more sharpness to some areas and less sharpness to other areas. This is the way I sharpen all my art prints. After running Unsharp Mask, you can also lessen the amount of sharpening by lowering the Opacity of the top layer.

USING SHARPEN ONLY EDGES BH AND UNSHARP MASK TO SHARPEN A FLATTENED VERSION OF THIS IMAGE

STEP 9: After saving my master image with all the layers, I use Image/Duplicate (F5), with the Duplicate Merged Layers Only checkbox on, to create a flattened version of this image. I use Image Size (F7) to set the resolution for my printer and resample if necessary. I then run the Sharpen Only Edges BH action script (Command-F5) which is described in detail in the large caption to the left. When this action script is completed, your image will be in LAB Color mode with two layers separated by a layer mask as shown to the right on the facing page. In the Channels palette, activate the Lightness channel for the top layer by clicking on the word Lightness while that top layer is active in the Layers palette. Now turn on the Eye icons, only, for the RGB, A and B channels then go into Filter/Sharpen/Unsharp Mask (F4). This will be only sharpening the Lightness channel but you will be seeing the results in color since the Eye icons are on for the other channels too. With the Preview button on in the Unsharp Mask filter, you can adjust the amount of sharpening until you think it is optimal for this image. When using one of these edge masks you can actually sharpen more than you would normally without grain appearing in flat areas, like skys. For the top layer here, I used an Amount of 400, a Radius of .75 and a Threshold of 0. Remember that you can turn the Preview checkbox in the Unsharp Mask filter off and on to see before and after this amount of sharpening. After choosing OK to the Unsharp Mask filter, if you Shift-click on the layer mask for the top layer, that will turn the mask off and you can actually see the large amount that this layer was actually sharpened. Shift-click again to turn the mask back on. Sometimes just sharpening the top layers Lightness channel is enough, especially when your original scan is tack sharp to the grain of the film. With this image I wasn't totally happy after sharpening the Lightness channel of the top layer. The original layer on the bottom didn't appear to have any grain pattern at all. Most digital files have a grain pattern you can see when you look at them at 100% on the screen. You don't want that grain pattern to be very heavy but if it is not there at all that may indicate that the image is a bit soft. You can also sharpen the Lightness channel of the image on the bottom of these two in the sharpening layers stack. Click on the

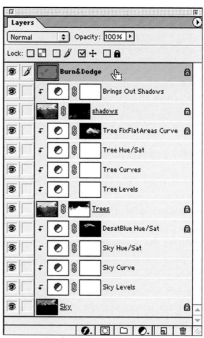

STEP 7: The final Layer palette for the master image of this composite. You can open my version of this file from the Extra Info Files folder inside the CD folder for this chapter.

Layer thumbnail for the bottom layer and activate only its Lightness channel in the Channels palette with just the Eye icons for the other channels on in the Channels palette. You also want the Eye icon to be on for the top layer in the Layers palette. Now go back into Unsharp Mask (F4) and sharpen this bottom Lightness channel but be careful not to sharpen it anywhere near as much as the Lightness channel in the top layer. I used settings of Amount at 150, Radius at 1 and Threshold at 2. While

doing this, you want to keep a careful eye on your sky and other areas of flat detail to make sure they don't get too grainy.

If you are going to print this Unsharp Mask layered image on the LightJet 5000 or an Epson printer, you should just leave it, or the flattened versions of it, in LAB color. You probably don't want to do yet another mode conversion back to, for example, Adobe RGB before printing. You can print LAB images to an Epson printer directly from Photoshop using the Auto settings in the print dialogs. If you have an ICC profile for your printer then you can use Image/Mode/Convert to Profile to convert from LAB color to that ICC profile. This converted file will probably be back in RGB color but in the color space specifically for that printer.

Another approach to using this Sharpen Only Edges BH action is to modify it to only create the edges mask that will separate the two sharpening layers. To do this, turn off the leftmost check column in the Actions palette for the "Duplicate current layer" step and then for all the steps after the "Gaussian Blur" step. That turns off those steps so now that action will only create the edge mask at the bottom of the Channels palette. You can then copy that mask and use it in a similar way between two RGB layers of your flattened final image. This allows your final image to avoid the mode conversion to Lab. Using it in that way, you could choose to sharpen just one of the RGB channels on the top layer, all of the RGB channels on the top layer or some combination of sharpening in both layers.

STEP 7: These are the Unsharp Mask layers used to produce the bottom final image. To do this sharpening, you start with a flattened copy of your master layer image and you run the Sharpen Only Edges BH action script on that. That converts the image into LAB color mode, copies the background layer to a 2nd layer on top which has a layer mask added to it containing the most crucial areas to be sharpened. For this image, I sharpened the Lightness channel on the bottom image by 150,1,2 and the Lightness channel of the top layer by 400,.75,0. The mask on the top layer combines the two to give you the final sharpening effect. To add even more sharpness in selective areas, use the Airbrush to paint white into the mask. To lessen the sharpness, paint black where you feel it is too sharp. You can lessen the overall sharpness by lowering the opacity of the top of the two layers.

The final version of the combined Mount Rainier image after spotting each layer, flattening and sharpening with the bottom Unsharp Mask layer's Lightness chanel sharpened at 150,1,2 with the entire layer being sharpened and the top masked layer's Lightness channel sharpened at 400,.75,0 with only the edge parts of that layer adding sharpness due to its layer mask that was created using the Sharpen Only Edges BH action.

Using Sharpen Only Edges BH and Unsharp Mask to Sharpen a Flattened Version of This Image

HANDS-ON SESSION: Bryce Stone Woman

Color correcting an image in LAB color, versus RGB, using
most of the techniques in this book.

The final Bryce Stone Woman image after correcting it in LAB color. You can see the "before" version of this image on the last page of this chapter.

This is one of my favorite photos of Bryce Canyon. The light rock formation in the front center, if you use your imagination a bit, could be a naked woman with long bushy hair sitting on the rock and admiring the view. Because the rocks are predominately red, it is hard to make the rocks look their best without making the green trees and shrubs look too dark and magenta. The solution is to use a layer mask to combine several versions of the image, one that optimizes the red parts and another that optimizes the green parts. You should read Chapter 14: "Color Spaces, Device Characterization and Color Management" to learn more about LAB color before doing this example. Also, this will not be a normal step-by-step example; because this is an example in LAB color, I decided to share the experience of creating the image with you instead of worrying about writing down every step. Therefore, to better understand this example, you should first do the examples in Chapters 21: "Yellow Flowers," 24: "Desert Al," 26: "Combining Bracketed Photos or Two Scans to

Increase Dynamic Range" and 28: "Rain in Costa Rica." These chapters use similar techniques but include all the details.

When I first got the scan for this image from Bill Atkinson and his Tango drum scanner, I converted it to RGB from the LAB format he had given it to me in and made a very nice LightJet 5000 print of it. When I started working on this example, I took my master RGB image from that print and thought I would start over with the original LAB scan to see if I could duplicate what I had done in RGB, using LAB this time. The following is the process I went through to arrive at the Layers palette, shown here, for the final LAB image printed on the previous page. **You should open my final LAB image, called BryceLAB.psd, from the folder for this chapter on the CD. You can then look at the layers setup on your screen and turn each layer on one at a time as we go through the purpose of each layer.**

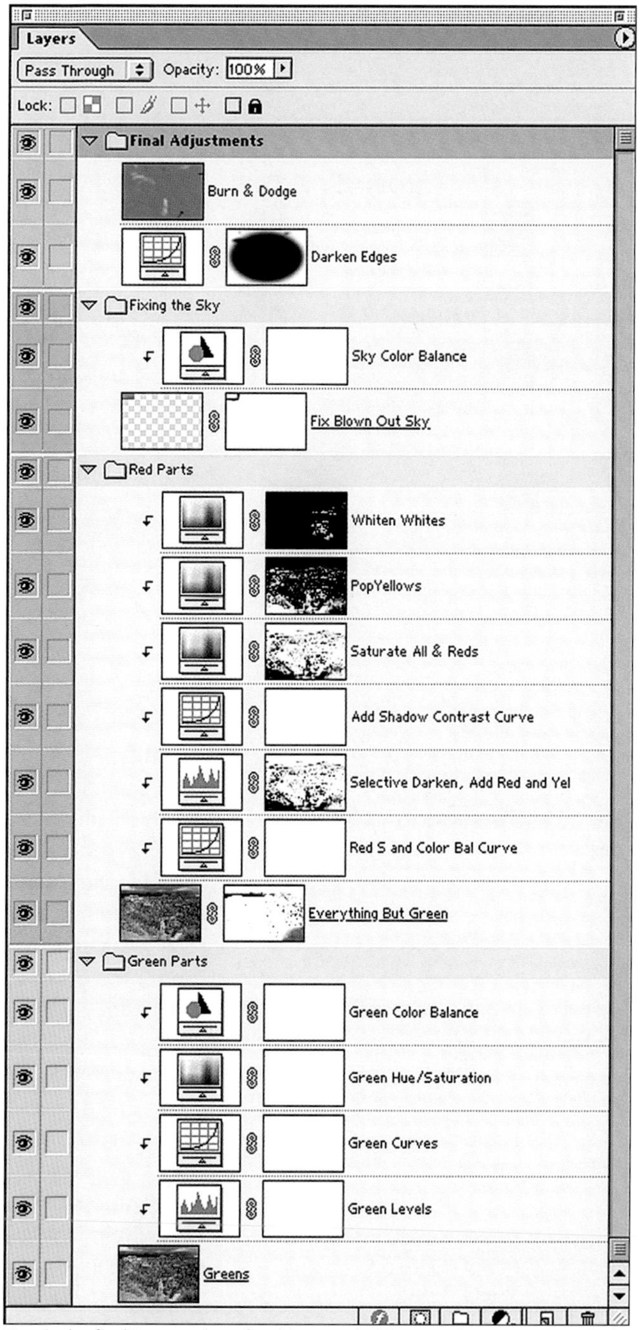

TRYING TO DUPLICATE WHAT I DID IN RGB

STEP 1: When I reopened the LAB scan, I realized that it was still uncropped and I had already cropped the RGB version I was trying to duplicate. I had not resampled the RGB image though, just done a crop, but I would need to line the two up. **To do this, I went into Image Size on the RGB version and noted the actual number of pixels in each dimension. This would be the crop size I would use on the LAB version too, so I set the Fixed Size Style on the Marquee to that width and height. When using the Marquee or Cropping tool, if you want a fixed size in pixels, you need to use Edit/Preferences/Units and Rulers to set the Ruler Units to pixels. Then the sizes in the Marquee and Cropping tool will show up in pixels instead of inches.**

Next, I copied the flattened version of my RGB image and pasted it on top of my LAB version, and of course, it was a bit smaller. I inverted this temporary RGB layer and set its Opacity to 50% because a positive and negative image on top of each other at 50% Opacity gives you 50% gray if they are perfectly lined up. If they are not lined up, you get an embossed effect. I then used the arrow keys while in the Move tool to nudge the inverted layer until the embossed effect went away and it lined up with the LAB image I had to crop underneath. At that point, I turned the Eye icon off for the the layer underneath and then clicked with the Mar- quee, which was already set for the correct size, and lined the Marquee up with the edges of the already cropped RGB image on top. Now my Marquee selection lines were lined up exactly, so I chose Image/Crop to do the crop and then threw away the temporary layer on top.

STEP 2: You might be wondering why I wanted to crop this LAB image so it lined up exactly with the RGB image I had made before. The reason is that there were some

Here is the final Layers palette for this example. We are going to go through the steps I went through in creating this image and all its layers. For Photoshop 6, we have added the layer sets to help delineate the four parts of this composition.

287

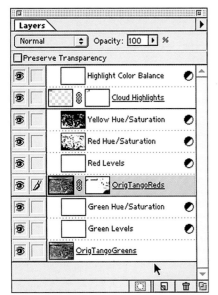

STEP 2: The Layers palette from my earlier RGB rendition of Bryce. Since I made sure the crop was exactly the same on my newer LAB version, I was able to reuse the layer mask separating the Red and Green elements as well as the Yellow Hue/Saturation mask and the Red Hue/Saturation mask, although the way I used them was sometimes different in LAB color.

STEP 2: The layer mask that separates the Green and non-Green layers in my RGB and LAB images. The white areas of the mask are where you will see the non-green areas from the upper of the two layers, and the black and gray parts of the mask are where you will see all or some of the image from the Green layer.

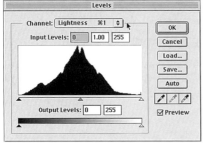

STEP 2: The Lightness channel for the Everything-ButGreen layer. This histogram looks very similar to a corrected RGB histogram. The Lightness channel contains the brightness and contrast information for a LAB image.

complex masks I had created for the RGB version of this image, and I was hoping to reuse them in doing the LAB version. Here is the Layers palette for my previous RGB version of this image, and I did reuse the masks as you will see.

My traditional overall color correction steps for an RGB image are to first use Levels to correct the histogram; then use Curves to adjust the contrast and then follow that with Hue/Saturation to saturate the colors. What I did in the RGB version, as you can see to the left here, is create one real layer, OrigTangoGreens, for the Green elements in the photograph and a second real layer, OrigTangoReds, on top of that, for the Red elements. The Layer mask to the right of the OrigTangoReds layer controls which parts of the image come from each of these two main layers. You'll notice several Grouped Adjustment layers above the OrigTangoGreens layer that set its Levels and Hue/Saturation settings. Then above the OrigTangoReds layer is the grouped Adjustment layer for the Reds Levels, and then two different Hue/Saturation Adjustment layers above that. For this image I used one Hue/Saturation layer to adjust the reddish tones and a separate one for the yellows, each with its own layer mask. Trying to do it all with one Adjustment layer caused too much crossover between the Red and Yellow areas especially where they mixed a lot. The layer mask that separates which part of the image comes from OrigTangoReds and which part from OrigTangoGreens was created using Image/Adjust/Threshold in a similar way that we created the Darken Sky mask with Levels in Chapter 20: "Correcting a Problem Image." To create the Red and Yellow Hue/Saturation masks, which are close to inverses of each other, I went into Select Color Range to create a selection of either the Red or Yellow areas and then used Select/Save Selection to save that selection in the Channels palette where I edited it, and then later used Load Selection to load it before creating my Red Hue/Saturation layer. For more details on this mask creation technique, see Chapter 21: "Yellow Flowers."

When I started working on the LAB version, I went ahead and created one layer for the Greens and a second layer for the Reds. You can see in the LAB Layers palette that these two layers, called Greens and Everything But Green, and the layer mask separating them remained. In the LAB version, I've put the layers that control the green appearance into a layer set called Green Parts and then put the layers that control the red appearance into a layer set called Red Parts. I tried to use Levels to do the initial overall color correction on the Red and Green layers. You can see these two layers, called Selective Darken Add Red and Yellow, and the other, Green Levels. I discovered that in LAB mode, the Lightness channel is great to work with for setting the highlight and shadow values because there are not color balance problems mixed in with setting the brightness and contrast values in the Lightness channel. The difficulty for me came when I went to the A and B channels within Levels and tried to adjust the color balance. Try this out for yourself using the BryceLab you have opened. Turn off all the Eye icons above the Everything But Green layer and activate that layer; then create a new Levels adjustment layer above it. You'll notice when you go into Levels that you are in the Lightness channel. This is a pretty normal histogram and you do the obvious thing of moving the endpoints in to where the data starts. Then use the middle slider to adjust the brightness. It is great to be able to adjust this separately from the color balance. Also, if you just sharpen the Lightness channel of a LAB image, you avoid the color shifts you can get when sharpening all the channels of an RGB image. There is no need to sharpen the A and B channels within a LAB image because they only contain color information and no brightness and contrast information as all the channels have in an RGB or CMYK image.

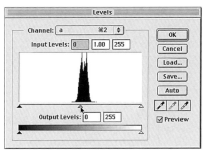

STEP 3: **Now choose the A channel. Moving the middle slider to the left makes the image more red, and moving it to the right makes the image more green. Try it and notice that moving this more than a small amount dramatically affects the color of the image.** That is because all the color information in this LAB image is squashed into that small area of the histogram spanning only about 51 in the A channel and 91 in the B channel of this image. The LAB color space spans all the colors that the human eye can see. That makes this space so large that the rest of the histogram, outside the range of 51 used in this image, is reserved for other colors that are not in this image. **Moving the Input Highlight slider of the A channel to the left makes the highlights more red and the Input Shadow slider to the right makes the shadows more green. Moving the Output Highlight slider of the a channel to the left makes the highlights more green, and moving the Output Shadow slider right makes the shadows more red.**

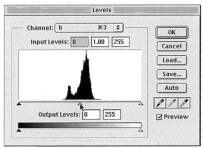

STEP 3: The a channel for the Everything But Green layer.

Now try out the B channel, where moving the middle slider to the left makes the image more yellow and moving it to the right makes it more blue. Try out the Input and Output Shadow and Highlight sliders to see what they do, too. Now hold down the Option key and choose Reset to put everything back where it started. Start with the Lightness channel, and adjust the brightness of the red and yellow parts of the image, actually everything but the greens. Then switch to the A and B channels and try to get the red and yellow colors the way you want them. You realize that the controls are quite different than when working in RGB or CMYK.

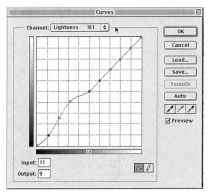

STEP 3: The b channel for the Everything But Green layer.

STEP 4: I duplicated the layer structure I had used in my RGB image. Of course, the adjustments I made, especially in Levels, were quite different, and I was able to get a LAB image that looked somewhat similar, but it didn't seem to have the same amount of contrast and separation of colors. **The layers I had created so far were Green levels and Green Hue/Saturation to adjust the Greens and Selective Darken, Add Red and Yellow (my Red levels layer), as well as Saturate All & Reds and Pop Yellows for the Everything But Green layer. Things looked a bit flat and muddy, and I could not get this image to look as good as the RGB one. Then I thought maybe Curves would work better, instead of Levels, as the initial adjustment for a LAB image, so I created the layers Red S and Color Balance Curve for the Everything But Green layer and Green Curves for the Greens layer. As you can see, the S curve I used for the Lightness channel of the Everything But Green layer helped increase the contrast and in the A channel, I moved the curve up and to the left to add red and I did the same thing in the B channel to add yellow. The Green Curves, as you can see, was mostly a move in the Lightness channel to lighten and brighten the greens by**

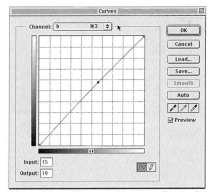

STEP 4: The Green Curves Lightness curve increases the slope of the curve, and thus the contrast, where most of the green values lie in the image.

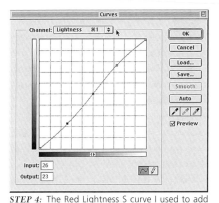

STEP 4: The Red Lightness S curve I used to add some contrast to everything but the greens.

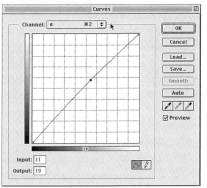

STEP 4: The Red a curve adds some red to the color balance. You want to be very subtle with your LAB a and b curve movements.

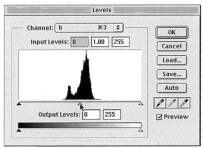

STEP 4: The Red b curve adds some yellow to the color balance.

289

increasing the slope of the curve where most of the green values were sitting, to the bottom left half of the curve. I initially turned off the Eye icons for my Levels adjustments and replaced them with these Curves adjustments, leaving the Hue/Saturation layers as they were. At some point though, I accidentally turned on all the layers, by Option-clicking the Eye icon of a layer, and noticed that the image looked even better with both the Levels and Curves layers on at the same time. I tweaked each layer a little further and was becoming happier with this image, except the shadow areas in the reds and yellows, which looked a little flat, and the color balance on the greens was not what I wanted.

STEP 5: **To solve this problem, I added the Add Shadow Contrast curve to the group of Everything But Green layers. This curve does a similar thing as the Green Curves on the previous page by increasing the slope of the part of the Lightness curve that corresponds to the tonal range of the image we wanted to modify. I added a Color Balance adjustment layer at the top of the Greens layers to just pop the greens, espe-**

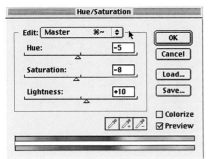

STEP 5: The Add Shadow contrast Curve helps the shadow areas in the Everything But Green layers of the image.

cially the green highlights, a bit. I didn't modify the pixels in the Greens or Everything But Green layers, so you can always throw my adjustment layers away, or turn their Eye icons off, and try your own adjustments, making your own adjustment layers.

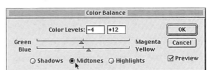

STEP 5: The Green Color Balance Adjustment layer. We also changed the Highlight and Shadows settings. You can check those out on your screen with my final BryceLAB image open.

FINE TUNING THE IMAGE

STEP 6: **By editing the PopYellows layer mask, I created a mask for the Whiten Whites Hue/Saturation adjustment layer. Its job is to take the pinkish cast out of rocks that I wanted to be white in the final image. The effect was mostly created by lowering the Saturation and increasing the Lightness on the Edit Master part of this Hue/Saturation dialog. The Hue shift here takes a little yellow out of the whites.**

STEP 6: The Whiten Whites Hue/Saturation settings.

STEP 7: **If you turn off the the Eye icon for the Fixing the Sky layer set, you'll notice that the sky in the top left corner is badly blown out. There wasn't a whole lot of detail in the original image or scan here anyway, so I created the Fix Blown Out Sky and Sky Color Balance layers specifically to patch that blown-out corner. Fix Blown Out Sky is just part of the sky to the right copied and edited to make it appear as though it were raining in that top left corner, as well. The color of this new sky area wasn't quite right, so I added a Grouped Color Balance adjustment layer just to tweak that sky part of the image. Remember that a Grouped adjustment layer is indented from the first real layer below it. It only affects the pixels in that real layer below it and the Grouped layer also gets its transparency from that real layer below. To created a Grouped adjustment layer, you need to turn on the Group With Previous Layer checkbox in the New Adjustment Layer dialog or Option-click the line between the already created adjustment layer and the real layer below it.**

STEP 8: **In the Final adjustments layer set, the Burn and Dodge layer is a normal layer, not an Adjustment layer, filled with 50% Gray using Edit/Fill, with its Blend mode set to Soft Light. Soft Light mode ignores 50% Gray but will darken the cumulative effect of all the layers underneath in areas that are darker than 50% Gray, and lighten those layers in areas that are lighter than 50% Gray. This allows you to burn and dodge the image using the Airbrush along with large, soft brushes having a low**

Chapter 27: Bryce Stone Woman

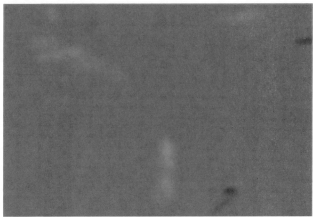

opacity. Before you start this type of work, type D to set the default colors of Black and White. Then you can type X, for eXchange, to toggle between painting on this Gray layer with either Black or White.

STEP 9: **As yet another final adjustment, we created a mask and adjustment layer curve to very slightly darken the outer parts of the image. We then edited this by hand with the Airbrush to re-lighten some of those darkened areas. To stop accidental movement of layers, notice that the position is locked in all the real layers as well as adjustment layers that contain masks.**

STEP 8: The Burn and Dodge layer. Areas that are darker than 50% gray will be darkened in the underlying layers, and areas that are lighter will be lightened.

We know that this has been a whirlwind tour of color correcting and editing using LAB images. I have corrected quite a few of my fine art prints using LAB color since many of the original scans were done with a Lino Tango scanner in LAB color. Sometimes it is harder to correct in LAB color and there are a few functions in Photoshop that don't work with LAB images but only work in RGB. Now I sometimes correct in LAB color and sometimes in Adobe RGB, depending on the image in question and where I got its scan.

If you get your original scans at 16 bits per channel, then doing a 16-bit per channel conversion between LAB and Adobe RGB should not lose detail information that will be noticeable. When working with 8-bit per channel images, you want to avoid doing mode conversions when possible. See Chapter 16: "Image Resolution, Scanning Film and Digital Cameras" for more information on the way to scan your images at 16 bits per channel, so you can work in LAB color, Adobe RGB or some other RGB space, and even do 16-bit per channel mode conversions without worrying about losing color information like in 8-bit per channel space.

STEP 9: The mask for the Darken Edges curves adjustment layer. This was a very subtle darkening of the Lightness channel curve.

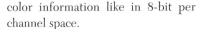
The original Bryce image before we made any color corrections.

COMPOSITING MULTIPLE IMAGES WITH LAYERS, ADJUSTMENT LAYERS, AND LAYER MASKS

USE THE PEN TOOL TO CREATE MASKS

USE FREE TRANSFORM TO SCALE AND MATCH PERSPECTIVES

REPLACE HEADS AND COLOR MATCH FACES

LEAN ADVANCED COMPOSITING TECHNIQUES

CREATE COMPLEX COMPOSITE ADVERTISEMENTS

The Burnley Graveyard in northern England, where my grandfather and uncle are buried, is on a cold windy hill in an old coal mining town. Originally a color 35mm photograph, creating this duotone version that accurately reflects my feelings when standing there was one of the most difficult Photoshop projects I've done, requiring an exact mask and several radical contrast adjustment curves.

HANDS-ON SESSION: Rain in Costa Rica

Using the Pen tool and a variety of selection and masking techniques to create a composite of four images, giving us a rainy street scene in San Jose, Costa Rica.

In this session, we will use the Pen tool and other selection and masking techniques to create a composite of a rain scene with rain photographs from San Jose, Costa Rica. We want this scene to appear as though you are looking at it through the front window of a bus that is coming onto this street. The bus front window shot was taken going down the highway in Costa Rica between San Jose and San Isidro, a road where I didn't want to drive myself since many buses and trucks pass each other even around curves sometimes. Costa Rica is a friendly and beautiful country to visit; I've been there three times!

SETTING UP THE FOUR FILES

STEP 1: **Open the four PSD files in the RainInCostaRica folder on the *Photoshop 6 Artistry* CD. Press the TAB key to get rid of your palettes from the screen. Click on the Blue Bus file to make it active; then type an F to put it in Full Screen mode followed by Command-0 to fill the screen with this file. We are going to move all the other images into this file, each as a separate layer. Switch to the Move tool (V) and activate the Red Car file from the Window menu. You should now see the Blue Bus file behind in Full Screen Mode and the Red Car file in front but within a window. While holding the Shift key down until after you release the mouse, click within the Red Car window and drag the Red Car image until the cursor has moved on top of the Blue Bus image. Release the mouse at that point, and you should have dragged and dropped the Red Car image as a new layer on top of the Blue Bus image. Doing this with the Shift key down should have caused the Red Car image to be centered on top of the Blue Bus image within the Blue Bus file. Now use the Window menu to make the Woman file active; then Shift-drag her image on top of the Blue Bus file in the same way you moved the Red Car over there. Now use the Window menu again to activate the Bus Window file and Shift-drag it onto the Blue Bus file. Your Blue Bus file should now have a Layers palette with Blue Bus on the bottom, then Red Car, then Woman and finally Bus Window on top. Choose File/Save As and save this as RainInCostaRicaLayers.psd.**

CROP AND COLOR CORRECT

STEP 2: **Turn off the Eye icons for the top three layers until you are just looking at the Blue Bus layer at the bottom of the Layers palette. Click on the words Blue Bus to activate that layer. Type a C to get the cropping tool and crop the black borders from the left,**

STEP 2: The crop you should make on the Blue Bus layer. Don't crop more than this.

bottom and right side. Be careful not to crop any more off than what you need to to remove the non-image black border from around the edge.

Choose Layer/New Adjustment Layer/Levels (Command-F2) to create the Levels adjustment layer and do Overall Color Correction on the Blue Bus image. Go through the process covered in Chapter 19: "Overall Color Correction" to do the Levels corrections on this image. With the highlights on this image, I actually left them as they were to keep the dull and rainy look the image has. If you'd like, you can load my Levels adjustments, called BlueBusLevels, from the RainInCostaRica/Extra Info Files folder on the CD. Choose OK when you are happy with your Levels adjustments; then use Command-F3 to create a new Curves adjustment layer. I use an S-Curve, called BlueBusCurves, to increase the contrast a bit. Choose OK on the S-Curve; then use Command-F4 to create a Hue/Saturation adjustment layer. What I did here is on the CD and is called BlueBusHueSat, so you can load that one and check it out, too. This example is mostly about compositing, not color correction, so I'm not spending a lot of time on the color correction aspects. At any time though, you can also open and look at my final version of this composite, called RainInCostaRicaFinalCC, from the Extra Info Files folder on the CD in the RainInCostaRica chapter.

Choose Layer/New/Layer Set and name the set Overall Color Correction. Drag the Layer thumbnail for each of the Levels, Curves and Hue/Sat adjustment layers and drop it on the Overall Color Correction Layer Set thumbnail. Make sure they are still in the same order within the set with Layers on the bottom, then Curves in the middle and Hue/Sat on the top. You can then close this layer set to make your Layers palette smaller.

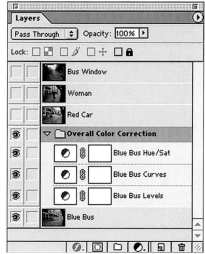

STEP 2: The Layers palette after doing the overall color correction on the Blue Bus image.

LEARNING ABOUT PATHS

STEP 3: Click on the word Bus Window to activate the Bus Window layer. If you already know how to use the Pen tool and Paths, you can skip steps 3 and 4. The Pen tool allows you to make selections, called paths, by clicking to create points between either straight or curved lines. If you click a point and immediately release the mouse, you create a corner point. If you click a point and drag before releasing the mouse, that point becomes a curve point. When you create or move a curve point, you get two lines coming out of the curve point; I call these handlebars. The handlebars control the shape of the curve. Try this out now! It's sort of like tracing—but more fun!

Type a P to get to the Pen tool. Click anywhere on top of the Bus Window image with the Pen tool and immediately release to create a corner point. Click four or five corner points to create a box. When you put the last corner point on top of the first, a little circle appears next to the arrow, indicating that you are closing the path. When you see the circle, click on top of the initial point again to close the path. If you're going to turn your path into a selection (as you are going to do here), you usually want the path to be closed. After closing the first box path, move the cursor down below that box, and in a new area, click and drag to create a curve point. Where you click is the location of the point, and dragging out the handlebar beyond the point affects the shape of the line segment between that point and the previous point as well as between that point and the next point. Draw an oval shape by clicking and dragging four curve points. Close the path by clicking again on the original point. You now have a box path made up of corner points and an oval path made up of curve points. If you bring up the Paths palette (Shift-F11), you can see them both in a new path called Work Path. Work Path is a temporary place where you can create a path without naming it. Actually, each of these two disjointed paths is a subpath of Work

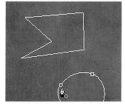

STEP 3: Clicking to enter corner points on a path.

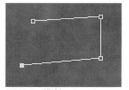

STEP 3: Clicking and dragging to enter curve points on a path. The handlebars should be in tangent to the curve shape you are trying to draw.

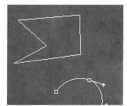

STEP 3: To close the curve, click the first point a second time when you see the small circle next to the Pen icon.

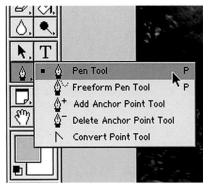

STEP 4: The Path Component Selection tool is for selecting and moving entire paths and the Direct Selection tool is for selecting and moving parts of paths.

STEP 4: The different tools available from the pop-out menu for Pen in the Tool palette. The Pen tool, and Freeform Pen tool are for entering points initially. To get the Magnetic Pen tool, first choose Freeform Pen Tool then choose Magnetic Pen Tool from the Options bar at the top of the screen. The Pen+ and Pen− tools are for adding and deleting anchor points, and the Convert Point tool is for changing points between corners and curves and for decoupling the handlebars.

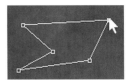

STEP 4: To move a corner point or a curve point, click it and drag.

STEP 4: To adjust the shape of the curve, first click the point whose handlebars affect the part of the curve you want to change. Second, click the end of the handlebar and make it longer or shorter or change its angle. This changes the shape of the curve.

STEP 4: Moving a curve point to make the oval longer.

STEP 4: Changing the shape of a curve segment by dragging one end of a handlebar.

Path. Double-click Work Path and rename it Play Path. After you name a path, any changes you make to it automatically save as part of that path.

STEP 4: Now select the Path Component Selection tool in the Tool palette by typing an A. See the diagrams on this page for the names of each of the Arrow and Pen tools. You can switch between the two different Arrow tools by using Shift-A. You can switch between the two Pen editing tools by typing Shift-P. Now try using the Path Component Selection tool, the black arrow, to edit the path. First click the box shape you made with the corner points. When you click the box shape, its points become highlighted. If you click and drag anywhere on the box, the entire box shape moves. To move one of these points in the box shape, type Shift-A to switch to the white Direct Selection Tool then click outside the box path to deselect the entire thing. Now to move a particular point, click back on that path to select it for point editing then click on the point you want to move, drag it to a new location, and then let go. This change updates automatically in your Play Path. Click the oval subpath now, still using the white Direct Selection tool, and its points become highlighted. If you want to move one of these curve points to elongate the oval, just click and drag it like you would a corner point. To adjust the shape of the curve, first click the point on one end of the curve segment that you want to change. This brings up the handlebars for that point. Now click the end of the handlebar next to the segment you want to change, and make it longer or shorter, or change its angle to change the shape of the curve. If you click, with this same white arrow tool, on a segment between two points, you can drag that segment to a new location or change the shape of a curved segment.

You can also add points with the Pen+ tool (the Add Anchor Point tool) and delete points with the Pen− tool (the Delete Anchor Point tool). To add a point, just click along the line segment where there currently isn't a point using the Pen+ tool. When over an existing point with the Pen+ tool, you will actually get the Direct Selection tool since you can't add a point where there already is one. When in the Pen− tool, you can click on any existing point to remove it but you will be in the Direct Selection tool when you are not over an existing point. If you are in the Pen− tool, the Option key will temporarily give you the Pen+ tool and vice versa. When you add a point with the Pen+ tool, it is a curve point. You can then change the shape of the curve by adjusting that point's handlebars with the Arrow tool. When in the Pen+ tool, holding down the Option key will give you the Pen− tool when over a point, but otherwise it will show you the White Arrow tool with a plus next to it. Clicking and dragging with that will make a copy of the entire path. When in the Pen− tool, holding down the Option key will give you the Pen+ tool unless you are over a point, in which case you get the White Arrow+ tool mentioned in the last sentence for copying the entire path.

If you want to change a curve point to a corner point, or vice versa, click it with the Convert Point tool. To change a corner to a curve, you click and drag the corner point to define the length and angle of your handlebars. You also can use the Convert Point tool to decouple a curve point's handlebars. Clicking either handlebar and moving slightly with this tool allows you to then use the White Arrow tool to drag each end of the handlebar to change its curve segment shape without changing the one on the opposite side of the handlebar's point. To recouple the handlebars together again, click and drag on the point between the handlebars using the Convert Point tool. You can also access the Convert Point tool from

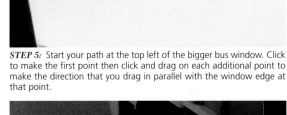

the White Arrow tool by holding down the Command and Option keys and putting the cursor over an existing point or handlebar end. Using the Pen tool in Photoshop is a lot like using the Pen tool in Illustrator, more so in Photoshop 6 than in earlier versions of Photoshop. To turn a path into a selection, choose Make Selection from the pop-up menu in the Paths palette. Click on the Play Path you just created in the Paths palette and drag it to the trash at the bottom right area of the Paths palette. If you made a selection, choose Command-D to deselect it.

STEP 5: Start your path at the top left of the bigger bus window. Click to make the first point then click and drag on each additional point to make the direction that you drag in parallel with the window edge at that point.

KNOCKING OUT THE BUS WINDOW

STEP 5: **Type a P to go back to the Pen tool and then Return to bring up its Options palette. Make sure the Rubber Band option is turned on.** As you are drawing a curve, this option will show you the line segment between the current existing point and the next point on the curve. I think it helps to make the curve more accurate. **Now press Tab to get rid of all your palettes; then use Command-0 to zoom the image up and fill the screen. If Tab doesn't get rid of your**

STEP 5: Here you can see the points we have placed at the bottom right of the large window. We are placing points as we work clockwise around the window.

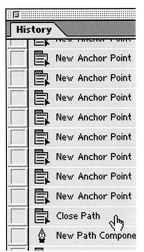

STEP 5: While working on a path in Photoshop 6, the History palette (F8) keeps track of each point that you enter. If you want to go back to redo several points, just click a few steps back in the History palette. The hand here is showing us the place where we closed the path on the big window and have just started the path on the smaller window to the left.

palettes, try Return and then Tab a few times until the Palettes disappear. The Bus Window layer should still be active and what you are seeing on your screen. Click down your first point at the top of the bigger window; then trace around the window clockwise placing points as you go. When you place points on a surface having subtle curves, you often want to click and drag which places the curve points with handlebars, allowing you to make subtle changes in the shape of the line segment between the last point and the point you are currently placing. If there is a long straight section, you can sometimes place regular corner points, by just clicking, within that section but you always want to use curve points whenever there is a curve. See the diagrams to the right for comments about drawing this path. **When you have traced all the way around, click again on the point you started the path with, which completes and closes this path.**

    Now trace a similar path around the smaller window to the left side. When this second subpath is closed, use Shift-F11 to bring up your Paths palette and double-click on the Work Path and name it Bus Windows. Now choose Make Selection from the pop-up menu on the Paths palette with the Feather set to 0,

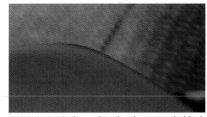

STEP 5: Once you have worked your way all around the window, place the cursor back on top of the first point you clicked and you will see a small circle next to the arrow at the lower right. When you see this circle, click once to complete the path.

STEP 5: A window edge that has an ugly black line showing. Using the Paintbrush and painting in the mask with black along this edge we removed it below. The trick is to click at one end of the part you want to remove then Shift-click on the other end to paint in a straight line with the brush and thus remove a straight piece of the window edge.

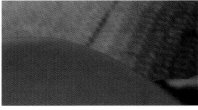

Anti-Aliased turned on and the New Selection choice active. This will turn your path into a selection. You are now going to choose Layer/Add Layer Mask/Hide Selection to remove the area of the window from view in this layer. Type a B to get the Paint-Brush and a D for default colors, giving you white. Select a small hard-edged brush; then zoom in to 200% and slowly look around the edge of the bus window for selection edges that don't look correct. Paint with black to remove more from the window frame edge and paint with white to bring some window edge back.

297

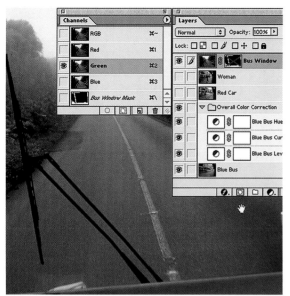

STEP 5: Here is the Layer and Channel setup for choosing the Green channel as the one to create our mask. Dragging it to the New Channel icon to the left of the Trash icon in the Channels palette will make a copy of this Green channel.

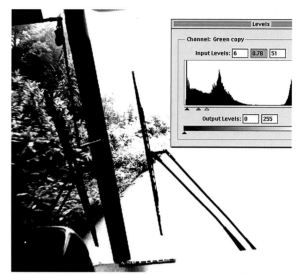

STEP 5: Here we are using Levels to separate the wipers from the rest of the image in this copy of the Green channel. These are the settings we used to separate the wipers.

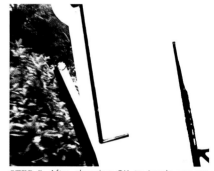

STEP 5: After choosing OK to Levels, we are painting using the Paintbrush with white in the Green copy channel to cleanly cut out the wipers.

Notice when you do this that it also removes the windshield wipers from the bus windows. We'd probably like to keep them in and on since the bus is going out into the rain. We could have selected those with the Pen tool also, but just to give you some other selection skills, we'll select those using a Levels mask. **To temporarily turn off the mask you just created, Shift-click on the Layer mask thumbnail, the rightmost one for this Bus Window layer. Now use Shift-F10 to bring up the Channels palette and look at each of the Red, Green and Blue channels by themselves to find the one that has the most contrast between the wipers and the background street scene. I chose the Green channel. Drag the Green channel to the New Channel icon to the left of the Trash icon at the bottom of the Channels palette. Now choose Image/Adjust/Levels to go into levels on that channel. Move the Highlight and Shadow sliders in towards the center left as you try to separate the wipers from all the noise in the window scene. The right wiper separates easily, so zoom in on it and get the settings that separate it as exactly as possible. Turn the Preview button off and then on again in the Levels dialog to make sure the mask you are creating correctly gets the edges of the wiper. Move the Shadow, Brightness and Highlight sliders of Levels as you are doing this to see what they do to the mask. Now look at the leftmost wiper and the metal bar that comes down into the window area on the left side. Get them as well as you can, but know that you will have to use the Paintbrush to clean up this mask. When the mask looks as good as you can get it, choose OK in Levels. Now type a B for the Paintbrush and a D for Default Colors, which will give you white as the foreground color. Paint with white at 100% to remove all the other parts of this mask that are not the wipers and that metal bar.** Remember that you can get a straight line with the brush by clicking at one end of a line and then Shift-clicking at the other end which draws the brush in a strait line between those two points. **When you are finished editing this mask, Command-click on this Green copy channel to load the white parts of it as a selection. You are actually loading everything but the wipers since the wipers were black in this channel. Choose Select/Inverse to invert the selection so the wipers are actually selected. Click back on the word RGB in the Channels palette and you will again be working on the Bus Window layer. Shift-click on the Bus Window layer mask thumbnail to turn the mask on again. Choose Select/Save Selection and set the Channel pop-up in the Save Selection dialog to Bus Window Mask. Choose the Add to Channel option; then click on OK to add in the wipers. Click on the rightmost Bus Window layer mask thumbnail to make sure you are editing the Bus Window Mask; then use the Paintbrush again to do any final mask cleanup on the ends of the wipers where they connect to the bottom of the dashboard.** I had to paint a little more white in the layer mask so the wipers looked connected to the dashboard. **Click in the Lock Position checkbox, the second checkbox from the rightmost padlock one at the top of the Layers palette, to lock the position of the Bus Window layer so it can't be accidentally moved with the Move tool. Click on the words Blue Bus to activate that layer; then lock its position also.**

STEP 5: Here we have loaded the wipers as a selection from the Green copy channel then we chose Select/Save Selection and are adding the wipers to the Bus Window mask using the Add to Channel option.

ADDING IN THE RED CAR

STEP 6: **Click on the name Red Car in the Red Car layer in the Layers palette. This should turn on that layer and it will appear in place of the Blue Bus layer, which is now obscured underneath. Type an L to switch to the Lasso tool; then type Return, type 3 and finally another Return. This will set the Feather of the Lasso to 3. The first Return selects the Feather text box, the 3 sets the Feather and the second Return deselects that feather text box so the next time you type a number it refers to the Opacity of the Red Car layer. Now type a 5, which should set the Opacity of this Red Car layer to 50%. You will now see the red car and the blue bus superimposed on each other. Hold down the Command key, while you click and drag the red car to the left so it looks like it is driving down the road in front of the bus. While holding down the Command key, you are put into the Move tool, which can accidentally move a layer if you click and drag by accident with the Command key held down. When in the correct position, you should see the red car within the left front window of the bus the viewer would be riding in. Getting the yellow curbs in the two images to line up is a good way to position the car on the road. Don't move the Blue Bus layer though; it should already be in the correct position. When the red car is approximately in the right place, type a 0 to set the Opacity of the Red Car layer back to 100%. Without the Command key down, you should still be in the Lasso tool and with that tool make a very loose selection around the red car. Make sure you include all of the red car's splash. Now choose Layer/Add Layer Mask/Reveal Selection, or just click on the second thumbnail from the left at the bottom of the Layers palette. This will add a layer mask removing the rest of the Red Car layer from this composite.**

STEP 6: This is the approximate initial selection you'll make on the red car. After making the layer mask from this selection you will paint white or black with the Paintbrush in that mask to add to or subtract from this selection.

STEP 6: Here is the red car in relationship to the blue bus before we scale the car.

STEP 6: Here is how they look after the car is scaled up by 145% and also moved to this new location further to the left and front.

STEP 6: The Red Car and Blue Bus after my final edits on the mask for the red car to tone down the splash a little. At this point, I have not yet added the Grouped Darken Car curve to the Red Car layer.

You'll notice that the color correction on the Red Car layer doesn't match, but that can actually be an asset at this point to make it easier to see what is coming from each layer. **Turn the Eye icon off for the Bus Window layer so you can concentrate on cleanly integrating the red car. Use Command-K to bring up the General Preferences and set the History States to 99.** You'll be doing a lot of blending here and if you don't like the direction it's going, you may want to back up a long way. It is amazing how quickly one can do more than 20 history clicks when retouching or blending a mask. **Use the Paintbrush (B), and paint in the Red Car layer mask to blend the red car and its splash into the Blue Bus scene. You'll probably want to set the Opacity of your brush to about 30%.**

I'm assuming here that you have BarrysPhotoBrushes loaded as explained in Chapter 3: "Setting System and Photoshop Preferences." If not, you may want to load those brushes from the Preferences folder on the CD. Use one of the brushes from the middle set, which have 80% hardness, painting with black to cleanly remove the original background from behind the roof of the red car. In front of the red car, you want to keep most of that car's splash but you want to use a soft brush, from the third set of brushes, to blend the splash and underside of the front of the car with the road in Blue Bus layer. When you have made some progress blending these, click on the Overall Color Correction Layer Set thumbnail and drag this up until the line above the Red Car layer is highlighted. Release the mouse at this point, and the color corrections you made to the Blue Bus layer are now applied to the Red Car layer as well. The two layers should now look good together, but if not, continue to work on the Red Car layer mask. If you are having trouble getting it to work, check out my version in the file called RainInCostRicaFinalCC.psd in the Extra Info Files folder for this chapter of your CD.

The red car may now look a little small because we have moved it in front of the blue bus and closer to your point of view so it needs to be a bit bigger in its relationship to the bus. **Click on the Red Car Layer thumbnail, to be sure that layer is active; then choose Edit/Free Transform (Command-T) so you can scale and move the Red Car. If you can't see the corner handlebars to do the transform, press the Escape key to get out of Free Transform while you close palettes, and put your window in Full Screen mode or whatever you need to do to have room to scale this layer. Once you are in Free Transform, you will want to hold down the Shift key while scaling the car so the scaling stays proportional. I held my Shift key down and then clicked and dragged the top right handlebar up and to the right to increase the size of the car. You can then release the mouse from the corner handlebar and move the red car's position by clicking and dragging in the center area of the scaling box. Scale the car and reposition it until you are happy with its size and location. The Options bar at the top of the screen gives you the amount of scaling you have done so far, and you can change this amount by just typing a new value into either the horizontal or vertical scale text box.** For a review of what Free Transform can do, see Chapter 9: "Transformation of Images." **When you are happy with the Free Transform, press Return to see it in full resolution. You will probably now want to click on the rightmost Layer Mask thumbnail in this Red Car layer so you can go back and edit this mask a bit more using black and white with the Paintbrush. To get my red car to look right, I actually scaled it up by 145% in width and height and also moved it further to the left and front until part of it was no longer visible. I also used Command-F3 at this point to add a Grouped Curves adjustment layer to the Red Car layer and then used**

STEP 7: The initial Lasso selection for the woman.

STEP 7: The tighter selection of the Woman made with the Wand and then the Lasso.

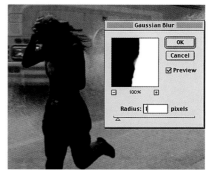

STEP 7: After saving the above selection to the Woman mask channel, then deselecting that selection, we Gaussian Blur the mask by 1 to soften the edges. The final step is to use the Airbrush with a low Opacity to blend the woman's hair and foot shadow with the Blue Bus layer's background.

this to darken the car a bit in relationship to the Blue Bus scene. You can load my Darken Car curve settings from the Extra Info Files folder for this chapter on the CD. Lock the position of the Red Car layer when you finish it.

ADDING THE RUNNING WOMAN

STEP 7: **Click on the word Woman in the Layers palette to activate that layer. Type L to go back to your Lasso tool and make sure the feather is still set to 3. Make a very loose selection around the edge of the woman, and the reflection of her feet and legs on the pavement. Make sure this selection is wide enough to be way more than the 3 pixel feather away from the edges of the woman. Click on the Add a Mask icon which is second from the left at the bottom of the Layers palette.** This just removes the parts of the woman layer you are sure you won't be using. Now you are going to refine the mask and then reposition and resize the woman if necessary. When you move or scale a layer that has a linked layer mask attached, the mask is also moved and scaled in the same ways. When you normally add a layer mask using the Add a Mask icon or the Layer/Add Layer Mask menu, that mask is linked to the layer. You can see the small Link icon between the layer's Layer thumbnail and its Layer Mask thumbnail.

Type a W to switch to the Magic Wand and make sure the Tolerance is set to 32. Click on the Layer thumbnail for the Woman layer and make a tighter selection on the woman by clicking several times in the black areas of her clothes. After selecting what you can this way with the Wand, type L to switch to the Lasso tool; then Return, 2 and Return again to set the Feather to 2. Now with the Shift key down, add in the areas that were not selected by the Wand. I've set the Feather to 2 because in the original image the woman is a bit soft along the edges since she is running. Choose Select/Save Selection and save to the Woman Mask channel using the

STEP 7: Here we see the composite with the running woman added into the original Blue Bus scene.

Replace Selection option. Now choose Select/Deselect to get rid of your selection since it has been already saved to a mask and we now are going to want to blur that mask. Choose Filter/Blur/Gaussian Blur and do a blur of 1 to make her edges a bit softer than the Magic Wand did. Now type a J to bring up the Airbrush and use soft brushes with an Opacity of about 07% to blend the woman's flopping black hair and foot shadow into the Blue Bus Layer's background. You should also drag the Overall Color Correction layer set up above the Woman layer so it is color corrected in the same way as the other two. Since all three of the Blue Bus, Red Car and Woman shots were taken at the same time with the same roll of film and only seconds apart, it is possible and even beneficial to use the same color corrections on all three layers. Keep working on the Woman layer mask until she blends in well.

FINISHING UP THE COMPOSITE

STEP 8: Now you can turn the Eye icon back on for the top Bus Window layer and your composite should be almost complete. I liked the location of the woman where she was, but if you don't, you can click on the word Woman in the Woman layer to reactivate it; then use the Move tool to move that layer around. When the location is final, lock the position of the Woman layer as you did the other layers earlier. Go ahead and drag the Overall Color Correction layer set to the very top of the Layers palette and you should find the look is complete.

STEP 8: This is the final composite with the Bus Window layer turned back on and the Overall Color Corrections layer set moved up to the top of the Layers palette so it corrects all these images in the same way. This has been a fun use of some of the pictures I took on my most recent trip to Costa Rica.

Chapter 28: Rain in Costa Rica

Using adjustment layers, layer masks, retouching and layer sets to color correct and composite the McNamaras' family portrait, where we need to move six smiling faces into the final image to create one where everyone is smiling.

I was an only child, so while growing up it was always more fun to go over to the McNamaras and play with their six kids. Now, as adults, we still get together a lot and I have had the joy of taking two of their five-year family portraits. Taking a family portrait of this many people, and especially this many kids along with their parents, is not the easiest task. I also wanted to use my 4x5 camera so there would be the maximum amount of detail in the image. All the kids are wiggling around, so it's hard to get them to smile at the camera, and then the parents often look down and give directions to their children at just that moment when all the children are actually looking at the camera. I knew this would be difficult to do with the 4x5, so I also brought along my trusty Canon F1 and shot two rolls of 35. With the 35mm stuff, I actually did get one picture where everyone was smiling and looking at the camera. That was the shot we used for the McNamara family. Still, though, I wanted to make a 4x5 version, because it would have so much more detail. Scans, with the Leaf 45 scanner, were made of enough of the 4x5 images that I had at least one smiling face of each person. Here we are going to composite all of them together to create the family portrait where everyone is smiling!

The images in this chapter were created using the ColorMatchRGB workspace, so just leave the images in that space in Photoshop 6 and work on them in Color-Match.

STEP 1: **Make sure that the version of Photoshop you are going to use for this example is already running. Bring up the General Preferences (Command-K) and set History States to 40.** This will help you undo any mistakes made when retouching to blend the new images in. If you have not used the History palette before, read Chapter 8: "History Palette, History Brush and Snapshots" because you will find the History palette very useful here. **Open each of the seven Photoshop files in the McNamaras folder on the *Photoshop 6 Artistry* CD,**

The original McNamaras image before color correction or the addition of the smiling faces.

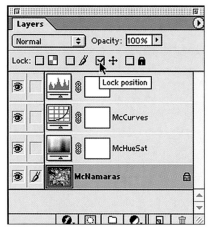

STEP 2: Locking the position of the McNamaras layer so it can't accidentally be moved.

STEP 2: The Layers palette after the McOverallCC set is created and set up.

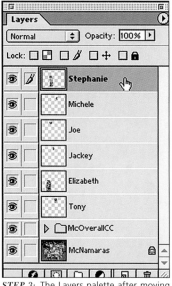

STEP 3: The Layers palette after moving all the smiling faces into the work file.

files that end in .psd, using the File/Open command in Photoshop. Choose the file McNamarasOrig from the Photoshop Window menu and put it in Full Screen mode by clicking on the middle icon at the bottom of the Tool palette or by typing F. Type C to bring up the Cropping tool and crop out any black or white borders around the image. Choose File/Save As and save it as McNamarasLayers.

STEP 2: **Choose Layer/New Adjustment Layer/Levels (Command-F2) to start the over-all correction for the McNamarasLayers image and call this first adjustment layer McLevels. Go through the basic levels adjustment, which you learned about in Chapter 19: "Overall Color Correction." You may want to review that chapter if you are not sure what to do here. I used the Highlight and Shadow Eyedroppers to set the highlight on Jackie's pants and the shadow in the darkest leaves along the top of the photo. If you want to check them out, you can look at my Levels settings and the Color Samplers I set for the highlights and shadows, in my McNamarasLayers file, from the Extra Info Files folder on the CD. When you are happy with the Levels color changes, press the Save button and save these as McLevels; then choose OK from your Levels adjustment layer.** We'll use the saved version later when we are working on the new faces. We did this using an adjustment layer so that we would have the option of changing it later after we get all the faces composited in.

Now use Command-F3 to create a Curves adjustment layer and adjust the con-trast of this image. It is sort of flat, especially for the people in the shadows in the back row. Use an S Curve to increase the contrast a bit. Again, if you are having trou-ble, check my McCurves layer from my final version of this chapter in the Extra Info Files folder for this chapter on the CD. Save your Curve changes as McCurves; then choose OK to finish up this adjustment layer.

Now use Command-F4 to create another adjustment layer of type Hue/Satu-ration, and call it McHueSat. Do the overall Saturation adjustments for the McNa-maras family like we did in Chapter 19. The contrast and saturation on this scan is flat with color casts. In fact, some of the separate face scans we are going to insert later look better, and you'll need to bring the McNamaras image up to their level. While the various photos were being taken, clouds were moving over, so some faces were in the sun and others in the shade. The people in the back all have dark flat color casts over their faces. In the end they will all just need to match and also make a pleasing color portrait. **When you are happy with the added saturation and tonal changes, use the Save button to save your Hue/Sat changes as McHueSat; then choose OK in the Hue/Saturation dialog box.** Since these are all adjustment layers, you can change them again later and probably will before this example is finished.

Double-click on the Background layer at the bottom of the Layers palette and rename it McNamaras. Turn on the new Photoshop 6 Lock Position icon to lock this layer against accidental movement. Now choose Layer/New/Layer Set and create a new layer set called McOverallCC. Drag that set to the top of the Layers palette and put the three adjustment layers inside it by dragging each layer's thumbnail and dropping it on top of the McOverallCC set's thumbnail. Make sure the order of the three layers stays the same inside this set. Now you can close the set to make more room in the Layers palette, which you will need.

ADDING THE SMILING FACES

STEP 3: **Type V to switch to the Move tool. Now use the Window menu to switch, one at a time, to each of the smiling face images you opened in step 1. For each separate smiling face image, drag and drop it with the Move tool on top of the same person's** face in your McNamarasLayers image. If you put the cursor on the nose in the smiling version, and then drag to the same person's nose in the McNamarasLayers file and release the mouse button at that point, you will have a good start on lining up the two heads. Go ahead and drag and drop each smiling person into their own layer; then Option-double-click on the layer thumbnail giving that layer the name for that person. The names of the smiling people's files are the actual names of that particular person. After dragging each person into their own layer, you can File/Close (Command-W) the file for that person. When you have moved all six people into their approximate position, go ahead and press Command-S to save

STEP 4: Here you see the two Jackeys before they are lined up. Pick an absolute position in the center of the image area, like her glasses' corner here, put the cursor on that position, and then drag the cursor to the same position in the other layer to move the Jackey layer and line them up. You can use the arrow keys to scroll by one pixel and fine-tune the positioning. After you adjust the position, you may have to rescale a bit, readjust a bit, and so on, until you get it right.

STEP 4: Here is how the two Jackeys look after they are lined up.

the McNamarasLayers with all their layers. Your Layers palette should now look like the one on the previous page.

STEP 4: Some of the smiling layers will overlap each other, but don't worry about that now, because we are going to work on each one of them separately to integrate it into the image in a custom way. **Turn off the Eye icons for all the smiling face layers except for Jackey. You still want the Eye icons on for the McNamaras layer and McOverallCC adjustment layer set. Click on the Jackey name in the Jackey layer to make it active, and then type a 5 to set its Opacity to 50%. You can now see 50% of the Jackey layer and 50% of the original image of Jackey underneath. Use the Move tool (V) to move the Jackey layer around a bit until you figure out which 50% comes from this layer. The face in the Jackey layer is a bit bigger than the original face underneath. Use the Move tool to line up the glasses and lips on each layer as best you can. Remember that you can use the arrow keys to move the Jackey layer one pixel at a time in any direction. Now choose Edit/Free Transform (Command-T) and use the Free Transform command to scale this Jackey layer exactly and move it into the exact position above the original head below. Remember to hold down the Shift key while clicking and dragging in one of the corner handles to make your scaling be proportional. To move the layer while in Free Transform, just click and drag in the middle of the box that defines the current image or use the arrow keys for fine adjustment. Press Return to end the Free Transform.** For a review of the Free Transform options, see Chapter 9: "Transformation of Images, Layers, Paths and Selections."

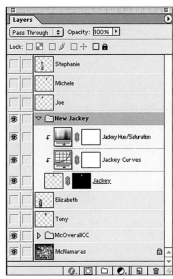

STEP 5: Make a Lasso selection (feather 2) of the inner area of Jackey's face; then click on the Layer Mask icon to create a layer mask only showing

STEP 5: **Type L to bring up the Lasso tool, and then press Return to bring up its Options palette. Now type a 2, and then press Return again to set the Feather at 2. Now make a selection around the inside of Jackey's face. This is the part of her face we are going to use from the Jackey layer. Now click on the Layer Mask icon (the second from the left most one at the bottom of the Layers palette) to add a layer mask isolating this selected area as the new face and blending it with the old face. You may notice a color difference between the skin and hair on the Jackey layer and the skin and hair in the original image. To fix this, add a Levels or Curves Adjustment layer above the Jackey layer and grouped with the Jackey layer. I added grouped**

STEP 5: The Layers palette after blending Jackey's better smile into her previous head and creating the New Jackey layer set.

STEP 7: Before Joe, Jackey, Tony, and Michele's heads are replaced by smiling versions.

STEP 7: After the smiling heads are installed.

Levels, Curves and Hue/Saturation adjustment layers above the Jackey layer and used them to match the color and contrast of Jackey's face and hair. I started by loading the McLevels, McCurves and McHueSat settings into each of these so the adjustments I made to Jackey's face were the same as I had made to the old version of her face. Since the initial contrast on the new face is different than the original one, this only serves as a starting point and the colors have to be tweaked to match. I also tweaked the original McCurves adjustment layer, above the McNamaras layer, to add a little more contrast to the McNamaras layer to better match Jackey. We may have to modify all of these as we add other smiling faces to the composite. After you get the colors to match fairly well, type a B to switch to the Paintbrush tool and then click on the Layer Mask thumbnail for the Jackey layer. Type a 0 (zero) to get 100% Opacity; then use a soft brush to paint in the layer mask to blend the two faces together even more. Paint with black to include more of the original Jackey face and paint with white to include more of the face from the Jackey layer. Sometimes you might want to paint with 50% Opacity to blend the two images together. I also used the Rubber Stamp tool to clone away a little of Jackey's hair at the top of her head in the original McNamaras layer.

Once you are happy with the new Jackey face, choose Layer/New/Layer Set and add a set called New Jackey. Click on the Layer thumbnail for the Jackey layer and lock the position for this layer as you did for the McNamaras layer in step 2. That will stop the Jackey layer, and those grouped with it, from being accidentally moved. Now drag and drop this Jackey layer on the thumbnail for the New Jackey layer set. This should move the Jackey layer and any adjustment layers grouped with the Jackey layer into this New Jackey layer set. You can then collapse this set to simplify your Layers palette before moving on to add some more of the new smiling faces. Turning the Eye icon off and on for this New Jackey layer set will toggle the entire image between having the original Jackey face and the new, bigger smile Jackey face. Now might be a good time to save the file (Command-S).

STEP 6: The original image of Joe was definitely not smiling very much. **Turn on the Eye icon for the Joe layer and you'll see that the new Joe definitely has a better smile. Now go through the sequence of adjustments you did for Jackey in steps 4 and 5, but this time do them for Joe and the Joe layer. You'll find that the area of each person's face that you have to change is different. Pull up the McNamarasLayers file from the Extra Info Files folder in the McNamaras example on the CD. This is my version of the final image. You can look at each of my layer masks and my adjustment layers to see what I did. Put all the Joe layers in a New Joe layer set as your did for Jackey's layers. Press Command-S to save your progressing McNamarasLayers file.**

STEP 7: **Let's do Tony next because he's actually standing behind Jackey. Click on the Tony layer in the Layers palette and drag it to below the Jackie layer in the Layers** palette. Now do steps 4 and 5 for the Tony layer. Don't worry about any overlap between Tony and Jackey; that will go away when you create the layer mask for the Tony layer. To get Tony's head to look right in the composite, I ended up adding first a Levels, then a Curves, and finally, a Hue/Saturation adjustment layer above Tony and grouped with Tony's layer. Stick all of Tony's layers in a New Tony layer set. To the right of Tony is Michele, so turn on the Eye icon for her layer and work with her after Tony. To get Michele to look right, I had to include part of her neck as well as her head. You have to rubber stamp her collar and neck a bit on the right side. Turn the Eye icon on and off for the Michele layer as well as Shift-clicking on her Layer Mask thumbnail in my final version of the McNamarasLayers to see what I did to make her look correct. Turning off the Eye icon for the Michele layer will let you see the original Michele; turning it on again allows you to compare the new version to the original to see if your composite is working. Shift-clicking on her Layer Mask Thumbnail turns off the Layer mask and shows you the entire new Michele layer. Toggling these back and forth can help you to see what you need to do to solve any problems. If you make a mistake while rubber stamping, use the History palette (F8) to go back a few steps, or you can also paint from an earlier state using the History Brush. See Chapter 8: "History Palette, History Brush and Snapshots" for more info on how to do this. For the color correction on Michele, I just used a Levels and a Curves adjustment layer. In a similar way as you did Tony and Michele, now you should turn on the Eye icon for the Stephanie layer and blend in the slightly better expression for Stephanie. Do steps 4 and 5 for her. I had to add Levels, Curves and Hue/Saturation adjustment layers to get her facial color to match the original. Each person's new layers should be put into a layer set for that person. Now might be a good time to save the file (Command-S).

STEP 8: You may notice that my final Layers palette, on the last page of this chapter, has two Curves adjustment layers on the top. One is called Open Up Parts, and the other is called Darken Parts. Although we didn't replace them, the faces of the three people at the top left of this family portrait are darker than many other faces in the image. Having these faces darker made it more difficult to match the new faces I was adding. I created the curve called Open Up Parts, which you see on this page, to allow me to brighten up those faces a bit. **To make such a curve, just click on the top-most layer set in the Layers palette to make it active. Choose Command-F3 to create a new Curves adjustment layer. Click in the center of the curve and drag it up and to the left until the darkest face that you want to change is plenty bright enough. If you are not sure, make it a bit brighter than you would like. Don't worry about the faces that are already bright enough; they will return to normal in a moment. Click on OK in the Curves dialog; then choose Image/Adjust/Invert (Command-I) to invert the mask for this layer causing it to now make no changes to the image. Select the Airbrush tool (J) from the Tools palette and set its Opacity to about 07%. Select a soft brush and type a D to make sure the foreground color is white. Now paint over the areas of the faces that you want to brighten up. The longer you hold the Airbrush down, the more white is slowly applied until you get the degree of brighter face that you want. If you overdo it, use Command-Z to Undo or type an X, and paint with black to go back the other way.** Using a similar technique, I also added the Darken Parts curve to fix the flat colors in the face of the woman to the top left with the red cloth belt. This curve is also used on several other faces to add some contrast where needed. Check these out along with their masks by looking at my final layers file on the book's CD.

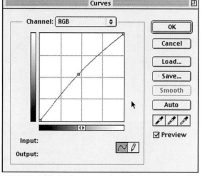

STEP 8: This is the curve I used to open up the dark faces a bit. It is only applied where the mask is not black.

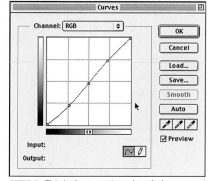

STEP 8: This is the curve I used to darken several faces. The S shape of the curve adds contrast, and moving the middle point down and to the right darkens the midtones as well. To this curve I also added some very minor color adjustments in the Green and Blue channels.

Adding the Smiling Faces

ADDING THE SMILING ELIZABETH

STEP 9: **The last person who needs a better smile is Elizabeth. Because her feet were in sort of a strange position in the original and she was sitting in the front, I decided to replace her entire body. The best way I found to line up the two images of Elizabeth was to make the chair she is sitting in line up between the two shots. Because there is quite a bit of movement between the two images of her, my initial Lasso selection included more than just the new Elizabeth. It also included the old Elizabeth. We will need to get rid of all of her from the original photo, so we might as well start by seeing how the locations where she was in the original photo look if used from the new photo. After making your Lasso selection, click on the Layer Mask icon to add a layer mask that includes only the selected area; then set the Opacity on the Elizabeth layer back to 100%. Now you need to use the Paintbrush tool in the layer mask, painting in either black, to remove the Elizabeth layer, or in white, to add parts of the Elizabeth layer. Do this until you get the two layers to merge the best that you can.**

STEP 10: **You will find there are some fringe areas that won't work from either the Elizabeth layer or the original McNamaras layer. You will have to use the Rubber Stamp tool (S) to clone some of what you need in those areas. Before you do this though, go ahead and add a Grouped Levels adjustment layer and get the color of the Elizabeth layer to match the original photo. A good place to compare is the white chair that Stephanie is sitting on behind and to the right of Elizabeth. Part of the armrest for this chair will come from the original image and part of it will come from the Elizabeth layer. Get those whites to match, and you will have the color pretty close. I also added Curves and Hue/Saturation adjustment layers above the Levels and grouped them with Elizabeth to fix her contrast and saturate her colors a bit. Now that the colors match pretty well, use the Rubber Stamp tool to clone the areas that won't work from either layer. For me, this was the top right edge of the lower left corner of Stephanie's dress, which came from the Elizabeth layer, and little sections of the pants on the boy to the left of Elizabeth. Remember, the Rubber Stamp tool even lets you clone from one layer onto another. Just have the first layer active when you Option-click to define where you are cloning from, and then activate the layer you are cloning to before you begin to paint in the clone. To get the part of Stephanie's dress that I used from the Elizabeth layer to match, I lassoed that part of the dress, then added a Curves adjustment layer (again, grouped with the Elizabeth layer), and used it to match the two dresses. Because I had the dress area selected when I created the new adjustment layer, this automatically made a layer mask that applied the Curves adjustments only in that dress area. As you rubber stamp and paint in the layers and layer masks to get Elizabeth to look correct, it is easy to get confused and forget which layer or layer mask you are using or which tool you are using. It is even hard for me sometimes when I'm doing something like this. Slow down and concentrate; think twice and make sure you are using the right tool in the correct state. Sometimes it helps you get your bearings if you turn off the Eye icon of a layer or Shift-click a Layer Mask thumbnail to see the image without a layer or a mask. You will be switching between the McNamaras and Elizabeth layers as you rubber stamp, and you'll also switch between rubber stamping on a layer and using the Paintbrush to edit a mask. Remember that you can always use the History palette or the History Brush to restore any layer, or just part of a layer, to a previous state.**

STEP 9: The initial Lasso selection for the Elizabeth layer with Opacity at 50%.

This example was in some previous versions of Photoshop Artistry, although we did rework and improve the file and text for Photoshop 6 Artistry. Elizabeth 's sister, Mary, was outside a Barnes and Noble bookstore one day, and she bet her friend $5 that her picture was in one of the books in the store. Her friend didn't believe her, so they went in and opened up a copy of Photoshop Artistry; then Mary made a quick $5. Pretty smart girl!

STEP 11: You now have all your smiling faces added and you have color corrected and masked them to match as best you can. Now it is time to look at the image as a whole and further tweak the color or contrast of any head that doesn't seem quite right. A particular person might seem slightly off color or have a different brightness or contrast than the rest. You might also decide to adjust the contrast or color balance of the entire McNamaras layer. Because you did all your color adjustments using adjustment layers, you can double-click on the Layer thumbnail of any of them and change the adjustment as many times as you like without degrading the original pixels in any of the layers. The final color changes to the pixels will not be made until you flatten the image; even better, use File/Save A Copy to create a flattened version. When I zoomed out and looked at the image, I ended up changing the Joe and Jackey heads a little to make them fit in better with the rest of the faces. I used Joe's Levels adjustment layer to make his face a little darker and warmer, and I used Jackey's Curves adjustment layer to make her face a little warmer. My final version, called McNamarasLayers, is on the CD in the Extra Info Files folder for this chapter. If you're having a problem with anything, pull up my version and see how I did it. Press Command-S to save your file when you finish it. Before printing this, I did Image/Duplicate to create a merged version, and then Unsharp Mask to sharpen it—and of course I converted it to CMYK.

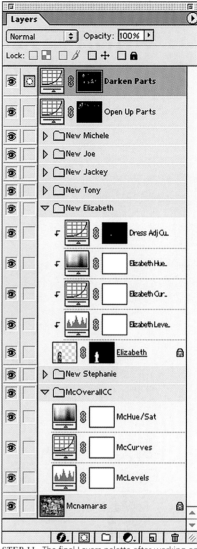

STEP 11: The final Layers palette after working on the new image of Elizabeth. This final McNamarasLayers file is in the Extra Info Files folder for the McNamaras chapter on the CD.

The final McNamaras' image after color correction and the addition of all the smiling faces. This was sharpened with Unsharp Mask at 150 percent, Radius of 1.5, and Threshold of 3.

Adding the Smiling Elizabeth

HANDS-ON SESSION: The PowerBook Ad

*Create an image from components for a specified canvas size,
like a magazine ad; work with drop shadows, knock-outs, the
Pen tool and linked layers for high-quality output.*

The final composite portable image. This is the image you will produce in this
example from the components shown below.

SETTING UP THE POWERBOOK IMAGE

STEP 1: I recently purchased this 500 MHz Apple
PowerBook portable and it has been a big help in
writing this book, since I was able to work while
on the road and can also easily carry it to different
places within our home. This allows me to work
late at night while also listening to my five-year-
old son sleep. I have also been testing an Epson
PhotoPC 3000Z 3.3 megapixel camera, which I
really like, and I was able to photograph the
PowerBook, for this example, using the camera
mounted on a tripod. I originally photographed
the PowerBook in color with the 3000Z then converted it to black-and-white for this example.

**Open the file PowerBook B&W.psd from the
CD folder called Ch30.The Power Book Ad.** Let's
say we want to use this to create an ad for a new
computer brochure. The ad needs to be 4.3 inches wide by 5
inches high for a 175-line screen print job. That means we

STEP 1:
The Tool
palette.

need to have an image that is
at least 1,505 pixels wide by
1,750 pixels high, since we
need 350 dpi to print at 175
line screen. The image we
are using is just slightly larger
than that.

CREATING A NEW BACKGROUND FOR THE POWERBOOK

STEP 2: **We want this to
be a color ad, so choose
Image/Mode/RGB to convert
the PowerBook into an RGB**

STEP 1: The menu bar.

STEP 1: The Banf Lake image that will be shown
on the PowerBook screen.

STEP 1: Here is the original PowerBook
grayscale image taken with the Epson 3000Z.

image. We need to create an image to go on the screen of the PowerBook as well as a background for it to sit on. First, let's work on creating a background. This black-and-white photo of the PowerBook still contains shooting setup objects around the actual computer. **Option-double-click on the one layer in the layers palette and name it My PowerBook. Use the Pen tool (P) to make a path around the outside edge of the PowerBook. Start at the top left edge of the PowerBook and click and drag curve points as you work your way around the computer, being careful to draw your path just a pixel or two inside the actual edge of the computer.** For more info about using the Pen tool and making paths, see the Pen tool part of Chapter 4: "The Tool Palette" or check out Chapter 28: "Rain in Costa Rica." **When you have drawn points all the way around the edge of the computer, click back again on the original point to complete the path. Bring up the Paths palette (Shift-F11) and double-click on the Work Path, renaming it to Portable Outline.**

STEP 2: Editing the clipping path with the white Arrow tool.

    Choose Layer/New Fill Layer/Solid Color to create a solid color fill layer and name it Background Color Fill. Choose a dark brown color when the Color Picker appears onscreen. Now drag that layer underneath the My PowerBook layer in the Layers palette. Bring up the Paths palette and click on your Portable Outline path to activate it. Now click back on the My PowerBook layer to activate it, and then choose Layer/Add Layer Clipping Path/Current Path. This clipping path should remove the background from around the PowerBook image. Type A to go to the Arrow tool then Shift+A until you get the white Arrow tool, called the Direct Selection tool. Click once on the path with this tool to bring up the path points, and then to edit a point, click and drag it to a new position. After editing the path, you can choose Command-H to see the PowerBook against the background

STEP 2: After using Command-H to hide the edges of the path so you can see any leftover white background around the edges of the PowerBook. If you do see some, Command-H again then use the white Arrow tool to fine tune the path.

without the path lines there. If you see a white line on the edge of the PowerBook, then you need to move the path in a bit until the white edge is gone. To do this, use Command-H again to bring your path back. Then edit it and use another Command-H to see if it now looks correct. Scroll around the entire edge of the PowerBook, editing the path until you see no white borders and the path is smooth and clean. If you want to compare your work to mine, my final file, with all its layers, is called PowerBookAdLayers.psd, and is in the the Extra Info Folder for this chapter on the CD. Being able to edit a path as it is applied to a layer as a clipping path, is a very useful new feature for Photoshop 6. Notice that this edited path shows up in the Paths palette whenever this layer is active. **Use Command-Shift-S to save this file on your hard disk in Photoshop format as PowerBookLayers.**

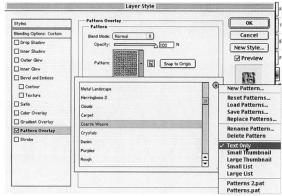

STEP 3: In the Layer Style dialog for the Background Color Fill layer, we clicked on Pattern Overlay to the left then used the pop-up menu to set the display of patterns as Text Only. This allows you to pick the Course Weave pattern without guessing which one it is from the Pattern icons.

ADDING EFFECTS TO YOUR BACKGROUND

STEP 3: **Double-click on the words Background Color Fill in the Layers palette to bring up the Layer Style palette for your Background Color Fill layer. First click on Pattern Overlay and choose the Course Weave pattern, as shown to the right. Then click on Color Overlay and change the Color and Opacity until you are happy with the color of your background with its Pattern Overlay. Choose OK in the Layer Style dialog and notice that the Course Weave pattern has no vanishing point.** If it were really sitting on a table and you were photographing it at an angle, as we are here, the pattern would seem closer together at the back of the table than it would at the front of

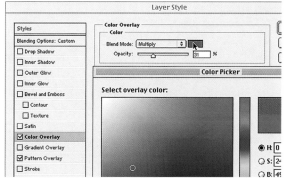

STEP 3: Choosing a color with Color Overlay.

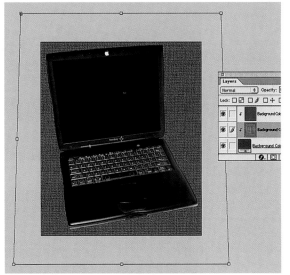

the table. Notice that Edit/Free_Transform is not currently an active option. **To add perspective to this pattern, you need to turn these effects into normal layers. Choose Layer/Layer Style/Create Layers, which will create a real layer to simulate each of your Layer Style effects. Click on the layer named Background Color Fill's Pattern Fill and zoom out so you can see the entire image plus some gray space around its edges. If not already in Full Screen mode with menu bar, type an F until you get there. You might also want to press Tab until all your palettes are removed from the screen. Choose Edit/Transform/Perspective then click and drag on the handles at the top of the screen towards the center to give the pattern the perspective that seems right to you. If those handles are outside of the screen's area, use Spacebar-Option-click to zoom until the handles are visible. After changing the perspective, you may need to use Spacebar-Command-click to zoom in until you can see the pattern sharply on the screen.**

STEP 3: Adding some perspective to the pattern.

MAKING THE LIGHTING MORE REALISTIC

STEP 4: **You may notice the bright highlight in the front-left corner of the PowerBook image. The light was coming from in front and above left. We want to make the background look as though it is lit in a similar way. Click back on the My PowerBook layer to activate it and choose Layer/New/Layer to create a new non-grouped layer named White. Choose Edit/Fill and fill this layer with 100% White. Now drag this layer down to the very bottom of the Layers palette. Click back on the Background Color Fill layer to activate it, and then choose Layer/Add Layer Mask/Reveal All. This will create a white layer mask on this layer, which can control the brightness of your background. Type a G to switch to the Gradient tool and choose the gradient named "Black, White" by clicking in the gradient area of the Options bar at the top left of your screen. Since you just added a layer mask, anything you do will now happen to that mask. Zoom way out; then click your gradient way below the image and drag upwards and slightly to the right until you reach the top of your background. When you release the mouse, this adds a gradient into the layer mask that is just a bit darker at the bottom than at the top. This reveals the White layer a bit towards the bottom of the image so you get the appearance of a light that is bright in front and fades towards the back. The brightness of the light in the front and how quickly it fades is determined by how you draw the gradient. To try different gradients, just keep drawing another one until you find the effect you like most.**

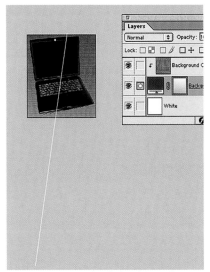

STEP 4: Here, using the Black, White gradient, we dragged the Gradient tool from way down at the bottom of the screen until it reached the top of the portable image. This makes a subtle gradient that is just a bit darker at the bottom than the top so it brightens up the bottom of the background pattern by revealing a bit of the White layer underneath.

ADDING A DROP SHADOW ON THE COMPUTER

STEP 5: **Click on the Layer thumbnail of the My PowerBook layer then double-click on the words My PowerBook to bring up the Layer Styles for this layer. Click on the word Drop Shadow towards the top left of the dialog to create a drop shadow.** When you are in Drop Shadow mode, you can move the cursor out on the screen and notice that it is in the Move tool. If you click and drag on your drop shadow, you can easily move it to the position you want, relative to the object you are adding the shadow to. This will change the Distance and Angle values in the Drop Shadow subdialog. You can use the Opacity slider to change the darkness of the shadow and you can use the Size slider to soften the edge of the shadow. The Spread controls how quickly the shadow blends into the background. You can also change the Blend mode of the shadow, although Multiply usually works quite well. Finally, if you click on the color box, you can bring up the Color Picker and change the hue of the shadow. **After adjusting your shadow as much as you can in the dialog, choose OK to add it to this layer as an effect. If you are not sure how dark to make it, it is better to make it darker than you think because you can always make it less dark later by lowering the opacity of the future Shadow layer. We need to turn this shadow into a regular layer because we will want to use Edit/Free Transform to make it match the lighting of this image.**

Now choose Layer/Layer Style/Create Layer to turn this drop shadow effect into a real layer. If you get a message saying that Some Aspects of the Effects cannot be Reproduced with Layers, just choose OK anyhow. Now you will have a new layer underneath your PowerBook layer named My PowerBook's Drop Shadow. Click on that new layer to make it active and choose Edit/Free Transform (Command-T). Zoom out so you can see the entire PowerBook and background. Holding the Command key down allows you to click in a handle and drag it in any direction to make the shadow look the way you think it should to match the lighting on the PowerBook. When you are finished with this step, press Return to complete the Free Transform. Using the slider at the top of the Layers palette, you can still lower the opacity of this layer. To change the color of the shadow, use the Color Picker to pick a new Foreground color and choose Edit/Fill (Shift-Delete on the Mac and Shift-Backspace with Windows). Fill with the Preserve Transparency checkbox turned on in the Fill dialog, and after the Fill you may want to readjust the opacity again. Remember that you can also change the Blend mode of this layer, which will also affect the appearance of the shadow.

COLORIZING THE COMPUTER

STEP 6: **Click the Layer thumbnail of the My PowerBook layer so the next layer you add is above this one. Choose Layer/New Adjustment Layer/Hue/Saturation (Command-F4) to create a Grouped adjustment layer on top of the PowerBook layer. Turn on the Colorize checkbox to the right of the Hue/Saturation dialog. Now lower the Saturation considerably and move the Hue slider until you get the color that you want.** Since this adjustment layer is grouped with the PowerBook (and the mask on the PowerBook layer isolates it from the background), only the Hue of the computer will change. Having objects that are neutral gray, like this PowerBook, make it easy to colorize them using a Hue/Saturation adjustment layer.

MAKING A PATH FOR THE COMPUTER SCREEN

STEP 7: **Type a P to switch to the Pen tool and create a path around the edge of the screen area on the PowerBook. Be careful to make the path accurately around the edge of the PowerBook's viewing area. Bring up the Paths palette (Shift-F11) and double-click on Work Path, naming it Screen.**

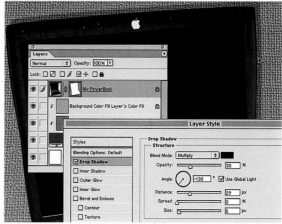

STEP 5: Here we see the setup for adding a drop shadow to the Power-Book using the Layer Style dialog. Notice the cursor to the top right of the screen where I can click and drag this shadow to whatever position I would like.

STEP 5: Here we are using Edit/Free Transform with the Command key down to adjust the shape of the shadow layer. If you don't want to keep the Command key down, you can just choose Edit/Transform/Distort.

STEP 6: The Layers palette setup for colorizing the PowerBook.

STEP 7: Use the Pen tool to create a path around the edge of the computer screen then name it Screen in the Paths palette.

STEP 8: Use the Marquee to select this rightside part of the menubar. Then choose Edit/Copy to copy it.

STEP 8: Use the Move tool to line the MenuBar up with the top and left of the screen.

STEP 8: After pasting the right part of the menubar down, use the Move tool to move it into position. Then use M to switch to the Marquee tool and select the part of this that covers the Help menu and remove it with the Delete key.

STEP 8: Using the Move tool with the Shift key down, click down in the BanfLake window then drag the cursor over on top of the RollerCoaster window where you should then release the Mouse button which will drop the BanfLake image as a new layer on top of the RolerCoaster image.

ASSEMBLING THE SCREEN'S IMAGES

STEP 8: **Choose File/Open four times and open the following files from the folder named Ch30.The Power Book Ad on the *Photoshop 6 Artistry* CD. Open the files named BanfLake.psd, RollerCoaster.psd, Tool Palette.tif and MenuBar.tif. Use the Window menu to bring the RollerCoaster image to the front, and then type F to put this file into Full Screen mode. Now use the Window menu to bring the BanfLake image to the front inside a normal window. Move the BanfLake window to the side so you can see part of the RollerCoaster image underneath. Type a V to switch to the Move tool; then, while holding the Shift key down, drag and drop the BanfLake image on top of the RollerCoaster image. Having the Shift key down will center the BanfLake image on top of the RollerCoaster image. See the illustration of this process to the left. Option-double-click on each layer in the Layers palette and name them with the correct names for that image. The bottom layer will be named RollerCoaster, and the next layer BanfLake.**

  Use the Window menu to choose the MenuBar image then drag and drop it so it is the layer on top of the BanfLake image. You'll get a message noting that the MenuBar image was created in the Color-Match color space, whereas the other two images are in Adobe RGB. Go ahead and choose OK to convert the Menu bar from ColorMatch to Adobe RGB color space. Option-double-click on this layer and name it MenuBar. You'll notice that the MenuBar image is wider than the canvas width of the RollerCoaster and BanfLake images. Use the Move tool to move the right side of the MenuBar to the right edge of the canvas. Type an M to switch to the Rectangular Marquee tool and select the rightmost part of the MenuBar and choose Edit/Copy. Now use the Move tool to move the MenuBar layer so the left edge and top of it line up with the left and top of the canvas. Now choose Edit/Paste to paste the right side of the MenuBar on top of this area. Move it so the rightmost part of it lines up with the top right edge of the screen. Now type M for the Marquee again and select the area you don't

want of this part of the menubar. The part you are selecting may be covering the Help menu. After selecting this part, press the Delete key to remove this part from this layer. Now choose Merge Down from the Layers palette pop-up menu to merge this edited right part of the MenuBar back with the left part of the MenuBar.

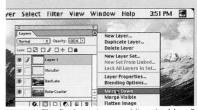

Use the Window menu to switch to the Tool Palette image then drag and drop it on top of the others. Use the Move tool to line the Tool Palette up below the MenuBar and along the left edge of the screen. Option-double-click on the Tool Palette layer and name it Tool Palette. Now click on the BanfLake layer to activate it; then click in the middle linking column for the other three layers in the Layers palette to link these other three layers to this BanfLake layer. Your Layers palette should

STEP 8: The final step in assembling the MenuBar layer is to use Merge Down to merge the two pieces of it together.

now look like the one shown here. Choose Select/All (Command-A) to make a selection going around the outside edge of the current image. Now choose Image/Crop to crop any parts of the MenuBar layer that may extend outside of the canvas area. Now choose Select/Deselect (Command-D) to get rid of this selection. Choose File/Save As and save this file as ScreenLayers. You can now use the Window menu to switch to each of the BanfLake, Tool Palette and MenuBar images and close them. Your PowerBookLayers and ScreenLayers files should still be open.

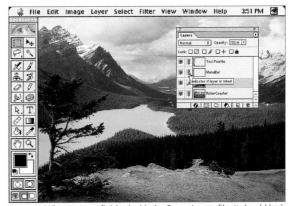

MOVING THE SCREEN IMAGES TO THE POWERBOOK FILE

STEP 9: The active layer on the PowerBookLayers file should be the top Color Computer layer and this file should be in Full Screen mode. Choose Layer/New/Layer Set and call this set Screen Simulation. Use the Window menu to activate the ScreenLayers file and type an F until it is no longer in Full Screen mode. The active layer in this file should be BanfLake. Move this window over to the left until you can see the Power-BookLayers image underneath. With the Move tool (M), click on the BanfLake image, inside the window for this file, and drag and drop it on top of the PowerBookLayers image. All four layers of the ScreenLayers image should move over to the PowerBookLayers image and be placed into the Screen Simulation layer set. Click on the words Screen Simulation to activate the layer set, and then use the Window menu or Shift-F11 to bring up the Paths palette. Click on the Screen path you made earlier to bring it up on your screen. From the pop-up menu of the Paths palette, choose Make Selection to turn this path into a selection with a feather value of zero and Anti-Aliased turned on. Now choose Layer/Add Layer Mask/Reveal Selection to add this to the Screen Simulation layer set as a layer mask. You'll notice that this entire ScreenLayers composite now appears as though it is inside the screen of the PowerBook computer. The only problem is the image is not lined up properly with the perspective of this PowerBook computer, whose screen is rotated back somewhat with the entire computer not directly facing the camera angle. There are various approaches to getting this image to look correct within the computer's screen area and most of them won't work that well. The method I eventually discovered for doing this, pointed out to me by a student of mine who also worked at Adobe at the time, is actually very simple and works better than anything else I had thought of.

STEP 8: When you are finished with the ScreenLayers file, it should look like this with the Layers palette shown here. Notice that the middle linking column of the Layers palette is pointed out here.

STEP 9: This is how things will look after adding the ScreenLayers layers to the Screen Simulation layer set.

STEP 10: This is how things will look after adding the ScreenLayers layers to the Screen Simulation layer set.

STEP 10: After you first go into Edit/Transform Distort, you'll see an outline of the entire ScreenLayers canvas area with handles on the corners.

STEP 10: The first step is to click on each of these corner handles and move it to a corner of the actual computer screen area.

GETTING THE IMAGES TO LOOK CORRECT WITHIN THE POWERBOOK'S SCREEN AREA

STEP 10: **The first thing you want to do is choose Filter/Blur/Gaussian Blur and put a 2-pixel blur on the layer mask you just added to the Screen Simulation layer set.** This will soften the transition between the edge of the screen and the images that will be displayed inside it. This will look like a shadow you might see around the edge of a computer screen. **Now click back on the BanfLake layer to make it active. Use the T ab key to get rid of your palettes. and then use Option-Spacebar-click to zoom out so you can see the entire image on the screen. Now choose Edit/Transform/Distort, which will bring up a frame around the edges of the canvas for your four screen layers. The cursor will have changed into a gray arrow, which you can use to click and drag the four corner handles around to distort this image. What you want to do is drag each of the four corner handles until they line up with the four corners of the actual computer screen. While zoomed out so you can see the entire top of the computer, move each of the corner handles to its perspective corner of the computer screen.**

Now use Command-Option-0 to zoom into 100% and look more closely at the top-left corner. Move the handle for that corner inward for a moment so you can clearly see the top left corner of the PowerBook's screen area. Now move the handle back so the corner of the image will be slightly to the left and above the corner of the PowerBook screen. This will allow the blurred edge mask to softly trim a little from the image and give the appearance of a slight shadow at the edge of the PowerBook screen area. Now move to the top right handle and do the same thing. Move it down and to the left of the actual corner and give the computer time to refresh the screen so you can actually see the corner. Now move the handle back into place getting it exactly where you want it so the mask gives it a slightly softer edge appearance, simulating a shadow there. As you work on each corner at 100% zoom factor, you can hold the Spacebar down to get the Hand tool and then click and drag when you want to scroll the image around inside Photoshop.

While within Transform/Distort, you can move each of these corners as many times as you want until you are happy with the results. After getting all four corners where you want them, press Return to complete the distort. You will notice that the image details are sharper now than with the preview you see using the Distort tool. **If you need to, you can use the Move tool (V) to move the image around within the Screen Simulation mask area. Once you are in the Move tool, you can use the Arrow keys to move this image one pixel at a time. When you are happy with its location, you should lock one of the layers, like the BanfLake layer for example. Since all four of these layers are linked together, locking one of them will lock them all.** Photoshop does not seem to give you the option of locking the Screen Simulation layer set, with its attached layer mask, that you would not want to be accidentally moved. **You can, however, activate the BanfLake layer and turn on**

the link column of the Screen Simulation layer set to link it to the four layers inside that set. This will stop it from being accidentally moved. You should also lock any of the other layers in this image that have pixel data or a mask in them. If you are not happy with the way the corners look on the PowerBook screen, you can change their shape by painting black with a soft brush in the corners of the MyPowerBook layer's layer mask.

Check out my version of this image in the file called Power-BookAdLayers inside the Extra Info Files folder for this chapter.

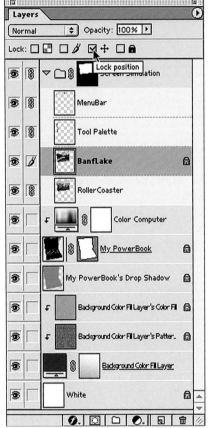

STEP 10: Here we see the final Layers palette for this composite image. It is a good idea to use the Lock Position icon at the top of the Layers palette to lock each layer that has a mask or some other element that you don't want to accidentally move. In the top five layers, we only had to lock the BanfLake layer since linking the other four to it also stops them from being moved.

STEP 10: While zoomed into 100% line up the top left corner so you can see the blurred mask acting like a shadow along the edge of your ScreenLayers image.

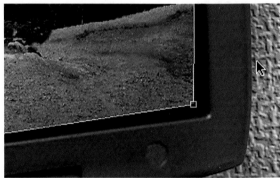

STEP 10: While zoomed into 100%, you can move a corner handle in a bit so you can see the details of the actual corner area of the computer screen. When you can clearly see those details then you can move that corner back to exactly where you want it, as we show below.

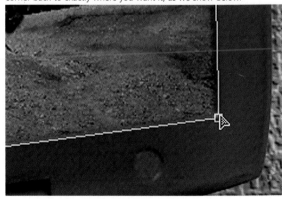

CALCULATIONS, PATTERNS, FILTERS, COMPOSITING AND EFFECTS

USE THE NEW TYPE TOOL AND LAYER STYLES

WORK WITH FILTERS, TEXTURES, PATTERNS, AND BITMAPS

USE PHOTOSHOP AND ILLUSTRATOR TOGETHER

UNDERSTAND THE BLEND MODES AND USE THEIR POWER

USING CALCULATIONS AND APPLY IMAGE

LEARN LAYER CLIPPING PATHS AND SHAPE LAYERS

Taken with my Canon EOS 10S on a backpacking trip in Yosemite, this sunset shot was scanned at 5000 dpi with a Tango Drum scanner and color corrected in Photoshop. As with all my images, Lightjet or Epson prints are available at www.barryhaynes.cm.

3 BLEND MODES, CALCULATIONS AND APPLY IMAGE

How each of the Blend modes work; the subtleties of using them in Calculations, Apply Image, Layers, Layer Styles, Layer Sets, Fill and the painting tools; when and how to use Calculations versus Apply Image versus Layers.

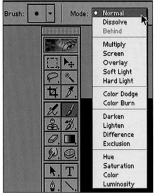

The Blend modes for the painting tools.

The Blend modes for the Fill command.

The Blend modes are used to determine how two groups of image information combine. The two groups of image information could be of various types within Photoshop. The first type could be a photographic image and the second a solid color that is painted or filled on top of the first image. You could do this using one of the painting tools or the Fill command. If you created a layer that was a solid color, you could also combine this layer with a photographic image on a second layer by using a Blend mode in the Layers palette. In the Layers palette, you can determine which Blend mode to use to combine two photographic images in the same layered Photoshop document. Blend modes appear in a variety of ways within the new Photoshop 6 Layer Styles palette. There they are usually affecting the way some sort of shadow or shading will look. You can use the Apply Image command with different Blend modes to combine two-color photographic images that are in separate documents and have the exact same pixel dimensions. Finally, you can use the Calculations command with Blend modes to combine two images of the same size when you want a black-and-white mask channel as a result. The Blend modes appear in the painting tools, the Fill tool, the Layers palette, the Layer Styles palette, the Apply Image command, the Calculations command, and the Stroke command. Not all of the Blend mode options are offered

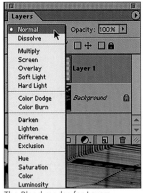

The Blend modes for Layers.

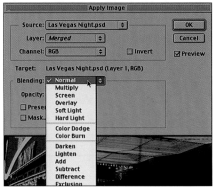

The Blend modes for the Apply Image command.

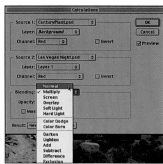

The Blend modes for Calculations.

in each of these areas. As we explain each Blend mode, you'll see why some of them make more sense in one area or another. Many of these options also offer you a way to use a mask as you combine the two groups of image information. The mask will affect the parts of the two groups that are combined.

THE TOOLS FOR BLENDING

First, we discuss the different tools and methods for blending and when it makes the most sense to use each of them. Later, we discuss each of the Blend modes and its unique applications within each of the different blending tools. You can find many of the images we use in this chapter in the Blend Modes Cals & Apl Im folder on the CD. Although this is not entirely a step-by-step hands-on session, we encourage you to play and explore these techniques with the images. By playing on your own, you learn new things, and you can have a lot of fun, too.

THE FILL COMMAND

The Edit/Fill command (Shift-Delete) is used to fill a selection, or the entire layer if there is no selection, with something like the foreground or background color, or from a pattern or the History Brush location. The Blend mode and Opacity in the Fill tool just determine how this filling image will combine with what was there before. Normal, at 100% opacity, completely covers what was there before with the new color, pattern or image. I mention image because you can change the "Use" pop-up to fill from the current History Brush setting or from a pattern. An opacity of 50% will give half what was there before and half the new filled image or color. We usually use Fill to completely cover a selection or the entire image with a solid color or a tint. We also use Fill a lot to revert the selected area to a Snapshot or other location in the History palette. When you use Fill, you need to pick a Source, Opacity, and Blend mode before you do the operation, and then you have to undo it if you want to change it. If you need to prototype the opacity or mode of your Fill, use the layer techniques we show you in this book because it is quicker to make variations in the Layers palette. We used Fill to get the highlight effects in the pop-up dialog boxes on the previous page. Because we wanted them all to look the same, we just used the Rectangular Marquee to select the Blend Mode pop-up menu, used Select/Inverse to invert that selection, and then used Fill with 40% black in Normal mode to get the effect.

THE PAINTING TOOLS

You use a painting tool when you want to apply an effect by hand and softly blend it in and out, like you would do with an airbrush or paintbrush. These tools in Photoshop have a lot more power, however, due to the magic of digital imaging and the blending modes. Go through Chapter 4: "The Tool Palette" to learn about the subtleties of each painting tool. With the Blend Mode options in the painting tools, you don't just lay down paint, or even a previous version of the image. Instead, you can control how this paint or image combines with what is already there. Add the Photoshop History palette and the ability to use the History Brush to paint from any step in the last 100 steps, and you have super power and flexibility. This History Brush also allows you to use the Blend modes. See Chapter 8: "History Palette, History Brush and Snapshots" for more information.

COMBINING IMAGES USING LAYERS

Layers and Adjustment layers are the most powerful ways to combine two or more images while keeping the most options open for further variations and many

Here's how we created the highlighted pop-ups on the previous page with Fill. We selected the pop-up with the Marquee tool and then used Select/Inverse followed by the above Fill command.

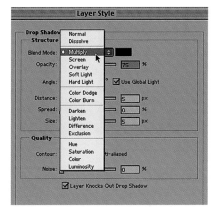

The Blend modes for layer styles appear in various places within the Layer Styles dialog but are usually the same set of Blend modes.

The Night Cab Ride image produced using many layers.

versions of your composite. Sometimes we use layers even when we are dealing with a pattern or solid color. The reason is that with layers, you can always go back and change something, move something, change the opacity or Blend mode without having to totally redo your image. Unlike the contents of the History palette, which go away when you close the file, layers stay around as long as you want. You can try an effect and be able to turn it on and off at will. Layers gives you the most sophisticated control of the Blend modes as well as many other abilities at the same time. If you don't understand layers, and if you haven't read Chapter 7: "Layers, Layer Masks and Adjustment Layers," you should read it now before you continue. When you use layers, your files may get much bigger because many layers add at least the original size of the file in that layer to your document size. Adjustment layers allow you to do color changes and some types of fills with a new layer without adding all the extra file size. Layered documents have to be saved in Photoshop format to maintain the flexible layer information. Still, layers are WAY COOL!

COMBINING IMAGES, LAYERS, AND CHANNELS USING APPLY IMAGE

The basic function of Apply Image is to copy one image, layer, or channel, called the Source image, and use it to replace another image, layer, or channel, the Target image, of exactly the same pixel resolution. To combine two items with Apply Image, they must be exactly the same width and height in pixels. The two images are combined using a blending mode and opacity that are chosen from the Apply Image dialog box. You can optionally choose a mask, which will combine the images only where the mask is white. Apply Image is useful when copying a channel or layer from one place to another, especially when you want to put it on top of an existing channel or layer and combine the two with a Blend mode.

Before you enter Apply Image, you should choose the Target image, layer, or channel. This will be modified when you leave Apply Image by choosing OK, so you may want to first make a copy of that target item.

The Las Vegas Night image.

The Century Plant image.

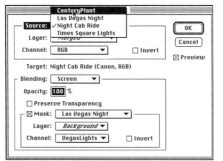

The Vegas Lights mask.

Here we see most of the possible options of Apply Image. Before we entered Image/Apply Image, we made Night Cab Ride the active document in Photoshop. Canon was the active layer within that document. This active item is always selected as the Target of Apply Image, so you will be changing that document, channel, or layer. The Source pop-up window shows you only documents that are the same pixel size and dimensions as the target document. Here, we chose the Century Plant as the Source. The Blending pop-up is where you choose the Blend mode. There is an optional mask, selected here, which causes the blending to happen only within the areas of the mask that are white. If the Preview button is on, you see the results of the Apply Image in the Target window. This lets you try different options and see what they do.

The results of the Apply Image settings shown in the previous illustration. The Century Plant image is brought into the Night Cab Ride composite where the Las Vegas Night mask was white. In that area, it is blended with the Canon layer using the Screen Blending mode.

Chapter 31: Blend Modes, Calculations and Apply Image

If the Preview button is on, you can see the results of the operation in the Target window. In choosing the source, you can pick any open document, layer, or channel, as long as it's the same exact pixel dimensions as the target. Like the source, the mask can be any open document, layer, or channel that is the same pixel dimensions as the target. The Preserve Transparency option, which is enabled if the target has transparent areas, will stop the Apply Image command from changing any transparent areas within a layer. Both the source and the mask have an Invert checkbox that you can check to turn that channel or layer to its negative.

In this chapter, we use three images that we have cropped to be exactly the same pixel size. They are the Las Vegas Night image, the Century Plant image, and a modified Night Cab Ride image. The Las Vegas Night image has a mask, called VegasLights, that is white where the neon lights are. There are no particular masks in the Century Plant image. Here are some other examples of using Apply Image, using the same three

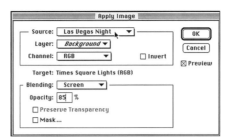

The Times Square Canon image.

The Las Vegas Night image.

Here we see a more simple application of Apply Image. The source, target, and resulting images are shown here. The Screen Blend mode is analogous to taking transparencies of the two images and projecting them onto the same screen from two different slide projectors. The light areas of the images are emphasized. Setting the opacity to 85% made the Las Vegas Lights a little less bright in the composite image below.

The composited image.

images, so you can get an idea what the command does. If you want to get a result that is more than one channel deep, you need to use Apply Image instead of Calculations. The effects you can create with Apply Image can also be achieved by using layers, by first copying the different components into a layer document. Layers give you more flexibility because the different layers don't have to start out being the exact same size and you can move them around side-to-side as well as above-and-below in relationship to each other. Effects within layers can also be done and undone in multiple combinations using the Eye icons.

You should use Apply Image mostly in cases where you already know the spatial relationship between the objects being combined, and you have to do the operation quickly for some production purpose. Motion picture and multimedia work (where you are compositing many frames of two sequences together that have been preshot in registration, to be lined up exactly) is a good example of how you would use Apply Image. This process could be automated over hundreds of frames by using actions with a batch or by using some other application automation software.

COMBINING CHANNELS USING CALCULATIONS

The main purpose of the Calculations command is to use the Blend modes to combine images, layers, or channels and end up with a single black-and-white channel as the result. When you need a color result, use Apply Image; when you need a channel result, use Calculations. Calculations provides for two source files, Source 1 and Source 2, and a Result file. When you enter Calculations, all three of these files are set to the active window within Photoshop. You can use the pop-up menus to change any of these files to any other open file that has the same pixel dimensions. The source files are the two that will be combined using the Blend mode that you choose. The Layer pop-up on each of these files is available for layered documents

The Tools for Blending

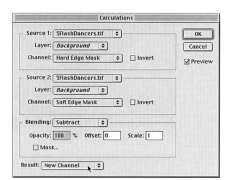

Here are the Calculations settings to produce the mask of the glow without the sign. When doing a Subtract, the item that you want to subtract should be in Source 1. The item you are subtracting from should be in Source 2. In this case, the result was a new channel. Depending on the choice we make for the Result, it could be a new channel in the existing file, a new file itself, or a selection in the existing file.

The Flashdancers sign where we want to make a mask of just the glow without the sign so we can have separate control over each.

We have a hard-edge mask of just the sign. We put this into Source 1.

We have a soft-edge mask of the glow, including the area of the sign. We put this into Source 2.

Here is the resulting glow mask where we subtracted the hard-edge mask from the soft-edge mask.

To move the sign to another background, we used the hard-edge mask to copy the text into one layer and the glow mask to copy the glow into another layer. We then had separate color, blending and blur control over each item in the sign that allowed us to get the result we wanted on the new background.

With the Channel pop-up, you can select any channel including Transparency and layer masks.

and allows you to choose the merged layer, which is the composite of all layers that currently have their Eye icons on or any other layer in the document.

The Channel pop-up allows you to choose any channel in the chosen file or layer. To access a layer mask channel, you need to first choose the layer that owns that layer mask. You can also choose the Transparency channel, which is a mask of any transparent areas in the chosen layer. This interface allows you to blend any two documents, layers, or channels that are open by using the blending modes, and to then put the result into a new channel, document or selection. These open items must have the same pixel dimensions as the active window. The blending interface also allows an optional mask, which will force the blending to happen only in the areas that are white in the mask. Both source items and the mask have an Invert checkbox to optionally invert any of them before doing the composite. You will learn more about Apply Image and Calculations as you go through each of the Blend modes next.

UNDERSTANDING EACH BLEND MODE

Let's start out with the Blend modes listed in the Edit/Fill command, which would have the same effect as the Blend modes used by the painting tools if you were painting with the same color, pattern, or image that you were filling with. When you use the Fill command, you fill a selected area. You can fill with the foreground or background colors as well as from the History palette or from a pattern. All these options are available to paint from by using different flavors of the painting tools. When you paint, you select your "fill area" as you paint instead of from a selection. In either case, the modes work the same. Some of these modes also apply to layers and to the Calculations and Apply Image commands.

Chapter 31: Blend Modes, Calculations and Apply Image

NORMAL

When painting or filling in Normal mode, you are filling the selected or painted area with the foreground or background color, the History palette, or a pattern. Normal mode for a top layer in the Layers palette means that the top layer will be opaque at 100% opacity. You will not see any of the layers below through this layer. You use Normal mode in Calculations or Apply Image to copy the source layer or channel to the target, or destination layer, or channel without any blending. This totally replaces the target, or destination, with the source.

DISSOLVE

Depending on the opacity of the dissolve, this mode appears to take the opacity as a percentage of the pixels from the blend color and place them on top of the base color. The base color is the color or image that was there before the dissolve. The blend color is the color or image that is being dissolved on top of the base color or image. Try this with two layers, setting the mode between them to Dissolve. If you set the opacity to 100%, you get all of the top layer and don't see the bottom layer. The same thing happens if you use a fill of 100% or paint at 100% in Dissolve mode. When you set the opacity to 50% and look at the pixels up close, you will see that there are about 50% pixels from the top layer and 50% from the bottom. If you set the opacity to 10%, only 10% of the pixels are from the top layer or color.

With Dissolve, the pixels seem to be entirely from one image or the other; there don't seem to be any blended pixels. If you want to achieve this type of look between two images but have more control over the pattern used to create the dissolve, create a layer mask on the top layer filled with solid white. Now, go into the Add Noise filter and add Gaussian noise to the layer mask. Where the noise is black, the bottom layer will show through and you will get an effect similar to Dissolve. This way you can use Levels or Curves or even a filter to change the pattern in the layer mask and thus change how the two images are combined. The more noise you add, the more you will see of the bottom layer. Also, in this case, some of the pixels can actually be blends between the layers, especially if you use Gaussian Blur to blur your layer mask too. Dissolve is not an option with Apply Image or Calculations, but you can get a similar effect here by using a Gaussian noise mask as you combine images, layers, and channels.

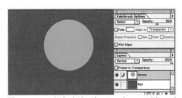

The green circle is in the top layer with red in the bottom layer. Now both layers' Eye icons are on.

Here is just the circle with the Red layer turned off. The transparent area shows up as a checkered pattern.

BEHIND

This Blend mode is used to paint into the transparent part of a layer. It is available only from Fill and the painting tools and only if the layer has a transparent area. It is not available if the Preserve Transparency checkbox is checked for that layer. Behind allows you to paint a shadow or color behind an object (like a circle) in the layer, using a painting tool or the Fill command. The actual image in the layer won't be affected because Behind only paints into the transparent area. Painting in Behind mode is like painting on the back of the acetate. Here we see a shadow that was added to a circle using the Paintbrush tool in Behind mode with a large soft brush.

We have painted black into this transparent area using Behind mode with a large soft brush.

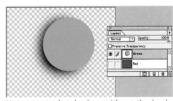

Here we see the shadow without the background color. When painting in Behind mode, we didn't have to worry about painting on top of the green. It is automatically masked out because it is not transparent.

Understanding Each Blend Mode

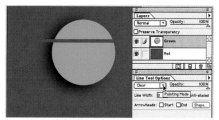

Here we used the Photoshop 5 Line tool to create the red line going across the circle by drawing the line in Clear mode. Clear mode is no longer available in the Photoshop 6 Line tool since it now creates a Shape layer where it used to be a pixel-based tool.

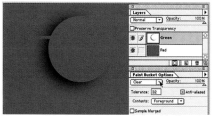

Here we clicked on the green circle with the Paint Bucket in Clear mode leaving only the shadow with this nice effect.

A Multiply of the Century Plant and Las Vegas Night images, from the third page of this chapter, emphasizes the darker areas of each image.

CLEAR

The Clear mode is available only when in a layered document from the Fill command and the Paint Bucket tool. It will fill the selected area with transparency. This is the little checkerboard pattern that means you can see the layers below through the transparent areas. Clear is also available as a menu item from the Edit menu, although Edit/Clear behaves a little differently depending on whether you are in a normal layer or a *Background* layer. When in a normal layer, Edit/Clear fills the selected area with transparency. When in a *Background* layer, Edit/Clear fills the selected area with the background color.

This brings up an interesting thing about Photoshop and how it deals with layers and the special layer called the *Background* layer. When you open a TIFF file or some other file that doesn't contain layers into Photoshop and then go into the Layers palette, you will notice that these files contain a single layer called *Background*. This isn't really a layer in the true sense of the word, because it is locked in that it can't have any transparent areas and you can't move it with the Move tool. You can paint on it though and if you make a selection in a Background layer of an image and then choose Edit/Clear, the selected area will be filled with the background color. You will notice that Clear does not show up as an available option for a Background layer within Fill or the Paint Bucket tools. If you double-click on this special Background layer within the Layers palette and rename it something else, it will turn into a normal layer. Now, Edit/Clear will fill a selection with transparency, and Clear is available in the Fill and Paint Bucket tools. You can also now move this newly created real layer with the Move tool! Until you rename the *Background* layer and make it a real layer, you can't interchange its order in the Layers palette with other layers.

MULTIPLY

Multiply is a very useful Blend mode that is available within all the Blend mode pop-ups. When you multiply two images together, it is analogous to what you would see if both the images were transparencies and you sandwiched them together and placed them on a light table or projected them onto a screen. Anything that was black in either image would be black in the resulting composite image. Anything that was white or clear in either image would let you see through it to what was in the other image in that area. When you multiply two images together, the 0–255 values of the corresponding pixels in each image are actually multiplied together using the following formula:

(Source 1) x (Source 2) / 255 = destination

Just like doing a multiply in mathematics, the order of the Source 1 and Source 2 images doesn't matter. Dividing by 255 at the end forces all the values to be in the 0–255 range. You can see that when either Source value is 0, black, you are going to get 0 as the result. When either Source value is 255, white, you are going to get the other Source value as the result, because 255/255 = 1, so you end up multiplying the other Source value by 1. Multiply is used as the default Blend mode for many of the blend mode pop-ups that occur in the Layer Styles palette. Its sister Blend mode, Screen, also shows up there as the default in some cases.

SCREEN

Screen is sort of the opposite of Multiply, in that when you do a Screen between two images, anything that is white in either of the images will be white in the resulting image. Anything that is black in either image will show the other image in that black area. Screen, like Multiply, is also available in all the different Blend mode pop-

The original Glow mask we want to drop a gradient into.

Doing a Load Selection on the glow, left, and dropping the gradient into the selected area, produces the halo around the glow at the right side.

Unwanted halo effect

Create the gradient in a separate mask channel and use Calculations to Multiply for the effect at right.

A Calculations Multiply of the Gradient and Glow mask channels drops the gradient into the glow area without a halo.

A powerful use for Multiply is to seamlessly add a gradient to an existing selection. Let's say we wanted to use the Glow mask to create a glow that was bright at the left side and fading toward the right. To do this, we would want to drop a gradient into this mask. If you do a Load Selection on the mask and then create the gradient within that selection, you will get a light halo around the edge of the gradient toward the right side. This is caused by the loaded selection. To avoid getting this halo, just create the gradient in a separate channel and then multiply the two channels together, giving you a better fade.

ups. When you Screen two images together, it is analogous to what you would see if both the images were projected from two different slide projectors onto the same screen. Here is the formula for Screen:

255 - ((255 - Source 1) x (255 - Source 2) / 255) = Destination

You can simulate the Screen command using the Multiply command if you first invert both of the Source images and then multiply them together, and finally, invert the result of that multiply. That is exactly what this formula for Screen does: (255 - Source1) does an Invert of Source 1. With the Screen formula then: The Invert of Source 1 is multiplied by the Invert of Source 2 and then is divided by 255. That part of the formula does the multiply of the two inverted images. Finally, subtracting that result from 255 at the end does the Invert of the result of that multiply, giving you a Screen. The important thing to remember between Screen and Multiply is that a Screen of two images will emphasize the lighter areas and a Multiply will emphasize the darker areas.

A screen of the Century Plant and Las Vegas Night images emphasizes the lighter areas of each image.

Soft Light

In Soft Light mode, the original image is blended with the blend color, pattern, or image by making the original image either lighter or darker depending on the blend image. If the blend image is lighter than 50% gray, the original image is lightened in a subtle way. Even where the blend image is pure white, the resulting image will just be lighter than before, not pure white. If the blend image is darker than 50% gray, the original image is darkened in a subtle way. Even where the blend image is pure black, the resulting image will just be darker than before, not pure black. The tonal values and details of the original are fairly preserved, just subtly modified by the blend image. If you add a 50% gray layer above an original image and set the Blend mode to Soft Light, you can then use a soft brush and paint or airbrush with white or black to dodge or burn the image by lightening or darkening this gray layer. Use less than 100% opacity on your brush to get more subtle effects. This is better than using the dodging or burning tool because it's infinitely adjustable since you're not actually changing the original image. You can easily get a 50% gray layer by clicking the New Layer icon in the Layers palette, choosing Edit/Fill, and filling at 100% Opacity with Use: 50% Gray and Mode: Normal.

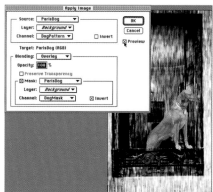

Apply Image was originally used to prototype the Paris Dog examples. The mask used to isolate the dog is seen here but we invert it to actually get the effect in the background.

The original ParisDog image.

The original Dog pattern.

The Dog mask before inverting.

To actually produce the final images, I set up a two-layer document and then used File/Save As to save each flattened TIFF version after changing only the Blend mode between each save. That was just a faster production choice.

The examples shown here use Apply Image and layers to combine my ParisDog image with a pattern that I created in Photoshop and a mask that stops the dog itself from being affected by the pattern. I initially tried this out using Apply Image. The original ParisDog image, the grayscale DogPattern, and the DogMask were all in the same file. Before entering Apply Image, I selected the RGB background layer of ParisDog; this made that the target. For the source, I selected the DogPattern, which applies the pattern on top of the ParisDog. I set the mode to Overlay to create the effect and then decided that I didn't want the pattern on the dog. Choosing the Mask option allowed me to pick the Dog mask, and the Invert checkbox was turned on because the mask was actually white in the dog area. Turning on Invert made the mask white in the background and the white area of the mask is where the DogPattern image is applied. With the Preview button on, I tried all the different Blend modes and could see that I wanted to use this as an example. At this point, I was going to have to produce five versions of this image, one for each Blend mode. When you use Apply Image, it actually changes the Target image, so to do five versions with Apply Image, I would have had to make five copies of the ParisDog, one for each Blend mode.

A more efficient way to do this, after prototyping the effect with Apply Image, was then to create the five versions from a layered document. The bottom layer was the ParisDog image. I added a layer above this for the Dog-Pattern, and to that layer I added a layer mask for the inverted DogMask channel. Now to produce the five different versions, all I had to do was change the Blend mode in the Layers palette, once for each version, and then choose File/Save As for each version to make a flattened TIFF copy with all channels and layers removed. For more information on using layer masks, see Chapter 30: "The PowerBook Ad" or Chapter 28: "The Rain in Costa Rica."

Again, Photoshop layers are a great prototyping and production tool! When I took this photo on a residential alley in Paris, the dog was in this pose as I walked by. I pointed and focused my camera, and then the dog went back inside just as I was about to shoot. I stood there for a bit with the camera ready, and, sure enough, the dog returned and posed for me. It has always been one of my favorite shots.

Overlay: This is contrasty but it still preserves some of the tone and detail from the original.

Multiply: Notice how dark the shadows are compared to Overlay.

Screen: Notice how bright the highlights are compared to Overlay.

Soft Light: This preserves the most tone and detail from the original.

Hard Light: The highlight and shadow values and the lightness values come pretty much directly from the pattern.

Understanding Each Blend Mode

Hard Light

In Hard Light mode, the original image is blended with the blend color, pattern, or image by making the original image either lighter or darker depending on the blend image. If the blend image is lighter than 50% gray, the original image is lightened and this lightening is a contrasty effect. If the blend image is pure white, the resulting image will be pure white. If the blend image is darker than 50% gray, the original image is darkened and this darkening is a contrasty effect. If the blend image is pure black, the resulting image will be pure black. In Hard Light mode, the resulting image seems to take its lightness value from the blend color, pattern, or image. Because the tonal values of the original are not very preserved, the adjustment is a radical one. If you add a 50% gray layer above an original image and set the Blend mode to Hard Light, you can then use a soft brush and paint with white or black to dodge or burn the image by lightening or darkening this gray layer. This will be a radical, contrasty dodge and burn. Use less than 100% opacity on your brush or you will get pure white or black. Remember that this effect is infinitely adjustable because you are not actually changing the original image. See the "Soft Light" section for how to get a 50% gray layer above the image.

Overlay

Overlay does a combination of Multiply and Screen modes. The dark areas of an original image are multiplied and the light areas are screened. The highlights and shadows are somewhat preserved, because dark areas of the image will not be as dark as if you were doing a Multiply and light areas will not be as bright as if you were doing a Screen. The tonal values and details of the original are preserved to some extent, but this is a more contrasty transition than Soft Light, just not as radical as Hard Light.

Darken and Lighten

The Darken and Lighten Blend modes are easy to understand. In the Darken mode, each of the corresponding pixels from the original image and the blend color, pattern, or image are compared, and the darker of the two is chosen for the result. In the case of Lighten, the lighter of the two pixels is chosen for the result. These Blend modes are most useful in combining masks to create new masks. An example of this, shown here, would be the situation in which you have pasted two objects into a composite scene and for each object you have a mask. When you paste in Photoshop, you always have a mask of the object, which is the transparency of the object's layer. You have a mask of each separate object, and now you need one mask that contains both objects at the same time.

Using Calculations to set the Blend mode to Lighten between the two masks will create the mask of both the objects. You can then use the inverse of this mask to give you a mask of the background. To

The shoes and the glasses have each been placed here separately.

You have one mask for the shoes.

Another mask for the glasses.

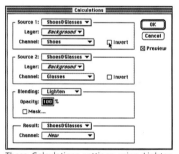

These Calculations settings using Lighten will create the new mask below to the left.

This mask of both shoes and glasses was created with Calculations using Lighten.

To create this background mask with a single calculation, invert both the source masks and use Darken instead of Lighten.

do this in one step, select the Invert checkboxes on both the Source channels in Calculations. Because both Source masks have now been inverted, you would have to use Darken to combine the two masks and get the final inverted mask with the white background.

DIFFERENCE AND EXCLUSION

Difference is one of the most useful blending modes. Difference compares two images and gives you a mask that is black where each of the two images are exactly the same and is nonblack and closer to white the more the images are different from each other. Here is the formula for Difference:

| Source 1 - Source 2 | = Destination

Difference is similar to Subtract but the results are never inverted; they are always positive because the two vertical bars stand for absolute value and therefore make the result positive. With a little photographic planning, you can use Difference to automatically separate an image from its background. Pick a background that is quite different in color and brightness from the objects to be shot. First, place the objects, adjust your lighting, and shoot them. Without moving the tripod or changing the lighting, shoot the background without the objects. If these two photographs are scanned in register, doing a Difference between them can often automatically give you a mask of just the objects. The two objects in the example here were shot on a tripod using a Kodak DCS electronic camera. When using an electronic camera, scanning the images in register is no problem because they are sent directly from the camera to the computer. In this case, we had the computer in the studio, so we could try Difference between the two images and then adjust the lighting and exposure to make sure we'd get the best knock-out. Actually, to create the final mask of the objects in this case, we used Calculations first to do a Difference between the Red channels of the two images; then we used Calculations again to Screen the results of the Difference with itself. Screening an image (or mask) with itself brings out the brighter parts of the image. We then brought this Screened mask into Levels and increased its brightness and contrast slightly again to darken the blacks and brighten the whites. Finally we did some quick editing of the masks of the actual objects. Still, this process was faster using Difference and Screen than if we had done the knock-out by hand. Using Difference to do knock-outs works even better for objects that have no shadows or where the shadow is not needed in the knock-out.

A digital camera hooked up to a computer is a reality for more and more photographers today, especially those who do a lot of repetitive catalog work. Also, consider the motion picture industry or multimedia applications where artists or technicians might

The objects as originally shot with the Kodak DCS system.

The background shot with the same lighting and camera position.

Difference between the Red channels of the background and the object shots. Try each channel and see which does the best job.

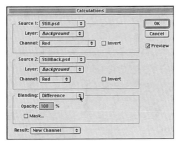
These Calculations settings using Difference will create the mask to the left.

Above mask after some quick edits and a brightness adjustment with Levels. Sometimes using Calculations to Screen a mask with itself will bring out the bright values even more. After that, Levels can by used to redarken the shadows, adjust the shadow midtones, and further brighten the highlights that represent the objects you are knocking out.

New background placed behind the objects using an inverted version of the mask to the left. Check out these images on the CD for this chapter in a folder named "Still, StillBk Difference Stuff." The Channels palette in the Still.psd file has these channels along with hints about how I made them. Try it yourself and have some fun!

The positive version of the image.

The negative version of the image.

Exclusion of the top Black to White layer with the positive image in the layer below.

Layer setup for Exclusion above.

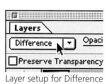

Layer setup for Difference below.

Difference of the top Black blending to White layer with the positive image in the layer below.

have to knock out hundreds or even thousands of frames to composite two sequences together. With Difference and a little computer-controlled camera work, this situation could also be automated. Say you're shooting some guys on horses riding across a field that you will later want to superimpose on another scene. Have a computer remember all the frame-by-frame motion of the camera while shooting the scene. Now immediately, while the lighting hasn't changed, use the computer to move the camera back to the original position at the beginning of the scene. With computer control, reshoot all those frames without the horses to just get the backgrounds. Now using Difference and an Actions Batch, to automate hundreds of frames, you can quickly create a knock-out of all those frames.

Exclusion is similar to Difference but not as intense. An Exclusion with black will do nothing to the image, as will a Difference with black. An Exclusion with white will invert the image completely, as will a Difference with white. An Exclusion with 50% gray leaves you with 50% gray, whereas a Difference with 50% gray still changes the image to make it appear partially negative. A Difference from black blending toward white is a slow transition from a positive image to a negative image with no gray section in the middle. In an Exclusion from black blending toward white, the portion from black to 50% gray is actually a transition from the positive image toward 50% gray. From 50% gray, the image turns more negative as we proceed toward white, where the image is totally negative.

ADD AND SUBTRACT

Add and Subtract are available only in Apply Image and Calculations. Add takes the corresponding pixels of the original and the blend image and adds them together using the following formula:

Add = (Source 2 + Source 1) / Scale) + Offset = Destination

Subtract takes the corresponding pixels of the original and the blend image and subtracts them using this formula:

Subtract = (Source 2 - Source 1) / Scale) + Offset = Destination

Scale and Offset are additional parameters that you use with these blending modes in Apply Image or Calculations. The normal values for Scale and Offset for both Add and Subtract are 1 and 0. The order of the Source 1 and Source 2 parameters doesn't matter with Add, but it definitely does with Subtract. The Source 1 parameter is always subtracted from the Source 2 parameter, and the result has to be in the 0–255 range. When Source 1 is white, 255, which represents a selection, the result of the Subtract will always be black. The effect of the Subtract is then to remove the selected areas of the Source 1 mask from the selected areas of the Source 2 mask. This is a very useful function. Of the two, Subtract is the Blend mode I use more often, and I usually do Subtracts between masks. See the example of Subtract with Calculations earlier in this chapter.

When doing either an Add or a Subtract, the Offset value will make the resulting mask lighter if the offset is positive, and darker if the offset is negative. The offset is a number, in the 0.255 range, that will be added to the result of each corresponding pixel's calculations. If we do an Add of two images and set the scale to 2, we are getting an average of the two. This would give us the same result having one image in a layer on top of the other with the top image having a Normal Blend mode and 50% opacity.

Chapter 31: Blend Modes, Calculations and Apply Image

HUE, SATURATION, COLOR, AND LUMINOSITY

These blending modes will affect the original image by using either the hue, saturation, color, or luminosity of the blend color, pattern, or image as the hue, saturation, color, or luminosity of the original image. In these examples, combining the two sides of the desert (the original desert Century Plant and Las Vegas), you can see how the Century Plant scene is modified by the hue, saturation, color, and luminosity of the Las Vegas Night scene. The Las Vegas scene has very intense hues that are also very saturated, so it is easy to see what happens with these two images. To get these different effects, we placed the Las Vegas scene as a layer on top of the Century Plant layer and just changed the layer Blend mode of the Las Vegas layer. In Hue mode, you see the hues from the Las Vegas scene, but the saturation and the intensity of those hues, and all the details, come from the Century Plant scene. In Saturation mode, the highly saturated values from the bright neon lights intensify the more subtle hues and details from the Century Plant scene. Color mode combines the hue and saturation from Las Vegas with the details, or luminosity, of Century Plant. When you put the Las Vegas scene in Luminosity mode, then you are seeing all the details from that Las Vegas scene but the more subtle hue and saturation values from the Century Plant. In the Las Vegas scene, there are large black areas. These have no hue or saturation values, which is why they show up as gray when in Hue, Saturation, or Color modes.

The Las Vegas Night image.

The Century Plant image.

A more interesting way to combine these two images is to double-click on the Las Vegas layer to bring up the Layer Style dialog. Moving the left, Shadow, slider to the right in the This Layer part at the bottom of the Advanced Blending area of Layer Style, removes the black part of the Las Vegas scene from the composite. In the final example of this image, we have used the Move tool to move the Las Vegas layer up a little bit. Now Las Vegas is at the end of the trail in the desert. We then double-clicked on the Las Vegas layer to bring up its Layer Style dialog. We are in Luminosity mode, but the colors of the Century Plant image show through in the black areas of Las Vegas because we have moved the Shadow sliders of This Layer over to the right.

First, we moved the Shadow slider of the This Layer slider to the right to 10. That removed all the digital values from 0 to 10 from the composite, allowing the Century Plant to show through. This produces jaggy edges on the transition between Las Vegas and the Century Plant backgrounds. By holding down the Option key and sliding the rightmost part of the Shadow slider further to the right, the Shadow slider has now split. We moved the rightmost part of this slider to 35. The meaning of this is that the black values in Las Vegas from 0 to 10 are completely removed, and the values from 11 to 35 are blended out making a softer edge between these two images.

The Las Vegas Hue with the Century Plant saturation and luminosity.

The Las Vegas Saturation with the Century Plant hue and luminosity.

The Las Vegas Color (hue and saturation), with the Century Plant luminosity.

The Las Vegas Luminosity with the Century Plant hue and saturation.

The Luminosity values in Las Vegas from 36 to 255 are still retained within this composite. For more information on this powerful Layer Style dialog box, see Chapter 7: "Layers, Layer Masks and Adjustment Layers," and Chapter 33: "Posterize, Bitmaps, Textures and Patterns."

COLOR DODGE AND COLOR BURN

Color Dodge brightens the original image as the blending color goes further toward white. A Color Dodge with black does nothing; then as the blending color gets lighter, the original image picks up brightness and color more and more from the blending color. Color Burn is similar but opposite. A Color Burn with white does nothing; then as the blending color gets darker, the original image picks up darkness and color more and more from the blending color

PASS THROUGH

Pass Through is a new Blend mode that was created to describe the behavior of layer sets. When you create a layer set, its default Blend mode is set to Pass Through. This means that the layers inside the set will appear in exactly the same way as they would if the set was not there. You can also set a layer set to a different Blend mode but this may dramatically change the total image appearance since this will cause all the layers in the layer set to be composited with themselves almost as if they were a separate image. Once the layers in the layer set are composited with themselves, the result of that composite is then composited, using the chosen Blend mode for the layer set, with the rest of the image as though the layers in the layer set were just a single layer. Choosing a Blend mode other than Pass Through stops the Blend modes of any of the layers inside the layer set from influencing any layers outside the layer set and it can make a big change.

Have fun with all the Photoshop Blend modes!

Here we see the results of using This Layer within Layer Style in Luminosity mode to completely remove the black values in the 0–10 range and to blend out the black values in the 11–35 range from the composite of Las Vegas and the Century Plant. We double-clicked on the Las Vegas layer to get the Layer Style dialog box.

The positive version of the image.

The Black to White layer by itself.

The Spectrum layer by itself.

Chapter 31: Blend Modes, Calculations and Apply Image

Color Burn of the top Black blending to White layer with the positive image in the layer below.

Color Dodge of the top Black blending to White layer with the positive image in the layer below.

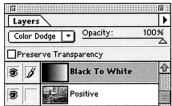

Layer setup for Black to White Color Burn and Dodge above.

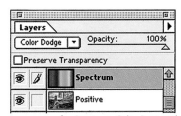

Layer setup for Spectrum Color Burn and Dodge below.

Color Burn of the top Spectrum layer with the positive image in the layer below.

Color Dodge of the top Spectrum layer with the positive image in the layer below.

Understanding Each Blend Mode

32 HANDS-ON SESSION: Layer Clipping Paths, Shape Layers and Layer Styles

Using Photoshop's new vector features to create a knockout using a layer clipping path; exploring shape layers and the infinite possibilities of layer styles.

The internet cafe image before applying the layer clipping paths. This file has three layers, one for the sign, one for the mural, and one for the night sky background.

Of the many new and enhanced features in Photoshop 6, the Layers palette has received several of the most publicized modifications. Improved vector support is provided by the new layer clipping paths and shape layers. A layer clipping path lets you use a path to directly specify areas of layer visibility. Shape layers, also new to this version, allow you to create object-oriented vector shapes that can be edited with all of the precision and flexibility usually found in drawing programs such as Adobe Illustrator. In addition to the standard collection of rectangles, ellipses and polygons, you can also access a preset library of custom shapes, or create and save your own custom shapes. And, if you feel that you need to add a little finesse to your newly created shape layer (or any other layer), the greatly expanded capabilities of layer styles are only a double-click away. This chapter combines a series of step-by-step exercises with explanations to help you get up to speed on the features of layer clipping paths, shape layers and layer styles.

LAYER CLIPPING PATHS

A clipping path is a vector-based outline of an image element that "clips" or excludes anything not within its borders. The advantages of using a clipping path versus a pixel-based selection, or layer mask, is that the vector qualities of clipping paths give them a much crisper and more precise edge when printed. Since they are vector based, you can also edit them easily if you need to perfect your initial outline. Clipping paths have been around in Photoshop for a long time. And though you could use them to create a knockout once an image was placed into a page layout program such as QuarkXPress, you couldn't apply them directly to a layer for the purpose of controlling which areas of a layer were visible. In previous Photoshops, you had to convert a path to a selection then convert that to a layer mask to get a similar effect. All that has now changed with Photoshop 6. Any path can be converted into a layer clipping path.

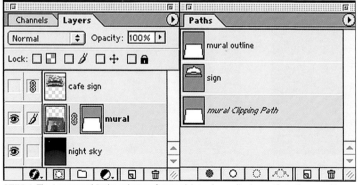

STEP 1: The Layers and Paths palettes after applying a layer clipping path to the mural layer.

STEP 1: **Open the Internet Cafe file from the Ch32LayerStyles folder on the *Photoshop 6 Artistry* CD.** We're going to create knockouts for the wall mural and the cafe sign using the two paths that have already been created for this image. **In the Layers palette, turn off the cafe sign layer temporarily by clicking its Eye icon. Click on the mural layer to make it the active layer. If your Paths palette is not already visible, open it (Window/Show Paths or Shift-F11) and click on the mural path to highlight it. Next, go up to the main menu and select Layer/Add Layer Clipping Path/Current Path.** A clipping path is added to the mural layer, trimming off a bit of the edges. Notice that in the Paths palette, a temporary path labeled mural clipping path shows up. This will only be visible in the paths palette when the mural layer is active.

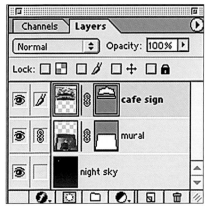

STEP 2: The Layers palette after applying a layer clipping path to the sign layer.

STEP 2: **Turn the Eye icon for the cafe sign layer back on and click on it to make it the active layer. In the Paths palette, click on the sign path to highlight it. Make a layer clipping path the same way as in Step 1 (Layer/Add Layer Clipping Path/Current Path)**. Everything outside the sign path is clipped, or excluded, from view. The important part is that all the pixel information for that layer is still there, it's just not visible when the clipping path is turned on.

STEP 3: **To temporarily turn off a layer clipping path, Shift-click on its thumbnail icon in the Layers palette. Shift-click it again to turn the path back on.**

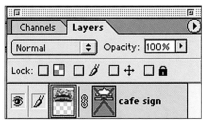

STEP 3: To temporarily turn off a layer clipping path, Shift-click its thumbnail in the layers palette. Shift click on it again to turn it back on.

STEP 4: If you look between the sign and mural layers and their layer clipping paths, you'll see that there is a Chain Link icon. This means that the layer is linked with its clipping path, so that if you move the layer, the clipping path moves with it. This is the default setting when you create a layer clipping path and in most cases you'll probably want to leave it that way. There are some imaging situations, however, where it might be advantageous to unlink the layer from its clipping path. **To get a feel for how this works, click on the link between the cafe sign layer and its clipping path to unlink them. Now, select the Move tool and move the layer around a bit. You'll see that it separates from its clipping path and ruins the effect we just created. Undo your layer movement by choosing Undo from the File menu, or by using the History palette if you've gone beyond a single level of Undo. Click back between the two icons to re-link them.**

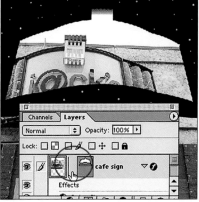

STEP 4: If you click on the chain link between a layer and its clipping path, you will unlink the layer from the path, allowing you to move the two independently. In some situations you may want to do this, but for this effect we need to have the layer linked with its clipping path. Click between the two again to re-link them.

STEP 5: **As a final touch, we'll add a glow effect to the sign. In the Layers palette, click on the small italicized f icon and choose Outer Glow from the drop down-menu. In the middle section of the Outer Glow controls, set the size of the glow to 60 pixels and then click OK.** We'll be going into layer styles in greater detail in the third part of this chapter.

If you find that your layer clipping path is not quite perfect, you can edit it using the same tools as you would with any Bezier path, refer to Chapter 4: "The Tool Palette" for more detailed coverage on creating and editing paths.

The internet cafe image with layer clipping paths applied to the sign and mural layers. For a final touch we used a layer style to add an outer glow around the sign.

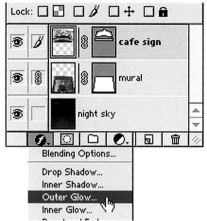

STEP 5: With the cafe sign layer active, click on the Layer Effects icon and choose Outer Glow from the popup menu.

WORKING WITH SHAPE LAYERS

Since version 2.0, Photoshop has provided vector support in the form of paths that could be created with the same type of precise Bezier drawing tools that are the bread and butter of illustration programs. Paths were, and still are, very useful for creating editable outlines that can be turned into selections for further pixel-based manipulations, or, with this latest version, for making layer clipping paths for specifying areas of layer visibility. Now, with the addition of vector shape layers, Photoshop adds a whole new level of functionality to its already impressive list of features.

Photoshop 6 added a new layer type called a Solid Color fill layer, which is like an Adjustment layer that is filled with a solid color. Like all adjustment layers, a Solid Color fill layer is very efficient because it actually doesn't have Red, Green or Blue channels or any actual pixels associated with it. To get a Solid Color fill layer, just choose Layer/New Fill Layer/Solid Color. A shape layer is actually just a Solid Color fill layer with a layer clipping path attached that describes the shape. The color only shows through the areas inside the path. Since the path, or shape, is vector-based, it remains editable long after its initial creation. You could start with a simple rectangle, for instance, and then, using the Direct Selection Arrow tool and some of its keyboard modifiers, transform the rectangle into a completely new shape.

Shape layers are easy and, once you get to know them, you'll soon see how useful they can be for certain image creation tasks. To familiarize yourself with how this new feature works, try going through the steps below. We'll start with some standard shapes and explore basic shape layer creation and modification.

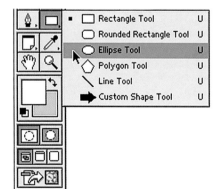

The Shape tools in the Tool palette.

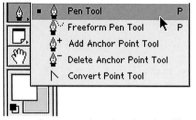

You can also create a shape layer by using either the Pen tool or the Freeform Pen tool to create a path and then by clicking on the Create Shape layer icon in the Options bar which will create a Shape layer with the shape of that path.

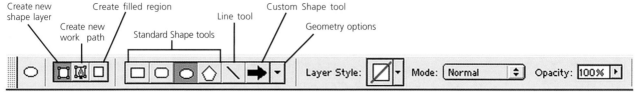

Create new shape layer
Create new work path
Standard Shape tools
Create filled region
Line tool
Custom Shape tool
Geometry options

The Options bar for the Shape tools. The first three buttons on the left allow you to use the shape tools to create a new shape layer, a new work path, or a rasterized filled region. The second set of buttons lets you select the type of tool used to create your shape. The first two buttons, for creating a shape layer or a new work path are also available when you have the Pen tool or Freeform Pen tool selected.

Later in the second part of the exercise, we'll use shape layers to create some Web page navigation elements and also delve into the greatly improved Layer Effects which are now in the Layer Styles palette.

STEP 1: **Use File/New to create a new file having a size of 800 pixels Width, 600 pixels Height and 72 pixels/inch Resolution in RGB mode with the Contents set to White**. This will serve as our canvas to try out some shape layer fundamentals. **Save the file in Photoshop format and call it ShapeLayers.**

STEP 2: **Select the Rectangle Shape tool from Shape pop-up in the tool palette. Check the Options bar at the top of your screen and make sure that the left-most button is selected (if you hover over it with your mouse for a second, a label will appear identifying it as the Create New Shape Layer icon), and click and drag in your image to create a shape.** As with Photoshop's selection marquees, if you hold down the Shift key, you will constrain the shape to a square, holding down the Option key will drag from the center out, and holding down the Spacebar, while in the middle of creating a shape, will let you move the shape on the canvas as you are creating it. The color of the shape will be whatever your foreground color is set to. Notice in your Layers palette that you now have a new layer, called Shape 1, above the white background. This layer has two parts to it, a Color Fill thumbnail on the left showing the actual color of the shape, and a Layer Clipping Path thumbnail on the right which shows the rectangle you created. The color is only showing through inside the bounds of the rectangle.

STEP 3: **Notice that the Options bar changed a bit after you drew the shape.** The first set of icons is different and they control how additional shapes will interact with the current shape. Whenever you see this state of the Options bar as a Shape tool or Pen tool is selected, it means that a shape layer is currently active, and any new shapes you draw will be affecting the current active shape, either by adding new area to your shape, subtracting from it, or modifying it using the Intersect and Exclude operations. We'll get to those options a bit later. **Use the Swatches palette or Color Picker to choose a new foreground color. To return the Options bar to its previous state and allow you to make a new, separate shape layer, simply click on the Shape 1 clipping path icon, the rightmost one, in the Layers palette.** If you click on it several times, you'll see that the Options bar toggles back and forth between the two states. Make sure that you have it set to the way it looked when you made the first shape (see the illustration at the top of the page). **Now select the Ellipse tool from the Tool Palette Shape pop-up; then click and drag out an oval shape on top of the rectangle. Try using the Shift key to constrain it to a circle, or the Option key to draw it from the center out.**

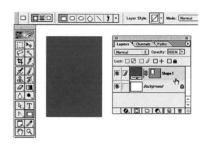

STEP 2: Select a Shape tool and drag out a shape on your image canvas. A shape layer is actually a Solid Color Fill layer with a vector clipping path attached that defines where the color is visible. The path "clips" the areas outside it so the color doesn't show there.

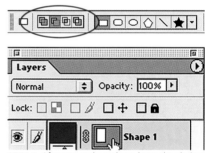

STEP 3: After you make a shape layer, the choices in the Options bar change slightly. The icons on the left control how a new shape will interact with an existing shape. To return the Options bar to its previous state in preparation for a creating a new, separate shape layer, click once on the clipping path icon for Shape 1.

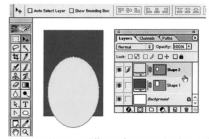

STEP 3:: Choose a different foreground color, and the Ellipse tool, and make a second shape layer.

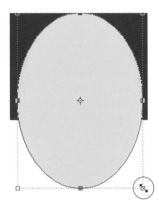

STEP 4: With the Move tool (V) selected and a layer active, you can show a rectangular bounding box around a layer's content.

STEP 4: With the bounding box showing, position your cursor over one of the handles until it changes to a small double-headed arrow and click once. You now have access to the numerous capabilities of Free Transform and Numeric Transform. For Free Transform, manipulate the handles, for Numeric, use the controls in the Options bar. Hit Enter or Return to apply your transformations.

STEP 5: The Direct Selection tool

STEP 4: The Layers palette now shows that you have two distinct shape layers, a rectangle (Shape 1) and an oval (Shape 2). If you switch to the Move tool (V), you can click and drag to move the active layer into a new position. With the Move tool selected and a layer active, you'll see that the Options bar has changed once again. Click the Show Bounding Box option in the Options bar. This places a rectangular bounding box around your layer content. The really cool thing about this, however, is that the handles on the bounding box give you immediate access to Photoshop's Free Transform tool and Numeric Transform controls. To transform the shape, simply position your cursor over one of the handles until you see it change to a small double-headed arrow, then click once. Using the handles on the box, you can now scale the shape larger or smaller, rotate it, skew it, shear it or distort it. To apply precise numeric transformations, use the controls that are now visible in the Options bar. To finalize your transformations, hit the Enter or Return keys. For a detailed explanation of the Transform features, Chapter 9: "Transformation of Images, Layers, Paths and Selections."

STEP 4: When you click on a corner of the layer content bounding box, the Options Bar gives you controls for precise numeric transformations.

MODIFYING SHAPES WITH THE DIRECT SELECTION TOOL

STEP 5: For more precise editing of a vector shape, you can use the Direct Selection tool. This tool gives you control over each individual point and the lines connecting the points. If you're familiar with editing Bezier paths in Illustrator or earlier versions of Photoshop, then this tool will be very familiar, although it has changed somewhat from the way it worked in Photoshop 5 or 5.5. **Select the tool by clicking and holding on the black arrow icon midway down the Tool palette and from the pop-out box, choose the white arrow icon representing the Direct Selection tool (or type A then Shift-A until you see the white arrow in the Tool palette).**

STEP 6: **Click on the visible path edge of the oval shape layer.** If no path is showing in your main document window, simply click inside the shape and it will become visible. Notice that the oval shape has four square points. Depending on the oval that you created, and how you may have modified it with Free Transform, you may see directional handles sticking out from some or all of the points. **Click on one of the points at the**

STEP 6: Clicking on the edge of the vector shape will activate the points and control handles.

STEP 6: Click on a point and drag to modify the shape.

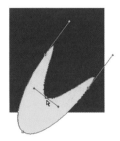

STEP 6: After dragging the point inward, the elliptical shape is beginning to look a bit like a Star Trek insignia.

STEP 6: Dragging the control handles on a point will reshape the curves on the line segments that branch out from it.

Chapter 32: Layer Clipping Paths, Shape Layers and Layer Styles

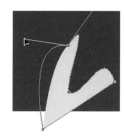

STEP 7: When you hold down the Command and Option keys, the Direct Selection tool changes to the Convert Point tool. If you click on a curve point, it will change it to a corner point. If you click on a corner point and drag out slightly, it will change to a curve point.

STEP 7: With the Direct Selection tool active, and the Command and Option keys held down, if you click on a directional handle, it will allow you to manipulate one side of a curve independently of the other side.

STEP 7: With the Command and Option keys down, click on all the points in the shape to turn them into corner points.

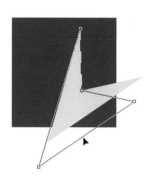

STEP 7: When the Direct Selection tool is used on a line segment, you are able to move that segment.

top of the oval and drag inward, as shown in the illustration. When you click on a point, it becomes solid, whereas the other points are "hollow." A solid, filled point indicates that it is selected. The Direct Selection tool lets you edit the individual points, line segments and directional handles that control the shape of a path.

STEP 7: **Next, hold down the Command and Option keys. The cursor changes to a slanted upside down V icon. This is the Convert Point tool. Clicking on one of the points will change it from a curve point to a corner point. If you click on it again and drag out slightly in the same motion, you'll return it to a curve point. With the Command and Option keys down, if you click on a directional handle, you are able to manipulate one side of a curve independently of the other side. Command-Option-click on all of the points in the former oval shape to turn them into corner points. To modify a line segment and the two points connected to it, use the Direct Selection tool with no keyboard modifiers and click and drag on a segment.**

MODIFYING A SHAPE USING ADD, SUBTRACT, INTERSECT, EXCLUDE AND COMBINE

So far, we've used the transformation commands and the Direct Selection tool to modify a shape, but there's another way to go about this that's also quite useful. It involves transforming a shape by drawing new shapes and using the settings in the Options bar for adding, subtracting, intersecting, excluding and combining.

STEP 8: **Turn off the Eye icon of the Shape 2 layer that we've been working with, and click on the Shape 1 layer (the rectangle) to make it the active layer. Select the Elliptical Shape tool. Check the Options bar for the Add, Subtract, Intersect and Exclude icons. If they don't show up, click on the clipping path thumbnail of the Shape 1 layer.** The left side of the Options bar should look like the illustration on the next page.

STEP 9: **In the Options bar, click the first icon so that the new shape you draw will be added to the existing shape. In the image, click and drag out a new oval so that part of it overlaps the rectangle.** Notice how the oval has been added to the rectangle, even though the outline of the two shapes can still be seen individually. **If you select the Path Component Selection tool (the black arrow), you can still select each shape and move them around.**

Modifying a Shape Using Add, Subtract, Intersect, Exclude and Combine

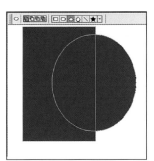

STEP 9: The oval added to the rectangle.

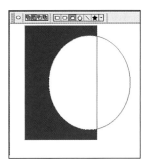

STEP 10: The oval subtracted from the rectangle.

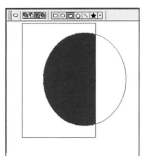

STEP 10: The oval intersected with the rectangle. The color only appears in the area where the two shapes intersect.

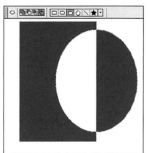

STEP 10: The oval shape with the operation set to Exclude. The color does not show where the two shapes overlap.

Add   Subtract   Intersect   Exclude

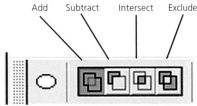

STEP 8: When you add a shape onto an active shape layer, you can choose from these operations in the Options bar: Add to the current shape; Subtract from the current shape; Intersect with the current shape; and Exclude from the current shape.

STEP 10: **Next, with the oval still added to the rectangle, try out the Subtract, Intersect and Exclude commands. You don't need to draw a new shape, simply click on the icons in the Options bar. Then, use the Black Arrow tool to click inside the oval shape and move it around. As you do, notice how it interacts with the rectangle.**

STEP 11: **With the oval selected, click on the Subtract button in the Options bar. This cuts the oval shape out of the rectangle. Next, use the Free Transform option to resize and position both the rectangle and the oval shape so that they are similar to the illustration at left. To resize the rectangle, click inside it with the black arrow and use the keyboard shortcut of Command-T to bring up Free Transform, or click the Show Bounding Box option in the Options bar and click once on one of the handles. Resize the rectangle with the handles and hit Enter or Return when you have it the way you like it.**

Use the same procedure to resize the oval shape. Now, with the Black Arrow tool, drag a box around both shapes to select them, and then click on the Combine button in the Options bar. This combines the subtracted oval and the rectangle into a single shape. Using multiple shapes along with the Add, Subtract, Intersect, Exclude and Combine operations is a very powerful and flexible way to create simple or complex shapes by starting out with basic primitives such as circles, rectangles, or polygons. In this case, we began with an oval and a rectangle and ended up with a simple arch.

STEP 11: After resizing both shapes with the Free Transform tool, the oval shape is positioned over the rectangle with its operation set to Subtract, and the Combine button is used to combine the two shapes into one element. With very little effort, we've taken a rectangle and an oval, and made a simple arch shape.

STEP 12: Now that we have the arch shape, we can easily copy it a few times and then combine the duplicate arches with the first arch to create a shape made up of three arches. **To copy the arch, use the Black Arrow tool. Hold down the Option key, click on the side of the arch and drag out to the right. The Option key tells Photoshop to make a copy of what you click on. If you add in the Shift key after you've begun the copy-drag motion, it will constrain the horizontal movement to a straight line. Drag the new arch into place and line it up side by side with the first one.**

Hold down the Option key again, click on the second arch and drag out a third copy. Line this up side by side with arch number two.

Finally, select all three arches using one of two methods: drag a box around them using the Black Arrow tool; or, using the same tool, click on one, and then

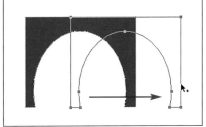

STEP 12: With the Path Component Selection tool (the black arrow), if you hold down the Option key while you click on a shape, you can drag out a copy of that shape. Here, we've created a duplicate copy of the arch.

STEP 12: After making three copies of the initial arch shape, we lined them up side by side, used the Path Component Selection tool to select them all by drawing a box around them, and then used Combine to create a single shape. With a little imagination, this could be the beginnings of an arched Roman bridge!

Shift-click on the other two until all are selected. Click on the Combine button in the Options bar to create a single element. Save your file. To add or subtract a point from a path using either the Path Component Selection tool or the Direct Selection tool (black or white arrows) just put the cursor where you want to add or subtract the point then Control-click to bring up a context-sensitive menu giving you those options.

CUSTOM SHAPES

So far we've been working with shapes derived from basic ovals and rectangles. As you can see, however, there is a wide range of possibilities even when starting out with these simple forms. In addition to the standard primitives in Photoshop's Shape tools, there's also the Custom Shape tool, which allows you to access a collection of preset shapes that ship with the program, as well as create and save your own custom shapes. The Custom Shape tool can be found in the Tool palette at the bottom of the pop-out menu for the Shape tools, or, once you've selected a shape tool, you can also find it in the Options bar for the Shape tools.

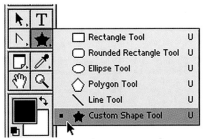

The Custom Shape tool.

STEP 1: **Select the Custom Shape tool, either from the Tool palette, or, if a Shape tool is already active, from the Options bar (just to the right of the Line tool). Move your cursor to the right and click on the second Custom Shape icon to open a drop-down collection of the custom shape presets that ship with Photoshop 6. Choose one that looks interesting, hit the Enter or Return key, and drag out a custom shape layer in your document.**

In your Layers palette, there is now a third shape layer. **You might want to temporarily turn off the arches layer while experimenting with the various custom shapes.** As you can see, a custom shape behaves no differently than a standard ellipse or rectangle. The only difference is that it can be stored in the presets and easily accessed whenever you need it. More importantly, you can also create your own custom shapes, directly in Photoshop or imported from Adobe Illustrator, and save them in a collection of presets for later use.

STEP 2: **Delete the custom shape layer and try out some of the other shapes in the custom shape preset collection.** As you make them, try to think how you might modify them using the Add, Subtract, Intersect, Exclude and Combine operations. Remember that any shape can be modified into an entirely new form.

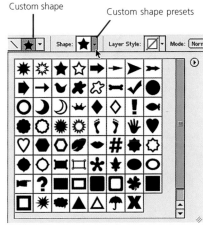

STEP 1: The presets collection of custom shapes that comes with Photoshop 6. You can add your own shapes into this library, or create specific collections for different uses. If you have a smaller set of shapes in your palette, choose Custom Shapes.csh after clicking on the pop-up arrow you see at the top right of this illustration and replace your smaller set with this one.

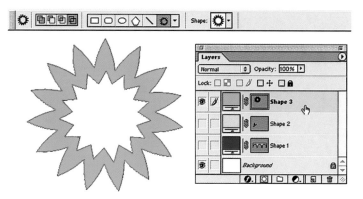

SAVING YOUR OWN CUSTOM SHAPES, CREATING AND EDITING NEW SHAPE COLLECTIONS

STEP 1: Apart from being a more complicated outline, a custom shape layer is no different from a standard elliptical or rectangle shape layer. As with the simpler shape layers, it is merely a color fill layer with a layer clipping path attached that defines where the color shows through. The truly useful thing abut custom shapes is that you can create your own, directly in Photoshop or imported from Adobe Illustrator, and save them in a collection of presets for later use.

STEP 3: As interesting as the default set of custom shapes may be, it's much more useful to be able to create your own shapes and save them in specific collections. You might have a collection of button shapes for Web projects, for instance, or graphic elements that you use often in illustrations. Now that we have a specialized shape of our own, the triple arch, we can save that as a custom shape and have it available for future use. **Click on the triple arch shape layer (Shape 1) to make it the active layer. Make sure that you can see the path highlighted around the shape in your image. If you don't see this, just click on the Shape Layer Clipping Path icon a second time. Next, go up to the main menu, click on Edit, and scroll down to Define Custom Shape. In the naming box that appears, give your shape a name, we called ours "roman bridge," and click OK. If you click on the Custom Shape tool now, and open up the collection of saved shapes, you'll see your new shape at the bottom of the list.**

STEP 4: Now that the Roman bridge shape has been added into the default custom shapes library, it will be saved with the program's preferences when you quit Photoshop and will appear in the collection when you start the program again. Any new shapes you save this way can still be lost, however, if at some point you reset the custom shapes to the default collection. To make sure this doesn't happen and ensure that your personal collection of custom shapes is not in danger of being erased, you need to save the current set of shapes under a new name. **To do this, click on the Shapes icon in the Options bar to open the Custom Shapes library and click on the arrow button at the top right of the collection. From the pop-out menu, choose Save Shapes. In the Save dialog, navigate to the Custom Shapes folder inside the Presets folder within the Adobe Photoshop 6 Application folder. Give the file a new name and click OK.** Saving the New Shapes library in the correct location will make it available at the bottom of the Shapes Collection pop-out menu the next time you start Photoshop.

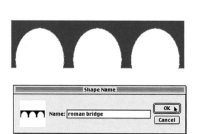

STEP 3: To save a shape layer as a custom shape, make its layer clipping path active and choose Edit/Define Custom Shape from the main menu.

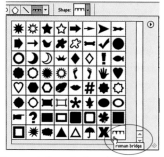

STEP 3: After you save and name the new shape, it will appear in the collection of saved shapes in the Options bar. To fully insure it against accidental loss, however, you should save the entire collection under a new name (see Step 4).

STEP 5: Even though we've just created a new shape collection, except for the addition of the roman bridge shape, it's essentially the same as the default shapes library. Fortunately, we can now edit our new collection and delete the shapes we don't want. **To delete a shape from the options bar pop-out collection, open the collection and Option-click on the shape you wish to delete. Another way to do this is to Control-click (right mouse-click on the PC) on the shape to call up the context sensitive menu and then choose the Delete option.** Although deleting shapes is undoable through the traditional Undo command or the History palette, if you make a

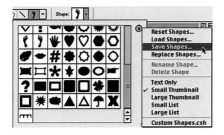

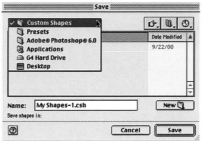

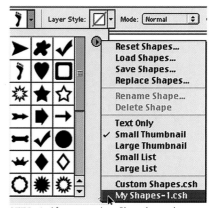

STEP 4: To create a new shape collection, just save the current group under a new name. After it's saved you can then delete the shapes you don't want and start adding your own.

STEP 4: Saving your new shapes collection in the right folder will make it available in the Shapes menu the next time you start Photoshop.

STEP 4: After restarting Photoshop, the new shapes collection we just saved, My Shapes-1, appears at the bottom of the Custom Shapes pop-out menu.

mistake and want to get back to where you were before you began throwing shapes away, simply load the library again and all your shapes will return. Deleted shapes are not erased in the actual shapes preset file on your hard disk until you save the library again.

EDITING SHAPE LIBRARIES WITH THE PRESETS MANAGER

STEP 6: Deleting shapes via the drop-down Shapes palette in the Options bar can be a bit tedious since you can only delete one shape at a time. A more flexible way to go about this is to use the new Presets Manager. In addition to custom shapes, you can also use this feature for managing brushes, gradients, swatches, styles, patterns and contours. **Go to the Edit menu and select the Presets Manager. From the drop-down menu at the top of the dialog, choose Custom Shapes. If you want to edit a specific shapes collection, click on the round arrow button, choose Replace Shapes and load the appropriate file. Click on a shape you wish to delete, and then Shift-click on any other shapes you want to remove. The shapes you have selected will be indicated by a bold outline. When you are done selecting the shapes, press the Delete button.**

If you click on Done after making your edits, the shapes will not be erased from the .csh file on your hard drive until you save the presets file again with the same name. Also, be aware that clicking the Load button in the Presets Manager will add any shapes you choose onto the existing shapes, so for editing purposes, it's best to choose Replace Shapes from the drop-down menu to be sure which shapes file you are working on. In future versions of the Presets Manager, we'd like to see some indication of which file you're editing as you're viewing the presets.

IMPORTING VECTOR SHAPES FROM ADOBE ILLUSTRATOR

If you're already accomplished with Bezier drawing tools, you may be more comfortable creating vector art in a program such as Adobe Illustrator and then importing it into Photoshop to make your custom shape. Since most vector art is created in programs with more full-featured vector capabilities than Photoshop, this is certainly a logical workflow, especially if it's one that you're used to. There are essentially four ways to import Illustrator art into Photoshop. Two of them will yield pixel-based image elements that are placed on a new layer, one will give you either a work path or add the art into an existing shape layer, and the fourth, and most flexible, gives you a choice of three different results.

Since we're dealing with vector shape layers here, we're not really concerned with creating pixel-based art in this section of the book, but we'll mention those methods anyway. The first way is to go to the File menu and choose Place. In the

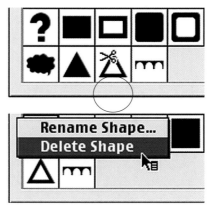

STEP 5: Two ways to delete a shape from the custom shapes collection in the Options bar: Option-click on it, or Control-click (right mouse-click on the PC) and choose Delete from the context sensitive menu.

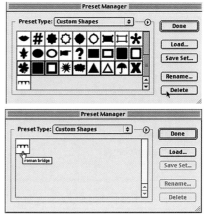

STEP 6: In the Presets Manager, we Shift-clicked on every shape except for the roman bridge (top), and pressed Delete. That left us with a shape library containing only our new custom Shape (bottom). We can now use this shape collection for any new shapes that we create in Photoshop.

345

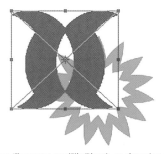

Placing Illustrator art (File/Place), or dragging and dropping it onto your Photoshop file will result in a pixel-based image element. You can scale the art with the bounding box before pressing Enter to rasterize it and place it on its own layer.

Open dialog which appears, find your Illustrator or EPS file and click Place. The vector art will appear in your image surrounded by a bounding box. While it is still in the bounding box, you can scale and transform it using commands like you would for Free Transform. At this point it's still resolution independent vector art. Once you press the Enter key, Photoshop rasterizes it into pixels and places it on its own layer.

The other way to bring vector art into your image as pixels is to drag and drop the file from Illustrator into Photoshop. Once in Photoshop, it will be governed by the same principles as if you had imported it through the Place command.

To import vector art as a work path, hold down the Command key as you drag from Illustrator and drop into Photoshop. Once it arrives, you will see a Bezier outline and there will be a new work path in the Paths palette. If the layer clipping path of a shape layer is active so you can see the actual path outline, and you press the Command key and drag and drop into Photoshop, the imported shape will be added into the shape layer that was active when you started the procedure.

Finally, in what is probably the most flexible method, select your artwork in Illustrator and copy it to the Clipboard. Then activate your Photoshop file and paste it down. When you do this, a small dialog will appear giving you the option of pasting as pixels, a work path, or a shape layer. If you paste as a shape layer, the color of the shape as it was in Illustrator will be replaced by the current Photoshop foreground color.

Once you have a vector version of your Illustrator art in Photoshop, either as a work path or a shape layer, you can create a custom shape from it by choosing Edit/Define Custom Shape.

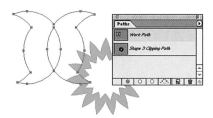

Holding down the Command key as you drag and drop from Illustrator into Photoshop will result in a new work path being created from the imported artwork.

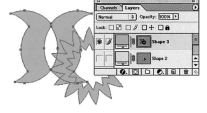

If a layer clipping path is active in Photoshop (so that you can see the clipping path outline), when you press the Command key and drag and drop from Illustrator, the imported shape will be added into the currently active shape layer.

THE INFINITE POSSIBILITIES OF LAYER STYLES

In Photoshop 5, Adobe introduced a feature called Layer Effects which allowed you to create editable effects such as drop shadows, bevels, embossing and glows. These effects worked with layers and updated themselves if you changed the layer's content. The flexibility and "live" nature of layer effects dramatically streamlined certain design production tasks such as the creation of text styling and adding a 3D look to Web navigation buttons. With version 6.0, layer effects have evolved into the new Layer Styles feature and have been significantly improved in terms of flexibility, features and customization. Now, in addition to applying the effects to a layer, you can combine several at once and save that specific mixture as a style which can then be applied very quickly to layers in the future. And with the Presets Manager you can save different collections of styles and distribute them within a production group, or share them with your friends and colleagues.

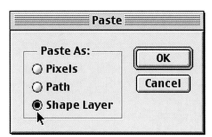

When you copy the artwork from Illustrator and then paste into Photoshop, you have three choices of how the vector art will be pasted.

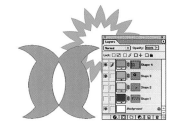

When you choose Paste As: Shape Layer, the Illustrator art is turned into a new shape layer. Any color that was present in the Illustrator art is replaced by the current Photoshop foreground color.

Chapter 32: Layer Clipping Paths, Shape Layers and Layer Styles

To explore the infinite possibilities that layer styles have to offer we're going to use a three-pronged approach. First, we'll take a look at what each of the individual effects do, then we'll work through a short step by step lesson applying some effects and creating and working with layer styles, and finally we'll go into the layer styles settings in greater detail.

LAYER EFFECTS: THE BUILDING BLOCKS OF LAYER STYLES

To use layer effects or styles, you first need to have a layer to apply them to. This can be any type of layer that contains a viewable image element, whether it be pixel-based, a vector shape, or a text layer. To access the layer styles, you can double-click on a layer's name, or go the the main Layer menu at the top of the screen, Layer/Layer Style, or click on the Effects icon (the italicized f at lower left) in the bottom of the Layers palette. This will bring up the Layer Styles dialog, which allows you to choose from a list of effects and modify settings for each of them.

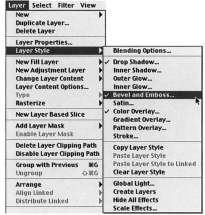

In addition to double-clicking on a layer's name to bring up the Style settings, you can also access it through the main Layer menu.

DROP SHADOW AND INNER SHADOW

Drop shadows are very useful for adding depth or providing visual separation between an image element and its background. The basic drop shadow effect is applied to layers beneath the target layer and you can easily control its distance from the layer and how hard or soft it is. An inner shadow makes it appear as if the layered element is recessed, or pressed down. The shading effect here is applied on top of the target layer.

The basic Drop Shadow effect is applied to any layers beneath the target layer.

An Inner Shadow makes it look as it the layered element is recessed (the classic pressed down effect of a web page button). With an inner shadow, the effect is applied in top of the target layer.

OUTER AND INNER GLOW

These effects apply either an outer or an inner glow to your layer. You can control the color, opacity, size, spread and numerous other aspects of the glow. An outer glow's effect covers part of the layers beneath the target layer, while an inner glow covers part of the target layer.

The list of available effects in the Layer Styles dialog box. Click on a name to apply it and gain access to its controls.

Outer Glow.

Inner Glow.

Inner Bevel. The effect is applied to the inside of the target layer.

Outer Bevel. The effect is applied to the outside of the target layer.

Emboss. This effect is like a combination of an inner and outer bevel.

Pillow Emboss creates an effect that looks as if the target layer has been stamped into the underlying layers.

Bevel with texture effect added.

Bevel with special edge contour applied.

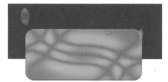

The new Satin effect.

The Gradient Overlay effect can be very simple, as in the black to white gradient above, or a more complex blend of several colors.

BEVEL AND EMBOSS

The Bevel and Emboss feature uses two main elements, a highlight and a shadow, to give the illusion that a layer has raised or recessed shape characteristics. This is most commonly seen in buttons or other navigational elements that give a Web page a subtle three dimensional look. The Bevel and Emboss feature has several "flavors" of effects that can be applied to a layer: Inner Bevel, Outer Bevel, Emboss, Pillow Emboss and Stroke Emboss (the latter is only available if a stroke effect is also applied). The look of a bevel or emboss can also be modified with additional technique settings, lighting angle and altitude controls, and contour adjustments. Some of these settings are all covered in greater detail at the end of this chapter.

The Bevel and Emboss styles also have two types of effects that can be used to further enhance the styling of your layered element. These are the Texture and Contour options. Texture lets you choose from a collection of texture presets (and, remember, you can always create your own) to add a textured feel to the layer. The look of the texture is further defined by the Lighting Angle and Depth settings you choose.

Contour allows you to change the default contour of a beveled edge by selecting from several presets, or by creating your own. The contour determines the exact nature of the raised and recessed regions (the hills and valleys) of an edge. In the example shown here, from the outside looking in, the edge appears to dip down, then rise up again, before finally sloping down into the interior of the button.

SATIN

This effect achieves its satiny look by applying shading to the interior of a layer. Since the form of the shading is created from the shape of the layer, the nature of the satin ripples and folds is different with every layer's shape. Other elements that influence the satin effect are the Distance, Size and Contour settings. Satin's Angle and Distance settings can also be adjusted by dragging in your image.

COLOR OVERLAY

A very basic, though highly useful, effect that overlays the layer with a specified color. Depending on the Blend mode and Opacity used, the color can totally replace the layer's original color and detail, or blend with it in a myriad of ways.

GRADIENT OVERLAY

The Gradient Overlay applies a gradient to the target layer. Depending on the particular gradient used, it can be a simple black to white gradient or a complex, multi-color blending effect.

PATTERN OVERLAY

This effect is similar to the Texture option in Bevel and Emboss, in that it uses a texture or pattern. The difference is that in the Bevel effect, the texture is applied

Chapter 32: Layer Clipping Paths, Shape Layers and Layer Styles

with Highlight and Shadow values so it looks as if the surface of the layer has a genuine textured surface. Here, the pattern is simply applied as an overlay. In Normal mode, it just looks as if you'd filled the layer with a pattern. Things get more interesting, however, when you branch out into some of the other Blend modes.

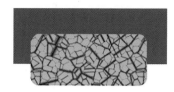

STROKE

Although quite simple and not visually as "cool" as some of the other styles available, this is actually a very useful effect. Being able to apply a Stroke to a shape, or to text, and still have it remain editable is a feature whose basic utility will find much use in every day design projects.

Strokes can be applied as a color, a gradient or as a pattern. And, if you have a Stroke effect applied to a layer, you can apply an Emboss to just the Stroke in the Bevel and Emboss settings.

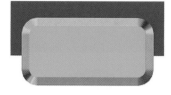

The Pattern Overlay.

A color Stroke applied.

A gradient Stroke applied.

A purple color stroke with a Stroke Emboss effect added.

WORKING WITH LAYER EFFECTS AND STYLES

STEP 1: Before we start in with layer effects and styles, we'll set the stage by creating a few vector shape layers to apply the styles to. This will also serve as a quick refresher in making shape layers. If you still have the shapes file open where we created the roman bridge, you can save and close it now. **Create a new file by going to the Photoshop File menu and choosing New. Set the size to 800 pixels wide, 600 pixels high, 72ppi, RGB mode and the contents set to White. Save your file in the Photoshop format and name it LayerStyles.**

STEP 2: **If they are not currently visible, use View/Show Rulers or Command-R to bring up the Rulers. Set the ruler units to pixels by control-clicking (Mac), or right mouse-clicking (PC) inside the rulers to open the context sensitive menu, and choose Pixels. From the top, horizontal ruler, drag out a guide down to approximately the 150 pixel mark.**

STEP 3: **In the Tool palette, select the Rectangular Shape tool and drag a rectangle shape layer across the top part of the file, stopping at the 150 pixel guide.** Since the shape layer color will be whatever you had your foreground swatch set to, you might want to choose a different color now, although the actual colors you use are not important for this exercise. **Double-click on the leftmost Solid Color layer thumbnail in the Layers palette to bring up the color picker. Choose a new color and click OK. Next, Option-double-click on the name "Shape 1" to bring up the Layer Properties dialog and rename the shape layer "Top Nav."**

With a shape layer, you get a different dialog box depending on where and how you click. Double-clicking the Solid Color thumbnail for the layer brings up the color picker so you can choose a new color. Double-clicking on the Layer Clipping Path thumbnail or the layer name will bring up the Layer Styles dialog, which is where

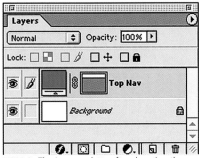

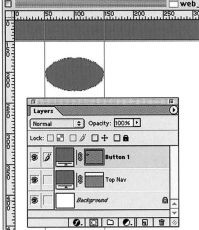

STEP 3: The Layers palette after changing the rectangular shape's color and renaming it "Top Nav."

STEP 4: After dragging out two vertical guides to help in sizing the button, a new elliptical shape layer is created.

STEP 6: You can also click on the Effects icon at the bottom of the Layers palette to apply an effect.

we'll be working shortly. Option-double-clicking on the layer name lets you give it a new name.

STEP 4: Before we start experimenting with the layer styles, let's add another shape element that might work as a Web page button. **From the vertical ruler, pull out a new guide to the 50 pixel mark, and another one to the 150 pixel mark. Select the Ellipse Shape tool, either from the Tool palette or from the Options bar. Look at the Options bar and make sure you can see the icon for creating a new shape layer. If you only see the Add, Subtract, Intersect and Exclude options, just click once on the layer clipping path for the Top Nav and that should reset the Option bar to the correct state. Refer back to the beginning of the shape layer section if you need to. With the Create Shape Layer option active, drag out an elliptical oval shape between the two vertical guides. This will be the starting point for our button shape. Option double click on the name of this new shape layer and rename it "Button 1."**

STEP 5: **Double-click the Solid Color Fill thumbnail for Button 1. This brings up the color picker and lets you to choose a new color. Choose a color that contrasts well with the color of the Top Nav layer and click OK.**

APPLYING SOME BASIC LAYER EFFECTS

STEP 6: Now that we have a couple of elements to start with, we're ready to start checking out layer styles. **Double-click on either the layer clipping path, or the name of Button 1 to bring up the Layer Styles dialog.** You may have already run into this several times by accident, especially if you're used to the Photoshop 5 shortcut for naming a layer, which was double-clicking on it. **You can also access the styles dialog from the main menu (Layer/Layer Style...), or by clicking on the Effects icon (the italicized f) at the bottom of the Layers palette.**

In the left-hand side of the Layer Style dialog, click in the checkbox labeled Drop Shadow to apply a shadow effect to the button.

STEP 7: Although clicking in the checkbox for Drop Shadow has applied the effect, we still don't have access to the controls that will modify the shadow's properties. If you look at the center section of the Layer Style dialog, you'll see the controls for general and advanced layer blending, but nothing pertaining to the shadow. **To display the controls for an effect, you have to click on the name of the effect to highlight it. Do this now to the Drop Shadow effect and you'll see the center section of the dialog change to display the Drop Shadow settings.**

STEP 8: **Go ahead and play around with some of the Drop Shadow settings to see how they affect your shadow.** Notice that you can put the cursor over the actual shadow and the Move tool appears which you can then use to actually position the shadow. This will may change the distance and angle parameters. We'll be covering some of the various layer style settings in more detail later in this chapter. **When you're done experimenting with the Shadow settings, hold down the Option key to change the Cancel button to a Reset button. Press the Reset button and then click the Drop Shadow name once again to apply the default settings.**

Now, let's add a Bevel effect to our button. In the left-hand panel of the Layer Style dialog, click on the Bevel and Emboss style and you'll see the center panel change to display the controls for bevel effects. If you look at your image, you'll also see that a Bevel has been applied to the button.

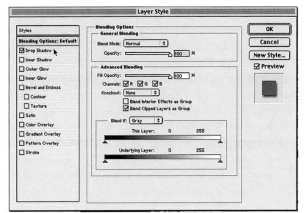

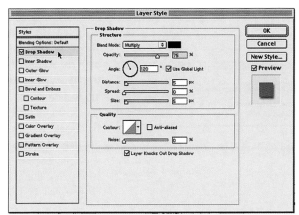

STEP 6: The Layer Style dialog box. The center section shows general and advanced blending options. The left side shows the available layer styles. By clicking in the checkbox for Drop Shadow, or on its name, that effect is applied to the layer.

STEP 7: Although clicking in the checkbox for Drop Shadow will apply the effect, you can't edit the properties of the effect until you click on the name of the effect to highlight it. Once this is done, the center panel changes, giving you access to controls that are specific to each effect.

To make your button to resemble ours, use the following settings:

Style: Inner Bevel; Technique: Smooth; Depth: 100%; Direction: Up; Size: 40px; Soften: 5px; Angle: 100°; Altitude: 50°. Leave the Gloss Contour and Highlight and Shadow settings as they are.

STEP 9: The last effect we'll apply to our button is to make it a specific color. **In the left side of the Style dialog, click on Color Overlay. In the center part of the dialog, click in the colored swatch next to the Blend Mode menu to bring up the color picker, and choose a light blue color. From the Blend Mode drop-down menu, select Color. Now we have used three separate layer effects to style our simple oval shape into a three dimensional button. Click OK to close the dialog box.**

If you look at your Layers palette now, you'll see that the Button 1 layer has the three effects added on underneath it. You can turn off the Eye icons for the entire group, or each effect individually. **If you want to edit any of these effects, simply double-click on them in the Layers palette and you'll be returned to the controls for that particular effect. Once in the Style dialog, you can move on to modify other effects, or add new ones, by clicking on their names in the left side panel.** The great thing about layer styles is that they are totally "live." This means that if you decide to change the shape of your button (or whatever layer content you've applied the style to), the effects will update automatically to reflect your changes.

CREATING A LAYER STYLE

If you're designing graphics for a Web site, chances are that you'll need to use the same effect many times throughout the site. The best way to do this is to save your particular mixture of effects as a layer style, so you can quickly apply it to new elements. In addition to saving you time and effort, if you're in a workgroup environment where more than one designer or production artist is creating graphics for a project, layer styles will help keep things consistent. Let's create a layer style now from the three effects we used on the blue beaded button.

STEP 10: **Double-click on the button layer name to bring up the Layer Style dialog again. In the upper right, click on the New Style button and give your style a**

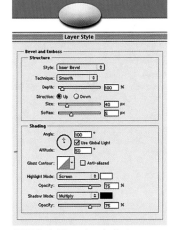

STEP 8: Adding a bevel effect.

STEP 9: The Layers palette after adding three different layer effects: a Drop Shadow, Inner Bevel, and a Color Overlay. To see a shape layer as it will actually appear on a Web page or when printed, click its Layer Clipping Path thumbnail until it loses the highlight around its edge. This de-activates the clipping path display on the screen which can sometimes make your object have unsightly edges.

STEP 10: After clicking on New Style in the Styles dialog, you can give your style a name.

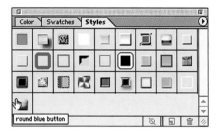

STEP 10: In the Styles palette, the new style, round blue button, appears at the end of the default collection of styles. You can now apply this to a layer simply by highlighting the target layer and clicking on the style. You can also drag and drop from the Styles palette onto the target layer in the Layers palette, or directly onto the layer in the document window.

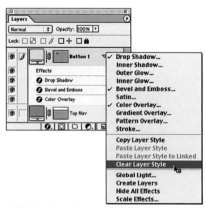

STEP 11: If you Control-click (Mac) or right-click (PC), on the Layer Effects icon, or on any of the currently applied styles, you can bring up the context sensitive menu. From here you have several options, including adding new effects, copying the current style, or clearing all layer effects.

descriptive name. We called ours "round blue button." Click OK and leave the Layer Style dialog. Next, go to the Window menu at the top of the screen and select Show Styles (if the Styles palette is already on screen somewhere, that choice will be Hide Styles). If you look at the bottom of the available styles, you should see the style you just created. Move your mouse over it and a label will pop out showing its name.

Even though your new layer style is now part of the Styles palette, keep in mind that if you choose to replace the current styles with another set of styles, or reset to the default group, you'll lose any new styles you've added. Just as with the custom shapes collections (or any of the presets), if you really want to protect your new styles from accidental erasure, you need to save the set under a new name. To do this, choose Save Styles from the Styles palette pop-up menu.

APPLYING A LAYER STYLE

If you look at the Styles palette when it's in the small thumbnail mode, it looks a bit like a box of brightly colored candy. Image candy, that is. Once you realize how easy it is to create and apply styles, it may be hard to keep your mouse out of the candy jar when you're playing around in Photoshop!

STEP 11: Before we experiment with applying some styles, let's clear the current effects from the oval shape. Make sure that the Button 1 layer is the active layer. **There are three ways we can clear the styling effects from a layer. You can do it from the main menu, Layer/Layer Style/Clear Layer Style. In the Layers palette, you can click on the word Effects just underneath the actual layer, and drag it to the small trashcan in the lower right of the palette. You can also Control-click (Mac), or right-click (PC) on the Effects icon on the layer, or on any of the individual effects that have been applied, and then choose Clear Layer Style from the context sensitive menu.**

STEP 12: Now that you have a button shape with no styles applied to it, **make a copy of the layer by going to the main menu and selecting Layer/Duplicate Layer. Call the new layer Button 2 and click OK. Select the Move tool in the Tool palette and move this layer to the right so you can see both buttons side by side.**

In the Styles palette, click once on the "round blue button" thumbnail to apply the style to Button 2. You can also drag and drop a style onto a layer in the Layers palette, or drag and drop onto actual pixel data in the document window. In the latter case, the style will be applied to the topmost layer containing pixels where the style is dropped.

APPLYING A LAYER STYLE AND PRESERVING EXISTING EFFECTS

Any time you apply a style onto a layer that already has a style applied, the newer style will overwrite the previous one. Fortunately, Photoshop provides a way around this situation by allowing you to hold down the Shift key as you apply a new style. Any existing effects which are not duplicated by the new style will be preserved. Effects which are present in both the current style and the new one will take on the properties assigned by the new style. Let's try this out, and along the way, explore a new type of layer effect, the Pattern Overlay.

Chapter 32: Layer Clipping Paths, Shape Layers and Layer Styles

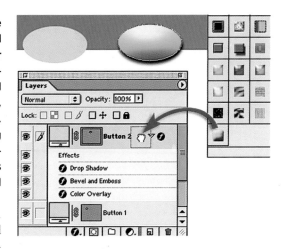

STEP 13: Click on Button 1 to make it the active layer. Next, click on the Effects icon (the italicized f) in the bottom of the Layers palette and select Pattern Overlay. The Styles dialog will appear with the controls for Pattern Overlay. Click on the Pattern thumbnail to open the default pattern presets. We chose the Clouds pattern at the end of the list, but feel free to chose another one if you like. Once you've selected the pattern, hit Enter or click back on the large thumbnail to close the pattern presets.

Directly beneath the Pattern thumbnail is a slider control for setting the Scale of the pattern. Move the slider to 50% and you'll see the pattern scaled down in the image. Next, move your cursor over the Clouds button in your image and click and drag to move the pattern around until you find a position that looks good. Click OK.

Now we have a button with a grayscale cloud pattern applied to it. Interesting, but not terribly exciting. Let's jazz it up by applying our round blue button style. We'll use the Shift key modifier as we do this to preserve the clouds pattern.

STEP 12: To apply a style to a layer, you can simply click on a style, or drag and drop onto a layer in the Layers palette. Here, we use the drag and drop method to apply the style to Button 2.

STEP 14: Hold down the Shift key and in the Styles palette, click once on the thumbnail for the round blue button style, or, hold down the Shift key and drag and drop the style onto the layer. That style is now applied to Button 1, but the clouds pattern effect has been preserved.

Apart from using the Shift key when we applied the layer style, the other main reason that the clouds are not obscured is because when we set the properties for the blue color overlay in the original style (step 9), we chose the Color Blend mode. This mode applies the hue and saturation of the selected color but does not modify the luminosity (the gray values) of whatever it's applied to. If we had left the Blend mode set to Normal, then the blue color would cover up the cloud pattern. To try this out, double-click on the color overlay effect for Button 1 and change its blend mode to Normal. When you're done, click Cancel to restore the Color Blend mode to the color overlay effect.

With the clouds blending into the blue beveled effect, we have an entirely different look for the button. Sort of a cross between seeing the sky reflected in a blue glass bead and a beautiful bird's egg. If you like this new style combination, you might want to save it as a new style.

STEP 13: With Button 1 as the active shape layer, click on the Add Layer Style icon in the Layers palette and choose Pattern Overlay.

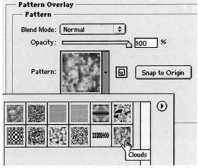

STEP 13: The Styles dialog with the Pattern Overlay settings. Click in the large Pattern thumbnail to display the current pattern presets (the ones here are the default) and select a pattern. Press the Enter key, or click the large thumbnail again to close the presets.

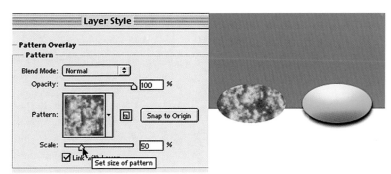

STEP 13: Using the Scale slider to make the make the pattern slightly smaller. You can also move your cursor into the image and click and drag to change the position of the pattern within your layer.

353

STEP 14: After Shift-clicking on the round blue button style in the Styles palette, it is applied to Button 1, but the clouds pattern is preserved. This is a pretty cool effect!

In the Styles palette menu, you can choose to view the styles as text only, thumbnails, or as a list. In list view the accompanying names might give you an idea of what to expect from a particular style. In the bottom of the palette menu are the styles presets that are installed with Photoshop.

DECONSTRUCTING LAYER STYLES TO SEE HOW THEY WORK

Photoshop comes with several collections of layer styles ready for you to use and one of the best ways to learn about how styles work is to look under the hood of some of these styles and see what individual effects are used and what their respective settings are. At the bottom of the pop-out menu for the Styles palette, you'll see a list of the available styles presets. These have names such as Buttons, Glass Buttons, Text Effects, and Image Effects that give you a good idea of where you might choose to use them. In the same pop-out menu, you can choose to view the styles as Text Only, two sizes of thumbnails, or two sizes of lists. The list views are helpful for determining what sort of an effect the style might produce as the names are usually descriptive in nature.

STEP 15: **Take some time to load some of the styles presets and apply them to your shapes, both the buttons and the rectangle. With each one, you'll see that it uses different combinations of individual effects. To gain further insight into how the effect is achieved, double-click on the effects that are listed below the layer in the Layers palette, and investigate the settings for each component of the style.** The great thing about deconstructing the existing styles that come with Photoshop, is that you can use them as a recipe book to help you understand them and then come up with your own styles.

THE LAYER STYLES CONTROLS

So far we've applied only a few of the many effects that are available in the Layer Style dialog box. If you're new to these features, you may be a bit overwhelmed at the many controls that some of them have. In the next section, we'll go over some of the styles settings and explain how they work. We won't be covering every single option, since many of them are pretty clear as to what they do. Since many of the settings are available in several of the effects, we'll be covering the settings and where they occur, rather than each individual effect's control panel.

ANGLE

This is one of the more common settings you'll run across, appearing in five of the ten available effects: Drop Shadow, Inner Shadow, Bevel and Emboss, Satin, and Gradient Overlay. This controls the lighting angle at which the effect is applied to the layer. The easiest way to understand this is to apply a Drop Shadow to one of the buttons in your styles test file and see how the Angle influences the shadow. If the "light source" is coming from above and to the left, then the shadow will appear below and to the right. In addition to controlling the angle from within the Style dialog box, you can also click and drag in your image, on a Drop Shadow for example, to change the angle.

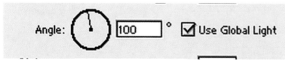

The Angle setting appears in several of the Layer Styles control panels. The Use Global Light option insures that all effects which use an angle value are consistent throughout your document. The Use Global Light option is checked by default.

USE GLOBAL LIGHT

This option insures that all layer effects which have a Lighting Angle setting use the same value throughout your document, giving the appearance of a consistent light source shining on the image. It is checked by default. You will find this option in the Drop Shadow, Inner Shadow and Bevel and Emboss controls. If you have Use Global Light on when changing the angle in any dialog, the angle will change for all dialogs where Use Global Light is

Chapter 32: Layer Clipping Paths, Shape Layers and Layer Styles

on in your document. You may not want this to happen so be aware when you make changes with Use Global Light on.

BLEND MODE

The Blend Mode settings are the same as those you find in the Layers palette, and they determine how a layer style will blend with the underlying layers, or with the active layer if the effect is normally applied to that layer (such as inner shadow). Generally, the default settings you see for the Blend modes will be the most appropriate for each effect. Don't let that stop you from playing around, however, as Blend modes can produce some very interesting effects. See chapter 31: "Blend Modes, Calculations and Apply Image" for more information on the Blend modes.

COLOR

Next to some controls in layer styles, you'll see a small color swatch box, usually filled with black, white (shadows and bevels) or a pale yellow (outer and inner glow). This is an easy one to overlook since it's not specifically labeled as a color setting. Clicking on it will bring you into the Photoshop color picker, allowing you to choose a new color. This setting lets you determine the color of a shadow, glow, highlight or stroke.

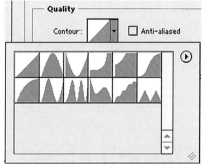

The Blend modes determine how a layer style interacts with the other styles applied to this layer and with underlying layers. Generally, the default blend modes are the most appropriate for each effect.

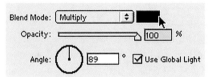

The Color swatch for the Drop Shadow effect.

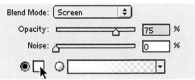

The Color swatch for the Glow effects. To the right of the color box, you can choose to have the glow color applied as a gradient, or choose from the gradients available in the presets collection.

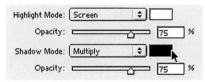

In the Bevel and Emboss controls, you can set the color separately for the highlight and shadow.

CONTOUR

Contour is a new setting with Photoshop 6, and it's definitely one of the coolest things about the expanded functionality of layer styles. Although it might be confusing at first, once you get used to it, you'll see that it's pretty useful and will greatly increase the types of effects you can achieve.

The exact result of the Contour setting will vary depending on the type of effect you're using, and the type of contour shape you choose. With shadows, Contour allows you to specify the fade of the shadow as the edge transitions from dark to light. In the Glow effects, you can make rings of transparency when combining certain contours with a solid color glow. With gradient-filled glows, you can create variations in the repetition of both gradient color and opacity. In the bevel and emboss controls, contour allows you to shape the ridges and valleys that are shaded by the embossing effect.

The default contour is a simple diagonal curve that generates an even transitional falloff for shadows, bevels, embossing and glows. To choose a different type of contour, click on the small downward-facing triangle next to the Contour thumbnail. This will open a drop-down menu showing the contour presets that ship with Photoshop 6. Click on a contour to select it and apply it to the effect you're working with.

The default contour is a simple diagonal curve, generating an even transitional falloff for shadows, bevels, embossing, and glows. To choose another type of contour, click on the small triangle next to it, and the contour presets will pop down. Clicking on the main Contour thumbnail itself will bring up the Contour Editing dialog. To edit any of the additional contours in the collection, double-click their thumbnails.

355

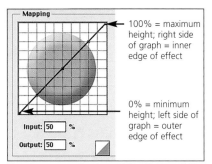

100% = maximum height; right side of graph = inner edge of effect

0% = minimum height; left side of graph = outer edge of effect

Input: 50 %

Output: 50 %

Here is a composite view of the Contour Editor showing the default contour for a bevel edge. The point at lower left is 0%, which represents the minimum height of the edge. In location terms, this left side of the graph controls the outer edge of the effect. The point at top right is 100% which represents the maximum height of the edge. The right side of the graph controls the inner edge of the effect.

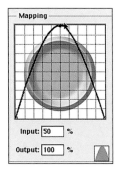

In this contour, the curve rises from 0%, or minimum height, up to maximum height at 100%, and then drops back down to 0%. Imagine the curve as a profile view, or cross section of the actual edge of the effect. Now look at the orange button shape and see how the shape of the curve is represented in the actual bevel edge. It rises up from the outer edge, comes to a peak, and then falls down before leveling out in the interior of the button.

Mapping

Input: 50 %

Output: 100 %

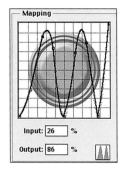

Here is a double ring contour. Again, look at it and try to imagine that it is a cross section side view of the edge contour. It rises up on the outside, reaches a peak, then falls down into a steep valley, rises to a second peak and then descends into a second valley before climbing up one more time to a point slightly higher than the first two peaks, and levels out to an even plateau on the top of the button.

Mapping

Input: 26 %

Output: 86 %

To modify a contour, double-click the large thumbnail to access the Contour Editor. In the Edit dialog box, there is a curve that you can manipulate by changing the placement and value of its points. The functionality of this curve is very much like the Curves dialog used for color and tonal correction. You click on the curve to choose a point, and drag to move it to another location. You can also highlight the point and then use numeric adjustments in the fields near the lower part of the dialog box. To remove a point from the curve, drag it out of the box.

The Contour Edit dialog is the same for each effect. Positions on the left side of the graph represent the outer edge of a contour, while positions on the right side control the inner edge. Values on the curve start at 0% at the bottom of the graph, and increase until they reach 100% at the top of the graph. Depending on the effect you're adjusting, these percentage values can mean different things. In a shadow, 0% equals the total absence of shading, and 100% equals a maximum shadow. A default shadow contour would be the straight diagonal line ranging from 100% in the upper right, down to 0% in the lower left, and producing an even falloff from the dark part of the shadow to where the shadow ends.

A Glow effect is similar to the shadow, except 100% here represents the glow color at maximum opacity, and 0% equals that part of the glow where it has faded out to complete transparency.

In a Bevel or Embossing effect, the contour represents the actual shape of the edge. As you look at the curve for a particular contour, think of it as a cross-section or profile view of the shape's edge. In this instance, 0% equals the minimum height of the edge and 100% equals the maximum height. To get a better idea of how this works, study the diagrams of the orange button shape and its associated contours. We've created a composite view of the Contour Edit dialog to help illustrate this point; in the actual Contour Editor you won't see a screened back view of your shape, or the small thumbnail in the lower right corner.

As with many Photoshop features, explanations such as this can only serve to illuminate certain aspects and provide some background on how you can use the settings to create a particular effect. To really begin to understand how it works on actual pixels, you just need to roll up your sleeves and dive in. Spend some time and take the contours for a spin on some test shapes and see what you come up with.

Gloss Contour

Yet another contour! You'll find this one in the the lower half of the Bevel and Emboss control panel. It creates a glossy, metallic appearance on the surface of the beveled layer. You apply this after the initial shading of the bevel or emboss has taken place. The choices of available contours, as well as the methods used to edit the contours, are the same as in the previous section.

Depth

In the Bevel and Emboss, and Texture controls, Depth adjusts the intensity of the shading and gives the illusion of more or less depth to a particular effect, be it a beveled or embossed shape, or a texture pattern.

Gradient

This setting appears in two of the layer styles, Gradient Overlay and Stroke. It allows you to specify the type of gradient being applied and fine tune several aspects of it, such as opacity, angle, size, and Blend mode. To choose a gradient, click on the small black triangle next to the sample gradient in the dialog box. This will open up the pop-out menu of Gradient presets. The Style drop-down list allows you to choose from five gradient styles such as Linear, Radial, Angle, Reflected and Diamond. If you click in the sample view of the selected gradient, it will bring up the Gradient Editor, which will allow you to modify the current gradient or create a new one. Refer to Chapter 4: "The Tool Palette," for a more detailed explanation of how the Gradient Editor works.

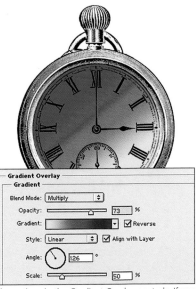

JITTER

Jitter appears only in the Outer and Inner Glow controls, and it varies the application of a gradient's color and opacity. When viewed close up, even small amounts as low as 1% or 2% will cause the gradient to appear as if it had been shaken vigorously, with the colors beginning to mix into each other. Higher amounts will create a speckled, noise effect. To see any result with jitter, you need to select the Gradient option for the glows, and choose a gradient other than the default pale yellow to transparent. Jitter does not work with solid color glows.

The options in the Gradient Overlay controls. If you click in the horizontal gradient sample, you can access the Gradient Editor which will allow you to modify the current gradient or create a new one. Clicking on the small, black triangle next to the gradient sample will open up the collection of gradient presets.

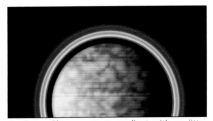

An Outer Glow spectrum gradient with no jitter applied.

The same Outer Glow with a jitter value of 20%.

A 300% zoom view of a jitter applied to a spectrum gradient outer glow. The jitter amount is only 2%, yet the shaken, "jittery" effect is already apparent.

RANGE

Range is another variable that appears only in the Outer and Inner Glow settings. It controls which portion or range of a glow is targeted for the selected contour. Beginning at 1%, the contour is applied to the outer edge of an outer glow first, and then moves inward as the range value increases. With an inner glow, the contour is applied to the inner edge first and then expands outward.

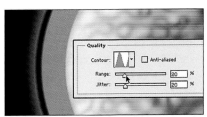

The Range setting determines which portion of a glow is targeted for application of a contour. In an outer glow, the range begins along the outer edge at 1% and then moves inward. Here, with the Range value set to 20%, the selected contour does not extend very far into the glow.

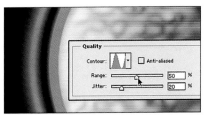

With the Range value increased to 50%, the contour moves inward and is applied to more of the glow. Since this is a solid color glow, the Jitter setting has no effect here.

3 HANDS-ON SESSION: Posterize, Bitmaps, Textures and Patterns

Create interesting texture effects using Posterize, bitmaps and patterns along with layers and Blend modes.

STEP 1: The original photo of the Packard.

STEP 1: Creating the new MezzoTint pattern.

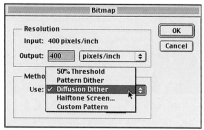

STEP 2: Here are the options when you choose Image/Mode/Bitmap.

There are many ways to create and integrate patterning into Photoshop images. Here we do it using more traditional Photoshop tools like bitmaps, filters and various layer options to add texture effects to images. There are also many new Photoshop 6 options using the Layer Styles palette which are described in Chapters 33 and 35.

STEP 1: Type the letter D to get the default colors. Open the Packard image in the Posterize Bitmaps & Patterns folder and bring up the Layers palette (F10 with ArtistKeys). Double-click on the Background layer and rename it Packard. Choose File/Save As and save this as PackardLayers. Choose Image/Duplicate (F5) and name the duplicate copy PackardStreaks. Use Image/Mode/Grayscale to change the mode on the duplicate copy to Grayscale and say OK to Discard Color Information. If you check the Don't Show Again checkbox in the Convert to Grayscale dialog, then next time you do this, Photoshop won't ask for your OK, it will just do the conversion. You will use PackardStreaks later. Do another Image/Duplicate, naming this one Packard/Mezzo. Choose Select All (Command-A), then Edit/Copy, and finally File/New (Command-N) to get a grayscale file the same size as the other Packard files. Before clicking on the OK button in the New dialog box, name the file MezzoTint and make sure that the White radio button is selected to fill this copy with white. Choose Filter/Noise/Add Noise and add 100 of Gaussian noise. This is sort of a mezzotint pattern. Press Command-A again to select all of the grayscale pattern. Now choose Edit/Define Pattern to make this a new pattern Photoshop can use. You should now have four windows on your screen. The original color Packard, now called PackardLayers, and the grayscale PackardStreaks, PackardMezzo, and the MezzoTint pattern.

DIFFUSION DITHER BITMAPS AND MEZZOTINT PATTERNS

STEP 2: **Return to the PackardMezzo window and choose Select/Deselect (Command-D). Now choose Image/Mode/Bitmap and say OK to the Flatten Layers question if you get it. You will get a dialog box having a pop-up with several options. Choose**

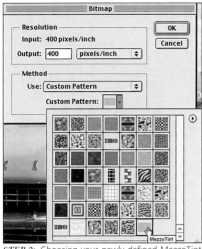

STEP 2: Choosing your newly defined MezzoTint pattern from inside the Pattern pop-up.

Diffusion Dither and say OK. Zoom the image in to 100% because diffusion dithers don't look right unless the image is seen at 100% or closer. A diffusion dither bitmap is an image made up of only black and white dots; there are no grays. The Bitmap mode contains one bit of information for each pixel; it is either on or off, black or white. These images are very compact, which is useful for the Web and multimedia. A regular grayscale image contains 8 bits per pixel, so each pixel can have 256 different gray values. Diffusion dithers are very universal because you can display them on any computer monitor and print them on any printer that can print black dots.

Now choose Command-Z to undo the diffusion dither, choose Mode/Bitmap again, and this time pick the Custom Pattern option in the pop-up. Doing this will highlight the pop-up Pattern menu which you need to click on and then choose the new pattern in the bottom of the menu. That will be the MezzoTint pattern you just defined. Press Return to get out of the dialog and you will see the image with this MezzoTint pattern. Choose Select All, go to Edit/Copy, and then use the Window menu to switch to your color PackardLayers image and do an Edit/Paste. Option-click on the name of this new layer to re-name it to MezzoPattern. Zoom in to 100%.

STEP 3: **With the MezzoPattern layer active and both Eye icons on, change the Opacity to 40%. Now you can see the original Packard layer with MezzoPattern on top of it. The colors on the Packard will be muted because you are in the Normal Blend mode. Change the Blend mode of the MezzoPattern layer in the Layers palette to Multiply to make the black dots more black and drop out the white parts of the pattern. It will also bring out better color saturation in the nonblack areas, and you will see better colors from the original Packard. Choose File/Save to update your file.**

STEP 3: A section of the image with the 40% MezzoTint pattern applied using Multiply mode. The Layers palette should look like this at this point.

A Subtle Posterize Effect

STEP 4: **Click on the Packard layer to make it the active layer, and then Option-drag it to the New Layer icon at the bottom of the Layers palette. Name the new layer Posterize and choose OK. Option-click on its Eye icon to turn off the other layers for now. Choose Image/Adjust/Posterize and set the Levels to 6.** This reduces each color channel in the Posterize layer to only six levels of gray and gives this layer a posterized look. **Now click on the Eye icon in the Packard layer to make that layer visible but leave the Posterize layer active (highlighted). Move the Opacity slider in the Layers**

STEP 4: After Option-clicking on the Posterize Eye icon, the other layers are not visible.

359

palette to 40%, which will show 60% of the original Packard layer from below. This will give you a subtle posterize effect while still maintaining most of the original image from below. To quickly see the image with and without this effect, click the Eye icon of the Posterize layer to turn it off and on again. **Now turn on the Eye icon of the MezzoPattern layer to see all three layers together.**

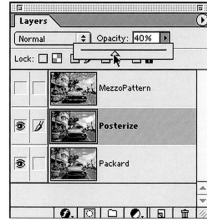

STEP 4: Seeing Posterize and Packard at the same time with Posterize being active at 40%.

STREAKED PATTERNS

STEP 5: Now we will create another pattern and add some more layers to give you other options with this image. **When we add the next layer, we want it to be added above the MezzoPattern layer, so click on the MezzoPattern layer to make it the active layer. Switch windows back to the MezzoTint file and zoom out so you can see the whole file onscreen. Use the Rectangular Marquee tool (M) to make a long, skinny selection on the left edge of the file the full height of the file. This rectangle should be about ¼ inch wide. Now use Edit/Transform/Scale and grab the middle-right handle and drag it across the screen to the right side of the window.** This stretches out _the dots within this ¼-inch selection and gives you a streaking pattern. **Press Enter or Return to finish the scale process. Command-Option-0 to zoom to 100%. Now choose Filter/Stylize/Emboss and emboss this pattern by 4 pixels, 150% at 135 degrees.** Notice how the pattern changes depending on the angle of rotation and the other Emboss parameters. **Choose OK from Emboss. Choose Select/All (Command-A) and then Edit/Define Pattern to define another pattern which you will call EmbossedStreaks. Use the Window menu to switch to the grayscale file PackardStreaks that you made in Step 1. Use Image/Mode/Bitmap to convert this to another bitmap again using the Custom Pattern option then choose EmbossedStreaks from the Pattern pop-up.** You will now get a streaked version of the Packard which looks best at 100% zoom factor. **Use File/Save As to save this as PackardStreaks.**

STEP 5: The long, skinny selection on the left edge.

STEP 6: **Choose Select/All and then Edit/Copy in the PackardStreaks document; then switch to PackardLayers and do an Edit/Paste.** This will make a new layer in the PackardLayers document above the MezzoPattern layer. **Option-double-click on this new layer and name it StreakPattern and choose OK. Now double-click on this StreakPattern layer name without the Option key and the Layer Style dialog box opens. Move this dialog box out of the way so you can see the PackardLayers document as well as this dialog box.** From the Layer Style dialog box, we can change the Opacity and Composite modes as well as do all the things we learned about in Chapter 32: "Layer Clip-

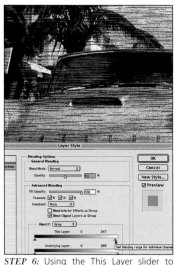

STEP 6: Using the This Layer slider to remove the whites from the pattern.

ping Paths, Shape Layers and Layer Styles." **At the bottom of the Advanced Blending area of this dialog is a very powerful feature that has been in Photoshop for a long time. There are two sets of slider bars that are very cool—this Layer, which allows you to remove some of the pixels in the 0–255 range from the active layer, and Underlying, which allows you to specify the pixels from the composite of all the layers that lie below this layer that will definitely be in the composite. Move the rightmost Highlight slider on This Layer until it says 247. This means that all the pixels from 248 through 255, the white pixels, will be removed from this layer in the composite. Now you see black streaks added to the composite image as the colors and pattern from below show through the white areas. Now change the General Blending Opacity to 50%, and the black steaks turn to gray. Click on the OK button, and then do a Save (Command-S).**

BLURRING BITMAPS TO ADD GRAY VALUES

STEP 7: **Click on the StreakPattern layer and Option-drag it to the New Layer icon at the bottom-right part of the Layers palette. Name this new layer, which should be above the StreakPattern layer, StreakPatBlur. Using the slider at the top of the Layers palette, set its Opacity back to 100% and then double-click on its name to bring up the Layer Style dialog. Move the rightmost This Layer slider back to 255. Click OK. Turn off the Eye icons on the StreakPattern and MezzoPattern layers but make sure the StreakPatBlur layer stays active. Choose Command-L to look at this layer in Levels and you will notice that, because this is a bitmap, only pure white and pure black values exist. Cancel from Levels. Use Filter/Blur/Gaussian Blur (Shift-F4) of 1 pixel to blur this StreakPatBlur layer. Look at it in Levels again and you will notice that the Gaussian Blur added many intermittent gray values. Now double-click on StreakPat-Blur to bring up the Layer Style dialog box again.**

STEP 8: Now we can use the This Layer slider bar to do a lot of different types of effects. **Zoom in to 100% (Command-Option-0) so you can see in detail what is happening. Move the left Shadow slider on This Layer to the right until it reads about 39. This removes the dark shadow values from 0 to 38. Now move the rightmost Highlight slider to the left until it reads about 226. This removes the bright highlight values from 227 to 255. Notice that this modified pattern contains jaggy edges where the whites and blacks have been removed. While holding down the Option key, click on the right side of the left Shadow slider and slide it to the right, which will split the slider in two. Drag the right side of the left slider to the right until it reaches 116. Option-click on the left half of the rightmost slider and drag it to the left until it reads 162. The numbers on the This Layer slider should now read, from left to right: 39, 116, 162, and 226.** This means the shadow values from 0 to 38 are completely removed. The values from 39 to 116 are blended out slowly, which removes the jaggy edges. The values from 117 to 161 are completely opaque. The values from 162 to 226 are blended out, and the values from 227 to 255 are completely removed. **Try changing the Blend mode between Normal, Multiply, Screen, Lighten, Darken, and Difference until you get the one you like best. You can also readjust the Opacity for each different Blend mode you try. Click on the OK button in the Layer**

STEP 8: The StreakPatBlur layer with its Layer options and the state of the Layers palette.

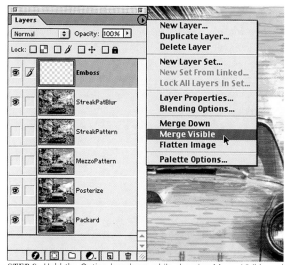

STEP 9: Hold the Option key down while choosing Merge Visible and leave it down until Photoshop stops working on its computations.

Options dialog box when you are happy with this layer's effect. Do Command-S to save this version of the document.

STEP 9: **You can obtain a very interesting effect by doing the following. Have the Packard layer at 100% Opacity and Normal Blend mode, the Posterize layer at 50% and Normal, and turn off the Eye icons for the MezzoPattern and StreakPattern layers. Now set StreakPatBlur to 40% and Multiply with the This Layer options, as shown in the Step 8 illustration. Option-click on the New Layer icon to the left of the trash can in the Layers palette and name the new layer Emboss. Make sure the new layer is above the StreakPatBlur layer. With the Emboss layer active, choose Option-Merge Visible from the Layers Palette menu to move all that you can now see into this Emboss layer. Make sure you leave the Option key down while Photoshop is doing the calculations. Now choose Filter/Stylize/Emboss and use the same settings you did in Step 5. Choose OK on the Emboss Filter; then change the Blend mode of the Emboss layer to SoftLight. If you now turn off the StreakPatBlur layer, you will notice that the pattern is embossed into the original colors without changing those colors much at all.** The Emboss layer has a lot of neutral gray in it and the Soft-Light Blend mode ignores neutral gray. **Try the Overlay and Hardlight modes that also ignore neutral gray. You can change the Opacity on the Emboss layer to lessen any of these effects.** See Chapter 31:"Blend Modes, Calculations and Apply Image" to understand how these Blend modes actually work.

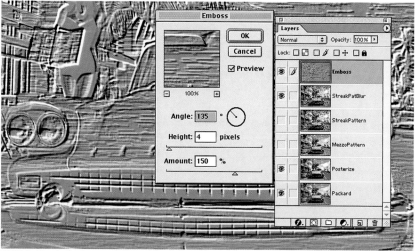

STEP 9: Here is the Layers palette and the Emboss filter while we are creating the Emboss effect.

TIME TO PLAY WITH LAYERS AND OPTIONS

STEP 10: Now you have several layers and effects that you can adjust until you get the final image you want. Remember that you can turn off any layer by clicking on its Eye icon. **Play with Opacity, Blend mode, the This Layer slider, and the Underlying slider in the Layer Style dialog for each layer until you get the final combined effect you like. Remember, the Underlying slider bar in the Layer Style dialog forces pixels of lower layers into the composite. In the StreakPatBlur layer, if you move the right-most Underlying slider to the left until it gets to 128, then all the values in the final**

Chapter 33: Posterize, Bitmaps, Textures, and Patterns

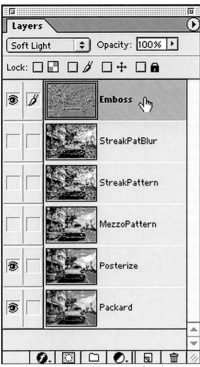

Here is the Layers palette setup for the image below.

composite from 128 to 255 will come from the lower layers, not from the StreakPatBlur layer. Play with these features until you understand them. When you are happy with a particular effect, you can use File/Save As with the Layers option turned off to save a flattened version of the file using only the layers that are currently visible. This way, you can save many variations of this multilayered document.

Before Photoshop had the Layer Style dialog and before it even had built in layer effects, like in Photoshop 6, Photoshop had the ability to create millions of interesting effects using this type of technique of stacking different versions of the same image on top of each other in different layers and then running filters and changing the Blend modes of each layer to create many of the effects that the current Layer Style dialog does in a more automatic way. Play with these features of Photoshop to prototype future effects that become the latest in your set of Photoshop surprises. I'm sure you can come up with something that looks great and nobody has ever tried before. The number of effect-combinations you can create is unlimited. HAVE FUN!

My favorite layer combination has the Packard Layer at 100% Normal, the Posterize layer at 50% Normal, the MezzoPattern, StreakPattern, and StreakPatBlur layers off, and the StreakPatBlur Emboss layer at 100% with its Blend mode set to SoftLIght.

34 HANDS-ON SESSION: Heartsinger CD Cover

*A tour of some of the more versatile Photoshop filters
as well as many useful layer and blending techniques
for getting the most out of all the filters.*

The best way to learn the simple filters is to play with them. Try out their features and compare different settings on the same image. Understand the range of possible things you can do with each filter. This is fun and easy, although you do need to give yourself a bit of time, as there are quite a few filters and lots of choices to make. There are many other Photoshop books, including the Photoshop manual, that have charts of each filter and what it looks like during one particular iteration. Photoshop comes with a set of over 75 filters, and with them and the rest of Photoshop, you can do millions of different effects. There are hundreds of other third-party filters on the market, and some of them are really unique, but a lot of them just give you a slightly easier way to do something that could already be done with the standard Photoshop filters by combining them with the other features of Photoshop.

In the rest of *Photoshop 6 Artistry,* we show you how to use the workhorse retouching filters in a lot of real-world examples. Here in this chapter, we are going to concentrate on how to use layers and masks to combine filters in interesting ways. We are also going to talk about some of the more complicated filters and how to understand them and make the best use of them. You need to play with all the filters and options because the possibilities for effects and combinations are in the millions; using the techniques we show you here, you can discover your own entirely new effects.

This example is the type of job that I normally would do using Photoshop, Painter and Illustrator. Painter is my primary tool for achieving painterly effects, Photoshop the tool for compositing and color correction and Illustrator the tool I'd use for type and shapes. To learn more about this type of work, check out *Photoshop, Painter, and Illustrator Side By Side.* For now, we'll show you how to set up the entire job in Photoshop.

GETTING MARGEE READY

STEP 1: **Open the file MargeeOrig.psd. Double-click on the Background layer to name it Layer 0.** We first have to knock Margee out of the garden background and do a bit of cleanup on a rather dirty scan. First, the cleanup. We start by using Dust & Scratches, which is useful for quick cleanup of this file because we are not going to be using a realistic version or the image. Then, we'll use Unsharp Mask, a filter that's explained in detail in Chapter 20: "Correcting a Problem Image."

Use Filter/Noise/Dust & Scratches and scroll around the picture to see areas that are dirty. I noticed areas in the hair and the lower-right side of the blue scarf that

STEP 1: Use Filter/Noise/Dust & Scratches to do an overall cleanup of the file.

were particularly noticeable. You want to set your filter high enough to rid the file of most of the noise, but not so high that you ruin details. In this case, **I used a Radius of 1 and a Threshold setting of 9**. This rids the file of all but the largest pieces of dust, yet doesn't soften the facial features too drastically. Any areas that are not cleaned by the filter would probably be better served by using the Rubber Stamp tool and cloning. Remember that you can use keyboard shortcuts to zoom in or out on the main window. By turning the Preview button on and off, you can see the effect your filter will have on the overall file.

STEP 2: After removing the dust, you'll need to resharpen the file to keep it from being too soft.

STEP 2: **Next, use Filter/Sharpen/Unsharp Mask** to bring back a bit of the detail in the photo. We're not going to do much. **Use between 125 and 135 for the Amount, 1 pixel for the Radius and 7 levels for the Threshold value.**

STEP 3: Highlight the edges of Margee's body and hair, making sure to overlap both the areas that you want extracted and the areas that you want to remove.

KNOCKING OUT THE BACKGROUND

STEP 3: Like most compositing jobs, we need to knock the figure out of its background before we start compositing. Photoshop 6 offers many ways to make a knock-out, but we're going to use the beefed up Extract command for this job.

First, you'll need to **make a copy of Layer 0** by dragging the layer name to the New Layer icon at the bottom of the Layers palette. **Hold down the Option key and double-click the Layer 0 copy to bring up the Layer Properties dialog and change the name of the layer to Extracted**. Please remember to always make a copy of the layer when you use the Extract command, as the command clears all the pixels that are left after the extraction. **Go to Image/Extract to bring up the Extract window and choose the first tool on the window's Tool palette, the Highlighter.**

Choose a width for your brush that allows you to cover the edge of Margee's body and hair with some overlap on both the body and the background. **I used 20**. Also, **change your highlight color from green to red** (or some custom color) to be able to see your highlight better against the primarily green background of the picture. Now you're simply going to **paint around the edges of the area that you want to extract from the background**, in this case, Margee. There's no need to paint around the bottom of the dress, but you do need to make sure your outline is solid—any gaps will cause the Fill tool to fill the entire file. Once you've made your outline, **choose the Fill tool**

STEP 3: Your file should look like this when you've completed highlighting.

STEP 3: If the blue filll spills over into the background, check your highlighted edges. When you use the Fill tool, Margee should be completely covered.

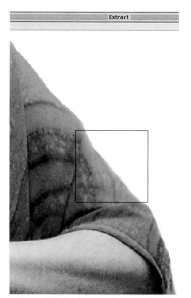

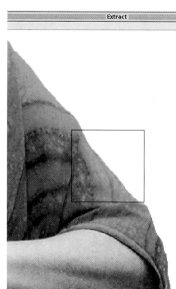

STEP 4: Here, I'm adding to the mask (making the deep blue edge more complete) by using Option with the Cleanup tool. Without the Option key, I can erase the errant blue pixels that you see in the white area.

STEP 4: This is the edge before using the Edge touch-up tool. It's a bit soft.

STEP 4: After using the tool, the edge is more well defined.

STEP 4: Check your edges against a black matte as well. You might be surprised at the pixels you missed using no matte or the white matte.

STEP 5: Resizing the file is a two-step process involving both Image Size (this dialog) and Canvas Size.

Step 6: The easiest way to set a new guide when you know the exact location you want is to use View/New Guide.

from the window's Tool palette and click inside the red highlighted area to fill the area of the extraction with blue fill. Click the Preview button when you're done with these steps.

STEP 4: **Set your Display Preview to White Matte and check the edges of your selection mask**. Chances are, you need to do some touch-up work. This is where the new capabilities of the Extract command come in very handy. First, we'll be working with the Cleanup tool. **Select the tool by clicking on the fifth icon on the Tool palette, or by typing C when you're in this dialog box** (all of the tools have keyboard shortcuts). **Use the tool to continue to delete unwanted areas by brushing over them, or use the Option key with the tool to bring back portions of the image that you want to keep.** You can change to opacity or brush size using the same keyboard shortcuts that you use with the regular painting tools. Once you've completed correcting the mask, **click the sixth tool in the palette to work with the Edge Touchup tool and sharpen the edges for a nice knock-out. Switch to Black Matte in the Display Preview to check your edges against a black background.** When you're happy with the preview, **click the OK button to make the knock-out.** Once you have this version on a separate layer, it can be used as it is, or to create a layer mask, as we will see later in this example.

STEP 5: At this point, we're going to set up the file for print size. This is the cover art and will bleed on three sides. **Go to Image/Image Size and make the Height 5 inches. Now go to Image/Canvas Size and make the Width of the canvas 4.85 inches. Position the existing artwork at the bottom-middle section.**

STEP 6: Now we need to set ruler guides for the edge of the CD cover and the text safety area. Adobe obviously listened to designers and added a new feature to the guides, allowing you to set guides numerically. This is good because they took away the Transform/Numeric feature, which allowed you to position items according to desired coordinates. Ah, well. **Go to View/New Guide and set the first horizontal guide at .125 inches. Set a second horizontal guide at .25 inches, a third at 4.625 inches and a forth at 4.75 inches.** Unfortunately, this command always defaults to a vertical guide (I suppose you do use those more than horizontal), so you have to **make sure you click the Horizontal button each time.** Now **set vertical guides** the same way but you only need guides on the right side **at 4.625 and 4.75 inches. Save this file as MargeeCDsize in Photoshop format.**

THE ARTISTIC FILTERS

Margee has requested that the photograph look more like a piece of artwork, and filtering is where we start to achieve that result. But many of the built in filters in Photoshop give you less than spectacular results if you rely on the default settings. One of the keys to successful filtering is exper-imentation. Change the options and see what happens. It helps to keep a notebook handy to record which filters and which settings give you results that are worth using. You don't want to endlessly repeat the process.

The Photoshop filters are arranged in groups that give you clues as to the function of the filters. In addition, the filters have names that sometimes clue you in to the result you can expect—Sometimes. In other cases, and the Artistic filters are a good example, if you go by name in choosing your filter, you'll most likely be dissapointed. Does this mean that the filters are useless? No, it means that you'll

STEP 7: The Dry Brush filter breaks up the photo but doesn't really give a spectacular look.

probably have to combine some filtered layers to get an effect that you like. And once again, don't forget to write it down. Or, name your layers with descriptive names that remind you what you did. I find that I most often use Overlay, Soft Light or Hard Light as the Blend mode for a layer filtered with the Artistic filters.

Now, on to filtering.

STEP 7: **Make a copy of the Extracted layer and name it Dry Brush. Go to Filter/Artis-tic/Dry Brush and use these settings: Brush Size, 2; Brush Detail, 8; and Texture, 1.** This will give you somewhat of a dry brush look, but it certainly isn't where we want to stop.

STEP 8: **Make a second copy of the Extracted layer, move it to the top of the Layers palette and call this one Colored Pencil.** If you use the default settings with this filter, you get a very strange gray overlay to areas of the file, which by itself is very ugly. If, however, you use that filtered layer with a Blend mode, you might get a result that looks a bit more like colored pencil. For this file **go to Filter/Artistic/Colored Pencil and use a Pencil Width of 3, a Stroke pressure of 12 and a Paper Brightness of 50.** This still doesn't give you what I'd call a colored pencil effect, but now **change the Blend mode of the Colored Pencil layer to Soft Light.** This is a much nicer effect than either filter by itself.

MORE FILTERS

STEP 9: **Make another copy of the Extracted layer. Move it to the top and call it Find Edges.** Now, I have to confess, the Find Edges filter is one of my favorites. In early versions of Photoshop it reminded me of those crayon drawings we did in elementary

STEP 8: Even though I changed the set-tings of the Colored Pencil filter, I didn't get what I'd call a true colored pencil effect.

STEP 8: When I changed the Blend mode to Soft Light, the effect became much nicer.

STEP 9: This is the result of the Find Edges filter.

STEP 9: Using the Find Edges layer in Overlay mode at 80% gives interesting detail and color to the artwork.

STEP 10: The Accented Edges layer in Soft Light mode at 60% adds yet another level of interest.

school, where you laid down colors, covered them with black crayon, then scraped through to reveal the underlying colors. The filter has changed in recent versions to an inverted version of the original, and that's fine because it really is a more useful filter that way. Still, it's a filter that's better used in conjunction with some changes in levels or Blend modes, than by itself. **Go to Filter/Stylize/Find Edges, and change the Blend mode to Overlay. Next, change the Opacity of the layer to 80%.** Open the History palette and click Blending Change (the state before the Opacity Change), and then click back on Opacity Change to see which effect you like the best. I left mine at 80%.

STEP 10: One final filter in this step, and yes, you need to **make an additional copy of the Extracted layer and move it to the top. Call this layer Accented Edges. Go to Filter/Brush Strokes/Accented Edges and use Edge Width: 5, Edge Brightness: 35 and Smoothness: 3. Change the Blend mode to Soft Light and make the Opacity 60%. Save your artwork.**

ADDING THE POSTER ARTWORK

STEP 11: Not only is Margee an excellent singer, she's also an accomplished artist. Because the songs on the CD are associated with the seven chakras, she wants to use a poster that she did a few years back as part of the CD cover. **Open the file, PosterOrig.psd. Go to Image/Image Size and make the height of the image 2.5 inches. Keep on Constrain Proportions and Resample Image.** This step is not absolutely necessary, but for me it's a bit easier than trying to do the entire resize with the Free Transform command. **Next, use the Move tool and move the entire layer over to the Margee file. Hold down the Shift key as you move the layer to have it placed in the middle of the window.** Before you continue working on the CD cover, **return to the PosterOrig.psd file and use File/Revert to bring it back to its original size.** You'll need it again later. **Now return to the Margee file.**

STEP 12: This is how the Poster Resize layer looks after you change its opacity.

STEP 12: Move only the bottom middle handle during the Free Transform to make the fourth heart fit at Margee's hands and the top heart fit at her shoulders.

STEP 12: This step is probably the hardest part of making this cover. The poster artwork has to fit a certain way over the body and hands. But the proportions of the poster are all wrong, so we're going to have to do some finagling to make things work. Be patient with this step. It's one of those things production artists have to do from time to time and it's not elegant work. Luckily we'll add some effects later that will disguise some of the problems.

Change the name of the layer to Poster Resize and change the Opacity to 60%. Here's where the fun begins. You have to **resize the poster so the fourth heart from the bottom fits over the porcelain heart that Margee is holding,** but at the same time, you have to **make the large heart at the top fit right at Margee's shoulders and throat.** So this is not going to be a uniform scale. **Go to Edit/Free Transform and use only the bottom-middle handle to make the scale. Press Enter to accept the transformation.**

STEP 13: Select only the part of the poster under Margee's hands for the next resize.

STEP 13: You don't need to extend the poster to the bottom of the blue scarf. It will fade out before then.

STEP 14: Select the right side of the poster for resizing.

STEP 14: Extend the artwork to Margee's elbow.

STEP 13: **Select the bottom portion of the poster under Margee's hands and use Edit/Free Transform and the bottom-middle handle to resize that portion to about 1 inch from the bottom of the window.** You don't need to cover the bottom of Margee's blue scarf, as we're going to fade the poster out before the bottom of the scarf. **Press Enter to accept this transformation.**

STEP 14: **Select the section of the poster to the right of the hearts and use Edit/Free Transform to extend the poster to the edge of Margee's scarf.** Use only the right-middle handle to avoid skewing the picture. **Select the left section and repeat the process, extending the artwork to the other elbow.**

STEP 15: **Bring the Opacity of the Poster Resize layer to 100%.** Now **Command-click on the Extracted layer** to load the silhouette as a selection. **Make the Poster Resize layer the active layer** and **click the Add Layer Mask icon on the bottom of the Layers palette** to make a layer mask. Once again, **save your file.**

STEP 16: Now we'll get rid of the lightest areas of the poster and leave only the color overlaying the dress and scarf. **Double-click the Poster Resize layer to bring up the Layer Styles dialog.** You may recognize the "Blend If" area, but you'll see that Photoshop 6 has added quite a bit of new functionality elsewhere in this dialog. **Start blend-**

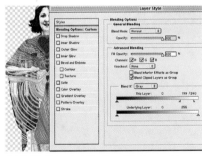

STEP 16: Using just the Gray This Layer slider you can remove most of the white pixels from the poster artwork without having to create a mask.

ing using the gray levels by moving the top Blend If slider down to 240. This gets rid of the majority of the light areas. **Hold down the Option key** to split the slider **and move the left half of the slider down to about 200**. This gives you a softer blend between the colored areas and the rest of the file.

Correcting the Poster Layer Mask

STEP 17: You probably noticed that the poster artwork ends rather abruptly before the bottom of the file. What we want is a gradual fade-out instead. **Command-click the Extracted layer to load that layer as a selection.** Now **Option-click the Layer Mask thumb-**

STEP 17: Option-drag the Margee tool to deselect the upper portion of the mask.

STEP 17: This is the section in which we will build the gradient.

369

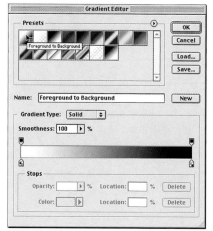

nail to see only that mask. We need to select the bottom portion of Margee's silhouette and add a gradient from white at the top to black at the bottom, in order to fade out the poster artwork. **Type M (or Shift-M) until you have the Rectangular Margee tool. Option-drag around the upper portion of the selection to delete it from the selected area.** You should leave only about one-third of the silhouette selected. **Type D to get the default colors and type G to get the Gradient tool.** Make sure you check the Tool Options bar for the current gradient before you start your blend. If you are not currently showing white to black, **click the gradient to bring up the Gradient Editor and select the Foreground to Background gradient. Start at the top of the selected area and drag about halfway down** to fade the poster artwork out completely before you reach the bottom of Margee's scarf. Click back on the Layer thumbnail to check the placement of your blend. If you are not happy, you can immediately redraw the blend to shorten or lengthen the exposed poster artwork. Deselect the bottom portion of the layer mask when you are happy with how the blend looks.

STEP 17: If you have any gradient besides White to Black here, click the gradient to get to the Gradient Editor.

STEP 17: Make sure that you are using the default colors and the Foreground to Background gradient.

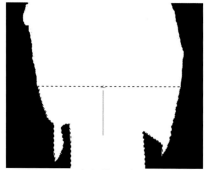

STEP 17: Drag only halfway down the selected area.

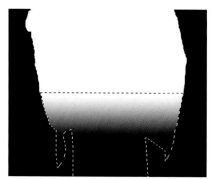

STEP 17: This is the resulting blend of the previous drag.

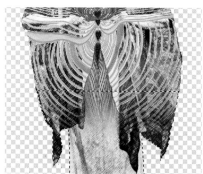

STEP 17: This is how the artwork looks when the blended mask is applied.

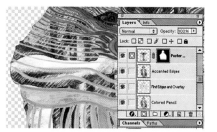

STEP 18: Make sure you are correcting the layer mask for the Poster Resize layer and not painting on the layer itself.

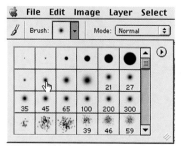

STEP 18: This is the Soft Round 9-pixel brush if you are using the default brushes.

STEP 18: There are a couple of other issues about the layer mask for the Poster Resize layer that need to be addressed. The yellow band under Margee's right arm is distracting and needs to be removed. Also, the top edge of the poster artwork above the largest heart is very straight-edged and rather artifical. We'll remove both by painting on the layer mask. **Use the Paintbrush tool (B or Shift-B) and click the Option arrow beside the Brush icon on the Tool Options bar to bring up the Brushes palette. Choose the Soft Round 9-pixel brush** (the second from the left on the second row if you are using the default brushes). Remember that Photoshop now increases or decreases your brush by 5 pixels when you use the Left and Right Bracket keys. You no longer scroll through the current Brushes palette. In this case, that will be really helpful. **Click the Layer Mask thumbnail for the Poster Resize layer so you work on the mask**, but make sure you are still viewing the artwork and not the mask. **Set your opacity on your brush to 100% by typing 0. Type X to exchange the foreground and background colors, and gently brush away the yellow band under the arm.** Increase or decrease the size of the brush as needed by using the keyboard shortcuts, and type X to paint the mask with white if you delete too much of the artwork.

STEP 19: **Scroll up to the top of the poster artwork** and look at the straight edge at Margee's neck. **Use the same brush with black to gently remove the edge.** Come in close to the heart and take away a bit on the shoulders to preserve a natural curve. **Now save your file again.**

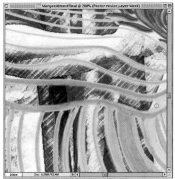

STEP 19: Use the same brush as before to remove the sharp edge at the neckline.

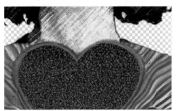

STEP 19: The finished product should look something like this.

STEP 18: The soft-edged brush helps you paint away the yellow band without harsh edges. Decrease the brush size with the keyboard shortcut as you get closer to the center of the poster.

MOVE THE LAYERS AND MAKE A LAYER SET

STEP 20: Remember that this CD cover bleeds on three sides. Right now we have Margee positioned in the center of the window, but that area includes .125 inches of bleed. She needs to be moved to the left a bit. The actual area of the front of the CD is 4.75 inches. **Use View/New Guide to place a vertical guide at 2.375 inches. Link Margee's filtered layers, the Extracted layer, the Original layer and the Poster Resize layer. Type V for the Move tool and use the Left Arrow key to move all the layers to the left about .125 inches. The hearts on the poster should be centered around the guide you just made.** In Photoshop 5 or 5.5, you could use the Free Transform/Numeric command to position the artwork exactly, but that command is gone and we'll just have to get by doing this visually. Now **unlink Layer 0 (the original layer), Extracted and Poster Resize.** The other four layers are going to become a layer set. Rather than creating a set and then dragging the layers to it, **use the Layers palette Options menu and use New Set from Linked (Shift-F12 with ArtistKeys). Name the new set MargeeArtwork, make the Blend mode Pass Through, and assign red as the color for the group.** Pass Through keeps the Blend mode of the layers within the set interactive with layers outside the set. **Save the file.**

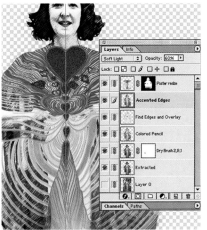

STEP 20: Link all the layers to move them as a group.

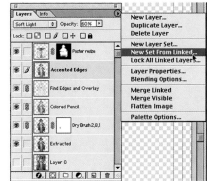

STEP 20: Unlink the three layers that are not filtered versions of Margee and create a layer set of the layers that are.

STEP 20: Once you've created a layer set you can assign a blend mode and opacity for the set as well as for each individual layer in the the set.

371

STEP 21: Select a portion that has the full range of colors.

STEP 21: Use Free Transform to stretch the color across the file.

STEP 21: Free Transform will give you an approximate preview until you hit Enter.

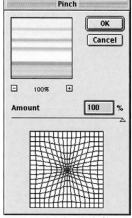

STEP 23: Set the Pinch filter to its maximum for the Pinch Filter layer.

CREATE THE BACKGROUND ARTWORK

There is still more work to be done with Margee, but we're going to take a break from working with her to work on the background.

STEP 21: **Reopen the PosterOrig.psd artwork** if you closed it earlier and **use Image/Image Size to make the height of the Poster 5 inches. Keep on Resample image.** Now **make a selection using the Retangular Marquee tool**. Your selection should be about **20-30 pixels wide and should cover the length of the artwork**. Choose an area that has a wide range of colors, as we will use this to create the background for the CD cover, but don't include any of the heart art towards the center of the poster. **Switch to the Move tool (type V) and Shift-drag this section over to the Margee file.**

STEP 22: The band will now be in the center of the Margee file. **Use the Move tool to place the band on the left edge of the window. Use Edit/Free Transform (Command-T) and drag the middle handle to the right to completely fill the window with color.** You may find that you have to drag the handle a bit past the actual window's edge on the right to keep the color from fading away before the edge. When you have resized the artwork to fit, **press Enter to accept the transformation. Option-double-click on the layer to rename it Background Lines, and move it to the bottom of the Layers palette.**

STEP 23: This looks okay, but it would be nice to have something a bit more fluid to harmonize with the curves of the poster artwork. So let's filter a bit. First, **make a copy of Background Lines by dragging it to the New Layer icon on the bottom of the Layers palette. Next, choose Filter/Distort/Pinch and set the amount to 100%. Say OK** and you have a really nice effect that gives you a sense of energy radiating from the center. **Name this layer, Pinch Filter.**

(Note: If you are following the bolded steps to create this example and you want to finish the necessary steps only, you can skip to Step 37 and continue.)

FILTERS AND BLEND MODES FOR FURTHER EFFECTS

STEP 24: Maybe you want something a little wilder. **Switch back to the Background Lines layer** and let's play a bit with the Wave filter. **Use Filter/Distort/Wave and input the settings shown in the illustration.** We're going to try the filter three different ways. **First use Sine as the Wave type.** By reducing the Number of Generators down to 1, you get a clearer picture of what the filter is actually doing to your file. **Say OK to this filter and view the results in the file.** If it helps, you can **click the Eye icon beside the Margee Artwork set, the Pinch Filter layer and the Poster Resize layer to view only the Background Lines layer. Now, Undo (Command-Z) the filter** to try another setting.

STEP 24: The result of the Wave filter using Sine as the wave type.

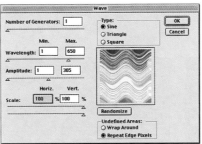

STEP 24: Set your filter options this way and get ready to run the filter several times.

STEP 25: **Make a copy of this layer and name it Triangle Wave. Return to the Wave filter** (you can use Command-Option-F to run the same filter with different options) and keep the same settings, but **use Triangle as the Wave type.** Once again, view the result in the file window.

STEP 26: **Return to the Background Lines layer and run the filter once again using Square as the Wave type. This time set the Amplitude to 250 Minimum and 500 Maximum. Rename the layer Square Wave.** We'll keep this version as well and do some further experimentation.

STEP 24: The result of the Wave filter using Triangle as the wave type. Don't adjust that dial!

STEP 24: The result of the Wave filter using Square as the wave type with adjusted settings.

STEP 27: **Turn on the Eye icons for the Pinch Filter and Square Wave layers only. Make sure the Square Wave layer is on top of the Pinch Filter layer. Now change the Blend mode of the Square Wave layer to Multiply.**

STEP 28: **Double-click the Square Wave layer** to bring up the Layer Effects dialog. We are once again going to use the Blend If section, but this time we are going to use only Color channels rather than the gray level for our blends. **Use the Channel pop-up and switch to the Red channel. Use the This Layer Highlight slider and move the slider left to**

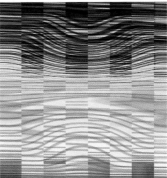

STEP 27: The Square Wave and Pinch Filter layers together with the Square Wave layer set to Multiply.

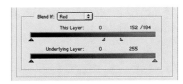

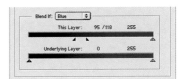

STEP 27: Use these settings in the Blend If area of the Square Wave layer blending options.

373

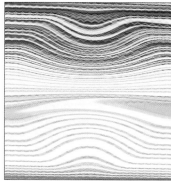

STEP 27: The result of the blending.

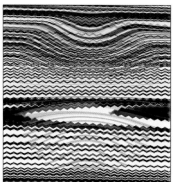

STEP 29: The Triangle Wave layer is above the Pinch Filter layer and set to Soft Light at 100%.

STEP 29: Here the Triangle Wave layer is set to Difference at 100%.

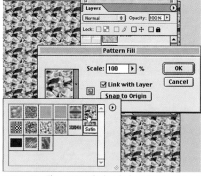

STEP 29: Here the Triangle Wave layer is set to Difference at 100%, but the Blend If Blue Highlight slider is set to 127 and 200.

184. Now hold down the Option key and split the slider, moving the left side down to 152. Switch to the Blue channel and use the This Layer Shadow slider. Move the slider right to 95, then hold down Option and move the right side of the slider to 118. Again, if you tried to do this with a layer mask, you'd make yourself crazy. I rely on Blend If a lot when I'm doing compositing.

STEP 29: **Turn off the Square Wave layer and turn on the Triangle Wave layer. Make sure that it is above the Pinch Filter layer. Set the Blend mode on this layer to Soft Light.** This gives you some nice textural effect. **Now set the Blend mode to Difference.** When I'm compositing, I generally try several of the Blend modes, usually Multiply, Overlay, Soft Light, Hard Light, Color Burn and Difference. I love Difference, just because you can end up with such funky colors. You can use Shift-+ or Shift-– to cycle through the Blend modes, and, with each Blend mode, try the Blend If command if you are looking for a special effect. **You can now throw away the Triangle Wave and Square Wave layers** unless you want to experiment more.

ADDING TEXTURE WITH LAYERS, FILTERS AND LIGHTING EFFECTS

STEP 30: Photoshop 6 has also added pattern layers, which can be used to quickly generate a texture and Gradient Map layers (which can give you unexpected and sometimes delightful color variations on a photo or layer). **Click the Pinch Filter layer** to make it active and **use the Layers palette New Fill Layer icon to create a new Pattern layer. Click the pattern swatch to show the currently loaded patterns.** This is such a treat to finally have more than one pattern available at a time to use with Photoshop. And, you can add pattern swatches, as we will see later in this example. For now, **click the rightmost swatch on the top row if you are using the default patterns.** This is the Satin pattern. **Say OK to this layer and set the Blend mode to Soft Light or Color Burn.** Both give you interesting texture. Now set the mode to Difference. This is pretty jumbled, but if you do some blending of the gray levels, you can get some cool effects. Another

STEP 29: Click and drag this icon to add a fill or adjustment layer. Option-click to bring up a dialog that allows you to group this layer with the one beneath it.

STEP 30: The currently loaded patterns appear when you click the pattern swatch. Choose the pattern you want then click back on the Pattern Fill dialog box to close the swatches.

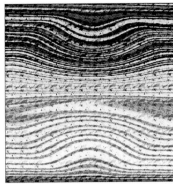

STEP 30: The Satin Pattern layer over the Pinch Filter layer in Color Burn mode.

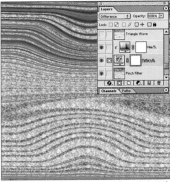

STEP 30: Though the Pattern layer is in Difference mode, I've blended out the highest gray values of the Pattern layer and added a Colorized Hue/Saturation layer on top.

possibility is to add a Hue/Saturation layer above the Pattern layer, grouped with the Pattern layer. Use the Colorize option to change to hue of the Pattern layer and see how it affects the Blend mode. Throw this Pattern layer away when you finish playing.

Step 31: Now let's use some filters to produce layers for texture. Click the New Layer icon on the Layers palette to make a new transparent layer. Use the Eyedropper to sample a medium blue color from the Pinch Filter layer. Now Command-Delete to fill the layer with that foreground color. Go to Filters/Texture/"Texturizer and choose Burlap from the pop-up menu. When you use the Texturizer, you can load textures from other places (such as the Pre-sets/Textures folder that ships with Photoshop 6), and you can create your own. Basically, any single layered Photoshop file can be used as a texture, but the tiling will look better if you use files created with use as a pattern or texture in mind. You can delete this layer when you finish playing with it.

STEP 31: The Texturizer filter can add texture to any layer or selection quickly. You can use a single layer file as a pattern.

STEP 32: **Use the same blue foreground color** that you chose before and **Option-click with the Eyedropper tool to select a light orange background color. Now go to Filter/Render/Clouds to create a Clouds layer**. If you hold down the Option key as you create this effect, you get a more contrasty version of the filter. For this layer, I liked **Exclusion for the Blend mode** with some heavy blending of the underlying layer to push the color stripes back through. Darken, Difference and Luminosity also gave interesting results.

STEP 31: My Burlap layer in Luminosity mode with some blending of the gray values.

STEP 32: The Clouds layer is set to Exclusion and the Blend If Underlying Layer Shadow slider settings are 165 and 215.

STEP 33: In the same group are two more filters that are invaluable for creating texture and effects: Filter/Render/Texture Fill and Filter/Render/Lighting Effects. First, Filter/Render/Texture Fill. You can use this filter in conjuction with a grayscale file to fill a layer or channel with texture. You could then use a layer created this way with Blend modes that give you textures similar to what we've been working with so far. But, if you use this filter to fill a channel, you have an added benefit in being able to use that channel with the Lighting Effects filter. This is where we're headed.

STEP 33: The Texture Fill filter works only with grayscale files. You can load one from the Presets/Textures folder or create your own before running the filter.

375

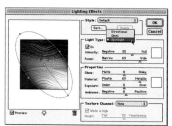

STEP 34: The Default light is a white spotlight with white ambient light and no texture channel chosen.

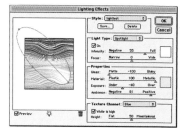

STEP 34: You can set up your own lighting situation and save it for later use.

STEP 35: I used these settings and the Snakeskin texture...

STEP 35: ...to achieve this effect.

STEP 35: The same settings as above used with the Puzzle texture.

Open the Channels palette and click the New Channel icon at the bottom of the palette to get a new channel. It will be completely black. Now **go to Filter/Render/Texture Fill and look in your Adobe Photoshop 6 folder to find the Presets/Textures folder. Choose the Snake Skin.psd file.** This will fill the channel with texture. **Double-click on the Alpha channel and name it Snakeskin.**

STEP 34: **Make a copy of your Pinch Filter layer, name it Lighting Effects and go to Filter/Render/Lighting Effects.** This is an enormous dialog box, but don't let it upset you. Like most things in Photoshop, if you work with one option at a time, you'll get the hang of it. First, notice the area named Light Type. There are three light types for you to choose from, and you can have any or all of them in any lighting situation that you set up. The Omni light is always round and shines from directly above the image. Directional lights shine from a distance, so the light is diffused and hits the entire image from the same direction. Spotlights are elliptical. The shape of that ellipses can vary from completely round to elongated, and is controlled via handles that appear when you click on the light source in the Preview window. The straight line defines the light direction and angle. The Focus slider (which only appears for this light type) controls how far towards the edges of the ellipses the beam is spread. The front edge is always at the gray circle at the end of the straight line. At its widest, the beam will spread so that it touches the middle handles of the ellipses. In all three light types, the color square in this area of the dialog defines the color of the current light, and you can change that color by clicking on the square to bring up the Color Picker. Each light in a setup can have its own color (but all lights in a setup have the same ambient color). The Intensity slider controls the brightness of the light with Full being 100% of the light color, and Negative being 100% of the complimentary color.

The Properties area controls the ambient light (chosen by clicking on the color square) and the reflective properties of the image. These controls remain the same for every light in a particular setup. Gloss controls how bright the hightlights will be. Material controls the reflection with Metallic reflecting more than Plastic. The Exposure slider controls the overall brightness of the image itself. Ambience controls how much of the light beam and the image are affected by the ambient light source, moving from Positive where the entire image is affected, to Zero where all ambient light is blocked out and only the color of the lights themselves shine on the image, into the Negative area where the light sources draw inward until they become only spots of color.

The Texture channel area is where you add texture, but unlike many of the other areas of Photoshop, where you can search for a file, you must have the texture available as a channel in the current file. If you use one of the color channels of the current document, you can achieve some impasto effects. If you use a Texture channel that you've created, you can simulate just about any texture imaginable.

STEP 35: **Choose the Snakeskin channel as the Texture channel and either use the settings shown in the illustration here or create your own. Click OK.** Try your same settings with a different Texture channel that you create (I used the Puzzle texture) and also with one of the Color channels of the document (Blue gives you a nice result).

LIQUIFY

STEP 36: And now for something completely different—Liquify. This modal dialog gives you many of the capabilities of Painter's liquid brushes, plus additional functionality. **Make a copy of the Pinch Filter layer and rename it Liquify; then go to Image/Liquify.** This new command in Photoshop 6 allows you to move the pixels of your image as if it were a pool of viscous liquid. If you make alterations that you really like, you can freeze areas that you want to leave undisturbed, continue working and thaw those areas later when you are ready to change them. You can reconstruct your file choosing different algorithms to give different effects. It's all pretty neat.

All the tools in the palette can use different size brushes and pressure. If you have a pressure sensitive tablet, you can also click a button to use pressure to change the brush size. However, I didn't find the tools particularly responsive and had better results setting the exact pressure I wanted to use. You can Shift-click with the tools, as you would regular painting tools, to make straight-line editing passes on the image, and you can select an area of the image with any selection tool or a mask before entering the Liquify dialog to edit a smaller area of the file. If you make an irregular shaped selection, Photoshop will give you a rectangular area in the dialog, but the area outside your selection will be frozen, so as not to be affected by your edits.

You'll probably use the Warp tool the most. This tool pushes the pixels as you drag. The Twirl Clockwise tool rotates pixels to the right. You might not notice a lot happening as you drag, but if you hold the mouse button down in one area, you'll see the pixels rotate around the center of your brush. Twirl Counterclockwise is the same, except the rotation is to the left.

The Pucker tool pulls the artwork toward the center of the brush, and the Bloat tool pushes away from the center of the brush. You want to play a little with both Pucker and Bloat to get a feel for how to paint with them. Although I started using both tools only in stationary positions, after a while I became pretty adept at moving the pixels while dragging. Once again, though, I set a specific pressure, rather that using pressure sensitivity.

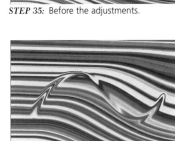

STEP 35: Before the adjustments.

STEP 36: Warp drag in a wavy line.

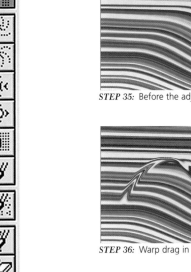

STEP 36: The Liquify tools and their keyboard shortcuts from top to bottom are: Warp (W), Twirl Clockwise (R), Twirl Counterclockwise (L), Pucker (P), Bloat (B), Shift Pixels (S), Reflection (M), Reconstruct (E), Freeze (F), Thaw (T).

STEP 36: Warp Shift-click horizontally.

STEP 36: Twirl Clockwise using a slow drag.

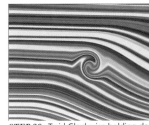

STEP 36: Twirl Clockwise holding down the mouse in one spot.

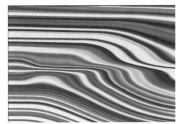

STEP 36: Pucker moving left to right.

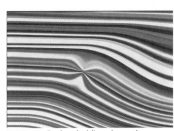

STEP 36: Pucker, holding down the mouse in one spot.

STEP 36: Bloat tool dragging.

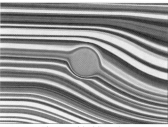

STEP 36: Bloat tool holding the mouse in one spot.

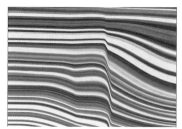

STEP 36: Here I used the Shift Pixels tool while dragging from top to bottom.

STEP 36: Here I've frozen the left half of Margee's face using the Freeze tool.

STEP 36: After three passes from top to bottom with the Reflect tool, I've basically brought the left half of her face to the right side.

STEP 36: Here I've thawed the area so you can better see the result.

Shift Pixels is bit difficult to understand at first. When you drag using this tool, pixels move perpendicular to the stroke direction. If you simply drag, pixels move to the left. If you Option-drag pixels move to the right. Here's a place where I felt Shift-clicking worked better than dragging.

The most difficult tool to work with is the Reflection tool. This tool takes pixels to the left of the brush area of a downward stroke and copies those pixels to the brush area. Option-dragging takes pixels to the right of the brush area to copy. A left to right stroke uses pixels below the brush for the copy. A right to left stroke uses pixels above the brush. Confused yet? Option-dragging takes pixels from the opposite direction. If you freeze the area that contains the pixels to be copied, you get a more controlled reflection of that area. Hopefully the illlustrations here will help you get an inkling of how to use the tool. It may be one of those things you just have to try until you get the "Aha!" response. Overlapping strokes create a watery reflection, but it may be easier to use one of Photshop's other filters.

The Reconstruction tool allows you to either revert or reconstruct the file. This tool works in conjuction with the Recontruction area of the dialog. If you choose Revert as the mode, the brush takes your artwork back to its original state as you stroke an area. But choose the other methods, and you can get some very interesting results. The Reconstruct button does the same thing to the entire artwork. You also have a Revert button that can take all of the artwork back to its original form in one click.

If you're an illustrator, you're going to absolutely love the Liquify command. It's worth the time it will take you to learn to use it. For the rest of us, a really neat trick is to make a bunch of alterations then hit the Reconstruct or Revert button and watch your screen do the magic dance. For once you can do what you'd really like to do to your client's job and not have the damage be permanent. **Play with this command and its tools.** Enjoy!

Chapter 34: Heartsinger CD Cover

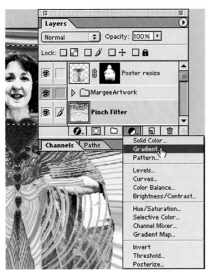

STEP 37: Click and drag the Fill and Adjustment Layer icon to the Gradient layer.

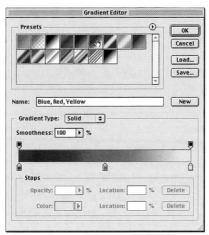

STEP 37: Once you choose a Gradient layer, you immediately go to the Gradient Editor to choose a gradient.

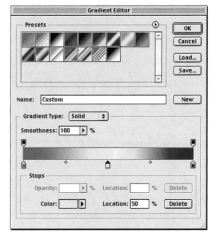

STEP 38: At any time you can edit the gradient you are using for your Gradient layer. Here, I've moved the color stops to create more of a natural spectrum.

ADD A GRADIENT LAYER

STEP 37: **Turn on the Margee Artwork set by clicking the Eye icon beside that folder. Return to the Pinch Filter layer.** We want to give a little color punch to this background, so **click and drag the Fill and Adjustment layer button on the Layers palette and to a Gradient Fill layer above the Pinch Filter layer. Click the gradient swatch to bring up the Gradient Editor and choose the Blue, Red, Yellow gradient. Say OK to both areas of this command. Now lower the opacity of this layer to 45%.** This is a good start, but we want the color to follow the spectrum of colors of the poster better, so we'll need to do a bit of editing.

STEP 38: **Double-click the icon for the Gradient Fill layer, and then click the gradient swatch. Move the Color Stop icons until Red is on the left, Yellow in the middle and Blue on the right.** Remember, if you inadvertently add an extra color stop, you can remove it by dragging it off the palette. If you need to get back to your last saved gradient, you can hold down Option and the Cancel button becomes Reset. **Say OK to both areas of this change.**

STEP 38: The new gradient is too yellow in the center.

ADD GRADIENT MASK TO GRADIENT LAYER

STEP 39: Now the color is basically correct and in the right areas, but the yellow in the center is a bit too intense and we want to take it out. We could edit the gradient again, maybe even add some transparency to the gradient. But because everything is pretty good the way it is, we'll elect to add a layer mask to the Gradient layer. **Click the Layer Mask icon on the Layers palette to add a new, blank mask. Type D for the default colors, and then X to swap the foreground and background colors. Now type G for the Gradient tool and choose the Reflected gradient type** (it's the forth icon on the Options bar). **Click and drag from the heart second from the bottom to about the tip of Margee's nose, while holding the Shift key to keep the blend straight up and down.** Because the blend is foreground (black) to background (white), the mask will be black in the center and white from the point you finished your drag. And as you are using the Reflected gradient, that pattern is reflected from the point of origin to

STEP 39: Adding a Gradient mask to the Gradient layer allows me to remove certain areas of the blend in a gentle way.

379

STEP 40: Here I've made a selection which I'll define as a pattern.

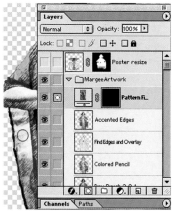

STEP 41: The new Pattern layer should be part of the Margee Artwork set.

STEP 43: Merge Layer Set collapses all the layers in the group into one layer.

the other side of the mask. This removes the yellow color in the center but leaves the gradient intact on both the top and bottom. Just right. **Save your file.**

ADD A PATTERN LAYER

STEP 40: The original photo of Margee was taken outside and the light shining through the blue scarf now looks awkward. We need to "add scarf" to the image. For this, we'll use a Pattern layer. When you define a pattern, you make a rectangular selection. All the layers that are turned on when you invoke the Define Pattern command will be part of the pattern. So, **turn on only the layers in the Margee Artwork set. Now make a selection in the blue scarf area under Margee's left arm.** Try not to take the darker blue vertical area, as that will make the pattern more noticeable when it tiles. When you are happy with your selection, **go to Edit/Define Pattern. The selected area will show in the swatch area. Name this Blue Scarf.**

STEP 41: **Click the Accented Edges layer** to make it active. Now **click and drag on the Fill and Adjustment Layer icon on the Layers palette to add a new Pattern layer.**

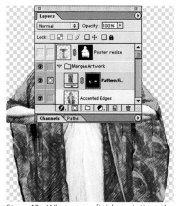

Step 42: When you finish painting the mask on the Pattern layer, the large white areas should be gone and the pattern of the scarf should look natural.

When the dialog box comes up, you should see the pattern that you just created. If not, click the pattern swatch and find the Blue Scarf pattern in the swatches area. **Say OK to fill this layer with the Pattern tile.** The Pattern layer automatically has a layer mask attached to it, and the layer mask will be active. If black is still your foreground color, **Option-Delete to fill the layer mask with black.** You are now looking at the Margee artwork, but we're going to paint on the Pattern layer mask.

STEP 42: **Type B to get the Paintbrush tool and choose the Soft Round 45-pixel brush** to start with. **Type D to get the default colors and 7 to paint at 70% opacity.** Now **paint over the white areas of the artwork,** and the Pattern layer will reappear where you paint out the mask. Use smaller brushes and less opacity when needed, and don't forget to switch colors and paint with black if you make mistakes that need correction.

ADD HANDS FROM MERGED LAYER SET

STEP 43: **Click the Margee Artwork layer set icon on the Layers palette.** When you are on a layer set layer in Photoshop 6, you have an additional Layer command, namely Merge Layer Set. The keyboard shortcut, Command-E, is shared by three commands: Merge Down, Merge Linked and Merge Layer Set. The setup of the Layers palette determines which command is currently available. **Use the Layers palette Options pop-up to choose Merge Layer Set.** The set becomes a layer with the name Margee Artwork. Convenient, huh?

STEP 44: **Make a rectangular selection of the arms and hands of the Margee Artwork layer and use Layer/New/Layer via Copy (Command-J) to copy those pixels to a new layer in exactly the same position. Option-double-click on this layer and rename it Hands. Move this layer to the top of the Layers palette. Make a selection of the**

hands and arms only, using whatever method is most comfortable and quickest for you. It doesn't have to be perfect, as you are going to have to do some painting on the layer mask anyway. But the better your selection, the less work later. I'm pretty handy with the Pen tool, so I made my selection that way. The Magnetic Lasso also made a decent selection without much trouble. **When you have a good, basic selection, click the Layer Mask icon to add a layer mask.**

STEP 44: Make a selection about this big to copy to a new layer.

STEP 44: The great thing about using Layer via Copy or Layer via Cut is they put the material on the new layer in exactly the same position as the old layer. This can be indispensible for compositing.

STEP 45: **Use a soft-edge brush to clean up your layer mask for the Hands layer.** It should look like the arms are coming out of the poster artwork, and like that artwork is printed on the blue scarf. I brought the Extracted layer to the top of my Layers palette and turned the Eye icon for that layer on and off to help me discern where the edges of the hands should be. You could also make that layer's opacity low and keep it on to guide you. **You should see the scarf artwork around the heart, and you also want to paint out the partial red heart just under Margee's thumbs. Save your work.**

STEP 44: Move the Hands layer to the top of the palette.

ADD HEART FROM ANOTHER FILE

STEP 46: The porcelain heart is an important element in this piece, so we have a separate file from which to place an unaltered version. **Open the file HandsSmall and open the Channels palette. Command-click the Heart Mask channel** to load it as a selection. Now **use the Move tool (V) and Shift-drag a copy of the heart to the Margee file. Option-double-click the layer; name it Heart and move it to the top of the Layers palette. Change the opacity of this layer to 60% and use Edit/Free Transform (Command-T) to resize the heart to slightly larger than the one in the Margee Artwork layer.** When you are happy with size and placement of the heart, **hit Enter to accept the transformation.** Return the opacity to 100% after the transform.

STEP 47: There's a shadow on the edge of the heart that makes it look like a composited item, so **add a layer mask to the Heart layer, use a soft-edge brush about 5 pixels at 30% opacity and gently brush any annoying edges away by painting the layer mask.**

STEP 44: This was my initial Pen Tool path.

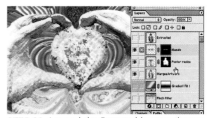

STEP 44: The Pen tool selection made a pretty good start at the layer mask.

ADD TEXT AND LAYER EFFECTS

STEP 48: Now we're ready to use Photoshop 6's new text handling ability. Though I normally eschew the Photoshop Type tool in favor of setting my type in Illustrator, the ability to add certain effects in Photoshop makes its Type tool more beguiling than ever. Both the tool and the interface have changed a lot, so take some time to familiarize yourself with the controls and how they work. You still **type T to access the Type tool,** and the current foreground color is still the color that the type will be built. But, you no longer have to wait for a dialog box to open; you type directly onto the file and a new Type layer is created. **Click the foreground color swatch on the Tool palette and choose a deep green for the first word: Heartsinger.** I set my Type specs before I started typing, but you could as easily type the word, highlight the letters and change the specs then. **I used ITC Benguiat Bold at 48 points.** You'll need to

STEP 36: I moved the Extracted layer to the top and turned it on and off to help me decide how to clean the Hands layer mask. Notice that I've painted out the red heart just under Margee's thumbs.

381

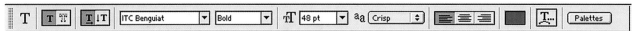

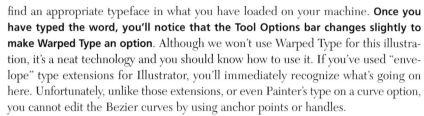

STEP 48: I moved the Extracted layer to the top and turned it on and off to help me decide how to clean the Hands layer mask.

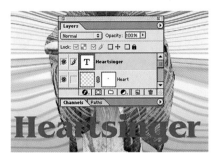

STEP 48: When you begin typing a new layer appears with a generic name, Layer #. As soon as you switch tools or layers, the word you typed becomes the layer name.

find an appropriate typeface in what you have loaded on your machine. **Once you have typed the word, you'll notice that the Tool Options bar changes slightly to make Warped Type an option.** Although we won't use Warped Type for this illustration, it's a neat technology and you should know how to use it. If you've used "envelope" type extensions for Illustrator, you'll immediately recognize what's going on here. Unfortunately, unlike those extensions, or even Painter's type on a curve option, you cannot edit the Bezier curves by using anchor points or handles.

STEP 49: **Make sure you are currently on the Heartsinger layer and in the Type tool. Click the Warp Type icon on the Tool Options bar.** A dialog appears with a pop-up where you choose the type of "envelope" you want to use. **Make sure you can see the type as you choose different envelopes and study their effects.** In my illustration, **I chose the Bulge effect.** The three sliders appear for each effect, as well as the Hori-

STEP 48: The Bulge Style with Horizontal Bend only looks like this.

STEP 48: The Bulge Style with Vertical Bend, Horizontal Distortion and Vertical Distortion.

STEP 48: The Bulge Style with Vertical Bend only.

zontal and Vertical buttons. The Bend slider controls where the effect will be most prominent, top or bottom, right or left, depending on the particular envelope you've chosen. The Horizontal slider controls which side of the envelope will be larger, with left being the left side of the type and right the right. The Vertical slider controls whether the top or bottom of the text will be spread wider. Left is the top of the text, right is the bottom. The two buttons control whether the primary effect is Horizontal or Vertical, and the change is sometimes radical. Depending on which buttons and slider you choose, you can bend, twist and flip the type over itself. This is an area you really want to explore if type effects are important to you. After you play with the effects, make sure you **Cancel or Undo (Command-Z) to bring the type back to its original shape.**

STEP 50: We're going to add a layer effect for the Heartsinger layer to make the text stand out from the background. **Double-click the Heartsinger layer in the Layers palette** to bring up the Layer Style dialog box. (Make sure you double-

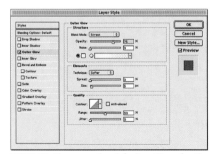

STEP 50: These are the default settings for the Outer Glow layer style.

STEP 50: These are the settings I used for the Outer Glow on the Heartsinger layer.

click the layer name and not the Layer thumbnail, which, in the case of a text layer, highlights all the text on that layer.) On the left side of this dialog is a list of default styles that ship with Photoshop. **Start styling this text by applying the Outer Glow style.** If you click the checkbox to the left of Outer Glow, you apply that style to the layer, but you do not see the controls for the style. Click the style name and the rest of the dialog box changes to show you the controls available for that style. **Situate the Layer Styles window so you can see the effect on the Heartsinger layer as you work.**

STEP 51: Using the default settings, you can just see a little yellow line around the type. It really doesn't stand out from the background. The first change we'll make is the size of the glow in number of pixels. **Use the Size slider or type 27 in the entry area to make the actual glow larger.** This makes the glow larger, but it's also blurred so much that it looks puny. So, **use the Spread slider or type 15 to expand the Type mask before the blurring happens.** Now the text is starting to stand out, but maybe more than we need on this already busy cover.

STEP 52: Now, **click the Contour pop-up** in the Quality area. This is a really mind-boggling new feature of Photoshop 6. The effects you achieve can range from subtle to very dramatic, depending on how you combine the contour you use with other settings in the dialog box. If you are using the default contours, **click the leftmost contour on the second row, the Half-Round contour.** This futher spreads the glow. Now **lower the Opacity to 55%** and **click the small yellow color swatch to open the Color Picker and warm the color towards orange.** If you'd like to continue to experiment, do so. If not, **click OK** and you're finished with this effect.

STEP 53: **Type T** to return to the Type tool and **click in the image below the word Heartsinger. Click the color swatch on the Tool Options bar and choose a deep blue color** for the text. **Type the words Margee Wheeler.** You will be using the same type specs that you used for the Heartsinger layer, so the text will be too large. **Double-click the Text icon for this layer in the Layers palette to highlight all of the text and use the keyboard shortcut (Command-shift-<) to resize the type until it almost fits under the word Heartsinger.** This should now be 36pt. text. There is no keyboard shortcut to scale the type one point at a time, so you'll have to **type 35 in the entry area for size on the Tool Options bar.**

STEP 54: The first thing you'll notice is that the type blends in with the bottom of the blue scarf. In the Layers palette, **click and drag the Outer Glow effect sublayer from the Heartsinger layer to the Margee Wheeler layer.** The entire effect is copied to the

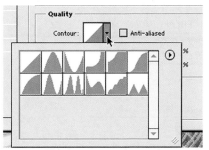
STEP 51: This is how the text looks after you use the Size and Spread sliders.

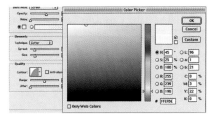
STEP 52: Click the small color swatch to bring up the Color Picker and change the color slightly.

STEP 52: Click the pop-up to give you the currently loaded contours. You can edit a contour by clicking on the Contour icon after you close the Contour Picker.

STEP 52: After changing the contour, color, and opacity the text is differentiated from the background but softly.

STEP 53: Make sure all the text is highlighted as you change the size of the characters.

STEP 54: You can simply drag and drop to copy the layer effect from one layer to another.

Add text and layer effects

layer. You can even drag an effect from one file to another. You can also use Layer/Layer Style/Copy Layer Style from the menu bar. Though this may seem to be more work, it gives you an advantage of being able to link several layers and then use Layer/Layer Style/Paste Layer Style to Linked to apply that style to several layers at once. **Turn on the guidelines (Command-') if they are not currently showing and position both text layers so they fit within the safety area.**

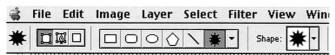

STEP 55: Choose the Custom Shapes icon from the Tool Options bar.

ADD HEARTS AND LAYER EFFECTS

STEP 55: To complete the Seven Chakras motif, we need to add a couple more hearts to the image—one at the third eye and one at the crown chakra. Luckily, Photoshop 6 makes this an absolute snap with the new Custom Shapes tool. First, **click the Eyedropper tool and make sure it is set to 3 by 3 Average** in the Tool Options bar. Now **sample the colors of the large heart at Margee's throat and shoulders until you find a deep red** that you like. Next, **type U for the Shape tool. In the Tool Options bar, click the icon for the Custom Shapes tool** (or you can type Shift-U until you get there). There is no Shape Editor attached to the options, so you can **click either the Custom Shape icon or the pop-up arrow** to get the palette of currently loaded shapes. **Choose the heart shape. Draw a small heart between and slightly above Margee's eyes.** Remem-

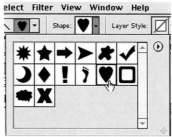

STEP 55: Click the heart to load this as the custom shape to draw.

ber, you can use the Option key to draw from the center out, and the Shift key to keep the drawing proportional. When you are happy with the size of the heart, **click the Checkmark button on the Tool Options bar.** If you do not click this button, subsequent shapes will be drawn to this same layer, which may be what you want sometimes, but not this time.

STEP 55: As you click and drag you see the path that forms the shape.

STEP 55: When you release the mouse after the drag the shape becomes filled with the current foreground color and a clipping mask is applied to the layer in the shape that you just built.

STEP 56: Align both hearts on the center guide.

STEP 56: This glow uses the Half Round contour.

STEP 56: This glow uses the Linear contour.

STEP 56: **Draw another heart above Margee's head. It should be slightly larger than the one for the third eye.** We drew these two hearts on different layers, even though they are the same color, because we want to add an effect to this heart and not the one at the third eye. Once again, **drag the Outer Glow effect from the Heartsinger layer (or the Margee Wheeler layer) to the Shape 2 layer**. The effect is pretty good, but a little too bright for this area. **Double-click the Outer Glow sublayer** to bring up the Layer Styles dialog box. **Click the Contour pop-up to choose the Linear contour.** This pulls the glow in and makes the effect more suitable to this heart.

Add Layer Styles to the Margee Artwork Layer

STEP 57: You're almost done! We only need to add a couple of layer styles to the Margee Artwork layer to make that layer stand apart from the background. First, **click the Margee Artwork layer to activate it, then double-click the layer to bring up the Layer Styles dialog. Click on Drop Shadow** (remember to click the name to bring up the options for that style). First, **change the angle to 90°** so the shadow will be on all sides of the artwork. Now **use the following settings** for the shadow itself: **Distance, 23 pixels; Spread, 23%; Size, 46 pixels. Lower the Opacity to 55% and click the color swatch to make the shadow color a deep indigo blue** rather than black. At the bottom of the dialog, you can **add Noise** to the shadow, and **I used 4%**—just a touch. I also felt the Half Round contour was a softer shadow than the Linear contour, but experiment with both, or click the contour swatch itself to edit the contour. **Choose the contour you prefer.**

STEP 58: Now, rather than say OK and leave the dialog, **click the Outer Glow style** name to switch to those options. **Bring the Opacity back up to 60% and click the color swatch to use the original color for Outer Glow. The RGB numbers for this yellow are 255, 255, 190.** We want this yellow to be brighter than the glows on the other layers. **Bring the Spread slider into 0 and the Size slider to 16.** And finally, **use the Linear contour** (the first one in the Contour Swatch palette) to keep this glow sharper than the glows on the text or hearts. **Say OK to this dialog** and check your work. You might want to turn the Eye icon for this particular effect on and off to see whether you like the effect or think the artwork is more natural without it. We printed the CD cover with the glow. So, you're finished with the CD cover. Now all you need to do to make this a real-world product is design the back cover of the four page brochure, the inside spread, the tray card and the CD itself. After this example, that should be a snap.

A Word about the Edit/Fade Command

When you run a filter in Photoshop, you have the option of Edit/Fade. after running the filter to change the effect of the filter before it is made permanent. Using Fade is sort of like running a filter on the image in a separate layer above the image. If you do that, you can always go back and change the Opacity or Blend mode of that layer to blend the filter with the original image underneath. Doing this with layers is a great approach, and we used it a lot, earlier in this chapter. The Edit/Fadecommand is like running the filter in this other layer, but if you don't adjust it before you do something else, it gets merged with the layer below. The feature says: "Let's give them one more chance to tweak this filter by changing the Opacity or Blend mode; then we'll make the effect permanent on the layer that was active when you ran the filter."

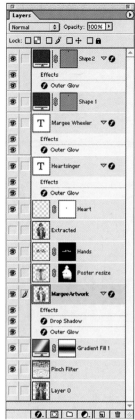

STEP 56: Align both hearts on the center guide.

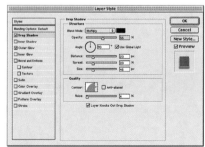

STEP 57: These are settings for the Drop Shadow style.

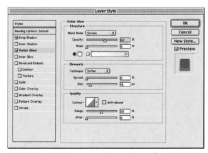

STEP 58: And these are the settings for the Outer Glow style.

385

You've built the front cover, now you can do the back cover, tray card and inside pages of the brochure.

To use Edit/Fadejust select it after running a filter and you will get the Fade dialog box. You can switch the Blend mode or Opacity, but you have no layer options or layer mask. You can then Undo and Redo the Fade, but when you do anything else that changes the Undo buffer, the ability to further change the Fade goes away, except by using the History Brush or Fill from History.

If you really want flexibility, just make a copy of the layer you were going to run the filter on, put that copy on top of the current layer and run the filter on the copy. Because this is a separate layer, you have all the capabilities of Fade, plus you have layer options, plus you can change it or undo it at any time, just by changing the Eye icon, Opacity, Blend mode or layer options. Even when you save the file and quit, you will later have these same options upon reopening the file.

35 HANDS-ON SESSION: South Africa in Focus

Building a flexible multilayered file to create various composite screens for multimedia use; layer styles, fill layers, clipping groups, text capabilities, and filters, help you get the job done.

When you work in multimedia you have to build many files to accomplish even the shortest project. How you set up your Photoshop files can make an enormous difference in how quickly you accomplish your tasks and how quickly you can adjust to the demands of a different application or end product. This chapter is a mere introduction to some of the issues that will crop up if you decide to use your Photoshop skills to do work for CD-ROMs, kiosks, or video.

BUILD THE BACKGROUND SCREEN

STEP 1: We'll be working on a project that is going to be used several different ways. There's going to be a video of the opening segment as well as an informative CD for educational use. Because we're unsure of exactly who's going to be doing the work with the files after we've done our Photoshop work, we want to build a file that has great flexibility to go out to other programs. **Use File/New to open a new file, 648 pixels by 486 pixels in RGB mode at 72 pixels per inch**. Although, 640x480 is the most common file size in multimedia, 648x486 works for most uses, and it's the preferred size for analog video transfers. You're working with low resolution-files because video, television (but not DTV), and computer monitors are low-resolution media. **Bring up the Color palette (Shift-F9), the Info palette (F9), and the Layers palette (F10) to assist you. Make sure your Info readout is in pixels by using the X and Y coordinates pop-up on the Info palette. Move the sliders on the Color palette to R-224, G-139, B-0 to set the foreground color. Now, Option-Delete to fill the entire screen with this foreground color. Save your file as In Focus.psd.**

The final composite we'll build during this session!

In the coming of DTV (Digital Television), HDTV is a component. However, all DTV signals will not include HDTV. Some will be SDTV (Standard Definition Television). How all this shakes down remains to be seen. For now, be prepared to need several different sizes for your graphics.

STEP 2: Now we'll add a bit of texture to the screen. **Choose Filter/Texture/Texturizer and use Sandstone as the texture. Choose 100 percent as the scaling, and Top as the Light Direction, but use a Relief of only 2.** Remember, there's going to be a lot happening on this screen; you want a little texture but you don't want the texture to compete with information or images that are truly important. **Double-click the**

STEP 2: The Texturizer filter has built-in textures, and there are additional textures in the Presets folder that loaded with Photoshop 6, or you can create your own.

Background layer and rename it Sandstone texture. By the way, if you haven't played with the Texturizer filter, now might be a good time to take a few moments to do so. You'll see when you choose your texture that you can load additional textures that came with Photoshop (look inside the Presets/Textures folder in your Photoshop folder), textures that you've purchased from third-party sources, or that you've scanned in or created from scratch. To create your own texture, use File/New to open a grayscale image filled with white that is the same size as your file. If your texture is smaller than your file, you might see tiling or repeating of the same pattern over and over again. You sometimes see this with the small textures that came with Photoshop. Now use Filter/Noise/Add Noise of about 50% Gaussian on your texture. Now use Filter/Brush Strokes and any of the Brush Stroke filters. Just play (Crosshatch is nice). When you have something you think looks interesting (hint: white and black areas remain flat when you Texturize), save the file with a meaningful name (like inktexture.psd) in Photoshop format. Go back to your In Focus.psd file and make a new layer by clicking the New Layer icon at the bottom of the Layers palette, and Option-Delete once again to fill this layer with the same background color that we used before. Go to Filter/Texture/Texturizer again; only this time choose Load Texture as your option and search for the grayscale file that you just created. You'll still get options of how much scaling and deep you want to make your texture. Experiment a bit and then say "OK," and take a look at what you've created. It's such fun that you can lose whole days creating textures and checking them out. If you've created a background that you like better than the one we made using the Texturizer and Sandstone, name it My Texture, keep it with the file on its own layer, and see how it works with the composite.

SET GUIDES TO ESTABLISH SAFE AREAS

One of the issues you have to deal with in multimedia is the overscanning (cropping) that happens when your pictures are displayed on a television screen. If you have text or images that are highly important (and which ones aren't?), you need to make sure that they appear in an area of the screen that will be readable. To make sure of accurate placement, we're going to build guides for both the *image safe* (the area that will display artwork accurately) and the *title safe* (the area that will display text legibly). Normal image safe on a 640x480 file that is the most common size used for this type of work is 33 pixels from each side of the frame and 25 pixels from the top and bottom. Title safe for the same size file is 65 pixels from each side and 49 pixels from top and bottom. As you can see, your live area diminishes a great deal when you start to put text onscreen.

About now you may be remembering that the file that we're working on is not 640x480 but rather 648x486. That's because the video editor who will be working with some of the files later has requested this size and we've built the file to accommodate her. However, we still need to set our safe areas for 640x480 because some of the files will be used in this format. So we're going to set guides for the smaller size file.

STEP 3: Photoshop 6 now lets you set your guides numerically, which is a much needed advance. Because we are using the 640x480 file as the basis for our guides, we need to add additional space to the safe areas to compensate. There are eight additional pixels of width and six additional pixels of height in our file, so we'll divide those numbers by two and make image safe 37 pixels from the left edge and 28 pixels from the top edge. Title safe will be 69 and 52 pixels respectively. **Use View/New**

Guide to set Vertical guides at 37 and 69. Then, use the same command again to set Horizontal guides at 28 and 52. It's so easy.

STEP 4: To set guides on the right side of the file we'll use subtraction: 648 minus 37 is 611, and 648 minus 69 is 579. **So, set your Vertical guides for the right side at 579 and 611. Horizontal guides are set at 458 (486 minus 28) and 434 (486 minus 52).**

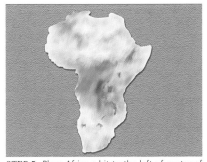

STEP 4: The View/New Guide command makes setting guidelines a breeze.

BRING IN AFRICA

STEP 5: Zoom out until you can see the entire screen. Open the file Africa.psd. Use the Move tool and drag the Africa layer into your file to create a new layer. Remember, if you **hold down the Shift key as you drag**, you automatically place the file in the middle of the screen, which is what we want to do here. You can place a guideline at the center of the file (324 pixels) to help you decide where you want to place Africa, but don't get too picky until you've put all the pieces together. If your guides are turned on (type Command-; on the Mac side or Ctrl+- on Windows if they're not), you can see how much of Africa is hanging over the image safe area. **The artwork will be larger than the background screen, so use Edit/Transform/Scale to scale it to fit. Remember to hold down the Shift key as you scale to scale the image proportionately.** You want the continent to "bleed" a bit, and I've placed it just a bit left of center, as there is more imagery on the right side of the final design than on the left.

Notice the Tool Options bar as you drag the handles and move the image. The bar tells you exactly how much you have scaled your image. At any time during the transformation, you can type in an exact location or scale percentage that you want; then press Return or Enter to accept the entire transformation. I used 80% as the amount of the scale.

When you work in multimedia (or do any complex artwork for that matter), it's a good idea to work with a notepad to write down what you're doing. Date the page and name the job you're working on. That way if you need to re-create a certain effect for another job, you have a record of how it was done. Also, save the layered version of your Photoshop file for reference.

STEP 5: Choose Edit/Transform/Scale to scale Africa by eye.

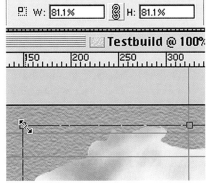

STEP 5: The Tool Options bar lets you know how much you've already scaled the item.

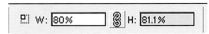

STEP 5: Double click an entry area to input a number manually.

ADD THE LAYER STYLE

STEP 6: We'll use one of Photoshop's layer styles, the Drop Shadow effect, for this layer. Because shadows sometimes need to be separated from the primary object, it's

STEP 5: Place Africa a bit to the left of center of the background. The shadow is a layer effect.

STEP 6: To style a layer use either Layer/Layer Style and choose the style you want…

STEP 6: …or, choose the style from the Layers palette.

STEP 6: Clicking the color square in the Layer Style dialog brings up the standard color picker.

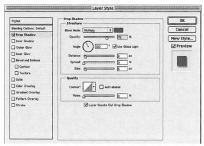

STEP 6: Your dialog should look like this for the Africa shadow.

not always possible to use this layer style for materials that go into other programs, but in this case, we'll be fine.

It's easy to add these quick effects, and, best of all, they remain completely interactive with the layer. You move the layer, the shadow goes with it; add or adjust the layer mask, the shadow changes. And if you don't like the color or angle or depth of the shadow at any time, it's a no-brainer to go in and fix it.

To add the shadow to Africa, **go to Layer/Layer Style/Drop Shadow** (or click the Add Layer Style button on the Layers palette and choose Drop Shadow) **and click the color square** to bring up the Color Picker. **Use a rich red-brown—I've used R:180, G:83, B:24—and keep the rest of the default settings.** You don't want a lot of shadow here because it might look too busy with all the other things going on. But remember, if you want to change it later, you can.

STEP 7: Option-drag to Solid Color to bring up the dialog allowing you to name your new layer.

STEP 7: When you choose New Fill Layer from the Layer menu, you automatically get the New Layer dialog box below.

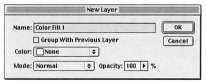

STEP 7: Type in the name, Animal Block, and change the Mode to Multiply.

BLOCK IN OTHER MAJOR ELEMENTS

STEP 7: Next, we're going to block in the three photos. I like to put placeholders down before I actually bring in the photos to have an idea of how much space I have to work with. So, **click the Foreground color swatch on the Tool palette or show the Color palette to choose a light brown.** Color doesn't really matter, we're eventually going to throw these layers in the trash; we just want to get a feeling for how things will lay out. **Type M or Shift-M to get the Rectangular Marquee tool. Draw a marquee about one-third of the width and one-third of the height of the file.** That's about 210 pixels by 150 pixels; there's not an exact size that we need. You can use the W and H measures in the bottom-right of the Info palette to see the size. **Option-drag the New Fill or Adjustment Layer icon at the bottom of the Layers palette to Solid Color to create a new layer called Animal Block.** This will fill the selection rectangle on that new layer with the light brown color you chose by creating a layer mask. **Change the Blend mode of the layer to Multiply.** This gives you the basic shape you'll be working with. **Option-drag that layer to the New Layer icon at the bottom of the Layers palette twice to create two** copies of the layer. Option-double-click on the layers to name one Art Block and the other People Block. (If you Option-drag the layer to the New Layer icon, the dialog allowing you to rename the layer appears automatically.) **Use the Move tool (V) to position each layer** where you'll want your photos to appear. **Animals will appear in the top-right section, People in the bottomright, and Art in the leftmiddle of the frame. Make sure your guidelines are showing (Command-;) so you can position the three photo blocks within the image safe for the most part.**

STEP 7: Your photo boxes should be placed something like this.

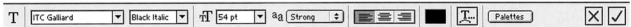

STEP 8: You can set most of the important text attributes on the Text Tool Options bar, but click the Palettes button for more detailed settings on the Character and Paragraph palettes.

TYPE IN THE TEXT

STEP 8: Next, let's type in the South Africa text. We're going to put each word on a separate layer, so we can move them independently of each other. **Type T to get the Text tool and make sure it's set to the regular, horizontal Text tool. Type D to get the default colors; then click in the upper left area of the file and type in the word "South."** I've used Galliard Black Italic at 54 points; you'll have to improvise depending on what typefaces you have installed in your system. The new Text tool works much more like Illustrator or a page layout application. The text is typed directly onto the file and you can edit without having to enter a modal dialog box. You can use the Backspace key just as you would in a word processor, but you have to highlight letters if you want to change size, tracking, baseline shift, or color.

I found that the spacing between the letters was good except between the S and the O and the OU combination. **To kern a letter pair, place the cursor between the two letters you want to tighten or loosen. Click the Palettes button on the Tool Options bar to bring up the Character palette. You can type a value in the Kerning box or use shortcut keys (Option plus right or left arrow) to move the letters. I used –30 to tighten the space between the S and O, and 20 to loosen the spacing between the O and U. When you like the way the text looks, click the checkmark to accept the text, or simply switch to another tool.** Notice the layer in the Layers palette now is named "South" and has a T on the far right side to let you know that this is a text layer and is still interactive. Although you can add layer styles to the the layer, certain operations, like filters, cannot be done to this layer until it is rendered.

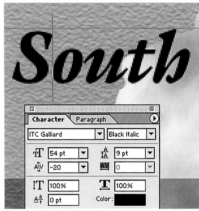

STEP 8: Onscreen kerning and dialog boxes that are more like Illustrator, make Photoshop 6 vastly better for working with text than previous versions. Here, I've kerned between the S and O by using keyboard shortcuts.

STEP 9: **Still in the Text tool, place the cursor at the end of the word, "South," and type a carriage return, and then type "Africa." If your letters are over the top of each other, check the leading. Make sure it's loose enough to give you a little air between the words. To change the leading, you must highlight at least two letters of a word on the line whose leading you want to change. Then choose a value from the pop-up menu** (48 worked nicely for me), **or highlight the input area and type in a value.**

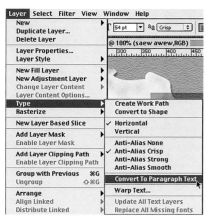

STEP 10: **Click the Palette tab to activate the Paragraph palette.** This may seem confusing for those of you who are used to page layout programs. If you try to indent the word, Africa, by choosing a first line indent, you'll see that both lines move over. This is because the type is currently set as point type. To make the text work as a paragraph, you must use the Text tool to build a bounding box before you set the type (do this by dragging with the tool), or select the layer in the Layers palette and then **use Layer/Type/Convert to Paragraph Text.** When you do this, you create a bounding box after the fact. **Click the word Africa and set a first line indent of about 60 points.** If the bounding box is now not large enough to encompass your text, use the handles to resize the box (if you don't see the bounding box, click in the text with the Text tool). You can also rotate the text. To skew the box, hold down the Command key, and to resize the type as you resize the box, add the Option key.

STEP 10: To access the power of the Paragraph palette, you must make sure that your text is Paragraph text.

STEP 10: When I changed the first line indent of the Africa paragraph, the word no longer fit in the bounding box. It was easy to grab a handle and open the box.

STEP 11: **Kern the word Africa.** Of course, it will depend on what typeface you are using, but I loosened the "fr" and "ic" combinations, and tightened up the "ca." There are no absolute rights or wrongs in kerning. I always think of kerning type in terms of music. The words have a rhythm and what you try to do is keep the rhythm consistent. Look at the negative space between the letters as well as the letterforms themselves.

STEP 12: Place the Adobe Illustrator logo, Focus.ai.

STEP 12: When you bring in vector artwork, you get a bounding box and a preview of how the art will look when rasterized. The arrow in the corner means you are ready to resize the art.

STEP 12: **Go to File/Place and place the Focus.ai logo.** This is an Adobe Illustrator file that we'll place, resize, and rasterize in Photoshop. When the logo comes in, it comes in at the size it was created in Illustrator. Photoshop gives you the opportunity to resize the logo before you rasterize it, avoiding any loss of clarity that might occur if you rasterize first and then resize. **Keep your eye on the Tool Options bar as you resize by Shift-dragging on a corner handle, and bring the logo down to about 70% of its original size. Then press Enter to accept the change and rasterize. Use the Move tool to move the artwork down and to the left a bit.**

BRING IN THE PHOTOS

STEP 13: It's time to start bringing in the photographs and setting up the text for the three main areas of our production, currently called "Animals," "Art," and "People." **Open the files Giraffe.psd, Ayanda.psd, and Masks.psd.** If you go to Image/"Image Size on any of these files, you'll notice that they are all considerably bigger than we need, but we won't worry about changing the resolution or image size in the original photos; we'll do all of our resizing in the In Focus file. **Start with the Giraffe.psd file**

and use the **Rectangular Marquee tool to select primarily the giraffe's head and neck with some of the foliage in the background. Take a bit more than you think you'll actually use. Command-C to copy the area; then switch to your In Focus file and Command-V to paste the giraffe as a new layer.** Your selection probably fills most of the screen because the Giraffe.psd file was at a much higher resolution than the 72dpi we're using. **Option-double-click on this layer and name it Giraffe.**

STEP 14: **In the Layers palette, move the Giraffe layer just above the Animals block layer. Option-click the line between the two to make a clipping group; that is, to clip the Giraffe layer to the shape of the the Animals block layer.** Because you already set the Blend mode of the Animals block layer to Multiply, the Giraffe layer will assume the same Blend mode. **To scale the Giraffe, choose Edit/Free Transform (Command-T) and hold down the Shift key while dragging the corners of the transform box inward. Click and drag in the middle of the box to move the image. When you're happy with the size and position, press Return or Enter to accept the transform.**

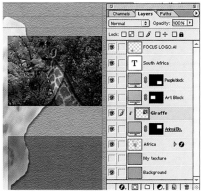

STEP 14: Your Layers palette and your artwork should look something like this after Step 14.

STEP 15: **Repeat the same basic process for Masks.psd and Ayanda.psd. Copy an area from the original file and paste it into the In Focus file as a new layer. Rename the layer and move it to above its corresponding block layer; then make a clipping group by Option-clicking the line between the layers. Use Edit/Free Transform to resize the artwork while holding down the Shift key to about 150% of the size of the block that "clips" it.** You want some extra because later we'll feather the mask to give the artwork softer edges. Wait for a few seconds after you make your transformation to get a preview of how the art will look before you **press Return to accept the transformation. When you are happy with the size of each image, click first on a block layer; then click the linking column (the middle column) of each image to link it with its block layer.** Now you can use the Move tool to move each two-layer group together.

BUILD THE TEXT AND TEXT EFFECTS

STEP 16: Now that the major elements are in place, we'll type in the text to finish up our original comp, and then we'll go back and finesse some of the elements after we get approval of the initial concept. **Make the Giraffe layer the active layer; then type I to get the Eyedropper tool and sample the light blue color on the Africa map to make that the foreground color. Type T to get the Text tool and click near the bottom of the Giraffe to place the insertion point there.** If the color square on the Tool Options bar is not the same as your foreground color, simply click the foreground color square on the Toolbox and that color will replace what was on the Tool Options bar. You can also click the color square on the Tool Options bar or Character palette to change the color of the type at any time, even while you are typing in letters. **I typed "nature" and used Frutiger Black at 40 points with tracking of 50 to give a little air between the letters.** If you don't have the same typeface, you can experiment with the type you have installed in your system and see the screen update as you change faces. Just remember that you need to highlight the text to change the typeface, or most other attributes, after you've typed it in. **When you're happy with the text, click the checkbox on the Tool Options bar.** Your layer will now automatically be named "nature."

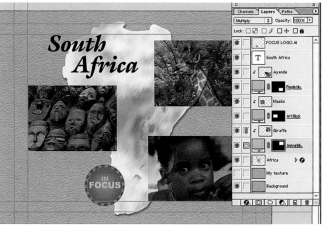

STEP 15: Your file and Layers palette should look something like this after Step 15. The arrow pointing down from a layer signifies a clipping group.

STEP 17: You can slide the Opacity slider back and forth to see what the glow will look like when it is animated.

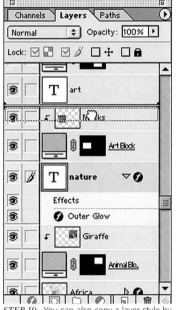

STEP 17: Save the glow you just created as a New Style.

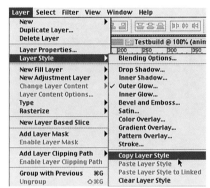

STEP 19: You can copy any style that you've already created from one layer and paste it to any other layer or group of linked layers in your file.

STEP 17: Let's go ahead and add the layer style to this text before we type in the other words. **Choose Layer/Layer Style/Outer Glow and use the default color and Mode, but change the Size to 10 pixels and the Opacity to 85%, and make the Contour Half Round. Click the New Style button and save this style with the name "85glow." Click OK to save the style and OK again to exit the Layer Style dialog box.**

STEP 18: We'll use two different methods to set the other two titles. Each way works just fine; it's up to you when you work which method to use. For "art," use the method to set the type that we just used; that is, **make the Masks layer active, use the Text tool (the settings that you last used will still be there), and simply type in the word "art" and click the checkmark on the Tool Options bar. Now, click on the "animals" text layer and go to Layer/Layer Style/Copy Layer Style.** After the effect has been copied, you can **click the "art" text layer and do Layer/Layer Style/Paste Layer Style** to get the same glow, color, and everything, that you used on the "animals" text layer.

STEP 19: The other way to do this is to **click the "art" text layer and drag that layer to the New Layer icon at the bottom of the Layers palette** to make a copy of the layer. **Use the Move tool (V) to move the text over the picture of Ayanda and, in the Layers palette, move that layer above the Ayanda layer. Now simply use the Text tool, double-click to highlight the current text, and replace it with the word "people."** You can copy any layer styles to other layers by dragging the effect you want to copy to the new layer.

STEP 19: You can also copy a layer style by dragging the style you want to the layer you want to apply it to.

FINESSE THE CLIPPING MASKS OR LAYER MASKS

STEP 20: After the original concept has been approved, you can start to add the touches that make your production stand out. First we're going to add a feathered edge to our masks for the three photographs. Depending on how you're sending out your files, you could work with the clipping group mask (in this case, the layer masks

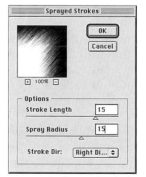

STEP 19: The basic elements are in place and the concept has been approved. Now it's time to get creative.

of the solid color layers). For our example, we are going to make black and white alpha channels that are employed as layer masks in Photoshop but will be used as alpha channels in Adobe Premiere through which video clips will be played. **Let's start with the "art" area. Command-click on the art block layer to load that shape as a selection. Show the Channels palette (Windows/Show Channels or Shift-F10). While the selection is active, click the Save Selection as Channel icon on the bottom of the palette (the second icon) and then deselect the area (Command-D).**

STEP 21: **Make sure Alpha 1 is the active channel by clicking on its name.** You should see only the black and white alpha channel at this point. When we feather the mask for the artwork, it's going to need to be about 10% bigger, so **go to Edit/Free Transform and type in 110% for both the width and height scaling in the Tool Options bar.**

STEP 22: **Go to Filter/Blur/Gaussian Blur (Shift-F4) and blur the entire channel by about 10 pixels. Next, go to Filter/Brush Strokes/Sprayed Strokes and set the Stroke Length and Spray Radius both to 15 with the Stroke Direction as Right Diagonal.** Preview your results in the window and make sure that you have enough feather. **When you're happy with the results, choose OK.**

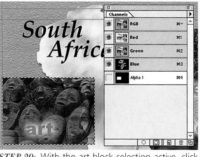

STEP 20: With the art block selection active, click on the Save Selection as Channel icon and you'll get Alpha1.

STEP 21: As soon as you begin your Free Transform, you can type in scaling values in the Tool Options bar.

STEP 20: After you have the new channel, deselect the area (Command-D) and you're ready to do the Free Transform and filtering.

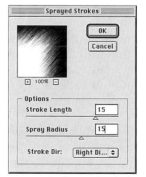

STEP 22: Set these options in the Sprayed Strokes dialog box and preview the edge to make sure you have enough feather.

Finesse the Clipping Masks or Layer Masks

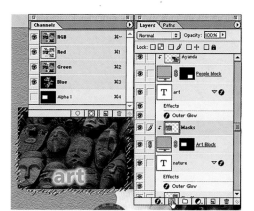

STEP 23: With the selection loaded and "masks" layer active, you're ready to make a layer mask by clicking the left-most icon at the bottom of the Layers palette.

With so many palettes open onscreen, you soon see why almost everyone who works in multimedia prefers a two-monitor setup. One monitor can run your production or your Photoshop file as you build it, while the other monitor holds all the palettes.

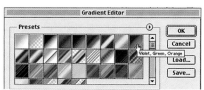

STEP 28: Click the color swatch on the Gradient Overlay dialog box to access the Gradient Editor, then choose the Violet, Green, Orange gradient.

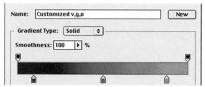

STEP 28: Customize the gradient by pulling in the violet and orange color stops toward the middle. Click the New button to add this variation to your Gradient palette.

STEP 23: We're now going to make a layer mask from this channel. **Command-click on the Alpha 1 channel** to load it as a selection; then switch over to the Layers palette. **Click on the "masks" layer to make it the active layer and click on the Add Layer Mask icon,** which is second from the left at the bottom of the Layers palette, **to add your selection as a layer mask.**

STEP 24: You now have a layer mask, but the artwork is still being clipped by the Art block layer below it. **Option-click on the line between the two layers to release the Clipping group. Click the Eye icon on the Art block layer to turn that layer off.** The Masks layer is now controlled by its layer mask. **Set the Blend mode on the Masks layer to Multiply and the Opacity to about 85%.** If you find that you have hard edges, or you don't like the placement of your artwork, click the Linking icon between the Layer thumbnail and the Layer Mask thumbnail. You can then move the layer and the mask separately from one another. If you still have a hard edge on part of your artwork, you may find that your artwork is simply not large enough to fill the entire mask area. Use Free Transform to make it slightly larger, but if your art is way too small you'll need to go back to the original Masks.psd file and make a new selection, bring it in, and resize it. At any rate, make sure you relink the layer to its layer mask before continuing.

STEP 25: **Repeat steps 20–24 for each of the other two photo layer groups. Command-click the clipping group block layer to select its shape, make a new channel of the selection, enlarge it 10%, blur it, and filter it with the Sprayed Strokes filter (steps 20–22). Then follow steps 23 and 24 to attach those channels as layer masks.**

MAKE THE MASKS LAYER MORE INTERESTING

STEP 28: To add a bit more visual interest to the Masks layer, **click on the Masks layer, and then use the Add Layer Style button on the bottom of the Layers palette to add a Gradient Overlay layer. Click the gradient color swatch** to bring up the Gradient Editor. **Choose the Violet, Green, Orange gradient; then use the violet and orange color stops below the color bar and drag each one a little towards the center of the color bar** to give you more pure violet and orange at the edges. If you want to save your gradient to the palette, simply give the gradient a name and click the New button. Remember to save the entire palette using the Save button if you build gradients that you want to keep long-term. **Say OK** to the changes you've made in the gradient. **In the Gradient Overlay dialog change the Opacity to 60% and the Angle and Scale both to 45%. Make sure the Blend Mode of the layer is set to Overlay.**

Although I've set my Blend mode of this layer to Overlay, you don't have to. This is a wonderful place to play with Blend modes and styles of gradients. There are illustrations of the ones I liked using the same settings except for the Blend mode. If you want to experiment further, you might try going back into the Gradient Editor and using a Noise gradient to add some variety.

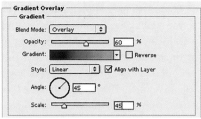

STEP 28: Type in these settings for the Gradient Overlay layer.

STEP 28: This is the result of using the above settings with Overlay as the Blend mode for the layer.

STEP 28: This is the result of using the above settings with Hard Light as the Blend mode for the Gradient Overlay layer.

STEP 28: This is the result of using the above settings with Color Dodge as the Blend mode for the Gradient Overlay layer.

STEP 28: This is the result of using the above settings with Difference as the Blend mode for the Gradient Overlay layer.

STEP 28: This is the result of using the above settings with Color as the Blend mode for the Gradient Overlay layer.

STEP 29: At this point, you really want to **show the History palette (F8)** because you'll be creating many different effects. **Take snapshots of versions of the file that you like by clicking the second icon on the bottom of the History palette and then click between snapshots to see which effects you like best.** When you click on the snapshot, your Layers palette and any effects you've added will return to the state they were when you made the snapshot. This is a great way to keep previous versions and continue experimenting. Double-click on the snapshots to give them meaningful names.

STEP 30: You might like to add some texture to the masks as well, and we'll do this by adding a Pattern Overlay layer effect to the layer. **Click the Add Layer Styles button on the Layers palette and drag to Pattern Overlay. I used the Nebula pattern, in Color Dodge mode with an Opacity of 35% and a Scale of 85%.** Once again, you can experiment by making snapshots and returning to previous versions to decide what works best.

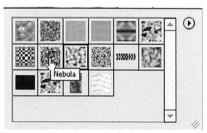

STEP 28: This is the result of using the above settings with Color as the Blend mode for the Gradient Overlay layer.

STEP 28: This is the result of using the above settings with Color as the Blend mode for the Gradient Overlay layer.

STEP 31: Another way to achieve effects rather than adding layer styles is to add fill layers above the current layer and group them so the clipping mask of the Masks layer defines the area of the fill. If you want to try this method, **turn off the layer styles for the Masks layer; then hold down the Option key, click the New Fill and Adjustment layer pop-up and drag to create a Gradient Map layer. Make sure you click the Group with Previous Layer button at the prompt.** When you do this, the colors of your chosen gradient are mapped to the luminosity values of the artwork. I

used the Yellow, Violet, Orange, Blue gradient. **Change the Blend Mode of this layer to Hard Light. Next, Option-drag to create a Pattern Fill layer. For this layer, use the Metal Landscape pattern, change the Opacity of the layer to about 25% and change the Blend mode to Hard Light.** Turn the layers on and off and take snapshots if you like. After looking at all my snapshots, I went with the fill layers rather than the layer styles. This is the final version that you saw at the opening of the chapter. On the CD I've included my final version, which also has layer styles for the Masks layer although the styles are turned off. There's lots of room for play on this example— make use of it!

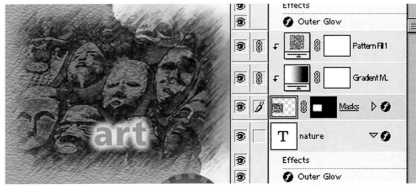

STEP 31: I turned off the layer styles and added two fill layers to achieve this effect.

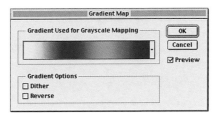

STEP 31: The Gradient Map layer is using this gradient.

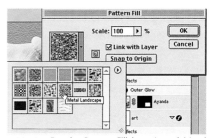

STEP 31: For the Pattern Fill layer I used Metal Landscape which ships with Photoshop 6.

It's useful to know that while in the Move tool, to quickly access any layer in the Layers palette, you can Control-click on the screen and get a menu of all layers having pixels at that location. Just choose the layer you want from the pop-up. If you are not currently in the Move tool, Command-Control-click does the same thing. For Windows, you use the right mouse button instead of the Control key when in the Move tool and Control-right mouse when not.

File size, naming conventions, and exact pixel dimensions and locations are all vitally important elements of a well-produced multimedia presentation. If you're building your own presentation, make sure you keep a log with all the vital information. And, if you know a good database program, here's where you want to use it.

Chapter 35: South Africa in Focus

HINTS FOR PREPARING GRAPHICS FOR AN ONLINE VIDEO EDIT

72ppi (pixels per inch) is the preferred resolution for videotape.

All of your images should be created at a 4:3 aspect ratio.

For nonbroadcast, 640x480 pixels is okay. However, as more people upgrade their computer systems, more multimedia productions are being built at higher resolutions, such as 800x600 and using thousands of colors rather than 256.

For transfer to D1 digital tape, images need to be 720x486.

For Broadcast spec, images must be 648x486 pixels (analog transfers), 720x486 pixels for digital transfers.

All your files should be the same resolution. It's a bad idea to give post-production facilities files of different resolutions (that is, 500x400, 640x480, and 32x200 pixels).

Most post-production facilities prefer that your graphics be either in the PICT format or QuickTime format. For PC graphics, facilities can usually handle TARGA, FLI, or FLC formats. If you are transferring an animation composed of numerous individual images, such as PICT or TARGA files, those files ideally should be numbered (that is, 001, 002, 003, 004, and so on). For PCs you will probably need files numbered with an extension after (that is, 001.tga, 002.tgs, 003.tga). Don't give the post-production facility a folder of images that all have different names such as Chip1, Chip1a, Fire1, Fire2, Dog, Today1. Just use numbers (not letters) if you have Mac files.

If you are importing Photoshop files into Adobe Premiere, you'll either have to flatten the image or import one layer at a time. If you import a single layer, Premiere will recognize the layer's transparency as an alpha channel. However, Premiere does not recognize layer masks or layer effects so you need to apply layer masks and create layers from any effects before importing.

You can import a layered file into Adobe After Effects, and After Effects will see all the layers, layer masks, layer transparency, and Blend modes. After Effects recognizes adjustment layers and precomposes them. The program does not currently recognize layer effects, so you need to create a separate layer using Layer/Layer Style/Create Layer.

Hints courtesy Nancy White, Lizmar Productions.

Make the Masks Layer More Interesting

IMAGES FOR THE WEB AND MULTIMEDIA

- NEW PHOTOSHOP 6 & IMAGEREADY 3 FEATURES
- ANIMATIONS, SLICES AND ROLLOVERS
- WHEN TO USE PHOTOSHOP VS IMAGEREADY
- WHEN TO CHOOSE GIF, JPEG OR PNG
- 4-UP DIALOGS TO OPTIMIZE WEB IMAGES
- WEB IMAGE GALLERIES AND PICTURE PACKAGES

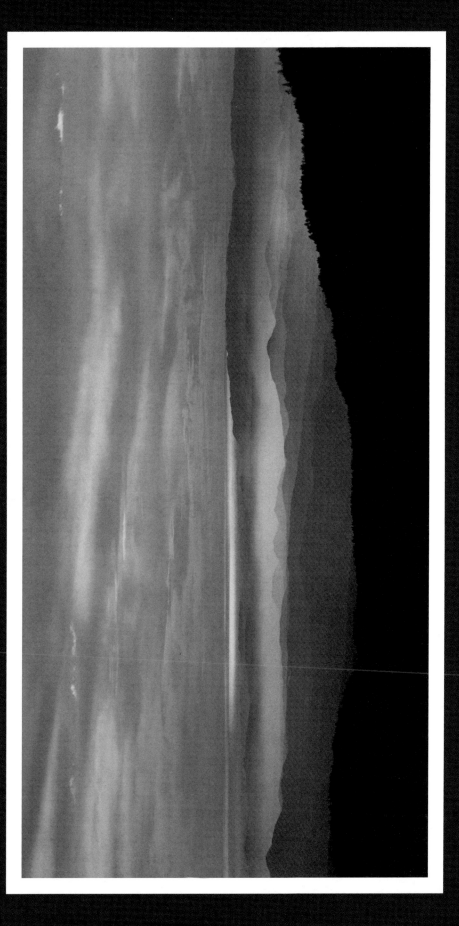

In college at UC San Diego, I always took perspective girlfriends on hikes up a grueling incline at San Jacinto state park west of Palm Springs. No significant relationships ever came from those hikes and much later I actually met my wife at a MacWorld con-ference. Walking back at the end of a long day on one of those hikes, I got this 35mm image looking west towards the ocean.

3 DIFFERENCES IN CREATING FOR THE WEB AND 8-BIT COLOR

What is different about the Web and
determining which viewers are most important.

WHY ARE THE WEB AND MULTIMEDIA DIFFERENT?

When I first started working with digital images in 1988, I was in the "Hypermedia Group" at Apple. We used to have the most fun in our weekly meetings, daydreaming about futures like digital virtual reality environments, sending color images over high-speed ISDN networks, computers that actually had built-in CD players as well as accelerated image compression and decompression, digital video and video conferencing, experiences like QuickTime VR, and many other things that were not possible at the time with our slow Mac IIx computers. The only thing that was just barely possible then was full-color, printed output from a Mac or PC. I could actually make color prints on Apple's $60,000 Dupont 4Cast dye-sub printer! All the 8-bit color stuff seemed low quality and of little interest to me. Back in 1988, there was no World Wide Web, as we know it.

Now, in 2001, most of the things we dreamed about back then have happened and are old news. Now we have the Web and multimedia applications where optimal JPEG compression and 8-bit color are important for delivering quality digital images. Even for photographers, who like seeing all the minute detail in a photograph, the current reality is that we often have to transmit digital comps to clients who want both print and Web versions of our images, and we probably want to create a Web site to advertise or display our own work. In making Web images for myself and my clients, I have realized that there is a real art to creating quality images for the Web and multimedia. Many of the techniques are the same that we use in creating images for print, but some very important differences can help you to make the transition between mediocre Web images and great Web images.

The Web is a rapidly changing environment. With constantly new features and possibilities on the Internet, you don't have to wait for a new book to be published or worry about the distribution channels to get the latest product. What I am telling you here in this book is based on what I know today and, in the world of the Web, that may easily change tomorrow or next week or a few months from now as new features appear. If you need to know the latest about the Web, then the Web is the best place to find that information because it can be updated any time. We've included some tips at the end of this chapter from our friend Ed Velandria, a true Web wizard. He gives you a couple of sites to visit to help you out. Our own Web site is www.maxart.com, and we place updated information, tips and articles there all the time. So check it frequently. You can send Wendy and I email at wendy@maxart.com or barry@maxart.com. We always enjoy hearing from our readers and try to answer questions when we can.

WHAT IS 8-BIT COLOR AND WHY IS IT SO IMPORTANT?

Eight-bit color is important for two reasons. First, some people have older computers that can see only 8-bit color on their monitors. New devices such as color handheld computers and Internet kiosks are also likely to only support 8-bit color. Second, 8-bit color images take up less space on disk than 24-bit color images of the same monitor display size. In most cases, this makes them faster to transmit over the Web and also allows you to store more of them on a multimedia CD. They are also faster to read from a CD and transmit to the screen.

To display color on a computer screen, you need a 24-bit digital value: 8 bits of Red, plus 8 bits of Green, plus 8 bits of Blue. These specify the exact color value of each pixel on a computer monitor. A 24-bit video card that places that color on the screen, needs enough memory to store one 24-bit value for each pixel on the screen. The 24-bit color values from your 24-bit color image get placed in the video card's memory buffer to display the part of the image you are currently seeing on the screen. This allows each pixel to be any one of 16,777,216 colors (256 ° 256 ° 256). Until recently, computer video memory was quite expensive, so many computer models were shipped with the cheaper 8-bit color instead. With 8-bit color, you can only see a total of 256 different colors on your computer screen at one time. Images that are 8-bit color store only 8 bits of information for each pixel in that image. Because of this, 8-bit digital images can have a total of only 256 distinct colors, but each 8-bit image can pick the 256 colors it will have out of the set of 16,777,216 colors. The particular set of colors that is chosen is called the Color palette for that image. A Color palette is a table of 256, 24-bit digital values.

When an 8-bit image is displayed on an 8-bit monitor, the 8-bit values of each pixel in the image are used as an index into a table of 256, 24-bit color values to drive the monitor. The monitor itself still gets 24-bit values from the 8-bit video card, but it gets only 256 different values at a time. When that 8-bit image is first displayed on the screen, this table is loaded from the Color palette of that image. There are 256, 24-bit values in a Color palette, and the index number (0–255) that represents each pixel in an 8-bit image is used to tell the video card which of those 256, 24-bit values in the table to display for that pixel. If the pixel's value is 0, the first entry in the table will be used. If the pixel's value is 5, the fifth entry will be used, and so on. This table lookup and display of the color pixels on the screen generally happens at least 60 times per second for each pixel on the screen. This is just one of the many things the computer has to do while you are just sitting there looking at it.

When loading from a CD or transferring over the Web, 8-bit color files can be faster because there are only 8 bits per pixel, versus 24, to load or transfer. One reason 8-bit video cards are cheaper is because they require only enough memory for 8 bits per pixel on the screen, plus the 256 entry 24-bit table, versus 24 bits per pixel on the screen. Now you know why the older computers with color monitors have had only 8-bit color. They were much cheaper to produce! In the last few years, though, computer memory has become less expensive, and most new video cards support 24-bit color.

8-bit image with one byte (8 bits) for each pixel

2	2	99	99	82	81
2	17	137	122	17	17
17	2	36	38	36	2
36	137	126	122	17	17
245	27	65	33	89	88
55	84	56	24	17	12

8-bit value is used as an index (lookup number) into the Color palette table

	RED 8-bit	GREEN 8-bit	BLUE 8-bit
0	27	59	222
1	69	159	38
2	122	161	16
3	65	16	200
4	47	58	166
253	56	17	8
254	197	22	78
255	56	147	59

256 entries in Color palette

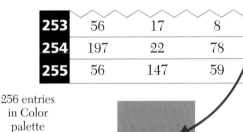

A 24-bit value is retrieved to light that pixel onscreen

About JPEG, GIF and PNG Files

JPEG, GIF and PNG file formats are all used in compressing images. The GIF and PNG-8 formats assume you start with an 8-bit image (or 7, 6, 5, or whatever). The trouble is that for photographs, a visible loss in quality occurs in converting a 24-bit image to an 8-bit or lower format. This is especially noticeable in areas that contain a subtle transition from one color or tone to another, such as in a gradient. After you have the 8-bit format, creating a GIF or PNG-8 will compress that, but the user will get the same 8-bit file when decompressed on the other end. No further loss will occur, but the main loss in a photograph has already occurred in converting from 24-bit to 8-bit. For graphic images with less than 256 colors in them to start with, GIF is great because the image can decompress back to the original with all its colors.

The JPEG and PNG-24 formats start with a 24-bit image and compresses it to make it smaller on the disk or for Web transfers. When the user opens it on the other end, they will also get a 24-bit image of the same opened size as the original, but the quality may be less than the original, with JPEG, due to the compression. The more compression you choose when you make the JPEG, the smaller the compressed file, but the lower the quality when reopened. The PNG-24 format has lossless compression but the files are considerably larger than JPEG compressed files. For more information on the JPEG and GIF file formats, see Chapter 10: "File Formats and Image Compression." JPEG is generally best for compressing 24-bit color photographs, and GIF is generally best for compressing graphics, such as logos. When you JPEG-compress graphics, the decompressed file will often not be as sharp as the original. PNG-24 is what you would have to use if you wanted a full 24-bit color transparency effect. This would allow an image that gradually fades into transparency to slowly fade into any background that is used on a Web page. Currently, however, not all browsers support this feature.

We sometimes end up compressing photographs using the GIF format because GIF gives you the option of having a transparent area surrounding a knocked-out photograph. This transparent GIF format, when displayed on a Web page, shows the background of the Web page in all the transparent areas. This allows transparent GIF images to be placed on any background and still, in theory, look fine. For this to work in practice, as we will show you, you need to be careful how you make your transparent GIF. Subtle gradient fades and drop shadow fades into different Web backgrounds can be tricky and may not give you what you would like. Another advantage of the GIF and PNG-8 formats is that they also support images that require even less than 8 bits of information per pixel. Many of the images I have created for commercial sites were GIF files that required only 5 bits per pixel. These files can be made very small and can also be transparent GIFs.

Designing for the Viewers You Care About the Most

When you, or your client, create a Web site or multimedia CD, it is important to consider who will be viewing it and what type of equipment those viewers might have. There is also the most important subset of those viewers, called "the ones you really care about." Those are the ones you want to design the site/CD for. In creating your Web/multimedia images, you want them to look best for these viewers, the ones you really care about. In creating the images for your project, you have to choose whether to use all 8-bit images, use all 24-bit images, use some of each, save your images in JPEG, GIF, PNG, PICT, Targa, or some other format, or use variations on each of these choices. Let's discuss how to simplify these decisions.

WHAT ABOUT PNG?

The PNG format uses lossless compression that can sometimes give you smaller files than GIF. It interlaces two dimensionally for faster loading, and can be stored at 8, 24, or 32-bits. PNG-24 supports alpha channel transparency, up to 256 levels of transparency, it is cross-platform, and it tags files with color space information, allowing viewing software to compensate for different monitor settings. Photoshop 6 and ImageReady 3 support PNG, but some browsers don't support all of PNG-24's features. Try it out and compare it to GIF for your images. Just make sure the browsers you care about support its features.

The average person who is browsing the Web may have a browser that uses a cheaper computer, or even his or her TV set, as the monitor environment (these are both 8-bit color) and a modem that is 28,800 kilobits/second in speed. Even with a 56kb modem, many local phone systems actually transmit at a slower speed. I found this out when I moved from Silicon Valley to Corvallis, Oregon. At 28kb, it takes about one-half second to download 1K (1,024 bytes) of information. The extra bits are taken up by software overhead, and the speed you actually get depends on a lot of issues, especially the performance of your Internet provider and the number of other people who are also trying to access information on that same site at the same time. If you create a 14K file, it will take these users about seven seconds to download and view that image. If you are creating a site for the average home Web user, say, the site for the Sears catalog, you can assume some of these people have 8-bit color. For them, you will want color photographs and graphics to be mostly 8-bit GIF files, which will look better on their 8-bit screens than 24-bit JPEG files, since 8-bit files generally look better on 8-bit monitors.

For our Web site, maxart.com, we make a different set of assumptions. We assume that the users we care most about are photographers, art directors, designers, and digital artists. These are the people who will be most interested in our books and services, and almost all of them have 24-bit color systems, 28.8 or faster modems, ISDN, DSL, cable modems or even T1 lines, and they want to see the best-quality images. For our site, we save most photographic images in JPEG format. Anything that is a photograph of nature or people, or a commercial composite example, is saved in JPEG format so it opens up in 24-bit color on the viewer's screen. We are more concerned about showing the users a high-quality image than creating an image that opens a few seconds faster. We may even show them small, lower-quality versions and give them the option of waiting a little longer to see a higher-quality version. The only time we use a GIF is for a graphic or illustration that started with less than 256 different colors, or for a small image that requires a transparent background. Our set of assumptions about the viewers we care most about are different than if we were creating a site for the average Web surfer. When creating images for a site, you need to know the type of visitor who is most important for that site and design for the lowest common denominator of your target audience. Make your images look best for that user.

To let your viewer see the highest quality images no matter what type of system they have, consider providing a choice on your home page to view either a site for users with 8-bit systems, or a site for users with 24-bit systems. You can then optimize the images on each branch of your main site to make each type of user happy.

HANDS-ON SESSION: Optimizing Images for the Web & Multimedia

Using the 4-Up dialogs, Master Color palettes and Weighted Optimization to create GIF, JPEG and PNG files.

USING THE 8.3 FILE NAMING CONVENTION.

We will be working on the files gc.psd, redac.psd, and macn.psd within the GIF JPEG and Color Palettes folder on your CD. The names of these files are abbreviations for Grand Canyon in Photoshop format, Red Acura in Photoshop format, and McNamaras in Photoshop format, respectively. When you are creating images to use on the Web, it's a good idea to use filenames that will work on any computer system. The names of your image files will also be embedded in your HTML code for your Web pages, and that code needs to work on any system. Older DOS Windows systems can't read files with names longer than eight characters, and most Windows systems use the three-character suffix at the end of the file name to decide what type of file it is. If you use file names with a maximum of eight characters and a three-character suffix, they will work on all Macs and all PCs. We will call this the 8.3 file name format. On UNIX systems, it can be even more complicated, because they see a difference between upper- and lowercase letters in file names. If you specify a file name in your HTML code that was both upper- and lowercase but the file on the UNIX volume was all in lowercase, when you run that code on a UNIX server, the system may not find your file. To be sure that your file names will work on all systems, use lowercase when naming images for the Web and be sure that any references to the images in your HTML code is also lowercase. And be sure to never use spaces between words in file names. If you must have a space, use the underscore character or a dash. That way, the code and the files will work together correctly, no matter what type of server your Web pages end up on.

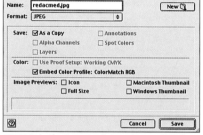

STEP 2: In the Save As dialog, choose JPEG from the Format menu, and click the As a Copy option to save the new JPEG to disk and leave your PSD file open and unaltered. Give your file a name in the 8.3 naming scheme that reveals the JPEG quality level. Here, we used "med" for medium.

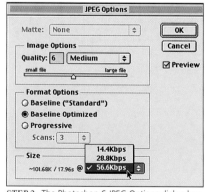

STEP 2: The Photoshop 6 JPEG Options dialog box. These options will appear after you have chosen the JPEG format and then pressed Save in the Save As dialog.

CREATING JPEGS IN PHOTOSHOP 6 VIA THE SAVE AS DIALOG

There are two routes within Photoshop to creating compressed images in the GIF and JPEG formats, and we'll cover both of them in this chapter. The method with the most functionality and options is the Save for Web dialog. This is a great part of the program that made its debut in version 5.5, and you may find that, once you become familiar with it, it's the best way to create GIFs and JPEGs. The other way to do this is how Photoshop users have been doing it for years, through the regular Save As dialog. Even though Save for Web has many more features available, if you just need to make a quick JPEG, then the "old fashioned" way is still perfectly valid. And for making a custom color palette that can be used for multiple GIFs, the Save for Web dialog is still lacking some important options that are very useful.

STEP 1: If you're primarily interested in how to optimize images for the Web, you could skip ahead a few pages to learn about creating Web images in the very useful

4-Up dialogs found in Photoshop 6 and ImageReady 3. You probably should read the next four pages anyway, though, as there is lots of useful information within them, especially concerning the creation of custom color palettes for multimedia projects. **Open the files gc.psd, redac.psd, and macn.psd from within the folder Ch37.GIF JPEG and ColorPalettes on your CD.**

STEP 2: **Make the redac.psd file active and go to File/Save As (Command-Shift-S). In the Save As dialog, choose JPEG from the drop-down Format menu and click in the As a Copy checkbox**. We're going to save a medium quality version of the file so choose an 8.3 format file name that reflects what you are doing. This is helpful for identification purposes when you're comparing different quality versions of the same image. For example, we used redacmed.jpg for the RedAcura file. Press the Save button and in the JPEG Options dialog that appears; experiment with different quality settings. With the Preview turned on, you can see how the different levels of compression affect the image quality. Since viewers of a Web site or a multimedia presentation are going to be seeing the images at 100%, be sure that you're zoomed in to 100% so you can accurately judge the compression/quality trade-offs. At the bottom of the dialog box, you can see how large the final JPEG will be when compressed, and also what the download time will be for various connection speeds (this information only appears if the Preview is turned on). You can also choose from three different format options: Baseline Standard, Baseline Optimized and Progressive. For most uses, Baseline Optimized will give you the best result and do a good job at compressing the image. The only very minor caveat with Baseline Optimized is that it may not be readable by some older browsers. If you want an image that appears in the browser gradually, looking chunky and pixelated at first and then getting better as more of it loads, choose Progressive. **Choose a Medium setting of 6 and click the OK button.**

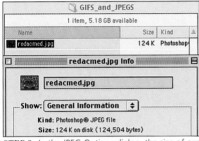

STEP 3: In the JPEG Options dialog, the size of our compressed file was forecast at about 102K, but in reality it turns out to be 124K because image previews and icons that were saved with the file increased its size.

STEP 3: **Next, take a look at the file in the Finder on a Mac, or in Windows Explorer on the PC, and see what the file size is.** In the JPEG Options dialog the previewed compressed size for a level 6 JPEG of the red Acura was about 102K, but our final result is 124K. The reason for the larger size is that image previews and icons were saved along with the file, making the final compressed size larger than expected. These extras are only seen when you are browsing your hard drive, or opening a file into an application that recognizes the thumbnail previews. For Web images or on a multimedia CD, they just take up extra space and make your file larger than it needs to be. Let's save another version without a preview.

First, go to the Preferences, **Edit/Preferences/Saving Files, and in the options for Image Previews, choose either Never Save, or Ask When Saving, and click OK. Next, choose Save As again (Command-Shift-S) and save the image as a JPEG with the same settings as in Step 2.** For identification purposes, we'll temporarily dispense with the 8.3 naming convention for this one, and call it "redacmed_nopreview." If you chose Ask When Saving for the image previews, make sure that the checkboxes at the bottom of the Save As dialog are all unchecked. In the JPEG Options dialog, choose a Level 6 quality setting, Baseline Optimized. After you save your file, compare the file size of the no preview image with the first JPEG you made. On my test, the file with no preview was reduced from 124K down to 104K, a savings of 20K or 16%! If you think that saving a mere 20K is not a big deal, let me assure you that when you're trying to make a Web page as small and fast-loading as possible, trimming 16% off a file's size becomes very significant.

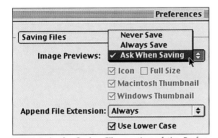

STEP 3: In the Saving Files section of the Preferences, you can control the saving of image previews and icons. These add file size to your image and should not be saved with Web images.

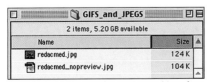

STEP 3: By eliminating the preview and icon from the second file shown above, I was able to save 20K, making the file 16% smaller than if the preview and icon had been included.

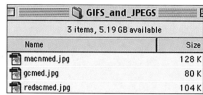

STEP 4: With JPEG compression, just because you use the identical settings on images that share the same pixel dimensions doesn't mean you'll end up with the same file size. The amount of compression you get depends on the visual complexity of each individual image. The more complex it is, the less compression you get; the more areas of flat color or repeated patterns, the better the compression. **Try this out for yourself by saving copies of the Grand Canyon and McNamara files with the same medium-quality JPEG settings we used for the Red Acura image.** These three images each started out with a pixel resolution of exactly 640x480, but they will yield different final JPEG file sizes. When you open them back up from JPEG compression, they will still be 640x480 pixels; their file size just gets compressed for saving on disk and transmitting over a network. With Windows and DOS, the file sizes displayed by the OS are quite close to the actual file sizes, and with Mac OS 8.1 or later and drives using the Mac Extended drive format, you will also get a very accurate display of Finder file sizes. If you're using Mac OS 8.0 or earlier, you need to first select that file in the Finder; then choose File/Get Info (Command-I) to bring up the Info dialog box for that file. The rightmost part of the Size line will have the actual bytes used in parentheses.

STEP 4: The actual amount of JPEG compression you get will vary, depending on the complexity of each image. All of these images were the same pixel dimension (640x480), and were all saved with the same, medium quality JPEG settings and no previews, yet each one is a different size.

A Cautionary Note: Since the JPEG format achieves its compression by discarding unnecessary pixel data, you should never use it as a file format for working on images. If you start out with a JPEG and then do some editing and save it repeatedly, every time you save in JPEG format, more data is being deleted, degrading image quality. Save your image in Photoshop format if you're going to be making major changes.

SAVING GIFS AND WORKING WITH COLOR PALETTES

As with JPEGs, a more full featured way of creating a GIF is to use the Save for Web dialog in Photoshop, or the 2-Up and 4-Up optimized tabs in ImageReady. We're definitely headed in that direction, but before we indulge ourselves there, we'll go over the other way you make a GIF, and also talk a bit about the color tables that are created with these files.

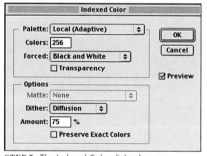

STEP 5: The Indexed Color dialog box.

STEP 5: **Make sure you have the original PSD versions open of the three files from the JPEG session we just finished. We are going to create GIF versions of all these images and take a look at their color tables. For each one, choose Image/Duplicate to make an onscreen copy of the image; then choose Image/Mode/Index Color. In the Indexed Color dialog box, select the Local (Adaptive) Palette, 256 Colors, Forced Black and White, No Transparency, and a Diffusion Dither of 75%. Now choose File/Save As and save each file with the Format set to CompuServe GIF. Give it a file name that identifies its color depth; for the Red Acura, we used redac256.gif. Redac tells us it's the Red Acura, and 256 tells us it has 256 colors.**

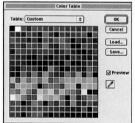

STEP 6: The Adaptive palette for the Red Acura image.

STEP 6: **Now make the redac256.gif image the active one by clicking its title bar, and choose Image/Mode/Color Table from the top menu bar.** The color table is the exact collection of 256 colors that were used to describe this image. Since we chose an Adaptive color palette, the 256 colors you see here were adapted from actual colors in the image. The first two pixels in the upper left are a result of choosing Forced Black and White, ensuring that the color table will have an absolute black and white included. **Now, switch to the other images and examine their color tables to see how a different set of 256 colors was used for each one.**

Compare each color table with the actual image' and you'll see that Photoshop did a very good job at choosing the 256 colors that best represent all of the colors in the image. For the Red Acura, there are lots of rich, saturated reds, as well as the purples, greens and blues that make up the streaked background. The Grand Canyon's color table has soft pastel blues, subtle greens and a range of reddish-brown earth tones. In the color table for the McNamaras image, a wide range of colors is used to describe the varying skin tones, clothing colors, and background vegetation. **When creating GIFS from photographic images, an Adaptive palette will usually give you the best results, since it is built from colors contained in the actual image.**

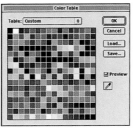

STEP 6: The Adaptive palette for the McNamaras image.

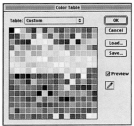

STEP 6: The Adaptive palette for the Grand Canyon image.

  You've probably noticed that, in addition to Adaptive, there are two other palette choices in the same section of the pop-up menu in the Indexed Color dialog. **Perceptual** creates a palette from colors in the image, but it gives priority to choosing those colors for which the human eye has greater sensitivity. **Selective** is similar to Perceptual, but it works better for images with broad areas of color and it favors the preservation of Web Safe colors. If you're making a GIF from an image that is not photographic, like a logo, or a graphic, then using the Selective palette will generally produce a better result.

THE SYSTEM PALETTE AND WEB PALETTE

STEP 7: The System palette was created to deal with the differences between Adaptive palettes of images that need to be displayed on the same page on an 8-bit monitor. A System palette contains a broad range of colors from all over the spectrum so that you can display any image and it will look reasonably okay. It won't usually look near as good as it would with its own Adaptive palette, but by using the System palette, you can display many different images at the same time with reasonable results. The problem for Web developers is that the Mac and Windows OS each have different colors in their System palettes. Fortunately, there are 216 colors in common between the two palettes. The palette with these common colors is called the Web palette. Photoshop 6 allows you to choose any of these palettes when creating 8-bit images. **Creating images using the Web palette allows them to display well on an 8-bit color monitor on the Mac and on the PC when using Netscape or Internet Explorer to browse your images. Having said that, you should still evaluate how much using these palettes will affect the color quality of your image, and also take into account your target audience.** Most desktop and laptop computers being sold today are shipping with the ability to display at least thousands of colors, so 8-bit color is not as crucial an issue as it once was. Where 8-bit color will probably continue to be important is in the color displays of Palm Pilots and other PDA devices. If you're creating a Web presentation of your photographs, then you're probably going to be more concerned about those viewers who have monitors that can display a quality image, rather than a handheld device. Besides, **for some images, using the Web or System palettes can make them look really bad, and the best choice would still be an Adaptive palette.**

> *When creating an Adaptive palette in Photoshop 6, to bias the color table toward particular colors in an image, make a selection of those color areas before you do the Index Color mode conversion. The color table will be more weighted to the selected area. You can also use the new Weighted Optimization feature that lets you use an Alpha Channel to specify which areas of an image should be given priority when building a color palette. See the last part of this chapter for a complete discussion of the weighted optimization features.*

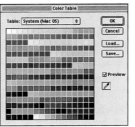

STEP 7: The Mac System palette.

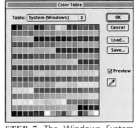

STEP 7: The Windows System palette.

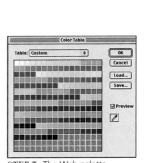

STEP 7: The Web palette.

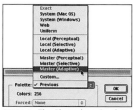

STEP 8: The Photoshop 6 palette choices in the Indexed Color dialog. The Master palette options are only available when you have more than one image open, and are used to create a common palette from colors in all of the open images.

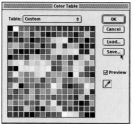

STEP 8: The custom palette created from all three of the open images, using the Master (Adaptive) setting. Click the Save button to save this palette for future use and call it "_all3.act."

STEP 6: When you save a custom palette in the Presets/Optimized Colors folder (left), it will be available in Photoshop's Save for Web dialog (right).

WHAT HAPPENED TO THE GIF89a EXPORT FILTER?

GIF89a Export used to be one of the more useful ways to create a GIF file in Photoshop. With the greatly expanded functionality of the Save for Web dialog, however, Adobe has downgraded GIF89a to an optional plug-in. If you want to use it for making your GIFs, you need to install it yourself. You can find it on the Photoshop CD in the Goodies, Optional Plug-ins folder.

CREATING A MASTER PALETTE FOR MULTIMEDIA USE

STEP 8: **When creating images for a multimedia CD where you have absolute control over your palettes, you can also create a custom palette for each group of images that would be on the screen at one time. To do this from Photoshop 6, make sure that the three original 24-bit PSD images are all open and choose one of them (it doesn't really matter which one you activate, but we'll do the Grand Canyon). Choose Image/Mode/Index Color and from the pop-up Palettes menu, pick Master (Adaptive).** The last time we used this dialog, we chose Local (Adaptive), which built a color table based on colors in the active image. With Master (Adaptive) selected, Photoshop will build a palette based on colors in all of the open images. **For the remaining settings in the Indexed Color dialog, choose 256 Colors, Forced Black and White, and 75% Diffusion Dither. Choose OK to convert to 8-bit color and then from the File menu, choose Save As and name the file gcall3.gif, to denote that we've used the color palette created from all three images.** Now that this custom table has been created, we can easily select it for the remaining two images. **Switch to one of the other two original 24-bit images and choose Image/Mode/Index Color, but this time, set the Palette type to Previous. This will use the same palette that was used for the previous image. Save this with another appropriate "all3" name like mcnall3.gif and then do the same thing with the third image.** You now have these images created with the same adaptive palette that was customized for just these three images. **With one of these new GIFs active, go into Image/Mode/Color Table and look at this common palette. It is a mixture of the three you saw on the last page. Click the Save button and save this palette as "_all3.act."** Now you can load this palette from the Color Table dialog box and also from the Save for Web dialog. If you need to make a lot of common palette images, you can create an action to do it to all the files in a folder and save yourself some time.

ImageReady also lets you create a master palette from multiple images, but the procedure is different than in Photoshop. Since the ImageReady process involves dealing with its optimized dialogs, we'll cover that first.

THE 4-UP DIALOGS IN PHOTOSHOP 6 AND IMAGEREADY 3

STEP 1: **Open the file redac.psd from the GIF JPEG and Color Palettes folder on your CD. Open the file in both Photoshop 6 and ImageReady 3, and then type F, for Full Screen Mode, in each of the programs.** We will use this file as we explore the different ways to make GIF, JPEG and PNG files with Photoshop 6 or ImageReady 3.

In Photoshop, choose File/Save for Web (Command-Option-Shift-S) to open the Save for Web dialog. Click on the 4-Up tab to choose the 4-Up view. This allows you to look at the original image and 3 different versions of the proposed Web file at the same time. Now switch to ImageReady 3, and you will notice that the different optimize options (Original, Optimized, 2-Up, 4-Up) are available all the time at the top left of the screen without going into the Save for Web modal dialog. This gives ImageReady the option of saving any version of an optimized image at any time without entering and then leaving the Save for Web modal dialog each time you choose OK to save from this dialog in Photoshop.

Original, Optimized, 2-Up, 4-Up

STEP 2: In either application, clicking on the Original tab will allow you to use the entire window space to look at the original image without any Web optimizations. Clicking on the Optimized tab allows you to use the entire window to look at the one Optimized version. The 2-Up view allows you to compare the Original to one optimization or to look at two optimizations at a time. The 4-Up view gives you the most options because it allows you to compare four versions of an image at a time, so we will start there. **Click on the 4-Up option in ImageReady; then click on the top left version of the red Acura image. Now switch back to Photoshop and click on the top left version of the red Acura image. Choose Original from the Settings pop-up in the top right of the window. This will continue to show you the original image in the top left window. Now click in the top, right window and change the set-**

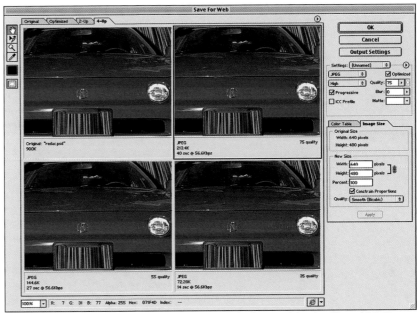

STEP 1: The Photoshop Save for Web dialog is a modal dialog box containing the different Web file types and optimize options in the upper right corner, the Image Size and Color Table information below that to the right side and the four views when looking at it in 4-Up mode. In Photoshop, you can only save one image at a time without re-entering this dialog and you can only see one Photoshop image within this dialog at a time.

tings to JPEG High to look at a JPEG version of the image. Photoshop will now create the JPEG version with the High quality setting and display it on the screen. Notice that below this top right subwindow on the left you also see the file size of this version and how long it will take to transfer over the Web using a certain speed of modem. You can use the Preview pop-up menu at the top right of this Save for Web dialog to change the speed of the Internet connection for these calculations and to also change the way Web images are displayed in Photoshop. We will explain the other settings in this Preview pop-up later. **To change the internet connection speed display calculations in ImageReady, you use the pop-up menus on the bottom left of the window.**

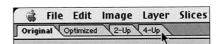

STEP 1: In ImageReady 3, the optimized views, Optimized, 2-Up, and 4-Up, are always available as tabs at the top left of the screen.

Making Your Own Optimize Settings

STEP 3: When you pick one of the Settings choices in either application, you are just choosing a predefined set for creating the Web image in this window. You can then customize that choice by changing any of the options like Quality, Blur and Matte that you see here. Photoshop and ImageReady come with several predefined settings choices, but you can also create your own settings once you have discovered which Save for Web options work best for your most common images. **To create your own settings file, just choose Save Settings from the Optimize pop-up menu to the right of the Settings menu. In order for your new setting to be available within the Save for Web setting menu, you need to save it within the Adobe Photoshop 6/Presets/Optimized settings folder on your hard disk. Now click in the bottom left window; then change the Quality slider to 51%. Choose the Save Settings pop-up and save this as "JPEG 51percent" within the above mentioned folder.** This setting will now be available to Photoshop. To make it available to ImageReady, you need to quit and then restart ImageReady.

STEP 2: The Preview menu in Photoshop's Save for Web dialog allows you to choose the color space used for image display within the dialog and also the speed of the Internet connection used to calculate Web file download times.

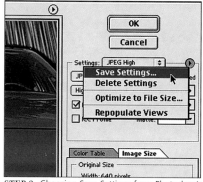

STEP 3: Choosing Save Settings from Photoshop's Save for Web dialog to save a particular set of JPEG file options. You need to save these settings within the "Adobe Photoshop 6 / Presets / Optimized Settings" folder on your hard disk.

PHOTOSHOP VS. IMAGEREADY WEB-OPTIMIZE LAYOUT

STEP 4: **Notice that in the Photoshop Save for Web dialog, you have all the Optimize settings options built into the top right corner, and then below that there is an Image Size section and a Color Table section.** You can use the Image Size section, while in Save for Web, to actually resample the file and make a smaller (or larger) Web image. That may seem convenient, but actually **it works better if you sharpen an image after it is resampled and before converting it to JPEG or GIF. Doing the resample within the Save for Web dialog doesn't give you that option**. In ImageReady, on the other hand, you have to use the Image/Image Size command to resample each image before you optimize it. This is probably better because you can then sharpen it before converting it to JPEG or GIF. You can do it the same way in Photoshop; you just need to remember to resample and sharpen the image before bringing up the Save for Web dialog. That means that for the sharpest Web images, you probably won't use the Image Size section of Save for Web. The Color Table section of Save for Web is only used when you are making GIF or PNG-8 files that will be using a color table. In ImageReady, the Color Table is a free-floating palette that you can access by choosing Window/Show Color Table. Even though Adobe is gradually increasing the number of ImageReady features available in Photoshop (the new slice capability, for instance) there are still functionality and feature gaps between the two programs, and from a workflow perspective it would be much more convenient if all of ImageReady's functionality is one day rolled into Photoshop.

Switch to ImageReady, and here you will need to use Window/Show Optimize to bring up the Optimize palette. Click on the top left image panel and choose Original from its Settings menu so that this view of the image shows you the original Red Acura. Click on the top right view and choose JPEG-High from the Optimize palette's setting menu to set it to the High quality JPEG option. Now change the Quality slider to 51, which I think is the best JPEG compromise for this image between image size and image quality. Choose File/Save Optimized As... and save this file as rdacIR51.jpg so you can look at it later. In the Format menu just below the Name field, be sure that Images Only is selected. This will save only the JPEG file and not an accompanying HTML file. To save the optimized image from the Photoshop Save for Web dialog, you would have to choose OK at the top right of the dialog while an optimized preview window with these options was selected. That would then take you out of Save for Web without the option of trying and saving further optimizations. To do more, you would have to then re-enter Save for Web, which takes extra time.

This is the ImageReady 4-Up view of the current file. In ImageReady, to see a 4-Up view of any file, all you have to do is switch to that file and then click on the 4-Up tab. Here in ImageReady, you can save as many variations as you want from any open file since the 4-Up choice is always there. To get the Optimize options or the Color Table in ImageReady, you need to choose Window/Show Optimize or Window/Show Color Table. To change the Image Size in ImageReady, you need to choose Image/Image Size, which is really a better way to do it than using the built-in Image Size option in Photoshop's Save for Web dialog since you will probably want to sharpen the image after resizing it and before saving it in a Web format.

COMPARING GIF TO JPEG

STEP 5: **Now, click in the bottom left view for the red Acura within ImageReady.**

Choose GIF 128 Dithered from the Settings menu in the Optimize dialog. You are now comparing the Original to a JPEG at quality 51 to a 128-color GIF file. Notice that the GIF file is very sharp, but the fine color transitions in the hood of the car look pixelated. **Use the Command-Spacebar-click shortcut to zoom into the Acura emblem and the color transitions on the hood of the car.** Notice that all four windows zoom in to the same place within the image for comparison. This is very cool, and the Save for Web dialog in Photoshop does it, too. Change the Palette options in the Optimize palette between Perceptual, Adaptive and Selective, and notice how the Color Table changes, within the Color Table palette. Notice how the Acura's pixelated hood changes, too. You can use this to get the best palette for each image. I think the

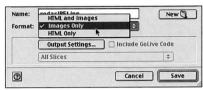

STEP 4: When saving the optimized image in this step, make sure that the Images Only option is selected in the Format menu below the Name field.

Adaptive looks the best here. If you need to scroll, just hold the Spacebar down; then scroll with the mouse just as you would within Photoshop. **Change the Colors pop-up to 64 and notice that the GIF file is still bigger than the 51 quality JPEG; you have to go down to 32 colors to make the GIF smaller, and by then it looks pretty bad. Choose File/Save Optimized As... to save this 32-color GIF just for fun. Now, go up to 256 colors and the GIF looks great, but it is now almost twice as big as the 51 JPEG—too big for an actual Web image. Move Colors back to 32 and the GIF is smaller, but then click on the bottom right window, choose JPEG and set the Quality to 25. Now this JPEG is twice as small as that very small and very ugly 32 GIF in the bottom left window.** With the exception of what happens to the Acura emblem below the 51 quality setting, JPEG does a much better job than GIF in size versus quality with this image.

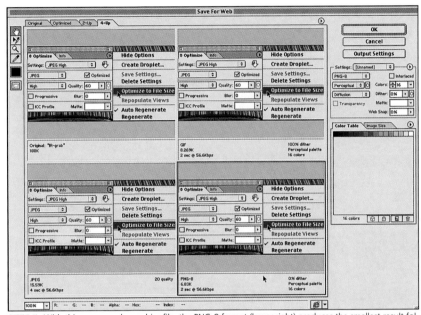

STEP 5: With this screen grab graphics file, the PNG-8 format (lower right) produces the smallest result followed closely by GIF. The JPEG format is well over twice the size of either of these 8-bit formats and still doesn't look quite as good. For an image such as this, with a limited color set to begin with, you'll want to use an 8-bit format like GIF or PNG-8, even for display on a full 24-bit monitor.

WHERE PNG-8 BEATS GIF AND GIF BEATS JPEG

I was looking for a good example of the type of image where GIF does a better job compressing than JPEG and I found a great example! You can see with the 4-Up dialog of the screen grab above that a good-looking GIF file is over twice as small as an acceptable JPEG and that the PNG-8 version is actually even smaller than the GIF for this image. **Images containing solid colors, straight lines, text and graphics are a great place to use the GIF and PNG-8 formats even when these 8-bit files will be displayed on a 24-bit, full-color display.**

By now you should be getting some idea about the power of using the 4-Up dialog within ImageReady and Photoshop to compare how different formats, color palettes and compression levels affect your image. It's a great tool for helping you decide just how to go about optimizing your files. ImageReady just has the edge of letting you do multiple saves while you are working. If you only save one image most of the time, then you can do all of your work, of this type, within Photoshop and you don't need ImageReady to make JPEG, GIF or PNG files. When you pick a particular set of options in either program, it appears that you get the same size and quality of image.

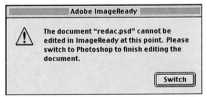

In either program, if you have entered a modal dialog, such as Save for Web in Photoshop, or Curves, or Levels, and you try to switch to the companion application to edit the same image, you will see a warning telling you that you must finish editing the image before you can move to the other program.

413

The 4-Up Dialogs in Photoshop 6 and ImageReady 3

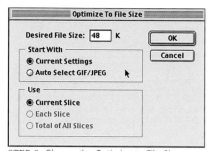

STEP 6: Choose the Optimize to File Size menu from either Photoshop or ImageReady to get this dialog and have the application choose the GIF or JPEG settings to get the file size you need. Current Settings will leave the format (GIF or JPEG) as you have it and just change the options of that format to arrive at the requested size.

STEP 6: In ImageReady, you can find Optimize to File Size in the pop-out menu of the Optimize palette.

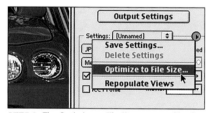

STEP 6: The Optimize to File Size command in Photoshop's Save for Web dialog.

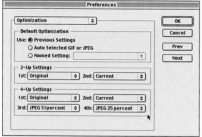

STEP 7: In ImageReady, you can use Edit/Preferences/Optimization to determine the settings you want for Default Optimization, the 2-Up and 4-Up views. If you set the first setting (the top left in the Optimize 2-Up and 4-Up views) to Original, then the next one has to be set to Current. In 4-Up view, you can set the third and fourth to whatever you want.

OPTIMIZE TO FILE SIZE

STEP 6: Another feature you might find useful sometimes is the Optimize to File Size command that is found in the Optimize palette pop-up in ImageReady and within the Optimize pop-up menu to the right of the Settings menu in Photoshop's Save for Web dialog. **With this feature you choose a desired file size and the application will use either JPEG or GIF to create a file with that size**. You can force it to choose one or the other format by being in that format when you enter the Optimize to File Size menu option, choosing Current Settings when you get there. If you don't care whether a GIF or JPEG is used, then choose Auto Select GIF/JPEG.

SETTING PREFERENCES FOR THE 4-UP DIALOGS

STEP 7: **With ImageReady you can use Edit/Preferences/Optimization to set up your preferences as to which choices you initially get when you enter the different Optimization dialogs.** You can see the dialog here with the preferences set to show different levels of JPEG quality. I use something like this as a starting point for a JPEG image; then I tweak the Quality slider until I get the quality I want at the size I need. You have to be careful not to completely rely on the optimization preferences because the current settings within the Optimize palette may override the preference settings for the Preview window that is currently active. If that happens, just use the Settings menu to put that window back where you want it. **In Photoshop if you set the top right Optimize view to a certain setting, like JPEG High, quality 60, and choose the Repopulate Views option from the pop-out menu next to the settings, Photoshop will automatically update the bottom left and bottom right views with JPEG settings that are 1/2 that quality, 30, and 1/4 that quality, 15.** Photoshop will then use that same set of quality settings for the next image that you open. In fact, it seems that Photoshop just uses the last settings you had in the Optimize part of the Save for Web dialog as the settings for the top right view and then repopulates the lower views with settings that are 1/2 and 1/4 of that top right setting. That seems to be the default behavior for the Photoshop 4-Up window, so you don't have the same amount of control here as in ImageReady.

UNDERSTANDING THE OTHER OPTIONS FOR OPTIMIZING WEB IMAGES

There are various options available for either JPEG, GIF or PNG that have some similarities and also some very important differences. To see all the options within the ImageReady Optimize palette, choose Show Options from the palette's pop-up menu. The same section of the Save for Web dialog in Photoshop always shows you all options. We will now explain the other JPEG options (Optimized, Progressive, ICC Profile, Blur and Matte) and the other GIF options (Lossy, Color Reduction Algorithm, Dither, Transparency, Interlaced, Matte and Web Snap). PNG-8 files have the same options as GIF but there is no Lossy option. Using the Lossy option can allow you to make a GIF file smaller than the corresponding PNG-8, but also of lower quality. We'll also cover how to create a Master Palette in ImageReady and the great new Weighted Optimization features that let you use an alpha channel to influence factors such as compression quality, dithering, and color palettes.

THE OTHER JPEG OPTIONS

OPTIMIZED, PROGRESSIVE AND ICC PROFILE

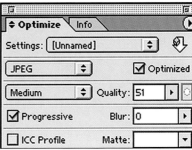

STEP 8: Here are all the JPEG options from within the ImageReady Optimize palette. Make sure you choose Show Options from the palette's pop-up menu to always see all the options for each format.

STEP 8: One of the other JPEG options here that we have not explored is Optimized, which creates a JPEG image with a little better compression than when Optimized is off. I have been using Optimized for quite a while with my JPEGs of photographs, and I'm very happy with the results. This is the same as choosing Baseline Optimized when you create a JPEG through Photoshop's Save As dialog. Progressive gives you a JPEG file that appears quickly on a Web page as a low-quality image that progressively gets better and sharper over time as the rest of the data downloads. **Make sure you are in ImageReady and then choose File/Open to open the file macn.psd on the CD within the McNamaras folder within the GIF JPEG and Color Palettes folder. Set the top right view to JPEG quality 60, the bottom left view to JPEG quality 51 and the bottom right view to JPEG quality 25. Notice for each of these JPEG versions that when you turn Progressive off, the file size actually gets a little bigger; when you also turn Optimized off, it gets bigger still.** Having Progressive on doesn't usually make the file much larger and, as you can see here, it can sometimes actually make the file smaller. Your choice of having Progressive on for an image should be based on the overall design of the Web page that the image appears on. You should also consider the time it will take for the full quality image to load. I don't like the initially blurry progressive images and would only use them when I expected a blank image box to sit for a long time while the full image loaded onto the page. I always choose Optimized, though.

The ICC Profile choice, if on, will embed in the JPEG file an ICC profile for the color space the image was created in. This will make the image a very small amount larger but is a good choice if you really care about the way images look on a viewer's screen. **For an embedded ICC profile to be of any use, of course, the person viewing the image needs to be using an ICC-aware application and, hopefully, a calibrated monitor.** If I were going to use a JPEG as a comp to send to an art director or an art dealer, I would turn ICC profile on. If you think there will be enough people looking at your site with calibrated monitors, browsers that make use of profiles, or if they are proofing an image directly in Photoshop or another ICC-aware application, then turn ICC profile on.

BLUR AND MATTE

STEP 9: The Blur option blurs the file with a Gaussian Blur of between 0 and 2 to minimize the artifacts caused by the lower-quality JPEG settings. This also blurs the entire image, however, so I usually don't use this option much for photographs. You might try it on problem text or graphics, like the Acura emblem in the redac image, to see if it can help the result. Blur settings below .5 are probably what you will want. **Use the Window menu in ImageReady to switch back to the redac image and set the Quality slider on both the top and bottom right views to 25. Make sure all the settings are the same. Now change the Blur setting on the bottom right image to 0.4, and you will notice as you compare the blurred bottom right to the unblurred top right that the size of the final JPEG gets smaller**. This is another possible use of Blur. The noise around the Acura emblem lessens somewhat, but the entire image also blurs a bit, too. **One thing to be aware of is that the Blur settings don't reset to 0 when you're finished saving an image.** When I was working on this example, the Blur value of 0.4 was still in place when I went to optimize another JPEG image. This could be a bug, or it could also be designed that way, but just be on the look out for it or you might inadvertently be blurring your JPEGs when you don't mean to.

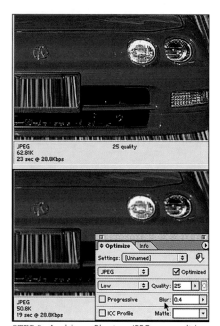

STEP 9: Applying a Blur to a JPEG can result in a smaller file and can also smooth obvious compression artifacts. In the lower image, a blur of 0.4 reduces the file size by 20% and also helps with the JPEG traces around the Acura emblem. The problem with this approach, of course, is that it blurs the entire image (note the reduced sharpness in the headlights).

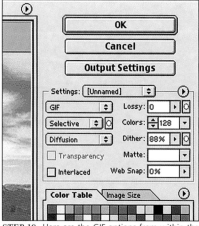

STEP 10: Here are the GIF options from within the Photoshop Save for Web dialog. In this dialog you always see all the options for each format.

The Matte option allows you to choose a Matte color to fill transparent areas of an image. You would only use this option if the image you were trying to compress had a transparent area that you wanted to fill with the background color of a Web page. The JPEG format, unlike GIF or PNG, doesn't allow for a transparent area that will later be filled with a Web site's background. With JPEG, however, you can choose a Matte color and then fill a transparent area with it when you save the optimized image. You need to know the site's background color ahead of time to do this. The JPEG matte will even give you soft shadows and nice things that you can't get with GIF transparency, but the catch is that if you later change the site's background color, you will have to re-create your JPEG files. That might be fine if you are generating your Web pages and their JPEG files automatically from a database using scripts and actions, like we often do. For more info about Transparency and Matte, see the discussion about these issues in a few pages at the end of the next GIF Options section.

The one JPEG option we haven't addressed here, Weighted Optimization using alpha channels, is covered at the end of this chapter.

THE GIF OPTIONS

STEP 10: **In ImageReady, use the Window menu to switch back to the macn.psd file and use the Settings menu in the Optimize palette to set the top left view to Original, the top right view to JPEG Medium, the bottom left view to GIF 128 Dithered and the bottom right view to GIF 64 Dithered.** One of the advantages of ImageReady over Photoshop is that you can look at 4-Up versions of more than one image at a time and just switch between them using the Window menu. Because Photoshop's 4-Up capabilities are within the Save for Web modal dialog, you don't have this capability in Photoshop. When you are in Photoshop 6's Save for Web modal dialog, you can't do anything else within Photoshop until you either exit the dialog using Cancel or make an optimization choice and then save the optimized image by exiting the dialog using OK. That's why we'll play with the GIF options using ImageReady.

Notice that for this file, the Medium 30 quality JPEG looks pretty good because it doesn't have a graphic like the Acura emblem in the redac image. Let's play with the GIF options and see if we can use them to reduce the size. **For this image, the GIF 64 Dithered version in the bottom right view doesn't look that bad. Click on the bottom left view and also set it to GIF 64 Dithered. Now click back into the bottom right view, and we'll play with the options and see how the file gets smaller and the quality degrades as we work.** When you convert an image into GIF (or PNG-8) format, it goes from having potentially millions of possible colors down to having 256 or fewer colors. In this case we have chosen 64 colors to reduce the size of the file. When you do the conversion to 256 or fewer colors, you sacrifice color information, but the GIF (or PNG-8) format will give you the best rendition of the image with that number of colors; either format will compress a reduced color image, and their file compression scheme is lossless. The initial information loss occurs by reducing the number of colors to 256 or less.

LOSSY AND COLOR REDUCTION

With the GIF format, you have the additional option of turning on the Lossy option, which allows some further loss in image quality with the gain of making the image smaller. **Changing the Lossy factor here to 80 will actually make this GIF version of the image about the same size as the JPEG 30, but it looks pretty bad. Setting the Lossy option to 35 here doesn't appear to do too much damage to the image, and it does reduce its size from 186.6K down to 132.8K.** In the end, it all comes down to what still looks acceptable to you and meets your file size requirements. As with many things in life, and certainly digital imaging, it's a big trade-off. The Lossy setting can also be influenced by the new Weighted Optimization feature which is covered at the end of this chapter.

As you are making these adjustments, you'll notice that if you use Spacebar-Command-click to zoom into 200% that many Web images look bad at that zoom factor. When I'm working on a high-quality art image that is not for the Web, I often zoom into 200% or higher to see all the details of what I'm doing. With Web images, I've found it is often better to do your final comparisons at 100% because that is what the user will see on the Web page. At 200% or higher, you often see a lot of problems that don't show up at 100% and so probably won't matter to the viewer of the Web site.

The second pop-up menu on the left, Color Reduction Algorithm, controls how the image is converted from 24-bit into 8-bit color and specifically how the palette is made. The default option for the GIF 64 Dithered setting is Selective, which we still see in the bottom left view. Try Perceptual and Adaptive in the bottom right view to see which one of the three works best. Perceptual gives priority to the colors the human eye is more sensitive to, Selective favors large areas of color and including more Web colors and it is the default, and Adaptive gives priority to the colors appearing most within the image. For this image, it is hard for me to tell the difference between them, but if you zoom into 200%, you can see pixels change as you switch between them. Adaptive seems to take up an extra K of image space but somehow, maybe just because I'm used to using it, I like it better here. If you choose Custom at this point, from this same pop-up menu, that option will preserve the current Selective, Perceptual, or Adaptive color table as a fixed palette and that palette will not change after you make further changes to the image. This may allow you to preserve a higher quality set of colors in the palette as you then go on and further refine the image to make it smaller. Choosing Mac OS gives you the standard Mac OS palette, Windows gives you the default Windows palette and Web gives you the Web palette, which contains the 216 colors that are common to both the Mac OS and Windows palette. Choosing Web avoids the possibility that a browser may dither your image when it's displayed on an 8-bit monitor, but the quality of the image may suffer from being converted to the Web palette. Black & White will simply make a color table of just those two colors and create a dithered bitmap rendition of your image, and Grayscale will turn it into a grayscale version.

The Dithering Options

Leave the Color Reduction Algorithm set to Adaptive and move down the pop-ups on the left side to the Dither Algorithm pop-up. The file seems to be the smallest leaving the setting at Diffusion. Both the Pattern and Noise choices make a much

bigger file without a noticeable difference at 100% viewing. Setting Dither Algorithm to No Dither does shave about 9K off the file size, but it also makes color transitions, especially on some of the shirts, clump up a bit. If you choose any of the dither types, you can also change the numeric Dither box to the right of this pop-up from the default 88% setting to a lesser amount of dithering. I tried turning Diffusion Dither

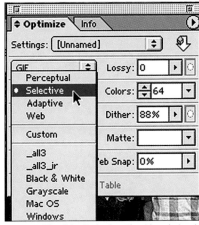

STEP 10: The Color Reduction Algorithm choices in ImageReady. Selective is the default setting. In the bottom section the all3 and all3_ir palettes are custom master palettes that I created in Photoshop and ImageReady.

STEP 10: The Dither choices in ImageReady.

STEP 10: Previewing the Bowser Dither in Photoshop's Save for Web dialog.

STEP 10: In ImageReady, you can preview the Browser Dither from the View menu.

back on and found that I needed a setting of about 50% before I noticed a difference between that and No Dither. **I've just decided to choose No Dither with this image in the quest for a smaller file. Try these same settings with the redac image, with its subtle color gradations on the car hood, and notice how bad the hood looks when you switch from 88% Diffusion Dither to No Dither.**

When images are viewed on an 8-bit display in a Web browser, the browser applies a dithering pattern. If you want to preview how a Web browser's dithering will affect the image, you can do this from Photoshop's Save for Web dialog by clicking on the top pop-up menu that is just above and to the right of the OK button and choosing Browser Dither. In ImageReady, this same option is found in the View menu under Preview.

TRANSPARENCY AND MATTE

STEP 11: The Transparency and Matte options control what will happen to images that contain transparent areas within their original RGB format. These options are also used in the next chapter, "Creating Your Own Web Photo Gallery." You'll notice that turning either option on or off while working on this macn image makes no difference in the size or appearance because this image contains no transparent areas. **For images that contain no transparent areas, just leave Transparency off and leave Matte set to None.**

To learn more about Transparency and Matte, switch to ImageReady and open the file Spherical Lock.psd from the Transparency and Matte folder inside the Ch37.GIF JPEG and ColorPalettes folder on your CD. We will use this file to explore the Transparency and Matte options within all the file formats.

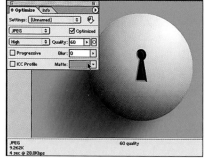

STEP 12: Here is the JPEG version of the spherical lock after we have set the Matte color to #339966. This file looks pretty good and is quite small in JPEG format.

STEP 12: **Turn off the white background layer by clicking its Eye icon. Type D to get the default colors and F for Full Screen mode; then close the Tool palette and any other palettes that are on the screen. Use Window/Show Optimize to bring up the Optimize palette. Make sure you have chosen to see all the options by choosing Show Options, the top Optimize palette menu choice. In this same menu, make sure that Auto Regenerate is also turned on with a check mark next to it. Click on the 4-Up tab and then click on the top left view and set it to Original using the Settings menu within the Optimize palette. Now click on the top right view and set the Settings to JPEG High.** Notice that the default for JPEG is to fill the transparent area, the checkerboard pattern, with the background color, white. JPEG format doesn't have a Transparency option, but it does allow you to fill the transparent parts of an image with a Matte color. If you choose the background color of your Web site as the Matte color, shadows within the JPEG file will look great, like they have 256 levels of transparency. You would have to re-create your JPEG file, however, each time you changed the background color on your Web page. **Click in the white box next to word Matte at the bottom right of the Optimize palette. This will allow you to choose a color for the JPEG Matte. Type in #339966 at the bottom right of the Color Picker dialog to insert this green color as your Matte color. This is what we would do to create a JPEG version of this image to sit on a Web page that had this green background color.**

STEP 13: **Now click in the bottom left view area and change the Settings for that view to GIF 128 Dithered. This setting starts out with the Matte color set to white and Transparency on. When Transparency is on with a GIF file and a Matte color is chosen, only the pixels that are 100% transparent will show the background of your**

Chapter 37: Optimizing Images for the Web & Multimedia

Web page. Areas that are partially opaque, like the ball's shadow, will be blended with the Matte color, which is now white. Click on the pop-up menu to the right of the Matte option and set the Matte to None. Now, with the Matte option off, opaque areas that are less than 50% opaque show up as transparent, and you will see your Web site's background in those areas. Areas that are more than 50% opaque, the darker shadow areas, now show up as black, which doesn't look convincing at all. There is no blending with GIF transparency!

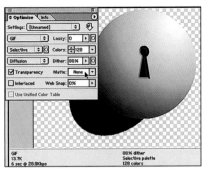

STEP 14: **Now turn Transparency off and you will get an even bigger black area. With Transparency off and no Matte color, areas that are totally transparent in the original are filled with white and areas that are partially opaque are filled with black. This is also of no use for our hypothetical Web page. Turn Transparency back on; then**

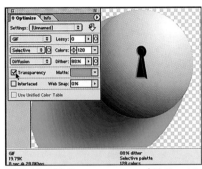

STEP 13: How our sphere's shadow looks with Transparency on and Matte set to None. This wouldn't look very good on our Web page!

click in the white box next to Matte and in the lower right of the color picker, set the Matte color to #339966. With these settings, the totally transparent areas of the image will be replaced by your site's background color or pattern, and the partially opaque areas will be blended with the Matte color. **If we now turn Transparency off,** the Matte color will blend with the shadow to give a natural look, but as with JPEG, you will need this Matte color to be the same as the background color of your Web page. **To**

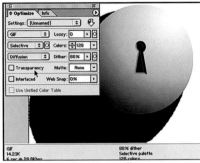

STEP 14: With Transparency off and Matte set to None, this is what we get when creating a GIF file.

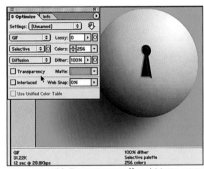

STEP 14: With Transparency on and Matte set to #339966, this is the result when creating a GIF file.

lessen the stepping of the sphere's gradations and of the shadow as it blends into the green background, set Colors to 256 and set the Color Reduction Algorithm to Adaptive. You might also want to set the Dither percentage up to 100%. Now your GIF file is almost three times as big as the JPEG version. If you want any random background pattern or color on your Web site to seamlessly blend with a soft shadow in your optimized image, neither GIF, PNG-8 nor JPEG format will work for you.

STEP 15: **Now click in the bottom right view and choose PNG-24 from the Settings menu. With Transparency on, the PNG-24 format will correctly show your 256 levels of shadow transparency onto any Web background color or pattern.** Notice that the size of this file is twice as big as the GIF and about six times bigger than the JPEG. The advantage of this extra size, though, is that the ball and its shadow will be decompressed losslessly onto your Web page. The problem with using PNG-24, besides the larger file size, is that not all browsers support the format and especially not its 256 levels of transparency—unless you have a PNG-24 plug-in installed. Check out the performance of PNG-24 images within the default versions of browsers and platforms you care about before you assume this file format will work for your site.

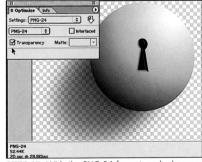

STEP 14: With Transparency off and Matte set to #339966, this is the result when creating a GIF file.

The Transparency and Matte options are also used in different ways within the next chapter, "Creating Your Own Web Photo Gallery." It's a good idea to check that out also.

INTERLACED AND WEB SNAP

STEP 16: **Use the Window menu to switch back to the macn image within ImageReady. If you're not currently viewing it in one of the Optimized panels, choose the 4-Up Optimized tab. Activate the top right panel and choose GIF 64**

STEP 15: With the PNG-24 format, and a browser that supports this format, the shadow should correctly blend with either the current solid color or pattern background on your Web site.

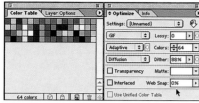

STEP 16: Here we see the GIF Color Table and Optimize options within ImageReady with Web Snap set to 0.

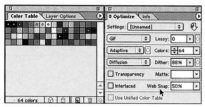

STEP 16: When we increase Web Snap to 50%, the colors in the Color Table that have been converted to Web colors are marked with small white diamonds.

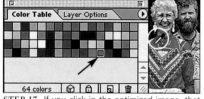

STEP 17: If you click in the optimized image, that color is highlighted in the Color Table.

Dithered from the Settings menu. In the lower part of the Optimized palette, turning on the Interlaced option will make the GIF image download in multiple passes from a poorer, low-res version to a final, higher quality version. This behavior is similar to the Progressive JPEG setting. Unlike the Progressive JPEG option, however, turning on Interlaced with GIF increases the file size by about 7K, so I'm leaving it off here. Again, if you feel it's really important for some sort of image to show up immediately when the page loads onto a user's machine, then you can use the Interlaced option.

Next to the Interlaced checkbox are the Web Snap controls. Changing the Web Snap option doesn't change the file size, but it does switch colors in your current color palette to colors within the Web palette based on the tolerance factor you choose. Open the Color Table palette from the Window menu so you can see the changes. With Web Snap set to 0, you'll notice here that none of the colors in this image's palette are common to the Web palette. When we change Web Snap to 50%, you'll see that some of the palette's colors have been changed to match similar Web palette colors (Web safe colors are denoted by the small, white diamond shape in the center of the swatch). The purpose for doing this is to make the image look better on 256-color systems where the browser is currently using the viewer's system palette. For this image I found that increasing the Web Snap to above 50% degraded the appearance of the image too much for my taste. One would be more likely to use the Web Snap option for a site whose target audience is users who only have 8-bit systems. Even then, **if optimum image fidelity is your paramount concern, then photographic images are usually not good candidates for using Web Snap.**

ADDITIONAL COLOR TABLE FEATURES

STEP 17: Since we have the Color Table palette already open, this is a good opportunity to point out some additional features that can be very useful. **First, press i on the keyboard to select the Eyedropper tool and click on a color in the optimized image. In the Color Table, you'll see that one of the colors is now highlighted by a light box. If you want to select multiple colors, hold down the Shift key as you click to add more colors into the selected group. You can even hold the Shift key down and drag through the image to quickly select a range of colors. If you click and hold on a color swatch in the Color Table, that color will be temporarily inverted in the optimized image, showing you where that particular color appears. Clicking and holding on a bright red swatch, for example, will turn parts of the red sweater in the center a cyan color.** Two out of three of these tricks will work in Photoshop's Save for Web dialog. The one that is left out in the cold is the last one, clicking and holding on a swatch to see that color highlighted in the image. This is another instance of the occasional interface inconsistencies that still exist between the two programs.

Once you have a color or group of colors selected in the Color Table, you can shift them to Web safe colors by clicking on the cube icon in the bottom of the palette. Web safe colors are denoted by the small, white diamond shape in the swatch. Clicking on the Padlock icon will lock or unlock selected colors so that they are protected against change or deletion if you want to try further experimentation while preserving the integrity of an important group of colors. Locked colors are indicated by a small white square with a dot in the center in the lower right corner of the swatch. Both the locking and shifting to Web safe colors behavior is the same in the Photoshop Save for Web dialog.

420

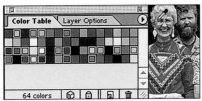

STEP 17: Shift-click on additional colors in the image, or Shift-drag through the image, to add more colors to your selection.

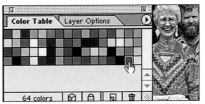

STEP 17: Click and hold on a swatch in the Color Table to see that color highlighted in the optimized image. The highlighted color is inverted; in this case, the red of the sweater is temporarily turned cyan.

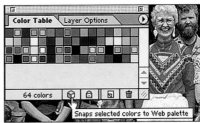

STEP 17: The Cube icon will shift all selected colors to their closest Web safe equivalents.

THE PNG-8 FORMAT

STEP 18: **Within ImageReady using the macn image, click back on the top right view and choose PNG-8 128 Dithered from the Settings menu in the Optimize palette. Now change the Colors to 64 and you'll notice that the PNG-8 file is slightly smaller than the original GIF 64 Dithered in the bottom left view.** You'll see that PNG-8 has the same options as GIF except PNG-8 doesn't have the Lossy option. With this image, the PNG-8 file seems to stay very slightly smaller than the GIF with the same settings, but when you turn on the 25% Lossy option in the GIF file, that makes the GIF significantly smaller. Be careful if you use the PNG-8 format because it is not supported by all browsers. Before you use it, be sure the versions of each browser you care about support this feature.

STEP 17: Locked colors are indicated by a small white square with a dot in the center.

ABOUT THE PNG-24 FORMAT

PNG-24 files only have the Interlaced, Transparency and Matte options. The PNG-24 format creates a lossless, 24-bit compressed image and has the capability to create an image with 256 levels of transparency, like you can have with a Photoshop mask channel. Using 256 transparency levels allows transitions, like subtle soft shadows, to seamlessly blend into any Web background. As you will see with GIF transparency in the next chapter, you cannot get seamless blends of soft transitions into various random Web backgrounds. PNG-24 images are also generally a lot larger than JPEG images, which are also in 24 bit, so usually the only reason you would create a PNG-24 image would be if you need a lossless 24-bit image or if you need to have 256 levels of transparency. If you need one of those features, then check out PNG-24; otherwise, you'll probably want to use JPEG, GIF or PNG-8. Be careful if you use the PNG-24 format because it and all its features, like 256 level transparency, are not yet supported by all browsers. Before you use it, be sure the versions of each browser you care about support it and the features you are using.

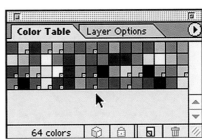

STEP 18: Here are all the PNG-8 options from within the ImageReady Optimize palette. Make sure you choose Show Options from the palette's pop-up menu to always see all the options for each format.

CREATING A MASTER PALETTE IN IMAGEREADY FOR MULTIMEDIA USE

Earlier in this chapter, we showed you how to use Photoshop's Indexed Color dialog box to create a Master color palette from all open images. This is useful for multimedia projects such as CD-ROMs, where you have control over the color palette that is used to display the images. ImageReady also allows you to do this, but it goes about it in a completely different way.

STEP 1: **Open the redac.psd, gc.psd, and macn.psd files from the Ch37.GIF JPEG and ColorPalettes folder on the CD. Click the Optimized tab for each image and choose**

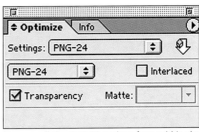

Here are all the PNG-24 options from within the ImageReady Optimize palette.

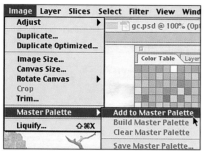

STEP 2: In ImageReady, adding colors from an optimized image to a Master palette.

STEP 3: After all color information from the three images has been added, the Master palette is built.

STEP 3: Before the new Master palette can be used, it must be saved first.

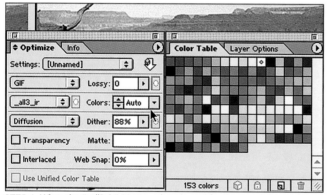

STEP 4: When the "_all3_ir" Master palette is used for the Grand Canyon image, the number of colors changes to Auto because ImageReady is only using a subset of the available colors to describe this particular image.

GIF 128 Dithered from the Settings menu. The exact GIF or dithering options you use here are important only in that they will determine how the color palette for each image is calculated. Since that information is then used to create the Master palette, you should first set up the individual images like you would if you were just creating a single optimized image.

STEP 2: **Make the Grand Canyon image active and from the main menu, select Image/Master Palette/Clear Master Palette if it is available. If there is nothing to clear, then this option will be grayed out. Clearing the Master palette ensures that you're only using colors from the current images. Next, go back into that same menu, but this time, choose Add to Master Palette. Switch over to the Red Acura image and, using the same menu command, add its colors to the Master palette. Finally, do the same for the McNamaras image. The color information for all three images has now been added to the data that will be used to create the Master palette.**

STEP 3: **Next, go back to the Image/Master Palette menu and choose Build Master Palette.** The Master palette has now been built based on the color information in our three images, although, somewhat frustratingly, there's no indication that anything has happened. To make it available to us, we first need to save it. **Return to the Image/Master Palette menu and select Save Master Palette. I called mine "_all3_ir.act." The ir tells me that it was made in ImageReady and distinguishes it from the earlier all3 palette I created in Photoshop. In order for this custom palette to show up automatically in ImageReady's menu, you need to save it in the following location on your hard drive: Adobe Photoshop 6/Presets/Optimized Colors.**

STEP 4: **Now, go back to the Grand Canyon image and from the Color Reduction Algorithm drop-down menu in Optimized palette, you should see the Master palette you just created. Select it and notice that the number of colors has changed to Auto.** If you study the Color Table, it probably seems that many of the very bright colors from the other two images are not represented here. This is kind of confusing at first, especially since it's not very well documented. What's happening is that **ImageReady is only using a subset of the Master palette's colors because it doesn't need to use all of them to describe this particular image.** If you switch over to the McNamaras or the Red Acura image and set their Color Reduction to the newly created Master palette, you'll see that more colors are being used in each image's Color Table.

WEIGHTED OPTIMIZATION

One of the great new features in Photoshop is the Weighted Optimization capability. This allows you to use an existing alpha channel in your image to customize settings such as JPEG quality, GIF lossiness, dither and color reduction. For those of you who want to have the most control in the quest for the smallest, yet best-looking Web images, weighted optimization will be a welcome addition to your imaging toolkit.

JPEG QUÏALITY MODIFICATION

STEP 1: **Switch to Photoshop and open the file Bodie Relic.psd from the Weighted Optimization folder within the Ch37.GIF JPEG and ColorPalettes folder on the** *Photoshop Artistry* **CD.** Bodie is a fascinating ghost town in California's eastern high desert that has been preserved as a state park and left much the way it was when it was abandoned. It's a bit of a drive off the beaten path and literally out in the middle of nowhere, but well worth the time if you ever get the chance to visit.

Click on the Car channel in the Channels palette, and you'll see that the foreground area, including the car, is white, and the background is black. We'll use this channel to explore the different ways of using weighted optimization.

STEP 1: Click on the Car channel for the Bodie Relic image.

STEP 2: **Click back on the RGB composite channel to return the image view to Normal and choose Save for Web from the File menu. Activate the 4-Up tab to see four different views of the image. In the top right view, select JPEG High from the drop-down Settings menu. Next, activate the lower right view and set it to JPEG High as well. Just to the right of the Quality field, click on the small Channel icon to bring up the weighted optimization settings for JPEG. This icon/button is only enabled if the image you are working with has an alpha channel.**

STEP 1: We can use the Car channel to apply different optimization settings based on the areas that are white and black.

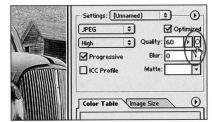

STEP 2: If the image you are optimizing has an alpha channel, the Channel button is enabled in Photoshop's Save for Web, and in ImageReady's Optimize palette. Click on it to open the weighted Optimization dialog.

STEP 3: **In the Modify Quality Setting dialog that appears, select Car from the pop-up channel menu. Now move the sliders to specify a minimum and maximum quality range. Notice that for the minimum setting, the slider is black, corresponding to the black areas in the channel, and the maximum slider is white, representing the white areas of the channel. In my first try with this image, I set the minimum to 8 and I left the maximum set to 60, which was determined when I initially chose the JPEG High setting.** The sliders control the quality settings for areas of the mask channel that are black, white, or some level of gray. In this case, areas of the image represented by black in the channel, the background, will be given a JPEG quality setting of 8, and areas where the channel is white will be compressed with a higher setting of 60. Any areas of gray (the transition between foreground grass and background on either side of the car) will receive some setting between 8 and 60 depending on their actual gray value.

As you move the sliders, you can see a preview of how the different quality values are affecting the image. Notice that the car and foreground always look pretty good, since they

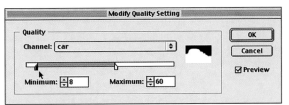

STEP 3: In the Modify Quality Setting dialog, the sliders determine the JPEG quality for the areas in the image represented by black and white in the mask channel. In this case, black areas receive a quality setting of 8 and white areas are set to 60.

STEP 3: A 200% view of how my initial settings affected the image (lower view). Although I did shave about 13K off the file size, the minimum quality level of 8 was a bit too rough on the background, causing severe edge pixilation on the houses.

STEP 4: After changing the minimum setting to 35, the JPEG artifacts in the background are greatly reduced and the file size has only increased by 1k. The Progressive option is on here as it seems to be very effective with weighted optimization images. In this case, with Progressive on, the file size is nearly 10K smaller than with it off.

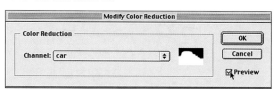

STEP 5: In the Modify Color Reduction dialog, you specify a mask channel and the resulting color table will be weighted towards colors that occur within the white areas of the mask.

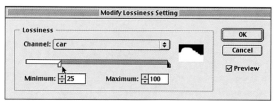

STEP 6: In the Modify Lossiness dialog, the white and black sliders are the exact opposite from the JPEG settings. White, and maximum quality (no lossiness) is on the left and black, representing minimum quality (more lossiness) is on the right.

STEP 6: The background of the image is very grainy because it is receiving a Lossy setting of 100, while the car and foreground are set to a Lossy value of 25.

are receiving a quality setting of 60. **Enter a setting of 8 for Minimum, leave Maximum at 60 and click OK.**

STEP 4: **Now, evaluate the quality trade-offs that our Minimum setting produced.** When I zoomed in to 200% in the Save for Web 4-Up views, it became apparent to me that 8 was too low and resulted in some serious edge pixelation in the houses in the background. **Click on the Channel icon in the JPEG settings (it's dark now, indicating that a channel is being used) to open up the Modify Quality dialog and change the minimum value to 35.** You should see a significant improvement in how the background looks, and the file size is only increased by about 1K. **Using the Progressive option seems to help reduce the file sizes when using this procedure with JPEGs. For this image, with my final settings of Minimum 35 and maximum 60, turning the Progressive option on reduced the file size by almost 10K!**

WEIGHTED OPTIMIZATION WITH GIFs & PNG-8 FILES

STEP 5: **In the Save for Web dialog, click on the upper right image to make it active. From the drop-down Settings menu, select GIF 128 dithered. For GIFs, you can use weighted optimization in three areas: Color Reduction, Lossiness, and Dithering. PNG-8 files behave the same as GIFs with the exception that they have no Lossy setting.**

Click on the Mask Channel icon next to the Color Reduction drop-down menu. For this setting, there are no sliders to adjust. You simply specify a channel, and Photoshop or ImageReady will weight the resulting color table more towards colors that appear within the white areas of the mask. **Move the Modify dialog so that you can see both the Color Table and the optimized view of the image and switch back and forth between None and the Car channel.** The differences are subtle, but when you specify the Car channel, the buildings in the background lose some of their reddish brown color. They actually take on a slight greenish tone due to the fact that all of the grasses in front of the car are influencing the colors that are being selected for the image. Watch how the Color Table changes as well. **Click Cancel in the Modify Color Reduction dialog to return to the Save for Web controls.**

This particular image doesn't necessarily benefit from weighted color reduction, but for some images this technique would work very well for favoring a certain range of colors in an image. **In previous versions of Photoshop, you could achieve this same effect by having a selection active when you optimized the image, and that method still works with version 6.**

STEP 6: **Next, in the Settings menu, select GIF-32 Dithered and then click on the Mask Channel icon next to the Lossy settings to bring up its Modify dialog box. As in the previous step, from the drop-down Channel menu, select the Car channel. The Lossy Modifier controls can be a little tricky at first because the white and black sliders and their corresponding numerical values are the exact opposite of the JPEG sliders.** On the left is the white slider and a value of 0, which represents no loss of quality. On the right is the black slider and a value of 100, which is the highest lossy setting. Remember that the color of the sliders corresponds to the colors in your mask channel. **So, if we set** the white slider to a value of 25 and leave the black slider at 100, it means that the white areas of the masked image will receive a lossy setting of 25 and the black areas will receive the highest setting of 100. With these settings the result is actually kind of interesting with a very grainy background and only a slightly grainy foreground.

STEP 7: **Click Cancel on the Modify Lossiness dialog and then click on the Mask Channel icon next to the Dither setting**. The minimum dither amount is controlled by the black slider and is applied to the areas represented by black in the mask, and the maximum is controlled by the white slider and affects the white areas of the mask. Experiment a bit with the Dither settings here and see how they affect both appearance and file size.

STEP 7: The Modify Dither dialog. White areas of the mask receive whatever maximum dither value you choose, and black areas are given the minimum dither setting.

The weighted optimization features in Photoshop 6 and ImageReady 3 are a great addition to an already powerful array of tools for creating images for the Web and multimedia. To the new user, the depth and complexity of the controls may seem a bit daunting at first, but the rewards are great if you take the time and get to know this part of both programs.

38 HANDS-ON SESSION: Creating Your Own Web Photo Gallery

Using Photoshop's automated features to make a Web photo gallery, picture packages and contact sheets.

CREATING WEB PHOTO GALLERIES

Photoshop 6 has greatly improved the Web Photo Gallery feature first introduced in version 5.5. You now have a choice of four gallery styles, the ability to set font attributes, control over exact image sizing and, for those who know how to tweak the code, the possibility of creating your own custom HTML templates that can be accessed from the Gallery Style's menu. Let's take the Web Photo Gallery feature for a spin and check it out. We'll use the same settings I used to create an image gallery on our Web site, www.maxart.com. To do this exercise, all you need is a collection of images gathered into a single folder. They can be your own images, or you can grab some of the image files from the *Photoshop Artistry* CD. Eight to ten images is a good number to start with.

STEP 1: **After you've placed the images into a folder on your hard drive, start Photoshop and go to File/Automate/Web Photo Gallery.** In the dialog that appears, there are several settings that will influence the appearance of our gallery. Before we do any of that, however, let's specify which images are going to be used. **At the bottom of the dialog box under the heading "Files," click on the Source button and find the folder where you've gathered your images. Highlight it and click the Choose button. Next, back in the main dialog, click on the Destination button and specify a location to place all the finished gallery files. It's best if you create a new folder for this and there is a button for that purpose. Once you have your destination folder, highlight it and click the Choose button.**

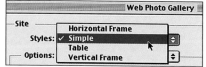

STEP 2: The default choices for Web gallery styles.

STEP 2: Now we can select the different options for the Web gallery. **Under the Style's drop-down menu, there are four different styles to choose from.** If you select each one in turn, you can see a thumbnail preview of the basic format of that style. **For this exercise, choose Simple. In the Banner section, enter a title for your gallery page and your name. For my version, I left the date blank. (The default behavior is for the current date to be in the Date field whenever you enter the dialog.) For the Font, choose Arial, and for the Font Size, enter a 5.**

STEP 3: The options for determining the size and quality of the larger gallery images. You can also specify a border setting here.

STEP 3: **Click in the Options drop-down menu and select Gallery Images.** These settings will affect the larger versions of your images, which will each appear on their own individual pages. **The Border setting allows you to specify a border around your images. The color of this border is based on the text color that we'll be setting shortly. For now, enter a value of 30 for the Border.** This will make the images look like a matted photograph. **Click in the Resize Images checkbox. If you had already prepared your images to be a specific size for your Web gallery, then you would**

leave this unchecked. For Image Size, choose Custom and enter a value of 475 pixels. This will make the longest dimension of the image 475 pixels. If we have a horizontal picture, it will be 475 pixels wide, and if we have a vertical image, it will be 475 pixels tall. **For JPEG quality, choose 7.**

STEP 4: **In the Options menu, move on to the next choice, Gallery Thumbnails. Under Captions, click Use Filename.** There can be drawbacks to this approach, which you may see in your finished gallery depending on the file names of your images. The main one is that Photoshop will add a file's three-letter format extension into the caption, so a file called Yosemite Falls.psd will end up with a caption that reads "Yosemite Falls.psd." **A more controlled way to handle captions, and the method which I employed here, is to use the File Info dialog that you can find in the File menu.** This lets you enter a specific caption, and Photoshop takes this information and uses it to write the image caption in the Web gallery. Entering the caption information for each file needs to be done prior to entering the Web Photo Gallery dialog. **Choose a Font and Font Size for the captions and set the size of the thumbnails to Custom, 117 pixels. As with the images, this makes the longest dimension of the thumbnail 117 pixels in length. Choose a column and row arrangement that is suitable for the number of images you have.** In the example I created here, I had ten images, so I chose 5 columns and 2 rows. **For the Border, enter a value of 10.**

STEP 5: **From the Options menu, choose Custom Colors.** Although the actual colors you end up using for your own Web galleries are up to you, it's wise to follow a few common rules. You should choose colors that are subtle and do not get in the way of the prime purpose of your gallery, which is showing your images. Ideally, neutral colors such as white, black or gray are the best for viewing photographs. For this exercise, use the same settings that I have here. **Click in the Background swatch and in the Color Picker, select Only Web Colors in the lower left. In the lower right, enter a hexadecimal value of #999999, and click OK. Follow the same procedure for the Banner color, except set it to be #333333. The Text, Link and Visited Link colors should all be set to white.** Normally, Web pages do use different colors to indicate visited links, but here, this setting also changes the border color of the thumbnails. If my visited link color were green, for instance, then the thumbnails would have green mattes around them if a person had already been to that page! Since that's not the effect I'm looking for, I'll leave them set to white. **The Active Link color is not that crucial here, but I chose a gray that was darker than the background gray. Now click the OK button and let Photoshop make a Web gallery for you! After it's done, it will automatically open up the new gallery in a browser.**

USING ACTIONS TO IMPROVE IMAGE SHARPNESS

The one thing that this automated Web gallery feature does not do is sharpen your images, and images that are made smaller for the Web always need careful sharpening to make them look their best. Unfortunately, we cannot really go back and sharpen the JPEGs that Photoshop created to make this gallery because then we would be compressing them a second time, which is not advisable for good-looking images. The solution to this situation is to go back and create a new set of images and

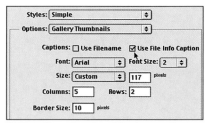

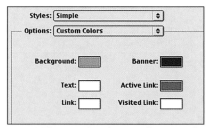

STEP 4: The options for setting how captions are generated, text characteristics for the captions, thumbnail size, visual layout of the thumbnails, and thumbnail borders.

STEP 5: These are the colors I used to create the example gallery in this chapter. Click in a color swatch to access the Color Picker.

STEP 5: The finished index page of the Web gallery that Photoshop created using the settings in these steps.

The Leaf image as the Web gallery automation treated it (left), and after some custom sharpening with the Unsharp Mask filter (right).

427

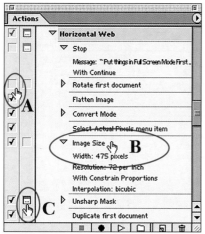

STEP 6: Customizing an existing action script: To turn off a particular step, click in the leftmost column (A) until the check mark is hidden. With an image open, double-click on a step (B) to change its settings; the action will record your changes and then stop. To pause the action with a dialog box open so you can adjust settings as the action is running, click in the second left column (C) to turn on the Dialog icon.

STEP 6: These are the files that were produced when I ran the Horizontal Web action on the Kansas image. The two top ones are the thumbnail-sized versions, as is clear from their file sizes. The bottom ones are the larger gallery images. The JPEGs will need to be renamed to the same filenames as those produced by the Web Gallery command. Once that is done, you can replace the first set of Web image files with the new sharpened versions.

STEP 7: This is the folder structure created by Photoshop's Web gallery automation.

thumbnails from the original files that are the same pixel dimensions as those that Photoshop produced, and run the Unsharp Mask filter on them. Doing this manually for each image would be pretty tedious. To make it go a bit faster, I created two special actions for creating sharpened Web images and their thumbnails. If you have the ArtistKeys loaded into the Photoshop Actions palette, you can find them listed as Horizontal Web and Vertical Web.

STEP 6: **In your original images folder that you used for the Web gallery, create another folder and separate your horizontal and vertical images.** The fastest way to create a new set of images with actions would be to run a batch process on an entire folder. You might want to open up a single image first, however, and run the action on it to become familiar with what it's doing. **Start with a horizontal image and go to the Actions Palette menu and highlight the Button Mode Setting until it shows the Actions as a named list. Find the Horizontal Web action (it's about 28th in the list) and click the triangle handle next to it to display all the steps for that action. Click the checkbox next to Rotate First Document to hide the check mark, and turn off that step.** This action was originally created for images that I had already rotated to vertical in preparation for making inkjet prints, so if your images are already horizontal, they won't need rotating.

The Horizontal and Vertical Web actions include steps for flattening layers and converting to RGB, so you don't need to do any special preparation to your files. **Click the Play button to run the action.** It will resize the file to 475 pixels wide (or tall if using the Vertical Web action), allow you to choose a sharpening value (or you can use the ones that I have already entered, they're pretty good for Web images), duplicate it, resize it to a thumbnail 117 pixels wide, then run the Unsharp Mask filter on the thumbnail. Finally, it will save a Photoshop format of the thumbnail (for generating future JPEGs), and then a final JPEG version. Then it will switch back to the larger image, save a PSD and JPEG versions of it and close the file when it's done. If you're using the Vertical Web action, there is no step for rotating that you have to turn off. When you apply these actions using a batch process, it's best to save them into a new folder. I also let the action give the file the default names, and then I renamed them after it was finished. For more detailed information on working with actions and batch processing, refer to Chapter 11: "Automating with Actions."

STEP 7: Once you've created the sharpened versions of the images and thumbnails, you need to give them the same names as the files that were produced by the Web gallery automation, and then replace those files with the newer, sharpened files. **Find the folder where Photoshop placed your Web gallery files. Inside it is a folder called Images and another called Thumbnails. Open up these folders so you can see what the filenames are. Rename the new sharpened files with exactly the same names. Once that is done, you can drag the new files into the appropriate Gallery folders and replace the versions that were created by the automation.** Just make sure you're putting thumbnails into the Thumbnails folder and the larger versions into the Images folder. **After you've replaced all the images and thumbnails, return to the browser page displaying your gallery and hit the Reload or Refresh button.** You should see a definite improvement in the sharpness of your images!

GETTING BETTER CAPTIONS AND CUSTOMIZING YOUR GALLERY

If you're less than thrilled with image captions that have a three-letter file format extension, try opening up each of your original images and going to File/File Info and entering in the title of the image in the top caption box. Then you can redo the Web gallery automation and check the "Use File Info Caption" choice in the Thumbnails options. Before you redo the entire gallery, however, make backup copies of the images and thumbnail folders that have the sharpened files, so you can replace the unsharpened images again. The automation will overwrite your sharpened versions each time you redo the gallery.

Even if you do get great captions using the File Info feature, however, the actual file name, minus the extension, still shows up as the image title in the banner on the individual image pages and in the top of the browser window. If you have a file name with no spaces between the words as in my example here, it looks a bit odd. (This type of file name format is actually recommended for the web—see the illustration below.) This is somewhat aggravating, especially since you can make sure you have the Use File Name option unchecked and it still shows up in these two places. To fix this involves a quick edit of the actual HTML code. Fortunately, it's not complicated and you can do it with a basic text editor such as Simple Text on the Mac or WordPad on the PC. (If you use Microsoft Word to make these edits, be sure to save as a Text file.) To modify my file, I opened up the page titled "BryceStoneWoman.htm" in Simple Text, found the lines of code with the title, changed them and then saved and closed the file. You can refer to the screenshot here to see the places in the code where I modified the text.

If you're experienced at editing HTML, you can now create your own custom Web gallery styles by duplicating one of the existing preset styles and modifying it to suit your needs. These files can be found in the Adobe Photoshop 6/Presets/Web-ContactSheet folder on your hard drive. Any new style you create will show up in the Web Gallery Styles menu as long as it remains in this folder.

CONTACT SHEETS AND PICTURE PACKAGES

In addition to Web galleries, Photoshop can also automate the creation of Contact Sheets and Picture Packages. Both of these are found under the File/Automate menu location. Since the controls for each procedure are pretty self explanatory, I won't go into great detail here. Improvements that have been made in Photoshop 6 include the ability to set font size for contact sheet image captions. You can still use the file name for the caption, but unlike Web galleries, you cannot use the File Info dialog. Hopefully, that will be added in the next version as it is a very useful feature.

The big improvement for picture packages is that Photoshop finally gives you the image sizes that it promises. In version 5.5, the automated packages included a white border around the images and calculated this into the image sizes, a quirk that definitely reduced its effectiveness in high volume production environments. Another welcome addition which owners of larger inkjet printers or professional labs will appreciate are four new package layouts designed to print on 11x17 paper. In all there are twenty different package layouts available.

Even though "Use Filename" for captions was not checked, it still appears in the banner on the individual image pages, and also in the page title at the top of the browser window.

```
<HTML>
<HEAD>

 <TITLE>BryceStoneWoman</TITLE>
 <META name="generator" content="Adobe Photoshop(R) 6.0 Web Photo Gallery">
 <META http-equiv="Content-Type" content="text/html; charset=iso-8859-1">
</HEAD>

<BODY bgcolor="#999999" text="#FFFFFF" link="#FFFFFF" vlink="#FFFFFF" alink="#666666" >

<TABLE border="0" cellpadding="5" cellspacing="2" width="100%" bgcolor="#333333" >
<TR>
 <TD><FONT size="5" face="Arial" >Photoshop Artistry / BryceStoneWoman<BR>Images by Barry Haynes<BR></FONT>
</TD>
```

Here is the HTML for the Bryce Stone Woman page opened up in Simple Text. I've highlighted two instances where I would go in and add spaces between the words. The top one is the title that appears in the top bar of the browser window, and the second one is where the title shows up in the banner on the actual Web page. Fortunately these Web pages have minimal display text, so finding what you need to edit in the code is pretty easy.

File names for the HTML gallery pages are derived from the image file names. One potential problem with the way Photoshop handles this is the inclusion of spaces between words in the file names. Files destined for the Web should always use an underscore or dash character between words instead of a space, as this can sometimes cause problems. To play it safe, we recommend that you avoid spaces in your image file names that are used for Web galleries. If you need your captions to look nice, use the File/File Info dialog to enter a caption prior to creating your Web gallery.

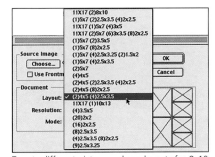

Twenty different picture package layouts for 8x10 and 11x17 size output are available in Photoshop's automated Picture Package feature.

429

39 HANDS-ON SESSION: Creating Slices, Rollovers and Animations in ImageReady 3

We'll use ImageReady to build a Web page from the ground up, with cool rollover effects and animations, and we won't have to write a single line of HTML or JavaScript.

MAKING A WEB PAGE USING IMAGEREADY

ImageReady is a great program for preparing Web graphics. With it you can automate many processes that used to entail lengthy and tedious procedures, or require knowledge of HTML and JavaScript. In addition to helping you optimize and compress images, you can slice an image up into several pieces to maximize optimization by using different formats and settings for different parts of the image (Photoshop 6 also features slicing capabilities). You can make animated GIFs with ImageReady, using the Layers palette as the basis for the animation frames. Rollover effects, such as when you move you mouse over a button and it lights up, have long been a staple on the Web. In image terms, a rollover is simply two different states of the same image slice: an off state and an over state. The actual rollover effect is created by using JavaScript in your HTML code to tell the browser to swap one image for another when the mouse rolls over a certain spot. Until programs like ImageReady came along, you had to know a bit about coding in order to create rollover effects. Fortunately, for those who'd rather not worry about learning HTML and JavaScript, ImageReady will write all of that code for you and present you with a finished Web page. And if you're already at home with the fine details of coding Web pages and prefer to write it yourself, you can still use ImageReady to quickly generate the basic image parts that you can then import into other programs such as Adobe GoLive, Macromedia Dreamweaver, or BBEdit for further customizing.

Lengthy animations of photographs take up a lot of disk space and, therefore, make a Web page load more slowly. When I first created this exercise, I had to down-size both the dimensions and number of frames in my animations several times before their size became acceptable. Creating an animation that will be downloaded from a Web page IS different from working with a QuickTime movie that is stored on your local hard disk. Say this to yourself many times so you don't make something that is too big! In the beginning, this was really hard for me, because I'm used to looking at large and very detailed photographic prints and digital images on my screen. My natural instinct is that bigger and more details are better. That may be so for images bound for fine prints or full screen displays, but after waiting a long time, over and over, for ImageReady to update your changes so you can preview your optimized Web page in a browser, smaller starts looking better all the time. More importantly, smaller files lead to faster download times so that viewers of your Web site don't become impatient waiting for images to load, throw up their hands in frustration and click out of your site. When you are doing most of your work in ImageReady and just using Photoshop from time to time, and the images you are working on are small Web images anyhow, change your memory allocation to give more memory to ImageReady than to Photoshop. It's amazing how quickly Photoshop, even with little memory, can open a complex ImageReady document while ImageReady takes longer to do almost anything with it. Of course, ImageReady does need to keep track of a lot more details in that document, including animations, rollovers, image maps etc., that Photoshop doesn't currently look at. When I was working on this example on my G4 400Mhz machine, I allocated 85Mb of RAM to ImageReady and it seemed to cruise along very well with that. Fortunately, Adobe seems to have improved ImageReady 3's overall performance and it is definitely faster and more responsive than version 2, which was incredibly sluggish at times.

For this example, we're going to create a Web page from the ground up that will demonstrate how to use some of the important features of ImageReady, such as slicing, creating rollover effects and making animated GIFs. Along the way, you'll also get some experience placing a pixel-precise set of guides from which you'll generate individual slices, creating layer effects, and working with layer sets to organize your layers into logical groups.

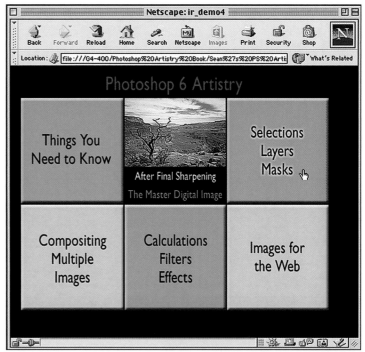

PREVIEWING THE END RESULT

Before we get into the actual exercise, let's preview what the final result will be so we know what we're working towards. To do this, you'll need to launch a Web browser. Once your browser is running, go to the File menu and choose the menu option that will allow you to open a file. In Netscape, this is called Open/Page in Navigator; in Internet Explorer it's simply Open File. Depending on the particular version of browser you're using, the exact language may be slightly different. In the Open dialog, navigate to the *Photoshop Artistry* CD.

Previewing the final HTML file in a Web browser. The Master Digital Image animation will begin playing after the entire page loads. Moving your mouse over the blue squares triggers the rollover effect, a subtle glow around the text. Click down on Things You Need to Know to see a second animation.

Inside the Ch39.Animations Slices RollOvrs folder, open the folder called Final_HTML and select the file ir_demo.html and open it into your browser. In the Finder or Windows Explorer view, you can also find the file on the CD and simply drag it into an open browser window. This Web page was originally created with the idea of showcasing the six different sections of the *Photoshop 6 Artistry* book. The Grand Canyon animation should begin shortly after the entire page loads. Move your mouse over the blue squares to see the rollover effects. Click down on the Things You Need To Know section to see another animation. We're going to build this starting with a blank file, and learn some cool new tricks along the way. Let's get started!

SETTING UP YOUR PAGE AND GUIDES

STEP 1: **Within ImageReady, type D for default colors, then X to exchange the colors, so that the background color is black. Choose File/New to create a new file that is 500 pixels by 375 pixels in size with Background Color selected to make it black.** Just for fun and also usefulness, let's set up our Swatches and Color palettes so they display

STEP 1: Creating the new 500 by 375 pixel document with a black background.

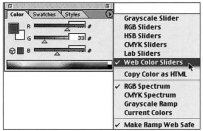

STEP 1: Setting up your Color palette for Web Safe colors, using Web Color Sliders, RGB Spectrum and Make Ramp Web Safe.

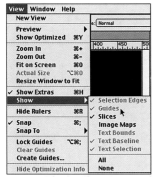

STEP 2: Selecting Show Extras, and Show Guides in the View menu. Make sure that Snap To/Guides is also checked.

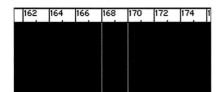

STEP 2: Zooming in on rulers to double-check the guide locations. You can also use the XY coordinates in the Info palette.

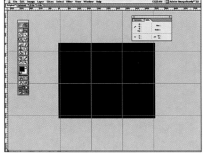

STEP 2: The way the document looks with all guides in place.

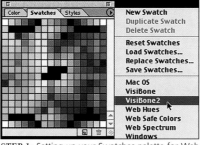

STEP 1: Setting up your Swatches palette for Web safe colors. I like the layout of Web safe colors offered by the VisiBone2 palette, which groups them by hue in an arrangement based on the color wheel.

colors from the Web palette only. Then the colors will show up without dithering when they are displayed on an 8-bit monitor. **Choose Window/Show Color; then choose Web Color Sliders, RGB Spectrum, and Make Ramp Web Safe from the Color palette's pop-up menu. Now bring up your Swatches palette, Window/Show Swatches, and from that palette's pop-up menu you can choose Web Safe Colors.** I also like to use the VisiBone2 palette because it has a more logical grouping of the Web colors that is based on the color wheel.

Press Tab to get rid of your palettes, F for Full Screen mode, then Command-Option-0 to zoom into 100%, and finally Command-R to bring up the Rulers. It's nice that many of these keyboard shortcuts work the same way in both ImageReady and Photoshop. Beware that not all of them do, however, and the most irritating one for long-time Photoshop users like me is that Command-Z in ImageReady does not toggle back and forth between Undo and Redo like Photoshop always has and still does in version 6 (although I should note that you can now customize this keyboard combination somewhat in Photoshop's Preferences). In ImageReady, repeated Command-Zs march back up the History palette, undoing state after state as they go. If this happens to you, as it did to me, just bring up the History palette and click back to where you wanted to be in the Undo state. In ImageReady's world, Undo is still Command-Z but Redo is now Command-Shift-Z, and if you want to continue to toggle back and forth between Undo and Redo, that is now Command-Option-Z.

STEP 2: **Choose View/Show and make sure that Guides is checked here and also in View/Snap to. Finally, in the View menu, select the Snap option so that it also has a check mark. Choose Window/Show Info and position this palette in the upper right portion of your screen. We are going to add some guides that will help us line things up. Using the Move tool (V), click in the vertical ruler on the left side of the document window and drag out to the right until your first guide lines up at X value 8. You can see the XY location of the guide in the Info window as you move the guide. Go back to the vertical ruler again, click down and drag out another guide; then place it at X position 168. This creates an 8-pixel border area on the left edge, then another area that is 160 pixels wide. We'll now create a 2-pixel border between this 160-pixel column and the next, so drag the next guide to position 170. The fourth guide goes at X value 170 + 160 = 330, and then put the fifth one at 332. Now put the final guide at 332+160 = 492. Now onto the horizontal guides. Click in the top horizontal ruler and drag down until you reach Y value 40; then release to place a horizontal guide there. Drag the next horizontal guide down to Y value 200, and then drag one down to Y value 202 and then another to 362. If you want to make sure your guides are in the right place, you can use Command-Spacebar-click and drag to zoom up on the guides at a high magnification and check their locations against the edges of the rulers.**

CREATING YOUR SLICES

In the Web world, the most common reason for slicing an image up into differ-ent pieces is to fit it into a specific HTML table structure that fulfills the design and technical requirements of the page. Slicing also allows you to apply individual opti-mization settings to different areas of the image which will result in smaller files and faster download times. A slice may contain a rollover or animation, or just a portion of an image. After you create your slices and save your optimized image, ImageReady not only cuts up the image according to your slice arrangement, it also creates an HTML table to hold it all together. Not every slice area needs to contain an actual piece of an image (the black borders around our composition, for example) so a slice can also be exported as a No Image slice. In the HTML file that ImageReady writes, a No Image slice will be replaced by a table cell that is filled with a specific color.

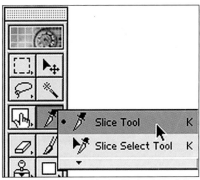

STEP 3: The Slice tool in the Tool palette. Below this is the Slice Select tool, which you use to select and adjust slices after you've created them.

STEP 3: **Choose the Slice tool from the Tool palette (it looks like an Exacto knife). You will use it to divide this image into 15 slices. With the Slice tool, click in the top left corner and drag a skinny vertical slice down to the bottom left corner and over 8 pix-els to that first vertical guide. This will be slice 1. You will notice that ImageReady has already positioned the starting place for slice 2 at the top to the right of slice 1. Click at the top just to the right of that first vertical guide and drag down and to the right until you reach the corner where the first horizontal guide and last vertical guide meet. This should be X value 492, Y value 40 (492,40). This is the bottom right of slice 2. Slice 3 will be the long vertical strip going from top to bottom of the image on the right side. Go ahead and create slice 3. Now slice 4 should be positioned at the top left corner at 8,40. Drag slice 4 down to the bottom right of this 160x160 box with its bottom right corner at 168,200. Slice 5 goes from a top left of 168,40 down to a bottom right of 170,200. Slice 6 coordinates are top left of 170,40 and bottom right of 330,200. Slice 7 is 330,40...332,200. Slice 8 is 332,40...492,200. Slice 9 is a long skinny horizontal slice from 8,200...492,202. Now slice 10 starts the bottom row of bigger boxes with positions 8,202...168,362. Slice 11 is 168,202...170,362. Slice 12 is 170,202...330,362, and slice 13 is 330,202...332,362. Slice 14 is 332,202...492,362 and, finally, slice 15, along the bottom is, 8,362...492,375.**

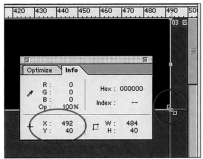

STEP 3: Creating precise slices by tracking the X and Y coordinates in the Info palette: Here we see a close-up view of the lower right corner of slice 2 and its XY coordinates, 492,40.

STEP 4: The Rectan-gle tool in the Tool palette (U).

STEP 4: **Choose File/Save As and save this docu-ment as ir_demo.psd on your local hard disk. Use Window/Show Layers to bring up the Lay-ers palette and Option Double-click on the Background to rename it to Root Image. In the Tool palette, choose the Rectangle tool (U); then click on the foreground color and use the Hexadecimal box at the bottom right of the ImageReady Color Picker to enter the color 6699CC, a medium blue. With the Rectangle tool, use the guides to create a blue shape layer exactly within the area of slice 4, the top left, large 160-pixel square box. Make another box layer exactly inside slice 8 on the top right and another inside slice 12 at the bottom in the middle. Click on the foreground color, or use**

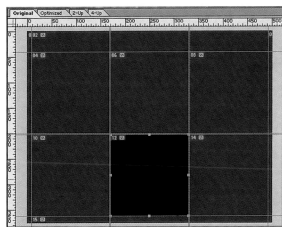

STEP 3: The document with all slices in place. When you are in Full Screen mode, ImageReady's status bar is at the very bottom of your screen. Make sure you don't cover that with a palette during a Save, Save Optimized or Preview In Browser. If the operation is taking a while to complete and you cannot see the progress status within that lower progress bar, you may actually think ImageReady has crashed. That blue strip progressing, sometimes very slowly, from left to right is the only sign that ImageReady is still working. I was hoping that with this new version of ImageReady, Adobe would place the progress bar in the center of the screen where it is more noticeable.

433

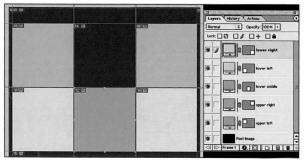

STEP 4: The document and Layers palette at the end of Step 4.

STEP 5: Adding a Bevel layer style.

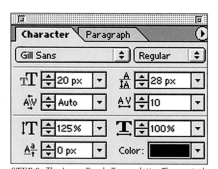

STEP 6: The ImageReady Type palette. The controls in the main palette from top left are: Type Size, Leading, Kerning, Tracking, Vertical Scale, Horizontal Scale, and Baseline Shift at the bottom left. Other type options, including the anti-aliasing settings, are available in the Options bar, and in the Palette menu (the triangle button at upper right).

STEP 7: Adding the Outer Glow effect to the type. This will serve as the "on" state for the rollover we will create.

Window/Show Color to bring up the Color palette; then choose 99CCFF, which is a lighter blue. Use the same Rectangle tool to draw similar light blue squares in slices 10 and 14.

After you've completed the five blue squares, Option-double-click on each layer and give it a descriptive name to make it easier to quickly differentiate between them. I named my layers by describing their location: lower right, lower left, lower middle, and so on.

STEP 5: Next, we'll add a simple layer effect to the blue squares to give them a bit of depth. At the bottom of the Layers palette, click on the Layer Style icon (the small, italicized f) and choose Bevel and Emboss from the pop-up menu. You could also do this by using the main menu Layer/Layer Style/Bevel and Emboss. The Layer Style palette should appear with the options for the bevel effect. We're going to leave them set at the default, which is a smooth inner bevel, size 5. You can see all the options in the illustration at left. Apply this same Layer Style to each of your blue shape layers. When you're done, click on the top blue square layer to make it the active layer.

ADDING THE TEXT INFORMATION

STEP 6: Press D on the keyboard to reset to the default colors, which will make the foreground color black. Type a T to choose the Type tool, click the cursor over the top left blue box, and type the words "Things You Need to Know," the name of the first section of *Photoshop 6 Artistry*. I put this on two lines with "Things You" on one line and "Need to Know" on the second line. Select the type you just entered by clicking at the end of the line and dragging across it. Using the Options bar at the top of the screen, I chose 20 px (pixel) Gill Sans regular for the typeface, but you may not have that font installed on your system, so choose something similar. Depending on the font you select, you may have to adjust the size up or down a bit. Just make it about the size of the type in the finished example at the beginning of this chapter. In the Options bar, click on the Palettes button on the far right to bring up the Type Character palette. Notice how you can now modify the Leading, Tracking and Kerning using the pop-ups within the Type palette. For my text, I set the Leading to 28, the Tracking to 10 and I entered a Vertical Scale value of 125% to make the letterforms a bit taller.

STEP 7: With the new Type layer active, use the Layer Style button at the bottom of the Layers palette to select Outer Glow. Set the Opacity and Intensity values in the Outer Glow palette each to 75 and the Blur value to 5. Click on the Color box and set the color of this glow to FFFF00, a bright yellow. Now turn off the Outer Glow by clicking the Eye icon next to the word Effects beneath the Type layer. This will be how the type will look for the normal or "off" rollover state; we will turn it on later when we create the "on" state of our rollover effect. Now, we can easily create the remaining text layers by simply copying this first type layer and then changing the words. To copy this Type layer, drag it down to the New Layer icon at the bottom of the Layers palette. Then use the Move tool (V) to drag that copy over the top of the appropriate blue box on the screen, and use the Type tool to select and change the actual type displayed over each box. Once you have changed the text and hit the Enter key, the name of the copy layer does not update to correspond to the new type, as it does in Photoshop. You have to double-click on its layer to change the

name of that layer to be the same as the type. This seems to be a bug, as it only happens on copy layers, and only in ImageReady. In Photoshop the Type layers update their names as you change the text. When you are finished, your screen should look like the illustration here and you should now have a Layers palette like the one pictured here. **Use the illustration at the right to see what type needs to be added over each box.** The two lines of orange and red type will be added in the next step.

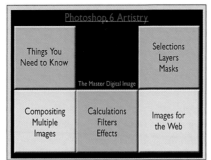

STEP 8: The ir_demo file after all the main type elements have been added.

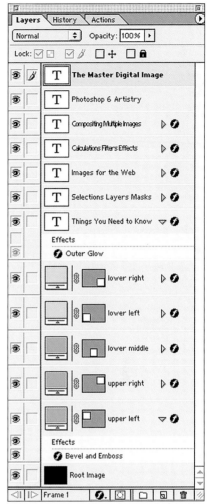

STEP 8: The Layers palette showing all of the blue boxes and the main Type layers.

STEP 8: **With the Type tool, click down in the top center of the screen, within slice 2, to create a new type layer. Since the background here is black and our previous type color was set to black, click in the color swatch in the Type Options bar and change it to FF0000, a bright red, and type the words "Photoshop 6 Artistry." Now select all this type with the Type tool and change its size to something similar to what you see in the illustration above.** My settings for this Type layer were 24 px for the size, leading of 28 and tracking of 20.

Now choose the Slice Select tool and click on the top middle 160x160 slice, slice number 6, which is the box that is still black. Choose Slices/Divide Slice from the main menu bar and choose the Divide Horizontally Into option and choose Pixels Per Slice under that. Type 130 into the box to the left of the words Pixels Per Slice. This will make the top slice, still number 6, be 130 pixels high and will create a new 30-pixel high slice, now number 9, below the newly shortened slice 6. Slices with numbers greater than 9 now get renumbered. Go back to the Type tool (T) and click down in the middle of the area of this new slice number 9. Click in the Type Options bar color swatch and set it to FF6633, a bright orange. Set the type size to a value that allows your text to stay within this slice (my Gill Sans size here was 14 px) and type the words "The Master Digital Image," which will represent the animation that will appear within slice 6 above.** You have now entered all the text

STEP 8: The Slice Select tool (K).

for the basic image layout.

STEP 9: **Choose File/Save As and save your document as ir_demo1.psd.** At this point, you might want to zoom in close and inspect each of the blue shape layers to make sure that they match up with the slices and guides. It's much easier to fix anything now, before we create rollovers, than afterwards. If you make any adjustments to the file, save it again. **Next, turn off the Eye icons in the Layers palette for all the Text layers. The Eye icons should now be on for just the five blue boxes and also the Root Image layer. Click on the Root Image layer, at the bottom of the palette, to make it the active layer and then choose Merge Visible from the Layers palette pop-up menu.** We do this to simplify the layer setup now, before we start to add rollover effects and animations to the demo. This will limit the number of layers that each animation frame and rollover needs to keep track of, and it will also simplify the Layers palette for us. **After doing that, turn on the Eye icons again for all the rest of the layers; then do a File/Save As again and save this as ir_demo2.psd.** That way if you

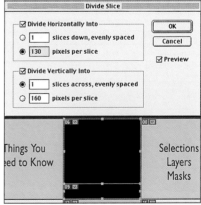

STEP 8: Dividing slice 6 into two slices. Choose the Pixels Per Slice option; then type 130 which will be the size of the top slice.

435

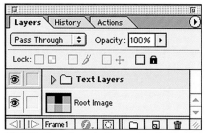

STEP 10: Making a layer set for all the Text layers.

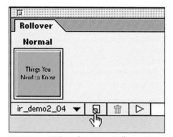

STEP 10: The color-coded layer set for the Text layers. The triangle handle is closed, hiding all those layers when we're not using them.

make a mistake when compressing layers, you can always go back to that earlier version and start over will all your layers still intact.

STEP 10: Once we add the animation later on, we're going to end up with several more layers in our file. **Let's simplify the Layers palette by using one of Photoshop's and ImageReady's great new features, layer sets. To easily add a layer set for the Text layers, click on the top Text layer and then click in the center column (between the Eye icon and the layer thumbnail) for all the other Text layers to link them together. From the pop-out Layers palette menu, choose New Layer Set From Linked. Once the set has been created, double-click on it to give it a name. I called mine "Text Layers" and gave it a blue label color to correspond to the blue boxes. Save your file after creating and naming the layer set.** Web page designs can generate many layers, and the Layers palette can get pretty confusing at times. I have friends in the Web design business, and they frequently work with files that have close to 100 layers! The new layer sets feature is a great way to organize your layers and make the Layers palette much easier to understand.

CREATING THE ROLLOVER EFFECTS

So far, we've been preparing our file by adding guides, layers, layer styles, and creating image slices, all procedures that we could do in Photoshop if we wanted to. Now we get to start playing around with rollovers and animations, two things that ImageReady is very good at. One reason we spent so much time preparing the file thus far is that each rollover state and frame of an animation is based on how your layers were set up at the exact moment you created the rollover or animation frame. If you find that you need to change something in the stationary elements after you've created your rollovers or animation, then it can be a real headache and a lot of work to go back and make sure that your change is reflected in every single animation frame or rollover state! It's best to have everything designed and laid out in detail before you begin making rollovers and animations.

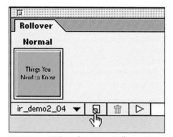

STEP 11: Using the New Rollover State icon in the Rollover palette.

STEP 11: Each of the five blue box slices has some text over it. We'll make rollovers for each text area so that when you move your mouse over the text, it will light up with a glow around it. **Use Window/Show Slice to bring up the Slices palette and Window/Show Rollover to bring up the Rollover palette. Choose the Slice Select tool (K) from the Tool palette; then click on slice 4 in the the top left corner and then also click on the Things You Need to Know layer in the Layers palette to activate that layer** (open your new layer set folder if you closed it during the last step). You may want to arrange your file and palettes as you see them in the illustration here so you can see what is happening in each at all times. **In the Rollover palette, choose New State from the pop-up menu or just click on the new Rollover icon to the left of the Trash icon at the bottom of the palette.** This will create a new Rollover state called Over. Any changes you now make to the file while this Over state is active in the Rollover palette, either within this slice or anywhere else in the image, will be recorded as the actual Over state when your image is exported as an HTML file. Since the Rollover palette keeps track of the current state of the layers in the Layers palette, you need to be careful that you're only making changes there that will reflect what you want to happen when the mouse moves over the slice and triggers the rollover effect in a Web browser.

Chapter 39: Creating Slices, Rollovers and Animations in ImageReady 3

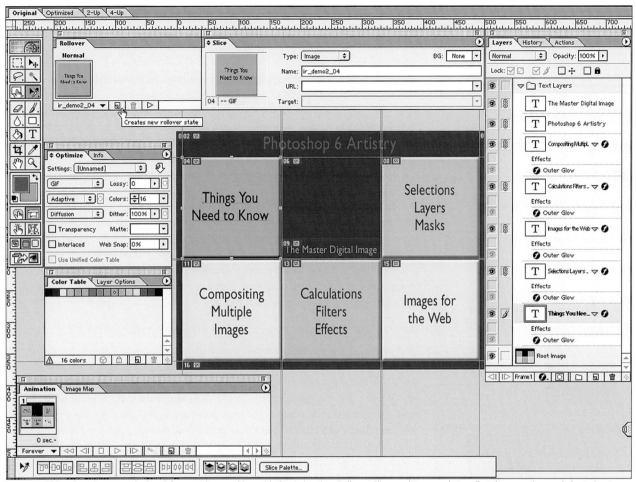

STEP 11: This palette layout worked well for me when working with the Animation, Rollover, Slices and Layers palettes all at the same time and also trying to see the Web page I'm working on. I typed F, for Full Screen mode, which centered my image on the screen, and also used View/Actual Size or Command-Option-0 (Zero) to zoom the page into 100%.

STEP 12: We already created the look we want our text rollovers to have back when we added the Outer Glow layer styling to the initial Text layer. Since we copied that first text layer to create all the others, the Glow effect was copied along with it. **Now, to create our rollover, all we need to do is turn on the Eye icon for the effects below the "Things You Need to Know" Text layer. Since the new Over state is active in the Rollover palette when we turn on the layer's outer glow effect, it is recorded as the Over state for that slice. Click back on the Normal state for this slice within the Rollover palette.** You want to return this slice to the Normal state so that when you set the Over state for the other slices, this slice appears normal within the other slices' Over states. **Now click on slice 11, called Compositing Multiple Images, and also click on the Compositing Multiple Images layer in the Layers palette. Use the Rollover palette to add an Over state to that slice; then turn that layer's effects Eye icon back on. Remember to click back on the Normal state within the Rollover palette after turning on the glow for this slice.**

Repeat this process to add the same Over effect to the correct layers for slices 8, 13 and 15. After creating each new rollover glow effect, remember to click back on the Normal state for each slice before moving on to the next step. When you're finished making all the rollover states, go the the File menu and select Save As. Save

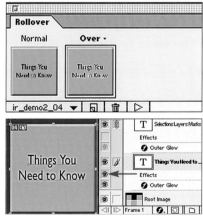

STEP 12: With the Over state active in the Rollover palette (top), turn on the Effects Eye icon for the appropriate layer in the Layers palette (bottom) to create the rollover effect.

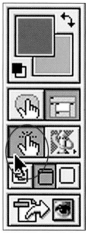

STEP 13: The Roll-
over Preview button.

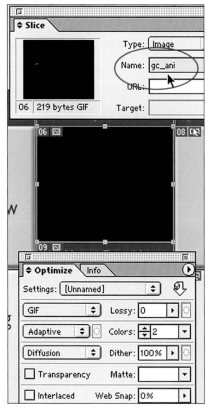

STEP 14: Renaming slice 6 to "gc_ani" will make it
easier to replace its optimized image slice with the
animated GIF we'll create later.

this version of the file as "ir_demo-ro." The "ro" tells us that this is the version with the rollovers.

STEP 13: Now that we have the rollovers created, let's test them to see how they look. One new improvement in ImageReady 3 is that you can now preview rollover effects directly in the program without loading the page into a Web browser. We'll try out both methods here. **First, to preview the rollovers within ImageReady, click on the Rollover Preview button near the bottom of the Tool palette, or press its keyboard shortcut, Y. Now, you should see the text glow effect turn on as your mouse moves over each text area.** Take a look at the Layers and Rollover palettes as you do this, and you'll see the glow effects turning on and off and the active rollover state switching from Normal to Over as you move through the image.

To see how this looks in a Web browser, click on the button just to the right of the Rollover Preview button to launch the default browser and display the page. Move your mouse around to test the rollovers. Underneath the display of the Web page is a copy of the actual HTML code along with the JavaScript used to make the rollovers work. **Close the browser window when you're done and return to ImageReady. If you found problems with any of the rollovers, refer to the previous steps and make the necessary corrections.**

OPTIMIZING THE ROLLOVER SLICES AND EXPORTING AN HTML FILE

STEP 14: Now that the rollovers are working, we can optimize the slices and export an HTML file of the demo Web page. **Make the Slice Select tool active and click on the 2-Up Optimized tab at the top of the screen (if you're still in Full Screen mode, the Options bar may be covering up the 2-Up and 4-Up tabs). Press the Tab key to hide your palettes; then bring up the Optimize palette (Window/Show Optimize), the Color Table (Window/Show Color Table), and the Slice palette (Window/Show Slice).** In the 2-Up view, the original image is displayed on the left and the optimized one on the right. In the Slice palette, notice that you can give each slice a Name and also enter a URL address for each slice if you want to link a click on that slice with a jump to another Web page. **With the Slice Select tool, click on slice 6, the empty black slice above the words "The Master Digital Image." In the Optimize palette, set the format to GIF, and the number of colors to 2. We will replace this slice later with an animation, so we need to give it a specific name. In the Slice palette, rename this slice to "gc_ani," for Grand Canyon animation.**

After doing that, go to each slice and set its Optimization settings. We don't need to rename the other slices in the file. Each slice has one possible Optimization setting for the entire slice, not one for each rollover state of each slice. **Within the Slice palette, set the Slice Type on slices 1, 3, 5, 7, 10, 12, 14 and 16 to No Image. For the very thin slices that form the gutter between the blue boxes (5, 7, 10, 12 & 14), you'll have to zoom in close to even see them.** Since those slices are just filled with black, using the No Image setting will cause ImageReady to create an empty table cell that displays black but that doesn't require any image. This will also make the final HTML page smaller since there will be fewer images. **Set the No Image slices Optimize settings to GIF, 2 Colors, No Dither, Selective palette. For slice 2, the title at the top of the Web page, the GIF 32 Dithered choice from the Settings menu seems to work well. For slices 4, 8, 11, 13 & 15, set Optimization to GIF 64 Dithered,** because GIF 32 Dithered for those slices doesn't provide enough color variation to do the subtle shading on the blue buttons without a noticeable stepping in the colors. Note that you can select multiple slices by holding down the Shift key when using the Slice Select tool.

STEP 15: The last step before we save an actual HTML version of our Web page is to set a specific background color for the final, saved file. **From the Window menu, choose Show Tools to bring the Tool palette back, and hit D on the keyboard to reset to the default colors. Choose File/Output Settings/Background and set the color to black by selecting Foreground Color from the drop-down menu.** If black wasn't either your foreground or background color, you could choose Other and then pick Black from the ImageReady Color Picker. This dialog is also the place where you'd specify an image to be used as the background for your Web page. **Before we export the Web page, save the file one more time.**

STEP 16: **From the File menu, choose Save Optimized As. In the Save dialog box, name the file "ir_demo1." For Format, make sure that HTML and Images is selected, and choose All Slices.** If you haven't made any changes to the program's defaults, then these last two settings should be in place when you enter the dialog. **To easily find our files again, create a new folder for this file and call it "ir_html-1." Click the Save button to export the HTML file and its image slices. To see how the final file is working, switch to a Web browser and open the file.** If you've followed these steps, you should be seeing the rollovers functioning like they did in the earlier preview.

Take a moment to look in the actual folder where you just saved this on your hard drive. ImageReady not only created the ir_demo1.html file, it also made a folder called images and inside that folder is where it placed all of the individual image slices that make up this Web page. **Since the HTML code looks for this images folder when it assembles the page in a browser, it's important to always keep its location in relation to the ir_demo1.html file the same in order for the images to be displayed properly.**

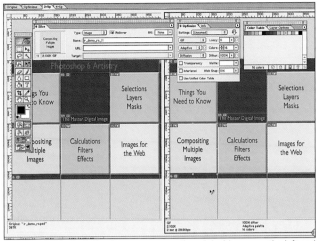

STEP 14: With the 2-Up view, you can see the original image on the left and compare that with the optimized version on the right. The Slice palette allows you to name the slice if you want, enter an HTML tag in the URL box if you want to jump to a URL when the slice is clicked, set a background color for the slice, and also set the Type to No Image if that slice doesn't contain an image.

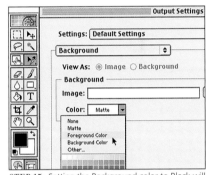

STEP 15: Setting the Background color to Black will generate HTML code that makes the entire Web page background black.

CREATING THE FIRST ANIMATION

Animations are somewhat like rollovers in that each animation frame represents a different combination of visible states in the Layers palette. But whereas the typical rollover has two to three states—a normal, a mouseover, and perhaps a mouseout or mousedown state—an animation can have many more individual frames. The more frames in your animation, the more complicated it gets to go back and change something once you've made all the frames. As with rollovers, it's best to do the animating at the end of your project, and not when you're still working on your overall design.

STEP 16: In the Save Optimized As dialog, these are the correct settings for saving both the optimized image slices and an HTML page to display them.

STEP 17: **In ImageReady, click back on the Original tab at the top left of your screen and choose File/Save As and spin off a new copy of this file called "ir_demo_ani.psd." With this new version of our file, we're only going to be working with, and then exporting, slice number 6, which will be an animated GIF.** The reason we are using a different file is to keep what we're doing with the animation separate from what we did with the rollovers. Since we've already exported the HTML file with the correct code for the rollovers, we can now concentrate on making the animation look good in slice 6 and not be concerned about accidentally messing with the rollover code in

439

STEP 18: The gc_animation file has five layers that will serve as a starting point for an animated GIF.

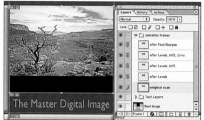

STEP 18: The ImageReady Layers palette and slice #6 after adding and aligning the five Grand Canyon layers.

STEP 19: The first animation title is added to the image.

the background. Trying to create rollovers, and an animation, and then export a single HTML file containing both that works like you want it to, can often be an exercise in extreme frustration.

STEP 18: Choose View/Show Guides to make sure your guides are up. Use Command-SpaceBar-click to zoom in to 200% centered on slice 6. If the slices are currently visible, then choose Hide Slices from the Slices menu, or use the Show/Hide Slices button near the bottom of the Tool palette to temporarily turn them off. Close the Text Layers set in the Layers palette and from the Layers palette menu, choose New layer Set. Name the new set "Animation Frames" and give it an orange label color. Now choose File/Open and from Ch39.Animations Slices RollOvrs folder on the *Photoshop Artistry CD*, open the file called gc_animation.psd.** If you look at the Layers palette for this file, you'll see that it consists of five linked layers, each one showing a different state in the color correction of an image. These five layers will be the starting point for our animated GIF. **Now use the Move tool (V) to drag and drop all these layers from this document onto your ir_demo_ani document. Just click down on top of the Grand Canyon image area; then hold, drag and release when the cursor is on top of the demo file image area. You should see all five of the Grand Canyon layers added to the Animation Frames layer set at the top of your ImageReady Layers palette. Use the Move tool to drag the Canyon layers so their top left corner is exactly in the top left corner of slice 6.** Having the Guides visible and also having Snap to Guides turned on will make lining this up correctly quite easy. The Canyon layers are already sized to exactly the 160-pixel width of this slice.

ADDING TEXT TITLES TO THE ANIMATION

STEP 19: Type F to go to Full Screen mode; then turn off the Eye icons of the top four canyon layers (but not the layer set containing those layers), and then click on the Original Scan layer within the Layers palette. Type D for default colors, then an X to exchange the colors, and make the Foreground color white. Select the Type tool and check the color swatch in the Options bar. If it's not white, open the drop-down menu by it and choose Foreground Color. Set the type size in the Type dialog to 14 px with the tracking set to 10; then click down in the black area below the Grand Canyon photo and above the orange "The Master Digital Image" and type the words "The Original Scan." For my file, using the Gill Sans typeface, 14 px worked well. If you're using a different font, you may end up using a different size for your text. **Use the Move tool to center this text beneath the canyon image** and notice that it has created a new layer above the Original Scan layer in the Layers palette. **With the new Type layer active, choose Duplicate Layer from the palette drop-down menu to make a copy of this layer. Turn off the Eye icons for the Original Scan layer and its title layer and drag the copy layer up above the After Levels layer. Use the Type tool to highlight the text and change it to "After Levels Adjustments". Double-click this Text layer and rename it so that its name is the same as the text it displays. If the new text runs into the blue box, use the Move tool (V) with the Shift key down to center it under the canyon image. The Shift key keeps it constrained to the same horizontal baseline. If it's still too big, use a smaller font size, but if you do, remember to go back to the Original Scan title and change its font size to match.** Creating the different Text layers this way keeps all the Text layers aligned and centered correctly and also keeps the font info and text color the same.

To make the third title, choose Duplicate Layer again. Turn off the Eye icon for the After Levels layer and its title and then drag the new copy layer up above the After Levels, H/S layer. Use the Type tool to highlight the text and change it to

440

"Adding Hue & Saturation." As before, once you've changed the text, double-click the layer in the palette to rename it to the same as the text it displays. Repeat this process adding a "A Curve to Pop Greens" Text layer above the After Levels, H/S, Crvs layer, and finally adding an "After Final Sharpening" Text layer above the After Final Sharpen layer. Do a File/Save to save this file and all the progress you have made so far.

STEP 20: **Click on slice 6 with the Slice Select tool (K). In the Layers palette click on the Original Scan layer to activate it and make sure that the Eye icon is also on for the "The Original Scan" Text layer above it. Turn off all the other canyon layers and their titles. This will be frame 1 of your animation. Bring up the Animation palette by accessing it from the Window menu. Under the thumbnail of the first frame, where it says 0 sec., open the Frame Delay pop-up menu, choose Other and then enter 3 seconds in the Frame Delay dialog.** This means that when the animation first appears on screen, this frame will display for 3 seconds before moving on the next frame.

   Now choose **New Frame from the Animation palette pop-up or click the New Frame icon at the bottom of the Animation palette.** This will create a second frame to the right of the first, and it will start out being a copy of the first frame. We now need to turn on the layers that will be visible during this second frame. **Turn off the Eye icons for the Original Scan layer and also for the "The Original Scan" Text layer; then turn on the Eye icons for the After Levels layer and the "After Levels Adjustment" text layer.** That is what is different about the appearance of frame 2 in this animation. **Now create a third frame by clicking on the New Frame icon in the Animation palette and for this frame turn off the Eye icons for the After Levels layer and the "After Levels Adjustment" Text layer. Turn on the Eye icons for the After Levels, H/S layer and the "Adding Hue & Saturation" text layer. Notice that the second and third frames already have their Frame Delay times set to 3 seconds because they were initially copies of the first frame. Now make a fourth frame in the same way. Turn off the Eye icons for the After Levels, H/S layer and the "Adding Hue & Saturation" Text layer, and turn on the Eye icons for the After Levels, H/S, Crvs layer and for the "Add Curve to Pop Greens" Text layer. Finally add a fifth animation frame, turn off the Eye icons for the After Levels, H/S, Crvs layer and the "Add Curve to Pop Greens" Text layer, and turn on the Eye icons for the After Final Sharpen layer and the "After Final Sharpen" Text layer.** You now have the five main frames of your animation, but it won't be very animated because each of those frames will play for 3 seconds before moving on to the next.

TWEENING FRAMES INTO THE ANIMATION

STEP 21: **Using the Slice Selection tool, click on slice 6 to make sure it is the current slice. The Rollover palette should be in the Normal state for this slice. Now click in**

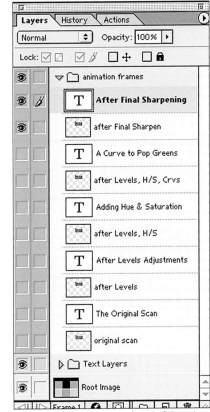

STEP 19: The Layers palette after all of the animation title layers have been added.

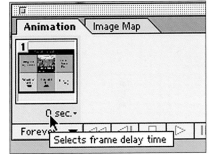

STEP 20: Clicking here allows you to set the Frame Delay for the first animation frame.

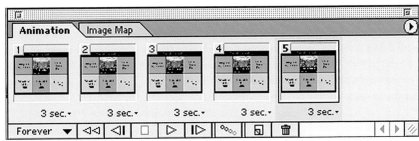

STEP 20: The first five animation frames seen here in the Animation palette.

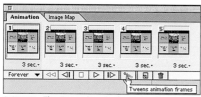

STEP 21: The Tween icon in the Animation palette.

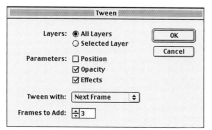

STEP 21: The correct settings for Tween in this example. We will use the Position setting later.

frame 1, the leftmost frame, in the Animation palette, and then choose Tween from the Animation palette pop-up menu. Tweening will allow you to automatically create frames between the existing frame 1 and frame 2 that will animate the state change between those two frames. Within the Tween dialog, choose All Layers, because you want to transition all the layers of each existing state, and also choose to tween the Opacity and Effects but not the Position. This will blend the way the two images look but not the location of the two images because they are actually already aligned. Set frames to Add to 3, which will add three frames between the current frame 1 and frame 2, and you are going to Tween with the Next Frame. Choose OK and notice the added frames. Now click back into frame 1; then click on the right arrow with the vertical bar to the left of it, the Select Next Frame icon, at the bottom of the Animation palette. This will advance to the next frame. Advance through the sequence and notice how the image slowly transforms from looking like frame 1 into looking like frame 5, which is the original frame 2. Notice, though, that frames 2–4 are dull looking compared with either frame 1 or 5. This is not what we want.

STEP 22: Let's click on frame 2 and see what the Tween actually did. With frame 2 active, notice that the Opacity of the Original Scan layer has been changed to 75% and the Opacity of the Levels adjustment layer has been changed to 25%. I noticed that if I changed the Opacity of the Original Scan Layer back to 100% that the effect worked better because then the new colors look more like they are being added to what was already there. In the Layers palette, change the Opacity of the Original Scan layer back to 100%, and also turn off the Eye icon for the Original Scan Text layer so we no longer see this text in frame 2. Both the Levels adjustment layer and the After Levels adjustment Text layer should still be set to 25% Opacity. Use the frame delay time pop-up at the bottom right of the frame 2 area to set the delay time for this frame to 0.2 seconds. Now move on to frame 3 and in that frame, turn off the Eye icon for the the Original Scan Text layer, set the opacity for the Original Scan layer to 100% and set the frame delay time to 0.2 seconds. Now move to frame 4, turn the Eye icon off for the the Original Scan Text layer and set the opacity for the Original Scan layer to 100% and set the delay time for this frame to 0.2 seconds.

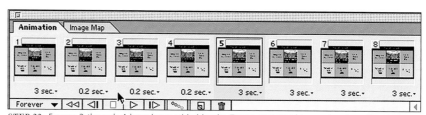

STEP 22: Frames 2 through 4 have been added by the Tween command to create a transition between frame 1 and frame 5 (originally frame 2). The frame delay for the new frames has been set to 0.2 seconds.

STEP 23: Now click on frame 5 in the Animation palette. We are going to tween it with frame 6. Select Tween from the Animation palette and choose the same settings you did before. Set the Frame Delay time in each of the new frames 6, 7 & 8 to 0.2 seconds and also turn off the Eye icon for the After Levels adjustment Text layer and set the Opacity for the Levels adjustment layer to 100% within each of those three frames. Now click on frame 9 and add a similar 3 frames between frames 9 and 10 except this time you will be turning off the Adding Hue & Saturation Text layer and setting the Opacity of the After Levels, H/S layer to 100%. Remember to set the new frames' delay time to 0.2 seconds. Finally, click on frame 13 and Tween it with frame

Chapter 39: Creating Slices, Rollovers and Animations in ImageReady 3

14. In the new tweened frames 14, 15 & 16, you'll be setting the Opacity of the After Levels, H/S, Crvs layer to 100%, turning the Eye icon off for the Curve to Pop Greens Text layer and setting each frame's delay time to 0.2 seconds. You should now have a total of 17 frames in your animation.

TESTING & OPTIMIZING THE ANIMATION

STEP 24: **Hide the slices and guides by pressing Command-H from the keyboard. If the slices are still visible, use the Show/Hide Slice button near the lower part of the Tool palette, or just use the keyboard shortcut, Q, to hide those as well. In the Animation palette, use the right-facing Play arrow button to play the animation sequence you've just created. If everything looks good, press the square Stop button and return to frame 1 by clicking on the frame 1 thumbnail. Now we can optimize the slice and export it as an animated GIF.**

Press the Tab key to get rid of your palettes; then use the Slice Select tool to click on slice 6 and bring up the Optimize palette. Set it to GIF, 128 colors, Adaptive palette, Lossy at 25 and Diffusion Dither at 100%. Now click on the 2-Up tab at the top of the screen to see the Original image on the left and the optimized one on the right. You'll notice, by looking at the bottom left corner of the right side optimized area that with these settings it will take about 148K to compress this entire animation. If you play with the GIF settings, you'll see that this size value, and the quality of the image, changes as you modify the settings. Slice 6 has to be a GIF because it contains an animation. The settings described above seemed to make the image look good, but this animation is still a bit larger than I would like. **Bring up the Slices palette and make sure that the name for slice 6 is still set to "gc_ani." This is very important because now we're going to replace the earlier optimized slice with that name, which was simply a black square, with this new one containing the animation.**

From the File menu, select Save Optimized As and in the dialog box that appears, choose Images Only from the Format menu, and make sure that the last available menu choice is set to Selected Slices. This will ensure that only slice 6, the gc_ani slice, is exported. By choosing Images Only we're telling ImageReady not to create an HTML file that will be associated with the image slice we are saving. **The place where you save this file is very important, so from within the Save Optimized As dialog, navigate to the "ir_html-1" folder where you saved the first HTML version of this file, the one that had the rollover effects. Inside that folder double-click the images folder to open it within the Save Optimized As dialog. This is where we'll save our new gc_ani slice.**

If you look at the illustration of the Save Optimized As dialog here, you may be confused by the fact that the file name is not "gc_ani.gif." Let me explain what's happening here, and why I'm not overly concerned with this detail: **The default way that ImageReady saves an HTML file is to give it the same name as your PSD file, which is what we see here. Since we're only saving a single slice, however, some additional preference settings take over. Click on the Output Settings button to see what I mean.** Under the Saving Files option, if an image slice doesn't have a specific name, it's given the document name, followed by whatever other name settings apply given the attributes associated with that slice. If a slice has been given a name, however, such as our own gc_ani slice, then the slice will be exported with that name. This is what will happen here if your settings are the same as mine. **Click OK to exit the Output Settings dialog and click Save in the Save Optimized As dialog. If you've chosen the correct folder to save the new slice in, then you should see a message asking if you really want to replace a previous file with the same name. Click Replace...we really do want to do this!** The previous gc_ani.gif file was created before we began

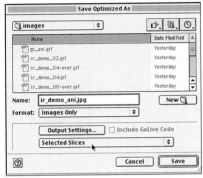

STEP 24: Before saving the optimized animation, double check that slice 6 is still named "gc_ani" in the Slice palette. This is important for replacing the previous slice that was exported with this same name.

STEP 24: The correct setup for saving the optimized gc_ani slice. I've navigated to the location where the images were saved when I last saved an optimized version of this file (the one with rollovers); I've chosen to save Images Only and Selected Slices. This last option ensures that only the gc_ani slice will be saved.

STEP 24: When exporting slices, the default Output Settings for saving files give priority to slices that have a specific name. This is why we do not have to give the file a specific name when we choose Save Optimized As.

STEP 24: If you've chosen the correct folder on your local hard disk, then you should get a message telling you that a file already exists with the name "gc_ani.gif." Clicking Replace here will overwrite the old slice, which was just a black box, with the new one containing the animation.

443

our animation, so it was just an empty, black area. By replacing it, our new slice, containing the animation, will show up in its place when the page is loaded into a Web browser.

If you don't get the Replace message, then either the file is being saved with a different name, or it's being saved in a different location than the first file. In the first scenario, simply find the file you just saved (try a sort by date to find the most recent), and rename it "gc_ani.gif." You might need to move it out of the Images folder to rename it, and then move it back again. In the second scenario, saving the file with the right name but in the wrong location, simply find the new file and drag it into the Images folder and overwrite the existing file of the same name.

STEP 25: **To test if the new animation image has successfully integrated into the previous file, switch over to a Web browser again and open the file ir_demo1.html.** This is the same HTML file that we saved when we created the rollovers several steps back. It may take a couple of seconds for the rollovers to start working while the mouseover states load into your browser's cache. When the entire page has loaded, you should be able to move your mouse over the text areas and trigger the rollover glow effects. The animation of the Grand Canyon image should play from start to finish, and then start over again, without being affected by any of the rollovers.

ADDING A SECOND ANIMATION TO ANIMATE POSITION

STEP 26: **Switch back to ImageReady and close the ir_demo_ani file. Open up the version where we set up the rollovers, ir_demo_ro.psd, and do a Save As and call this new version "ir_demo_ro2.psd."** We're going to add a new rollover state and a second animation to one of the slices and I want to preserve all the functioning rollover work we did in the first file. **Click on slice 4, with the Slice Select tool. This is the "Things You Need To Know" slice, and we are going to add an**

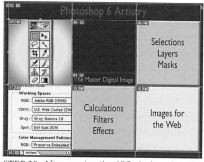

STEP 26: After copying the AllGrabs layer into the main file, and positioning it inside slice 4, this is what your file should look like.

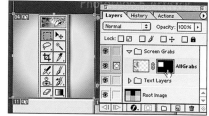

STEP 26: The Layers palette after you have added the layer mask to the AllGrabs layer.

animation to it that will run when you click down on this slice. Click on the New State icon at the bottom of the Rollover palette or choose New State from its pop-up menu. Because you already have a Normal and Over rollover state, this new state will automatically be set to Down. You could change that with the pop-up where you see Down, but don't. In the Layers palette, click on the topmost layer set to make it active and then, from the palette pop-up menu, choose New Layer Set. Name the set "screen grabs" and click OK.

Use File/Open and from the Ch39.Animations Slices RollOvrs folder on the *Photoshop Artistry CD*, open the ScreenGrabs.psd file. Click on the All Grabs layer to make it active and use the Move tool (V) to drag and drop this layer onto your ir_demo_ro2 document. The copied layer should show up at the top of the Layers palette, inside of the new layer set. Choose View/Show Guides to turn on your guides and make sure View/Snap to Guides is turned on. Now drag the AllGrabs layer, within the document window, until the top of it, showing the Tool palette, lines up exactly over the ThingsYouNeedToKnow slice, slice 4. When you get it into place, the lower portion of the layer will be extending beyond the bottom of your view area because it is taller than the main file. Choose Select/Create Selection from Slice to get a selection exactly around the edge of this slice. Now choose Layer/Add Layer Mask/Reveal Selection from the main Layer menu to add a layer mask to the All Grabs layer, which will only reveal the part within slice 4. This will now be frame 1 of your animation. Set the frame delay time to 0.5 seconds using the pop-up at the bottom right of the frame.

DOING THE POSITION TWEEN

STEP 27: In the Animation palette, click on the New Frame button to make frame 2 of your animation. In the Layers palette, click on the Layer thumbnail, the leftmost one, of the All Grabs layer. Now turn off the link, the icon between the Layer thumbnail and the Layer Mask thumbnail, between the layer and its mask. This will allow you to move the layer without moving the mask. With the Shift key held down to constrain the motion to a vertical line, use the Move tool (V) to drag the All Grabs layer up until you reach the last screen grab panel within that layer (it's the red-tinted view showing the available profiles for Epson Stylus printers). We are now going to do a Tween between these two animation frames, so choose Tween from the Animation palette pop-up. Tween with the Previous Frame using Position only, adding 4 frames. See the Tween dialog settings here to the right. When the new frames have been added, click back on the Normal state within the Rollover palette and then do a File/Save.

To preview the interactive effects in ImageReady, click on the Rollover Preview button (Y) near the bottom of the Tool palette. You should be able to trigger all the existing text rollover effects that we added earlier, and when you click down and hold on the Things You Need to Know area, it should play the six frames of the new animation. Everything worked fine with my file, but I found that in a couple of the frames, the position of the AllGrabs layer was just a bit off, leaving a sliver of the previous or next screen grab panel visible. To fix this, I clicked on the frame that I wanted to adjust, and then used the Move tool and the up/down arrow keys on the keyboard to move the layer one pixel at a time until it looked right.

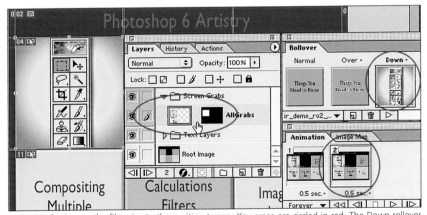

STEP 27: Setting up the file prior to the position tween: Key areas are circled in red. The Down rollover state is active in the Rollover palette; the layer has been unlinked from its layer mask and the Layer thumbnail is the active element (see the Paintbrush icon by the layer); frame 2 is the selected frame in the Animation palette.

STEP 27: While holding down the Shift key to constrain the motion to a vertical line, use the Move tool (V) to drag the AllGrabs layer up until you reach the last screenshot (above). This is the correct state for frame 2 before we use the Tween command.

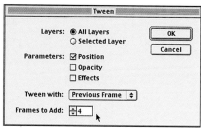

STEP 27: The correct settings for the position tweening of the second animation.

Click back on the Preview button to turn off the Preview mode and make any adjustments to the individual frames if you feel they are needed. From the File menu, choose Save Optimized As. Since we don't want to overwrite our earlier version, give this file a new name, ir_demo2, and create a different folder on your hard drive for it. Call the new folder "ir_html-2." Choose the HTML and Images, and All Slices options and click Save to export the files. Open this new file into a browser and test it out. If something doesn't work properly, just remember that it is easy to leave one of the palettes, either rollover, animation or layers, in the wrong state at some stage of the process. If that happens, look at what is happening in your browser and think about what state each slice needs to be in at that moment to get the behavior you desire. This will usually give you a hunch about what may be wrong and you can go back to ImageReady and find the problem.

STEP 28: The last step to pull all of our elements together into a single file is pretty easy compared to all the intricate hoops we've been jumping through to get to this point! Find the folder with the first ir_demo1.html file and open up its images folder. Make a copy of the gc_ani.gif file and move that copy to the images folder inside the new folder you made for the ir_demo2 file that we just saved. On a Mac, Option-dragging the file from one folder to another will copy it and move it at the same time. On a PC, right-click and choose Copy; then move to inside the destination folder, right-click again and choose Paste. This will replace the black rectangle gc_ani slice that was exported with the new HTML file, with the finished canyon animated GIF that we made in the third part of this exercise. Now, when you preview the ir_demo2.html file in a browser, the canyon animation should be playing independently in the top center square, the text area rollovers should all work, and when you click down on Things You Need to Know and leave your cursor over that area, you should see the Photoshop screen grab animation. Pretty cool, especially when you consider that we didn't have to write a single line of HTML or JavaScript code!

ADDITIONAL ANIMATION SETTINGS

Several Animation settings can be important to set when working with ImageReady. One that may be influential for a particular effect is the Frame Disposal Method. This decides if you should throw out the current frame in an animation before displaying the next frame. To set this for a particular frame in an animation, Control-click, or right-click on a PC, on that frame within the Animation palette. The Restore to Background option will completely toss the current frame before displaying the next one. This will stop the current frame from appearing through any transparent areas of the next frame. If you use Restore to Background, you will see white, or the current background color, through those transparent areas. The Do Not Dispose option will leave the current frame visible as the next one is displayed so you will see the current frame through the transparent areas of the next frame. The Automatic option will automatically choose a method for each frame transition. Automatic will discard the current frame if the next frame contains any transparency; otherwise it won't do the discard. Within this example, I left the Frame Disposal Method set to Automatic.

LAYER-BASED SLICES AND IMAGE MAPS

Two other very useful Web features are layer-based slices (Photoshop and ImageReady) and image maps (ImageReady only). If you have a document with layers, you can turn a layer into a layer-based slice. This is a special slice that is created

446

based on the pixel data in the layer, so if you change that layer, then the slice will automatically change its dimensions to always conform to what is on the layer. This is especially helpful with Text layers where the actual copy may be changed several times throughout the design process. Image maps let you specify a precise area of an image that will contain an HTML link to another Web page, either within your own site, or out on the Web somewhere. Both layer-based slices and image maps are very easy to create, so let's take a brief tour of them now.

CREATING A LAYER BASED SLICE

STEP 1: **In ImageReady, navigate to the Ch39.Animations Slices RollOvrs folder of the *Photoshop 6 Artistry* CD and open the file called gallery_nav_layers.psd. Each of the Website areas here is a separate Text layer. Click on the Artist's Statement layer in the Layers palette to make it active. To make a slice based on this layer, go to the Layer menu and choose New Layer-Based Slice. A new slice is automatically created for you.** The process for making a layer-based slice is the same in Photoshop.

STEP 2: Now, let's change the words on the Type layer. **Select the Type tool (T), and delete the word "Artist's" from the layer, so it just reads "Statement." The slice automatically updates as you make your changes.**

MAKING AN IMAGE MAP

STEP 1: **From the CD, open the file called gallery_nav_imagemap.psd.** This is the same list of Web page navigation links as in the previous example, except in this file, all the text is on a single layer. An image map is a set of instructions that describes an area of the Web page with a set of XY coordinates and a size of the defined area. This works by telling the browser that X pixels down from the top of the page, and Y pixels in from the left edge is an area that is a certain dimension, and any click inside this area will link to a specific Web page. Let's see how to set this up.

In the Tool palette, choose the Image Map Select tool (just under the Lasso, at the bottom of the pop-up list) and notice that the top four lines of text have boxes around them. Click in the one for Black & White and then bring up the Image Map palette (Window/Show Image Map). Here you'll see the XY coordinates and dimensions of this mapped area, the Name of the map, the URL that this map links to and an Alt field where you can enter a line of alternative text that displays when the image loads, and in some browsers, when the viewer moves their mouse over it, a label will pop out after a few seconds. The Target value is for determining how the new page will load in a browser window.

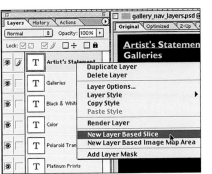

STEP 1: To make a layer-based slice, you can control-click on the layer in the palette (right-click on the PC) to access the contextual menu; or, from the main Layer menu, choose New Layer Based Slice.

STEP 1: A layer-based slice created from the "Artist's Statement" Text layer.

STEP 2: With a layer-based slice, when you make changes to the layer, then the slice updates to reflect the new boundaries of the layer. Here we've removed the word "Artist's" and the slice has updated to reflect the new size of the layer.

The Image Map tools in the Tool palette.

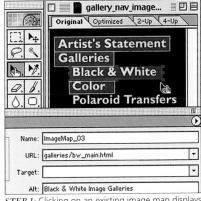

STEP 1: Clicking on an existing image map displays its attributes in the Image Map palette. In this case, the link would lead to a file within this same site called bw_main.html located in the galleries folder.

STEP 2: Using the Image Map rectangle tool to create a map for the Contact link.

STEP 2: **Select the Image Map Rectangle tool and drag a box around the text for "Contact" at the bottom of the list. To edit the shape of the box, go back to the Image Map Select tool.** If this were an actual Web page design, and you were using ImageReady to generate all the HTML, you would enter the desired link address in the URL field at this point. **Just remember that, for this to work, ImageReady has to create all the code for the Web page, and the image map has to be part of an entire page design, not just a small portion as we have here.** You also cannot specify an image map in ImageReady and then use the individual image slice in a Web page that has been created in another authoring program because the image map is part of the HTML code the program generates, and not the image.

In addition to layer-based slices, ImageReady also has layer-based image map areas. These work the same as a layer-based slice. The size and shape of the map is generated by the actual layer, so if you increase the size of a layer, or change the words in a Text layer, the image map will update to reflect those changes. Image maps are only available in ImageReady. To make a layer-based image map, select the layer you want in the Layers palette and from the main Layer menu, or by using the contextual menu, choose New Layer-Based Image Map Area.

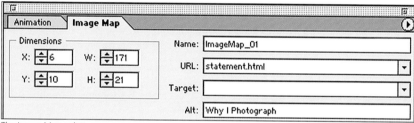

The Image Map palette.

Another thing to know about ImageReady is that although adjustment layers can only be added and updated in Photoshop, they will remain in place when you open the file in ImageReady. Like Photoshop 6, ImageReady 3 also has a very useful online help system that you can access by going to Help/Help Topics. You can also check our Web site, www.maxart.com, for additional and new update information about Photoshop, ImageReady and digital photography.

BIBLIOGRAPHY

PUBLICATIONS

Adams, Ansel with Mary Street Alinder. *Ansel Adams: An Autobiography*. Boston, MA: New York Graphic Society Books, 1985.

Adams, Ansel with Robert Baker. *Ansel Adams: The Camera*. Boston, MA: New York Graphic Society Books, 1980.

Adams, Ansel with Robert Baker. *Ansel Adams: The Negative*. Boston, MA: New York Graphic Society Books, 1981.

Adams, Ansel with Robert Baker. *Ansel Adams: The Print*. Boston, MA: New York Graphic Society Books, 1983.

Blatner, David, and Bruce Fraser. *Real World Photoshop 6: Industrial Strength Production Techniques*. Berkeley, CA: Peachpit Press, 2001.

Blatner, David, Phillip Gaskill, and Eric Taub. *QuarkXPress Tips & Tricks: Industrial-Strength Techniques, 2nd Edition*. Berkeley, CA: Peachpit Press, 1994.

Booth, Sara, ed. *Step-by-Step Electronic Design*. Peoria, IL: Step-by-Step Publishing.

Burns, Diane and Sharyn Venit. *The QuarkXPress 4.0 Handbook*. New York, NY: Random House Electronic Publishing, 1994.

Margulis, Dan. *Professional Photoshop 6, The Classic Guide to Color Correction*. New York, NY: John Wiley & Sons, Inc., 2000.

McClelland, Deke. *Macworld Photoshop 6 Bible*. Foster City, CA: IDG Books Worldwide, 2001.

Rich, Jim and Sandy Bozek. *Photoshop 5 in Black-and-White: An Illustrated Guide to Producing Black-and-White Images Using Adobe Photoshop*. Berkeley, CA: Peachpit Press, 1998.

Weinman, Lynda. *Creative HTML Design.2*. Indianapolis, IN: New Riders Publishing, 2001.

Weinman, Lynda, and John Warren Lentz. *Deconstructing Web Graphics.2*. Indianapolis, IN: New Riders Publishing, 1998.

Weinman, Lynda. *Designing Web Graphics.3*. Indianapolis, IN: New Riders Publishing, 1999.

Weinman, Lynda, and Bruce Heavin. *Coloring Web Graphics*. Indianapolis, IN: New Riders Publishing, 1996.

Wilhelm, Henry with Carol Brower. *The Permanence and Care of Color Photographs: Traditional and Digital Color Prints, Color Negatives, Slides, and Motion Pictures*. Grinnell, IA: Preservation Publishing Company, 1993.

WEB SITES (SEE WWW.BARRYHAYNES.COM FOR INFO RELATING TO *Photoshop 6 Artistry*)

Atkinson, Bill. *www.Natureimages.com*. Bill Atkinson Photography.

Cramer, Charles. *www.charlescramer.com*. Charles Cramer Photography.

Haynes, Barry and Wendy Crumpler. *www.Maxart.com, www.barryhaynes.com*. Photographers, Imaging consultants and *Photoshop 6 Artistry* authors. See our site for Workshops, Art Gallery, Print Sales and free Latest Tips.

Lawler, Brian P. *www.Callamer.com/BPLawler*. Graphic Arts Consultant.

Velandria, Ed. *www.tarantula.com*. Award-winning Web designer and creative director at Tarantula.

Weinman, Lynda. *www.Lynda.com*. Web books and information.

White, Nancy and René White, *www.lizmar.com*. Media designers for video, multimedia and the Web.

Wilhelm, Henry. *www.wilhelm-research.com*. Color permanence information.

INDEX

COLOPHON

This book was produced almost entirely by the authors on two machines: first, a Mac Power PC 8600/300 with a Sonnet 400 MHz G3 accelerator, a 34Gb internal hard disk, 288Mb RAM, built-in video with an Apple Colorsync 17 display, ZIP transportable drive; and second, a Mac Power PC G3 with 26Gb internal, 288 Mb RAM, PressView 21 SR monitor, ZIP transportable drive; and third, a 500 MHz Mac G3 Powerbook with 256 Mb RAM, 12 Gig Hard Drive, Zip, etc. CD backups were burned using a Micronet Master CD Plus 2x4 CD burner.

Each chapter of this book was set up as a separate document in QuarkXPress. The text was input directly into Quark using a template document with Master pages and style sheets. Charts were done in Adobe Illustrator and color correction and separation was done, of course, from Photoshop 5 and 6 using the methods and settings described in this book.

Screen captures were done with Snapz Pro, and the Mac's Command-Shift-3 command. Low-res RGB captures were placed in the original documents and sized in Quark. After design decisions were made as to final size and position, the resolution was changed to 350 dpi and photos were resampled, sharpened, separated, and saved as CMYK TIFFs in Photoshop. They were then reimported into Quark at 100%.

Most photographs in this book are from Lino Tango Drum scans done by Bill Atkinson Photography, Imacon scans, UMax Powerlook 3000 scans and Photo CD or Pro Photo CD scans from 35mm slides done primarily by Palmer Photographic in Mountain View, CA.

Most pages were output at 2400 dpi using a 175-line screen. Critical color proofing was done using Spectrum Digital Match Print proofs and less critical color was proofed with Fuji First Look proofs. We used the techniques explained in this book, as well as our GTI Soft-View D5000 Transparency/Print Viewer, to calibrate Photoshop 6 separations on our Apple Colorsync 17 and our PressView 21 SR monitors to color proofs for critical color pages and the cover.

Transfer of files was done primarily using CDs and Iomega ZIP disks which were sent via Airborne Express between the authors and the printer. Files were sent as Quark documents with high-res photos in position. Film was set in signatures of 16 pages starting with the most color-critical signatures first. In time critical instances, images and Quark files were sent via internet between the authors and the publisher.

Printing was done by GAC Shepard Poorman in Indianapolis, direct to plate with a Creo platesetter, then printed on Heidelberg Speed Master sheet fed presses. The book is printed on 70lb Productolith Dull and the cover is 12pt C1s with a lay-flat gloss laminate.

Typefaces are New Caledonia, New Caledonia SC&OSF, and Frutiger from Adobe and, on the cover, ITC Orbon from International Typeface Corporation.

PHOTO AND ILLUSTRATION CREDITS

The first or most prominent occurance of each art piece is listed.

Wendy Crumpler (541-754-2219)
© 2001, Wendy Crumpler, All Rights
   Reserved
Fish Art: 34
Tree: 35
Happy Valentine: 45
Starry Night: 42
Heartsinger CD Cover: 386
South Africa Composite: 387
Ayanda: 393
Giraffes: 393
Mask: 393

Sean Duggan (530-477-8596)
© 2001, Sean Duggan, All Rights Reserved
Brooklyn: xxviii
Man Sitting: 85
Grid World: 96
Jacks Internet Cafe: 336
Spherical Lock: 418
Bodie Relic: 423

Barry Haynes (541-754-2219)
©2001, Barry Haynes, All Rights Reserved
Sienna: Cover
Half Dome in Fog: 1
Golden Gate: 7
7A: 37
Costa Rica Scenes: 69
Self Portrait: 92
Victorians: 100
Crater Lake: 109
Bandon Harbor: 182
Florida Swamp Scenes: 195
The Dogs: 209
Banf Lake: 218
Kansas: 238
Yellow Flowers: 250
English Church: 261
Burnley Graveyard: 262, 293
Al: 266
Mount Rainier: 285
Bryce Stone Woman: 286
McNamaras: 303

Yosemite Sunset: 319
The Packard: 358
San Jacinto Sunset: 401

Adams Collection (561-694-2000)
© 2001, Adams Collection, All Rights
   Reserved
Cochrane Train Station by Arthur F.
   Lynch Jr.: 270

Margee Wheeler
© 2001, Margee Wheeler, All Rights
   Reserved
Self Portrait: 365
Poster Artwork: 372

NEW RIDERS HAS WHAT YOU NEED TO MASTER PHOTOSHOP 6.

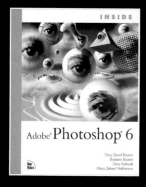

Inside Adobe Photoshop 6
Gary Bouton, Barbara Bouton
ISBN: 0735710384
$44.99

Photoshop Photo-Retouching Secrets
Scott Kelby
ISBN: 0735711461
$39.99

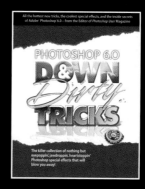

Photoshop 6 Down & Dirty Tricks
Scott Kelby
ISBN: 073571147X
$39.99

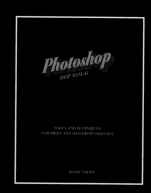

Photoshop Shop Manual
Donnie O'Quinn
ISBN: 0735711305
$40.00

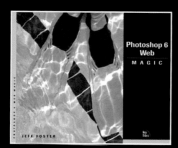

Photoshop 6 Web Magic
Jeff Foster
ISBN: 0735710368
$45.00

Bert Monroy: Photorealistic Techniques with Photoshop and Illustrator
Bert Monroy
ISBN: 0735709696
$49.99

Photoshop 6 Effects Magic
Rhoda Grossman, Sherry London
ISBN: 073571035X
$45.00

New Riders

WWW.NEWRIDERS.COM

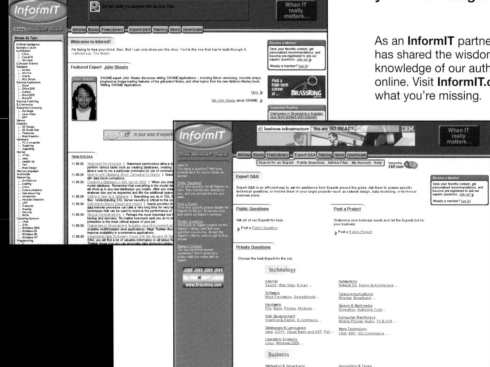

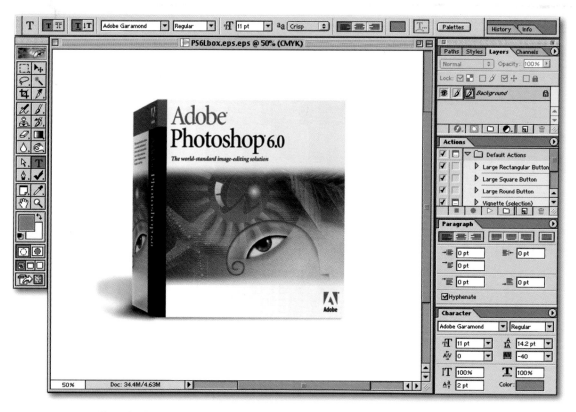

If Adobe® started shipping Photoshop® 6.0 in October 2000...how did NAPP members learn to use 6.0's new features three weeks before it shipped?

Nearly a month before the general public started getting their copies of the most expansive Photoshop update in years, members of the National Association of Photoshop Professionals (NAPP) already knew what the new features were. And better yet, they already knew how to use them.

How's this possible? Well, it's because NAPP, with Adobe's help, created a special all-Photoshop 6.0 issue of their highly acclaimed "how-to" magazine *Photoshop User*. The day Adobe announced Photoshop 6.0, it was already on its way to NAPP members, over a month before 6.0 actually shipped. In this special 6.0 issue, NAPP members learned all the new features, including Layer Styles, the new Web tools, the new type features, vector shapes, and tons more. And on top of that, the minute Adobe made their announcement, every member had access to QuickTime videos, feature articles, and discussion forums all on 6.0 from the members-only Web site. That's an example of how the NAPP keeps its members on the cutting edge.

The NAPP is an educational organization just for people who use Adobe Photoshop. And joining this ever-expanding global community can change the way you use Photoshop forever. Membership is open to anyone using Photoshop and is essential for graphic designers, ad agencies, photographers, Web designers, educators, print shops, publications, or anyone who realizes that there's more to learn about Photoshop than there is time to learn.

Join today, and we'll include that special all-Photoshop 6.0 issue in your new member kit. Plus, as a member, you'll also enjoy a host of member benefits, including:

- A free subscription to *Photoshop User*, the highly acclaimed Adobe Photoshop "how-to" magazine
- Big discounts on software, hardware, upgrades, peripherals seminars, videos, Web hosting, graphics magazine subscriptions, and even car rentals, hotel discounts, and more!
- Access to the private members-only Web site—the #1 Photoshop resource on the entire Web
- Expert Photoshop tech support and real-world advice just for members
- Invitation to PhotoshopWorld, the NAPP's annual convention and the largest Photoshop event anywhere in the world

Plus there's so much more. We invite you to join the thousands of people in 64 different countries who have made the NAPP the most complete resource for Photoshop training, education, and news in the world.

The National Association of Photoshop® Professionals
The Photoshop® Authority

A one-year membership is only $99 (U.S.funds)
Join today by calling **800-738-8513**
or enroll online at **www.photoshopuser.com**

Corporate and International memberships available. Photoshop and Adobe are registered trademarks of Adobe Systems, Inc.

USE YOUR INFLUENCE

Have you ever said, "If only there were a book that…" or "I'd like like to have a book that told me how to…" If so, we want to hear from you.

Our next book is:

Making The Digital Print There are many steps in achieving a great digital print, having to do with properly calibrating the scanner, monitor & printer, making the scan, color correcting and sharpening the file, as well as setting it up for the printer, that are common with almost all digital printers. You'll learn how to get the best results on the latest models of the most popular printers available for photographs. For the first edition of this book, printers like the Epson Stylus Photo 1270, 2000, 7500 and 9500, the Fuji Pictrography printers, and the Lightjet 5000, will be covered. We'll talk about permanence of colors using different types of inks and papers. Hybrid digital printing methods, like creating a piece of film that can be more easily printed in the traditional darkroom, or outputting to an imagesetter and making black and white darkroom contact prints, will also be discussed. This book will also point you towards the 3 or 4 best desktop film scanners and show you how to use each one to get the highest quality scans.

LET US KNOW WHAT YOU WANT!

Please let me know when you ship:

☐ **MAKING THE DIGITAL PRINT**

Actually, I'm more interested in a book about _____

_____

and I'd like to be on you course mailing list. Here's my important information:

Name _____

Address _____

City _____ *State* _____ *Zip* _____

Phone _____ *Fax* _____ *E-mail* _____

See the next page for information about our Photoshop workshops for Photographers

Photoshop 6 Workshops for Photographers by Barry Haynes:
(for details see www.barryhaynes.com)

Barry Haynes teaches small custom hands-on Photoshop 6 workshops in his studio. These courses are for a maximum of five photographers at a time!

Check www.barryhaynes.com for course descriptions and the latest schedules.

Check www.barryhaynes.com for Barry and Wendy's gallery, book and print sales, free Photoshop, calibration and Epson printing tips, book errata, and information about new versions of Photoshop.

If you want to be on our mailing list, please send your e-mail address to barry@maxart.com with a request to be on the mailing list.

The 5-day/4-evening printmaking course:
• Printmaking for Photographers (Photoshop 6)

In the 5-day courses, Barry helps you with your projects or questions during the day, then you solidify new techniques during the evening studio time. Each class has a minimum of three students and maximum of five. A creative place with small class size that encourages student-student-instructor interactions. We want you to learn the most in the least amount of time and enjoy the process.

www.barryhaynes.com or call us at 541-754-2219

Stamp
Please

Barry Haynes and Wendy Crumpler
2222 NW Brownly Hts. Dr.
Corvallis, OR 97330

Hey, I'd also like to know more about

☐ THE PRINTMAKING FOR PHOTOGRAPHERS COURSE

☐ WENDY's *Photoshop, Painter and Illustrator Side-By-Side* BOOK

☐ BARRY's UPCOMING *Making the Digital Print* BOOK

Check our Web site at www.barryhaynes.com for detailed course descriptions, schedules and locations.

Fold this side up first, staple or tape the edge, and send it on!

Quotes from Photoshop Instructors:

"I teach online for The New School University in New York City so my students come from all over the States and all over the world. It's critical that I have a "text book" that students can follow easily. The "Artistry" book is the best book I have found to teach the intermediate to advanced courses. Students find the examples useful because they are "real-life" problems they will have to solve. An excellent book by authors who are willing to spend time answering your questions and emails afterwards!"

Marion Suro

"Hi, Barry and Wendy. We are using *Photoshop 5 Artistry* for our digital class here at Northern Kentucky University. It is a fountain of information that will serve students well long after the class is finished... I basically learned Photoshop via your first book; I don't think it's an exaggeration to say I couldn't have done it without you. Thanks."

Barry Andersen, Professor of Art, Northern Kentucky University

"Dear Barry, Just a line to say thanks and congratulations on the *Photoshop 4 Artistry* book. A couple of years ago, I hit an extended period of ill health, which limited my mobility for a time. I turned to digital imaging to keep my mind active, bought a copy of your book (just about the only one anyone really needs) and have enjoyed hundreds of hours of fun ever since. I've recently had some images published in a number of British magazines—which is largely thanks to the excellent examples in *Artistry* … I've just gotten *Photoshop 5 Artistry* (and congratulations, it's even better than the PS4 version) … I have a fairly large personal library of PS books and, for what it's worth, I think *Photosho 5 Artistry* is one of the two best books currently available on the subject —anywhere!"

With great appreciation, Kindest regards, Bob Rowe ARPS

"Barry, we are anxiously awaiting *Photoshop 5 Artistry*! When will it be available? We use it as the primary text in our Intro to Digital Imaging course and love it. When I began using Photoshop 5, I went through each chapter to see if we would need to make any changes from procedures in the *Artistry 4* book....Thanx again to you and Wendy for the great book."

Stan Shire, Chair, Department of Photographic Imaging, Community College of Philadelphia

Quotes from Photographers:

"Simply, *Photoshop Artistry* is a book that will open the full potential of Photoshop to the user. There are theoretical sections, but the book is mainly concerned with a series of hands-on tutorials that will take you right around Photoshop and make you a competent user; the book is always there for reference if you should need it!"

With Regards, Ahmno "Himalaya CyberLink"

"Hi Barry and Wendy. I just wanted to send you both a very big 'Thank you' across the ocean for the wonderful book *Photoshop 4 Artistry*. I found the book in a Barnes & Noble bookstore in Poughkeepsie, NY, while on a vacation trip. I immediately fell in love with your book and could barely wait to return to my home in Germany. In the meantime, I started studying it and worked through most of the hands on examples. No trouble so far; everything is nicely explained. And I have had so much fun and learned so much about Photoshop in such a short time."

Joachim Hoegner, Sindelfingen Germany

"Barry, yours is by far the best of the Photoshop adjunct books... Wish I could come to your workshops. I continue to use your book to refresh basics... We missed meeting in Camden, Maine. Kodak invited me as an artist-in-residence and suggested that I take your Photoshop offering. I was using an Amiga at the time. Had a one-person show at the Neikrug with some of those images. Am really a photojournalist (past stringer for *Life*, *People*, *Time*, etc.) … Look forward to many of your future books."

Judith Gefter, a few credentials: Life member of ASMP, listed in 15 Who's Who's including WW in American Art.

More Quotes from Photographers:

"Did you ever pick up a book and hear the author's voice behind your ear and know you know the voice? Well that about describes how I met you two. I've started reading, and I just needed to say how pleased I am. I'm a computer professional, system architect, and have been doing serious nature photography for five years. I recently decided to extend my photo activities through a digital darkroom. I greatly enjoyed visiting your site; it transpires the same warmth and good feeling I found in your book."

Milicska Jalbert, Montreal, Quebec

"Dear Barry and Wendy, I rate your *Photoshop 5 Artistry* the best Photoshop book I have seen. Indeed it is kept beside my bed for every evening reading so good it is!"

Richard Kenward ABIPP, Richard Kenward Digital Imaging

"Your book is GREAT!! For a beginner in digital imaging but an experienced photographer, it has been unbelievably helpful. Thanks."

VIC, Victor Smole

"For a complete novice to the computer and Photoshop it is essential to study and learn by using the best material. Ph.5 Artistry is a book that appeals to the budding artist in that it immediately reveals the beauty of playing about with colour and form, giving your material its own unique expression. My field is in judging sighthounds and also providing people with a true - albeit optimized - (digital) photo of their great dog, which I have put through all the digital finesse of Photoshop and Illustrator. Ph.5 Artistry is phenomenal in helping me along from basics to advanced steps."

Birgit Wamberg, Fairway Whippets, Denmark.

"I am enjoying your book Photoshop 5 Artistry very much - by far the best to help a newcomer to Photoshop."

Petra Campbell, Canberra, Australia

"Dear Barry and Wendy, You have the best book on the market, Photoshop 5 Artistry. I have learned so much and am so grateful to you for creating such an informative, well-written manual. As I learn, I'll be thinking to myself, "Why did they do that?" and just like THAT, the book says, "You do that because...""

Thanks again, Karen G.

Quotes About Our Workshops:

"Barry is the best hands-on instructor I've ever had. His book reads like a good conversation and his teaching style is equivalent. He listens well. I liked almost everything about the workshop, especially the opportunity to watch him work on my images and also to help me as I worked on them. The 9 to 5 plus 7 to 10 days in the Printmaking for Photographers course were wonderful to really intensely focus. I would Absolutely recommend this workshop to others."

Jon Veigel

"I think Barry did an excellent job. The Printmaking for Photographers course really moved me up on the learning curve by the number of hours we were able to devote to Photoshop. Loved the total emersion. I would recommend this workshop to others with enthusiasm."

Mike Greenberg

Check our web site at www.barryhaynes.com for more quotes from workshop students and Photoshop Artistry readers.